(京)新登字041号

图书在版编目(CIP)数据

青岛统计年鉴. 2006/青岛市统计局编.
——北京：中国统计出版社，2006.6
ISBN 7-5037-4970-9

Ⅰ. 青…
Ⅱ. 青…
Ⅲ. 统计资料—青岛市—2006—年鉴
Ⅳ. C832.523-54

中国版本图书馆CIP数据核字(2006)第028144号

青岛统计年鉴－2006

作　　者/ 青岛市统计局
责任编辑/ 蔡启新
E-mail/ yearbook@stats.gov.cn
责任校对/ 林玉森　苏延玲
封面设计/ 青岛天之韵广告文化传播有限公司
彩页设计/ 青岛天之韵广告文化传播有限公司
出版发行/ 中国统计出版社
通信地址/ 北京市西城区三里河月坛南街75号　中国统计出版社
邮　　编/ 100826
电　　话/ (010)63376907
印　　刷/ 青岛星球印刷有限公司
经　　销/ 新华书店
开　　本/ 890x1240毫米1/16
字　　数/ 1180千字
印　　张/ 27
印　　数/ 1-1000册
版　　别/ 2006年7月第1版
版　　次/ 2006年7月第1次印刷
书　　号/ ISBN 7-5037-4970-9/F.2317
定　　价/ 200.00元

◎ 全市生产总值（亿元）

Gross Domestic Product (100 million yuan)

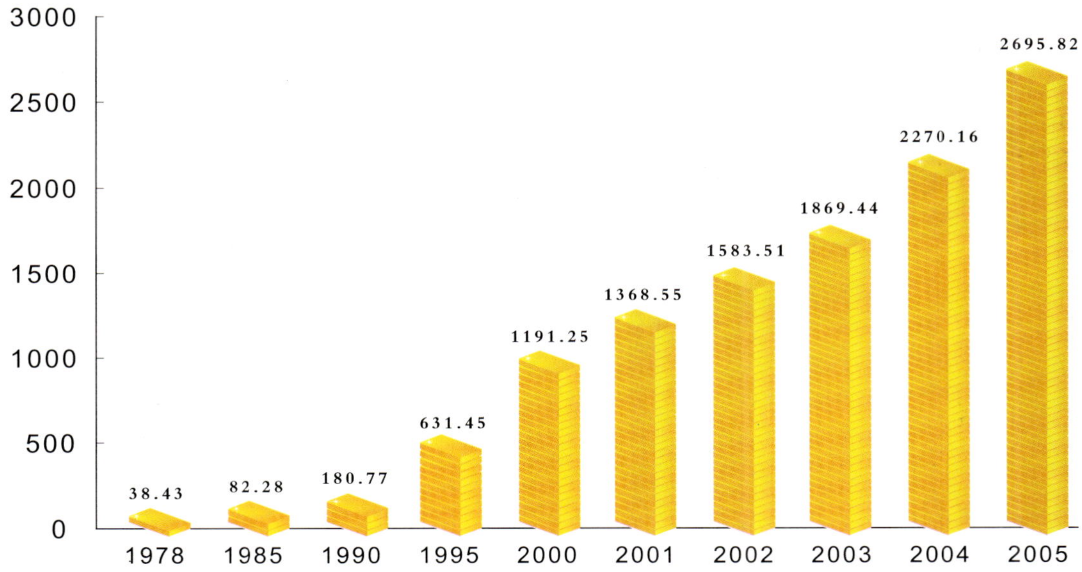

◎ 人均生产总值（元）（按常住人口计算）

Per Capita GDP(yuan) (at Constant Population)

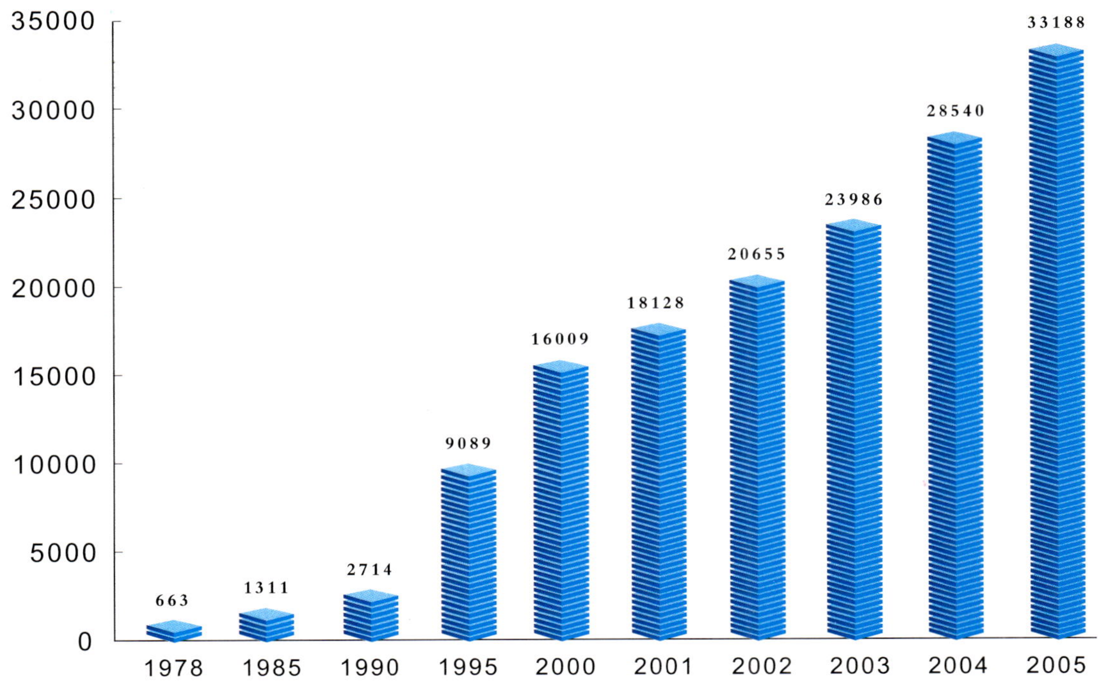

三次产业比例
Composition Of Gross Domestic Product

一产比例 Primary Industry　　二产比例 Secondary Industry　　三产比例 Tertiary Industry

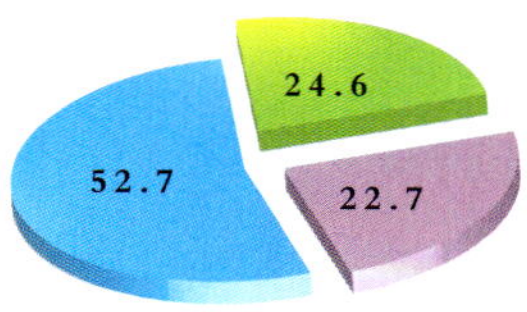

1978

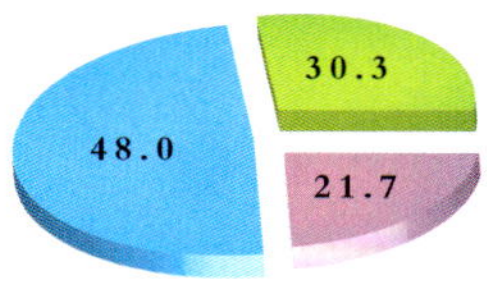

1990

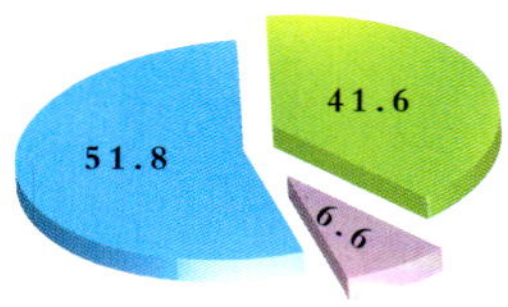

2005

青岛的一天 (2005)
Daily Economic Indicators Of Qingdao (2005)

- 全市生产总值73858万元
  GDP 738.58 million yuan
- 地方财政一般预算收入4831万元
  General Budget Revenue of Local Finance 48.31 million yuan
- 工业总产值137035万元
  Gross Output Value of Industry 1370.35million yuan
- 农业总产值8781万元
  Gross Output Value of Agriculture 87.81 million yuan
- 接待国内外游客68972人次
  Overseas and Domestic Tourists 68972 person-times
- 外商直接投资1002万美元
  Direct Foreign Investment 10.02 million USD
- 港口货物吞吐量513055吨
  Cargo Handled at Ports 513055 tons
- 用电量5384万千瓦时
  Daily Electricity Consumption 53.84 million kwh
- 社会消费品零售总额23723万元
  Total Retail Sales of Consumer Goods 237.23 million yuan
- 口岸进出口总额18994万美元
  Total Imports and Exports Through Custom 189.94 million USD
- 房屋竣工面积37775平方米
  Floor Space of Residential Buildings completed 37775 sq.m
- 供水量91万吨
  Daily Water Supply 0.91 million tons
- 液化气供应量214吨
  Supply Volume of Liquefied Gas 214 tons
- 煤气供应总量454055立方米
  Supply Volume of Gas 454055 cu.m
- 新增移动电话用户3430户
  Cell Phone Users Newly Increased 3430 users
- 全社会固定资产投资39906万元
  Total Investment in Fixed Assets 399.06 million yuan

农林牧渔业总产值（亿元）
Gross Output Value of Agriculture (100 million yuan)

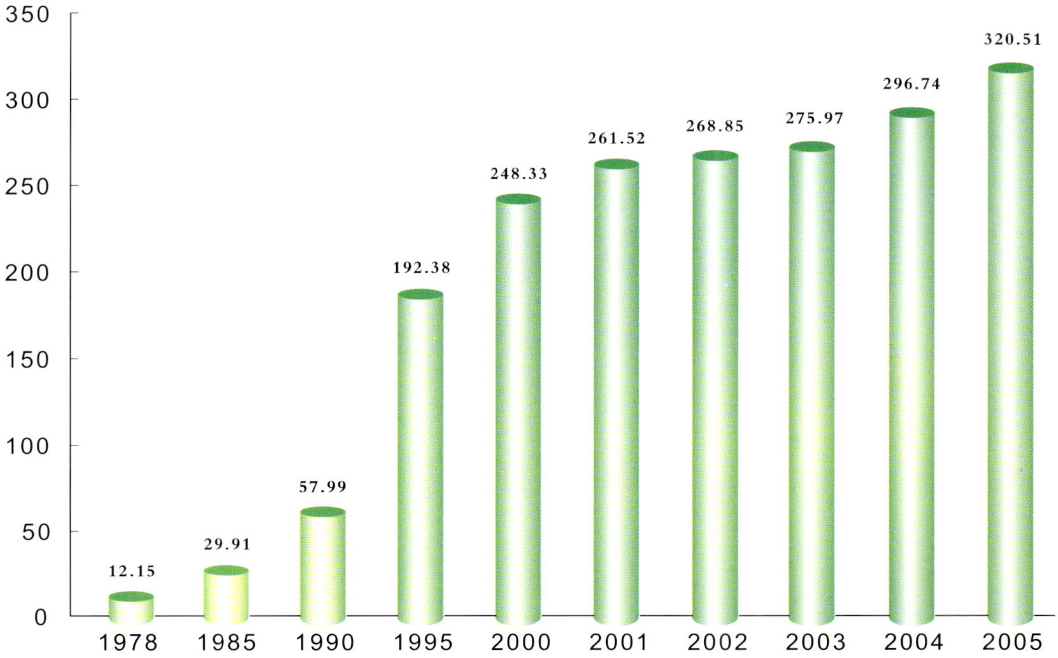

主要农产品产量（万吨）
Yield Of Farm Crops (10000 tons)

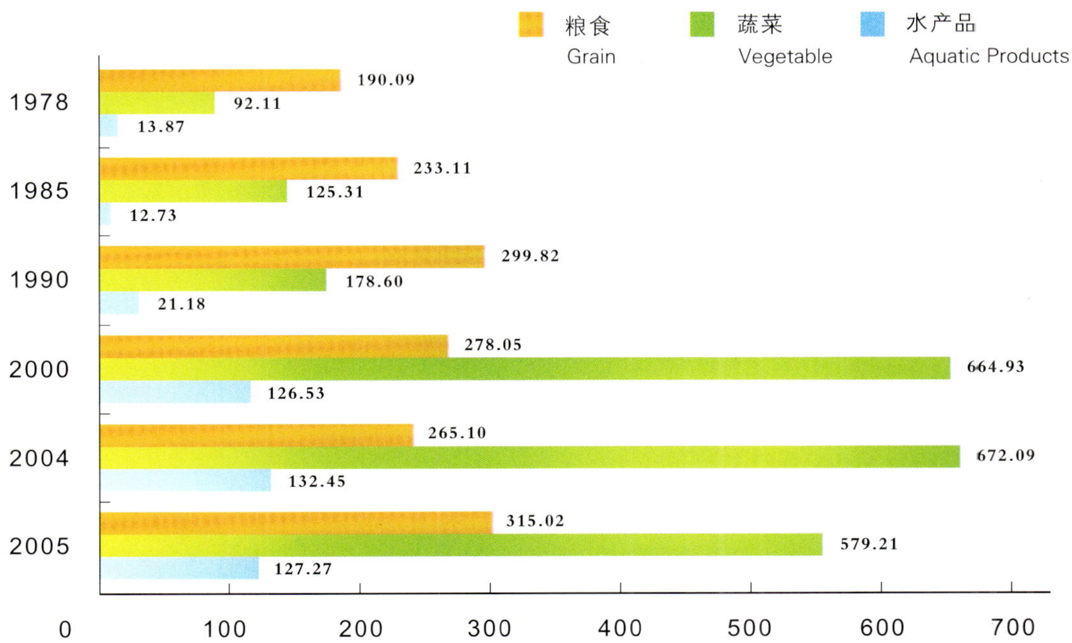

◎ 工业总产值（亿元）
Gross Output Value of Industry (100 million yuan)

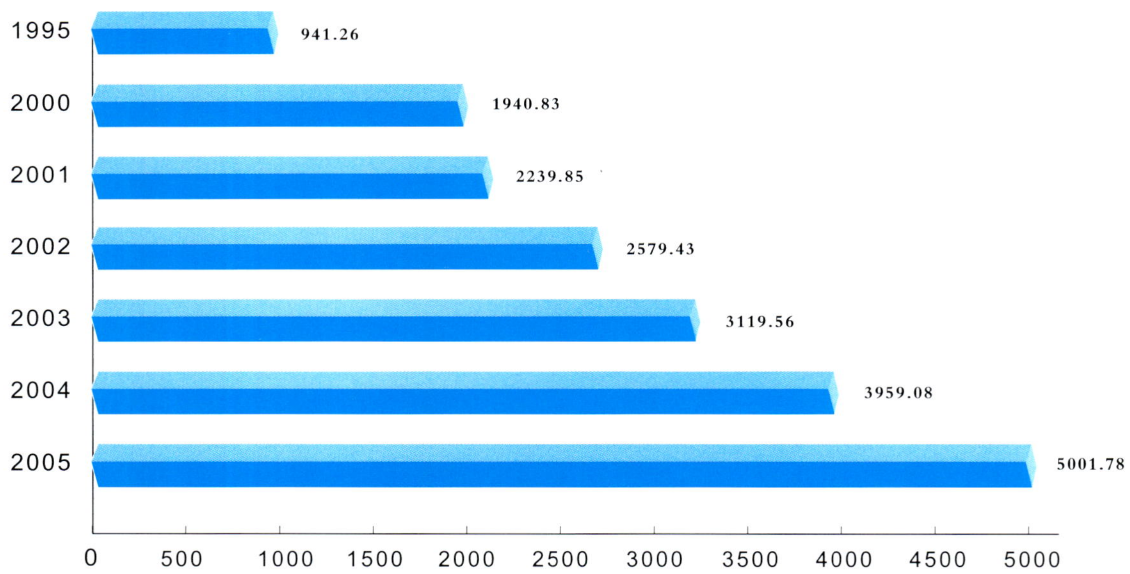

◎ 规模以上工业实现利税总额（亿元）
Total Profits And Tax of Industry Above Scale(100 million yuan)

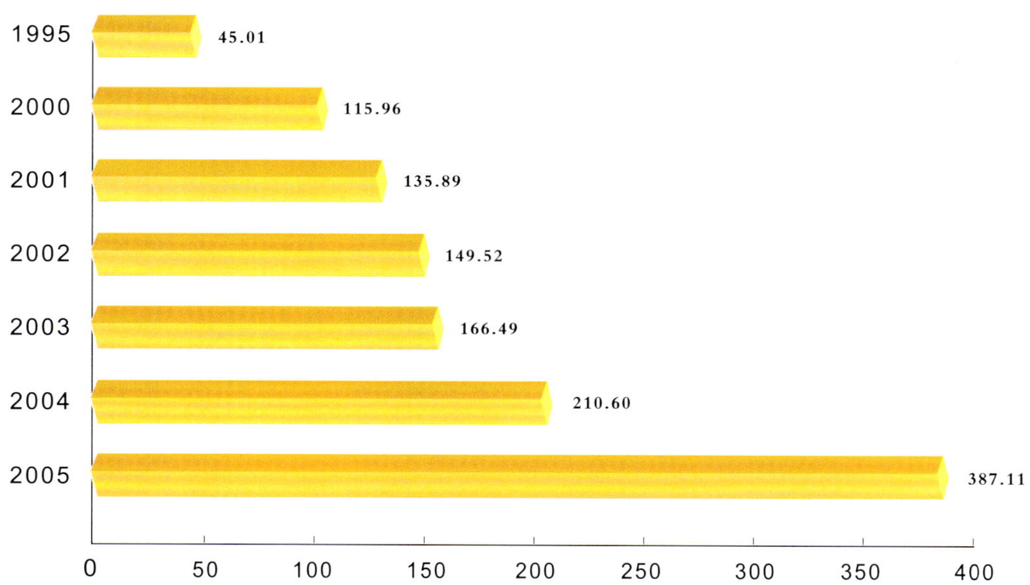

全社会固定资产投资（亿元）
Total Investment In Fixed Assets(100 million yuan)

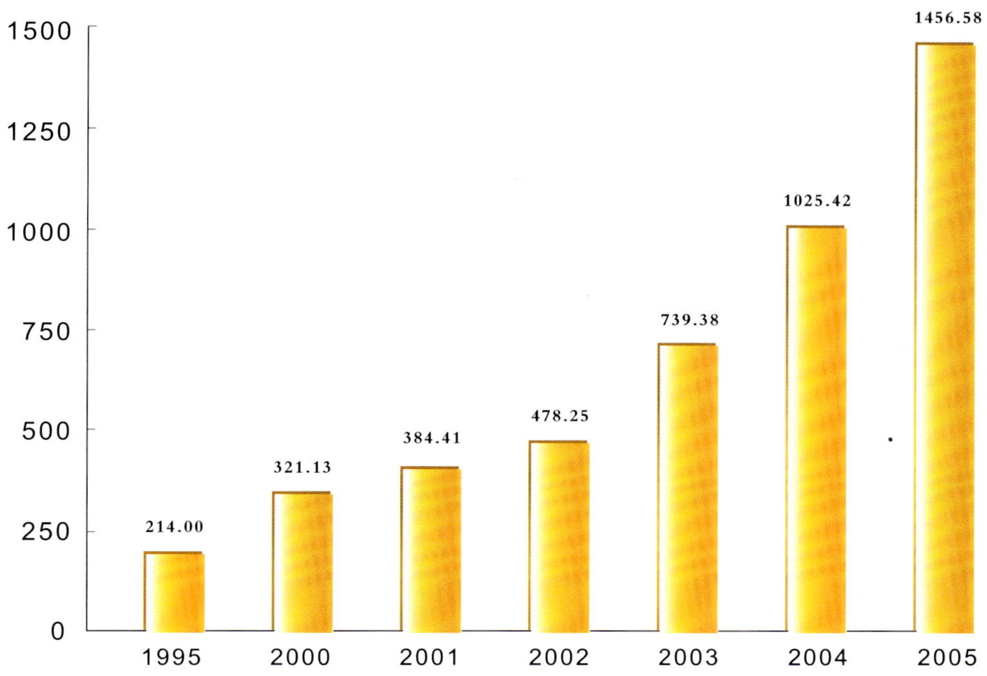

房屋竣工面积、住宅竣工面积（万平方米）
Floor Space Of Building Completed,Floor Space Of Residential Buildings Completed(10000 sq.m)

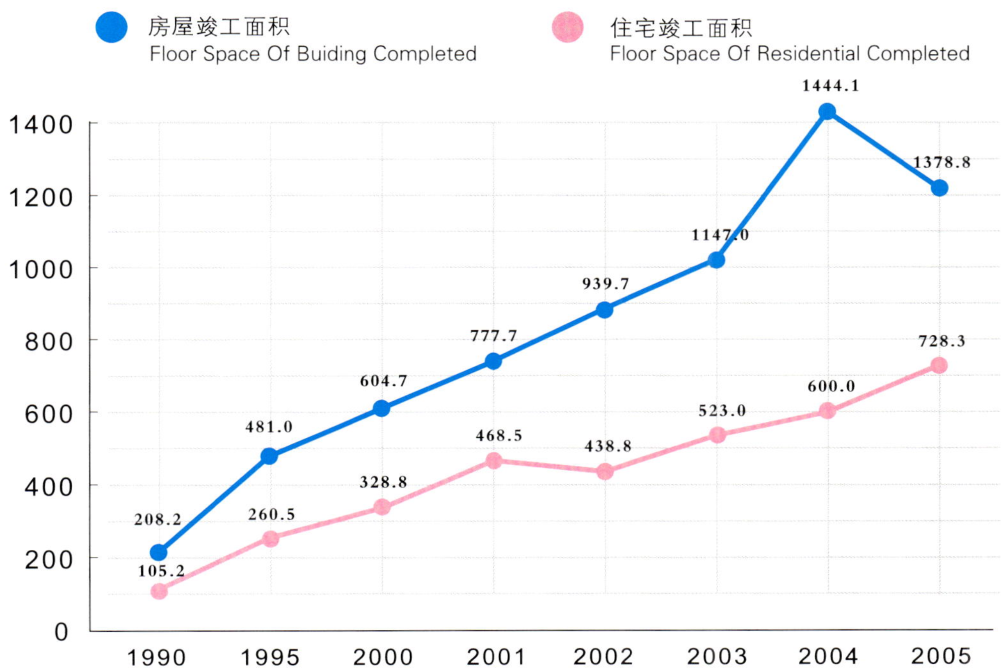

◎ 社会消费品零售额（亿元）

Total Retail Sales Of Consumer Goods(100 million yuan)

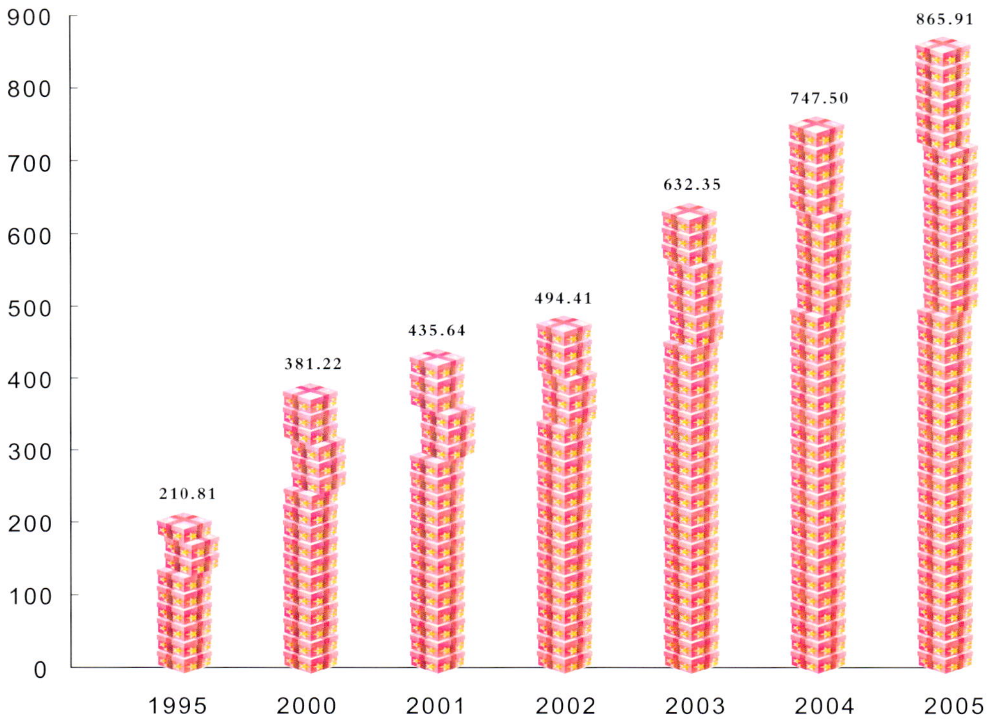

◎ 消费构成（%）

Composition Of Total Retail Sales Of Consumer Goods(%)

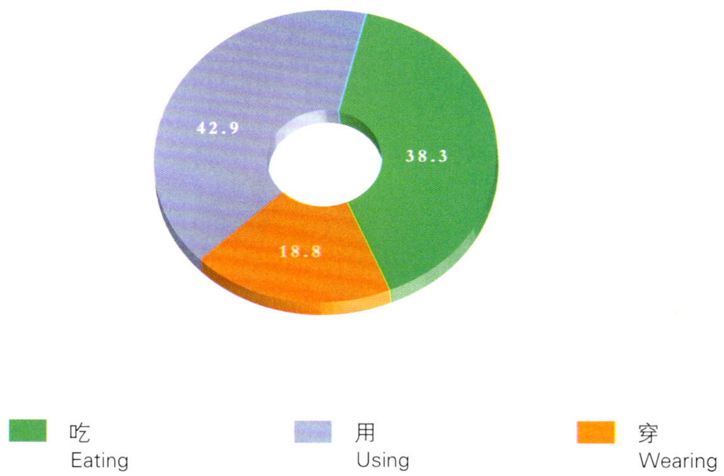

◎ 地方财政收入（亿元）
Government Revenue(100 million yuan)

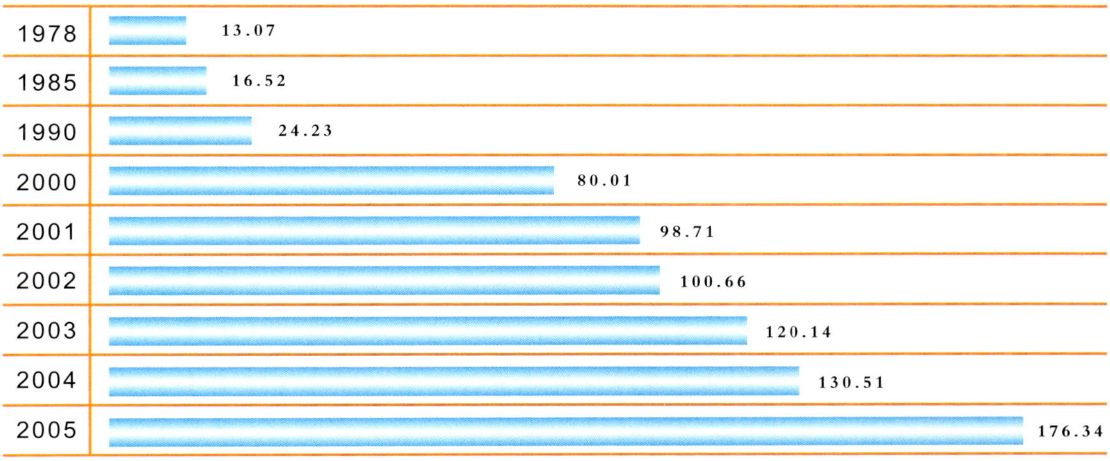

注：2002年以后财政收入为一般预算收入数
Note:Since 2002,government revenue refers to general budget revenue

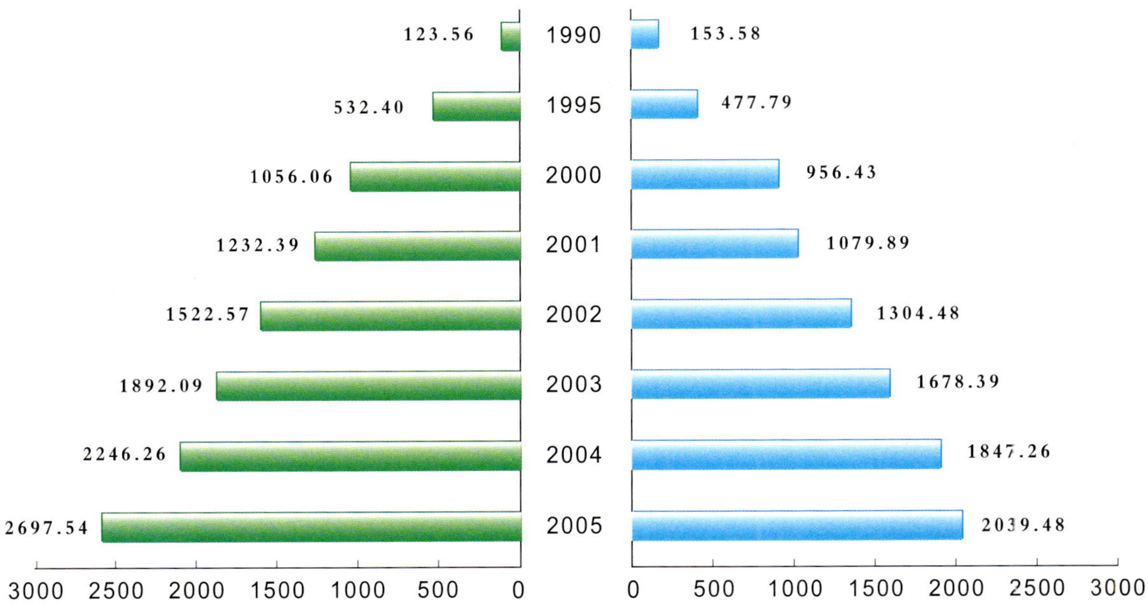

金融机构年末人民币存款余额（亿元）
Year-end Savings Deposits (RMB) Of Financial Institution (100 million yuan)

金融机构年末人民币贷款余额（亿元）
Year-end Loans (RMB) Of Financial Institution (100 million yuan)

进出口总额（亿美元）
Total Imports And Exports Goods(100 million USD)

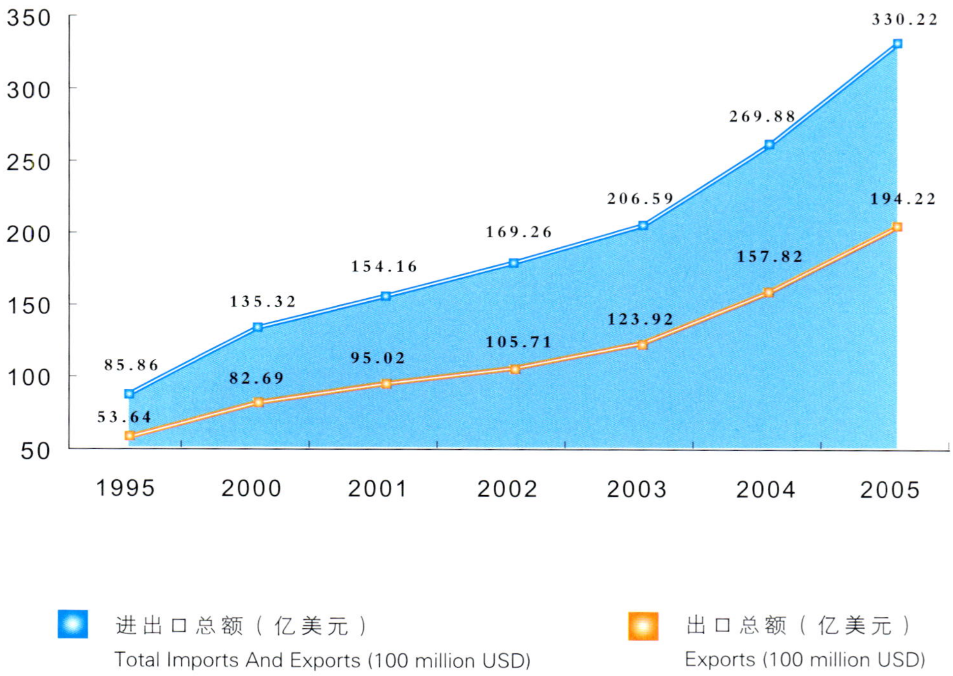

旅游人数（万人次）
Number Of Tourists (10000 person-times)

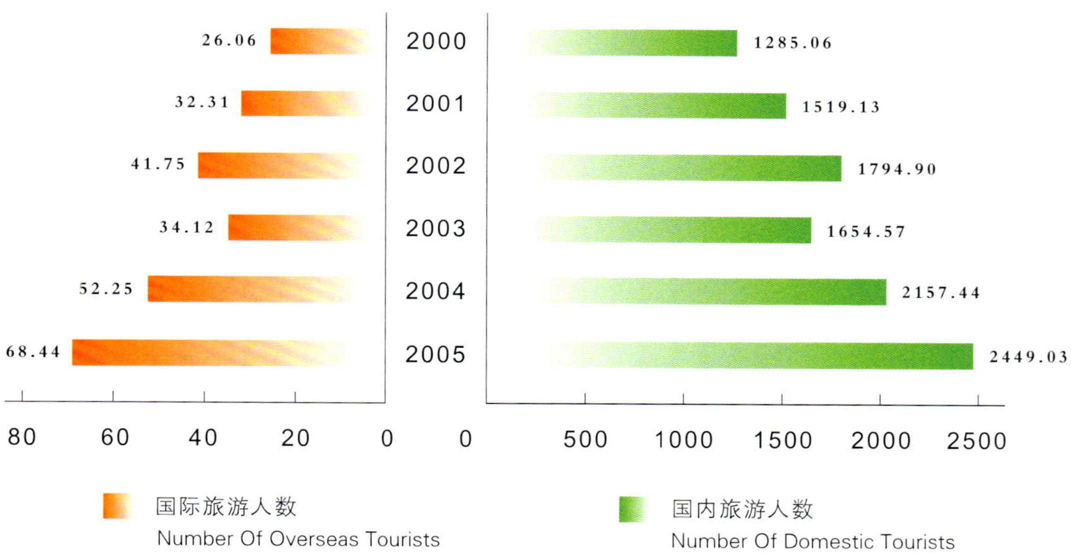

主要年份城市铺装道路长度、面积
Major Year's Length And Area Of Road

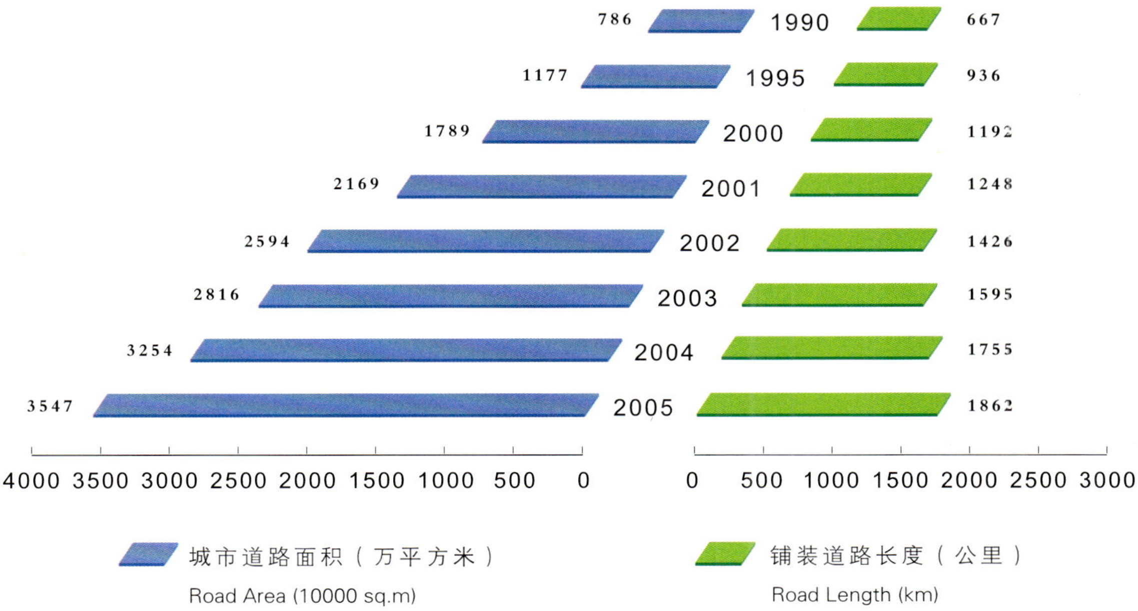

市区居民人均住宅建筑面积（平方米）
Per Capita Construction Space Of Residential Buildings In Urban Area(sq.n)

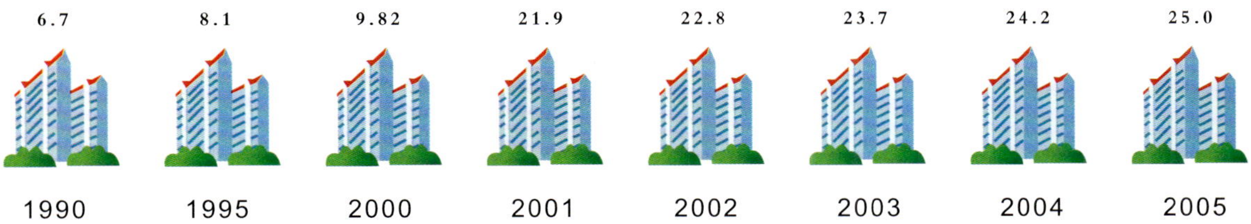

注：2000年以前人均住宅面积为人均居住面积。
Note:Before 2000,per capita space of residential building refers to living space.

建成区绿化覆盖率（%）
Coverage Rate Of Green Areas In Constructed Area(%)

◎ 授权专利（件）

Patent Applications Granted(item)

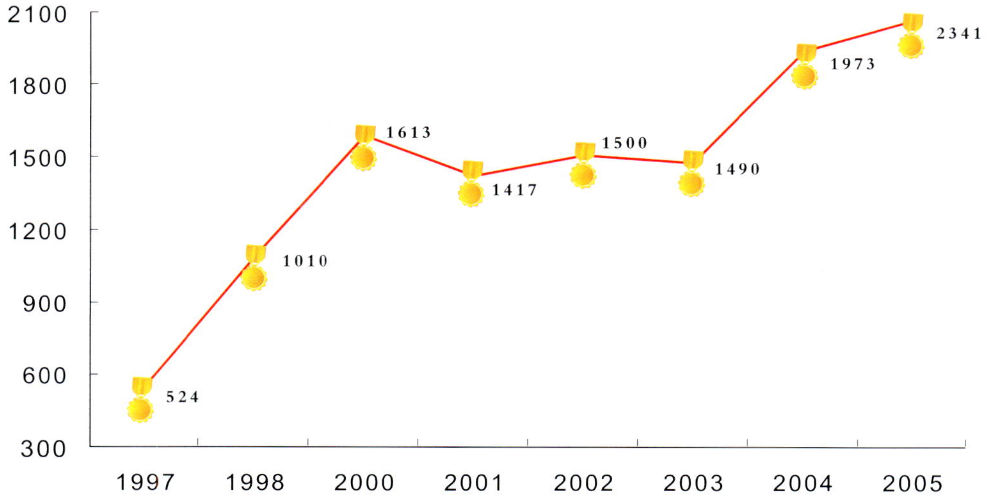

◎ 普通高校在校人数（万人）

Students Enrollment Of Regular Institutions Of Higher Education(10000 persons)

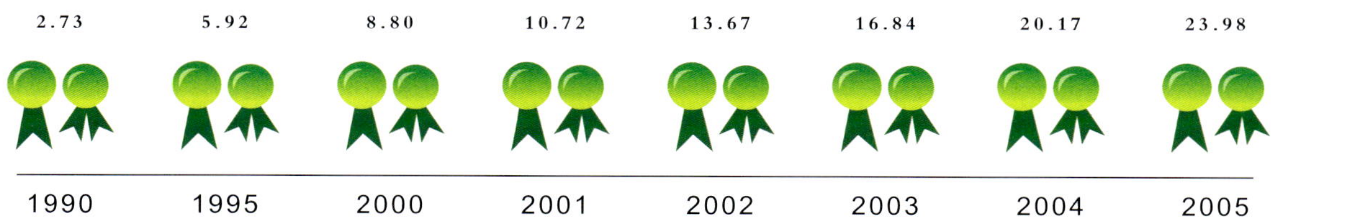

◎ 卫生医疗机构（个）

Health Care Institutions(unit)

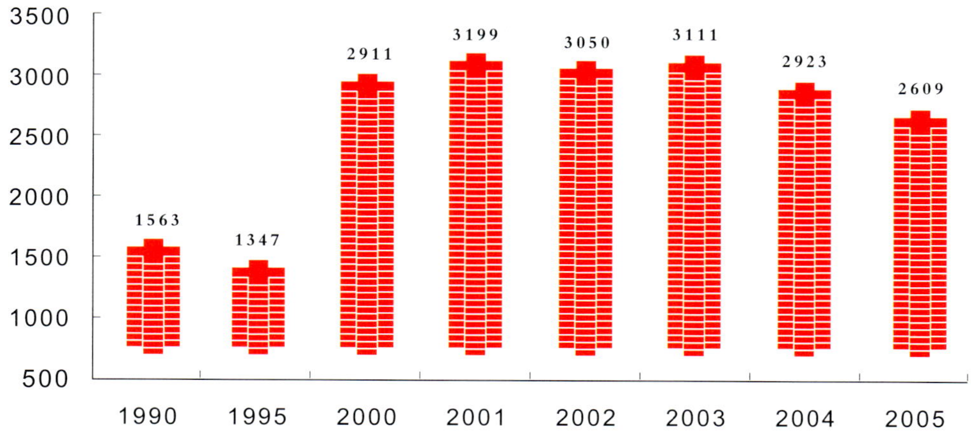

城乡居民收入（元）
Income of Urban And Rural Residents(yuan)

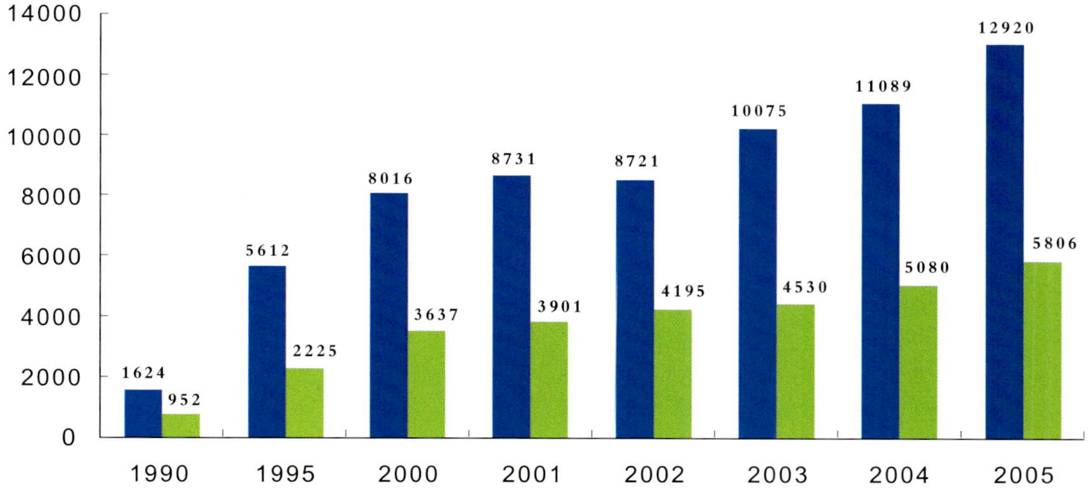

注：2002年开始城市居民人均可支配收入为新口径，与往年不可比。
Note: Since 2002,new calibre has been adopted in per capita disposale income of urban residents.

城市居民人均可支配收入（元）
Per Capita Disposable Income Of Urban Residents(yuan)

农民人均纯收入（元）
Per Capita Net Income Of Rural Residents(yuan)

城乡居民储蓄余额（亿元）
Savings Deposits(100 million yuan)

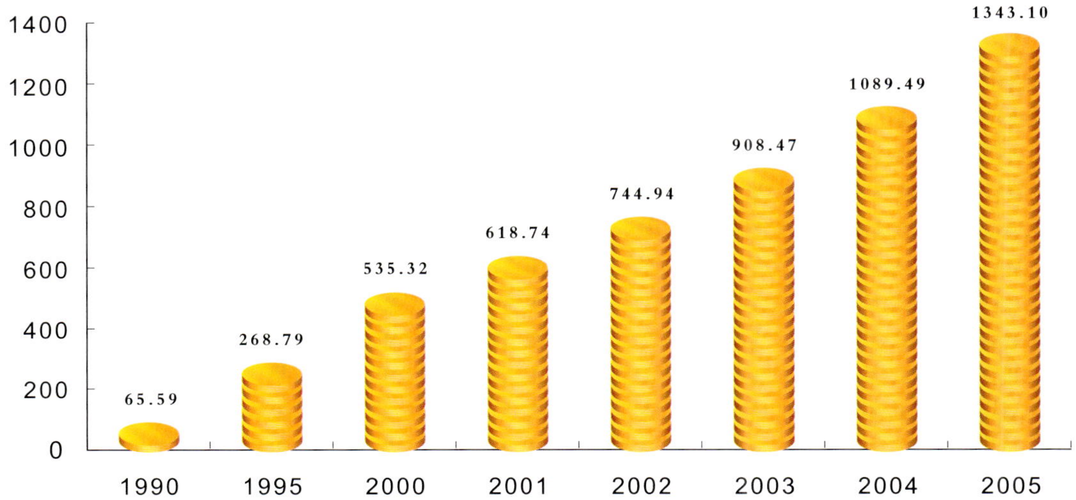

青岛统计年鉴(2006)

编辑委员会

QINGDAO STATISTICAL YEARBOOK(2006)

EDITORIAL BOARD

编者说明

一、《青岛统计年鉴-2006》是一本信息高度密集的资料工具书。本书收录了2005年青岛的经济和社会等各方面的统计数据，以及重要年份和改革开放以来的主要统计数据。

二、全书内容分为十八部分，包括：综合、人口、从业人员及职工工资、固定资产投资、能源消耗、财政金融和保险业、物价、人民生活、城市建设和环境保护、农业、工业、建筑业、运输邮电、国内贸易、对外经济贸易和旅游、教育科技文化体育、卫生和民政司法及企业调查。为方便读者正确地使用年鉴资料，书末还附有主要统计指标解释。

三、根据国家统计局有关规定，本年鉴依据第一次经济普查结果，对2004年以前全市生产总值历史数据和1993-2004年社会消费品零售总额等历史数据作了修订。

四、本年鉴数据均为新行政区划统计口径。读者在使用历史数据时，凡与本年鉴有出入的，均以本年鉴为准。

五、本年鉴中的符号说明：

"-"表示无该项统计数据；

"…"表示数据不足本表最小单位数；

"#"表示其中的主要项；

空白栏表示该项统计数据不详

六、《青岛统计年鉴》自公开出版以来，受到社会各界的关心和支持，对于年鉴的内容和编辑工作提出了许多宝贵的意见，对此我们深表谢意。限于我们的水平，欢迎读者继续对年鉴的不足之处给予批评和指正，帮助我们进一步改进年鉴编辑工作，以期更好地为广大读者服务。

Editor's Note

Ⅰ. Qingdao Statistical Yearbook 2006 is a very important reference book, which contains High-density information. The book contains all kinds data of Qingdao' s social and economic development in 2005,and data in significant year or data since the beginning of reform and opening up.

Ⅱ.The book is composed of 18 parts, including: General Survey; Population; Employment and Wages of Staff and Workers ;Investment in Fixed Assets; Consumption of Energy; Finance ,Banking and Insurance ;Price ;People' s Livelihood ;City Construction and Environ-ment Protection; Agriculture; Industry; Construction; Transportation, Posts and Telecommunications; Domestic Trade; Foreign Economic Trade and Tourism; Education, Science and Culture; Sports, Health Care, Civil Administration and Judicature; Enterprises Survey. Meanwhile interpretation of major statistical indicators has been attached for readers to use the data correctly.

Ⅲ. According to national statistical regulation, historical data of Gross Domistic Product before 2004 and Total Retail Sales of Consumer Goods between 1993 to 2004 have been adjusted on the basis of statistics of first economic census.

Ⅳ.All of the data in the book are in accordance with new administrative division. In any case the data of this book shall be deemed as the authertic ones.

Ⅴ. Marks in this book:

"–" indicates that the data is not available;

"…" indicates that the figure is not large enough to be measured with the smallest unit in the table;

"#" indicates the major items of the total;

"(blank)" indicates that the data is unknown.

Ⅵ. Previous editions of Qingdao Statistical Yearbook have won wide acclaim among the readers. In order to excel, we welcome all candid comments and criticism from our readers.

目　　录

一、综　　合

二、人　　口

三、从业人员及职工工资

四、固定资产投资

五、能源消耗

六、财政、金融和保险业

七、物　　价

八、人民生活

九、城市建设、环境保护

十、农　　业

十一、工　　业

十二、建筑业

十三、运输、邮电

十四、国内贸易

十五、对外经济贸易和旅游

十六、教育、科技和文化

十七、体育、卫生和民政、司法

十八、企业调查

附　　录

CONTENTS

Chapter 1. GENERAL SURVEY

Chapter 2. POPULATION

Chapter 3. EMPLOYMENT AND WAGES OF STAFF AND WORKERS

Chapter 4. INVESTMENT IN FIXED ASSETS

Chapter 5. CONSUMPTION OF ENERGY

Chapter 6. PUBLIC FINANCE, BANKING AND INSURANCE

Chapter 7. PRICE

Chapter 8. PEOPLE'S LIVELIHOOD

Chapter 9. CITY CONSTRUCTION AND ENVIRONMENT PROTECTION

Chapter 10. AGRICULTURE

Chapter 11. INDUSTRY

Chapter 12. CONSTRUCTION

Chapter 13. TRANSPORTATION, POSTAL AND TELECOMMUNICATIONS SERVICES

Chapter 14. CIVIL TRADE

Chapter 15. FOREIGN TRADE AND TOURISM

Chapter 16. EDUCATION, SCIENCE AND CULTURE

Chapter 17. SPORTS, HEALTH CARE, CIVIL ADMINISTRATION AND LAW

Chapter 18. ENTERPRISES SURVEY

APPENDIX

2005年
青岛市国民经济和社会发展
统计公报

青岛市统计局

（2006年2月13日）

2005年，全市人民在市委、市政府的正确领导下，认真贯彻落实科学发展观，围绕建设全国重点中心城市和世界知名特色城市的目标，进一步加强宏观调控，努力克服经济发展中的各种矛盾和困难，促进了全市经济的持续快速协调健康发展和各项社会事业的全面进步，确保了“十五”计划主要目标的完成。繁荣青岛、平安青岛、文明青岛建设取得了巨大成就。

一、综合

全市经济保持较快增势。初步核算，全市实现生产总值（GDP）2695.5亿元，增长16.9%，比上年提高0.1个百分点，为1994年以来的最高增幅。其中,第一产业增加值174.64亿元，增长0.4%，第二产业增加值1399.75亿元，增长20.0%，第三产业增加值1121.11亿元，增长16.0%。三次产业的比例关系调整为6.5：51.9：41.6。

宏观经济效益稳步提高。2005年全市实现地方财政一般预算收入176.34亿元，增长35.1%；地方财政一般预算支出203.06亿元，增长23.4%。税收保持较快增长，全年国税系统组织税收收入（含海关代征）393.01亿元,增长15.1%;地税税收收入120.88亿元,增长20.0%。宏观经济景气保持高位运行。反映企业家对宏观经济环境信心与预期的企业家信心指数年末达到130.37，反映企业综合生产经营状况和经济效益的企业景气指数为147.65。

市场物价小幅上升。全年居民消费价格总指数102.3,比上年上升2.3%，其中，食品、衣着、娱乐教育文化用品及服务、居住分别上升2.1%、8.3%、0.4%、7.7%，烟酒及用品、家庭设备用品及维修服务、医疗保健和个人用品、交通和通讯分别下降0.2%、0.7%、0.6%、1.9%。主要工业品出厂价格指数101.39，上升1.39%；原材料、燃料、动力购进价格指数106.52，上升6.52%。房屋销售价格指数110.9，上升10.9%，土地交易价格指数103.4，上升3.4%,房屋租赁价格指数103.3，上升3.3%。

国民经济和社会发展存在的主要问题是：经济增长方式转变和经济结构调整步伐有待进一步加快，第三产业比重仍然偏低，消费需求对经济增长的拉动作用相对较弱；社会低收入群体收入增长相对缓慢；经济社会持续发展面临的资源、环境、劳动力等方面压力加重等。

二、农业

2005年，我市各级党委、政府认真贯彻落实“三农”政策，采取有力措施确保农业增产、增效，积极推进城乡统筹发展。全市认真落实种粮、良种和农机具购置补贴等各项惠民政策，全面取消了农业税，历史上首次实现了农民“零负担”。农林牧渔业生产在结构调整中继续保持平稳增长，农业基础设施和生产条件不断改善，基础地位得到进一步强化。

粮食生产丰收。全市粮食播种面积748.88万亩，增长20.6%,亩产达到421公斤，总产量达到315.02万吨，这是从1999年以来相隔六年，我市粮食总产再次超过三百万吨。2005年末，全市实有耕地面积42.1万公顷，减少0.4%。

主要农产品产量如下:

	2005年(万吨)	比上年+-%
粮食总产量	315.02	18.8
其中: 小麦	153.55	18.0
玉米	147.86	23.0
花生	50.39	-13.2
蔬菜(不含果用瓜)	579.21	-13.8
水果	73.73	-1.5

全年完成造林面积1.61万公顷，下降50.5%；森林覆盖率31.7%，提高1.9个百分点。全年完成幼林抚育面积2.29万公顷，下降30.8%。

畜牧业生产持续稳定发展。畜牧业生产紧紧围绕农民增收和农村经济发展的目标，突出结构调整、示范园区建设和新技术推广应用等重点工作，加快产业化经营和标准化生产步伐。

主要畜产品产量如下：

	2005年（万吨）	比上年+－%
肉类总产量	81.94	8.4
其中：猪肉	28.07	5.5
牛、羊奶	50.82	6.0
禽蛋	38.63	1.7

渔业生产产量下降。水产品总产量127.27万吨，下降3.9%，其中，捕捞产量40.06万吨，下降8.9%；养殖产量87.21万吨，下降1.4%。海、淡水养殖面积6.47万公顷，增长1.6%。

农村基础设施和生产条件明显改善。2005年末，全市自来水受益村达5320个，全市拥有农业机械总动力619.69万千瓦。农用拖拉机16.3万台，农用载重汽车1.16万辆；农村用电量37.26亿千瓦时，增长12.7%；地膜覆盖面积17.51万公顷，增长3.7%。

三、工业与建筑业

全市工业经济保持了较快增长，结构更趋优化。2005 年全市完成工业增加值 1266.79 亿元，增长 21.0%。国有及年产品销售收入 500 万元以上的非国有工业企业（以下简称规模以上工业企业）完成增加值 1063.3 亿元，增长 29.4%。其中，国有及国有控股企业完成 217.4 亿元，增长 16.1%；集体企业完成 147.5 亿元，增长 6.0%；股份制企业完成 453.7 亿元，增长 33.4%；外资及港澳台企业完成 318.1 亿元，增长 42.6%；其他经济类型企业完成 46.9 亿元，增长 67.0%。轻、重工业协调发展，轻工业增加值 525 亿元，重工业增加值 538.3 亿元，分别增长 27.7%和 29.4%，轻重工业的比例为 49.4:50.6。

2005 年，全市“四大工业基地”和“六大产业集群”集群效应逐步呈现，有力促进了工业的快速发展。四大工业基地完成工业总产值 2334.7 亿元，占规模以上工业总产值的 54.33%；六大产业集群完成总产值 1685.86 亿元，占 39.2%。

规模以上工业主要产品产量如下：

	2005 年	比上年+－%
纱	7.2 万吨	4.0
布	5.1 亿米	-0.8
化学纤维	9.6 万吨	9.9
卷烟	753.6 亿支	2.4
啤酒	435.2 万千升	11
原盐	10 万吨	-16.7
发电量	98.6 亿千瓦时	11
钢材	330.3 万吨	43.9
原油加工量	378.9 万吨	-21.9
烧碱	16.1 万吨	8.2
纯碱	62.5 万吨	2.6
化学农药	6524 吨	74.5
染料	13979 吨	17.7
轮胎外胎	3967.3 万条	96.9
水泥	210.8 万吨	19.9
汽车	31055 辆	-50.4
彩色电视机	1324.3 万台	38.2
家用电冰箱	908.8 万台	11.5
房间空调器	983.6 万台	0.6

规模以上工业运行质量显著提高。2005 年实现利税总额 373.3 亿元，利润 186.4 亿元。产品销售收入 4266.8 亿元，增长 28.5%。工业经济效益综合指数为 173，比上年提高 22.6 个百分点。资本保值增值率为 122.55%，产品销售率为 98.1%。

产品结构调整取得明显成效，高新技术产品为全市工业经济提供了新的发展动力。全年规模以上工业企业共完成高新技术产品产值 1296.16 亿元，比上年增长 14.77%，占工业总产值的比重 30.16%。

建筑业生产稳定增长。全年实现增加值 132.96 亿元，增长 9.2%。实现利税总额 19.5 亿元，增长 34.5%。

四、固定资产投资

2005 年，全社会固定资产投资完成 1456.6 亿元，增长 45.0%。规模以上固定资产投资 1403.3 亿元，增长 45.6%。投资结构不断优化。在规模以上投资中，第一产业投资 29 亿元，比上年增长 5%；第二产业投资 789.2 亿元，增长 45.9%，第三产业投资 585.1 亿元，增长 40.7%。2005 年，我市一批重量级项目步入施工阶段，带动投资增长，海湾大桥（北桥位）、滨海公路北段、浮山湾奥林匹克中心项目、青岛市即墨至平度高速公路（青银二期）、青岛临港产业加工区海尔工业园、招商局国际码头、青岛发电厂烟气脱硫工程等亿元以上大项目投资贡献明显。

全年规模以上固定资产投资施工项目 5617 个，新开工项目 4945 个，竣工项目 681 个；在建项目计划总投资规模 3243.5 亿元，增长 54.6%。全年新增固定资产 611.4 亿元，项目建成投产率 12.1%，固定资产交付使用率 43.6%。

全市各类房屋竣工面积 1378.8 万平方米，下降 4.5%，其中，商品房竣工面积 811.2 万平方米，增长 13.1%。商品房销售面积 739.9 万平方米,增长 27%。

全市固定资产投资新增主要生产能力和效益：

卷烟	万箱/年	11.3
合成橡胶	吨/年	2000
轮胎外胎	万条/年	339.6
候机楼	座	1
	万平方米	10
移动电话机（手持机）	万部/年	480
移动通信基站	个/年	102
高等院校：学生席位	个	15570
建筑面积	万平方米	19.5

五、交通运输、邮电和旅游业

基础设施建设力度加大。公路建设成效显著，高速公路总里程 525 公里。港口建设取得新进展，全年港口吞吐量 1.87 亿吨,增长 14.9%;外贸吞吐量 1.4 亿吨,增长 14.8%;集装箱吞吐量 631 万标准箱，增长 22.8%。

各种运输方式完成的运输量：

	2005年	比上年＋－%
客运周转量	72.5亿人公里	5.74
铁路	16.8亿人公里	2.96
公路	54.6亿人公里	6.52
水运	1.1亿人公里	11.44
货运周转量	3314.1亿吨公里	37.58
铁路	69.9亿吨公里	28.23
公路	88.8亿吨公里	2.97
水运	3155.4亿吨公里	39.12

航空运输保持稳步增长。年末拥有国内航线72条，国际（地区）航线14条，全年航空旅客吞吐量达到555.04万人次，增长15.43%；航空行货邮吞吐量12.34万吨，增长18.1%。

邮电通信业快速增长。全年完成邮电业务总量97.02亿元，增长32.4%。其中，邮政业务总量5.77亿元，增长16.2%；电信业务总量91.25亿元，增长33.6%。信函8011.83万件，增长5.97%；网络信息技术不断普及和提高，2005年互联网用户累计达84.3万户，增长27.7%，使用时长达275.6亿分钟。年末市话交换机总容量达320.16万门；年末市话用户达到227.48万户，其中新装电话21.9万户；全市移动电话发展到383.64万户，其中年内新增125.2万户。

旅游业强劲增长。全市旅游总收入达 256.58 亿元，增长 23.6%，其中国内旅游总收入 222.59 亿元，增长 21.1%；国际旅游收入 4.15 亿美元，增长 44.3%。全年共接待国内外游客 2517.47 万人次，增长 13.9%；其中国内游客 2449.03 万人次，增长 13.5%；海外游客 68.44 万人次，增长 31.0%。

六、国内贸易

2005 年，在居民收入增加、消费能力提升和旅游、会展经济的带动下，城乡消费品市场规模进一步扩大。全年实现社会消费品零售额突破 800 亿大关，达 865.91 亿元，增长 15.8%。城乡市场协调发展，城市市场实现零售额 668.21 亿元，增长 16.9%，农村市场实现零售额 197.7 亿元，增长 12.5%。

商品交易市场规模扩大。全市商品交易市场（含集市贸易市场）830 处，增加 6 处。其中：消费品市场 763 处，增加 3 处；生产资料市场 67 处，增加 3 处。

居民消费结构升级明显加快，餐饮、汽车、文化娱乐、旅游等成为消费市场的主要拉动力量。全年餐饮业实现零售额 105.1 亿元，增长 15.1%；限额以上汽车零售额达到 62.3 亿元，增长 35%；通讯器材零售额 10.9 亿元，增长 44.3%。

七、对外经济

2005 年，全市对外开放水平继续提高，在更大范围和更深程度参与国际经济竞争与合作，进一步构筑全方位、多层次、宽领域的对外开放新格局。

对外贸易实现较快增长。青岛地区（含中央、省公司）实现外贸进出口总额330.22亿美元，增长22.4%；其中，出口额194.22亿美元，增长23.1%，进口额136.00亿美元，增长21.4%。青岛市（不含中央、省公司）实现外贸进出口总额304.55亿美元，增长25.2%；其中，出口额175.88亿美元，进口额128.67亿美元，分别增长26.4%和23.5%。外商投资企业是全市外贸出口的主体，出口额107.25亿美元，增长20.3%,占全市出口额的比重为61.0%。

据青岛海关统计，青岛口岸对外贸易进出口总额 693.29 亿美元，增长 22.1%，其中出口额 395.99 亿美元，进口额 297.3 亿美元，分别增长 23.8%和 19.9%。

利用外资稳步提升。全年共批准利用外资项目 2530 个，增长 4.4%，合同外资 95.45 亿美元，增长 42.1%，外商直接投资达到 36.56 亿美元，增长 13.1%。

对外经济技术合作步伐加快。全年完成对外承包工程、劳务合作和设计咨询合同金额2.81亿美元，增长33.5%，营业额2.73亿美元，增长32.2%；共外派人员6377人次，增长33.9%。

对内招商引资发展迅速。2005 年全年引进内资 258.75 亿元，增长 34.2%，其中，引进亿元以上内资项目 32 个，实际到位内资 65 亿元。

八、金融和保险业

金融业健康运行。年末金融机构本外币存款余额达2849.24亿元，比年初增加428.15亿元，其中，人民币存款余额2697.54亿元，比年初增加420.92亿元。城乡居民储蓄继续增加，本外币储蓄达1413.33亿元，其中人民币存款余额达1343.10亿元，比年初增加253.61亿元。各项贷款稳定增长，信贷结构得到优化。金融机构本外币贷款余额达2232.81亿元，比年初增加319.06亿元，其中，人民币贷款余额2039.48亿元，比年初增加280.14亿元。在人民币贷款中，短期贷款余额981.51亿元，比年初增加91.7亿元；中长期贷款余额807.35亿元，比年初增加123.15亿元。

保险业平稳发展。全年实现保费收入49.57亿元，增长4.2%，其中：财产保费收入15.98亿元，增长16.8%；人身保费收入33.59亿元，下降0.9%。赔款支出金额14.41亿元，其中财产险赔付金额9.27亿元，人身险赔付金额5.14亿元。

九、科学技术和教育

科技事业加快发展。初步统计，2005年全市共取得重要科技成果438项。获得国家级科技奖励4项，其中，国家发明奖1项，科学技术进步奖3项；获得省级科技奖励71项，其中，科学技术最高奖1项，自然科学奖4项，技术发明奖3项，科学技术进步奖63项。全年研发经费占GDP比重达到2.2%。

科技市场交易活跃。全年共成交技术合同项目1414项,成交额4.3亿元。全年专利申请量5603件，授权专利2341件。

教育事业稳步发展。2005年末，全市共有各类大专院校28所（含民办高校），其中普通高校25所，在校学生22.2万人，增长20.7%。中等学校395所，其中，普通中学317所，在校学生39.11万人，下降10.3%；中等专业学校和技工学校78所，在校学生17.81万人，增长9.5%。接受中等职业教育的学生占高中阶段在校生的56.1%。共有小学1004所，在校学生47.98万人，增长0.6%。学龄儿童入学率100%，初中入学率达99%以上。

十、文化、卫生和体育

文化事业繁荣发展。全市共有各类文化机构489处。其中，影剧院29处，电影队214个，文化馆（站）172处，博物馆8处，公共图书馆13处，艺术表演团体12个，广播电台1座、12套节目，电视台1座、15套节目，全市有线电视用户达到176.6万户，并提前完成了市区60万有线电视用户的数字化整体转换。全市出版各类杂志1734万册，出版报纸54897万份。全年共创作发表文艺作品420篇（件、幅），获得省以上奖励53项。全市共有档案馆14处。

卫生事业稳步发展。年末全市共有卫生机构（含诊所）2632处，其中，医院、卫生院232处，卫生防疫机构20处，妇幼保健机构10处，门诊部（所）、卫生保健所、医务室1858处。年末各类卫生技术人员3.4万人，其中，医生1.5万人。全市拥有医疗床位3万张，其中，医院、卫生院床位2.8万张。

体育事业取得新的进步。全市运动员在各项比赛中共获得金牌263枚，银牌227枚，铜牌179枚。共打破全国纪录2项，全省纪录3项。全市共有体育专业队7个，队员107人。重点体校13所，学员2374人，业余体校5所，学员7840人。群众体育和全民健身运动广泛开展。

十一、城市建设与环境保护

城市平均每天供水量91万吨，增长8%。城市全年实际用水量2.9亿吨，增长8.8%，其中生产用水和生活用水分别为1.23亿吨和1.67亿吨。

城市使用液化气、煤制气、天然气的总户数达到105.2万户，增长13.9%。全年供应液化气总量7.95万吨，增长35.8%，供应煤制气总量16573万立方米，增长6.9%。供应天然气总量7455.6万立方米，增长175%。城市气化率达到100%。

全社会用电量193.8亿千瓦时，增长15.4%。其中，工业用电127.8亿千瓦时，城乡居民生活用电33.8亿千瓦时，分别增长13.5%和42.9%。

全年新增供热面积683.2万平方米，累计供热面积达到2804万平方米，增长32.2%。

年末市区公共汽、电车线路187条，较上年持平。共有营运的公交汽、电车3911辆，增长1.6%。年末全市共有出租汽车8121辆,增长0.3%。

年末城市道路总长度1978.63公里，增长12.7%。扩建、翻建道路224条。城市下水道总长度2160.3公里，增长7.9%。

环境保护得到加强。全年市区空气质量功能区达标率100%；市区空气质量优良天数达到331天，占90.7%，比上年提高0.3个百分点。市区区域环境噪声平均值53.4分贝，市区交通干线噪声平均值68.3分贝。市区共植树199.3万株。建成区绿化覆盖率达到38.8%，比上年提高0.8个百分点；市区园林绿地面积达11140.2公顷，增长10.9%；新增公共绿地292.6公顷，人均占有公共绿地11.8平方米，增长7.2%。市区现有公园、动物园47个。

十二、人口、人民生活和社会保障

人口增速加快。年末全市总人口为740.9万人（户籍人口），增长1.3%。其中，市区265.43万人，增长2.7%；五市（县级）475.47万人，增长0.6%。全年新出生人口75530人，出生率为10.26‰；死亡人口48109人，死亡率为6.54‰；全年净增人口97824人，人口自然增长率为3.72‰。

城乡居民生活水平显著提高。市委、市政府采取各项措施提高城乡居民特别是低收入群体的收入水平，城市居民人均可支配收入 12920 元，增长 16.5%；人均消费性支出 9883 元，增长 9.8%；城市恩格尔系数 37.6%，下降 0.4 个百分点。农民人均纯收入 5806 元，增长 14.3%；人均生活消费支出 3737 元，增长 11.4%；农村恩格尔系数 37.5%，下降 1.2 个百分点。社会职工平均工资 15616 元，增长 16.1%，其中，在岗职工平均工资 16015 元，增长 15.0%。

城乡居民居住条件进一步改善。据抽样调查，年末城市人均现住房建筑面积22.96平方米，增加1.75平方米；农民人均住房使用面积29.54平方米，增加1.55平方米。

就业局势稳定，社会保障水平不断提高。2005年末全市单位从业人员224.3万人,增长8.3%。全年通过各种渠道共安排失业人员实现就业15.4万人，组织4.5万人次失业人员参加就业培训，组织农村劳动力转移培训4.8万人。年末全市城镇登记失业率为2.96%，下降0.14个百分点。2005年末全市参加基本养老保险人数为131.1万人，参加失业保险人数为105.1万人，全年累计领取失业保险金的人数为8.9万人，下降8.5%。

社会福利事业成效显著。2005年全市各类社会福利院床位达14371张，收养8092人。

注：

1. 公报中部分统计数据为初步统计数。
2. 公报中全市生产总值、各产业增加值、按经济类型分组的增加值绝对数按现价计算，增长速度按可比价计算。
3. 根据经济普查数据并按照新的核算方法计算，全市2004年GDP总量调整为2270.16亿元。其中第一产业为163.49亿元，第二产业为1149.94亿元，第三产业为956.73亿元。
4. 部分工业产品产量系集团口径。
5. 规模以上投资统计范围包括城镇、农村 50 万元以上投资项目。
6. 市话交换机总容量包括小灵通容量。
7. 社会职工平均工资：各单位职工在一定时期内平均每人所得的工资额。包括：国有经济、集体经济、联营经济、股份制经济、外商和港、澳、台投资经济、私营经济单位等。在岗职工平均工资：各单位在岗职工在一定时期内平均每人所得的工资额。
8. 城乡居民住房面积分别根据城乡住户抽样调查取得，由于方法改变，城市居民住房面积数据与以往口径不同。
9. 自 2005 年 8 月起，实际利用外资统计数据采用商务部确认的外商直接投资（FDI）数据。

Qingdao Statistics Bureau - Statistics Communiqué
Qingdao's Economic and Social Development during 2005

February 13, 2006

Thanks to the local government's faithfulness to a scientific development approach that focused on building Qingdao into "one of China's major regional centers and internationally-known metropolises", the city, during 2005, achieved and sustained a harmonious, healthy and rapid economic growth and social progress in all fields as well as overcoming various difficulties and problems in its economic development.

I. General

Qingdao maintained a rapid economic growth momentum. Preliminary statistics showed a gross domestic product (GDP) of 269.55 billion RMB, up 16.9% or 0.1 percentage points over the previous year. The increase was the largest since 1994. Primary industries contributed 17.464 billion RMB in added value, up 0.4%. Secondary industries contributed 139.975 billion RMB, up 20.0%. And tertiary industries contributed 112.111 billion RMB, up 16.0%. The percentage of primary, secondary and tertiary industries was 6.5, 51.9 and 41.6 respectively.

The macro economy grew steadily. In 2005, Qingdao realized 17.634 billion RMB in the local government's general budget revenue, up 35.1% and 20.306 billion RMB in the general budget expenditure, up 23.4%. Tax revenue grew at a high rate. The national tax revenue (including those collected by customs) rose 15.1% to 39.301 billion RMB and local tax revenue increased 20.0% to 12.088 billion RMB. The macro economy continued to experience high prosperity. The entrepreneur's confidence index reflecting entrepreneurs' confidence and expectations for the macro economy was 130.77 while the business prosperity index reflecting companies' overall production and operation status was 147.65.

Prices picked up by a small margin. The total consumer price index was 102.3, up 2.3% from the previous year. The price of food, clothes, entertainment, educational and cultural products and services increased by 2.1%, 8.3%, 0.4% and 7.7% while that of tobacco and wine, household appliances and repair services, medical care and personal articles and transportation and communications decreased by 0.2%, 0.7%, 0.6% and 1.9% respectively. The factory price index for main industrial products was 101.39, up 1.39%. The purchase price index for raw materials, fuels and power was 106.52, up 6.52%. The housing price index was 110.9, up 10.9%. The land trading price index was 103.4, up 3.4%. The house rental price index was 103.3, up 3.3%.

Main problems that existed in economic and social development included: transformation in economic growth pattern and economic restructuring needs for acceleration; the percentage of tertiary industry needed to be increased; the driving effect of consumer demands on the economic growth was relatively weak; the growth in income for the low-income group was relatively slow; and pressures on resources, environment, workforce and other elements for the sustained economic and social development were on rise.

II. Agriculture

Active actions were taken to ensure an increase in agricultural production and efficiency and rural and urban areas developed in a planned way. Various preferential policies were carried out for farmers to grow crops, fine breed and purchase farming machinery. Agricultural tax was removed to unburden farmers for the first time in history. Agriculture, forest, animal husbandry and fish production continued to increase steadily during structural adjustments. Agricultural infrastructure and facilities and production conditions were continuously improved and the agricultural foundation was further consolidated.

The crop harvest was good. In 2005, the sown area for crops totaled 7,488,800 *mu* (499,253 hectares), up 20.6%. The grain output reached 421 kg per *mu*. Total grain output reached 3,150,200 tons, exceeding 3,000,000 tons again in the past 6 years since 1999. By the end of 2005, Qingdao had 421,000 hectares of cultivated land, down 0.4%.

Output of Major Farm Products:

	2005 (ton)	+/-% over the previous year
Total grain output	3,150,200	18.8
Including: wheat	1,535,500	18.0
corn	1,478,600	23.0
Peanuts	503,900	-13.2
Vegetables (excluding melons)	5,792,100	-13.8
Fruits	737,300	-1.5

16,100 hectares of trees were planted in the year, down 50.5%. Forest coverage reached 31.7%, up 1.9 percent. 22,900 hectares of young growth were cultivated, down 30.8%.

Steady growth was seen in animal husbandry. Concentration was made on increasing farmers' income and the economy of rural areas. Key works included the sector restructuring, development of demonstration areas, and new technology promotions to speed up industrialized operations and standardized production.

Output of Major Livestock Products:

	2005 (ton)	+/-% over the previous year
Meats	819,400	8.4
Including: pork	280,700	5.5
Cow and goat's milk	508,200	6.0
Fowl eggs	386,300	1.7

Fishery production decreased. The total output of aquatic products increased 3.9% to 1,272,700 tons. Of the total, 400,600 tons were from fishing, down 8.9% and 872,100 tons were from farmed fish, a decline of 1.4%. The combined seawater and freshwater farming area was 64,700 hectares, up 1.6%.

Agricultural infrastructure and production conditions were significantly improved. By the end of 2005, there were 5,320 villages with running water. Power from farming machines totaled 6,196,900 KW. Farming tractors totaled 163,000 units and heavy farming trucks totaled 11,600 units. Rural power consumption totaled 3.726 billion KWh, up 12.7%. Total greenhouse area was 175,100 hectares, up 3.7%.

III. Industry and Construction

Industry grew rapidly and its infrastructure optimized. In 2005, Qingdao realized an industrial added value of 126.679 billion RMB, up 21.0%. The added value generated by state-owned enterprises and non-state owned enterprises with an annual sales revenue over 5 million RMB (hereinafter referred to as the industrial enterprises above designated size) totaled 106.33 billion RMB, up 29.4%. Of the total, 21.74 billion was finished by the state-owned and controlled enterprises, up 16.1 %; 14.75 billion by collective enterprises, up 6.0%; 45.37 billion by shareholder enterprises, up 33.4%; 31.81 billion by enterprises invested by foreign companies and by compatriots from Hong Kong, Macao and Taiwan, up 42.6%; and 4.69 billion by other types of businesses, up 67.0%. Both light and heavy industries grew relationally. Light industry finished 52.5 billion RMB in added value, up 27.7% and heavy industry generated 53.83 billion RMB, up 29.4%. The ratio of light to heavy industry was 49.4:50.6.

In 2005, Qingdao's 4 largest industrial bases and 6 industrial cluster areas took shape and became a driving force for its rapid industrial growth. The former generated 233.47 billion RMB in industrial added value, accounting for 54.33% of the total industrial output value; and latter finished at 168.586 billion RMB, accounting for 39.2%.

Output of Major Industrial Products by Industrial Enterprises above Designated Size:

Product	2005	+/− % over the previous year
Yarn	72,000 tons	4.0
Cloth	510,000,000 meters	-0.8
Chemical fiber	96,000 tons	9.9
Cigarettes	75.36 billion pieces	2.4
Beer	4,352,000 kilolitres	11
Raw salt	100,000 tons	-16.7
Hydro Electricity	9.86 billion kWh	11
Steels	3,303,000 tons	43.9
Crude oil processed	3,789,000 tons	-21.9
Caustic soda	161,000 tons	8.2
Soda ash	625,000 tons	2.6
Chemical pesticide	6,524 tons	74.5
Dye stuffs	13,979 tons	17.7
Tire casings	39,673,000 pieces	96.9
Cement	2,108,000 tons	19.9
Motor vehicles	31,055 units	-50.4
Color TV sets	13,243,000 sets	38.2
Household refrigerators	9,088,000 sets	11.5
Room air conditioners	9,836,000 sets	0.6

Industrial enterprises above the designated size performed well. In 2005, total pre-tax profits were 37.33 billion RMB with after-tax profits of 18.64 billion RMB. Sales income rose 28.5% to 426.68 billion RMB. The total industrial enterprise performance index was 173, up 22.6 percent over the previous year. The capital maintenance and appreciation was 122.55 %. The sales ratio was 98.1%.

The achievement was significant in product mix and industry restructuring. High concentrated technology and new products were new driving forces for the industrial sector. Industrial enterprises above the designated size turned out new and high-tech products worth 129.616 billion RMB, up 14.77% year-to-year, accounting for 30.16% of the total turnover for the industrial sector.

The construction industry grew steadily. In 2005, the industry generated 13.296 billion RMB in added value, up 9.2% and 1.95 billion RMB in pre-tax profit, up 34.5%.

IV. Fixed Assets Investment

The fixed asset investment in 2005 totaled 145.66 billion RMB, up 45.0%. Investment made by the industrial enterprises above the designated size totaled 140.33 billion RMB, up 45.6%. The investment structure continued to be optimized. Of that figure, 2.9 billion RMB was made in primary industries, up 5%, 78.92 billion RMB in secondary industries, up 45.9% and 58.51 billion RMB in tertiary industries, up 40.7%. A number of key projects went into construction phase, which absorbed a large investment. Large investment projects with an investment of over 100 million RMB each contributed significantly to the investment, including the Bay Bridge (north part), the North Part of the Seaside Highway, the Olympic Sailing Center at Fushan Bay, the Jimo-Pingdu Expressway (Second Phase of the Qing-Yin Expressway), Qingdao Haier Industrial Park Port Industry Processing Area, the Investment Bureau's International Wharf and the Qingdao Power Plant Desulfurizing Project.

The fixed assets investment construction projects above the designated size numbered 5,617. New start-up projects numbered 4,945 and completed projects numbered 681. The amount of investment in projects in progress was 324.35 billion RMB, up 54.6%. Another 61.14 billion RMB was invested in fixed assets for the whole year. The project completion ratio was 12.1% and the fixed asset delivery ratio was 43.6%.

13,788,000 square meters of buildings were completed in Qingdao, down 4.5%. Of the total, 8,112,000 were commercial buildings, up 13.1%. Commercial buildings floor space sold was 7,399,000 square meters, up 27%.

Newly increased capacities through investment in fixed assets:

Description	Measurement unit	Increased capacities in 2005
Cigarettes	box/year	113,000
Synthetic rubber	ton/year	2,000
Tire casings	piece /year	3,396,000
Airport departure terminal	building	1
	square meter	100,000
Mobile phones (handsets)	unit/year	4,800,000
Mobile communication base station	number of station/year	102
Higher education schools:	student places	15,570
	square meter of floor space	195,000

V. Transportation, Post, Telecommunications and Tourism

Infrastructure investment was increased and highway construction enjoyed remarkable achievements. Qingdao expressways totaled 525 km in length. New progress was made in port construction. Port throughput totaled 187,000,000 tons for the whole year, up 14.9%, with 140,000,000 tons handled for foreign trade, up 14.8%. Container throughput reached 6,310,000 TEUs, up 22.8%.

Volume completed by various transportation means:

	2005	+/− % over the previous year
Passenger volume	7.25 billion person-km	5.74
Railways	1.68 billion person-km	2.96
Highways	5.46 billion person-km	6.52
Waterways	110,000,000 person-km	11.44
Cargo volumes	331.41 billion ton-km	37.58
Railways	6.99 billion ton-km	28.23
Highways	8.88 billion ton-km	2.97
Waterways	315.54 billion ton-km	39.12

Air transportation maintained a steady growth. By the end of the year, there were 72 domestic airlines and 14 international and regional airlines in operation. The airport passenger throughput for the whole year reached 5,550,400 person-times, up 15.43% and air cargo and mail throughput was 123,400 tons, up 18.1%.

The post and telecommunication industries grew quickly. Postal and telecommunication service business transactions in 2005 totaled 9.702 billion RMB, up 32.4%. Of the total, 577,000,000 were from the postal service, up 16.2%, and 9.125 billion from the telecommunication service, up 33.6%. The total number of letters handled was 80,118,300, up 5.97%. Access to Internet and other information technologies improved and experienced a widespread increase. In 2005, Internet users numbered 843,000, up 27.7% and time online reached 27.56 billion minutes. The total capacity of telephone exchanges reached 3,201,600 lines. At the end of the year, fixed-line telephone users numbered 2,274,800, of which 219,000 were new users. Mobile phone users numbered 3,836,400, of which 1,252,000 were new users.

The tourism industry maintained a strong growth momentum. Tourism income for the year totaled 25.658 billion RMB, up 23.6%. Of the total, 22.259 billion was from domestic tourism, up 21.1% and 415 million USD from international tourism, up 44.3%. Tourists to Qingdao duing the year totaled 25,174,700 person-times, up 13.9%. Of the total, 24,490,300 were domestic tourists, up 13.5% and 684,400 overseas tourists, up 31.0%.

VI. Domestic Trade

Consumer markets in both rural and urban areas expanded in size due to an increase in individual income and consumption and travel and conference and exhibition events. In 2005, total retail sales of consumer goods increased by 15.8% to 86.591 billion RMB, exceeding the 80 billion RMB mark. Of the total, 66.821 billion was generated by the urban market, up 16.9% and 19.77 billion by the rural market, up 12.5%.

The size of the commodity exchange markets increased. There were 830 marketplaces for commodity exchange in Qingdao and the number was increased by 6. Of the total, 763 were for consumer goods and increased by 3 and 67 for production materials and increased by 3.

The pace of residents' consumption upgrades was significantly quickened. Catering, cars, culture and entertainment and tourism have become driving forces in the consumer market. The catering industry generated 10.51 billion RMB in retail sales, up 15.1. The retail sales of motor vehicles above the limited value reached 6.23 billion RMB, up 35%; and retail sales of communications equipment amounted to 1.09 billion RMB, up 44.3%.

VII. Foreign Trade

The economy was further exposed to the outside world. Participation in international competition and cooperation widened and deepened. The development of an all round open economy and in a wide field are building up at many levels.

Foreign trade saw a rapid growth. Qingdao's import and export volume (including that of companies directly controlled by provincial and central governments) was 33.022 billion USD, up 22.4% over last year, with exports amounting to 19.422 billion USD, up 23.1% and imports amounting to 13.600 billion USD, up 21.4%. Excluding companies directly controlled by provincial and central governments trade volume was 30.455 billion USD, up 25.2%, with exports amounting to 17.588 billion USD, up 26.4% and imports amounting to 12.867 billion USD, up 23.5%. Foreign investment enterprise played a leading role in exports, which amounted to 10.725 billion USD, up 20.3%, accounting for 61.0% of Qingdao's total exports.

According to Qingdao Customs' statistics, imports and exports registered at Qingdao ports totaled 69.329 billion USD, up 22.1%. Of the total, 39.599 billion were exports, up 23.8% and 29.73 billion were imports, up 19.9%.

Foreign investment increased steadily. In 2005, Qingdao approved 2,530 foreign investment projects, up 4.4%. Contractual investment amounted to 9.545 USD, up 42.1%. Direct foreign investment reached 3.656 billion USD, up 13.1%.

Overseas economic and technical cooperation were stepped up. Total contracted value of overseas contractor projects, personnel and design consulting services was 281 million USD, up 33.5%. Turnover amounted to 273 million USD, up 32.2%; the number of personnel sent overseas reached 6,377, up 33.9%.

Domestic investment increased rapidly. In 2005, Qingdao attracted a total investment of 25.875 billion RMB, up 34.2%. There were 32 new domestic investment projects each with an investment of over 100 million RMB. The actual domestic investment amounted to 6.5 billion RMB.

VIII. Finance and Insurance

The finance sector was in healthy operation. At year-end, the balance of local and foreign currencies on the deposit accounts with financial institutions in Qingdao stood at 284.924 billion RMB, an increase of 42.815 billion RMB from the beginning of this year. The balance of deposits in local currency (RMB) was 269.754 billion, an increase of RMB42.092 billion from the beginning of the year. Resident savings in rural and urban areas continued to increase. Savings of local and foreign currencies reached 141.333 billion RMB. The balance of savings in local currency (RMB) was 134.310 billion, an increase of 25.361 from the beginning of the year. Various loans increased steadily and the credit mix was optimized. The loan balance in local and foreign currencies reached 223.281 billion RMB, an increase of 31.906 billion RMB from the beginning of this year. The loan balance in local currency (RMB) was 203.948 billion, an increase of 28.014 billion RMB from the beginning of the year. Of the total loans in RMB, 98.151 billion was in short-term loans, an increase of 9.17 billion RMB from the beginning of the year; and 80.735 billion RMB in medium- and long-term loans, an increase of 12.315 billion RMB from the beginning of the year.

The insurance industry grew steadily. The insurance premium totaled 4.957 billion RMB, up 4.2%. Of the total, 1.598 billion was for property insurance, up 16.8%; 3.359 billion RMB for personal insurance, down 0.9%. Expenses for claims amounted to 1.441 billion RMB. Of this figure, 927 million was for property claims and 514 million for personal claims.

IX. Science, Technology and Education

The science and technology sector developed at a fast pace. Preliminary statistics show that Qingdao achieved 438 key scientific and research results in 2005 and received four (4) national scientific and technological prizes. One (1) was for national invention and three (3) were for scientific and technological progress; it also received 70 provincial-level scientific and technological prizes. Of them, one (1) was the top scientific and technological prize, two (2) were for natural science, three (3) were for technological inventions and sixty-three (63) were for scientific and technological progress. The annual research and development budget accounted for 2.2% of the GDP.

The technology market is brisk. In 2005 there were a total of 1,414 technology transfer contracts completed with a value of 430 million RMB; 5,603 patents were pending and 2,341 more were granted with patent certificates

The education sector developed at a steady pace. By the end of 2005, there were 28 higher education schools (including private schools) including 25 ordinary colleges and universities. There were 222,000 students enrolled, up 20.7%. Secondary schools numbered 395. Of them, 317 were ordinary middle schools enrolling 391,100 students, down 10.3%; technical secondary schools and vocational schools numbered 78, enrolling 178,100, up 9.5%. The number of vocational secondary students accounted for 56.1% of the number of senior middle school students. There were 1,004 primary schools enrolling 479,800 pupils, up 0.6% and 100% of pre-school aged children were schooled. The schooling of youngsters for junior middle school was over 99%.

X. Culture, Public Health Services and Sports

The cultural sector was prosperous and continually growing. There were a total of 489 cultural institutions in Qingdao, including 29 cinemas, 214 movie-projecting teams, 172 cultural centers, 8 museums, 13 public libraries, 12 performing arts troupes, one radio and broadcasting station with 12 programs and one TV station with 15 programs. Cable TV users numbered 1,766,000. The digitalization was completed in advance, serving 600,000 cable TV users in urban areas. 17,340,000 magazines and 548,970,000 were published. 420 artistic works were produced and published. 53 prizes from the provincial-level and above were received. There were 14 archives in Qingdao.

Public health institutions grew steadily. At the end of the year, there were 2,632 public health institutions including

232 hospitals, 20 epidemic prevention institutions, 10 children and women's health care centers and 1,858 clinical and medical health locations. There were 34,000 medical professionals, including 15,000 doctors. Medical beds numbered 30,000, with 28,000 beds in hospitals and clinics.

New progress was made in the area of sports. Qingdao athletes won 263 gold medals, 227 silver medals and 179 bronze medals in various games, creating 2 new national records and 3 new provincial records. There were 7 professional sport teams totaling 107 members. Sports schools numbered 13, enrolling 2,374 students. Part-time sports schools numbered 5, enrolling 7,840 students. Mass sports and fitness exercise programs were very popular and enjoyed all over Qingdao.

XI. Urban Construction and Environmental Protection

Urban water supply averaged 910,000 tons per day, up 8%. The actual water consumption for the year totaled 290 million tons, up 8.8%, including 123 million tons for production use and 167 million tons for residential use.

Liquefied petroleum fuel, coal energy and natural gas users numbered 1,052,000, up 13.9%. The total liquefied petroleum fuel supply for the year was 79,500 tons, up 35.8%. The total coal energy supply was 165,370,000 cubic meters, up 6.9%. The total natural gas supply was 74,556,000 cubic meters, up 175%. The urban fuel coverage was 100%.

Total electricity consumption was 19.38 billion kWh, up 15.4%, including 12.78 billion kWh for industrial use, up 13.5% and 3.38 billion kWh for residential use, up 42.9%.

Total heating space increased by 6,832,000 square meters to 28,040,000 square meters, up 32.2%,

There were 187 public bus lines and trolleys operating in urban areas, an equal number to last year. 3,911 public buses and trolleys were in operation, up 1.6%. Taxicabs numbered 8,121, up 0.3%.

Distance covered by roads in urban areas totaled 1,978.63 km, up 12.7%, 224 roads were expanded and rebuilt. The total length of underground sewers was 2,160.3 km, up 7.9%.

Environmental protection measures were strengthened. The air quality of functional regions all reached the desired standards. Acceptable air quality percentages in urban areas reached 331 days, accounting for 90.7% of the whole year, an increase of 0.3 percentage points over the previous year. Environmental noise pollution in urban areas averaged 53.4 dB. Noise pollution at traffic trunk lines averaged 68.3 dB. 1,993,000 trees were planted in urban areas with "green area" coverage of 38.8%, up 0.8%. The "green area" of parks and gardens totaled 11,140.2 hectares, up 10.9%. The increase in public "green area" was 292.6 hectares. Per capita "green area" was 11.8 square meters, up 7.2%. There are 47 parks and zoos in the City of Qingdao.

XII. Population, Lifestyle and Social Security

Qingdao's population is on the rise. At the end of the year, the total population was 7,409,000 (with permanent residence), up 1.3%. Of the total, 2,654,300 represent the population of the City of Qingdao, up 2.7%; 4,754,700 represent the population of the Greater Qingdao regions, up 0.6%. New births in 2005 totaled 75,530, a birth rate of 10.26‰. The number of deceased persons totaled 48,109, a percentage rate of 6.54‰. The population increased by 97,824 with a natural growth rate of 3.72‰.

Living standards improved significantly. Various measures were taken by local governments to increase residents' income, especially among low-income groups. The per capita average disposal income was 12,920 RMB, up 16.5%. The per capita consumption expense was 9,883 RMB, up 9.8%. The Engel Coefficient for urban areas was 37.6%, down 0.4 percentage points. The average net income among farmers was 5,806 RMB, up 14.3%; per capita consumption expense was 3,737 RMB, up 11.4%. The Engel Coefficient for rural areas was 37.5%, down 1.2 percentage points. Employees' average wage was 15,616 RMB, up 16.1%. The average wage was 16,015 RMB, up 15.0%.

Residents dwelling conditions in urban and rural areas were further improved. A survey showed that the per capita average floor space in urban areas was 22.96 square meters, an increase of 1.75 square meters; and the per capita average floor space for rural residents was 29.54 square meters, an increase of 1.55 square meters.

The employment situation was stable and the social security level continued to increase. At the end of 2005, the number of people employed in Qingdao was 2,243,000, up 8.3%. In 2005, of the 154,000 people unemployed, 45,000 were trained and 48,000 of the work force in rural areas were also trained to be farm-turned workers. At yearend, the registered urban unemployment rate was 2.96%, down 0.14 percentage points. People who benefited from the basic endowment insurance plan numbered 1,311,000, people who participated in the unemployment insurance program numbered 1,051,000, and people who received payment from the unemployment insurance program numbered 89,000, down 8.5%.

The social welfare sector made significant achievements. Nursing homes registered 14,371 beds with 8,092 residents.

Note:

1. Some figures are preliminary statistics.
2. Qingdao's total production value, industries' added value and the absolute added value grouped by the types of economy were calculated at current prices and growth rates were calculated at comparable prices.
3. According to economic census data and the new accounting method, Qingdao's GDP during 2004 was adjusted to 227.016 billion RMB, of which, 16.349 billion was from primary industries, 114.994 billion from secondary industries and 95.673 billion from tertiary industries.
4. Part of the industrial output was the group coverage.
5. Investment statistics on the above-designated size included rural and urban investment projects of at least 500,000 RMB.
6. The total exchanger capacity for local calls included Xiaolingtong or Smart Phones.
7. Employees' average wage means the average wage paid at a certain time to employees by employers of such ownership types as the state-owned, collectively-owned, joint operation, shareholding, privately-owned and investment by foreign business people and by compatriots from Hong Kong, Macao and Taiwan. The average wage referred to the average wage paid at a certain time to "on the job" employees.
8. Figures relating to floor space among urban and rural dwellers were based on a survey. Coverage statistics were different from previous ones in terms of floor space due to a change in methodology.
9. As of August 2005, the data on direct foreign investment (DFI) verified by the Ministry of Commerce is used for actual foreign investment statistics.

Note: If there is any contradiction between the English, Japanese and Korean versions of this report and the Chinese one, the Chinese version prevails.

2005年
青島市国民経済と社会発展官報統計

青島市統計局

（2006年2月13日）

2005年、市民は市委員会、市政府の正しい指導の下で、全国重点中心都市と世界的に著名な特色ある都市建設の目標を実現するために、科学的発展観にたって徹底的に推進してきている。マクロコントロールをいっそう強化し、経済発展の中でのいろいろな対立と困難を克服して努力している。市経済の急速かつ健全で調和のとれた持続的発展と各社会事業の全面的な進歩を促進させてきている。「十五」の主要計画目標を完成している。

青島の繁栄、青島の平安、青島の文明建設に大きな業績を上げてきている。

一、総　合

市経済わりに速い増大を維持

初歩的な計算で、市総生産（GDP）は、2695.5億元で16.9%増、昨年比0.1%の伸び、1994年以来最高の伸びであった。

その中、第1次産業の増加額は、174.64億元、0.4%増。第2次産業の増加額は1399.75億元、20.0%増、第三次産業の増加額は1121.11億元、16.0%増である。

第3次産業との比例の割合は、6.5：51.9：41.6である。

マクロ的経済効果は着実に伸びている。

2005年の市地方財政一般予算は、収入176.34億元、35.1%増。支出203.06億元、23.4%増である。

税収はわりに速い増加を維持し、年国税系統組織税収入は（税関を含む）393.01億元、15.1%増。地税収入は120.88億元、20.0%増である。

マクロ経済景気は高水準を維持

企業家に対するマクロ経済環境の自信と企業家の予測信頼指数の反映は、年末に130.37まで達した。企業総合生産経営状況と企業景気指数の経済効果の反映は147.65である。

市場物価は小幅の上昇

年消費者物価総指数は、102.3、昨年比2.3%上昇している。その中、食品、服装、娯楽教育文化用品とサービス、居住は2.1%、8.3%、0.4%、7.7%それぞれ上昇している。タバコと酒と日用品、家庭用品とメンテナンス「サービス、医療の保健と個人用品、交通と通信はそれぞれ0.2%、0.7%、0.6%、1.9%に下がっている。

主要な工業製品出荷価格指数は、101.39、1.39%上昇している。原材料、燃料、動力価格指数は、106.52購入、6.52%上昇である。

家屋販売価格指数は、110.9、10.9%上昇、土地の取引の価格指数は、103.4、3.4%上昇、家屋賃貸価格指数は、103.3、3.3%上昇である。

国民経済と社会発展にもたらす主要問題は、経済成長方式の転換と経済構造調整の足並みの一層の加速を待たなければならない。第三次産業の比重は依然として偏りがあり、低く、消費需要対経済成長の牽引作用が比較的弱い。社会低収入集団の収入増加は比較的緩慢であり、経済社会を持続発展するために直面する資源、環境、労働力等の面に圧力が加わっている。

二、農業

2005年、市の各級党委員会、政府は“三農業”の政策を徹底的に実行し、力強い措置をとり、農業の増産に効果をあげ、積極的に都市と農村の全体を発展させる計画をすすめた。

市は真剣に食糧、優良品種と農業機械補助金などの各恵民政策を取り入れ、農業税を全面的になくし、歴史上初めて農民“0負担”を実現した。

農業、林業、漁業、牧畜の生産は、構造調整の中で穏やかな増加を引き続き維持し、農業インフラと生産条件を絶えず改善し、基礎固めを一歩前進させてきた。

糧食生産は豊作

市の食糧作付面積は、748.88 万ムー、20.6%増。1 ムー当たりの収穫量は 421 キログラムまで達し、総生産量は 315.02 万トンである。これは 1999 年以来 6 年ぶりで、市食糧総生産量は再度 3 百万トンを超えた。

2005 年末、市実用耕地面積は、42.1 万ヘクタール、0.4%減である。

主要な農産物の生産高は次の通り。

	2005 年(万トン)	昨年比+-%
食糧の総生産量	315.02	18.8
その中小麦	153.55	18.0
トウモロコシ	147.86	23.0
落花生	50.39	-13.2
野菜(果実含まず、ウリ含む)	579.21	-13.8
果物	73.73	-1.5

年造林面積は、1.61 万ヘクタール、50.5%減、森林被覆比率 31.7%、1.9 パーセント増。

年植林面積は、2.29 万ヘクタールで、30.8%の減。

牧畜業生産は、持続的に安定し発展

牧畜業生産は、確実に農民の収益増加と農村経済発展の要となり、構造調整、模範園区の建設と新技術の応用を推し広める等重要な業務、企業的経営と生産の標準化の足並みを加速させている。

主要な畜産品の生産高は次の通り

	2005 年（万トン）	昨年比＋－%
肉類の総生産量	81.94	8.4
その中　ブタ肉	28.07	5.5
牛、羊の乳	50.82	6.0
家禽卵	38.63	1.7

漁業生産高は減少

水産物の総生産量は、127.27 万トン、3.9%減、その中、漁獲高は 40.06 万トン、8.9%減。養殖生産高は、87.21 万トン、1.4%減である。

海淡水養殖面積は、6.47 万ヘクタール、1.6%増である。

農村のインフラと生産条件、改善顕著

2005 年末、全市水道水の受益村は 5320 に達し、全市農業用機械総動力は、619.69 万キロワットである。

農業用トラクターは、16.3 万台、農業用トラックは、1.16 万台。農村の電力使用量は、37.26 億キロワット時、12.7%増。マルチフィルムカバー面積は、17.51 万ヘクタール、3.7%増である。

三、工業と建築業

全市工業経済は、わりに速い増加を維持し、構成は、更に優れた方向になっている。

2005 年全市の工業増加額は、1266.79 億元、21.0%増。

国有および年製品販売収入 500 万元以上の私有工業企業（以下が規模以上工業企業と略称）増加値は、1063.3 億元、29.4%増である。

その中、国有および国有持株企業は、217.4 億元で、16.1%増。集団企業は、147.5 億元、6.0%増。株式制企業は、453.7 億元で、33.4%増。外資と香港┌マカオ┌台湾企業は、318.1 億元、42.6%増。その他の経済類型企業は、46.9 億元、67.0%増である。

軽、重工業は歩調を合わせて発展し、軽工業増加額は、525 億元。重工業増加額は、538.3 億元、それぞれ 27.7%と 29.4%に増である。軽重工業の割合は、49.4:50.6 である。

2005 年、全市“四大工業基地”と“六大産業集団”集団効果が徐々に現れ、強力に工業化強力に進み、ハイスピードの発展を促進した。

四大工業基地の工業生産総額は、2334.7 億元、規模以上工業生産総値の 54.33%を占める。六大産業集団の生産総額は、1685.86 億元で、39.2%を占める。

規模以上工業の主要な製品の生産高は次の通りである。:

	2005 年生産額	昨年比＋－%
紗	7.2 万トン	4.0
布	5.1 億メートル	-0.8
化学繊維	9.6 万トン	9.9
巻きたばこ	753.6 億本	2.4
ビール	435.2 万千リットル	11

未精製塩	10 万トン	−16.7
発電量	98.6 億キロワット時	11
鋼材	330.3 万トン	43.9
原油加工量	378.9 万トン	−21.9
苛性ソーダ	16.1 万トン	8.2
純炭酸ソーダ	62.5 万トン	2.6
化学農薬	6524 トン	74.5
染料	13979 トン	17.7
タイヤ	3967.3 万本	96.9
セメント	210.8 万トン	19.9
自動車	31055 台	−50.4
カラーテレビ	1324.3 万台	38.2
家庭用電気冷蔵庫	908.8 万台	11.5
室内エアコン	983.6 万台	0.6

規模以上工業の質量向上顕著

2005 年の利益納税総額は、373.3 億元、利潤 186.4 億元。製品販売収入は、4266.8 億元、28.5%増。

工業経済効果総合指数は 173 で、昨年比 22.6%高まる。資本価値保持増大率は 122.55%で、製品販売率は 98.1%である。

製品の構造調整は明らかな効果があり、ハイ・テクノロジーの製品は市工業経済の新しい発展の原動力となった。

年規模以上工業企業のハイ・テクノロジーの製品生産額は、1296.16 億元、昨年比 14.77%増で、工業生産総額の比重は 30.16%を占めている。

建築業は、安定した成長

年増加額は、132.96 億元、9.2%増である。利益納税総額は、19.5 億元、34.5%増である。

四、固定資産投資

2005 年、固定資産投資は、1456.6 億元、45.0%増である。

規模以上企業の固定資産投資額は、1403.3 億元、45.6%増である。

投資構造は絶えず優れたものに

規模以上企業投資の中で、第 1 次産業は 29 億元、昨年比 5%増。第 2 次産業は 789.2 億元、45.9%増。第三次産業は 585.1 億元、40.7%増である。

2005 年、当市のいくつかのヘビー級プロジェクトは、施工段階、浮山湾オリンピックセンタープロジェクト、青島市即墨から平度への高速道路（青銀の 2 号）、青島臨港産業加工区ハイアール工業園、企業誘致局国際埠頭、青島発電所排煙脱硫工程等億元以上の大プロジェクトが投資に貢献しているのは明らかである。

年規模以上企業固定資産投資の工事プロジェクトは、5617 個、新規着工の項目は、4945 個、竣工プロジェクトは、681 個である。建設中プロジェクト計画総括的投資規模額は、3243.5 億元、54.6%増である。

年固定資産は、611.4 億元新たに増加し、プロジェクト竣工投産率は、12.1%で、固定資産交付使用率は、43.6%である。

市各種家屋竣工面積は、1378.8 万平方メートル、4.5%減であった。その中、分譲住宅竣工面積は、811.2 万平方メートル、13.1%増である。

分譲住宅販売面積は、739.9 万平方メートル、27%増である。

市固定資産投資により、新たに増加した主要生産能力と利益効果：

巻きたばこ	万箱/年	11.3
合成ゴム	トン/年	2000
タイヤ	万本/年	339.6
空港ターミナルビル	席	1
万平方メートル	10	
携帯電話	万本/年	480
移動通信ターミナル	個/年	102
大学・高等専門学校：	学生定員/個	15570
建築面積	万平方メートル	19.5

五、交通運輸、郵便・電信と観光業

インフラ建設力増大

道路建設は著しい効果を現し、高速道路総距離数は、525 キロメートル。

港湾建設は新たな進展を見せ、年港湾取扱量は、1.87 億トン、14.9%増。外国貿易の取扱量は、1.4 億トン、14.8%増。；コンテナ取扱量は、631 万 TU、22.8%増である。

各種運送の総輸送量：

	2005 年	昨年比＋－%
旅客輸送の取扱量	72.5 億人キロ	5.74
鉄道	16.8 億人キロ	2.96
道路	54.6 億人キロ	6.52
水運	1.1 億人キロ	11.44
貨物運送回転量	3314.1 億トンキロ	37.58
鉄道	69.9 億トンキロ	28.23
道路	88.8 億トンキロ	2.97
水運	3155.4 億トンキロ	39.12

航空輸送は着実に増大

年末の国内線は 72 便、国際（地区）線は 14 便、年航空旅客取扱量は、555.04 万延べ人数、15.43%増である。航空貨物郵便取扱量は、12.34 万トン、18.1%増である。

郵便・電信・通信業は急速に増大

年郵便・電信業務総量は、97.02 億元、32.4%増である。

その中、郵政業務の総量は、5.77 億元、16.2%増。電気通信業務の総量は、91.25 億元、33.6%増である。

書簡は、8011.83 万件、5.97%増。ネットワークの情報技術は絶えず普及、成長し、2005 年インターネットユーザーは、84.3 万戸累計に達し、27.7%増。使用時間は、275.6 億分である。

年末市の電話交換台総容量は、320.16 万である。年末市電話ユーザーは、227.48 万戸であり、その中の新規加入電話は、21.9 万戸。市携帯電話は、383.64 万戸まで伸び、その中年内に新たに増加したのは、125.2 万戸である。

観光業は、力強い伸び

全市観光旅游総収入は、256.58 億元、23.6%増。その中国内旅行総収入は、222.59 億元、21.1%増、国際旅行総収入は、4.15 億ドル、44.3%増である。

年国内外観光旅客数は、2517.47 万延べ人数、13.9%増である。その中、国内観光客は、2449.03 万延べ人数、13.5%増大。海外観光客は、68.44 万延べ人数、31.0%増である。

六、国内貿易

2005 年、住民の収入は増加し、消費能力向上と旅游、会議・展示経済の動きにより、都市と農村の消費財市場規模はいっそう拡大している。

年社会消費財小売額は、800 億の大台を突破、865.91 億元に達し、15.8%増である。

都市と農村市場は歩調を合わせた発展となり、都市市場小売額は、668.21 億元、16.9%増。農村市場の小売額は、197.7 億元、12.5%増である。

商品取引市場の規模は拡大

市商品取引市場（定期市の売買市場を含む）は、830 所、6 所増。

その中、消費財市場は、763 所、3 所増。生産手段市場は、67 所、3 所増。

住民消費構造はランクアップし、加速している。飲食、自動車、文化娯楽、旅行等は消費市場引き上げの主力である。

年飲食業小売額は、105.1 億元、15.1%増。定額以上の自動車小売額は、62.3 億元、35%増である。通信器材小売額は、10.9 億元、44.3%増である。

七、対外経済

2005 年、市対外開放は一定の水準で引き続き向上している。更に広範囲で深さのある国際経済競争に参加し、合作することで、全方位、多方面、広領域の対外開放の新局面を開いていくことである。

対外貿易は比較的速いペースで増加

青島地区（中央、省会社を含む）は、外国貿易の輸出入貿易総額 330.22 億ドル、22.4%増。その中、輸出額は、194.22 億ドル、23.1%増、輸入額は、136.00 億ドル、21.4%増である。

青島市（中央、省会社を含まない）は、外国貿易の輸出入貿易総額は、304.55 億ドル、25.2%増。その中、輸出額は、175.88 億ドル、輸入額は、128.67 億ドル、それぞれ 26.4%と 23.5%増である。

外国投資企業は市の外国貿易輸出の主体で、輸出額は 107.25 億ドル、20.3%増。市の輸出額に占める比重は 61.0%である。

青島税関の統計によると、青島港の対外貿易輸出入貿易総額は、693.29 億ドル、22.1%増。その中、輸出額は、395.99 億ドル、輸入額は、297.3 億ドル、それぞれ 23.8%と 19.9%増である。

外資を利用して着実に伸長

年外資利用プロジェクトは、2530件許可、4.4%増である。契約外資は、95.45億ドル、42.1%増。外国投資家の直接投資は、36.56億ドル、13.1%増である。

対外経済・技術協力の足並は加速

年対外工事・労務請負契約、労務協力と設計コンサルティング契約した金額は、2.81億ドル、33.5%増である。売上げは、2.73億ドル、32.2%増。国外派遣人員は、6377延べ人数、33.9%増である。

国内企業誘致、資金導入により迅速に発展

2005年国内資本は、258.75億元導入、34.2%増。その中、億元以上の国内資本プロジェクトは32件導入、実際に利用された国内資本は65億元である。

八、金融と保険業

金融業は健全に進んでいる。

年末金融機関当外貨預金残高は、2849.24億元、年初比428.15億元増。その中、人民元預金残高は、2697.54億元、年初に比べ420.92億元増である。

都市と農村の個人預金残高は引続き増加している。当外貨預金は、1413.33億元、その中、人民元預金残高は、1343.10億元、年初比253.61億元増である。

各貸付けは安定して伸びている。信用貸付機構は優良

金融機関当外貨貸出残高は、2232.81億元、年初比319.06億元増。その中、人民元貸出残高は、2039.48億元、年初比280.14億元増である。

人民元貸付けの中で、短期貸出残高は、981.51億元、年初比91.7億元増。中長期貸出残高は、807.35億元、年初比123.15億元増である。

保険業はゆるやかに発展

年保険掛金は49.57億元、4.2%増。その中、財産保険掛金は、15.98億元、16.8%増。生命保険掛金は、33.59億元、0.9%減である。

賠償額は、14.41億元。その中、財産保険賠償額は、9.27億元。生命・人身賠償金は、5.14億元である。

九、科学技術と教育

科学技術事業は加速発展

初歩的な統計によると、2005年市重要科学技術の成果は、438項。

国家級科学技術の奨励賞獲得は、4項、その中、国家発明賞1項、科学技術進歩賞3項。省クラス科学技術奨励賞獲得は、71項。その内訳は、科学技術グランプリ1項、自然科学賞4項、技術発明賞3項、科学技術進歩賞63項である。

年経済研究・開発費のGDP比重は、2.2%。

科学技術市場での交易活発。

年間技術契約プロジェクトは、1414項成立、取引高は4.3億元。

年間特許出願は、5603件、特許権は、2341件付与。

教育事業着実に発展

2005年末、市各種総合大学と単科大学は28校（私立大学含む）、その中、普通大学は、25校、在校生22.2万人、20.7%増。

中等学校は395校、その中、普通中学校は317校、在校生39.11万人、10.3%減。中等専門学校と技術工学校は78校、在校生17.81万人、9.5%増。

中等職業教育の学生は、高校段階の在校生の56.1%を占める。

小学校は、1004校、在校生47.98万人、0.6%増。

学齢児童就学率は、100%、初級中学入学率は99%以上。

十、文化、衛生とスポーツ

文化事業は繁栄・発展

市各種文化機関は、489所。

その中、映画館は、29所。映画撮影団体は、214。文化会館（站）は、172所。博物館は8所。公共図書館13所。芸術出演団体は、12団体。ラジオ放送局は、1局、12番組。テレビ局は1局、15番組。市ＣＡＴＶユーザーは176.6万戸。早期に市街区有線ＣＡＴＶデジタル化転換ユーザーは、60万戸。

市各種雑誌出版 1734 万冊、新聞は、54897 万部発行。

年創作文芸作品は、420 編を発表、省以上奨励賞獲得は 53 項。

市書類保存館は、14 所

衛生事業は、着実な発展。

年末市の保健・医療施設（診療所を含む）は、2632 所、その中、病院、診療所は、232 所、衛生防疫機関は 20 所、婦人・子供保健機関は、10 所、外来診察所、衛生保健所、医務室は、1858 所。

年末各種医療技術者数は、3.4 万人、その中、医者は 1.5 万人。

全市医療ベッド数は、3 万床、その中、病院、診療所のベッド数は、2.8 万床。

スポーツ事業は新たに前進

市スポーツ代表選手は各試合で金メダル 263 枚、銀メダル 227 枚、銅メダル 179 枚獲得。

全国記録 2 種目、全省記録 3 種目。

市スポーツ専門チーム 7 団体、メンバー107 人。

重点体育学校 13、学生 2374 人、アマチュア体育学校 5 校、学生 7840 人。

大衆スポーツと国民トレーニングを広範に展開している。

十一、都市建設と環境保護

都市 1 日当たりの給水量は、91 万トン、8%増。

都市年実水使用量は、2.9 億トン、8.8%増である。その中、生産用水と生活用水はそれぞれ 1.23 億トンと 1.67 億トンである。

都市の液化ガス、石炭ガス、天然ガスの総使用戸数は、105.2 万戸、13.9%増である。

年液化ガス供給総量 7.95 万トン、35.8%増。石炭ガス供給総量は、16573 万立方メートル、6.9%増である。天然ガス供給総量 7455.6 万立方メートル、175%増である。

都市気化率は、100%である。

全電力使用量は、193.8 億ｋｗ. 15.4%増である。

その中、工業用電力は、127.8 億ｋｗ. 都市と農村の住民生活用電力は、33.8 億ｋｗ. それぞれ 13.5%と 42.9%の増である。

年新供熱増加面積は、683.2 万㎡、累計の供熱面積は、2804 万㎡で、32.2%増である。

年末市街区公共バス、電車路線 187 本は、昨年同様の水準を維持

公共バス、電車は、3911 台、1.6%増。

年末市タクシーは、8121 台、0.3%増。

年末都市道路総距離数は、1978.63 キロメートル、12.7%増。

拡張、改修した道路は、224 本。

都市下水道総距離数は、2160.3 キロメートル、7.9%増。

環境保護は強化されている

年市街区空気質量正常機能基準到達率は、100%。市街区の空気質量優良日数は、331 日であり、90.7%に到達している。昨年比 0.3 パーセント向上している。

市街区地区環境雑音平均値は、53.4 デシベル、市街区交通幹線地雑音平均値は、68.3 デシベルである。

市街区 199.3 万本植樹

区緑化率、38.8%、昨年比 0.8 パーセント向上。市街区緑地面積は、11140.2 ヘクタールに達し、10.9%増。公共緑地、292.6 ヘクタール新たに増し、1 人当りの公共緑地面積は、11.8 平方メートルであり、7.2%増である。

市街区の公園、動物園は 47 所

十二、人口、暮らしと社会保障

人口増加速度は加速している

年末市総人口は、740.9 万人（戸籍の人口）、1.3%増。

その中、市街区は 265.43 万人、2.7%増。5 市（県レベル）は 475.47 万人、0.6%増である。

年新生児は、75530 人、出生率は、10.26‰。死亡人口は、48109 人、死亡率は 6.54‰。年人口増は、97824 人で、ひたすら増えている。自然人口増率は、3.72‰である。

都市と農村の住民生活水準は著しく向上

市委員会、市政府は、都市と農村の住民特に低収入層の収入増のためにいろいろな措置をとってきている。都市住民 1 人当たりの収入は、12920 元となり、16.5%増である。1 人当たりの消費額は 9883 元、9.8%増である。都市エンゲル係数は、37.6%、0.4%減である。

農民1人当たり純収入は、5806元、14.3%増。1人当たり生活消費額は、3737元、11.4%増である。農村のエンゲル係数は、37.5%、1.2%減である。

労働者平均賃金は、15616元、16.1%増。その中、部門労働者の平均賃金は、16015元、15.0%増である。

都市と農村住民の居住条件は一層改善

サンプリング調査によると、年末都市1人当たり住宅面積は、22.96㎡、1.75㎡増である。農民1人当たり住宅使用面積は、29.54㎡、1.55㎡増である。

就業情勢安定、社会保障は絶えず向上

2005年末市部門従業員は224.3万人、8.3%増。

年各種方法で、失業者に就業させた数は、15.4万人。4.5万延べ人数の失業者が、就業育成訓練に参加している。農村労働力の転業を組織し、そのための育成訓練を受けた者は、4.8万人である。

年末市都市と町、登録失業率は、2.96%、0.14%減である。

2005年末全市基本的養老保険加入者は、131.1万人であり、失業保険加入者は、105.1万人である。年累計失業保険受給者は、8.9万人で、8.5%減である。

社会福祉事業の効果顕著

2005年全市各種社会福祉ベッド数は、14371床、8092人引取り、養育。

注：

1. 官報の中の部分統計データは、初歩統計数による。
2. 官報の中の全市総生産は、各産業の増加額、経済タイプグループに分けた増加額の絶対数によって価格の計算を現している。増長速度はレートに計算したものである。
3. 全面調査した経済データを根拠に新しい計算方法によって調整計算した、2004年市GDP総額は2270.16億元である。
   その中の第1次産業は163.49億元、第2次産業は1149.94億元、第三次産業は956.73億元である。
4. 部分工業製品生産高はグループ幅による。
5. 規模以上投資統計範囲は、都市と町、農村の50万元以上の投資項目を含むものである。
6. 市電話交換台総容量は「小霊通」の容量を含む。
7. 社会労働者平均賃金は、各部門従業員の一定時期内所得の1人平均賃金高である。
   包含：国有経済、集団経済、共同経営経済、株式制経済、外国投資家と香港、マカオ、台湾経済、私営経済の部門等である。
   各部門で働いている労働者の平均賃金は、各部門で働いている従業員一定時期内所得の1人平均賃金高である。
8. 都市と農村の住民住宅面積は、それぞれ都市と農村の居住所帯のサンプリング調査によって得たものである。方法を変えたので、都市住民住宅面積のデータは以前のとは異なる。
9. 2005年8月から、実際の外資利用統計データは、商務部が確認した外国投資家直接投資のデータを（FDI）採用している。

注釈：英文、日本語、韓国語の訳文の内容が中国文と一致しない場合は、中国文によることとする。

2005 년
청도시 국민경제 및 사회발전 통계

청도시 통계국

(2006 년 2 월 13 일)

2005 년 청도시 시민은 시위, 시정부의 확고한 지도하에 과학의 발전관을 철저히 실행, 전국 중점 도시 및 세계적인 유명특색도시 건설을 목표로 거시경제 조정을 강화, 경제발전에서의 다양한 모순과 어려움을 극복함으로써 청도시 경제의 지속적인 발전과 각종 사회사업의 전면적인 진보를 가져왔다. 아울러 "十五"기획의 주요 목표 달성을 확보하였으며 '번영청도', '평안청도', '문명청도' 건설에서 커다란 성과를 달성하였다.

1. 종합

청도시 경제는 비교적 빠른 증가추세를 유지하였다. 초보적인 계산에 따르면 청도시 GDP 는 2695.5 억元에 달하여 16.9%가 증가, 전년 대비 0.1%증가, 1994 년 이래 가장 높은 증가폭을 기록하였다. 그 중, 제 1 차 산업의 증가치는 174.64 억元으로 0.4% 증가, 제 2 차 산업의 증가치는 1399.75 억元으로 20.0% 증가, 제 3 차 산업의 증가치는 1121.11 억元으로 16.0%증가하였으며 3 차 산업의 비율 관계는 6.5 : 51.9 : 41.6 으로 조정 되었다.

거시경제의 효익이 안정적으로 향상 되었다. 2005 년 청도시 지방재정의 일반 예산 수입은 176.34 억元으로 35.1%증가, 지방재정의 일반 예산 지출은 203.06 억元으로 23.4%증가하였다. 세수방면은 비교적 빠른 증가추세를 유지하였다. 지난해 국세 수입(해관 징수 포함)은 393.01 억元으로 15.1%증가, 지세 수입은 120.88 억元으로 20.0% 증가했다. 거시경제 경기는 높은 위치에서 운영되었다. 기업가들의 거시경제 환경의 믿음과 예상을 반영하는 기업가 믿음지수는 연말까지 130.37 포인트에 달하였으며 기업의 종합 생산 경영 현황과 경제 효익을 반영하는 기업 경기 지수는 147.65 포인트에 달하였다.

시장물가가 소폭 인상하였다. 지난해 주민 소비가격 총 지수는 102.3 포인트로 전년 대비 2.3% 상승하였다. 그 중, 식품, 의류, 오락 교육문화 및 서비스, 거주영역이 각각 2.1%, 8.3%, 0.4%, 7.7% 상승하였으며 담배와 술 및 생필품, 가정시설용품 및 A/S 서비스, 의료보건 및 개인용품, 교통 및 통신 분류가 0.2%, 0.7%, 0.6%, 1.9%씩 각각 하락하였다. 주용 공업품 출고 가격 지수는 101.39 포인트로 1.39%상승; 원자재, 연료, 동력 구매 가격 지수는 106.52 포인트로 6.52% 상승하였다. 부동산 판매 가격 지수는 110.9 포인트로 10.9%상승, 토지 거래 가격 지수는 103.4 포인트로 3.4%상승, 주택 임대 가격 지수는 103.3 포인트로 3.3% 각각 상승하였다.

국민경제 및 사회발전에서 존재하는 주요 문제는 경제 성장방식의 변화와 경제구조 조정의 속도가 보다 빠른 추세로 변환해야 하며, 제 3 차 산업의 비중이 여전이 낮고, 소비 수요가 경제성장을 추진하는 힘이 상대적으로 미약하다는 것이다. 또한 사회 저소득층의 수입 증가가 상대적으로 느리며 경제사회의 지속적인 발전에 필요한 에너지, 환경, 노동력 등 방면의 부담이 심화되고 있는 점 등이 문제점으로 지적된다.

2. 농업

2005 년, 청도시 각 급 당위, 정부는 "三农"정책을 철저히 실행하고 다양한 대책을 통하여 농업의 생산증가, 효익증가를 확보하였으며 도시농촌(城鄉)발전을 적극적으로 추진하였다. 청도시는 양식재배, 우량 종자와 농기구 구매 등 다양한 혜택을 농민들에게 제공하고 농업세의 취소는 역사상 최초로 농민들에게 "무부담"을 안겨주었다. 농업, 임업, 목축업, 어업의 생산은 구조 조정에서 안정된 증가 추세를 유지하였으며 농업 기초시설과 생산 환경은 지속적으로 개선되어 기초적 지위는 더욱 강화 되었다.

곡식 생산 수확. 청도시 곡식 파종면적은 748.88 만무(1亩=666.66M^2)로 20.6% 증가하였으며 한무당 생산량은 421Kg, 총 생산량은 315.02 만톤에 달하여 1999 년부터 시작하여, 6 년 동안의 청도시 곡식 총 생산량은 300 만톤을 재차 돌파하게 되었다. 2005 년 말까지, 청도시 경지 면적은 42.1 만 헥타르로 0.4% 감소 되었다.

주요 농산품 생산량은 아래와 같다.

	2005 년(만톤)	전년대비 +-%
곡식 생산 총량	315.02	18.8
그 중 : 밀	153.55	18.0
옥수수	147.86	23.0
땅콩	50.39	-13.2

야채(과일용 미포함)	579.21	-13.8
과일	73.73	-1.5

지난해 완성한 조림 면적은 1.61 만헥타르로 50.5% 하락, 삼림 피복율은 31.7%로 1.9% 상승하였다. 지난해 완성한 유림(幼林) 재배 면적은 2.29 만헥타르로 30.8% 하락하였다.

목축업의 생산은 지속적으로 안정된 발전을 유지하였다. 목축업 생산은 농민 수입의 증가와 농촌 경제 발전의 목표를 필두로 구조조정, 시범구 건설 및 신기술 응용 등 중점적인 작업을 통하여 산업화 경영과 표준화 생산의 속도를 가속화 하였다.

주요 목축업 제품의 산량은 아래와 같다

	2005 년(만톤)	전년대비 +-%
육류 총 생산량	81.94	8.4
그 중 ; 돼지고기	28.07	5.5
소, 양 유지류	50.82	6.0
달걀류	38.63	1.7

어업 생산량은 하락 현상을 보였다. 수산물 총 생산량은 127.27 만톤으로 3.9% 하락, 그 중, 연근해 생산량은 40.06 만톤으로 8.9% 하락, 양식 산량은 87.21 만톤으로 1.4% 하락하였다. 바다, 내수면 양식 면적은 6.47 만헥타르에 달해 1.6% 증가하였다.

농촌 기초시설과 생산 조건은 현저한 개선을 가져왔다. 2005 년 말까지 청도시 상수도 사용 촌은 5,320 개에 달했고, 청도시에서 보유하고 있는 농업기계 총 동력은 619.69 만 kw, 경운기 16.3 만대, 농업용 차량 1.16 만대, 농촌 전기 사용량 37.26 억 kw/h 로 12.7%증가하였으며 지막피복 면적은 17.51 만헥타르로 3.7% 증가하였다.

3. 공업과 건축업

청도시 공업경제는 비교적 빠른 증가 추세를 유지하였으며 구조가 보다 정예화 되었다. 2005 년 청도시에서 달성한 공업 증가치는 1266.79 억元으로 21.0% 증가하였다. 국유 및 연간 매출수입이 500 만元이상의 비국유 공업기업(규모이상 공업기업으로 약칭)이 달성한 증가치는 1063.3 억元에 달하여 29.4% 증가하였다. 그 중, 국유 및 국유 주식기업은 217.4 억元을 달성해 16.1% 증가, 집체기업은 147.5 억元으로 6.0% 증가, 주식기업은 453.7 억元으로 33.4%증가, 외상투자 및 홍콩, 마카오, 타이완 기업은 318.1 억元으로 42.6% 증가, 기타 경제형 기업은 46.9 억元으로 67.0%증가하였다. 경, 중공업은 조화롭게 발전하여 경공업 증가치는 525 억元, 중공업 증가치는 538.3 억元에 달하여 각각 27.7%, 29.4%씩 증가하였으며 경, 중 공업의 비율은 49.4 : 50.6 으로 나타났다.

2005 년 청도시 "4 대 공업기지"와 "6 대 산업공동화"의 효과가 점차적으로 두드러져 공업의 급속한 발전을 추진하였다. '4 대 공업기지'가 달성한 공업 총 생산치는 2334.7 억元으로 규모이상 공업 총 생산치의 54.33%를 차지하였으며 '6 대 산업공동화'가 달성한 공업 생산치는 1,685.86 억元으로 39.2%를 차지하였다.

규모이상 공업의 주요 제품 산량은 아래와 같다.

	2005 년	전년대비 +-%
사(紗)	7.2 만톤	4.0
포(布)	5.1 억 M	-0.8
화학섬유	9.6 만토	9.9
담배(卷煙)	753.6 억대	2.4
맥주	435.2 만 kL	11
천일염	10 만톤	-16.7
발전량(发电量)	98.6 억 Kw/h	11
강재	330.3 만톤	43.9
원유 가공량	378.9 만톤	-21.9
수산화나트륨	16.1 만톤	8.2
탄산나트륨	62.5 만톤	2.6
화학농약	6524 톤	74.5
염료	13979 톤	17.7
타이어	3967.3 만대	96.9
시멘트	210.8 만대	19.9
자동차	31055 대	-50.4
칼라 TV	1324.3 만대	38.2
가정용 냉장고	908.8 만대	11.5
가정용 에어컨	983.6 만대	0.6

규모이상 공업기업의 운영 수준이 현저히 향상되었다. 2005 년 달성한 세금 총액은 373.3 억元, 이윤액은 186.4 억元,

제품 매출은 4,266.8 억元으로 28.5%증가했다. 공업경제 효익의 종합 지수는 173 포인트로 전년대비 22.6% 상승하였으며 자본금의 평가절상 비율은 122.55%, 제품 매출율은 98.1%에 달했다.

제품의 구조조정은 현저한 효과를 거두었다. 하이테크 제품은 청도시 공업경제에 새로운 발전 동력을 제공하였다. 청도시 규모이상 공업기업이 완성한 하이테크 제품 생산치는 1,296.16 억元으로 전년 대비 14.77%가 증가하여 공업 생산치 비중의 30.16%를 차지했다.

건축업 생산은 안정된 증가세를 보여 지난해 증가치는 132.96 억元으로 9.2%증가하였으며 세금 총액은 19.5 억元으로 34.5% 증가했다.

4. 고정자산 투자

2005 년 전 사회 완성한 고정자산 투자는 1,456.6 억元으로 45.0% 증가했다. 규모이상 고정자산 투자는 1,403.3 억元으로 45.6% 증가했다. 투자구조가 끊임없이 정예화 되어 규모이상 투자 중, 제 1 차 산업의 투자는 29 억元으로 전년 대비 5%증가, 제 2 차산업의 투자는 789.2 억元으로 45.9% 증가, 제 3 차 산업의 투자는 585.1 억元으로 40.7% 증가했다. 2005 년, 청도시 일부 대규모 프로젝트가 시공단계에 들어서서 투자 증가를 추진하였으며 해상대교(북쪽다리), 해빈도로 북쪽, 푸산만(浮山灣) 올림픽센타 프로젝트, 즉묵(即墨)-평도(平度)고속도로(청은그속도로 2 기), 청도 임항(臨港)산업가공구 하이얼(海爾)공업원, 초상국 국제부두, 청도 발전공장의 연기탈황 프로젝트 등 투자규모가 억元이상에 달하는 대규모 투자의 공헌이 두드러졌다.

지난해, 규모이상 고정자산 투자 시공 프로젝트는 5,617 개, 새로 시공한 프로젝트는 4,945 개, 준공 프로젝트 681 개에 달했으며 시공 단계인 프로젝트의 기획 투자 규모는 3,243.5 억元으로 54.6%증가, 전년도 새로 증가한 고정자산은 611.4 억元, 완공 프로젝트의 투입율은 12.1%, 고정자산 교부 사용율은 43.6%에 달했다

청도시 각종 부동산 준공 면적은 1,378.8 만평방미터로 4.5%의 하락을 보였으며 그 중, 분양주택의 준공 면적은 811.2 만평방미터로 13.1%가 증가하였다. 분양주택의 판매 면적은 739.9 만평방미터로 27%가 증가했다.

청도시 고정자산 투자에서 새로 증가한 주요 생산능력 및 효익 :

담배(卷煙)	만박스/년	11.3
합성고무	톤/년	2,000
타이어	만대/년	339.6
탑승 대기 건물	개	1
만평방미터	10	
휴대폰	만대/년	480
이동통신기지	년	102
	좌석/개	15570
고등대학원	건축면적/만평방미터	19.5

5. 교통운수, 우전(郵電) 및 관광업

기초시설 건설이 강화 되었다. 도로 건설의 성과가 현저하며 고속도로의 총 길이는 525 킬로미터에 달하였다. 항구건설은 새로운 진전을 가져와 지난해 항구 물동량은 1.87 억톤에 달해 14.9%증가, 대외무역 물동량은 1.4 억톤으로 14.8%증가, 컨테이너 물동량은 631 만 TEU 에 달해 22.8%가 증가했다.

각종 운송 방식이 완성한 운송량 :

	2005 년	전년대비 +-%
승객 운송량	72.5 억인 KM	5.74
철도	16.8 억인 KM	2.96
도로	54.6 억인 KM	6.52
수운	1.1 억인 KM	11.44
화물 운송량	3,314.1 억톤 KM	37.58
철도	69.9 억톤 KM	28.23
도로	88.8 억톤 KM	2.97
해상	3,155.4 억톤 KM	39.12

항공운송은 안정된 증가세를 유지하였다. 작년말까지 국내 노선 72 선, 국제(지역)노선 14 선를 확보하였으며 전년도 항공 여객 수송은 555.04 만명으로 15.43%증가, 항공 화물부문 물동량은 12.34 만톤으로 18.1% 증가했다.

우편통신(郵電)업이 급성장 하였다. 지난해 달성한 우편통신(郵電)업무 총량은 97.02 억元으로 32.4% 증가하였으며 그

중, 우편(郵政)업무 총량은 5.77 억元으로 16.2%증가, 전신(電信)업무 총량은 91.25 억元으로 33.6% 증가하였다. 사서함(信函)은 8,011.83 만건으로 5.97%증가하였으며 네트워크 기술의 지속적인 보급과 향상에 따라 2005 년 인터넷 사용가구는 누계 84.3 만가구로 27.7%증가, 인터넷 사용시간은 275.6 억분에 달하였다. 작년말까지 전화교환기의 총 사용량은 320.16 만개, 고정 전화기 227.48 만가구, 그 중, 새로 안장한 전화가 21.9 만가구에 달했다. 휴대폰 사용량은 383.64 만대, 그 중, 지난해에 새로 증가한 수량이 125.2 만대에 달했다.

관광업은 고속성장을 보였다. 지난해, 청도시 관광업의 총 수입은 256.58 억元으로 23.6%증가하였다. 그 중, 국내 관광 수입은 222.59 억元으로 21.1%증가, 해외 관광 수입은 4.15 억달러로 44.3%나 증가했다. 지난해 맞이한 국내외 관광객은 총 2,517.47 만명으로 13.9%증가, 그 중 국내 관광객은 2,449.03 만명으로 13.5%증가하고 해외 관광객이 68.44 만명으로 31.0% 증가했다.

6. 국내무역

2005 년 주민소득 증가, 쇼핑능력 향상, 활발한 관광 및 전시회 경제로 인하여 교외(城鄕)소비품 시장 규모가 확대 되었다. 지난해 사회 소비품 소매액은 800 억元을 돌파한 865.91 억元으로 15.8% 증가하였다. 교외(城鄕)시장은 조화롭게 발전하여 도시시장의 매출액은 668.21 억元으로 16.9% 증가, 농촌시장의 매출액은 197.7 억元을 달성하여 12.5% 증가했다.

상품 거래 시장의 규모가 확대 되었다. 청도시 상품 거래 시장<정기개장(集市)무역 시장 포함>은 830 곳으로 6 곳이 증가 되었다. 그 중, 소비품 시장이 763 곳으로 3 곳이 증가하고 생산자재 시장이 67 곳으로 3 곳이 증가 되었다.

주민 소비구조의 업그레이드가 가속화되는 현상이 현저하였다. 요식, 자동차, 문화 오락, 관광 등 소비시장이 주요 역할을 하였으며 지난해, 요식업의 소매액은 105.1 억元으로 15.1%증가, 자동차 수입쿼터의 소매액은 62.3 억元으로 35%증가, 통신제품 소매액은 10.9 억元으로 44.3% 증가했다.

7. 대외경제

2005 년, 청도시 대외개방 수준은 지속적으로 향상되고 보다 넓은 범위와 심도 있는 수준에서 국제경제와 경쟁 및 합작하여 넓은 영역의 대외개방 체제를 구축하였다.

대외무역은 비교적 빠른 증가추세를 보였다. 청도지역(중앙, 성 소속회사 포함)의 대외무역 수출입 총액은 330.22 억달러로 22.4%증가하였으며, 그 중 수출액은 194.22 억달러로 23.1% 증가, 수입액은 136.00 억달러로 21.4% 증가했다. 청도시(중앙, 성소속회사 미포함)의 대외무역 수출입 총액은 304.55 억달러로 25.2% 증가, 그 중, 수입액은 175.88 억달러, 수입액은 128.67 억달러로 26.4%, 23.5%씩 각각 증가하였다. 외상투자기업은 청도시 대외무역 수출의 주체로서 수출액은 107.25 억달러로 20.3%증가하였으며 청도시 수출액 비중의 61.0%를 차지하였다. 청도해관의 통계에 따르면 청도항구의 대외무역 수출입 총액은 693.29 억달러로 22.1%증가하였으며 그 중, 수출액은 395.99 억달러, 수입액은 297.3 억달러로 23.8%, 19.9%씩 각각 증가하였다고 나타났다.

이용 외자는 안정적으로 향상 되었다. 지난해 허가받은 이용 외자 프로젝트는 총 2,530 개로 4.4%증가, 계약 외자 금액은 95.45 억달러로 42.1% 증가하였으며 외상 직접투자 금액은 36.56 억달러로 13.1% 증가하였다.

대외경제 기술 합작은 빠른 진보를 보였다. 지난해 달성한 대외 청부 공정, 노동합작 및 디자인 자문 계약 금액은 2.81 억달러로 33.5%증가했으며 매출액은 2.73 억달러로 32.2%증가, 해외파견 인원은 6377 명으로 33.9%가 증가했다.

국내 투자유치도 급속한 발전을 가져왔다. 2005 년 한 해에 유치한 국내 금액은 258.75 억元으로 34.2%증가, 억元단위 이상 국내 프로젝트는 32 개로 실제 도착한 내자 금액은 65 억元으로 나타났다.

8. 금융 및 보험업

금융업은 양호한 운영상태를 유지하였다. 작년말까지 금융기구의 인민폐 및 외화 예금여액은 2,849.24 억元에 달해 연초대비 428.15 억元 증가하였다. 그 중, 인민폐 예금여액은 2,697.54 억元으로 연초대비 420.92 억元 증가하였다. 교외(城鄕)주민들의 예금율이 지속적으로 증가하여 인민폐 및 외화 예금여액 1,413.33 억元, 그 중, 인민폐 예금여액은 1,343.10 억元으로 연초대비 253.61 억元 증가하였다. 각종 대출은 안정적으로 증가하였다. 신용대출 구조가 정예화 되어 금융기구의 인민폐 및 외화 대출여액은 2,232.81 억元에 달해 연초대비 319.06 억元 증가하였으며 그 중, 인민폐 대출여액은 2,039.48 억元으로 연초대비 280.14 억元 증가하였다. 인민폐 대출에서 단기 대출여액은 981.51 억元으로 연초대비 91.7 억元증가, 중장기 대출 여액은 807.35 억元으로 연초대비 123.15 억元 증가하였다.

보험업은 안정적으로 발전하였다. 지난해 완성한 보험 수입은 49.57 억元으로 4.2% 상승, 그 중, 재산보험 수입은 15.98 억元으로 16.8%증가하였으며 생명보험 수입은 33.59 억元으로 0.9% 하락하였다. 재무지출은 14.41 억元으로 그 중, 재산보험 배상 금액은 9.27 억元, 생명보험 배상 금액은 5.14 억元으로 나타났다.

9. 과학기술과 교육

과학기술 사업은 신속한 발전을 가져왔다. 초보적인 통계에 따라 2005 년 청도시에서 달성환 주요 과학기술 성과는 438 개로, 국가급 과학기술상은 4 개로 나타났다. 그 중, 국가급 과학 발명상 1 개, 과학기술 진보상이 3 개 이다. 성급 과학기술상은 71 개로 그 중, 과학기술 최고상이 1 개, 자연 과학상이 4 개, 기술 발명상이 3 개, 과학기술 진보상이 63 개로 나타났으며 전년도 연구개발 비용은 GDP 총량의 2.2%를 차지하였다.

과학기술 시장이 활발하였다. 지난해 계약된 기술 프로젝트는 1,414 개, 거래액은 4.3 억元에 달하였으며 전년도 특허신청량은 5,603 개, 특허 수여량은 2,341 개로 나타났다.

교육사업은 안정적으로 발전하였다. 2005 년 말까지 청도시 각종 대학교 28 곳(민반(民辦)대학 포함), 그 중, 일반 대학이 25 곳, 재교학생은 22.2 만명으로 20.7% 증가하였다. 초중고가 395 개, 그 중, 중학교 317 개, 재교학생이 39.11 만명으로 10.3% 하락하였으며 직업 전문학교 및 기공학교가 78 곳, 재교학생이 17.81 만명으로 9.5% 증가하였다. 직업 전문 교육을 받고 있는 학생수량이 고등학교 학생수량의 56.1%를 차지하였으며 초등학교 1,004 곳, 재교학생이 47.98 만명으로 0.6%증가, 취학전 아동의 입학율은 100%, 중학교 입학율은 99%이상에 달하였다.

10. 문화, 위생 및 체육

문화사업은 번영 발전하였다. 청도시의 각종 문화기구는 489 곳으로 그 중, 영화관 29 곳, 방영팀 214 개, 문화관(站)172 곳, 박물관 8 곳, 공공 도서관 13 곳, 예술표현 단체 12 개, 라디오 방송국 1 개, 12 개 채널, TV 방송국 1 개, 15 개 채널에 달하며 청도시 유선 TV 를 설치한 가구는 176.6 만 가구에 달하였으며 市區 60 만 가구의 유선 TV 에서 디지털 TV 로 전환하는 계획을 앞당겨 완성하였다. 청도시에서 출판한 각종 잡지는 1,734 만부, 신문 54,897 만부에 달하였으며 전년도 발표한 문예작품은 420 편(건, 폭)에 달하고 53 가지의 성급이상 장려를 수여받았으며 14 곳의 檔案館을 보유하고 있다.

위생사업은 안정적으로 발전하였다. 작년말까지 청도시 위생기구(진료소 포함)는 총 2,632 곳으로 그 중, 병원 및 위생원(衛生院)이 232 곳, 위생방역(防疫)기구가 20 곳, 부유(婦幼)보건기구 10 곳, 진료부(소), 위생보건소 및 의무실(醫務室)이 1,858 곳을 보유하고 있다. 연말까지 각종 위생기술 인원수는 3.4 만명으로 그 중, 의사 1.5 만명을 차지했다. 청도시 보유하고 있는 의료 병상 3 만장으로 그 중, 병원, 위새원 (衛生院)의 병상이 2.8 만장에 달하였다.

체육사업은 새로운 진전를 거두었다. 청도시 운동선수들은 각종 경기에서 금메달 263 매, 은메달 227 매, 동메달 179 매를 획득하였으며 2 가지 중국 최고 기록, 3 가지 산동성 최고 기록을 돌파하였다. 청도시는 전문 체육팀은 7 개, 선수 107 명을 보유하고 있으며 중점학교 13 곳, 학생수 2,374 명, 아마추어 학교 5 곳, 학생수는 7,840 명을 확보하고 대중체육 및 건강운동이 광범위하게 전개 되었다.

11. 도시건설 및 환경보호

도시 일일 평균 물공급량은 91 만톤으로 8% 상승하였다. 전년도 실제 용수량은 2.9 억톤으로 8.8% 상승하였으며 그 중, 생산용수와 생활용수는 각각 1.23 억톤, 1.67 억톤으로 나타났다.

LPG 가스, COG 가스, LNG 가스, 사용수는 105.2 만가구로 13.9%증가하였으며 연간 LPG 의 공급량은 7.95 만톤으로 35.8%증가, COG 가스의 공급량은 16,573 만립방미터로 6.9%증가, LNG 가스의 공급량은 7,455.6 만립방미터로 175%증가하였고 가스 사용율은 100%에 달했다.

전기 사용량은 193.8 억 kwh/h 로 15.4% 상승하였으며 그 중, 공업용 전기 사용량은 127.8 억 kwh/h, (城鄉)주민 생활용 전기 사용량은 33.8 억 kwh/h 로 각각 13.5%, 42.9%씩 상승하였다.

지난해 새로 증가한 열공급 면적은 683.2 만평방미터로 누계 열공급 면적은 2,804 만 평방미터에 달해 32.2% 증가했다.

작년말까지 市區 공공버스, 전차선로는 187 갈래로 전년 수치와 동일했으며 총 3,911 대의 공공버스 및 전차가 운영하여 1.6%증가, 택시수량은 연말까지 8,121 대에 달하여 0.3% 증가했다.

연말까지 도시 도로의 총 길이는 1,978.63 킬로미터로 12.7%증가, 확장 및 재수리 도로는 224 갈래에 달했다. 도시 하수도 길이는 2,160.3 킬로미터로 7.9% 증가했다.

환경보호는 더욱 강화되었다. 2005 년 市區 공기질량 기능구역의 합격율은 100%, 市區 공기질량이 우수한 날짜는 331 일에 달해 90.7%를 차지하였으며 전년 대비 0.3% 상승하였다. 市區구역 생활잡소리의 평균치는 53.4db, 市區 교통잡소리의 평균치는 68.3db 에 달하였으며 市區 식수 수량은 199.3 만 그루에 달했다. 도시 녹화 피복율은 38.8%에 달해 전년 대비 0.8% 상승, 市區 원림 녹지 면적은 11,140.2 헥타르로 10.9% 상승, 새로 증가한 공공 녹지면적은 292.6 헥타르, 일인당 점유하고 있는 공공 녹지 면적은 11.8 평방미터로 7.2% 상승하였으며 현재까지 市區에는 47 개의 공원, 동물원을 보유하고 있다.

12. 인구, 인민생활 및 사회보장

인구증가 속도가 빨라졌다. 2005 년 말까지 청도시 총 인구는 740.9 만명(청도호구)으로 1.3%증가하였으며 그 중, 市區인구는 265.43 만명으로 2.7% 증가, 五市 (縣級) 인구는 475.47 만명으로 0.6% 증가하였다. 지난해 신생아는 75,530 명, 출생율은 10.26%, 사망인구는 48,109 명으로 사망률은 6.54‰를 차지하였으며 인구 증가수량은 97,824 명, 인구 자연 증가율은 3.72%를 차지하였다.

교외(城鄕)주민들의 생활 수준이 현저히 향상하였다. 시위, 시정부는 각종 대책을 실시하여 교외(城鄕)주민, 특히 저소득층의 수입수준을 향상시켰으며, 도시주민의 가처분소득은 12,920 元으로 16.5%증가하였다. 일인당 소비성 지출은 9,883 元으로 9.8%증가, 도시 엥겔지수는 37.6%로 0.4%하락, 농민들의 일인당 평균 순수입은 5,806 元으로 14.3%증가, 일인당 생활 소비지출은 3,737 元으로 11.4% 증가하였으며 농촌 엥겔지수는 37.5%로 1.2% 하락하였다. 사회 공인들의 평균 봉급은 15,616 元으로 16.1% 증가하였으며 그 중, 재직 직원들의 평균 봉급은 16,015 元으로 15.0%증가하였다. 교외주민들의 거주 조건이 개선 되었다. 일부 조사결과 2005 년 말까지 도시 주택의 일인당 건축면적은 22.96 평방미터로 1.75 평방미터, 농촌 주택의 일인당 주택 사용면적은 29.54 평방미터로 1.55 평방미터가 증가 되었다.

취업형세가 안정되고, 사회보장 수준이 지속적으로 향상되었다. 2005 년 말까지 청도시의 기업 근로자는 224.3 만 명으로 8.3% 증가하였다. 지난해 각종 루트를 통하여 15.4 만 명의 실업자들에게 취업자리를 마련, 4.5 만 명의 실업자들에게 취업 교육을 실시하였으며 4.8 만 명의 농촌 노동력에 대한 교육을 진행하였다. 2005 년 말까지 청도시 등기한 실업률은 2.96%로 0.14%하락하였으며 양로보험에 참가한 인수는 131.1 만 명, 실업보험 참가자는 105.1 만 명에 달했다. 지난해 실업보험금 배당 수는 8.9 만 명으로 8.5% 하락하였다.

사회 복리사업의 성과와 효과가 두드러졌다. 2005 년 청도시 각종 사회복리원의 병상은 14,371 장으로 8.092 명을 받아들였다.

주 :

1. 상기 발표 내용 중 일부 통계수치는 초보적 통계수치 임.
2. 상기 발표 내용 중 청도시 GDP, 각종 산업 증가치, 경제유형에 따라 구분된 증가치의 절대치는 현 가격으로계산하였으며 증가속도는상대치를 기준으로 계산하였음.
3. 경제조사 및 새로운 계산방법에 따르면 청도시시 2004 년 GDP 총량은 2,270.16 억元으로 수정되며 그 중, 제 1 차산업은 163.49 억元, 제 2 차산업은 1,149.94 억元, 제 3 차산업은 956.73 억元임.
4. 일부 공업제품 생산량은 그룹에 따름.
5. 규모이상 투자 통계 범위는 도시, 군급 농촌의 50 만元이상 투자 프로젝트 포함
6. 전화 교환기의 총량은 샤오링통(小靈通)용량까지 포함
7. 사회 공인들의 평균 봉급 : 각 단위 공인들이 일정한 기간 내에 평균적으로 받는 급여. 국유기업, 집체경제, 연합경제, 주식경제, 외상투자 및 홍콩, 타이완, 마카오, 자영경제 단위 등을 포함. 재직 직공의 평균 급여는 각 단위 재직 직공이 일정한 기간 내에 평균적으로 수령한 급여 액수 임.
8. 교외(城鄕)주민 주택 면적은 교외주민들 중 일부 조사한 결과이며 조사 방법의 변동에 따라 도시 주민들의 주택 면적 데이터도 예전과 다를 수 있음.
9. 2005 년 8 월부터 실제이용 외자 통계 데이터는 상무부에서 확인한 외상 직접투자(FDI)데이터를 채용

주 : 영,일,한 번역문 내용과 중문이 부합되지 않는 곳은 중문 원고를 기준으로 한다.

CHAPTER 1

第一篇

综　合

GENERAL SURVEY

1－1 行政区划(2005 年底)

ADMINISTRATIVE DIVISION(END OF 2005)

单位:个(unit)

市、区名称	Region	街 道 Subdistrict	镇 Town	社区居委会 Community Neighborhood Committee	村民居委会 Villager Neighborhood Committee
		小计 Sub-total	小计 Sub-total		
全　市	**Whole Municipality**	**99**	**79**	**1193**	**5 494**
市　区	Urban Area	74	–	950	44
市南区	Shinan District	14	–	81	–
市北区	Shibei District	16	–	107	–
四方区	Sifang District	15	–	91	–
李沧区	Licang District	11	–	123	–
城阳区	Chengyang District	8	–	234	9
黄岛区	Huangdao District	6	–	168	35
崂山区	Laoshan District	4	–	146	–
胶州市	Jiaozhou	5	13	61	811
即墨市	Jimo	5	18	35	1 028
平度市	Pingdu	4	26	58	1 785
胶南市	Jiaonan	6	11	51	965
莱西市	Laixi	5	11	38	861

# 1 -2 气象情况(2005 年)
METEOROLOGY(2005)

市、区名称	Region	平均气温（摄氏度） Average Temperature (centigrade)	极端气温 Extreme Temperature (centigrade)		降水量（毫米/年） Precipitation (millimeter/year)	日照时数（小时/年） Sunshine Hours (hour/year)	平均气压（百帕） Average Atmospheric Pressure(100 pa)
			最高(摄氏度) Maximum(centigrade)	最低(摄氏度) Minimum(centigrade)			
市　　区	Urban Area	12.8	32.8	-7.7	830.8	2 355.1	1 008.4
崂山区	Laoshan District	13.4	35.0	-8.5	825.1	2 148.7	1 011.5
胶州市	Jiaozhou	12.9	39.0	-10.3	942.7	2 508.6	1 015.4
即墨市	Jimo	13.0	36.9	-10.1	907.8	2 316.5	1 013.7
平度市	Pingdu	12.3	38.7	-12.1	733.7	2 635.9	1 011.0
胶南市	Jiaonan	13.0	36.1	-9.0	937.1	2 197.2	1 015.8
莱西市	Laixi	12.3	39.8	-12.1	841.1	2 537.7	1 010.2

1 -3 市区分月气象情况(2005 年)
MONTHLY METEOROLOGY OF URBAN AREA(2005)

月　份	Month	平均气温（摄氏度） Average Temperature (centigrade)	降水量（毫米） Precipitation (millimeter)	日照时数（小时） Sunshine Hours (hour)
一　月	Jan.	-0.7	0.0	201.8
二　月	Feb.	-0.9	29.0	151.9
三　月	Mar.	4.7	8.9	235.4
四　月	Apr.	12.5	10.5	256.6
五　月	May	16.5	53.1	278.8
六　月	Jun.	22.3	83.7	209.2
七　月	Jul.	25.2	63.2	160.9
八　月	Aug.	24.3	256.7	165.3
九　月	Sept.	21.5	290.9	138.1
十　月	Oct.	16.4	21.5	210.7
十一月	Nov.	11.5	5.8	174.5
十二月	Dec.	0.4	7.5	171.9
全　年	**Annual Total**	**12.8**	**830.8**	**2 355.1**

1 -4 各部门基层单位数(2005 年底)

NUMBER OF BASIC UNITS IN EACH DEPARTMENT(END OF 2005)

项　目	Item	单位	unit	数　量 Number
一、农村基层单位	**Rural Basic Units**			
镇 政 府	Town Government	个	unit	79
乡村户数	Households of Village	万户	10000 households	151.06
二、工业企业单位	**Industrial Enterprises**	**个**	**unit**	**69 948**
规模以上	Above Scale	个	unit	3 697
#国　有	State-owned	个	unit	76
集　体	Collective-owned	个	unit	87
三　资	Hong Kong, Macao and Taiwan Funded	个	unit	1 399
规模以下	Under Scale	个	unit	66 251
三、交通运输单位	**Units of Transportation**			
铁　路	Railway	个	unit	–
公　路	Highway	个	unit	42
水　运	Waterway	个	unit	7
四、邮电局(所)	**Post Offices**	**处**	**place**	**718**
五、建筑业施工企业(总承包、专业承包企业)	**Construction Working Enterprises**	**个**	**unit**	**602**
国有企业	State-owned Enterprises	个	unit	36
城镇集体企业	Collective-owned Enterprises	个	unit	42
其　他	Others	个	unit	524
六、批发和零售业、住宿和餐饮业	**Wholesale & Retail Trade Accommodation and Catering Trade**			
限额以上批发贸易业	Wholesales Trade above Level	个	unit	317
限额以上零售贸易业	Retail Sales Trade above Level	个	unit	275
星级以上住宿业	Accommodation above Star-rated	个	unit	95
限额以上餐饮业	Catering Trade above Level	个	unit	179

1 -4 续表
continued

项　目	Item	单位	unit	数　量 Number
七、各级各类学校	**Various Schools**			
普通高等学校	Institutions of Higher Education	所	place	25
中等专业学校	Specialized Secondary Schools	所	place	7
普通中学	Regular Secondary Schools	所	place	317
小　学	Primary Schools	所	place	1 004
幼 儿 园	Kindergartens	所	place	2 235
八、科研机构	**Science Research Organizations**	**个**	**unit**	**50**
中央属	Central Level	个	unit	7
省　属	Provincial Level	个	unit	8
市　属	Municipal Level	个	unit	32
县级市属	County Level	个	unit	3
九、文化事业机构	**Cultural Institutions**	**个**	**unit**	**221**
#艺术事业	Art	个	unit	27
图书馆事业	Libraries	个	unit	13
十、电影发行放映机构	**Institutions of Distribution and Projection of Films**	**个**	**unit**	**257**
#电影院	Cinemas	个	unit	24
#影剧院	Theatres	个	unit	15
十一、广播、电视事业	**Broadcasting and Television**			
广播电台	Broadcasting Stations	个	unit	1
电视台	Television Stations	个	unit	1
十二、卫生事业机构	**Health Care Institutions**	**个**	**unit**	**2 609**
#医　院	Hospitals	个	unit	235
十三、社会福利事业机构	**Institutions of Social Welfare**	**个**	**unit**	**212**

1 -5 国民经济主要平均指标
MAIN AVERAGE INDICATORS OF NATIONAL ECONOMY

指　　标	Indicators	单 位	Unit	1990 年	1995 年	2000 年	2004 年	2005 年
人口密度	Density of Population	人/平方公里	person/sq. km	626	643	664	686	695
每户年平均人口	Average Annual Persons Per Household	人	person	3.57	3.29	3.14	3.11	3.12
职工年平均工资	Average Annual Wage of Staff and Workers	元	yuan	2 400	6 164	10 072	15 950	19 086
城市居民人均年可支配收入	Per Capita Annual Disposable Income of Urban Households	元	yuan	1 624	5 612	8 016	11 089	12 920
农民人均年纯收入	Per Capita Annual Net Income of Rural Residents	元	yuan	952	2 225	3 637	5 080	5 806
每一播亩平均粮食产量	Output of Grain Per Mu of Sowing Area	千克	kg	351	409	411	429	421
每亩蔬菜平均产量	Average Output of Vegetables Per Mu	千克	kg	3 017	3 274	2 735	2 971	2 985
每亩茶叶平均产量	Average Output of Tea Per Mu	千克	kg	35	8	8.1	25.07	16.5
每亩花生平均产量	Average Output of Peanut Per Mu	千克	kg	244	311	298	325	327
每亩棉花平均产量	Average Output of Cotton Per Mu	千克	kg	55	39	83	76	74
每台拖拉机负担耕地面积	Cultivated Area Ploughed by Per Tractor	亩/台	mu/set	135	129	56	38	39
每亩耕地施用化肥量(折纯)	Chemical Fertilizer Consumption Per Mu(convert to pure amount)	千克	kg	27	43	45	51	52
每人平均消费品零售额	Per Capita Retail Sales of Consumer Goods	元	yuan	995	3 093	5 409	10 298	11 765
城市每天平均生活用水量	Residential Use of Water Per Day	万吨	10000 tons	11.7	22.6	33.33	32.04	34.35
城市每人平均绿化面积	Per Capita Green Area	平方米	sq. m	3.7	5.4	8.5	11	11.82
城市每人平均住宅建筑面积	Per Capita Construction Space of Residence	平方米	sq. m	14.16	17.12	20.76	24.22	25.01
每万人拥有医疗床位	Hospital Beds Owned by Every 10000 Persons	张	bed	35.3	36.93	34.5	34.8	41.3
每万人拥有医生数	Doctors Owned by Every 10000 Persons	人	person	20.6	20.2	21	19.1	20.3
每万人中高等学校学生数	Students Enrollment of Institutions of Higher Education Per 10000 Persons	人	person	23	36	65	276	324
每万人中中等学校学生数	Students Enrollment of Secondary Schools Per 10000 Persons	人	person	527	658	704	819	768
每万人中小学学生数	Students Enrollment of Primary Schools Per 10000 Persons	人	person	948	870	757	652	648

注:职工年平均工资为城镇单位职工年平均工资。

Note: Average annual wage of staff and workers refers to average wage of staff and workers of units in town.

1－6 主要年份社会经济主要指标

MAJOR YEAR'S MAIN INDICATORS OF SOCIETY AND ECONOMY

指　　标	Indicators	单　位	Unit
年末总人口	Year-end Population	万人	10000 persons
平均人口	Average Population	万人	10000 persons
出生人数	Population of Birth	人	person
死亡人数	Population of Death	人	person
总户数	Total Households	万户	10000 households
社会从业人员	Employees	万人	10000 persons
全市单位从业人员	Population of Staff and Workers	万人	10000 persons
全市生产总值(当年价)	Gross Domestic Product(the current price)	亿元	100 million yuan
工农业总产值(当年价)	Gross Output Value of Industry and Agriculture(the current price)	亿元	100 million yuan
农业总产值(当年价)	Gross Output Value of Agriculture(the current price)	亿元	100 million yuan
工业总产值(当年价)	Gross Output Value of Industry(the current price)	亿元	100 million yuan
运　输	Transportation		
铁路货运量	Total Cargo Transport of Railway	万吨	10000 tons
公路货运量	Total Cargo Transport of Highway	万吨	10000 tons
水运货运量	Total Cargo Transport of Waterway	万吨	10000 tons
民航货邮吞吐量	Total Cargo and Postal Matter Transport of Civil Aviation	万吨	10000 tons
全社会固定资产投资总额	Investment in Fixed Assets	亿元	100 million yuan
社会消费品零售总额	Total Retail Sales of Consumer Goods	亿元	100 million yuan

注:1. 全市生产总值2004年以前历史数据根据经济普查结果进行了修订。
2. 社会消费的零售总额1993年—2004年历史数据根据经济普查结果进行了修订。
3. 单位从业人员2004年以前为职工人数(不含私营企业)。
4. 2004年底青岛铁路分局撤销,2005年铁路货运量数据为济南铁路局反馈数据,与往年口径不同。

Note:1. Historical data of Gross Domistic Product has been adjusted on the basis of statistics of first economic census.
2. Historical data of Total Retail Sales of Consumer Goods between 1993 to 2004 has been adjusted on the basis of statistics of first economic census.
3. Before 2004, the data of population of staff and workers refer to number of staff and workers(decluding private enterprises).
4. Qingdao railway station has been cancelled in the end of 2004. Cargo Transport of Railway in 2005 is fedback by Jinan railway station and its calibra is diffierent from the preceding year.

1952 年	1978 年	1990 年	1995 年	2000 年	2004 年	2005 年
423.36	585.33	666.65	684.63	706.65	731.12	740.91
420.34	584.17	661.9	681.58	704.81	725.9	736.01
155 141	85 537	114 300	81 520	73 141	79 341	75 530
54 738	36 481	43 541	45 152	49 465	49 230	48 109
93.96	131.17	186.79	208.13	224.73	235.29	237.35
163.94	256.66	352.82	374.15	397.6	458.81	471.03
23.36	70.7	103.2	111.58	118.26	207.1	224.3
6.74	38.43	180.77	631.45	1 191.25	2 270.16	2 695.82
10.87	68.7	415.17	1 133.64	2 189.16	4 255.82	5 322.29
2.44	12.15	57.99	192.38	248.33	296.74	320.51
8.43	56.55	357.18	941.26	1 940.83	3 959.08	5 001.78
447	2 917.00	3 741	4 205	4 256	5 119	2 299
399	1 561	6 433	8 912	17 234	29 937	31 009
44	528	1 556	2 112	2 998	3 503	4 471
–	–	0.22	2.1	4.84	10.45	8.91
–	2.97	28.46	214	321.1	1 025.4	1 456.6
2.61	10.03	65.82	210.81	381.22	747.50	865.9

1 -6 续表
continued

指　　标	Indicators	单 位	Unit
对外贸易	Foreign Trade		
进出口总额(不含中央、省公司)	Total Value of Imports and Exports(decluding central and provincial companies)	亿美元	100 million USD
#出口总额	Exports	亿美元	100 million USD
财政	Public Finance		
地方财政一般预算收入	General Budget Revenue of Local Finance	亿元	100 million yuan
地方财政一般预算支出	General Budget Expenses of Local Finance	亿元	100 million yuan
#文教、科学、卫生事业费	Operating Expenses for Culture,Education,Science and Health Care	亿元	100 million yuan
教育、文化、卫生	Education,Culture and Health Care		
小学在校学生数	Students Enrollment of Primary Schools	万人	10000 persons
普通中学在校学生	Students Enrollment of Regular High Schools	万人	10000 persons
高等学校在校学生	Students Enrollment of Institutions of Higher Education	万人	10000 persons
小学专任教师	Teachers of Regular High Schools	万人	10000 persons
普通中学专任教师	Teachers of Regular High Schools	万人	10000 persons
电影院、影剧院	Cinema and Theatre	个	unit
医生总数	Doctors	万人	10000 persons
医院床位数	Hospital Beds	万张	10000 beds
人民生活	People's Livelihood		
职工工资总额	Total Wage Bill of Staff and Workers	亿元	100 million yuan
城市居民人均可支配收入	Per Capita Disposable Income of Urban Residents	元	yuan
城市居民人均消费支出	Per Capita Consumption Expenditure of Urban Residents	元	yuan
#食品支出	Expenditure of Food	元	yuan
每百户拥有彩色电视机	Number of Color TV Set Owned Per 100 Households	台	set
每百户拥有电冰箱	Number of Refrigerator Set Owned Per 100 Households	台	set
农民人均纯收入	Per Capita Net Income of Rural Residents	元	yuan
城乡居民储蓄余额	Household Saving Deposits	亿元	100 million yuan
物价指数	Price Indexes		
居民消费价格指数(以 1950 年为 100)	General Consumer Price Index(1950 = 100)	%	%
商品零售价格指数(1950 年为 100)	General Retail Price Index(1950 = 100)	%	%
食品价格指数(1950 年为 100)	Food Price Index(1950 = 100)	%	%

1952年	1978年	1990年	1995年	2000年	2004年	2005年
–	–	4.16	37.64	108.31	243.32	304.55
–	–	3.35	24.51	61.14	139.12	175.88
1.98	13.07	24.23	29.48	80.01	130.51	176.34
0.22	1.94	13.39	37.7	87.87	164.62	203.03
0.04	0.52	2.61	6.75	18.82	34.33	45.31
41.33	83.49	63.23	59.59	53.49	47.69	47.98
2.42	45.75	29.62	37.23	39.85	43.61	39.11
0.28	0.35	1.54	2.49	4.61	20.17	23.98
1.18	3.2	3.15	3	3.17	3.16	3.17
0.11	2.42	2.04	2.26	2.63	3.04	2.97
20	29	106	61	45	29	39
0.16	0.59	1.39	1.38	1.49	1.4	1.5
0.17	1.07	1.66	1.81	2.01	2.35	2.86
1.14	4.02	24.39	68.3	120.4	200.7	250.7
–	336	1624	5 357	8 016	11 089	12 920
–	321	1 507	4 606	6 677	9 002	9 883
–	186	880	2 416	2 835	3 424	3 719
–	–	68	100	120	123.5	118.3
–	–	62	89	94.3	92.5	94.8
–	–	952	2 225	3 637	5 080	5 806
0.18	2.15	65.59	268.79	535.32	1 089.50	1 343.1
110.3	128.9	272.3	593.1	718.9	743.5	760.6
110.3	128.9	264.2	525.3	509.9	488.4	485.0
104.8	138.8	333.5	792.8	800.4	854.3	872.2

1 -7 国民经济主要比例关系
PRINCIPAL RATIO OF MAJOR ECONOMIC INDICATIORS

单位:%

指　　标	Indicators	1990 年	1995 年	2000 年	2004 年	2005 年
一、全市生产总值中一、二、三产业比例	**Structure of GDP**					
第一产业	Primary Industry	21.7	17.8	11.8	7.2	6.6
第二产业	Secondary Industry	48.0	46.6	46.6	50.7	51.8
第三产业	Tertiary Industry	30.3	35.6	41.6	42.1	41.6
二、工业总产值中轻重工业比例	**Structure of Gross Output Value of Industry**					
轻工业	Light Industry	61	59.3	64.1	54.2	49.4
重工业	Heavy Industry	39	40.7	35.9	45.8	50.6
三、农林牧渔业总产值中农林牧渔业比例	**Structure of Gross Output Value of Agriculture**					
农　业	Farming	58.92	42.45	39.9	33.15	33.17
林　业	Forestry	1.42	0.9	0.8	1.09	0.82
牧　业	Animal Husbandry	18.74	26.42	28.1	33.93	35.80
渔　业	Fishery	20.92	30.23	31.2	31.83	30.21
四、固定资产投资中生产性与非生产性比例	**Structure of Investment in Fixed Assets**					
生产性	Productive	74	56.13	54	64.4	65.4
非生产性	Non-productive	26	43.87	46	35.6	34.6
五、粮食与经济作物播种面积比例	**Structure of Sown Areas of Farm Crops**					
粮食作物	Grain Crops	74.2	70.17	58.9	58.0	66.6
经济作物	Economic Crops	20.2	20.45	18.3	19.8	15.9
其他作物	Others	5.6	9.38	22.8	22.2	17.5
六、一、二、三产业人员比例	**Employment Structure of Industry**					
第一产业	Primary Industry	44.36	41.52	36.4	24.8	22.2
第二产业	Secondary Industry	34.93	35.39	33.9	39.4	41.8
第三产业	Tertiary Industry	20.71	23.09	29.7	35.8	36.0

1－11 主要年份全市生产总值构成(以全市生产总值为100)
COMPOSITION OF MAJOR YEAR'S GROSS DOMESTIC PRODUCT(GROSS DOMESTIC PRODUCT＝100)

年份 Year	全市生产总值 GDP	第一产业 Primary Industry	第二产业 Secondary Industry	#工　业 Industry	第三产业 Tertiary Industry
1952	100	26.1	48.2	43.8	25.7
1957	100	18.5	53.3	49.8	28.2
1962	100	11.4	48.3	44.1	40.3
1965	100	11.6	57.8	54.7	30.6
1970	100	13.6	62.2	59.7	24.2
1975	100	23.9	52.9	50.5	23.2
1978	100	22.7	52.7	49.8	24.6
1980	100	21.0	54.0	49.9	25.0
1985	100	25.9	45.6	41.4	28.5
1988	100	22.9	49.2	44.4	27.9
1989	100	19.3	51.4	46.6	29.3
1990	100	21.7	48.0	43.7	30.3
1991	100	20.9	48.1	43.6	31.0
1992	100	16.8	49.8	45.0	33.4
1993	100	16.7	49.3	44.2	34.0
1994	100	16.7	47.8	42.8	35.5
1995	100	17.8	46.6	41.8	35.6
1996	100	18.7	45.2	40.6	36.1
1997	100	14.7	47.1	42.7	38.2
1998	100	15.6	45.5	41.0	38.9
1999	100	13.6	46.0	41.6	40.4
2000	100	11.8	46.6	42.3	41.6
2001	100	10.6	47.0	42.6	42.4
2002	100	9.3	47.9	43.4	42.8
2003	100	8.0	49.4	44.5	42.6
2004	100	7.2	50.7	45.5	42.1
2005	100	6.6	51.8	46.9	41.6

注:本表根据经济普查结果,对2004年以前全市生产总值构成历史数据进行了修订。
Note:Historical data before 2004 have been adjusted according to data of economic census.

1－12 主要年份全市生产总值发展速度(以上年为基数)

GROWTH RATE OF MAJOR YEAR'S GROSS DOMESTIC PRODUCT(PRECEDING YEAR＝100)

单位:%

年份	Year	全市生产总值 GDP	第一产业 Primary Industry	第二产业 Secondary Industry	第三产业 Tertiary Industry
1979	1979	12.0	10.6	12.9	11.4
1980	1980	10.4	4.3	13.1	10.3
1981	1981	-2.0	-9.1	-2.4	4.7
1982	1982	4.1	5.5	-0.2	11.9
1983	1983	16.9	42.8	9.3	12.7
1984	1984	13.0	18.9	11.5	10.3
1985	1985	9.9	5.4	5.8	21.3
1986	1986	9.2	2.6	12.1	10.0
1987	1987	12.0	3.6	16.0	12.0
1988	1988	13.8	-0.3	21.5	11.2
1989	1989	5.1	-0.8	4.6	9.9
1990	1990	9.3	9.8	7.3	12.2
1991	1991	10.6	9.9	11.0	10.5
1992	1992	18.1	2.7	23.5	20.7
1993	1993	22.4	20.5	21.1	25.6
1994	1994	14.4	3.6	14.7	20.2
1995	1995	12.0	10.9	12.1	12.4
1996	1996	7.2	7.7	7.6	6.4
1997	1997	11.5	-10.6	16.8	14.6
1998	1998	12.9	17.6	11.3	13.4
1999	1999	13.9	4.1	15.5	15.3
2000	2000	15.2	6.5	16.4	16.4
2001	2001	13.7	2.3	16.3	14.2
2002	2002	14.5	3.2	16.9	14.6
2003	2003	16.3	2.5	20.1	14.9
2004	2004	16.7	2.7	20.3	15.2
2005	2005	16.9	0.4	20.0	16.0
1978－2005 平均每年增长	1978－2005 Average Year Increase Rate	12.1	6.1	13.0	13.6
1991－2005 平均每年增长	1991－2005 Average Year Increase Rate	14.4	5.4	16.2	15.3
1996－2005 平均每年增长	1996－2005 Average Year Increase Rate	13.8	3.4	16.1	14.1
2001－2005 平均每年增长	2001－2005 Average Year Increase Rate	15.6	2.2	18.7	15.0

注:本表根据经济普查结果,对 2004 年以前全市生产总值发展速度历史数据进行了修订。

Note:Historical data before 2004 have been adjusted according to data of economic census.

1－13 分市、区生产总值(2005 年)
GROSS DOMESTIC PRODUCT BY REGION(2005)

单位:亿元(100 million yuan)

市、区名称	Region	地区生产总值 GDP	第一产业 Primary Industry	第二产业 Secondary Industry	#工业 Industry	第三产业 Tertiary Industry
市南区	Shinan District	229.01	–	34.42	24.61	194.59
市北区	Shibei District	153.48	–	54.17	45.79	99.31
四方区	Sifang District	86.92	–	46.23	43.24	40.69
李沧区	Licang District	141.25	0.16	95.09	89.99	46.00
黄岛区	Huangdao District	358.64	3.97	244.66	227.76	110.01
崂山区	Laoshan District	197.03	5.70	120.74	110.71	70.59
城阳区	Chengyang District	306.04	13.95	194.31	182.02	97.78
胶州市	Jiaozhou	292.11	24.17	166.19	150.69	101.75
即墨市	Jimo	300.94	29.84	158.22	140.55	112.88
平度市	Pingdu	272.75	45.31	138.15	128.35	89.29
胶南市	Jiaonan	288.65	29.86	170.98	156.88	87.81
莱西市	Laixi	198.79	25.36	88.13	77.74	85.30

注:1. 本表按当年价格计算。
　2. 三次产业分类采用《国民经济行业分类》(GB/T4754－2002)标准。

Note:1. The data are calculated at current prices.
　2. Three Industries are grouped by "Classification and code of the Sectors of the National Economy"(GB/T4574－2002).

1－14 按支出法计算的全市生产总值(2005 年)
GROSS DOMESTIC PRODUCT BY EXPENDITURE APPROACH(2005)

单位:亿元(100 million yuan)

项　目	Items	2005 年 2005	2004 年 2004	2005 年为 2004 年% 2005/2004(%)
支出法计算的全市生产总值	**Gross Domestic Product by Expenditure Approach**	**2 695.82**	**2 270.16**	**116.9**
(一)最终消费	Final Consumption	988.57	841.42	114.9
1. 居民消费	Resident Consumption	708.94	613.69	113.0
农村居民	Rural Residents	129.46	116.45	108.4
城镇居民	Urban Residents	579.48	497.24	114.2
2. 政府消费	Government Consumption	279.63	227.73	120.0
(二)资本形成总额	Total Capital Formed	1 465.67	1 161.12	120.9
1. 固定资产形成总额	Fixed Assets	1 391.30	1 010.72	132.3
2. 存货增加	Stock Increased	74.38	150.40	48.0
(三)货物和服务净流出	Net Outflows of Goods and Services	241.58	267.62	105.8

注:绝对额按当年价格计算,速度按可比价格计算。

Note:The absolute numbers are calculated at current prices, their speed of increase is calculated at constant prices of 1990.

1 -15 全市生产总值构成(2005 年)
COMPOSITION OF GROSS DOMESTIC PRODUCT(2005)

指　　标	Indicators	增加值(亿元) Added Value (100 million yuan)	2005 年为 2004 年% 2005/2004(%)
全市生产总值	**GDP**	**2695.82**	**116.9**
第一产业	Primary Industry	178.33	100.4
(1)农林牧渔业	Farming, Forestry, Animal Husbandry and Fishery	178.33	100.4
第二产业	Secondary Industry	1396.25	120.0
(2)工　业	Industry	1263.29	121.0
(3)建筑业	Construction	132.96	109.2
第三产业	Tertiary Industry	1121.24	116.0
(4)交通运输、仓储及邮政业	Transportation, Storage and Post	287.35	118.1
(5)信息传输、计算机服务和软件业	Information Transmission, Computer Services and Software Industry	47.43	119.5
(6)批发和零售业	Wholesale and Retail Trade	211.80	106.2
(7)住宿和餐饮业	Accommodation and Catering Trade	67.35	115.7
(8)金融业	Banking	64.61	123.4
(9)房地产业	Real Estate	92.89	115.6
(10)租赁和商务服务业	Rental and Business Services	45.75	115.1
(11)科学研究、技术服务和地质勘查业	Scientific Research, Technical Services and Geology Exploration	33.37	128.3
(12)水利、环境和公共设施管理业	Water Conservancy, Environmental and Public Facilities Manage	7.54	101.1
(13)居民服务和其他服务业	Residental Services and Other Services	49.74	107.9
(14)教育	Education	65.50	118.9
(15)卫生、社会保障和社会福利业	Health Care, Social Security and Social Welfare	37.28	122.2
(16)文化、体育和娱乐业	Cluture , Sport and Entertainment	15.24	119.7
(17)公共管理和社会组织	Public Management and Social Organizations	95.39	126.0

注:表中绝对数按现行价格计算;相对数按可比价格计算。

Note: The absolute numbers are calculated at current prices, the relative numbers are calculated at comparable prices.

1－16 主要年份工农业总产值(按当年价格计算)

MAJOR YEAR'S GROSS OUTPUT VALUE OF AGRICULTURE AND INDUSTRY (THE CURRENT PRICE)

单位:万元(10 000 yuan)

年份 Year	工农业总产值 Gross Output Value of Agriculture and Industry	农业总产值 Gross Output Value of Agriculture	占比重(%) Percentage(%)	工业总产值 Gross Output Value of Industry	占比重(%) Percentages(%)
1949	38 116	16 511	43.3	21 605	56.7
1952	108 723	24 428	22.5	84 295	77.5
1957	169 109	26 189	15.5	142 920	84.5
1962	136 094	15 356	11.3	120 738	88.7
1965	240 659	26 123	10.4	215 536	89.6
1970	389 290	44 078	11.3	345 212	88.7
1975	495 754	93 213	18.8	402 541	81.2
1978	687 000	121 497	17.7	565 503	82.3
1980	827 126	149 436	18.1	677 690	81.9
1985	1 413 030	299 139	21.2	1 113 891	78.8
1986	1 641 688	325 458	19.8	1 316 230	80.2
1987	2 082 811	378 981	18.2	1 703 830	81.8
1988	2 959 547	447 953	16.1	2 481 594	83.9
1989	3 655 595	463 952	12.7	3 191 643	87.3
1990	4 151 722	579 877	14.0	3 571 845	86.0
1991	4 651 206	664 779	14.3	3 986 427	85.7
1992	5 617 685	703 433	12.5	4 914 252	87.5
1993	8 280 202	989 763	12.0	7 290 439	88.0
1994	12 518 645	1 424 074	11.4	11 094 571	88.6
1995	11 336 406	1 923 771	17.0	9 412 635	83.0
1996	13 643 196	2 317 434	17.0	11 352 762	83.0
1997	15 752 447	2 047 712	13.0	13 704 735	87.0
1998	18 180 409	2 386 303	13.1	15 794 106	86.9
1999	19 204 756	2 382 320	12.4	16 822 436	87.6
2000	21 891 594	2 483 256	11.3	19 408 338	88.7
2001	25 013 692	2 615 228	10.5	22 398 464	89.5
2002	28 482 856	2 688 532	9.4	25 794 324	90.6
2003	33 955 287	2 759 692	8.1	31 195 595	91.9
2004	42 558 172	2 967 389	7.0	39 590 783	93.0
2005	53 222 886	3 205 057	6.0	50 017 829	94.0

CHAPTER 2

第二篇

人 口

POPULATION

编辑单位：人口和社会科技统计处
编　　委：高明辉
编　　辑：王　磊
校　　对：关　静
电　　话：85912263

2－1 主要年份全市总人口数
MAJOR YEAR'S GROSS POPULATION

单位:人(person)

年　份 Year	总人口 Population	按性别分 Grouped by Sex 男 Male	女 Female	平均人口 Average Population
1949	4 056 550	1 997 293	2 059 257	4 054 431
1952	4 233 586	2 125 392	2 108 194	4 203 428
1957	4 822 756	2 424 729	2 398 027	4 773 862
1962	4 627 432	2 319 658	2 307 774	4 578 313
1965	4 901 670	2 461 629	2 440 041	4 859 712
1970	5 391 852	2 720 633	2 671 219	5 337 282
1975	5 742 206	2 904 347	2 837 859	5 717 456
1978	5 853 321	2 959 800	2 893 521	5 841 638
1980	5 961 129	3 015 357	2 945 772	5 937 187
1985	6 267 223	3 185 409	3 081 814	6 253 157
1988	6 516 920	3 319 534	3 197 386	6 474 541
1989	6 571 597	3 348 454	3 223 143	6 544 259
1990	6 666 482	3 392 253	3 274 229	6 619 040
1991	6 709 277	3 411 776	3 297 501	6 687 880
1992	6 731 072	3 420 886	3 310 186	6 720 175
1993	6 753 497	3 431 149	3 322 348	6 742 285
1994	6 785 291	3 446 019	3 339 272	6 769 394
1995	6 846 346	3 476 300	3 370 046	6 815 819
1996	6 902 677	3 502 600	3 400 077	6 874 512
1997	6 954 391	3 527 588	3 426 803	6 928 534
1998	6 995 666	3 545 403	3 450 263	6 975 029
1999	7 029 707	3 561 061	3 468 646	7 012 687
2000	7 066 481	3 577 367	3 489 114	7 048 094
2001	7 104 875	3 595 652	3 509 223	7 085 678
2002	7 156 537	3 619 778	3 536 759	7 130 706
2003	7 206 806	3 644 032	3 562 774	7 181 672
2004	7 311 228	3 692 991	3 618 237	7 259 017
2005	7 409 052	3 740 309	3 668 743	7 360 140

2 -2 主要年份全市户数、人口数、人口密度
MAJOR YEAR'S HOUSEHOLDS, POPULATION AND DENSITY OF POPULATION

年 份 Year	总户数(万户) Total Households (10000 households)		总人口(万人) Total Population (10000 persons)		平均每户人口(人) Average Persons Per Household (person)		人口密度(人/平方公里) Density of Population (person/sq. km)	
	全 市 Whole Municipalit	市 区 Urban Area	全 市 Whole Municipalit	市 区 Urban Area	全 市 Whole Municipalit	市 区 Urban Area	全 市 Whole Municipalit	市 区 Urban Area
1949	90.64	21.68	405.66	103.69	4.48	4.78	381	941
1952	93.96	22.70	423.36	107.62	4.51	4.74	397	977
1957	102.56	27.41	482.28	134.76	4.70	4.92	453	1 223
1962	106.11	29.29	462.74	137.86	4.36	4.71	434	1 251
1965	105.31	29.64	490.17	146.74	4.65	4.95	460	1 332
1970	113.07	32.14	539.19	150.81	4.77	4.69	506	1 369
1975	123.18	36.56	574.22	161.13	4.66	4.41	539	1 462
1978	131.27	40.08	585.33	168.00	4.46	4.19	549	1 525
1980	138.44	43.03	596.11	175.27	4.31	4.07	560	1 591
1985	157.06	53.43	626.72	190.87	3.99	3.57	588	1 732
1988	169.72	58.95	651.69	201.38	3.84	3.42	612	1 827
1989	177.47	61.57	657.16	203.63	3.70	3.31	617	1 848
1990	186.79	63.94	666.65	205.78	3.57	3.22	626	1 867
1991	192.46	67.15	670.93	207.22	3.49	3.09	630	1 880
1992	199.08	68.94	673.11	209.28	3.38	3.04	632	1 899
1993	201.36	70.13	675.35	212.06	3.35	3.02	634	1 924
1994	204.05	71.24	678.53	214.97	3.33	3.02	637	1 951
1995	208.13	72.53	684.63	218.38	3.29	3.01	643	1 982
1996	212.40	75.11	690.27	223.86	3.25	2.98	648	2 032
1997	215.12	76.39	695.44	227.22	3.23	2.97	653	2 062
1998	218.59	77.90	699.57	229.58	3.20	2.95	657	2 084
1999	222.61	79.27	702.97	231.94	3.16	2.93	660	2 105
2000	224.73	80.46	706.65	234.60	3.14	2.92	664	2 129
2001	227.43	81.41	710.49	237.60	3.12	2.92	667	2 156
2002	229.67	82.85	715.65	241.74	3.12	2.92	672	2 194
2003	232.26	84.15	720.68	246.77	3.10	2.93	677	2 240
2004	235.29	86.93	731.12	258.40	3.11	2.97	686	2 229
2005	237.35	87.99	740.91	265.43	3.12	3.02	695	2 290

2 -3 分市、区户数与人口数(2005 年底)
TOTAL HOUSEHOLDS AND POPULATION BY REGION(END OF 2005)

市、区名称	Region	户数(户) Households (household)	人口(人) Population (person)	按性别分 Grouped by Sex 男 Male	女 Female	平均人口(人) Average Population (person)
总　　计	**Total**	**2 373 458**	**7 409 052**	**3 740 309**	**3 668 743**	**7 360 140**
市　　区	Urban Area	879 921	2 654 340	1 340 442	1 313 898	2 619 157
市南区	Shinan District	159 548	505 789	253 485	252 304	497 600
市北区	Shibei District	176 586	473 207	237 147	236 060	473 104
四方区	Sifang District	131 140	389 079	204 166	184 913	386 387
李沧区	Licang District	105 470	290 848	147 995	142 853	288 689
城阳区	Chengyang District	158 084	480 475	235 515	244 960	472 096
黄岛区	Huangdao District	79 152	300 308	155 743	144 565	290 111
崂山区	Laoshan District	69 941	214 634	106 391	108 243	211 171
胶州市	Jiaozhou	239 211	777 593	389 330	388 263	773 558
即墨市	Jimo	331 772	1 090 075	547 294	542 781	1 086 141
平度市	Pingdu	418 163	1 353 594	686 258	667 336	1 349 715
胶南市	Jiaonan	263 718	811 318	411 158	400 160	809 878
莱西市	Laixi	240 673	722 132	365 827	356 305	721 692

2 -4 分市、区土地面积、人口和人口密度(2005 年底)
LAND AREA, POPULATION AND DENSITY OF POPULATION BY REGION(END OF 2005)

市、区名称	Region	土地面积 Land Area		年末人口 Year-end Population		人口密度(人/平方公里) Density of Population (person/sq. km)
		面积(平方公里) Area(sq. km)	比重(%) Percentage(%)	人口(人) Population(person)	比重(%) Percentage(%)	
总　　计	**Total**	**10 654**	**100.00**	**7 409 052**	**100.00**	**695**
市　　区	Urban Area	1 159	10.88	2 654 340	35.82	2 290
胶州市	Jiaozhou	1 210	11.36	777 593	10.50	643
即墨市	Jimo	1 727	16.21	1 090 075	14.71	631
平度市	Pingdu	3 166	29.72	1 353 594	18.27	428
胶南市	Jiaonan	1 870	17.55	811 318	10.95	434
莱西市	Laixi	1 522	14.28	722 132	9.75	474

2－5 主要年份人口自然变动
MAJOR YEAR'S NATURAL CHANGE OF POPULATION

年份 Year	出生 Birth			死亡 Death			自然增长 Natural Growth		
	人数(万人) Population (10 000 persons)	出生率(‰) Birth Rate (‰)	#市区 Urban Area	人数(万人) Population (10 000 persons)	死亡率(‰) Death Rate (‰)	#市区 Urban Area	人数(万人) Population (10 000 persons)	增长率(‰) Natural Growth Rate(‰)	#市区 Urban Area
1949	11.62	28.66	31.86	6.10	15.03	11.25	5.52	13.62	20.61
1952	15.51	36.91	39.60	4.97	11.83	9.18	10.54	25.08	30.42
1957	17.82	37.34	42.40	6.38	13.37	8.82	11.44	23.97	33.58
1962	17.29	37.77	35.75	5.82	12.70	8.08	11.47	25.07	27.67
1965	17.63	36.28	27.18	4.66	9.59	5.61	12.97	26.69	21.57
1970	17.65	33.06	23.79	3.79	7.11	5.55	13.86	25.95	18.24
1975	10.55	18.45	17.52	3.95	6.90	5.67	6.60	11.55	11.85
1978	8.55	14.64	11.64	3.65	6.24	5.53	4.90	8.40	6.11
1980	8.00	13.48	11.28	3.77	6.35	5.73	4.23	7.13	5.55
1985	5.82	9.31	10.37	3.88	6.21	5.64	1.94	3.10	4.73
1988	10.22	15.79	15.39	4.17	6.44	5.29	6.05	9.35	10.10
1989	10.37	15.85	14.13	3.88	5.93	5.48	6.49	9.92	8.65
1990	11.44	17.28	11.68	4.35	6.58	5.78	7.09	10.70	5.90
1991	7.98	11.93	8.17	4.15	6.21	5.56	3.83	5.72	2.61
1992	6.17	9.18	8.65	4.54	6.75	6.14	1.63	2.43	2.51
1993	5.95	8.82	8.49	4.44	6.59	6.01	1.51	2.23	2.48
1994	6.92	10.22	8.66	4.71	6.96	6.40	2.21	3.26	2.26
1995	8.15	11.96	9.03	4.52	6.62	6.08	3.63	5.34	2.95
1996	8.40	12.21	8.98	4.83	7.03	6.38	3.57	5.18	2.60
1997	7.80	11.26	8.76	4.80	6.93	6.33	3.00	4.33	2.43
1998	7.51	10.77	8.62	4.68	6.71	6.12	2.83	4.06	2.50
1999	6.48	9.24	8.05	4.56	6.50	6.05	1.92	2.74	2.00
2000	7.31	10.38	9.25	4.95	7.02	6.33	2.37	3.36	2.92
2001	6.74	9.51	8.37	4.64	6.54	6.17	2.10	2.97	2.20
2002	7.54	10.57	9.24	4.74	6.65	6.12	2.80	3.92	3.12
2003	5.11	7.11	5.89	4.81	6.70	6.12	0.30	0.41	-0.23
2004	7.93	10.93	8.93	4.92	6.78	6.03	3.01	4.15	2.90
2005	7.55	10.26	7.84	4.81	6.54	6.10	2.74	3.72	1.74

2-6 分市、区人口出生率、死亡率、自然增长率(2005 年底)

RATE OF BIRTH, DEATH AND NATURAL GROWTH IN POPULATION BY REGION(END OF 2005)

市、区名称	Region	出生 Birth		死亡 Deathv		自然增长 Natural Growth	
		人数(人) Population (person)	出生率(‰) Birth Rate (‰)	人数(人) Population (person)	死亡率(‰) Death Rate (‰)	人数(人) Population (person)	增长率(‰) Natural Growth Rate(‰)
总　计	**Total**	**75 530**	**10.26**	**48 109**	**6.54**	**27 421**	**3.72**
市　区	Urban Area	20 532	7.84	15 966	6.10	4 566	1.74
市南区	Shinan District	3 153	6.34	2 557	5.14	596	1.20
市北区	Shibei District	2 856	6.04	3 497	7.39	-641	-1.35
四方区	Sifang District	2 132	5.52	2 547	6.59	-415	-1.07
李沧区	Licang District	2 265	7.85	1 859	6.44	406	1.41
城阳区	Chengyang District	5 009	10.61	3 002	6.36	2 007	4.25
黄岛区	Huangdao District	3 127	10.78	1 160	4.00	1 967	6.78
崂山区	Laoshan District	1 990	9.42	1 344	6.36	646	3.06
胶州市	Jiaozhou	10 095	13.05	4 886	6.32	5 209	6.73
即墨市	Jimo	13 056	12.02	7 618	7.01	5 438	5.01
平度市	Pingdu	15 331	11.36	8 268	6.13	7 063	5.23
胶南市	Jiaonan	8 941	11.04	6 279	7.75	2 662	3.29
莱西市	Laixi	7 575	10.50	5 092	7.06	2 483	3.44

2-7 分市、区人口机械变动(2005 年底)

MECHANICAL CHANGE OF POPULATION BY REGION(END OF 2005)

市、区名称	Region	迁入人数(人) Inflows(person)	迁出人数(人) Outflows(person)	增(+)、减(-) Increase(+), Reduction(-)
总　计	**Total**	**121 925**	**53 279**	**68 646**
市　区	Urban Area	89 606	24 336	65 270
市南区	Shinan District	19 099	7 263	11 836
市北区	Shibei District	5 022	2 750	2 272
四方区	Sifang District	14 871	5 277	9 594
李沧区	Licang District	6 578	2 045	4 533
城阳区	Chengyang District	16 329	2 106	14 223
黄岛区	Huangdao District	21 275	3 800	17 475
崂山区	Laoshan District	6 432	1 095	5 337
胶州市	Jiaozhou	6 185	4 228	1 957
即墨市	Jimo	7 601	5 294	2 307
平度市	Pingdu	7 820	7 125	695
胶南市	Jiaonan	6 344	6 126	218
莱西市	Laixi	4 369	6 170	-1 801

2 -8 计划生育情况(1978 -2005 年)
PLANNED PARENTHOOD(1978 -2005)

年 份 Year	已婚有生育能力的人数(人) Married and Fertile Persons(person)	节育人数(人) Persons under Birth Control(person)	节育率(%) Contraceptive Prevalence Rate(%)	四项手术人数(人) Persons Performed Four - operation(person)	#放环人数 Persons Set Contraceptive Rings
1978	694 292	571 077	82.25	125 913	68 475
1980	763 226	673 069	88.19	180 979	70 927
1985	1 017 649	929 284	91.32	146 742	67 234
1990	1 258 232	1 165 216	92.61	149 327	70 964
1991	1 319 722	1 219 795	92.43	153 970	77 406
1992	1 348 503	1 256 271	93.16	90 107	56 226
1993	1 380 717	1 271 884	92.12	76 783	45 492
1994	1 400 425	1 268 378	90.57	73 169	41 482
1995	1 427 442	1 285 264	90.04	84 099	52 716
1996	1 459 465	1 316 516	90.21	84 370	57 648
1997	1 482 204	1 340 399	90.43	76 579	55 285
1998	1 505 499	1 367 648	90.84	74 199	50 526
1999	1 523 471	1 378 131	90.46	73 663	44 976
2000	1 521 331	1 371 447	90.15	74 285	45 999
2001	1 514 274	1 360 543	89.85	70 205	43 601
2002	1 541 855	1 400 145	90.81	50 575	45 453
2003	1 518 448	1 354 917	89.23	57 458	47 953
2004	1 540 706	1 357 703	88.04	52 934	42 859
2005	1 590 476	1 417 755	89.14	58 097	49 716

2 -9 分市、区计划生育情况(2005 年)
PLANNED PARENTHOOD BY REGION(2005)

市、区名称	Region	计划生育率(%) Planned Parenthood Rate(%)	计划内出生(人)		计划外出生(人)		多胎(人) Babies
			一胎 First Baby	二胎 Second Baby	一胎 First Baby	二胎 Second Baby	
总　计	**Total**	**99.53**	**53 308**	**19 495**	**22**	**228**	**93**
市　区	Urban Area	99.89	16 762	2 387	1	16	4
市南区	Shinan District	99.84	2 434	99	_	4	_
市北区	Shibei District	99.59	2 358	73	_	9	1
四方区	Sifang District	100.00	1 918	97	_	_	_
李沧区	Licang District	99.91	2 015	172	_	1	1
城阳区	Chengyang District	99.94	3 758	1 188	1	1	1
黄岛区	Huangdao District	99.97	2 598	470	_	1	_
崂山区	Laoshan District	99.95	1 681	288	_	_	1
胶州市	Jiaozhou	99.48	6 817	2 980	5	34	12
即墨市	Jimo	99.71	9 121	3 802	1	24	13
平度市	Pingdu	99.46	9 155	5 528	3	56	20
胶南市	Jiaonan	99.79	6 429	2 580	4	10	5
莱西市	Laixi	98.17	5 024	2 218	8	88	39

CHAPTER 3

第三篇

从业人员及职工工资

EMPLOYMENT AND WAGES OF STAFF AND WORKERS

编辑单位：人口和社会科技统计处
编　　委：高明辉
编　　辑：秦　浩
校　　对：关　静
电　　话：85912263

3 -1 社会从业人数(1978—2005 年)
SOCIAL LABORERS(1978 - 2005)

单位:万人(10 000 persons)

年 份 Year	合 计 Total	第一产业 Primary Industry	第二产业 Secondary Industry	第三产业 Tertiary Industry
1978	256.70	157.4	65.6	33.7
1979	265.60	156.1	72.2	37.3
1980	270.10	153.6	82.1	43.2
1981	278.90	153.6	82.1	43.2
1982	282.70	151.1	86.2	45.4
1983	289.60	156.4	85	48.1
1984	304.20	149.2	97.7	57.4
1985	315.30	149.2	104.5	61.7
1986	326.40	149.6	112.1	64.6
1987	334.80	149.9	120.2	64.7
1988	336.50	147.6	123.2	65.7
1989	344.20	152.5	122.1	69.6
1990	352.80	156.5	123.3	73.1
1991	361.20	161.9	124.3	74.9
1992	370.30	161.7	127.8	80.8
1993	365.70	160.5	128.8	76.4
1994	367.60	157.1	129.4	81.2
1995	374.20	155.4	132.4	86.4
1996	381.50	152.2	137.1	92.2
1997	388.70	155.2	138.1	95.3
1998	393.10	154.8	138.6	99.7
1999	396.10	150.3	142	103.8
2000	397.60	144.7	134.91	117.99
2001	400.50	133.9	142.3	124.3
2002	413.31	121.38	153.85	138.08
2003	438.96	119.91	163.93	155.12
2004	458.81	113.98	180.63	164.2
2005	471.03	104.48	196.8	169.75

3－2 主要年份全市单位从业人员人数

MAJOR YEAR'S NUMBER OF STAFF AND WORKERS IN THE WHOLE CITY

单位:万人(10 000 persons)

年　份 Year	合　计 Total	#市　区 Urban Area	#国有单位 State-owned Units	#集体单位 Collective-owned Units
1949	14.8	13.4	9.3	5.5
1952	23.4	20.1	18.3	5.1
1957	29.7	24.5	24.1	5.6
1962	32.3	26.8	24.5	7.8
1965	36.7	30.6	26.8	9.9
1970	45.6	37.4	32.2	13.4
1975	53.4	43.5	38.0	15.4
1978	70.7	54.5	49.2	21.5
1980	79.2	61.5	55.0	24.2
1985	88.8	66.7	59.8	28.9
1988	98.2	70.0	66.7	31.2
1989	99.2	70.4	67.7	31.0
1990	103.2	70.6	69.5	32.9
1991	105.4	78.4	71.5	32.5
1992	108.2	80.4	73.6	32.8
1993	109.4	80.8	75.3	29.5
1994	110.1	80.2	72.4	28.3
1995	111.6	80.2	72.4	27.5
1996	118.4	81.1	71.6	26.0
1997	117.1	78.1	69.0	22.6
1998	116.2	75.6	64.2	19.0
1999	119.0	78.3	60.4	16.6
2000	118.3	76.6	57.6	14.2
2001	117.5	75.1	53.2	12.2
2002	119.1	75.2	49.5	10.3
2003	118.0	74.3	47.2	8.9
2004	207.1	111.1	43.7	18.0
2005	224.3	122.3	43.9	18.2

注:2004 年以前为职工人数(不含私营企业)。

Note: Before 2004, the data refer to number of staff and workers (decluding private enterprises).

3-3 城镇单位分行业职工人数(1978—2002年)

MAJOR YEAR'S NUMBER OF STAFF AND WORKERS IN TOWN(1978-2002)

单位:万人(10 000 persons)

年 份 Year	合 计 Total	农林牧渔业 Farming, Forestry, Animal Husbandry and Fishery	工 业 Industry	建筑业 Construction	地质勘察水利管理业 Geological Prospecting and Water Conservancy Administration	交通运输仓储邮电通信业 Transportation, Storage, Postal and Telecommunications	批发零售贸易、餐饮业 Wholesale, Retail and Catering Business
1978	70.7	1.5	41.3	3.4	0.2	4.2	9.4
1980	79.2	1.6	46.8	3.9	0.1	4.9	9.9
1985	88.8	1.3	51.9	3.8	0.2	5.2	10.1
1990	103.2	1.1	58.2	4.2	0.3	6.0	11.8
1991	105.4	1.4	57.9	4.7	0.3	6.1	12.5
1992	108.2	1.5	57.7	5.2	0.3	6.2	13.4
1993	109.4	1.3	57.6	5.5	0.5	6.1	13.4
1994	110.1	1.4	57.0	5.0	0.3	6.4	13.7
1995	111.6	1.2	58.3	4.9	0.3	6.3	13.4
1996	118.4	0.9	63.8	4.8	0.3	6.5	13.7
1997	117.1	0.9	62.5	4.3	0.3	6.3	13.3
1998	116.2	0.9	61.5	4.6	0.3	6.1	12.4
1999	119.0	0.9	65.2	4.4	0.3	6.1	11.6
2000	118.3	0.9	65.2	4.5	0.3	6.0	10.6
2001	117.5	0.8	65.6	4.2	0.3	5.9	9.7
2002	119.1	0.8	66.8	5.0	0.3	5.6	8.8

注:本表按旧行业划分标准(GB/T4754-94)分类职工人数(不含私营企业)。

Note: Numbers of staff and works are according to old classification of the sectors (decluding private enterprises).

3 –3 续表
Continued

单位:万人(10 000 persons)

年 份 Year	金 融 保险业 Banking and Insurance	房 地 产 业 Real Estate	社 会 服务业 Social Services	卫生体育社会 福利业 Health Care. Sports and Social Welfare	教育文化艺术 广播电影电视业 Education,Culture. Art Broadcasting. Film and Television	科学研究和综 合技术服务业 Scientific Research and Polytechnical Services	国家机关政党 机关社会团体 Government Institutions, Party and Social Organizations	其 他 行 业 Others
1978	0.4	0.4	1.2	1.9	4.1	0.4	2.3	–
1980	0.5	0.4	1.3	2.0	4.7	0.5	2.6	–
1985	0.8	0.2	2.5	2.4	5.7	0.8	3.8	–
1990	1.3	0.5	3.7	2.8	7.2	1.1	5.0	–
1991	1.3	0.5	4.0	3.0	7.4	1.1	5.2	–
1992	1.5	0.6	4.3	3.1	7.9	1.1	5.4	–
1993	1.6	0.9	5.0	3.1	7.8	1.1	4.9	0.6
1994	1.8	1.1	5.1	3.2	8.2	1.4	5.1	0.4
1995	2.0	1.2	5.2	3.3	8.4	1.4	5.3	0.4
1996	2.1	1.1	5.5	3.4	8.5	1.4	6.1	0.3
1997	2.2	1.2	5.5	3.5	8.9	1.4	6.5	0.3
1998	2.3	1.1	5.7	3.6	9.7	1.3	6.4	0.3
1999	2.3	1.1	5.6	3.6	10.0	1.2	6.3	0.4
2000	2.4	1.1	6.1	3.7	10.1	1.1	6.3	0.2
2001	2.4	1.1	6.1	3.7	10.1	1.1	6.3	0.2
2002	2.4	1.4	6.1	3.7	10.2	1.1	6.6	0.3

3-4 全市单位国民经济各行业从业人员人数(2005年)

NUMBER OF STAFF AND WORKERS IN THE WHOLE CITY IN EACH SECTOR OF NATIONAL ECONOMY(2005)

单位:万人(10 000 persons)

		2005年		2004年	
		合计 Total	女性 Female	合计 Total	女性 Female
总计	**Total**	**224.3**	**93.9**	**207.1**	**88.6**
1. 农、林、牧、渔业	Farming, Forestry, Animal Husbandry and Fishery	1	0.4	1	0.3
2. 采矿业	Excavation	2.1	0.3	1.8	0.3
3. 制造业	Manufacturing	125.9	62.3	114.8	58
4. 电力、煤气及水的生产供应业	Power, Gas and Water Production and Supply	2.3	0.6	2.1	0.6
5. 建筑业	Construction	21.8	2.3	19.8	2.5
6. 交通运输、仓储及邮政业	Transportation, Storage, Postal and Telecommunications	8.9	2.1	8.6	2.2
7. 信息传输、计算机服务和软件业	Information Transmission, Computer Service and Software Service	1.2	0.4	1	0.4
8. 批发和零售业	Wholesale and Retail Trade	15.8	6.2	15.7	6.2
9. 住宿和餐饮业	Accommodation and Catering Trade	3.6	1.8	3	1.5
10. 金融业	Banking	3.1	1.6	3.1	1.6
11. 房地产业	Real Estate Trade	3	1	2.7	0.9
12. 租赁和商务服务业	Leasing Trade and Commercial Service	4.8	1.6	4.5	1.5
13. 科学研究、技术服务和地质勘察业	Scientific Research, Technical Service and Geological Prospecting	2.3	0.6	2	0.6
14. 水利、环境和公共设施管理业	Water Conservancy, Environment and Administration of Public Facilities	1.8	0.6	1.6	0.6
15. 居民服务和其他服务业	Resident Services and Other Services	0.7	0.3	0.6	0.3
16. 教育	Education	13.2	6.8	12.4	6.4
17. 卫生、社会保障和社会福利业	Health Care, Social Protection and Social Welfare	4.6	2.9	4.5	2.7
18. 文化、体育和娱乐业	Culture, Sports and Recreation	1.1	0.4	1.2	0.4
19. 公共管理和社会组织	Public Administration and Social Orgnization	7.1	1.7	6.7	1.6
20. 国际组织	International Orgnization	0	0	0	0

3 -5 全市单位分市、区国民经济各部门从业人员人数(2005 年)

NUMBER OF STAFF AND WORKERS IN THE WHOLE CITY IN EACH SECTOR OF NATIONAL ECONOMY BY REGION(2005)

单位:万人(10 000 persons)

市、区名称	Region	合计 Total	农林牧渔业 Farming, Forestry, Animal Husbandry and Fishery	采矿业 Excavation	制造业 Manufacturing	电力燃气和水生产供应业 Power, Gas and Water Production and Supply	建筑业 Construction
总　计	**Total**	**224.3**	**1**	**2.1**	**125.9**	**2.3**	**21.8**
#城 阳 区	Chengyan District	26.7	0.1	0.3	21.5	0	1
黄 岛 区	Huangdao District	15.9	0	0	10.1	0.3	1.5
崂 山 区	Laoshan District	12.5	0	0	7.6	0	0.7
胶 州 市	Jiaozhou	26.7	0.3	0	16.4	0.1	5
即 墨 市	Jimo	24.1	0.1	0.1	18.4	0.1	1.4
平 度 市	Pingdu	19.7	0.2	1.2	10.5	0.2	3.6
胶 南 市	Jiaonan	17.1	0.1	0.3	11.1	0.2	1.9
莱 西 市	Laixi	14.4	0	0.2	9.7	0.2	1.5

3 -5 续表 1

Continued

单位:万人(10 000 persons)

市、区名称	Region	金融业 Banking	房地产业 Real Estate	租赁和商务服务业 Leasing Trade and Commercial Service	科学研究技术服务和地质勘察业 Scientific Research, Technical Service and Geological Prospecting	水利环境和公共设施管理业 Water Conservancy, Environment and Administration of Public Facilities
总　计	**Total**	**3.1**	**3**	**4.8**	**2.3**	**1.8**
#城 阳 区	Chengyan District	0.1	0.1	0.9	0.3	0.1
黄 岛 区	Huangdao District	0	0.4	0.3	0	0.2
崂 山 区	Laoshan District	0.1	0.6	0.3	0.3	0.1
胶 州 市	Jiaozhou	0.2	0.2	0.1	0.3	0.1
即 墨 市	Jimo	0.2	0.1	0.1	0	0.1
平 度 市	Pingdu	0.2	0.1	0.2	0	0.1
胶 南 市	Jiaonan	0.1	0.1	0.2	0.1	0.1
莱 西 市	Laixi	0.1	0.1	0.1	0	0.2

单位:万人(10 000 persons)

交通运输仓储及邮政业 Transportation, Storage, Postal and Telecommunications	信息传输计算机服务软件业 Information Transmission, Computer Service and Software Service	批发和零售业 Wholesale and Retail Trade	住宿和餐饮业 Accommodation and Catering Trade
8.9	**1.2**	**15.8**	**3.6**
0.5	0	0.3	0.1
0.5	0.2	0.8	0.2
0.2	0.1	1	0.2
0.3	0	0.9	0.3
0.1	0	0.6	0.2
0.1	0.1	0.6	0.1
0.2	0	0.6	0.1
0.1	0	0.5	0.1

单位:万人(10 000 persons)

居民服务其他服务业 Resident Services and Other Services	教育 Education	卫生社会保障和社会福利业 Health Care, Social Protection and Social Welfare	文化体育和娱乐业 Culture, Sports and Recreation	公共管理和社会组织 Public Administration and Social Orgnization	国际组织 International Orgnization
0.7	**13.2**	**4.6**	**1.1**	**7.1**	**0**
0	0.7	0.3	0	0.4	0
0	0.9	0.1	0	0.4	0
0.2	0.5	0.2	0.1	0.3	0
0	1.4	0.3	0	0.6	0
0	1.5	0.4	0	0.9	0
0	1.4	0.3	0	0.8	0
0	1.1	0.3	0	0.6	0
0	0.8	0.3	0	0.5	0

3 -6 全市单位分市、区全部从业人员人数(2005 年底)

TOTAL NUMBER OF STAFF AND WORKERS IN THE WHOLE CITY BY REGION(END OF 2005)

单位:万人(10 000 persons)

市、区名称	Region	年末人数 Year-end Population	国有单位 State-owned Units	集体单位 Collective-owned Units	其他经济类型单位 Others
总　计	**Total**	**224.3**	**43.9**	**18.2**	**162.2**
市　区	Urban Area	122.3	27.2	11.2	83.9
#城阳区	Chengyang District	26.7	1.8	2.5	22.4
黄岛区	Huangdao District	15.9	1.7	1.1	13.1
崂山区	Laoshan District	12.5	1.3	2.9	8.3
胶州市	Jiaozhou	26.7	5.2	0.9	20.6
即墨市	Jimo	24.1	3.1	2.5	18.5
平度市	Pingdu	19.7	3.5	0.9	15.3
胶南市	Jiaonan	17.1	2.4	1.9	12.8
莱西市	Laixi	14.4	2.5	0.8	11.1

3 -7 全市在岗职工工资总额、平均工资(2001—2005 年)

TOTAL WAGE BILL AND AVERAGE WAGE OF STAFF AND WORKERS IN WORKERS(2001 - 2005)

年份 Year	工资总额(万元) Total Wage Bill(10000 yuan)		平均工资(元) Average Wage(yuan)	
	全社会单位 All Units	其中:城镇单位 of which:Units in Town	全社会单位 All Units	其中:城镇单位 of which:Units in Town
2001	-	1 293 684	-	12 722
2002	-	1 469 247	-	14 114
2003	2 256 034	1 603 371	12 597	15 335
2004	2 804 932	1 933 541	13 932	17 190
2005	3 594 799	2 427 971	16 015	20 022

3－8 全市职工工资总额、平均工资(1978—2005 年)

TOTAL WAGE BILL AND AVERAGE WAGE OF STAFF AND WORKERS(1978－2005)

年 份 Year	工资总额(万元) Total Wage Bill(10000 yuan)		平均工资(元) Average Wage(yuan)	
	全社会单位 All Units	其中:城镇单位 of which:Units in Town	全社会单位 All Units	其中:城镇单位 of which:Units in Town
1978	–	40 161	–	584
1979	–	48 005	–	662
1980	–	59 503	–	782
1981	–	63 498	–	778
1982	–	65 914	–	785
1983	–	68 640	–	809
1984	–	89 673	–	1 041
1985	–	96 049	–	1 103
1986	–	118 352	–	1 311
1987	–	142 138	–	1 519
1988	–	179 770	–	1 862
1989	–	207 263	–	2 120
1990	–	243 864	–	2 400
1991	–	264 061	–	2 553
1992	–	317 550	–	2 970
1993	–	403 568	–	3 694
1994	–	595 085	–	5 455
1995	–	682 953	–	6 164
1996	–	782 257	–	6 640
1997	–	825 299	–	7 030
1998	–	871 805	–	7 518
1999	–	1 000 932	–	8 405
2000	–	1 203 991	–	10 072
2001	–	1 357 786	–	11 426
2002	–	1 538 475	–	12 839
2003	2 326 424	1 674 429	12 007	14 162
2004	2 882 933	2 007 102	13 445	15 950
2005	3 678 422	2 506 705	15 616	19 086

3-9 全市职工工资总额、平均工资指数(1978—2005年)
INDEXES OF TOTAL WAGE BILL AND AVERAGE WAGE OF STAFF AND WORKERS(1978-2005)

年份 Year	工资总额 Total Wage Bill		平均工资 Average Wage	
	全社会单位 All Units	其中:城镇单位 of which:Units in Town	全社会单位 All Units	其中:城镇单位 of which:Units in Town
1978	-	120.8	-	104.66
1979	-	119.53	-	113.36
1980	-	123.95	-	118.13
1981	-	106.71	-	99.49
1982	-	103.8	-	100.9
1983	-	104.14	-	103.06
1984	-	130.64	-	128.68
1985	-	107.11	-	105.96
1986	-	123.22	-	118.86
1987	-	120.1	-	115.87
1988	-	126.48	-	122.58
1989	-	115.29	-	113.86
1990	-	117.66	-	113.21
1991	-	108.28	-	106.38
1992	-	120.26	-	116.33
1993	-	127.09	-	124.38
1994	-	147.46	-	147.67
1995	-	114.76	-	113
1996	-	114.54	-	107.72
1997	-	105.5	-	105.87
1998	-	105.64	-	106.94
1999	-	114.81	-	111.8
2000	-	120.29	-	119.83
2001	-	112.77	-	113.44
2002	-	113.31	-	112.37
2003	111.98	108.84	109.4	110.30
2004	128.65	119.87	111.98	112.63
2005	127.59	124.89	116.15	119.66

3 -10 分市、区职工工资总额(2005 年)
TOTAL WAGE BILL OF STAFF AND WORKERS BY REGION(2005)

单位:万元(10 000 yuan)

市、区名称	Region	合计 Total	#工业 Industry	国有单位 State-owned Units	#工业 Industry	集体单位 Collective-owned Units	#工业 Industry	其他所有制单位 Other Ownership Units	#工业 Industry
总计	**Total**	**3 678 422.1**	**1 717 107.2**	**1 310 756.0**	**167 780.6**	**238 846.7**	**106 616.3**	**2 128 819.4**	**1 442 710.3**
市区	Urban Area	2 335 159.1	926 921.6	894 782.6	142 671.2	117 470.2	66 229.1	1 322 906.3	718 021.3
#城阳区	Chengyang District	378 648.9	272 717.7	72 028.0	1 959.7	31 321.6	16 701.9	275 299.3	254 056.1
黄岛区	Huangdao District	278 445.9	154 022.4	74 247.0	10 204.6	15 187.6	7 833.2	189 011.3	135 984.6
崂山区	Laoshan District	219 630.9	114 802.6	57 803.3	985.9	32 386.4	20 316.7	129 441.2	93 500.0
胶州市	Jiaozhou	364 122.7	194 286.6	116 517.6	6 064.6	10 842.9	6 716.5	236 762.2	181 505.5
即墨市	Jimo	316 652.5	220 693.7	71 146.0	4 365.7	23 177.9	15 123.5	222 328.6	201 204.5
平度市	Pingdu	223 079.9	112 585.5	63 197.5	5 448.1	9 942.3	5 604.4	149 940.1	101 533.0
胶南市	Jiaonan	240 399.2	144 470.1	60 750.0	3 918.4	26 643.3	10 655.7	153 005.9	129 896.0
莱西市	Laixi	199 008.7	118 149.7	46 559.0	5 312.6	18 383.7	2 287.1	134 066.0	110 550.0

3 -11 分市、区职工平均工资(2005 年)
AVERAGE WAGE BILL OF STAFF AND WORKERS BY REGION(2005)

单位:元/年(yuan/year)

市、区名称	Region	合计 Total	#工业 Industry	国有单位 State-owned Units	#工业 Industry	集体单位 Collective-owned Units	#工业 Industry	其他所有制单位 Other Ownership Units	#工业 Industry
总计	**Total**	**15 616**	**12 575**	**26 837**	**17 660**	**10 792**	**9 692**	**12 934**	**12 485**
#城阳区	Chengyang District	15 134	13 534	35 129	12 112	11 950	11 528	13 542	13 929
黄岛区	Huangdao District	17 925	15 368	41 567	25 973	13 071	15 646	14 996	15 034
崂山区	Laoshan District	17 997	15 281	41 373	15 825	11 417	10 849	17 297	16 883
胶州市	Jiaozhou	13 543	11 482	21 647	13 852	10 048	8 228	11 567	11 628
即墨市	Jimo	12 568	11 344	22 262	17 869	8 532	8 144	11 524	11 600
平度市	Pingdu	10 897	9 354	16 737	11 448	7 760	8 768	9 729	9 288
胶南市	Jiaonan	11 903	10 183	23 613	12 664	10 038	8 360	10 431	10 344
莱西市	Laixi	12 173	11 368	17 180	9 380	10 128	7 033	11 320	11 581

CHAPTER 4

第四篇

固定资产投资

INVESTMENT IN FIXED ASSETS

编辑单位：	固定资产投资统计处	农村社会经济调查队
编　　委：	王金峰	纪中锐
编　　辑：	王之钰　孙辉	王爱卿
校　　对：	王之钰　孙辉	王爱卿
电　　话：	85912252	82869356

4－1 主要年份固定资产投资

MAJOR YEAR'S INVESTMENT IN FIXED ASSETS

单位:万元(10 000 yuan)

年 份 Year	全社会固定资产投资 Total Investment in Fixed Assets	规模以上固定资产投资总额 Investment in Fixed Assets above the Set Scale	按用途分 Grouped by Use		
			生产性投资 Productive Investment	非生产性投资 Non- productive Investment	#住宅投资 Residential Housing Investment
1949	–	16	12	4	3
1952	–	3 097	1 368	1 729	1 007
1957	–	5 923	3 947	1 976	1 151
1962	–	2 747	2 049	698	192
1965	–	5 481	4 155	1 326	375
1970	–	6 100	5 813	287	154
1975	–	15 839	13 548	2 381	1 064
1978	–	29 660	23 499	6 161	3 203
1980	–	47 499	33 865	13 634	9 335
1985	–	107 421	60 643	73 424	19 058
1989	–	262 214	190 950	71 264	26 592
1990	–	284 576	210 453	74 123	38 898
1991	–	349 031	256 633	92 398	51 898
1992	–	583 068	420 748	162 320	83 844
1993	1 269 000	953 274	511 684	441 590	162 419
1994	1 795 000	1 329 716	728 532	601 184	324 094
1995	2 140 000	1 648 281	925 194	723 087	390 206
1996	2 100 000	1 610 562	972 398	638 164	285 412
1997	2 102 000	1 611 902	932 207	679 695	278 951
1998	2 423 000	1 909 711	1 125 821	783 890	316 999
1999	2 789 478	2 205 891	1 246 328	959 563	421 151
2000	3 211 270	2 426 820	1 311 538	1 115 282	470 963
2001	3 844 127	2 934 728	1 487 762	1 446 966	729 181
2002	4 782 532	3 683 623	1 962 588	1 721 035	765 030
2003	7 393 766	5 475 526	3 023 930	2 451 596	1 038 304
2004	10 254 204	9 845 646	6 336 279	3 509 367	1 608 738
2005	14 565 808	14 032 960	9 172 206	4 860 754	1 841 644

注:规模以上固定资产投资数据2003年以前为城镇以上统计范围。

Note:The data of investment above the set scale refer to investment above city and town level before 2003.

4 –1 续表
continued

单位:万元(10 000 yuan)

年　份 Year	按构成分 Grouped by Composition 建筑安装工程 Construction and Installation	设备工器具购置 Purchase of Equipment and Instruments	其他费用 Others	按资金来源分 Grouped by Capital Source 国家投资 Investment of State	国内贷款 Domestic Loans	利用外资 Utilization of Foreign Capital	自筹及其他 Self-raised and Other Capital
1949	11	3	2	16	–	–	–
1952	2 146	870	81	1 512	–	–	1 585
1957	2 853	2 773	297	3 816	–	–	2 107
1962	1 631	984	132	2 205	–	–	542
1965	3 346	1 859	276	4 451	–	–	1 030
1970	3 136	2 835	129	2 721	–	–	3 379
1975	7 489	8 133	217	9 378	1 362	–	5 099
1978	19 968	9 124	568	16 828	1 601	–	11 231
1980	30 993	15 541	965	10 371	12 925	1 420	22 783
1985	64 665	35 100	7 656	17 377	35 888	1 136	53 020
1989	141 821	95 333	17 269	38 747	79 999	25 081	114 939
1990	167 731	91 305	25 540	24 687	91 895	23 688	144 306
1991	196 212	108 929	43 890	22 615	131 676	38 325	156 415
1992	304 060	208 384	70 624	22 660	213 217	89 130	258 061
1993	600 011	225 555	127 708	23 736	208 672	94 469	626 397
1994	842 809	272 126	214 781	26 062	318 334	221 265	764 055
1995	1 020 484	385 934	241 863	25 683	379 198	328 124	915 276
1996	929 735	458 284	222 543	35 639	444 443	310 722	819 758
1997	875 057	485 122	251 723	27 928	297 089	363 789	923 096
1998	1 034 500	574 852	300 359	67 762	491 812	170 709	1 179 428
1999	1 456 473	459 596	289 822	128 603	584 120	145 589	1 347 579
2000	1 476 397	652 640	297 783	75 978	489 697	164 175	1 806 238
2001	1 781 235	744 549	408 944	93 491	620 562	217 526	2 157 787
2002	2 328 492	796 685	558 446	78 775	719 677	411 704	2 831 288
2003	3 544 790	1 133 333	797 403	127 861	989 178	722 644	4 237 643
2004	6 413 046	2 312 139	1 120 461	85 549	1 100 297	1 016 145	8 245 272
2005	8 949 231	3 141 732	1 941 997	136 632	1 250 343	1 850 921	11 540 604

4 -2 主要年份固定资产投资构成(以投资总额为 100)

COMPOSITION OF MAJOR YEAR'S INVESTMENT IN FIXED ASSETS(TOTAL INVESTMENT = 100)

年份 Year	按用途分 Grouped by Use		
	生产性投资 Productive Investment	非生产性投资 Non-productive Investment	#住宅投资占非生产性比重 Proportion of Residence Investment in Non-productive Investment
1949	75	25	75
1952	44.17	55.83	58.24
1957	66.64	33.36	58.25
1962	74.59	25.41	27.51
1965	75.81	24.19	28.28
1970	95.3	4.7	53.66
1975	84.97	15.03	44.69
1978	79.23	20.77	51.99
1980	71.3	28.7	68.47
1985	56.45	43.55	40.74
1989	72.82	27.18	37.3
1990	73.95	26.05	52.5
1991	73.53	26.47	56.17
1992	72.16	27.84	51.65
1993	53.68	46.32	36.78
1994	54.79	45.21	53.91
1995	56.1	43.9	54
1996	60.4	39.6	44.7
1997	57.8	42.2	41
1998	59	41	16.6
1999	56.5	43.5	19.1
2000	54	46	19.4
2001	50.7	49.3	50.4
2002	53.3	46.7	44.5
2003	55.2	44.8	42.4
2004	64.4	35.6	45.8
2005	65.4	34.6	37.9

4－2 续表
continued

年份 Year	按构成分 Grouped by Composition			按资金来源分 Grouped by Source			
	建筑安装工程 Construction and Installation	设备工器具购置 Purchase of Equipment and Instruction	其他费用 Others	国家投资 Investment of State	国内贷款 Domestic Loans	利用外资 Utilization of Foreign Capital	自筹及其他 Self-raised and Other Capital
1949	68.75	18.75	12.5	100	-	-	-
1952	69.29	28.09	2.62	48.82	-	-	51.18
1957	48.17	46.82	5.01	64.43	-	-	35.57
1962	59.37	35.82	4.81	80.27	-	-	19.73
1965	61.05	33.92	5.03	81.21	-	-	18.79
1970	51.41	46.48	2.11	44.61	-	-	55.39
1975	47.28	51.35	1.37	59.21	8.6	-	32.19
1978	67.32	30.76	1.92	56.74	5.4	-	37.86
1980	65.25	32.72	2.03	21.83	27.21	2.99	47.97
1985	60.2	32.68	7.12	16.18	33.41	1.06	49.35
1989	54.08	36.36	6.59	14.78	30.51	9.56	45.15
1990	58.94	32.08	8.98	8.68	32.29	8.32	50.71
1991	56.22	31.21	12.57	6.48	37.73	10.98	44.81
1992	52.15	35.74	12.11	3.89	36.56	15.29	44.26
1993	62.94	23.66	13.4	2.49	21.89	9.91	65.71
1994	63.38	20.46	16.16	1.96	23.94	16.64	57.46
1995	61.9	23.4	14.7	1.6	23	19.9	55.5
1996	57.7	28.5	13.8	2.2	27.6	19.3	50.9
1997	54.3	30.1	15.6	1.7	18.4	22.6	57.3
1998	54.2	20.8	15.7	3.5	25.8	8.9	61.8
1999	66	20.8	13.2	5.8	26.5	6.6	61.1
2000	60.8	26.9	12.3	3.1	20.2	6.8	74.4
2001	60.7	25.4	13.9	3	20.1	7	69.9
2002	63.2	21.6	15.2	1.9	17.8	10.2	70.1
2003	64.7	20.7	14.6	2.1	16.3	11.9	69.7
2004	65.1	23.5	11.4	0.8	10.6	9.7	78.9
2005	63.8	22.4	13.8	0.9	8.5	12.5	78.1

4-3 全社会固定资产投资
TOTAL INVESTMENT IN FIXED ASSETS

单位:万元(10 000 yuan)

指　标	Indicators	2005 年 2005	2005 年比 2004 年增长% Growth of 2005 Compared to 2004
总　计	**Total**	**14 565 808**	**45**
其中:规模以上单位投资	Units above the Set Scale	14 032 960	45.6
第一产业	Primary Industry	289 887	5
第二产业	Secondary Industry	7 892 555	45.9
#工业	Industry	7 555 770	54.4
第三产业	Tertiary Industry	5 850 518	40.7

注:本表中的投资增长速度为调整 2004 年投资基数以后的口径。
Note: The growth rate of investment in the form is calculated according to the adjusted data in 2004.

4-4 分市、区固定资产投资额(2005 年)
INVESTMENT IN FIXED ASSETS BY REGION(2005)

单位:万元(10 000 yuan)

市区名称	Region	全社会固定资产投资额 Investment in Fixed Assets	#房地产开发 Investment in Real Estate Development
总　计	**Total**	**14 565 808**	**2 238 370**
市　区	Urban Area	6 304 202	1 753 732
#城阳区	Chengyang District	1 628 026	170 281
黄岛区	Huangdao District	1 708 417	181 756
崂山区	Laoshan District	726 645	366 419
胶州市	Jiaozhou	1 968 640	108 123
即墨市	Jimo	1 813 173	142 527
平度市	Pingdu	1 324 930	52 394
胶南市	Jiaonan	1 971 985	134 630
莱西市	Laixi	1 182 878	46 964

4-5 规模以上固定资产投资(2005 年)
INVESTMENT ABOVE THE SET SCALE IN FIXED ASSETS(2005)

单位:万元(10 000 yuan)

项目	Items	合计 Total	#房地产开发 Investment in Real Estate Development
一、本年施工项目(个)	**Projects Under Construction of the Year**	**5 631**	
#本年新开工(个)	Newly Operating Projects of the Year	4 962	
二、本年建成投产项目(个)	**Projects Completed and Put into Use of the Year**	**1 710**	
三、本年完成投资	**Investment Completed of the Year**	**14 032 960**	**2 238 370**
1. 按构成分	Grouped by Composition		
#建筑工程	Construction Projects	8 244 384	1 430 146
安装工程	Installation Projects	704 847	149 734
设备工器具购置	Purchase of Equipment and Instruments	3 141 732	29 332
#用于更新的设备	Equipment Used in Updates	146 807	
2. 按建设性质分	Grouped by Type of Construction		
#新　建	New Construction	8 062 740	
扩　建	Reconstruction	2 520 686	
改　建	Expansion	786 735	
3. 按隶属关系分	Grouped by Administrative Relationship		
中央单位	Central Govemment Units	348 058	7 792
地方单位	Local Units	13 684 902	2 230 578
4. 按国民经济行业分	Grouped by Economis Sector		
(1)农、林、牧、渔业	Farming, Forestry, Animal Husbandry and Fishery	242 052	
农　业	Farming	26 635	
林　业	Forestry	11 740	
畜牧业	Animal Husbandry	50 387	
渔　业	Fishery	134 795	
农、林、牧、渔服务业	Farming, Forestry, Animal Husbandry and Fishery Services	18 495	
(2)采矿业	Excavation	95 973	
煤炭开采和洗选业	Coal Mining and Dressing	1 900	
石油和天然气开采业	Petroleum and Natural Gas Extraction	1 100	
黑色金属矿采选业	Ferrous Metals Mining and Dressing	51 067	
有色金属矿采选业	Nonferrous Metals Mining and Dressing	12 781	
非金属矿采选业	Nonmetal Minerals Mining and Dressing	29 125	
其他采矿业	Other Minerals Mining	-	

4 -5 续表
continued

单位:万元(10 000 yuan)

项　　目	Items	合计 Total	#房地产开发 Investment in Real Estate Development
(3)制 造 业	Manufacturing	7 180 877	
农副食品加工业	Agriculture Non-staple Food Processing	526 596	
食品制造业	Food Manufacturing	250 330	
饮料制造业	Beverage Manufacturing	63 627	
烟草加工业	Tobacco Processing	43 382	
纺 织 业	Textile Industry	414 463	
纺织服装、鞋、帽制造业	Textile, Chothing and Footwear Production	517 179	
皮革、毛皮、羽毛(绒)及其制品业	Learthers, Furs, Down and Related Products	202 156	
木材加工及木、竹、藤、棕、草制品业	Timber Processing, Bamboo, Cane, Palm Fiber and Straw Products	88 140	
家具制造业	Furinture Manufacturing	190 814	
造纸及纸制品业	Papermaking and Paper Products	125 077	
印刷业和记录媒介的复制	Printing and Record Medium Reproduction	123 355	
文教体育用品制造业	Stationary, Education and Sports Goods	127 504	
石油加工、炼焦及核燃料加工业	Petroleum Processing, Coking and Nuclear Fuel Processing	97 288	
化学原料及化学制品制造业	Raw Chemical Materials and Chemical Products	551 020	
医药制造业	Medical and Pharmaceutic Products	65 313	
化学纤维制造业	Chemical Fibers	18 312	
橡胶制品业	Rubber Products	214 303	
塑料制品业	Plastic Products	214 930	
非金属矿物制品业	Nonmetal Mineral Products	381 968	
黑色金属冶炼及压延加工业	Smelting and Processing of Ferrous Metals	46 641	
有色金属冶炼及压延加工业	Smelting and Processing of Nonferrous Metals	48 371	
金属制品业	Metal Products	599 317	
通用设备制造业	General-purpose Equipment Manufacturing	566 743	
专用设备制造业	Special-purpose Equipment Manufacturing	468 574	
交通运输设备制造业	Transportation Equipment Manufacturing	344 157	
电气机械及器材制造业	Electric Equipment and Machinery Manufacturing	314 081	

4－5 续表 1
continued

单位：万元(10 000 yuan)

项 目	Items	合计 Total	#房地产开发 Investment in Real Estate Development
通信设备、计算机及其他电子设备制造业	Communication Equipment, Computers and Other Electronic Equipment Production	325 551	
仪器仪表及文化、办公用机械制造业	Instruments, Meters, Cultural and Office Facilities Manufacturing	49 214	
工艺品及其他制造业	Handicraft Articles and Other Goods Production	175 921	
废旧资源和废旧材料回收加工业	Discarded Resources and Waste Materials Recovery and Processing	26 550	
(4)电力、燃气及水的生产和供应业	Electric Power, Gas, Water Production and Supply	278 920	
电力、热力的生产和供应业	Electric Power, Steam, Hot Water Production and Supply	218 344	
燃气生产和供应业	Gas Production and Supply	25 058	
水的生产和供应业	Tap Water Production and Supply	35 518	
(5)建 筑 业	Construction	336 785	
(6)交通运输、仓储及邮政业	Transportation, Storage, Postal and Telecommunications	497 305	
铁路运输业	Railway Transportation	655	
道路运输业	Highway Transportation	189 563	
城市公共交通业	Urban Public Transit	3 307	
水上运输业	Waterway Transportation	189 237	
航空运输业	Air Transportation	0	
(7)信息传输、计算机服务和软件业	Information Transmission, Computer Service and Software Service	22 798	
(8)批发和零售业	Wholesale and Retail Trade	420 856	
(9)住宿和餐饮业	Accommodation and Catering Trade	136 223	
(10)金融业	Finance	5 858	
(11)房地产业	Real Estate	2 712 275	2 238 370

4 -5 续表 2
continued

单位:万元(10 000 yuan)

项　　目	Items	合计 Total	#房地产开发 Investment in Real Estate Development
(12)租赁和商务服务业	Leasing Trade and Commercial Service	91 505	
(13)科学研究、技术服务和地质勘察业	Scientiffic Research, Technical Service and Geological Prospecting	37 078	
(14)水利、环境和公共设施管理业	Water Conservancy, Environment and Administration of Public Facilities	959 213	
水利管理业	Administration of Water Conservancy	47 835	
环境管理业	Administration of Environment	47 905	
公共设施管理业	Administration of Public Facilities	863 473	
(15)居民服务和其他服务业	Residents Services and Other Social Services	45 461	
居民服务业	Residents Services	30 887	
其他服务业	Other Services	14 574	
(16)教育	Education	181 625	
(17)卫生、社会保障和社会福利业	Health Care, Social Protection and Social Walfare	73 620	
卫生	Health Care	61 206	
(18)文化、体育和娱乐业	Culture, Sports and Recreation	180 132	
新闻出版业	News and Publish	1 294	
广播、电视、体育和音像业	Broadcast, TV, Sports and Audio-video	27 344	
文化艺术业	Culture and Art	12 406	
体育	Sports	56 232	
娱乐业	Recreation	82 856	
(19)公共管理和社会组织	Public Administration and Social Ognization	534 404	
国家机构	Government Instiutions	285 287	
群众团体、社会团体和宗教组织	Mass, Social and Religion Organizations	786	
基层群众自治组织	Mass Autonomic Organizations	248 331	
(20)国际组织	International Ognization	-	
国际组织	International Ognization	-	

4－5 续表3
continued

单位：万元(10 000 yuan)

项　目	Items	合计 Total	#房地产开发 Investment in Real Estate Development
四、本年新增固定资产	**Newly Increased Fixed Assets of the Year**	**7 767 271**	**1 511 949**
(1)农、林、牧、渔业	Farming, Forestry, Animal Husbandry and Fishery	125 516	
(2)采 矿 业	Excavation	79 401	
(3)制 造 业	Manufacturing	4 199 657	
(4)电力、燃气及水的生产和供应业	Power, Gas and Water Production and Supply	55 384	
(5)建 筑 业	Construction	210 797	
(6)交通运输、仓储和邮政业	Transportation, Storage, Postal and Telecommunication	166 398	
(7)信息传输、计算机服务和软件业	Information Transmission, Computer Service and Software Service	6 395	
(8)批发和零售业	Wholesale and Retail Trade	191 487	
(9)住宿和餐饮业	Accommodation and Catering Trade	59 772	
(10)金融业	Banking	5 858	
(11)房地产业	Real Estate Trade	1 694 919	1 511 949
(12)租赁和商务服务业	Leasing Trade and Commercial Service	15 420	
(13)科学研究、技术服务和地质勘察业	Scientific Research, Technical Service and Geological Prospecting	9 073	
(14)水利、环境和公共设施管理业	Water Conservancy, Environment and Administration of Public Facilities	456 616	
(15)居民服务和其他服务业	Resident Services and Other Services	14 758	
(16)教育	Education	115 070	
(17)卫生、社会保障和社会福利业	Health Care, Social Protection and Social Welfare	19 422	
(18)文化、体育和娱乐业	Culture, Sports and Recreation	64 459	
(19)公共管理和社会组织	Public Administration and Social Ognization	276 869	
(20)国际组织	International Ognization	0	
五、本年资金来源合计	**Total Capital Source of the Year**	**15 779 797**	**3 453 969**
上年末结余资金	A Balance at End of Previous Year	1 001 297	696 087
本年资金来源小计	Sub-total Capital Source of the Year	14 778 500	2 757 882
国家预算内资金	Capital Within the State Budget	136 632	1 600
国内贷款	Domestic Loans	1 250 343	508 617
债　券	State Treasury Bond	500	0
利用外资	Foreign Investment Used	1 850 921	702
自筹资金	Self-raised Capital	9 953 807	1 102 619
其他资金来源	Other Capital	1 586 297	1 144 344

4-6 规模以上投资项目新增主要生产能力(或工程效益)(2005年)

PRODUCTION CAPACITY(OR BENEFIT) NEWLY INCREASED OF INVESTMENT PROJECTS ABOVE THE SET SCALE(2005)

分组指标	Indicators in Groups	本年新增能力 Newly Increased Capacity
洗煤(万吨/年)	Dressing Coal(10000 tons/year)	120
焦炭(万吨/年)	Coke(10000 tons/year)	60
铁矿开采(原矿)(万吨/年)	Iron ore mining (10000 tons/year)	60.2
炼钢(万吨/年)	Steel - making(10000 tons/year)	73.39
火力发电(万千瓦)	Thermal Power Generation(10000 kw)	13
水泥(万吨/年)	Cement(10000 tons/year)	102.4
平板玻璃(万重量箱/年)	Plate Glass(10000 wt. cases/year)	107
石墨及炭素制品(吨/年)	Graphite and charcoal plain products(ton/year)	71 470
烧碱(吨/年)	Caustic Soda(ton/year)	2 000
塑料树脂及共聚物(吨/年)	Plastic Resin(ton/year)	5 500
轮胎外胎(万条/年)	Tires(10000 lines)	1 095
化学原料药(吨/年)	Chenical Medicines(Raw Materials)(ton/year)	530
中成药(吨/年)	Proprietary Chinese Medicines(ton/year)	200
内燃机(台/年)	Internal Combustion Engines(set/year)	21
金属切削机床制造(台/年)	Metal - cutting Machines(set/year)	1 610
载货汽车制造(辆/年)	Freight Trucks(vehicle/year)	100
化学纤维(吨/年)	Chemical Fibers(ton/year)	220
食用植物油(日处理原料:吨)	Vegetable Oil(Daily Treatment of Row Material:ton)	330
卷 烟(箱/年)	Cigarette(case/year)	112 800
房间空气调节器(万台/年)	Air Conditioner(10000 units/year)	40
新建公路(公里)	Newly - built Highway(km)	598
改建公路(公里)	Revamped Highway(km)	251
一级公路(公里)	Class 1 Highway(km)	25
新(扩)建港口码头(年吞吐量:万吨)	Newly Built(or Expanded) Port(Yearly Handled Volume:10000 tons)	102
新(扩)建港口码头(泊位:个)	Newly Built(or Expanded) Port(Berth:unit)	15
新(扩)建客、货运站(个)	Newly Built(or Expanded) Passenger and Freight Station(unit)	1
新(扩)建客、货运站(平方米)	Newly Built(or Expanded) Passenger and Freight Station(sq. m)	23 292
候机楼(座)	Airport Departure Buliding(place)	1
候机楼(平方米)	Airport Departure Buliding(sq. m)	8 000
造林面积(万亩)	Forestation Area(10000 mu)	0.21
有效灌溉面积(万亩)	Effective Irrigated Area(10000 mu)	5.5
商业冷藏库(万吨)	Commercial Refrigerator(10000 tons)	10.36
水产冷藏库(万吨)	Aquatic Refrigerator(10000 tons)	0.02

4-6 续表
continued

分组指标	Indicators in Groups	本年新增能力 Newly Increased Capacity
高等院校:学生席位(个)	Institution of High Learning:Student Enrollment(seat)	12 130
建筑面积(平方米)	Construction Area(sq. m)	223 931
中等学校:学生席位(个)	Secondary Schools:Student Enrollment(seat)	6 504
建筑面积(平方米)	Construction Area(sq. m)	168 177
小学校:学生席位(个)	Primary Schools:Student Enrollment(seat)	6 760
建筑面积(平方米)	Construction Area(sq. m)	24 691
其他学校:学生席位(个)	Other Schools:Student Enrollment(seat)	1220
建筑面积(平方米)	Construction Area(sq. m)	29 080
公共图书馆:藏书量(万册(件))	Public Library:Collection Books(10000 copies)	100
阅览室座席(个)	Seat in Reading room(seat)	200
建筑面积(平方米)	Construction Area(sq. m)	10 200
医院病床(张)	Beds in Hospitals(bed)	2 088
宾馆、旅馆、招待所客房数(间)	Guest Rooms of Hotels,Restaurants & Hotels(room)	1 092
宾馆、旅馆、招待所客房数(平方米)	Guest Rooms of Hotels,Restaurants & Hotels(sq. m)	40 268
城市自来水供水能力(万吨/日)	Capacity of Tap Water Supply(10000 tons/day)	59
城市自来水管道长度(公里)	Length of Tap Water Pipes:steam(km)	61.5
城市煤气生产能力(万立方米/日)	Capacity of Gas Product(10000 cu. m/day)	2
城市天然气储气能力(万立方米/日)	Capacity of Natural Gas Store(10000 cu. m/day)	5
城市供热能力:蒸汽(吨/小时)	Capacity of Heat Supply:Steam(ton/hour)	800
热水(兆瓦/小时)	Hot Water(mega-w/hour)	613
城市道路扩建长度(公里)	Length of Expanded Roads(km)	80.2
城市道路扩建面积(万平方米)	Area of Expanded Roads(10000 sq. m)	66.5
城市排水管道铺设长度(公里)	Length of Sewage Pipes(km)	109.9
城市污水处理能力(万吨/日)	Capacity of Waste Water Treatment(10000 tons/day)	8
城市永久性桥梁(座)	Permanent Bridge(place)	2
客车制造(辆/年)	Bus Manufacturing(vehicle/year)	8 000
电视机(万部/年)	Television Set(10000 sets/year)	410
移动电话机(手持机)(指生产能力)(部/年)	Cell Phone(portable) (referring to the production)(set/year)	4 800 050
二级公路(公里)	Class 2 Highway(km)	133
钢材(万吨/年)	Rolled-Steel(10000 tons/year)	37
发电机组容量(万千瓦)	Power Generation Set(10000 kw)	13
汽车制造(辆/年)	Automobile Manufacturing(vehicle/year)	8 100
乳制品(吨/年)	Milk Product(ton/year)	9 300
酒(万吨/年)	Liquor(10000 tons/year)	22.21

4-7 主要年份房地产开发投资
MAJOR YEAR'S INVESTMENT IN REAL ESTATE DEVELOPMENT

单位:万元、万平方米(10 000 yuan、10 000 sq. m)

年 份 Year	房地产开发投资额 Investment in Real Estate Development	房屋施工面积 Floor Space Under Construction	房屋竣工面积 Floor Space Completed	房屋实际销售面积 Floor Space of Buildings Sold	房屋实际销售额 Sales of Buildings
1995	562 861	1 008	240	103	185 384
1996	455 765	748	203	80	125 150
1997	426 570	675	237	113	216 311
1998	438 059	742	259	178	351 805
1999	629 717	900	474	240	430 123
2000	675 142	1 047	352	301	550 401
2001	925 153	1 374	532	406	802 364
2002	1 036 476	1 417	537	427	933 031
2003	1 277 969	1 765	552	469	1 121 885
2004	1 626 965	2 101	635	516	1 530 964
2005	2 238 370	2 363	811	740	2 666 738

4 -8 房地产开发投资情况(2005 年)

INVESTMENT IN REAL ESTATE DEVELOPMENT(2005)

单位:万元(10 000 yuan)

指标名称	Indicators	合计 Total	按经济类型分 Grouped by Economic Types		
			国有经济 State-owned	集体经济 Collective-owned	其他经济 Others
本年完成投资额	**Investment Completed in the Year**	**2 238 370**	**113 551**	**112 108**	**2 012 711**
#土地开发投资额	Investment in Lands Development	63 146	3 291	4 687	55 168
1. 住　宅	Residential Housing	1 620 904	92 904	95 122	1 432 878
2. 办公楼	Office Building	138 630	3 158	1 770	133 702
3. 商业营业用房	Commercial Building	180 071	4 485	2 665	172 921
4. 其　他	Others	298 765	12 923	12 551	273 291

4 -8 续表

continued

单位:万元(10 000 yuan)

指标名称	Indicators	按资质等级分 Grouped by Grades					
		一级 1 Class	二级 2 Class	三级 3 Class	四级 4 Class	暂定 Provisional	其他 Others
本年完成投资额	**Investment Completed in the Year**	**199 828**	**540 578**	**466 546**	**355 093**	**627 095**	**49 230**
#土地开发投资额	Investment in Lands Development	24 579	13 102	13 814	10 192	145	1 314
1. 住　宅	Residential Housing	179 411	358 836	309 882	264 428	475 367	32 980
2. 办公楼	Office Building	32 891	2 627	83 773	9 580	500	9 259
3. 商业营业用房	Commercial Building	4 197	28 562	34 068	43 175	64 986	5 083
4. 其　他	Others	15 720	150 553	38 823	37 910	53 851	1 908

4-9 房地产施工、竣工面积及竣工价值(2005 年)
FLOOR SPACE UNDER CONSTRUCTION AND COMPLETED AND COMPLETED VALUE OF REAL ESTATE(2005)

单位:万平方米(10000 sq. m)

施工、竣工房屋面积及竣工价值	Indicators	施工面积 Floor Space Under Construction	#新开工 Newly Operating	竣工房屋 Floor Space Completed	竣工房屋价值(万元) Completed Value (10000 yuan)
房屋建筑面积总计	**Floor Space of Buildings**	**2 362.7**	**1 213.2**	**811.3**	**1 302 556**
住　宅	Residential Housing	1 862.8	979.3	578.3	1 060 948
其中:经济适用房	of which: Residental Housing for the Low-income Households	240.1	73.6	72.2	-
办公楼	Office Building	93	47	7.7	9 237
商业营业用房	Commercial Building	227.1	89.6	81.4	158 036
其　他	Others	179.8	97.3	43.9	74 335

4-10 商品房屋销售情况(2005 年)
SALES OF COMMERCIAL HOUSES(2005)

单位:万平方米(10000 sq. m)

商品房屋销售情况	Sales of Commercial Houses	实际销售 Actual Sales	空置 Vacancy	实际销售额(万元) Actual Sales Volume (10000 yuan)
房屋面积总计	**Floor Space of Buildings**	**739.9**	**113.6**	**2 666 738**
住　宅	Residential Housing	650	61.5	2 252 945
经济适用房	of which: Residental Housing for the Low-income Households	40.8	-	-
办公楼	Office Building	9	13.7	69 392
商业营业用房	Commercial Building	65.2	30.5	283 984
其　他	Others	15.7	7.9	60 417

4－11 农村非农户固定资产投资(2005 年)

INVESTMENT IN FIXED ASSETS OF NON-AGRICULTURAL RESIDENTS(2005)

市区名称	Region	新增固定资产原值(万元) Newly Increased Fixed Assets (10000 yuan)	固定资产投资额(万元) Investment in Fixed Assets (10000 yuan)	施工房屋面积(万平方米) Floor Space Under Construction (10000 sq. m)	竣工房屋面积(万平方米) Floor Space Completed (10000 sq. m)	#住 宅 Residential Housing
总　计	**Total**	**298 112**	**298 112**	**120.97**	**99.21**	**18.47**
胶州市	Jiaozhou	56 502	56 502	32.33	32.33	
即墨市	Jimo	74 569	74 569	13.93	13.59	
平度市	Pingdu	79 673	79 673	27.95	12.47	
胶南市	Jiaonan	56 497	56 497	18.68	18.42	
莱西市	Laixi	30 872	30 872	28.08	22.40	18.47

4－12 农户固定资产投资(2005 年)

INVESTMENT IN FIXED ASSETS OF AGRICULTURAL RESIDENTS(2005)

单位:万元(10 000 yuan)

市区名称	Region	新增固定资产原值 Newly Increased Fixed Assets	固定资产投资额 Investment in Fixed Assets	#自筹资金 Private Capital	#建筑工程 Construction Projects	#住宅 Residential Housing	#农业 Agriculture
总　计	**Total**	**234 736**	**234 736**	**228 290**	**131 526**	**87 681**	**65 300**
胶州市	Jiaozhou	44 713	44 713	44 713	26 037		18 812
即墨市	Jimo	48 408	48 408	41 962	30 579	21 138	4 291
平度市	Pingdu	60 168	60 168	60 168	29 538	25 939	13 370
胶南市	Jiaonan	30 503	30 503	30 503	10 345	10 345	8 623
莱西市	Laixi	50 943	50 943	50 943	35 026	30 259	20 204

CHAPTER 5

第五篇

能源消耗

CONSUMPTION OF ENERGY

编辑单位：工业交通统计处
编　　委：吴加琪
编　　辑：王福临　于泳洋
校　　对：王福临　于泳洋
电　　话：85912257

5-1 规模以上工业主要能源消费与库存(2005年)
CONSUMPTION AND STOCK OF MAJOR ENERGY OF INDUSTRY ABOVE THE SET SCALE(2005)

名　称	Name	计算单位	Unit	年初库存 Year-beginning Stock	本年消费 Consumption in the Year	#工业 Industry	#非工业 Non-industry	年末库存 Year-end Stock
原　煤	Raw Coal	吨	ton	938 827	13 042 275	12 765 673	276 602	1 024 670
焦　炭	Coke	吨	ton	19 812	1 742 424	1 742 261	163	5 293
焦炉煤气	Coking Gas	万立方米	10000 cu. m	0	524	523	1	0
其它煤气	Other Gas	万立方米	10000 cu. m	0	4 283	3 062	1 221	0
原　油	Crude Oil	吨	ton	85 559	2 076 284	2 076 219	65	34 919
汽　油	Petrol	吨	ton	662	106 198	85 915	20 283	7 807
煤　油	Kerosene	吨	ton	177	14 005	12 167	1 838	128
柴　油	Diesel Oil	吨	ton	2 870	219 650	185 963	33 687	4 650
燃料油	Fuel Oil	吨	ton	46 624	1 837 102	1 836 907	195	68 361
液化石油气	Liquefied Petroleum Gas	吨	ton	136	14 301	7 568	6 733	174
炼厂干气	Refinery Dry Gas	吨	ton	0	58 962	58 962	0	1
热　力	Heat	百万千焦	million kJ	0	27 363 579	26 474 367	889 213	0
电　力	Electricity	万千瓦时	10000 kwh	0	1 461 595	1 434 332	27 263	0

补充资料:2005年综合能源消费量13517585吨标准煤,工业总产值43166128万元。

Note: In 2005, the consumption of synthetical energy is 13517585 tons SCE, and the gross output value of industry is 431661.28 million yuan.

5－2 规模以上工业主要能源分行业消费量(2005 年)

MAJOR ENERGY CONSUMPTION BY SECTORS OF INDUSTRY ABOVE THE SET SCALE(2005)

		原煤 (吨) Raw Coal (ton)	焦炭 (吨) Coke (ton)	其他煤气 (万立方米) Other Gas (10000 cu. m)	原油 (吨) Crude Oil (ton)	汽油 (吨) Petrol (ton)
总　计	**Total**	**13 042 275**	**1 742 424**	**4 283**	**2 076 284**	**106 198**
采掘业	Excavation	24 977	0	0	0	742
制造业	Manufacturing	5 076 717	1 742 424	4 283	2 076 284	97 709
电力煤气及水生产供应业	Power Gas and Water Production and Supply	7 940 581	0	0	0	7 747

5－2 续表

continued

		煤油(吨) Kerosene (ton)	柴油(吨) Diesel Oil (ton)	燃料油(吨) Fuel Oil (ton)	液化石油气 (吨) Liquefied Petroleum Gas (ton)	热　力 (百万千焦) Heat (million kJ)	电　力 (万千瓦时) Electricity (10000 kwh)
总　计	**Total**	**14 005**	**219 650**	**1 837 102**	**14 301**	**27 363 579**	**1 461 595**
采掘业	Excavation	395	8 727	7	0	0	25 542
制造业	Manufacturing	10 595	196 025	1 832 959	11 368	26 143 250	1 213 943
电力煤气及水生产供应业	Power Gas and Water Production and Supply	3 015	14 898	4 136	2 933	1 220 329	222 110

5－3 重点耗能工业企业能源加工转换(2005年)

ENERGY PROCESSING TRANSFER OF MAJOR CONSUMPTION INDUSTRIAL ENTERPRISES(2005)

		单 位	Unit	能源消费合计 Total Energy Consumption	#转换投入 Transfer Input	火电 Thermal Power	供热 Heat Supply	炼油 Oil Refining	制气 Gas Making	能源转换产品 Transfer Output of Energy
原 煤	Raw Coal	吨	ton	9 266 826	7 680 153	5 442 127	2 238 026	0	0	0
洗精煤	Dressing Coal	吨	ton	617 282	617 282	0	0	0	617 282	0
型 煤	Held Coal Briquette	吨	ton	0	0	0	0	0	0	0
焦 炭	Coke	吨	ton	0	0	0	0	0	0	461 987
其他焦化产品	Other Coking Products	吨	ton	0	0	0	0	0	0	23 716
焦炉煤气	Coking Gas	万立方米	10000 cu. m	0	0	0	0	0	0	14 628
其他煤气	Other Gas	万立方米	10000 cu. m	0	0	0	0	0	0	2 000
原 油	Raw Oil	吨	ton	2 043 064	2 043 064	0	0	2 043 064	0	0
汽 油	Petrol	吨	ton	12 033	0	0	0	0	0	555 632
煤 油	Kerosene	吨	ton	3 000	0	0	0	0	0	0
柴 油	Diesel Oil	吨	ton	16 608	2 226	2012	199	15	0	883 693
燃料油	Fuel Oil	吨	ton	1 482 265	1 482 265	0	0	1 482 265	0	818 977
液化石油气	Liquefied Petroleum Gas	吨	ton	2 933	2 933	0	0	0	2 933	155 800
炼厂干气	Refinery Dry Gas	吨	ton	47 553	47 553	0	0	45 557	1 996	1 875
其他石油制品	Other Petroleum Products	吨	ton	0	0	0	0	0	0	399 036
热 力	Heat	百万千焦	million kJ	14 060 905	0	0	0	0	0	40 733 263
电 力	Electricity	万千瓦时	10000 kwh	249 948	0	0	0	0	0	800 874
其他燃料	Other Fuel	吨标准煤	ton SCE	0	0	0	0	0	0	0
能源合计	**Total**	**吨标准煤**	**ton SCE**	**13 127 258**	**11 163 748**	**3 895 268**	**1 596 866**	**5 107 895**	**563 718**	**6 719 322**

5. 能源消耗

5 -4 主要能源工业消费量(2005 年)

MAJOR ENERGY CONSUMPTION OF INDUSTRY(2005)

		原煤(吨) Raw Coal (ton)
总　计	**Total**	**13 042 275**
煤炭开采和洗选业	Coal Mining and Dressing	0
石油和天然气开采业	Petroleum and Natural Gas Extraction	0
黑色金属矿采选业	Ferrous Metals Mining and Dressing	660
有色金属矿采选业	NonFerrous Metals Mining and Dressing	4 516
非金属矿采选业	Nonmetal Minerals Mining and Dressing	19 801
其他采矿选业	Other Minerals Mining and Dressing	0
农副食品加工业	Agricultural Non – staple Food Processing	183 491
食品制造业	Food Production	80 277
饮料制造业	Beverage Production	225 316
烟草制品业	Tobacco Production	0
纺织业	Textile Industry	266 787
纺织服装、鞋、帽制造业	Textile, Clothing and Footwear Production	81 657
皮革、毛皮、羽毛(绒)及其制品业	Leathers, Furs Down and Related Products	48 087
木材加工及木、竹、藤、棕、草制品业	Timber Processing Bamboo Cane Palm Fiber and Straw Products	9 648
家具制造业	Furniture Manufacturing	23 985
造纸及纸制品业	Papermaking and Paper Products	132 145
印刷业、记录媒介的复制	Printing and Record Medium Reproduction	9 395
文教体育用品制造业	Cultural, Educational and Sports Goods	22 116
石油加工、炼焦及核燃料加工业	Petroleum Processing Coking and Nuclear Fuel Processing	25
化学原料及化学制品制造业	Raw Chemical Materials and Chemical Products	2 207 620
医药制造业	Medical and Pharmaceutic Products	9 951
化学纤维制造业	Chemical Fibers	3 432
橡胶制品业	Rubber Products	376 262
塑料制品业	Plastic Products	43 942
非金属矿物制品业	Nonmetal Mineral Products	535 621
黑色金属冶炼及压延加工业	Smelting and Processing of Ferrous Metals	358 776
有色金属冶炼及压延加工业	Smelting and Processing of Nonferrous Metals	6 589
金属制品业	Metal Products	61 975
通用设备制造业	General – purpose Equipment Manufacturing	92 694
专用设备制造业	Special – purpose Equipment Manufacturing	11 457
交通运输设备制造业	Transportation Equipment Manufacturing	89 219
电气机械及器材制造业	Electric Equipment and Machinery	134 394
通信设备、计算机及其他电子设备制造业	Communication Equipments Computers and Other Electronic Equipment Products	25 680
仪器仪表及文化、办公用机械制造业	Instruments Meters Cultural and Office Machinery	7 084
工艺品及其他制造业	Handicraft Articles and Other Goods Production	28 458
废弃资源和废旧材料回收加工	Discarded Resources and Waste Materials Recovery and Processing	634
电力、热力的生产和供应业	Power and Heat Production and Supply	7 725 972
燃气生产和供应业	Gas Production and Supply	214 250
水的生产和供应业	Water Production and Supply	359

洗精煤（吨）Dressing Coal(ton)	其他洗煤（吨）Other Dressing Coal(ton)	型煤（吨）Held Coal Briquette(ton)	焦炭（吨）Coke (ton)
622 707	**8 195**	**10 072**	**1 742 424**
0	0	0	0
0	0	0	0
0	0	0	0
0	0	0	0
0	0	403	0
0	0	0	0
7	0	753	1 309
0	0	320	46
0	0	0	145
0	0	0	0
24	1 015	7	45
960	1 810	52	939
5	40	29	7 030
0	0	0	0
0	0	70	8
0	1 240	338	28
0	0	99	0
600	5	85	77
5	0	0	3
0	0	28	197
5	0	360	102
0	0	20	0
765	0	0	21
50	8	0	0
0	0	902	1 874
0	0	0	1 688 172
0	0	0	241
1 980	3 706	365	7 023
800	281	5 957	25 013
0	0	190	6 667
3	0	27	3 157
34	90	20	172
0	0	0	17
0	0	22	0
187	0	25	138
0	0	0	0
0	0	0	0
617 282	0	0	0
0	0	0	0

5－4 续表
continued

		焦炉煤气 （万立方米） Coking Gas （10000 cu. m）
总　计	**Total**	**524**
煤炭开采和洗选业	Coal Mining and Dressing	0
石油和天然气开采业	Petroleum and Natural Gas Extraction	0
黑色金属矿采选业	Ferrous Metals Mining and Dressing	0
有色金属矿采选业	NonFerrous Metals Mining and Dressing	0
非金属矿采选业	Nonmetal Minerals Mining and Dressing	0
其他采矿选业	Other Minerals Mining and Dressing	0
农副食品加工业	Agricultural Non－staple Food Processing	0
食品制造业	Food Production	4
饮料制造业	Beverage Production	0
烟草制品业	Tobacco Production	45
纺织业	Textile Industry	0
纺织服装、鞋、帽制造业	Textile, Clothing and Footwear Production	0
皮革、毛皮、羽毛(绒)及其制品业	Leathers, Furs, Down and Related Products	0
木材加工及木、竹、藤、棕、草制品业	Timber Processing, Bamboo, Cane, Palm Fiber and Straw Products	0
家具制造业	Furniture Manufacturing	0
造纸及纸制品业	Papermaking and Paper Products	0
印刷业、记录媒介的复制	Printing and Record Medium Reproduction	0
文教体育用品制造业	Cultural, Educational and Sports Goods	0
石油加工、炼焦及核燃料加工业	Petroleum Processing, Coking and Nuclear Fuel Processing	0
化学原料及化学制品制造业	Raw Chemical Materials and Chemical Products	0
医药制造业	Medical and Pharmaceutic Products	0
化学纤维制造业	Chemical Fibers	0
橡胶制品业	Rubber Products	0
塑料制品业	Plastic Products	0
非金属矿物制品业	Nonmetal Mineral Products	0
黑色金属冶炼及压延加工业	Smelting and Processing of Ferrous Metals	0
有色金属冶炼及压延加工业	Smelting and Processing of Nonferrous Metals	0
金属制品业	Metal Products	0
通用设备制造业	General－purpose Equipment Manufacturing	300
专用设备制造业	Special－purpose Equipment Manufacturing	0
交通运输设备制造业	Transportation Equipment Manufacturing	175
电气机械及器材制造业	Electric Equipment and Machinery	0
通信设备、计算机及其他电子设备制造业	Communication Equipments, Computers and Other Electronic Equipment Products	0
仪器仪表及文化、办公用机械制造业	Instruments, Meters, Cultural and Office Machinery	0
工艺品及其他制造业	Handicraft Articles and Other Goods Production	0
废弃资源和废旧材料回收加工	Discarded Resources and Waste Materials Recovery and Processing	0
电力、热力的生产和供应业	Power and Heat Production and Supply	0
燃气生产和供应业	Gas Production and Supply	0
水的生产和供应业	Water Production and Supply	0

其他煤气 （万立方米） Other Gas （10000 cu. m）	原油 （吨） Crude Oil（ton）	汽油 （吨） Petrol （ton）	煤油 （吨） Kerosene （ton）
4 283	**2 076 284**	**106 198**	**14 005**
0	0	0	0
0	0	0	0
0	0	6	0
0	0	324	0
0	0	411	395
0	0	1	0
0	299	7 878	230
0	0	4 862	31
0	992	2 841	16
0	0	224	1
0	0	7 619	533
0	1 021	3 128	1 048
0	0	2 361	2 141
0	0	430	44
0	18	729	213
0	10	2 417	47
0	0	619	250
20	5	770	158
0	1 986 915	705	7
1 887	32	9 137	57
0	0	926	0
0	0	76	0
0	221	13 095	467
1	3	2 630	10
0	86 206	3 478	63
0	0	2 948	1 000
0	0	353	687
539	441	2 755	166
10	0	6 708	1 708
30	13	3 826	123
296	21	6 684	156
0	54	5 282	288
0	21	1 753	153
0	12	1 517	207
1 500	0	1 954	791
0	0	4	0
0	0	6 962	3 011
0	0	324	0
0	0	461	4

5－4 续表 1
continued

		柴油（吨）Diesel Oil（ton）
总　　计	**Total**	**219 650**
煤炭开采和洗选业	Coal Mining and Dressing	0
石油和天然气开采业	Petroleum and Natural Gas Extraction	0
黑色金属矿采选业	Ferrous Metals Mining and Dressing	112
有色金属矿采选业	NonFerrous Metals Mining and Dressing	539
非金属矿采选业	Nonmetal Minerals Mining and Dressing	8 046
其他采矿选业	Other Minerals Mining and Dressing	30
农副食品加工业	Agricultural Non－staple Food Processing	10 263
食品制造业	Food Production	10 204
饮料制造业	Beverage Production	33 680
烟草制品业	Tobacco Production	144
纺织业	Textile Industry	9 516
纺织服装、鞋、帽制造业	Textile, Clothing and Footwear Production	4 993
皮革、毛皮、羽毛（绒）及其制品业	Leathers, Furs, Down and Related Products	4 263
木材加工及木、竹、藤、棕、草制品业	Timber Processing, Bamboo, Cane, Palm Fiber and Straw Products	481
家具制造业	Furniture Manufacturing	1 209
造纸及纸制品业	Papermaking and Paper Products	7 141
印刷业、记录媒介的复制	Printing and Record Medium Reproduction	1 201
文教体育用品制造业	Cultural, Educational and Sports Goods	1 761
石油加工、炼焦及核燃料加工业	Petroleum Processing, Coking and Nuclear Fuel Processing	458
化学原料及化学制品制造业	Raw Chemical Materials and Chemical Products	12 827
医药制造业	Medical and Pharmaceutic Products	1 565
化学纤维制造业	Chemical Fibers	270
橡胶制品业	Rubber Products	4 889
塑料制品业	Plastic Products	22 398
非金属矿物制品业	Nonmetal Mineral Products	19 862
黑色金属冶炼及压延加工业	Smelting and Processing of Ferrous Metals	8 141
有色金属冶炼及压延加工业	Smelting and Processing of Nonferrous Metals	1 572
金属制品业	Metal Products	4 450
通用设备制造业	General－purpose Equipment Manufacturing	8 328
专用设备制造业	Special－purpose Equipment Manufacturing	1 706
交通运输设备制造业	Transportation Equipment Manufacturing	14 033
电气机械及器材制造业	Electric Equipment and Machinery	4 954
通信设备、计算机及其他电子设备制造业	Communication Equipments, Computers and Other Electronic Equipment Products	2 272
仪器仪表及文化、办公用机械制造业	Instruments, Meters, Cultural and Office Machinery	382
工艺品及其他制造业	Handicraft Articles and Other Goods Production	3 062
废弃资源和废旧材料回收加工	Discarded Resources and Waste Materials Recovery and Processing	0
电力、热力的生产和供应业	Power and Heat Production and Supply	12 975
燃气生产和供应业	Gas Production and Supply	1 682
水的生产和供应业	Water Production and Supply	241

燃料油 (吨) Fuel Oil (ton)	液化石油气 (吨)Liquefied Petroleum Gas(ton)	炼厂干气 (吨) Refinery Dry Gas(ton)
1 837 102	**14 301**	**58 962**
0	0	0
0	0	0
0	0	0
0	0	0
7	0	0
0	0	0
86 010	312	1 384
52 000	317	0
5 636	0	0
0	0	0
9 611	48	0
9 637	25	0
19 457	23	9 985
5	0	0
20	0	0
1 755	0	0
17	15	0
724	362	0
6 024	0	45 557
15 934	369	0
0	1	0
0	0	0
8 244	0	0
665	38	0
1 587 559	905	0
21 520	504	0
0	5	0
2 428	789	40
1 695	272	0
83	112	0
117	6 550	0
69	583	0
0	0	0
33	0	0
3 716	138	0
0	0	0
0	0	0
4 136	2 933	1 996
0	0	0

5 -4 续表 2
continued

		其他油制品（吨）Other Petroleum Products(ton)
总　计	**Total**	**15 149**
煤炭开采和洗选业	Coal Mining and Dressing	0
石油和天然气开采业	Petroleum and Natural Gas Extraction	0
黑色金属矿采选业	Ferrous Metals Mining and Dressing	0
有色金属矿采选业	NonFerrous Metals Mining and Dressing	0
非金属矿采选业	Nonmetal Minerals Mining and Dressing	0
其他采矿选业	Other Minerals Mining and Dressing	0
农副食品加工业	Agricultural Non - staple Food Processing	0
食品制造业	Food Production	0
饮料制造业	Beverage Production	0
烟草制品业	Tobacco Production	0
纺织业	Textile Industry	1
纺织服装、鞋、帽制造业	Textile, Clothing and Footwear Production	3 371
皮革、毛皮、羽毛(绒)及其制品业	Leathers, Furs, Down and Related Products	0
木材加工及木、竹、藤、棕、草制品业	Timber Processing, Bamboo, Cane, Palm Fiber and Straw Products	0
家具制造业	Furniture Manufacturing	0
造纸及纸制品业	Papermaking and Paper Products	0
印刷业、记录媒介的复制	Printing and Record Medium Reproduction	0
文教体育用品制造业	Cultural, Educational and Sports Goods	0
石油加工、炼焦及核燃料加工业	Petroleum Processing, Coking and Nuclear Fuel Processing	1 420
化学原料及化学制品制造业	Raw Chemical Materials and Chemical Products	3 763
医药制造业	Medical and Pharmaceutic Products	0
化学纤维制造业	Chemical Fibers	0
橡胶制品业	Rubber Products	11
塑料制品业	Plastic Products	0
非金属矿物制品业	Nonmetal Mineral Products	6 550
黑色金属冶炼及压延加工业	Smelting and Processing of Ferrous Metals	0
有色金属冶炼及压延加工业	Smelting and Processing of Nonferrous Metals	0
金属制品业	Metal Products	17
通用设备制造业	General - purpose Equipment Manufacturing	4
专用设备制造业	Special - purpose Equipment Manufacturing	0
交通运输设备制造业	Transportation Equipment Manufacturing	8
电气机械及器材制造业	Electric Equipment and Machinery	0
通信设备、计算机及其他电子设备制造业	Communication Equipments, Computers and Other Electronic Equipment Products	0
仪器仪表及文化、办公用机械制造业	Instruments, Meters, Cultural and Office Machinery	4
工艺品及其他制造业	Handicraft Articles and Other Goods Production	0
废弃资源和废旧材料回收加工	Discarded Resources and Waste Materials Recovery and Processing	0
电力、热力的生产和供应业	Power and Heat Production and Supply	0
燃气生产和供应业	Gas Production and Supply	0
水的生产和供应业	Water Production and Supply	0

热　　力 （百万千焦） Heat （million kJ）	电　　力 （万千瓦时） Electricity （10000 kwh）	其他燃料 （吨标准煤） Other Fuel （ton SCE）
27 363 579	**1 461 595**	**67 769**
0	0	0
0	0	0
0	308	0
0	12 114	0
0	13 101	0
0	20	0
344 353	64 246	15 930
36 474	28 620	0
764 443	17 050	0
425 479	3 189	0
4 983 109	84 695	0
246 635	39 572	0
219 076	30 475	56
2 779	4 192	0
18 549	7 577	0
163 149	20 990	3 600
12 270	3 769	0
79 377	11 465	54
0	12 856	0
17 210 131	241 605	40 043
158 537	7 049	0
58 194	13 316	0
159 659	47 824	0
7 861	37 415	3 937
117 214	72 709	1 897
2 259	149 543	0
104 831	13 636	0
20 161	62 891	0
22 962	40 787	0
120 941	22 562	0
538 543	39 605	0
287 960	79 542	0
22 836	39 992	800
0	2 608	0
15 469	13 279	20
0	883	0
1 220 329	209 373	16
0	808	0
0	11 930	1 416

CHAPTER 6

第六篇

财政、金融和保险业

PUBLIC FINANCE,BANKING AND INSURANCE

编辑单位：国民经济核算处
编　　委：刘建华
编　　辑：陈　强　陈旭亮
校　　对：陈旭亮
电　　话：85912239

6 -1 主要年份地方财政收支

MAJOR YEAR'S FINANCIAL BALANCE

单位：万元(10 000 yuan)

年份 Year	财政收入 Financial Revenue	财政支出 Financial Expenditure	#基本建设 Capital Construction	#城市维护费 City Maintenance	#行政管理 Administration	#文教卫生 Culture, Education and Health Care
1949	1 527	306	–	–	183	113
1952	19 809	2 226	733	272	735	423
1957	29 875	3 556	–	241	1 145	1 665
1962	32 869	4 327	11	11	112	2 064
1965	47 682	6 280	1	573	1 242	2 239
1970	95 778	7 825	1 504	636	1 366	2 495
1975	90 220	11 966	183	746	1 750	4 118
1978	130 749	19 427	548	957	2 392	5 172
1980	124 835	20 064	1 120	2 467	2 888	7 419
1985	165 155	41 996	2 233	3 716	5 245	14 262
1988	201 206	93 931	4 730	8 706	11 401	20 073
1989	221 183	113 585	6 197	12 971	9 440	23 208
1990	242 303	133 875	7 180	13 872	10 576	26 143
1991	259 377	137 716	6 831	14 770	12 206	29 022
1992	275 589	155 696	18 514	16 049	15 662	33 790
1993	182 348	211 938	26 850	20 121	18 370	39 761
1994	227 490	277 331	32 567	20 443	24 509	58 898
1995	294 771	376 982	72 585	30 952	28 673	67 494
1996	379 674	469 569	113 244	35 601	37 035	65 777
1997	476 804	564 787	129 089	44 599	43 061	77 360
1998	580 434	678 575	157 146	62 563	50 324	116 353
1999	680 089	740 937	151 802	60 373	62 701	141 032
2000	800 120	878 702	134 437	60 566	80 296	186 841
2001	987 080	1 097 848	201 995	61 365	101 240	232 569
2002	1 006 616	1 243 880	198 502	80 847	126 855	274 606
2003	1 201 398	1 471 747	282 040	89 874	148 904	304 661
2004	1 305 136	1 646 214	237 107	114 987	174 683	340 773
2005	1 763 412	2 030 622	289 346	132 247	240 732	449 549

注：1. 1993 年以后实行新制度，财政收入数与历年不可比。

2. 2002 年以后，财政收入、支出为一般预算数。

Note: 1. Since 1993, new regulations have been adopted in calculating financial revenue, The figures are not comparable with those over the years.

2. Since 2002, financial revenue and financial expenditure refer to general budget revenue and expenditure.

6－2 分市、区地方财政一般预算收入(2005 年)
GENERAL BUDGET REVENUE OF LOCAL FINANCE BY REGION(2005)

单位:万元(10 000 yuan)

市、区名称	Region	财政收入 Financial Revenue	#城建税 City Construction Tax	#增值税 Value-added Tax	#营业税 Sales Tax
总　计	**Total**	**1 763 412**	**97 522**	**265 650**	**495 568**
市　区	Urban Area	593 326	35 859	100 652	169 746
#城阳区	Chengyang District	70 086	8 098	15 107	15 818
黄岛区	Huangdao District	116 945	8 028	19 460	33 190
崂山区	Laoshan District	117 948	5 226	16 436	22 716
胶州市	Jiaozhou	91 195	3 819	15 500	16 465
即墨市	Jimo	93 577	5 423	17 119	19 590
平度市	Pingdu	91 840	3 484	10 985	11 992
胶南市	Jiaonan	120 835	4 969	12 835	18 693
莱西市	Laixi	56 344	2 510	7 907	8 558
市本级	Municipal Level	716 295	41 458	100 652	250 524

6－2 续表
continued

单位:万元(10 000 yuan)

市、区名称	Region	#企业所得税类 Enterprise Income Tax	#国有企业计划亏损补贴类 Planning Subsidies to Loss-making State-owned Enterprises	#基金收入类 Funds Revenue	#农牧业税和耕地占用税类 Farming&Animal Husbandry Tax and Land Occupation Tax
总　计	**Total**	**219 069**	**－10 000**	**287 171**	**104 379**
市　区	Urban Area	90 170	0	43 582	27 431
#城阳区	Chengyang District	7 805	0	8 013	4 110
黄岛区	Huangdao District	17 913	0	17 168	0
崂山区	Laoshan District	18 959	0	16 941	4 927
胶州市	Jiaozhou	5 948	0	1 523	17 101
即墨市	Jimo	2 457	0	2 355	11 626
平度市	Pingdu	4 832	0	4 088	13 945
胶南市	Jiaonan	8 132	0	4 172	28 032
莱西市	Laixi	1 915	0	6 222	6 244
市本级	Municipal Level	105 615	－10 000	225 229	0

6-3 分市、区地方财政一般预算支出(2005 年)

GENERAL BUDGET EXPENDITURE OF LOCAL FINANCE BY REGION(2005)

单位:万元(10 000 yuan)

市、区名称	Region	财政支出 Financial Expenditure	#基本建设支出类 Capital Construction	#企业挖潜改造资金类 Technical updates and Transformation of Enterprises	#科技三项费用类 Science and Technology Promotion	#农林水气事业费 Supporting Agricultural Production	#城市维护费类 City Maintenance
总计	**Total**	**2 030 622**	**289 346**	**91 787**	**34 918**	**82 833**	**132 247**
市区	Urban Area	709 969	118 722	40 509	20 448	27 579	73 875
#城阳区	Chengyang District	138 050	10 615	260	3 609	11 276	25 628
黄岛区	Huangdao District	168 881	41 417	14 343	6 856	6 190	7 593
崂山区	Laoshan District	146 487	40 297	11 310	3 788	9 643	8 982
胶州市	Jiaozhou	115 168	21 316	471	2 261	7 266	4 263
即墨市	Jimo	125 815	9 367	7 780	546	7 489	7 753
平度市	Pingdu	133 612	11 061	4 125	1 628	9 397	7 404
胶南市	Jiaonan	146 785	16 234	7 249	4 126	9 492	12 954
莱西市	Laixi	82 619	2 773	3 113	146	9 676	3 638
市本级	Municipal Level	716 654	109 873	28 540	5 763	11 934	22 360

6-3 续表

continued

单位:万元(10 000 yuan)

市、区名称	Region	#文教卫生事业费类 Culture, Education and Health Care	#科学事业费类 Science	#抚恤和福利费类 Pensions and Relief Funds	#行政管理费类 Administration	#政策性补贴支出类 Price Subsidies	#基金支出 Funds Expenditure
总计	**Total**	**449 549**	**3 503**	**62 299**	**240 732**	**3 184**	**286 301**
市区	Urban Area	146 679	971	15 449	91 988	1 350	71 693
#城阳区	Chengyang District	34 316	338	2 079	16 646	488	14 653
黄岛区	Huangdao District	24 978	236	1 493	20 523	392	17 233
崂山区	Laoshan District	24 020	353	1 654	12 519	470	29 627
胶州市	Jiaozhou	32 250	223	3 767	21 699	180	6 462
即墨市	Jimo	38 350	156	4 047	21 950	376	7 067
平度市	Pingdu	54 356	159	5 028	14 167	296	9 377
胶南市	Jiaonan	44 019	227	4 165	19 954	139	3 293
莱西市	Laixi	25 697	125	4 421	12 284	116	15 179
市本级	Municipal Level	108 198	1 642	25 422	58 690	727	173 230

6 -4 主要年份金融系统人民币存贷款(年末余额)

MAJOR YEAR'S SAVING DEPOSITS AND LOANS OF BANKING SYSTEM (YEAR - END BALANCE)

单位:万元(10 000 yuan)

年份 Year	存款合计 Total Saving Deposits	#企业存款 Enterprise Deposits	#城乡储蓄存款 Urban and Rural Saving Deposits	贷款合计 Total Loans	#工业流动短期贷款 Short-Term Loans to Industrial Sector	#商业流动短期贷款 Short-Term Loans to Commercial Sector
1949	693	239	28	278	11	234
1952	9 093	4 308	1 838	3 322	1 154	1 921
1957	10 372	3 359	4 037	30 690	3 388	25 099
1962	20 040	8 579	3 279	73 601	17 952	50 322
1965	27 331	11 830	6 347	64 555	9 172	49 544
1970	38 264	13 024	7 576	126 382	35 686	84 058
1975	60 622	22 568	15 637	207 006	38 314	165 109
1978	66 523	21 004	21 455	297 184	52 441	237 796
1980	120 644	38 105	38 609	379 666	68 989	294 970
1985	344 760	99 736	155 604	452 142	126 604	188 880
1988	754 442	206 541	366 483	955 351	290 776	273 984
1989	932 430	245 529	481 692	1 174 448	381 231	330 629
1990	1 235 562	321 542	655 895	1 535 751	513 363	403 939
1991	1 553 564	411 417	824 428	1 871 462	610 814	468 654
1992	2 076 667	612 868	1 044 165	2 352 449	724 318	560 225
1993	2 747 294	835 617	1 372 239	2 940 658	885 049	713 779
1994	3 769 019	1 399 110	1 918 734	3 610 564	993 369	841 404
1995	5 324 026	2 030 382	2 687 888	4 777 864	1 223 130	1 021 518
1996	6 991 289	2 630 958	3 499 219	5 941 281	1 510 652	1 209 667
1997	7 385 092	2 885 632	4 060 259	6 508 776	1 664 348	1 407 476
1998	8 183 471	3 018 063	4 591 012	7 239 231	1 923 279	1 377 769
1999	9 160 001	3 454 570	4 978 045	8 945 730	2 045 861	2 401 172
2000	10 560 624	4 386 316	5 353 215	9 564 293	2 130 183	2 112 002
2001	12 323 942	4 955 336	6 187 409	10 798 871	2 428 417	2 167 471
2002	15 225 733	5 819 655	7 449 408	13 044 792	2 965 019	2 085 739
2003	18 920 868	7 027 227	9 084 693	16 783 917	3 042 596	2 247 226
2004	22 462 592	7 924 690	10 894 941	18 472 613	3 306 830	1 628 161
2005	26 975 372	8 226 661	13 431 016	20 394 792	3 068 744	1 296 981

6-5 金融系统人民币存贷款(年末余额)

SAVING DEPOSITS AND LOANS OF BANKING SYSTEM (YEAR-END BALANCE)

单位:万元(10 000 yuan)

项　目	Items	2005 年 2005	2004 年 2004	2005 年为 2004 年% 2005/2004(%)
一、存款总计	**Total Saving Deposits**	**26 975 372**	**22 766 154**	**118.5**
企业存款	Enterprise Deposits	8 226 661	7 958 972	103.4
财政存款	Fiscal Deposits	541 793	489 625	110.7
城乡储蓄存款	Urban and Rural Saving Deposits	13 431 016	10 894 937	123.3
#活期储蓄	Demand Deposits	4 501 555	3 846 199	117.0
定期储蓄	Time Deposits	8 929 461	7 048 739	126.7
农业存款	Rural Deposits	539 025	509 209	105.9
二、贷款总计	**Total Loans**	**20 394 792**	**17 593 365**	**115.9**
短期贷款	Short-Term Loans	9 815 113	8 898 101	110.3
#工业	Loans to Industrial Sector	3 068 744	3 117 946	98.4
商业	Loans to Commercial Sector	1 296 981	1 202 433	107.9
建筑业	Loans to Construction Sector	458 725	328 528	139.6
乡镇企业	Loans to Township Enterprises	540 031	480 380	112.4
农业贷款	Loans to Agricultural Sector	894 445	824 956	108.4
中长期贷款	Medium & Long-term Loans	8 073 532	6 842 012	118.0

注:2004 年数据已调整为可比口径。

Note: The calibre in 2004 has been adapted to comparable calibre.

6 -6 主要年份银行现金收支

MAJOR YEAR'S CASH BALANCE OF BANK

单位:万元(10 000 yuan)

年　份 Year	现金收入 Cash Revenue	#商品销售 Commodity Sales Income	#服务事业 Service Undertaking Incom	现金支出 Cash Payment	#工资性 Wage Payment	#行政管理 Administrative Payment	现金投放(+)回笼(-) Cash Issuance(+) & Withdrawn(-)
1949	3 119	-	-	3 236	-	-	117
1952	28 804	-	-	28 287	-	-	-517
1957	45 077	-	-	44 608	-	-	-469
1962	56 188	34 524	5 500	52 522	23 283	1 826	-3 666
1965	56 851	37 919	4 092	57 013	25 064	2 095	162
1970	66 130	47 520	4 651	63 976	26 324	2 000	-2 154
1975	91 815	67 664	6 179	92 100	34 648	3 391	285
1978	113 340	82 479	8 017	113 947	45 981	5 086	607
1980	173 520	120 406	10 971	178 729	73 397	7 657	5 209
1985	598 363	223 521	25 444	595 731	134 624	19 039	-2 632
1988	1 398 031	429 809	55 593	1 417 676	263 138	52 162	19 645
1989	1 656 601	460 190	71 033	1 658 737	317 850	64 680	2 136
1990	1 876 881	469 615	87 866	1 906 673	363 904	80 351	29 792
1991	2 283 805	545 935	106 979	2 322 834	414 840	101 651	39 029
1992	3 079 322	706 552	148 343	3 144 721	510 471	156 282	65 399
1993	5 193 485	1 029 624	236 637	5 256 445	672 287	310 720	86 930
1994	6 294 925	1 186 501	336 485	6 453 386	900 221	463 399	196 356
1995	8 764 491	1 467 021	422 847	9 004 585	1 185 977	577 619	196 356
1996	11 156 505	1 658 193	549 176	11 484 504	1 207 512	700 358	318 652
1997	15 373 658	2 045 935	690 023	15 508 138	1 219 955	804 803	411 518
1998	16 964 006	2 251 331	899 472	17 333 720	1 561 412	1 019 060	400 945
1999	20 976 030	2 651 046	1 080 667	20 976 030	1 791 625	1 248 999	521 976
2000	24 930 720	3 251 409	1 323 025	25 356 500	2 091 646	1 540 663	425 780
2001	28 448 088	3 466 253	1 478 646	28 960 617	2 174 856	2 059 759	512 529
2002	29 132 065	4 032 095	1 729 895	29 795 311	2 018 679	2 579 733	663 246
2003	36 734 943	4 924 862	1 975 237	37 567 906	2 189 917	3 228 401	833 579
2004	47 393 355	5 879 881	2 392 491	48 216 917	2 777 982	3 975 391	823 562
2005	54 644 469	6 252 843	2 545 605	55 743 626	3 523 460	4 160 210	1 099 157

6-7 银行现金收支
CASH BALANCE OF BANK

单位：万元(10 000 yuan)

项目	Items	1996年	2000年	2004年	2005年
一、现金收入总计	**Total Cash Income**	**11 156 505**	**24 930 720**	**47 393 355**	**54 644 469**
商品销售收入	Commodity Sales Income	1 658 193	3 251 409	5 879 881	6 252 843
服务业收入	Service Undertaking Income	549 176	1 323 025	2 392 491	2 545 605
税款收入	Tax Payment Income	32 158	145 562	244 599	229 054
城乡个体经营收入	Urban and Rural Private-owned Business Income	103 289	491 422	973 301	1 145 178
储蓄存款收入	Saving Income	6 757 851	16 890 798	34 853 757	40 603 804
其他金融机构收入	Other Income of Financial Institutions	377 920	154 499	46 194	85 310
汇兑收入	Remittance Income	114 710	433 098	268 035	424 482
有价证券收入	Marketable Securities Income	106 135	221 238	211 025	141 064
其他收入	Other Income	1 079 251	1 721 358	1 750 918	2 417 826
二、现金支出总计	**Total Cash Payment**	**11 484 504**	**25 356 500**	**48 216 917**	**55 743 626**
工资性支出	Wage Payment	1 207 512	2 091 646	2 777 982	3 523 460
#部队存款支出	Army Saving Payment	67 065	87 487	99 929	100 852
农副产品采购支出	Agricultural Sideline Product Stock Payment	215 947	426 928	1 084 962	1 084 928
行政事业管理费支出	Administrative Payment	700 358	1 540 663	3 975 391	4 160 210
城乡个体经营支出	Urban and Rural Private-owned Business Payment	176 812	785 720	1 710 734	1 684 463
储蓄存款支出	Saving Payment	6 696 168	17 615 049	36 178 727	42 054 685
其他金融机构支出	Other Payment of Financial Institutions	177 279	126 099	41 584	86 948
汇兑支出	Remittance Payment	106 859	249 955	112 847	95 605
有价证券支出	Marketable Securities Payment	124 284	176 138	140 537	97 310
其他支出	Other Payment	1 348 789	1 651 363	1 252 218	2 015 517

6-8 国内保险业务(1990-2005年)

DOMESTIC INSURANCE BUSINESS(1990-2005)

单位:万元(10 000 yuan)

		1990年	1995年	2000年	2004年	2005年
一、国内保险总值	**Total domestic insurance Value**	**4 392 323**	**11 256 080**	**38 357 485**	**73 037 741**	**91 691 581**
二、国内业务收入	**Domestic Business Income**	**17 177**	**107 159**	**220 780**	**475 792**	**495 701**
1. 保费收入	Premium Income	12 085	81 976	218 714	475 792	495 701
#财产险	Property Insurance	10 417	51 808	85 161	136 822	159 746
农业险	Agriculture Insurance	145	142	18	-	12
人身险	Personal Insurance	1 523	30 026	133 535	338 970	335 943
2. 储金	Reserve	5 092	25 183	2 066	-	-
#财产险	Property Insurance	659	12 583	1 900	-	-
农业险	Agriculture Insurance	-	408	-	-	-
人身险	Personal Insurance	4 433	12 192	166	-	-
三、国内业务支出	**Domestic Business Payment**	**5 449**	**40 115**	**94 877**	**187 518**	**214 148**
1. 赔款支出	Indemnity Expenditure	4 735	32 105	62 275	97 169	111 385
#财产险	Property Insurance	4 145	29 420	58 361	82 053	92 700
农业险	Agriculture Insurance	129	24	5	-	11
人身险	Personal Insurance	461	2 661	3 909	15116	18 674
2. 满期给付	Expiry Payment	509	7 652	27 955	31 414	32 739
3. 退保	Surrender	205	358	4 647	58 935	70 024

注:2004年数据已调整。

Note: The calibre in 2004 has been adapted.

CHAPTER 7

第七篇

物价

PRICE

编辑单位:	城市社会经济调查队消价处	城市社会经济调查队生价处
编　　委:	于　青	赵素欣
编　　辑:	王道君　赵　伟	高义茂　迟　波
校　　对:	王道君　赵　伟	高义茂　迟　波
电　　话:	82870297	82871663

7－1 主要年份物价指数(以上年价格为100)
MAJOR YEAR'S PRICE INDEXES(PRECEDING YEAR＝100)

年份 Year	商品零售价格指数 General Retail Price Index	居民消费价格指数 General Consumer Price Index	#食品类 Food	#衣着类 Clothing	#服务项目价格指数 Services Price Index	原材料、燃料、动力购进价格指数 Purchasing Price Indexes Of Raw Materials, Fuels And Power	工业品出厂价格指数 Factory Price Indexes Of Industrial Products	房地产销售价格指数 Sales Price Index of Real Estate
1951	100.5	110.5	105.2	112.4	–	–	–	–
1952	99.8	99.8	99.6	98.7	–	–	–	–
1957	101.4	101.4	101.3	101.4	99.3	–	–	–
1962	102.6	102.6	102.0	100.2	99.9	–	–	–
1965	101.2	101.2	101.3	98.8	96.9	–	–	–
1970	98.9	98.9	99.7	100.0	99.5	–	–	–
1975	100.3	100.3	100.1	100.0	100.0	–	–	–
1978	100.5	100.5	100.2	99.8	100.0	–	–	–
1980	105.5	105.2	108.5	100.3	100.0	–	–	–
1985	110.9	110.4	115.2	102.3	102.7	–	–	–
1987	109.8	109.4	112.5	106.8	102.5	–	–	–
1988	120.9	120.7	125.2	117.3	118.3	–	–	–
1989	114.4	115.3	109.2	121.1	130.2	–	–	–
1990	103.6	104.5	103.4	103.4	118.8	108.6	104.3	–
1991	106.8	107.0	107.0	112.1	109.6	108.1	101.7	–
1992	110.8	111.4	115.1	108.6	119.9	107.1	105.5	–
1993	119.8	123.9	120.9	119.0	158.5	126.9	115.5	–
1994	122.8	126.9	135.2	130.1	117.9	120.3	121.6	–
1995	114.2	116.2	118.1	122.8	123.2	114.3	112.7	–
1996	106.0	112.6	110.1	104.3	130.4	103.3	103.8	–
1997	100.2	104.0	101.2	102.3	120.8	101.9	100.2	–
1998	94.9	100.0	93.7	94.5	136.2	92.8	95.0	100.1
1999	96.6	100.2	96.7	97.1	115.6	95.9	96.9	103.7
2000	99.7	103.3	100.0	108.3	112.0	106.8	101.9	102.3
2001	98.9	101.0	100.6	98.0	108.7	97.8	98.0	104.1
2002	99.5	98.9	97.8	100.2	101.0	96.8	97.4	107.6
2003	98.3	101.4	104.3	98.4	101.7	106.5	101.0	114.6
2004	99.0	102.1	104.0	103.6	104.7	113.6	102.9	115.2
2005	99.3	102.3	102.1	108.3	101.4	106.5	101.4	110.9

7－2 主要年份物价指数(以1950年价格为100)

MAJOR YEAR'S PRICE INDEXES(1950＝100)

年份 Year	商品零售价格指数 General Retail Price Index	居民消费价格指数 General Consumer Price Index	#食品类 Food	#衣着类 Clothing	#服务项目价格指数 Services Price Index
1951	100.0	100.0	100.0	100.0	100.0
1952	110.5	110.5	105.2	112.4	－
1957	119.4	119.4	120.7	115.3	91.6
1962	127.1	127.1	128.8	115.1	94.2
1965	133.1	133.1	138.8	108.4	81.5
1970	128.8	128.8	137.7	110.3	76.7
1975	128.7	128.7	138.2	110.0	75.7
1978	128.9	128.9	138.8	109.8	75.7
1980	137.9	137.4	154.2	109.3	75.7
1985	163.9	162.3	196.2	103.8	80.0
1987	189.8	187.2	235.9	113.5	84.7
1988	229.5	226.0	295.3	133.1	100.2
1989	255.0	260.6	322.5	161.2	130.5
1990	264.2	272.3	333.5	166.7	155.0
1991	282.2	291.4	356.8	186.9	169.9
1992	312.7	324.6	410.7	203.0	203.7
1993	374.6	402.2	496.5	241.6	322.9
1994	460.0	510.4	671.3	314.3	380.7
1995	525.3	593.1	792.8	386.0	469.0
1996	556.8	667.8	872.9	402.6	611.6
1997	557.9	694.5	883.4	411.9	738.8
1998	529.4	694.5	827.7	389.2	1 006.2
1999	511.4	695.9	800.4	377.9	1 163.2
2000	509.9	718.9	800.4	409.3	1 302.8
2001	504.3	726.1	805.2	401.1	1 416.1
2002	501.8	718.1	787.5	401.9	1 430.3
2003	493.3	728.2	821.4	395.5	1 454.6
2004	488.4	743.5	854.3	409.7	1 523.0
2005	485.0	760.6	872.2	443.7	1 544.3

7-3 居民消费价格分类指数(2005年)
CONSUMER PRICE INDEXES BY CATEGORY(2005)

项　目	Items	指 数 Indexes
居民消费价格总指数	**General Consumer Price Index**	**102.3**
非食品价格指数	Non-Food Price Index	102.4
服务项目价格指数	Services Price Index	101.4
扣除鲜菜鲜果总指数	General Price Index Without Fresh Vegetables & Fresh Fruits	102.1
消费品价格指数	Consumer Goods Price Index	102.5
一、食品	**Food**	**102.1**
1. 粮食	Grain	103.7
2. 淀粉及薯类	Starch and Yam	105.9
3. 干豆类及豆制品	Dried Beans and Bean Products	106.2
4. 油脂	Oil or Fat	102.8
5. 肉禽及其制品	Meat Poultry and Their Products	101.1
6. 蛋类	Eggs	110.5
7. 水产品	Aquatic Products	94.0
8. 菜	Vegetables	99.7
9. 调味品	Flavoring	116.8
10. 糖	Sugar	99.2
11. 茶及饮料	Tea and Beverages	100.8
12. 干鲜瓜果类	Dried and Fresh Fruits	113.8
13. 糕点饼干面包	Pastry, Biscuit and Bread	98.1
14. 奶及奶制品	Milk and Milk Products	98.9
15. 在外用膳食品	Food of Dining out	100.9
16. 其它食品及食品加工服务	Other Food and Food Processing Services	104.0
二、烟酒及用品	**Tobacco & Liquor and Articles**	**99.8**
1. 烟草	Tobacco	101.7
2. 酒	Liquor	99.2
3. 吸烟饮酒用品	Smoking and Drinking Articles	95.2

7 –3 续表
continued

项　　目	Items	指　数 Indexes
三、衣着	**Clothing**	**108.3**
1. 服装	Garments	109.4
2. 衣着材料	Clothing Materials	102.7
3. 鞋袜帽	Shoes, Socks and Hats	105.4
4. 衣着加工服务	Clothing Processing Services	105.4
四、家庭设备用品及维修服务	**Household Facilities and Articles**	**99.3**
1. 耐用消费品	Durable Consumer Goods	97.9
2. 室内装饰品	Interior Decorations	100.8
3. 床上用品	Bed Articles	93.3
4. 家庭日用杂品	Daily Use Household Articles	100.8
5. 家庭服务及加工维修服务	Household Services and Maintenance Services	108.1
五、医疗保健和个人用品	**Medicines and Medical Articles**	**99.4**
1. 医疗保健	Medicine and Medical Services	100.2
2. 个人用品及服务	Personal Articles and Services	97.1
六、交通和通讯	**Means of Transportation and communication**	**98.1**
1. 交通	Transportation	100.5
2. 通讯	Communication	95.8
七、娱乐教育文化用品及服务	**Recreation, Education and Culture Articles and Services**	**100.4**
1. 文娱用耐用消费品及服务	Durable Consumer Goods for Recreational Use	96.4
2. 教育	Education Articles	102.4
3. 文化娱乐用品	Recreation and Culture Articles	101.0
4. 旅游及外出	Tourism and Going outside	96.5
八、居住	**Residence**	**107.7**
1. 建房及装修材料	House Building and Decoration Materials	104.4
2. 租房	House Rent	100.0
3. 自有住房	Personal House	108.9
4. 水、电、燃料	Water, Electricity and Fuels	110.0

7 -4 商品零售价格分类指数(2005 年)
RETAIL PRICE INDEXES BY CATEGORY(2005)

项　目	Items	指　数 Indexes
商品零售价格总指数	**General Retail Price Index**	**99.3**
一、食品	**Food**	**103.0**
1. 粮食	Grain	103.9
2. 淀粉及薯类	Starch and Yam	105.9
3. 干豆类及豆制品	Dried Beans and Bean Products	105.9
4. 油脂	Oil or Fat	102.4
5. 肉禽及其制品	Meat Poultry and Their Products	102.1
6. 蛋	Eggs	110.5
7. 水产品	Aquatic Products	101.4
8. 菜	Vegetables	99.8
9. 调味品	Flavoring	116.3
10. 糖	Sugar	98.5
11. 干鲜瓜果	Dried and Fresh Fruits	114.8
12. 糕点饼干面包	Pastry, Biscuit and Bread	98.4
13. 奶及奶制品	Milk and Milk Products	99.1
14. 在外用膳食品	Food of Dining out	100.9
15. 其他食品	Other Food	104.0
二、饮料、烟酒	**Tobacco & Liquor and Articles**	**100.8**
1. 茶及饮料	Tea and Beverages	101.3
2. 烟草	Tobacco	101.9
3. 酒	Liquor	99.2
三、服装、鞋帽类	**Clothing**	**107.6**
1. 服装	Garments	108.2
2. 鞋袜帽	Shoes, Socks and Hats	105.5
3. 其他	Other	83.8
四、纺织品类	**Textiles**	**93.2**
1. 衣着材料	Clothing Materials	101.1
2. 床上用品	Bed Articles	91.7
五、家用电器及音像器材	**Household Appliances and Stereos**	**96.1**
1. 家庭设备	Household Facilities	97.6
2. 文娱用耐用消费品	Recreation, Education and Culture Articles and Services	94.1
3. 音像器材类	Sound and Video Equipment	96.5

7 -4 续表
continued

项　　目	Items	指　数 Indexes
六、文化办公用品	**Culture and Office Articles**	**84.9**
七、日用品	**Daily Use Articles**	**96.4**
1. 日用百货	Daily Use Goods	98.1
2. 日用杂品	Daily Use Groceries	99.4
3. 洗涤用品	Detergents and Cleaning Products	102.7
4. 其他日用品	Other Daily Use Articles	93.8
八、体育娱乐用品	**Sports and Recreation Articles**	**99.6**
1. 体育用品	Sports Articles	103.0
2. 娱乐用品	Recreation Articles	98.2
九、交通、通信用品	**Transportation and Communication Articles**	**86.7**
1. 交通运输机械	Transportation Machines	91.7
2. 通讯器材类	Communication Equipment	73.7
十、家具	**Furniture**	**100.4**
十一、化妆品类	**Cosmetics**	**96.1**
十二、金银珠宝类	**Jewelry**	**104.7**
十三、中西药品及医疗保健用品	**Medicines and Medical Articles**	**100.3**
1. 医疗器具及用品	Medical Articles	105.0
2. 中药材及中成药	Chinese Herbal Medicines and Chinese Patent Medicines	100.6
3. 西药	Western Medicines	99.4
4. 保健器具及用品	Health Care Articles	101.1
十四、书报杂志及电子出版物	**Books, Newspapers, Magazines and Electronic Publications**	**99.8**
1. 教材及参考书	Teaching Material and Reference Books	104.8
2. 书报杂志	Books, Newspapers and Magazines	100.2
3. 电子音像制品	Electronic Sound and video Products	95.3
十五、燃料类	**Fuels**	**112.2**
1. 煤炭及制品类	Coal and Its Products	116.1
2. 石油及制品类	Petroleum and Its Products	111.9
十六、建筑材料及五金电料类	**Building Decoration Materials**	**103.6**
1. 建筑装璜材料	Building Decoration Materials	102.3
2. 五金电料类	Hardware and Electrical Materials	105.5

7－5 房地产价格指数(以上年价格为100)

REAL ESTATE PRICE INDEXES(PRECEDING YEAR＝100)

房地产销售价格指数	Sales Price Index of Real Estate	2005年
总计	**Total**	**110.9**
一、商品房	**Sales of Commodity Housing**	**112.2**
(一)住宅	Residence	112.7
1.经济适用房	Residential Buildings for the Low-income Households	109.8
2.普通住宅	Common Residence	113.0
(1)多层住宅	Multi-storey Residence	113.5
(2)高层住宅	High Residence	111.9
3.高档住宅	Luxurious Residence	113.1
(二)非住宅	Non-residence	109.4
#商业娱乐用房	Commercial Entertainment Housing	114.5
二、二手房	**Second-hand House**	**109.3**
(一)住宅	Residence	109.7
(二)非住宅	Non-residence	107.6

7－5 续表

continued

房地产租赁价格指数	Rental Price Index of Real Estate	2005年
总　计	**Total**	**103.3**
一、住宅	**Residence**	**103.8**
(一)普通住宅	Common Residence	105.2
(二)高档住宅	High Standard Residence	105.2
(三)经济适用房	Residential Buildings for the Low－income Households	115.1
(四)廉租房	Inexpensive Rental Housing	100.0
二、办公楼	**Office Building**	**102.9**
(一)写字楼	Office	103.5
(二)普通办公用房	Common Office Building	100.6
三、商业娱乐用房	**Commercial Entertainment Housing**	**102.7**
四、工业仓储用房	**Industrial Workshop and Storehouse**	**100.0**
(一)工业厂房	Industrial Workshop	100.0
(二)仓库	Storeshop	100.0

7－6 主要原材料、燃料、动力购进价格指数(以上年价格为100)

PURCHASING PRICE INDEXES OF MAJOR RAW MATERIALS, FUELS AND POWER(PRECEDING YEAR＝100)

名　称	Names	1990年	1995年	2000年	2004年	2005年
总　指　数	**General Index**	**108.64**	**114.25**	**106.81**	**113.62**	**106.52**
1. 燃料、动力类	Fuel, Power	97.94	109.96	113.82	113.61	117.34
2. 黑色金属材料类	Ferrous Metals	113.94	97.00	102.66	132.28	107.84
#钢材	Rolled-steel	–	98.86	105.44	125.1	106.57
其他	Others	–	93.76	101.10	160.52	112.88
3. 有色金属材料及电线类	Nonferrous Metals and Electric Wire	97.97	128.79	106.75	114.8	108.06
4. 化工原料类	Chemical Raw Materials	98.35	129.93	106.90	109.95	112.47
5. 木材及纸浆类	Wood and Paper Pulps	98.57	109.68	108.98	108.47	103.80
6. 建筑材料及非金属矿类	Building Materials and Nonmetals	144.52	93.94	99.50	123.65	115.54
7. 其他工业原材料及半成品	Other Industrial Raw and Proceed Materials	–	97.04	105.32	104.58	97.87
8. 农副产品	Farm and Sideline Products	115.72	134.17	92.73	118.73	101.55
9. 纺织原料类	Textile Raw Material	112.47	99.25	104.03	107.66	98.15

7－7 主要工业品出厂价格指数(以上年价格为100)

FACTORY PRICE INDEXES OF MAJOR INDUSTRIAL PRODUCTS(PRECEDING YEAR＝100)

名　称	Names	1990年	1995年	2000年	2004年	2005年
总　指　数	**General Index**	**104.33**	**112.7**	**101.89**	**102.92**	**101.39**
#轻工业	Light Industry	106.19	115.33	98.50	101.09	99.78
重工业	Heavy Industry	102.06	108.61	105.62	106.26	104.32
生产资料	Means of Production	102.78	110.20	105.03	104.8	103.24
(1)采掘	Excavation	113.17	119.02	95.67	107.00	114.74
(2)原料	Raw Materials	108.80	109.54	113.82	107.45	106.91
(3)加工	Processing	99.71	110.29	97.58	103.64	101.45
生活资料	Consumer Goods	105.83	114.77	98.25	100.63	99.13
(1)食品	Food	108.04	116.48	96.59	104.65	98.80
(2)衣着	Clothing	109.27	117.60	99.37	104.49	101.48
(3)一般日用品	General Consumer Goods	104.16	117.65	104.52	101.54	101.97
(4)耐用消费品	Durable Consumer Goods	96.72	103.25	97.70	96.42	97.43

CHAPTER 8
第八篇

人民生活
PEOPLE'S LIVELIHOOD

编辑单位：	城市社会经济调查队住户处	农村社会经济调查队
编　　委：	张茂海	纪中锐
编　　辑：	邱黎明　吕东海	唐　东
校　　对：	邱黎明　吕东海	唐　东
电　　话：	82872312	82869356

8-1 人民生活基本情况(1990-2005年)
BASIC STATISTICS OF PEOPLE'S LIVELIHOOD(1990-2005)

		单位	Unit	1990年	1995年	2000年	2004年	2005年
一、城乡居民收入	**Income of Urban and Rural Residents**							
农民年人均纯收入	Per Capita Annual Net Income of Rural Residents	元	yuan	952	2 225	3 637	5 080	5 806
职工年平均工资	Average Annual Wages of Staff and Workers	元	yuan	2 400	6 164	10 072	15 950	19 086
城市居民年人均可支配收入	Per Capita Annual Disposable Income of Urban Residents	元	yuan	1 624	5 612	8 016	11 089	12 920
二、城乡居民消费	**Expenditure of Urban and Rural Residents**							
城市:粮食	Urban:Grain	千克	kg	114.48	75.6	69.6	82.49	83.66
食用植物油	Vegetable Oil	千克	kg	6.96	6	8.4	8.95	8.9
鲜蛋	Fresh Eggs	千克	kg	18.48	24	25.2	18.9	19.59
鱼	Fish	千克	kg	11.52	13.2	15.6	12.16	12.68
农村:粮食	Rural: Grain	千克	kg	248.33	185.01	216.45	153.12	155.79
食用油	Edible Oil	千克	kg	6.56	7.54	9.03	6.74	6.01
肉类	Meat	千克	kg	9.22	9.62	12.36	20.95	23.53
水产品	Aquatic Products	千克	kg	4.44	10.77	13.54	13.48	14.28
三、城市居民人均住宅建筑面积	**Per Capita Construction Area of Urban Residents**	**平方米**	**sq. m**	**14.16**	**17.12**	**20.76**	**24.22**	**22.96**
农村居民人均居住面积	Per Capita Living Area Of Rural Residents	平方米	sq. m	19.6	23.03	25.88	27.99	29.54
四、城市每万人拥有公共车辆	**Public Buses Owned by Every 10 000 Persons**	**辆**	**vehicle**	**6.38**	**13.18**	**19.95**	**20.32**	**20.63**
五、城乡居民储蓄余额	**Urban and Rural Saving Deposits**	**亿元**	**100 million yuan**	**65.59**	**268.79**	**535.32**	**1 089.49**	**1 343.1**
人均储蓄余额	Per Capita Saving Deposits	元	yuan	984	3 926	7 575	14 902	18 128
六、学龄儿童入学率	**Attendance Rate of School age Children**	**%**	**%**	**99.84**	**99.82**	**99.99**	**99.99**	**99.99**
每万人口中大学在校学生	Students Enrollment of University Per 10 000 Persons	人	person	23.15	36.38	65.28	276	324
七、城市每百户拥有彩色电视机	**Color TV Sets Owned by Every 100 Households**	**台**	**set**	**68**	**100**	**120**	**123.5**	**118.25**
城市每百户拥有电冰箱	Household Refrigerators Owned by Every 100 Households	台	set	62	89	94.3	92.5	94.5
八、每万人口拥有医疗床位	**Hospital Beds Owned by Every 10 000 Persons**	**张**	**bed**	**35.3**	**36.93**	**34.5**	**34.8**	**41.3**
每万人口拥有医生	Doctors Owned by Every 10 000 Persons	人	person	20.6	20.22	21	19.1	20.3
九、城市每一就业者负担人数(包括本人)	**Persons Supported by Each Urban Employee (including oneself)**	**人**	**person**	**1.72**	**1.58**	**1.82**	**1.86**	**1.97**
农村每一就业者负担人数(包括本人)	Persons Supported by Each Rural Employees(including oneself)	人	person	1.6	1.41	1.33	1.35	1.33
十、农民、城市居民人均年收入对比	**Contrast of Rural and Urban Residents in Per Capita Annual Income**			**1:1.7**	**1:2.4**	**1:2.2**	**1:2.2**	**1:2.2**
农民、城市居民人均年生活费支出对比	Contrast of Rural and Urban Residents in Per Capita Annual Consumption			1:2.4	1:2.7	1:2.8	1:2.7	1:2.6

注:1. 自2002年起城市居民年人均可支配收入为新口径。农民与城市居民人均年收入对比,农民以纯收入,城市居民以可支配收 入计算。
2. 职工年平均工资为城镇单位职工年平均工资。

Note:1. Since 2002, new calibre has been adopted in per capita annual disposable income of urban Resident. The calculation of contrast of rural and urban residents in per capita annual income is using net income of rural residents and disposable income of urban residents.
2. Average annual wage of staff and workers refers to average wage of staff and workers of units in town.

8 -2 城市居民家庭基本情况 (2005 年)
BASIC STATISTICS OF URBAN HOUSEHOLD(2005)

项　目	Items	单位	Unit
调查户数	Households Surveyed	户	household
平均每户人口数	Average Number of Persons Per Household	人	person
户均有收入者人数	Average Number of Persons Having Income Per Household	人	person
户均就业人口数	Average Number of Employees Per Household	人	person
#国有经济单位职工人数	Staff and Workers in State-owned Units	人	person
集体经济单位职工人数	Staff and Workers in Collective-owned Units	人	person
聘留离退休人员数	Number of Retired Persons Employed Again	人	person
户均离退休人数	Average Number of Retired Persons Per Household	人	person
户均其他有收入者人数	Average Number of Other Persons Having Income Per Household	人	person
户均无收入者人数	Average Number of Persons Having No Income Per Household	人	person
平均每人期初手存现金	Average Cash on Hand Term-beginning Per Capita	元	yuan
平均每人每年家庭总收入	Average Yearly Income Per Capita	元	yuan
#平均每人每年可支配收入	Average Yearly Disposable Income Per Capita	元	yuan
平均每人每年出售财物收入	Average Yearly Income of Selling Properties Per Capita	元	yuan
平均每人每年借贷收入	Average Yearly Savings and Lending Income Per Capita	元	yuan
平均每人每年家庭总支出	Average Yearly Expenditure Per Capita	元	yuan
#平均每人每年消费支出	Average Yearly Consumption Expenditure Per Capita	元	yuan
平均每人每年储蓄借贷支出	Average Yearly Savings and Lending Expenditure Per Capita	元	yuan
平均每人期末手存现金	Average Cash on Hand Term – end Per Capita	元	yuan
平均每一就业者负担人口(包括本人)	Persons Supported by Each Employee (including oneself)	人	person

全市平均 Total Average	最低收入户 Lowest Income	低收入户 Low Income	较低收入户 Medium-low Income
400	40	40	80
2.82	3.29	3.01	2.79
2.18	1.98	2.16	2.18
1.43	1.13	1.28	1.42
0.82	0.46	0.72	0.83
0.12	0.20	0.15	0.16
0.05	0.03	0.03	0.10
0.66	0.54	0.69	0.66
0.09	0.31	0.18	0.10
0.64	1.31	0.86	0.61
490.82	240.00	210.86	301.85
13 864.96	4 849.97	7 077.77	9 360.49
12 919.84	4 449.14	6 494.41	8 608.53
2.59	0.31	14.35	0.74
1 976.38	519.75	697.53	1 221.64
11 836.80	4 878.70	6 964.47	8 903.69
9 883.45	4 236.79	6 099.98	7 567.22
3 432.20	240.74	341.52	1 175.78
993.71	534.72	613.72	834.98
1.97	2.91	2.35	1.96

8 -2 续表
continued

项　目	Items	单位	Unit
调查户数	Households Surveyed	户	household
平均每户人口数	Average Number of Persons Per Household	人	person
户均有收入者人数	Average Number of Persons Having Income Per Household	人	person
户均就业人口数	Average Number of Employees Per Household	人	person
#国有经济单位职工人数	Staff and Workers in State-owned Units	人	person
集体经济单位职工人数	Staff and Workers in Collective-owned Units	人	person
聘留离退休人员数	Number of Retired Persons Employed Again	人	person
户均离退休人数	Average Number of Retired Persons Per Household	人	person
户均其他有收入者人数	Average Number of Other Persons Having Income Per Household	人	person
户均无收入者人数	Average Number of Persons Having No Income Per Household	人	person
平均每人期初手存现金	Average Cash on Hand Term-beginning Per Capita	元	yuan
平均每人每年家庭总收入	Average Yearly Income Per Capita	元	yuan
#平均每人每年可支配收入	Average Yearly Disposable Income Per Capita	元	yuan
平均每人每年出售财物收入	Average Year Income from Selling Properties Per Capita	元	yuan
平均每人每年借贷收入	Average Yearly Savings and Lending Income Per Capita	元	yuan
平均每人每年家庭总支出	Average Yearly Expenditure Per Capita	元	yuan
#平均每人每年消费支出	Average Yearly Consumption Expenditure Per Capita	元	yuan
平均每人每年储蓄借贷支出	Average Yearly Savings and Lending Expenditure Per Capita	元	yuan
平均每人期末手存现金	Average Cash on Hand Term – end Per Capita	元	yuan
平均每一就业者负担人口(包括本人)	Persons supported by Each Employee(including oneself)	人	person

中间收入户 Medium Income	较高收入户 Medium - high Income	高收入户 High Income	最高收入户 Highest Income
80	80	40	40
2.80	2.86	2.56	2.40
2.18	2.30	2.19	2.18
1.60	1.62	1.41	1.18
0.93	1.03	0.77	0.67
0.11	0.06	0.11	0.04
0.00	0.02	0.13	0.05
0.53	0.64	0.72	0.99
0.04	0.03	0.06	0.01
0.62	0.56	0.37	0.22
614.65	665.60	738.43	655.61
12 252.50	17 197.25	22 898.39	34 140.92
11 343.78	15 873.45	21 748.64	32 461.50
0.44	0.31	1.21	7.75
2 376.77	2 748.03	2 165.27	4 755.76
11 222.08	14 795.25	17 726.76	24 198.42
9 506.12	11 628.73	15 158.27	20 309.15
2 872.79	4 400.23	6 472.47	13 999.04
932.00	1 371.04	1 551.36	1 172.96
1.75	1.76	1.82	2.03

8－3 农村居民家庭基本情况（1990－2005年）
BASIC STATISTICS OF RURAL RESIDENTS(1990－2005)

项　　目	Items	单位	Unit
调查户数	**Households Surveyed**	**户**	**household**
常住人口	**Permanent Persons**	**人**	**person**
平均每户常住人口	Average Number of Permanent Persons Per Household	人	person
平均每户整半劳力	Total and Semi-labor Per Household	人	person
平均每个劳动力负担人口(含本人)	Persons Supported by Each Laborer(including oneself)	人	person
总收入	**Total Income**	**元**	**yuan**
工资性收入	Wage	元	yuan
家庭经营收入	Household Business Income	元	yuan
财产性收入	Property Income	元	yuan
转移性收入	Transfer Income	元	yuan
现金收入	**Cash Income**	**元**	**yuan**
工资性收入	Wage	元	yuan
家庭经营收入	Household Business Income	元	yuan
财产性收入	Property Income	元	yuan
转移性收入	Transfer Income	元	yuan
总支出	**Total Expenditure**	**元**	**yuan**
家庭经营费用支出	Household Business Expenditure	元	yuan
购置生产性固定资产	Buying Productive Fixed Assets	元	yuan
税费支出	Tax and Fee Payment	元	yuan
生活消费支出	Life Expenditure	元	yuan
转移性和财产性支出	Transfer Expenditure	元	yuan
现金支出	**Cash Expenditure**	**元**	**yuan**
家庭经营费用支出	Household Business Expenditure	元	yuan
购买生产性固定资产	Buying Productive Fixed Assets	元	yuan
税费支出	Tax and Fee Payment	元	yuan
生活消费支出	Life Expenditure	元	yuan
转移性和财产性支出	Transfer Expenditure	元	yuan
平均每人年纯收入	**Annual Net Income Per Capita**	**元**	**yuan**
工资性收入	Wage	元	yuan
家庭经营纯收入	Household Business Income	元	yuan
财产性收入	Property Income	元	yuan
转移性收入	Transfer Income	元	yuan

1990 年	1995 年	2000 年	2004 年	2005 年
2 300	**770**	**820**	**860**	**860**
9 598	**2 919**	**2 856**	**2 976**	**2 964**
4.17	3.79	3.48	3.46	3.45
2.6	2.69	2.61	2.55	2.59
1.6	1.41	1.33	1.35	1.33
1 398	**3 516**	**5 394**	**7 299**	**8 370**
267	816	1 481	2 161	2 402
1 095	2 600	3 802	4 869	5 565
36	42	32	155	236
	58	79	114	167
1 087	**2 126**	**4 554**	**6 261**	**7 403**
267	816	1 479	2 157	2 400
784	1 207	2 428	3 838	4 603
	31	24	152	233
36	72	135	113	167
1 104	**3 093**	**4 223**	**5 656**	**6 363**
349	1 127	1 536	1 950	2 244
21	59	144	162	192
74	98	103	45	27
633	1 723	2 380	3 353	3 737
27	86	60	146	162
1 004	**2 377**	**3 883**	**4 874**	**5 700**
224	539	941	1 506	1 833
20	59	144	162	192
66	98	96	42	27
494	1 295	2 080	3 018	3 486
34	78	117	147	162
952	**2 225**	**3 637**	**5 080**	**5 806**
267	816	1 481	2 161	2 402
655	1 320	2 059	2 668	3 026
–	42	32	155	236
30	47	65	96	142

8-4 城市住户每百户家庭主要耐用品拥有量（1980-2005年）

POSSESSION OF MAJOR DURABLE CONSUMER GOODS PER 100 URBAN HOUSEHOLDS(1980-2005)

年份 Year	家用电脑（台）Personal Computer	钢琴（架）Piano	空调器（台）Air Conditioner	淋浴热水器（台）Water Heater	洗衣机（台）Washing Machine	电冰箱（台）Household Refrigerator	家用汽车（辆）Household Automobile	彩色电视机（台）Color TV Set	移动电话（部）Cell Phone	照相机（架）Camera
1980	-	-	-	-	-	-	-	-	-	2
1981	-	-	-	-	12	-	-	1	-	2
1982	-	-	-	-	22	-	-	2	-	4
1983	-	-	-	-	27	1	-	6	-	6
1984	-	-	-	-	30	2	-	8	-	8
1985	-	-	-	-	35.5	3.5	-	17.5	-	13.5
1986	-	-	-	-	40	4.5	-	24.5	-	15
1987	-	-	-	-	51.5	18	-	33.5	-	17.5
1988	-	-	-	-	60.5	33	-	47	-	20.5
1989	-	-	-	-	67	50	-	59	-	22
1990	-	-	-	-	66	62	-	68	-	26
1991	-	-	-	-	70	76	-	82	-	33
1992	-	1	0	12.5	72.5	83	-	81	-	38.5
1993	-	2	0.5	18	82.5	85.5	-	87.5	-	49.5
1994	-	4	1	17	81	88.5	-	92	-	51
1995	-	4	3	33.5	81.5	89	-	100	-	60.5
1996	-	4.5	6.5	39.5	83	91.5	-	105	-	63
1997	1	4.5	9	46.5	83	93	-	110.5	2.5	63
1998	8.3	5.3	16.5	53	83	91.8	-	110.8	6.8	69.4
1999	10.5	3.8	21.8	61.3	83	93.5	-	117.3	15	68.5
2000	19.3	2	24.5	65.8	83.3	94.3	-	120	30.3	69.5
2001	20	2.3	24.3	65.8	84	92.8	-	127.5	36	68.5
2002	31.5	2.3	38.3	75.3	89.3	93	0.5	123.3	80	72.8
2003	40.8	3.3	47.5	76.3	90.5	92.8	0.3	124.8	105.5	70
2004	46	3	55	79	92.5	92.5	2	123.5	128	68.3
2005	55	4.3	69.3	83.8	91.8	94.8	3.8	118.3	152.8	72.3

8-5 城市居民家庭消费构成
COMPOSITION OF URBAN HOUSEHOLD CONSUMPTION

项目	Items	2005年		2004年	
		年人均支出金额(元) Annual Expenditure Per Capita (yuan)	占消费支出的比重(%) Percentage in the Consumption Expenditure(%)	年人均支出金额(元) Annual Expenditure Per Capita (yuan)	占消费支出的比重(%) Percentage in the Consumption Expenditure(%)
消费支出	**Consumption Expenditure**	**9 883.45**	**100.0**	**9 002.32**	**100**
一、食　品	**Food**	**3 718.88**	**37.6**	**3 423.60**	**38**
#1. 粮　食	Grain	259.4	2.6	253.54	2.8
2. 油　脂	Oil or Fat	116.19	1.2	98.14	1.1
3. 肉禽及其制品	Meat Poultry and Their Products	652	6.6	583.17	6.5
4. 蛋　类	Eggs	123.75	1.3	111.48	1.2
5. 水产品	Aquatic Products	487.62	4.9	413.13	4.6
6. 菜　类	Vegetables	330.31	3.3	281.54	3.1
7. 烟　草	Tobacco	112.08	1.1	101.31	1.1
8. 酒和饮料	Liquor and Beverages	224.5	2.3	204.66	2.3
9. 干鲜果品	Dried and Fresh Fruits	322.48	3.3	289.71	3.2
10. 奶及奶制品	Milk and Milk Products	202.61	2.0	209.65	2.3
二、衣着	**Clothing**	**1 041.7**	**10.6**	**898.65**	**10**
#(1)服装	Garments	705.74	7.1	630.15	7
(2)衣着材料	Clothing Material	8.35	0.1	11.65	0.1
三、家庭设备用品及服务	**Household Facilities, Articles and Services**	**656.94**	**6.6**	**553.5**	**6.1**
#日用耐用消费品	Daily Use Durable Consumer Goods	313.6	3.2	285.89	3.2
四、医疗保健	**Medicines and Medical Services**	**804.75**	**8.2**	**678.22**	**7.5**
五、交通与通讯	**Traffic and Communications**	**988.28**	**10.0**	**914.1**	**10.2**
六、娱乐教育文化服务	**Education, Cultural and Recreation Services**	**1 435.28**	**14.5**	**1 414.52**	**15.7**
1. 文化娱乐用品	Cultural and Recreational Goods	423.13	4.3	371.07	4.1
2. 文化娱乐服务	Recreation and Culture Services	353.89	3.6	275.55	3.1
3. 教育	Education	658.27	6.7	767.9	8.5
七、居住	**Residence**	**951.56**	**9.6**	**872.33**	**9.7**
八、杂项商品与服务	**Miscellanecus Commodities and Services**	**286.07**	**2.9**	**247.4**	**2.8**

8 -6 城市居民家庭年人均消费支出（2005 年）

AVERAGE ANNUAL CONSUMPTION EXPENDITURE OF URBAN HOUSEHOLD PER CAPITA(2005)

项　目	Items	全市平均 Total Average	最低收入户 Lowest Income	低收入户 Low Income
一、食品	**Food**	**3 718.88**	**2 214.35**	**2 967.46**
㈠粮油类	Grain and Oil	450.18	396.91	449.62
1.粮食	Grain	259.40	226.52	250.47
2.淀粉及薯类	Starch and Yam	33.54	28.08	34.62
3.干豆类及豆制品	Dried Beans and Bean Products	41.05	30.65	36.46
4.油脂类	Oil or Fat	116.19	111.66	128.08
㈡肉禽蛋水产品类	Meat, Poultry, Eggs and Aquatic Products	1 263.37	802.71	1 087.32
1.肉类	Meat	552.95	370.99	516.32
2.禽类	Poultries	99.05	72.54	70.11
3.蛋类	Eggs	123.75	95.23	115.23
4.水产品类	Aquatic Products	487.62	263.96	385.65
㈢蔬菜类	Vegetables	330.31	249.94	293.84
1.鲜菜	Fresh Vegetable	298.75	229.87	263.52

单位:元(yuan)

较低收入户 Medium-low Income	中间收入户 Medium Income	较高收入户 Medium-high Income	高收入户 High Income	最高收入户 Highest Income
3 332.95	**3 707.07**	**4 050.24**	**4 958.28**	**5 843.86**
464.36	422.96	436.29	490.01	555.84
265.16	254.12	246.23	298.68	309.40
34.10	29.15	34.07	38.64	43.09
41.87	39.15	41.79	52.63	50.89
123.24	100.55	114.21	100.07	152.46
1 166.09	1 205.79	1 350.46	1 737.66	1 849.80
530.93	540.50	594.90	669.87	732.20
85.24	107.51	101.45	155.19	123.12
126.79	131.27	114.53	145.72	150.69
423.12	426.51	539.59	766.88	843.80
329.40	306.34	350.44	395.53	441.79
301.24	279.40	315.91	352.99	390.32

8－6 续表 1
continued

项　　目	Items	全市平均 Total Average	最低收入户 Lowest Income	低收入户 Low Income
2.干菜	Dried Vegetables	22.96	14.00	23.44
3.菜制品	Vegetable Products	8.59	6.08	6.87
㈣调味品	Flavoring	57.04	39.44	54.70
㈤糖烟酒饮料类	Suger, Tobacco, Liquor and Beverages	366.81	178.64	314.33
1.糖类	Suger	30.22	15.25	23.66
2.烟草类	Tobacco	112.08	67.33	91.18
3.酒类	Liquor	130.45	57.20	127.20
4.饮料	Beverages	94.05	38.86	72.29
㈥干鲜瓜果类	Melons and Fruits	322.48	175.54	237.05
1.鲜果	Fresh Fruits	192.22	111.77	143.10
2.鲜瓜	Fresh Melons	49.72	27.31	32.59
3.干果	Dried Fruits	16.33	8.42	8.36
4.瓜果制品	Melons and Fruits	10.33	6.09	7.16
5.坚果及果仁	Nuts	53.88	21.94	45.84
㈦糕点、奶及奶制品	Pastry, Milk and Milk Products	302.91	164.76	217.66
1.糕点	Pastry	100.31	54.68	70.75
2.奶及奶制品	Milk and Milk Products	202.61	110.07	146.91
㈧其他食品	Other Food	84.45	46.84	70.65
其中:半成品	of which: Semi-finished Products	10.82	5.57	7.11

单位:元(yuan)

较低收入户 Medium-low Income	中间收入户 Medium Income	较高收入户 Medium-high Income	高收入户 High Income	最高收入户 Highest Income
20.52	17.56	25.17	32.47	39.83
7.64	9.38	9.37	10.07	11.64
49.51	55.59	66.29	60.59	83.18
339.42	346.63	397.45	439.22	692.52
32.06	31.19	33.72	35.98	39.45
121.78	119.12	126.00	75.87	173.28
113.28	107.17	136.74	180.94	278.97
72.30	89.15	101.00	146.43	200.82
282.33	347.39	374.67	408.27	476.17
170.03	214.50	211.85	248.61	270.00
40.08	52.57	62.52	62.47	78.37
17.92	13.26	16.21	21.84	37.20
9.71	10.00	13.15	12.44	14.09
44.60	57.06	70.94	62.92	76.51
263.08	325.36	347.10	390.50	466.65
86.89	110.48	120.66	121.56	143.99
176.18	214.88	226.44	268.94	322.66
71.69	82.65	98.67	104.47	140.24
8.77	12.00	14.11	12.29	16.28

8－6 续表 2
continued

项　　目	Items	全市平均 Total Average	最低收入户 Lowest Income	低收入户 Low Income
㈨饮食服务	Catering Services	541.33	159.56	242.27
1.食品加工服务费	Food Processing Service Charges	0.65	0.07	0.00
2.在外饮食	Dining Out	540.68	159.49	242.27
非食品类	**Non-food**	**6 164.57**	**2 022.44**	**3 132.52**
二、衣着	**Clothing**	**1 041.70**	**373.40**	**604.94**
㈠服装	Garments	705.74	236.21	373.21
㈡衣着材料	Clothing Material	8.35	9.37	10.76
㈢鞋类	Shoes	238.98	106.97	166.31
㈣其他衣着用品	Other Clothing Articles	78.79	19.36	44.61
㈤衣着加工服务费	Clothing Processing Service Charges	9.84	1.49	10.06
三、家庭设备用品及服务	**Household Facilities, Articles and Services**	**656.94**	**135.34**	**278.58**
㈠耐用消费品	Durable Consumer Goods	313.60	31.21	82.22
1.家具	Furniture	65.39	1.97	1.15
2.家庭设备	Household Facilities	248.20	29.24	81.07
(1)洗衣机	Washing Machine	36.19	0.00	0.00
(2)电风扇	Electric Fans	3.53	6.19	5.31
(3)电冰箱	Household Refrigerator	44.28	0.00	12.41
(4)冰柜	Freezer	2.04	0.00	0.00
(5)微波炉	Microwave Oven	5.99	6.81	5.63
(6)空调器	Air Conditioner	63.98	0.00	16.54
(7)电炊具	Electric Cooking Utensils	8.28	2.71	7.99
(8)淋浴热水器	Water Heater	18.35	0.00	5.48
(9)排油烟机	Cooking Soat Inducer	10.59	0.00	0.00
(10)吸尘器	Vacuum Cleaner	1.76	0.00	0.00
(11)消毒碗柜	Sterilized Cabinet	2.40	0.00	0.00

单位:元(yuan)

较低收入户 Medium-low Income	中间收入户 Medium Income	较高收入户 Medium-high Income	高收入户 High Income	最高收入户 Highest Income
367.07	614.37	628.86	932.02	1 137.66
0.07	1.68	0.92	0.98	0.25
367.00	612.69	627.95	931.04	1 137.41
4 234.27	**5 799.06**	**7 578.49**	**10 199.99**	**14 465.29**
767.49	**1 008.01**	**1 352.46**	**1 597.93**	**2 043.59**
503.67	696.54	930.51	1 103.65	1 407.75
6.28	6.88	8.78	7.83	12.16
171.83	221.22	305.79	372.59	439.30
76.41	76.55	97.94	98.08	158.62
9.29	6.83	9.43	15.77	25.76
457.17	**549.55**	**819.87**	**979.86**	**1 996.03**
199.56	276.30	367.50	581.94	1 016.35
40.09	19.76	52.63	183.88	331.27
159.47	256.53	314.86	398.07	685.08
15.61	33.91	66.45	50.07	108.32
0.17	1.81	4.56	2.00	9.30
7.15	53.12	32.45	149.95	139.37
0.00	0.00	0.00	0.00	26.24
3.03	11.00	6.65	0.00	5.45
58.02	55.05	115.25	51.87	149.76
4.49	7.13	10.47	22.97	7.57
14.90	24.37	14.23	58.51	22.07
4.17	9.85	17.39	5.68	48.68
0.00	0.00	0.85	3.90	15.90
0.00	2.35	1.29	10.47	9.35

8 -6 续表3
continued

项　　目	Items	全市平均 Total Average	最低收入户 Lowest Income	低收入户 Low Income
⑿洗碗机	Dishwasher	0.00	0.00	0.00
⒀饮水机	Drinking Machine	8.10	0.00	1.99
⒁取暖器	Heater	5.41	0.00	8.48
⒂其他	Others	37.31	13.54	17.24
㈡室内装饰品	Interior Decorations	27.19	4.13	9.45
1.纺织装饰品	Textile Decorations	4.08	0.21	0.19
2.装饰灯具	Decoration Lights	5.93	1.19	1.01
3.其他装饰品	Other Decorations	17.18	2.73	8.25
㈢床上用品	Bed Articles	51.41	6.42	24.18
㈣家庭日用杂品	Daily Use Household Articles	237.92	89.62	156.50
1.厨、餐、茶具	Cooking, dinner and Tea sets	37.78	3.94	20.24
2.家用工具	Household Tools	4.33	0.87	1.39
3.家居清洁用品	Cleaning Articles	44.89	29.10	37.89
4.其他日用杂品	Other Daily Use Articles	150.92	55.70	96.97
㈤家具材料	Furniture Material	7.95	0.03	0.04
㈥家庭服务	Household Services	18.87	3.93	6.20
1.家政服务	Household Management Services	6.77	0.59	0.55
2.加工维修服务费	Processing and Mending Service Charges	12.10	3.34	5.64
四、医疗保健	**Medicines and Medical Services**	**804.75**	**203.23**	**251.79**
㈠医疗器具	Medical Articles	6.55	0.33	0.03
㈡保健器具	Health Protection Articles	18.33	7.31	1.37
㈢药品费	Medicines	308.90	86.47	98.61
㈣滋补保健品	Health Protection Products	171.51	33.92	21.03
㈤医疗费	Medical Services	281.56	72.79	125.78
㈥其他	Others	17.90	2.41	4.96
五、交通和通讯	**Traffic and Communications**	**988.28**	**354.45**	**592.90**
㈠交通	Traffic	388.28	93.05	228.15
1.家庭交通工具	Traffic Instruments	69.66	0.29	2.24
(1)摩托车	Motor	0.62	0.00	0.00
(2)自行车	Bicycle	1.87	0.29	1.32
(3)助力车	Motorbike	0.00	0.00	0.00
(4)家用汽车	Household Car	66.44	0.00	0.00
(5)其他交通工具	Other Traffic Instruments	0.73	0.00	0.92

单位:元(yuan)

较低收入户 Medium-low Income	中间收入户 Medium Income	较高收入户 Medium-high Income	高收入户 High Income	最高收入户 Highest Income
0.00	0.00	0.00	0.00	0.00
2.34	5.48	0.88	2.43	76.20
5.55	3.33	7.90	4.89	8.76
44.05	49.15	36.50	35.34	58.11
30.60	13.79	44.55	17.43	79.65
1.36	3.46	8.30	2.30	15.47
10.70	3.27	2.59	9.16	19.20
18.55	7.07	33.66	5.97	44.99
30.50	26.25	60.15	47.09	261.20
184.60	204.81	322.56	301.09	514.85
20.15	33.25	64.18	51.58	88.58
6.42	2.62	6.95	6.56	3.30
27.78	43.77	52.43	47.41	104.68
130.26	125.16	198.99	195.53	318.30
4.92	8.02	6.68	14.72	34.39
6.99	20.39	18.43	17.59	89.59
1.49	3.09	4.28	7.00	54.51
5.50	17.30	14.15	10.59	35.09
576.85	**627.41**	**1 019.40**	**1 152.18**	**2 600.98**
4.86	4.54	11.96	11.86	14.69
2.75	10.32	16.64	62.89	72.90
265.59	266.47	314.04	418.53	1 026.75
56.61	80.94	235.46	304.60	808.60
230.67	243.64	423.80	337.13	621.65
16.37	21.51	17.51	17.17	56.40
689.05	**873.84**	**1 155.16**	**2 357.99**	**1 575.16**
198.18	279.25	409.72	1 373.79	645.14
2.47	0.20	9.04	738.69	2.26
0.00	0.00	3.10	0.00	0.00
2.47	0.00	4.69	0.78	2.26
0.00	0.00	0.00	0.00	0.00
0.00	0.00	0.00	734.09	0.00
0.00	0.20	1.25	3.82	0.00

8 -6 续表4
continued

项　　目	Items	全市平均 Total Average	最低收入户 Lowest Income	低收入户 Low Income
2. 车辆用燃料及零配件	Fuel and Automobile Spare Parts	35.42	1.59	15.57
(1)燃料	Fuel	31.25	0.09	4.73
(2)零配件	Automobile Spare Parts	1.20	0.01	0.00
(3)其他	Others	2.97	1.50	10.84
3.交通工具服务支出	Expenditure for Traffic Instrument Services	30.18	0.07	5.33
(1)维修费	Mending Cost	16.71	0.07	4.75
(2)车辆使用税费	Tax Payment of Automobile Use	9.76	0.00	0.00
(3)其它车辆使用费用	Other Cost of Automobile Use	3.71	0.00	0.58
4.交通费	Transportation	253.01	91.09	205.00
(1)飞机	Air Plane	11.31	0.00	0.00
(2)火车	Train	21.07	2.60	10.03
(3)长途汽车	Long-distance Bus	11.60	8.41	6.52
(4)市内公共交通	Bus	148.88	70.50	137.88
(5)出租汽车费	Taxi	44.74	7.99	20.94
(6)其他交通费	Other Transportation	15.42	1.59	29.64
(二)通信	Communications	600.00	261.41	364.75
1.通信工具	Communication Instruments	147.04	50.18	18.72
(1)电话机	Telephone	3.39	3.48	0.81
(2)移动电话	Cell Phone	141.09	46.50	17.13
(3)寻呼机	Pager	0.00	0.00	0.00
(4)传真机	Fax Machine	0.00	0.00	0.00
(5)其他通信工具	Other Communication Instruments	2.55	0.19	0.78
2.通信服务	Communication Services	452.96	211.23	346.03
(1)电信费	Telecommunications	428.97	203.80	340.70
(2)邮费	Postage	3.05	1.15	0.01
(3)其他	Others	20.95	6.28	5.32
六、教育文化娱乐服务	**Education, Cultural and Recreation Services**	**1 435.28**	**428.78**	**686.81**
(一)文化娱乐用品	Cultural and Recreational Articles	423.13	91.08	279.68
1.彩色电视机	Color TV Set	64.91	10.25	16.97
2.影碟机	Video Disc Player	7.09	0.00	0.00
3.录放像机	Video Recorder	0.79	0.00	4.12
4.家用电脑	Computer	109.57	2.20	131.48
(1)整机电脑	Entire Computer	99.65	0.00	131.01

单位:元(yuan)

较低收入户 Medium-low Income	中间收入户 Medium Income	较高收入户 Medium-high Income	高收入户 High Income	最高收入户 Highest Income
0.97	5.19	58.45	128.99	115.47
0.78	4.43	47.76	126.46	111.99
0.00	0.12	5.67	0.08	0.51
0.19	0.64	5.03	2.45	2.97
3.93	2.23	39.00	145.91	94.71
0.86	1.11	27.31	40.72	85.72
0.84	0.60	0.51	103.48	0.00
2.23	0.51	11.18	1.71	8.99
190.80	271.64	303.23	360.20	432.71
0.00	11.58	18.31	24.47	40.26
12.42	17.01	31.17	40.29	49.85
7.76	14.96	13.98	18.46	10.89
140.62	163.57	166.39	173.55	196.06
21.03	50.01	60.36	54.16	132.37
8.97	14.51	13.04	49.27	3.27
490.86	594.59	745.44	984.21	930.02
108.27	124.33	199.01	383.99	225.04
7.98	5.36	0.47	1.01	0.00
93.76	117.10	196.49	381.47	222.62
0.00	0.00	0.00	0.00	0.00
0.00	0.00	0.00	0.00	0.00
6.54	1.87	2.06	1.51	2.42
382.59	470.25	546.43	600.22	704.98
357.18	437.03	507.29	573.73	698.76
2.35	9.98	1.43	1.22	0.52
23.06	23.25	37.71	25.26	5.69
923.02	**1 602.41**	**1 854.47**	**2 352.83**	**2 802.99**
179.76	590.98	530.39	734.96	706.86
0.00	215.04	8.86	95.90	108.93
3.68	3.55	7.69	28.66	19.32
1.72	0.00	0.00	0.00	0.00
8.10	119.12	142.14	260.93	228.68
6.50	93.16	133.51	248.01	213.29

8－6 续表5
continued

项　目	Items	全市平均 Total Average	最低收入户 Lowest Income	低收入户 Low Income
(2)计算机外部设备	External Equipment	2.39	0.00	0.25
(3)各种零配件及耗材	Various Spare Parts	7.53	2.20	0.23
5.组合音响	Hi-Fi Stereo Component System	4.11	0.00	0.00
6.录音机	Tape Recorder	3.39	1.60	0.00
7.摄像机	Pickup Camera	5.48	0.00	0.00
8.照相机	Camera	33.65	0.00	0.00
9.钢琴	Piano	0.00	0.00	0.00
10.其他中高档乐器	Other Medium and Top Grade Music Instruments	5.33	0.00	0.00
11.健身器材	Body Building Equipment	10.43	0.00	0.00
12.电子辞典	Electronic Dictionary	4.76	0.00	0.00
13.音像制品及软件	Audio-visual Products and Software	7.01	0.42	4.42
14.体育用品	Sports Goods	1.38	0.14	0.12
15.书报杂志	Books, Newspapers and Magazines	67.77	40.90	64.03
16.纸张文具	Paper and Stationery Goods	17.33	9.54	10.74
17.其他文娱用品	Other Recreation and Culture Articles	80.13	26.03	47.82
(二)文化娱乐服务	Recreation and Culture Services	353.89	35.00	101.55
1.参观游览	Visit	43.65	9.08	24.25
2.健身活动	Body Building Activities	7.47	0.47	0.00
3.团体旅游	Team Tour	217.70	0.34	44.97
4.其它文娱活动	Other Recreation and Culture Activities	78.23	20.79	23.81
5.文娱用品修理服务费	Service Charges for Recreation and Culture Articles Mending	6.85	4.32	8.51
(三)教育	Education	658.27	302.70	305.58
1.教材	Teaching Material	46.18	33.59	30.20
(1)课本及参考书	Text Books and Reference Books	36.89	29.73	28.23
(2)教育软件	Teaching Software	0.54	0.00	0.00
(3)其它教材	Other Teaching Material	8.75	3.86	1.97
2.教育费用	Education Cost	612.09	269.12	275.37
(1)非义务教育学杂费	Tuition Fee for Noncompulsory Education	246.64	101.58	126.68
(2)义务教育学杂费	Tuition Fee for Compulsory Education	48.70	51.56	75.92
(3)托幼费	Child-care Fee	37.07	47.25	23.13
(4)成人教育费	Adult Education Expenses	78.22	1.61	1.38
(5)家教费	Family Education Expenses	27.32	25.86	7.53
(6)培训班	Training Fee	79.72	19.61	9.48

单位:元(yuan)

较低收入户 Medium-low Income	中间收入户 Medium Income	较高收入户 Medium-high Income	高收入户 High Income	最高收入户 Highest Income
0.26	6.49	3.52	3.33	0.10
1.34	19.47	5.11	9.60	15.28
3.00	4.44	3.09	22.02	0.00
2.99	0.00	10.08	2.58	4.30
0.00	0.00	27.40	0.00	0.00
11.27	40.81	50.87	86.13	67.39
0.00	0.00	0.00	0.00	0.00
6.20	0.00	20.35	0.00	0.00
0.00	25.64	17.73	0.00	22.68
0.00	12.66	5.74	0.00	14.01
5.60	7.94	7.61	17.22	8.77
1.06	2.15	0.69	2.22	4.68
54.78	61.01	89.76	86.75	87.63
16.59	11.77	33.23	15.96	15.45
64.77	86.86	105.15	116.59	125.02
199.25	317.20	392.51	446.50	1 491.65
21.74	49.00	54.29	82.89	94.94
1.60	13.44	6.55	4.26	34.84
94.09	180.87	215.79	261.59	1 167.64
76.36	68.10	108.46	93.78	177.58
5.47	5.79	7.43	3.98	16.65
544.00	694.22	931.58	1 171.38	604.48
69.50	45.01	47.19	37.05	37.44
51.69	36.72	39.11	25.43	29.08
0.39	1.75	0.27	0.59	0.00
17.42	6.54	7.81	11.04	8.36
474.50	649.21	884.39	1 134.32	567.04
226.34	254.95	305.20	525.09	194.46
49.16	47.47	40.02	50.00	29.49
22.54	31.30	39.43	88.86	27.09
29.60	124.57	129.84	181.73	58.55
23.93	25.91	33.65	35.74	43.32
28.87	89.07	108.23	193.76	173.55

8 -6 续表6
continued

项　目	Items	全市平均 Total Average	最低收入户 Lowest Income	低收入户 Low Income
(7)学校住宿费	Accommodation Expenses at School	17.52	1.61	4.97
(8)其他	Others	76.90	20.03	26.29
七、居住	**Residence**	**951.56**	**480.57**	**595.36**
(一)住房	Housing	237.56	45.07	28.63
1.租赁房房租	House Rent	21.90	26.67	0.12
2.自有房租金折算	Private House Convert to House Rent	0.00	0.00	0.00
3.住房装潢支出	Decoration Expenses	185.21	13.80	0.00
4.维修用建筑材料	Construction Material for Mending	13.28	1.92	12.90
5.其他	Others	17.18	2.68	15.60
(二)水电燃料及其他	Water, Electricity, Fuel and Others	639.37	414.05	539.22
1.水	Water	39.21	31.46	31.63
2.电	Electricity	267.45	167.01	220.58
3.燃料	Fuel	189.00	152.50	198.38
(1)煤炭	Coal	53.35	42.63	68.08
(2)液化石油气	Liquefied Petroleum Gas	55.27	53.06	67.63
(3)管道煤气	Pipeline Gas	60.82	40.05	50.19
(4)其他燃料	Other Fuel	19.55	16.76	12.48
4.其他	Others	143.70	63.08	88.63
(三)居住服务费	Residence Service Charges	74.62	21.44	27.51
1.物业管理费	Property Management Fee	20.96	4.71	11.15
2.维修服务费	Mending Service Charges	5.62	0.45	0.34
3.其它	Others	48.05	16.27	16.03
八、杂项商品和服务	**Miscellanecus Commodities and Services**	**286.07**	**46.67**	**122.15**
(一)杂项商品	Miscellanecus Commodities	215.83	36.70	92.02
1.金银珠宝饰品	Jewellery	61.65	3.18	0.52
2.手表	Watch	4.83	0.48	0.10
3.理发美容用具	Haircut and Cosmetology Articles	5.01	1.27	3.57
4.化妆品	Cosmetics	72.39	13.37	31.22
5.其他杂品	Other Miscellanecus Commodities	71.95	18.40	56.60
(二)服务	Services	70.23	9.97	30.13
1.旅馆住宿费	Accommodation Expenses at Inn	6.33	0.00	1.65
2.理发洗澡费	Washing and Haircut Service Charges	21.35	7.05	9.84
3.美容费	Cosmetology Service Charges	14.95	0.14	2.25
4.其他服务	Other Services	27.60	2.78	16.39

单位:元(yuan)

较低收入户 Medium-low Income	中间收入户 Medium Income	较高收入户 Medium-high Income	高收入户 High Income	最高收入户 Highest Income
36.62	13.31	24.42	15.66	4.56
57.44	62.62	203.61	43.48	36.01
620.98	**883.61**	**1 028.18**	**1 298.85**	**2 617.99**
62.82	116.83	277.65	298.48	1 421.11
5.51	30.79	36.70	25.57	22.37
0.00	0.00	0.00	0.00	0.00
39.83	51.53	201.90	221.63	1 348.08
8.84	4.22	17.31	38.02	27.18
8.64	30.29	21.74	13.27	23.47
520.24	695.27	665.69	848.01	986.86
38.30	39.39	41.92	40.71	54.97
231.72	269.97	298.82	314.60	440.25
196.15	194.11	178.84	203.49	210.14
61.61	69.74	36.92	32.01	52.99
63.62	54.43	43.54	51.77	56.14
56.56	55.49	67.97	78.75	93.46
14.37	14.45	30.41	40.96	7.54
54.07	191.79	146.12	289.21	281.50
37.92	71.51	84.84	152.36	210.02
12.07	12.90	28.52	28.02	76.17
5.99	6.90	4.64	7.66	16.82
19.85	51.71	51.69	116.68	117.03
199.72	**254.21**	**348.95**	**460.35**	**828.55**
159.99	180.74	255.42	298.56	703.98
19.54	55.56	38.58	78.94	402.47
3.46	3.73	11.79	3.42	8.30
3.10	5.41	7.92	4.26	10.22
42.10	52.76	103.92	158.59	169.54
91.79	63.29	93.22	53.35	113.44
39.73	73.47	93.53	161.79	124.58
0.17	0.71	14.39	14.58	22.98
13.95	28.18	26.13	32.08	36.58
1.87	19.38	18.50	37.35	43.31
23.73	25.20	34.51	77.77	21.71

8-7 城市居民家庭年人均购买主要商品(2005年)
AVERAGE ANNUAL PURCHASES OF MAJOR COMMODITIES OF URBAN HOUSEHOLD PER CAPITA(2005)

项　目	Items	单位	Unit	全市平均 Total Average	最低收入户 Lowest Income	低收入户 Low Income
粮　食	Grain	千克	kg	83.66	82.16	85.35
#大　米	Rice	千克	kg	20.93	20.15	21.26
面　粉	Flour	千克	kg	15.10	19.80	19.39
其他粮食	Other Grain	千克	kg	5.61	4.91	5.54
粮食制品	Grain Products	千克	kg	42.02	37.30	39.16
淀粉及薯类	Starch and Yam	千克	kg	12.80	10.71	14.06
食用植物油	Vegetable Oil	千克	kg	8.90	8.64	10.02
猪　肉	Pork	千克	kg	20.32	16.04	21.61
牛　肉	Beef	千克	kg	1.62	1.16	1.39
羊　肉	Mutton	千克	kg	1.78	1.19	1.38
其他肉	Other Meat	千克	kg	0.84	0.60	0.85
肉制品	Meat Products	千克	kg	11.20	6.79	9.04
禽　类	Poultries	千克	kg	7.48	6.12	5.59
#鸡	Chicken	千克	kg	4.42	4.13	4.02
蛋　类	Eggs	千克	kg	21.37	17.03	20.12
#鲜蛋	Fresh Eggs	千克	kg	19.59	15.93	18.72
水产品类	Aquatic Products					
#鱼	Fish	千克	kg	12.68	10.19	11.97
虾	Shrimp	千克	kg	4.12	3.21	2.94
干　菜	Dried Vegetables	千克	kg	0.65	0.35	0.77
白　酒	White Spirit	千克	kg	2.24	1.42	2.76
果　酒	Wine	千克	kg	0.36	0.05	0.48
啤　酒	Beer	千克	kg	13.09	6.15	14.23
其他酒	Other Liquor	千克	kg	0.63	0.33	0.28

较低收入户 Medium-low Income	中间收入户 Medium Income	较高收入户 Medium-high Income	高收入户 High Income	最高收入户 Highest Income
87.78	79.62	76.50	91.34	92.75
21.40	20.43	20.14	20.88	23.82
14.64	12.31	14.18	13.42	14.65
5.79	5.24	5.46	5.64	7.70
45.96	41.64	36.72	51.40	46.57
14.52	11.10	11.65	13.81	15.90
9.48	7.76	8.61	7.80	11.18
20.48	18.95	21.08	23.33	22.84
1.40	1.33	1.94	2.03	2.65
1.52	1.62	2.06	2.45	2.88
0.84	0.77	0.81	1.12	1.18
10.34	12.33	11.74	13.73	16.08
6.54	8.03	7.43	11.34	8.87
4.12	4.57	4.02	5.83	5.19
22.10	22.52	19.72	24.77	25.21
20.97	19.86	18.18	22.23	22.68
13.01	12.17	12.88	14.43	15.46
3.65	3.63	4.68	5.41	6.69
0.57	0.54	0.65	0.91	1.17
3.31	1.55	1.77	2.03	3.27
0.25	0.31	0.31	0.44	1.15
11.30	10.89	14.67	19.81	20.74
0.58	0.69	0.93	0.90	0.44

8－7 续表
continued

项　目	Items	单位	Unit	全市平均 Total Average	最低收入户 Lowest Income	低收入户 Low Income
碳酸饮料	Carbonated Beverage	千克	kg	2.57	1.11	1.25
果蔬饮料	Fruit and Vegetable Juice Beverage	千克	kg	1.49	0.49	0.97
瓶装饮用水	Bottled Drinking Water	千克	kg	9.58	2.10	3.17
茶　叶	Tea	千克	kg	0.51	0.38	0.67
鲜　果	Fresh Fruits	千克	kg	49.98	32.74	41.38
鲜　瓜	Fresh Melons	千克	kg	23.57	12.66	16.62
干　果	Dried Fruits	千克	kg	1.23	0.70	0.77
瓜果制品	Melons and Fruits	千克	kg	0.99	0.68	0.75
坚果及果仁	Nuts	千克	kg	3.98	1.91	3.75
糕　点	Pastry	千克	kg	9.43	6.25	7.05
鲜乳品	Fresh Milk Products	千克	kg	32.30	20.11	24.13
奶　粉	Milk Power	千克	kg	0.51	0.24	0.93
酸　奶	Yoghurt	千克	kg	4.85	1.83	2.64
服　装	Garments	件	article	6.16	3.03	4.42
1.男士服装	Men's Garments	件	article	2.49	1.57	1.72
2.女士服装	Women's Garments	件	article	3.12	1.20	2.28
3.童　装	Children's Garments	件	article	0.55	0.26	0.42
鞋　类	Shoes	双	pair	3.11	1.99	2.79
水	Water	吨	ton	18.59	14.50	15.00
电	Electricity	度	watt-hour	488.72	301.59	406.45
煤　炭	Coal	千克	kg	140.22	95.24	162.49
液化石油气	Liquefied Petroleum Gas	千克	kg	11.14	10.79	13.80
管道燃气	Pipeline Gas	立方米	cu. m	52.75	33.31	39.15

较低收入户 Medium-low Income	中间收入户 Medium Income	较高收入户 Medium-high Income	高收入户 High Income	最高收入户 Highest Income
2.40	2.84	2.59	3.29	5.47
0.82	1.79	1.57	2.35	3.52
6.60	12.33	10.32	8.11	30.68
0.45	0.43	0.49	0.59	0.80
48.44	55.83	51.21	63.05	59.26
20.43	25.65	28.96	29.05	32.79
1.40	0.94	1.15	1.54	2.88
1.01	1.00	1.12	1.23	1.10
3.66	3.96	5.06	4.50	5.10
8.76	10.37	10.49	10.90	12.56
29.55	35.56	34.11	40.20	47.43
0.41	0.34	0.31	0.78	1.18
3.65	4.54	6.83	7.45	8.39
5.58	6.29	7.72	7.88	8.62
2.29	2.56	3.17	2.90	3.15
2.77	3.13	3.92	4.29	4.70
0.51	0.59	0.64	0.69	0.78
2.81	2.74	3.80	3.98	4.28
17.90	19.21	19.56	19.34	26.79
421.26	493.79	546.68	578.52	803.89
179.42	187.74	92.96	71.05	156.27
12.89	10.82	8.86	10.23	11.11
45.33	49.31	63.92	71.05	80.10

8-8 每百户城市居民家庭年末耐用品拥有量
YEAR-END POSSESSION OF DURABLE CONSUMER GOODS PER 100 URBAN HOUSEHOLDS

项　目	Items	单位	Unit	全市平均 Total Average	最低收入户 Lowest Income	低收入户 Low Income
成套家具	Complete Sets of Furniture	套	set	72.25	68.29	60.00
摩托车	Motor	辆	vehicle	7.75	4.88	10.00
自行车	Bicycle	辆	vehicle	29.00	29.27	30.00
助力车	Motorbike	辆	vehicle	2.25	4.88	2.50
家用汽车	Household Car	辆	vehicle	3.75	2.44	0.00
洗衣机	Washing Machine	台	set	91.75	63.42	82.50
电风扇	Electric Fans	台	set	108.75	92.68	100.00
电冰箱	Household Refrigerator	台	set	94.75	75.61	90.00
冰柜	Freezer	台	set	22.75	14.63	15.00
彩色电视机	Color TV Set	台	set	118.25	104.88	105.00
影碟机	Video Disc Player	台	set	49.50	21.95	30.00
录音机	Tape Recorder	台	set	54.50	31.71	37.50
录放像机	Video Recorder	台	set	28.25	14.63	17.50
家用电脑	Computer	台	set	55.00	24.39	40.00
组合音响	Hi-Fi Stereo Component Systen	套	set	27.75	12.20	22.50
摄像机	Pickup Camera	架	set	8.25	7.32	5.00
照相机	Camera	架	set	72.25	48.78	57.50
钢琴	Piano	架	set	4.25	0.00	2.50
其他中高档乐器	Other Medium and Top Grade Music Instruments	件	article	8.50	0.00	7.50
微波炉	Microwave Oven	台	set	73.00	56.10	57.50
空调器	Air Conditioner	台	set	69.25	26.83	45.00
取暖器	Heater	台	set	51.50	21.95	47.50
电炊具	Electric Cooking Utensils	台	set	66.75	24.39	42.50
淋浴热水器	Water Heater	台	set	83.75	78.05	75.00
排油烟机	Cooking Soat Inducer	台	set	92.25	82.93	95.00
消毒碗柜	Sterilized Cabinet	台	set	5.25	2.44	2.50
洗碗机	Dishwasher	台	set	1.25	0.00	0.00
饮水机	Drinking Machine	台	set	61.25	58.54	37.50
吸尘器	Vacuam Cleaner	台	set	39.00	21.95	22.50
健身器材	Body Building Equipment	套	set	6.25	0.00	0.00
普通电话	Telephone	部	set	97.00	92.68	92.50
移动电话	Cell Phone	部	set	152.75	92.68	112.50
传真机	Fax Machine	部	set	3.50	2.44	5.00

较低收入户 Medium-low Income	中间收入户 Medium Income	较高收入户 Medium-high Income	高收入户 High Income	最高收入户 Highest Income
65.85	72.15	77.50	82.50	81.58
3.66	8.86	10.00	10.00	7.90
24.39	39.24	27.50	32.50	15.79
2.44	2.53	1.25	2.50	0.00
1.22	1.27	5.00	7.50	13.16
92.68	89.87	98.75	100.00	110.53
104.88	100.00	123.75	112.50	126.32
92.68	94.94	98.75	105.00	105.26
19.51	21.52	31.25	22.50	31.58
113.42	118.99	123.75	132.50	128.95
43.90	53.17	58.75	65.00	68.42
53.66	60.76	60.00	77.50	50.00
21.95	30.38	36.25	40.00	34.21
45.12	68.35	70.00	65.00	55.26
20.73	25.32	37.50	32.50	44.74
6.10	6.33	8.75	12.50	15.79
62.20	74.68	80.00	95.00	89.47
1.22	2.53	8.75	7.50	7.90
9.76	5.06	17.50	5.00	7.90
70.73	74.68	80.00	80.00	86.84
59.76	75.95	77.50	85.00	113.16
45.12	53.17	55.00	75.00	65.79
62.20	78.48	76.25	102.50	65.79
79.27	83.54	87.50	92.50	92.11
85.37	96.20	92.50	100.00	97.37
2.44	2.53	5.00	12.50	15.79
0.00	1.27	2.50	2.50	2.63
51.22	55.70	73.75	67.50	89.47
34.15	37.98	41.25	62.50	57.90
3.66	7.60	6.25	12.50	15.79
98.78	96.20	98.75	97.50	100.00
125.61	173.42	186.25	180.00	176.32
2.44	1.27	3.75	7.50	5.26

8-9 分市、区农村住户基本情况(2005年)

BASIC STATISTICS OF RURAL HOUSEHOLD BY REGION(2005)

指　标	Indicators	青岛市 Qingdao	#黄岛区 Huangdao District
调查户数(户)	Households Surveyed(household)	860	60
平均每户常住人口(人)	Average Number of Permanent Persons Per Household (person)	3.45	3.23
平均每户整半劳动力(人)	Total and Semi-labor Per Household(person)	2.59	2.33
全年纯收入	Annual Net Income Per Capita	5 806.42	6 496.24
生活消费支出	Life Expenditure	3 736.88	3 772.42
1.食品消费支出	Food	1 402.73	1 611.45
2.衣着消费支出	Clothing	341.71	506.37
3.居住消费支出	Residence	670.8	327.92
4.家庭设备、用品消费支出	Household Facilities and Articles	201.93	151.14
5.交通和通讯消费支出	Traffic and Communications	381.23	558.91
6.文化教育、娱乐消费支出	Culture,Education and Recreation	464.08	410.3
7.医疗保健消费支出	Medicines and Medical Services	202.56	127.42
8.其他商品和服务消费支出	Other Goods and Services	71.84	78.92
平均每户年内新建(购)房屋面积(平方米)	Newly Building Area Per Capita in the Year(sq.m)	0.99	0
平均每户年末使用房屋面积(平方米)	Living Area Per Capita Year-end(sq.m)	29.54	29.22

单位:元(yuan)

崂山区 LaoshanDistrict	城阳区 ChengyangDistrict	胶州市 Jiaozhou	即墨市 Jimo	平度市 Pingdu	胶南市 Jiaonan	莱西市 Laixi
50	90	130	140	170	110	110
3.08	3.31	3.54	3.44	3.48	3.57	3.56
2.36	2.50	2.78	2.64	2.58	2.55	2.67
6 712.78	5 964.58	5 806.52	5 735.99	5 545.03	5 733.82	5 542.08
6 483.14	4 336.4	4 418.53	3 363.88	3 016.6	3 465.48	3 201.4
2 254.16	1 477.31	1 502.89	1 340.93	1 184.99	1 416.69	1 180.98
837.99	467.86	283.53	362.31	229.29	303.26	220.32
1 196.21	888.25	1 052.48	617.52	475.81	435.41	616.37
309.38	253.77	305.28	199.74	166.61	134.02	148.2
676.9	410.58	453.53	323.21	287.85	360.57	302.8
721.84	510.34	463.33	290.16	501.6	578.01	398.19
447.57	244.34	250.52	152.13	139.58	179.26	235.77
39.09	83.94	106.97	77.87	30.86	58.26	98.77
0	1.83	1.5	0.67	1.03	1.27	0.64
36.33	31.84	36.43	28.17	27.18	26.08	25.91

8 -10 农村住户基本情况(1990 -2005 年)

BASIC STATISTICS OF RURAL HOUSEHOLD(1990 -2005)

项　目	Items	单位	Unit
调查户数	**Households Surveyed**	**户**	**household**
常住人口	**Permanent Persons**	**人**	**person**
一、平均每户常住人口	**Average Number of Permanent Persons Per Household**	**人**	**person**
1. 年龄结构	Age Distribution	人	person
(1)6 岁及以下	6 Year-old and Under	人	person
(2)7 -15 岁	Between 7 and 15 Year-old	人	person
(3)16 -60 岁	Between 16 and 60 Year-old	人	person
(4)61 岁及以上	61 Year-old and Above	人	person
2. 在校学生人数	Students Enrollment	人	person
其中:7 -15 岁在校学生人数	of which:Between 7 and 15 Year-old	人	person
3. 平均每户整半劳动力	Total and Semi-labor Per Household	人	person
(1)整劳动力	Total-labor	人	person
(2)半劳动力	Semi-labor	人	person
整半劳动力占常住人口的比重	Proportion of Total and Semi-labor in the Permanent Persons	%	%
平均每个劳动力负担人口	Persons Supported by Each Laborer	人	person
二、平均每户常住人口中职工人数	**Average Number of Staff and Workers in Permanent Persons Per Household**	**人**	**person**
职工人数占常住人口的比重	Proportion of Staff and Workers in the Permanent Persons	%	%
平均每户常住人口中乡村企业从业人员	Countryside Enterprise Employment in the Permanent Persons Per Household	人	person
乡村企业从业人员占常住人口的比重	Proportion of Countryside Enterprise Employment in the Permanent Persons	%	%
三、平均每百个劳动力中	**Among Per 100 Laborers**		
文盲半文盲人数	Illiterate and Semiliterate	人	person
小学程度人数	Primary School	人	person
初中程度人数	Junior High School	人	person
高中程度人数	Senior High School	人	person
中专程度人数	Secondary School	人	person
大专程度人数	Junior College	人	person
四、经营耕地面积(人均)	**Business Cultivated Area(per capita)**	**亩**	**mu**
#承包耕地面积	Contract Cultivated Area	亩	mu
占经营耕地面积的比重	Proportion in Business Cultivated Area	%	%
#自留地面积	Private Plot Area	亩	mu
占经营耕地面积的比重	Proportion in Business Cultivated Area	%	%

1990 年	1995 年	2000 年	2004 年	2005 年
2 300	**770**	**820**	**860**	**860**
9 598	**2 919**	**2 856**	**2 976**	**2964**
4.17	**3.79**	**3.48**	**3.46**	**3.45**
–	–	–	140	132
–	–	–	300	283
–	–	–	2 348	2354
–	–	–	188	195
–	–	–	528	518
–	–	–	299	283
2.6	2.69	2.61	2.55	2.59
1.95	2.11	1.78	1.69	1.73
0.65	0.58	0.83	0.86	0.86
62.35	71	75	73.82	75.1
1.6	1.41	1.33	1.35	1.33
0.1	**0.1**	**0.12**	**–**	**–**
2.49	2.9	3.57	–	–
0.37	0.32	0.31	0.48	–
8.91	8.5	8.79	13.78	–
9	4.7	2.99	1.78	2.07
38	31.5	23.03	17.39	15.72
42	47.2	53.9	56.26	54.04
10	14.4	15.83	18.02	21.61
1	2	3.22	4.64	4.27
–	0.2	1.03	1.91	2.29
1.62	**1.45**	**1.49**	**1.36**	**1.4**
1.39	1.39	1.47	1.36	1.4
85.8	95.9	98.95	100	100
0.14	0.06	0.02	–	–
8.64	4	1.05	–	–

8－10 续表

continued

项　目	Items	单位	Unit
五、平均每户年末生产性固定资产原值	**Productive Original Value of Fixed Assets Per Household(year-end)**	**元**	**yuan**
1. 役畜、产品畜	Draught Animal and Commodity Animal	元	yuan
2. 大中型铁木农具	Large and Medium Iron and Wooden Farm Tools	元	yuan
3. 农林牧渔业机械	Agricultural Machinery	元	yuan
4. 工业机械	Industrial Machinery	元	yuan
5. 运输机械	Transport Machinery	元	yuan
6. 生产用房	Buildings for Production	元	yuan
7. 其他	Others	元	yuan
六、平均每户年末拥有汽车	**Possession of Automobiles Per Household(year-end)**	**辆**	**vehicle**
大中型拖拉机	Large and Medium Tractors	台	set
小型和手扶拖拉机	Small and Walking Tractors	台	set
七、期末住房情况	**Housing Condition Term-end**	**–**	**–**
1. 人均住房面积	Living Area Per Capita	平方米	sq. m
2. 每平方米住房价值	Housing Value Each Square Metre	元	yuan
3. 住房类型	Housing Type	–	–
(1)人均楼房面积	Apartment Area Per Capita	平方米	sq. m
(2)人均砖瓦平房面积	Brick Bungalow Area Per Capita	平方米	sq. m
(3)人均其它住房面积	LivingArea of Other Housing Per Capita	平方米	sq. m
4. 住房结构	Structure of Housing	–	–
(1)钢筋混凝土结构面积	Reinforced Concrete Structure	平方米	sq. m
(2)砖木结构面积	Brick and Wood Structure	平方米	sq. m
(3)其它	Others	平方米	sq. m
八、期内新建(购)住房情况	**Condition of Newly Building(Buying) Housing During the Term**	**–**	**–**
1. 新建(购)住房面积	Area of Newly Building(Buying) Housing	平方米	sq. m
2. 每平方米新建(购)住房价值	Value of Newly Building(Buying) Housing Each Square Metre	元	yuan
3. 新建(购)住房类型	Type of Newly Building(Buying) Housing	–	–
(1)楼房面积	Apartment Area	平方米	sq. m
(2)砖瓦平房面积	Brick Bungalow Area	平方米	sq. m
(3)其它	Others	平方米	sq. m
4. 新建(购)住房结构	Structure of Newly Building(Buying) Housing	–	–
(1)钢筋混凝土结构面积	Reinforced Concrete Structure	平方米	sq. m
(2)砖木结构面积	Brick and Wood Structure	平方米	sq. m
(3)其它	Others	平方米	sq. m

1990 年	1995 年	2000 年	2004 年	2005 年
1 081.1	**3 165.1**	**5 458.2**	**10 712**	**13 844.9**
207.8	530	477.5	917.4	1 102.8
92.8	163.5	276.7	604.8	216.6
410.3	1 105.8	2 370.2	2 843.8	3 204.3
35.1	265.1	244	707.3	1 246.5
175.7	662.4	765.5	1397.8	1623.3
63.3	405.1	495.8	2 212.8	3 745.7
96.2	33.2	828.5	216	314.7
–	**0.01**	**0.03**	**0.04**	**0.04**
0.01	0.02	0.04	0.06	0.05
0.05	0.11	0.25	0.29	0.31
–	–	–	–	–
–	–	–	28	29.5
–	–	–	380.61	394.47
–	–	–	–	–
–	–	–	3.24	3.42
–	–	–	24.75	25.85
–	–	–	–	0.26
–	–	–	–	–
–	–	–	5.7	6.53
–	–	–	22.29	23
–	–	–	–	–
–	–	–	–	–
–	–	–	0.38	0.99
–	–	–	778.05	512.16
–	–	–	–	–
–	–	–	0.19	0.29
–	–	–	0.19	0.7
–	–	–	–	–
–	–	–	–	–
–	–	–	0.3	0.67
–	–	–	0.08	0.31
–	–	–	–	–

8－11 农村住户人均总收入和纯收入(2005 年)
TOTAL INCOME AND NET INCOMEOF RURAL HOUSEHOLD PER CAPITA(2005)

单位:元(yuan)

项　目	Items	金额 Sum
一、总收入	**Total Income**	**8 370.18**
(一)工资收入	Wage	2 402.07
1.在非企业组织中劳动得到收入	Gained from Non-enterprise Organization	452.99
2.在本乡地域内劳动得到收入	Gained in Local Area	1 434.26
(1)在企业中劳动得到收入	Gained From Enterprises	1 294.83
(2)在国家投资基建项目得到收入	Gained From Capital Construction Programs Invested by State	17.79
(3)提供其他劳务收入	Other Labour Services	121.65
3.外出从业得到收入	Gained from Out-city Enterprise by Permanent Person	514.82
(1)在乡外县内从业得到收入	Out of Countryside and in County	357.18
(2)在县外省内从业得到收入	Out of County and in Province	112.6
(3)在省外国内从业得到收入	Out of Province and in County	11.67
(4)在国外从业得到收入	From Abroad	33.37
(二)家庭经营收入	Household Business Income	5 564.96
1.第一产业收入	Primary Industry	3 872.55
(1)农业收入	Farming	2 536.27
(2)林业收入	Forestry	38.14
(3)牧业收入	Animal Husbandry	1 146.89
(4)渔业收入	Fishery	151.25
2.第二产业收入	Secondary Industry	756.35
(1)工业收入	Industry	626.27
(2)建筑业收入	Construction	130.08

8 -11 续表
continued

单位:元(yuan)

项　目	Items	金额 Sum
3.第三产业收入	Tertiary Industry	936.07
(1)其他产品收入	Other Products	2.12
(2)第三产业服务性收入	Services of Tertiary Industry	933.94
①交通、运输和邮电业收入	Transport and Postal Services	249.78
②批发零售贸易、餐饮业收入	Wholesale,Retail and Catering Business	404.23
③社会服务业收入	Social Services	121.87
④文教卫生业收入	Culture,Education and Health Care	21.33
⑤其他行业收入	Other Household Business	136.74
(三)财产性收入	Property Income	235.52
#1.利息	Interest	6.69
2.租金(包括农业机械)	Rental (including agricultural machinery)	101.50
3.土地征用补偿收入	Compensation for Land Requisition	100.60
4.转让承包土地经营权收入	Making over Business Power of Land	5.94
5.其他投资收益	Others	0.07
(四)转移性收入	Transfer Income	167.64
其中:1.家庭非常住人口寄回	Of which:Income from Outside City	12.09
2.城市亲友赠送收入	Presentation from relatives and Friends	9.92
3.农村亲友赠送收入	From Outside The Country	25.06
4.退耕还林还草补贴收入	Subsidy For Giving back Cultivation to Forest or Grass	1.63
二、全年人均纯收入	**Annual Net Income Per Capita**	**5 806.00**

8－12 农村住户人均总支出(2005 年)

TOTAL EXPENDITURE OF RURAL HOUSEHOLD PER CAPITA(2005)

单位:元(yuan)

项 目	Items	金额 Sum
总支出	**Annual Total Expenditure**	**6 362.92**
(一)家庭经营费用支出	**Household Business Expenditure**	**2 243.72**
1. 第一产业生产费用支出	Primary Industry	1 695.43
(1)农业生产费用支出	Farming	926.11
(2)林业生产费用支出	Forestry	28.61
(3)牧业生产费用支出	Animal Husbandry	696.29
(4)渔业生产费用支出	Fishery	44.42
2. 第二产业生产费用支出	Secondary Industry	252.6
(1)工业生产费用支出	Industry	237.71
(2)建筑业生产费用支出	Construction	14.89
3. 第三产业生产费用支出	Tertiary Industry	295.7
(1)交通、运输和邮电业生产费用支出	Transport and Postal Services	80.78
(2)批发贸易餐饮业生产费用支出	Wholesale, Retail and Catering Business	176.81
(3)社会服务业生产费用支出	Social Services	18.69
(4)文教卫生业生产费用支出	Health Care	5.97
(5)其他行业生产费用支出	Other	13.44
(二)购置生产用固定资产支出	**Buying Productive Fixed Assets**	**191.81**
(三)建造生产性固定资产雇工支出	**Employee of Building Productive Fixed Assets**	**0.91**
(四)税费支出	**Tax and Fee Payment**	**27.42**
1. 第一产业税	Primary Industry	1.1
2. 第二产业税	Secondary Industry	13.54
3. 第三产业生产税	Tertiary Industry	6.65
4. 其他各种收费	Other Various Payment	6.13

8 -12 续表
continued

单位:元(yuan)

项 目	Items	金额 Sum
(五)生活消费支出	**Life Expenditure**	**3 736.88**
1. 食品消费支出	Food	1 402.73
2. 衣着消费支出	Clothing	341.71
3. 居住消费支出	Residence	670.8
4. 家庭设备、用品消费支出	Household Facilities, Articles and Services	201.93
5. 交通通讯消费支出	Traffic and Communications	381.23
6. 文化教育、娱乐消费支出	Cultural, Education and Recreation Articles and Services	464.08
7. 医疗保健消费支出	Medicines and Medical Services	202.56
8. 其他商品和服务消费支出	Other Commodities and Services	71.84
(六)财产性支出	**Property Expenditure**	**4.34**
1. 宅基地有偿使用费	Unfree Use of Land for Building House	0.36
2. 承包其他农户转让费	Expenditure for Making Over	2.8
3. 其 他	Others	1.18
(七)转移性支出	**Transfer Expenditure**	**157.83**
1. 寄给带给家庭非常住人口	Expenditure to Outside City	29.89
2. 赠送农村亲友	Presentation to Relatives and Friends in Rural Area	52.03
3. 赠送城市亲友	Presentation to Relatives and Friends in Urban Area	6.19

8 -13 农村住户人均生活消费支出(2005 年)

CASH CONSUMPTION EXPENDITURE OF RURAL HOUSEHOLD PER CAPITA(2005)

单位:元(yuan)

项　目	Items	金额 Sum
生活消费支出	**Life Expenditure**	**3 736.88**
(一)食品	**Food**	**1 402.73**
1. 购买食品支出	Buying Food	1 275.46
2. 食品消费服务性支出	Services of Food Consumption	127.27
(二)衣着	**Clothing**	**341.71**
1. 购买衣着支出	Buying Clothing	339.91
2. 衣着消费服务性支出	Services ofClothing Consumption	1.8
(三)居住	**Residence**	**670.8**
1. 购买居住消费品支出	Buying Residential Consumption	496.22
2. 居住消费服务性支出	Services for Residential Consumption	174.58
(四)家庭设备、用品及服务	**Household Facilities, Articles and Services**	**201.93**
1. 购买家庭设备、用品支出	Buying Household Facilities and Articles	193.73
2. 家庭设备服务消费支出	Services for Household Facilities	8.2
(五)交通和通讯	**Traffic and Communications**	**381.23**
1. 购买交通和通讯用品支出	Buying Traffic and Communications Articles	168.64
2. 交通和通讯服务消费支出	Services for Traffic and Communications	212.59
(六)文化教育、娱乐用品及服务	**Recreation, Education and Culture Articles and Services**	**464.08**
1. 购买文化教育、娱乐用品	Culture, Education and Recreation Articles	95.85
2. 教育服务消费	Services for Education	321.24
3. 文化体育、娱乐服务消费	Services for Culture, Sports and Recreation	46.99
(七)医疗保健	**Medicines and Medical Services**	**202.56**
1. 购买医疗保健用品	Buying Articles of Medicines and Medical Services	98.58
2. 医疗保健服务消费支出	Services for Health care	103.98
(八)其他商品和服务	**Other Goods and Services**	**71.84**
1. 购买其他商品支出	Goods	51.44
2. 其他消费服务支出	Services	20.4

8－14 农村住户人均年购买消费品情况（2005 年）
CONSUMER GOODS PURCHASING OF RURAL HOUSEHOLD PER CAPITA(2005)

商品名称	Name	计量单位	Unit	数量 Amount
蔬　菜	Vegetables	千克	kg	41.58
豆制品	Beans	千克	kg	2.72
猪　肉	Pork	千克	kg	11.81
牛羊肉	Beef and Mutton	千克	kg	0.76
食　糖	Sugar	千克	kg	0.52
糕　点	Pastry	千克	kg	22.44
糖　果	Sweet	千克	kg	4.72
卷　烟	Cigarette	盒	case	24.36
酒	Liquor	千克	kg	20
#啤　酒	Beer	千克	kg	12.6
茶　叶	Tea	千克	kg	0.51
水　果	Fruits	千克	kg	19.48
服　装	Garments	件	article	3.09
购买洗衣机	Washing Machine	台	unit	0.01
购买电风扇	Electric Fan	台	unit	0.01
购买电冰箱	Refrigerator	台	unit	0.01
购买手机	Cell Phone	部	unit	0.04
购买彩色电视机	Color TV Set	台	unit	0.01
购买照相机	Camera	只	unit	–
购买家用计算机（电脑）	Personal Computer	台	unit	–

注：抽样调查资料。
Note: The data is from sampling

8－15 农村住户每百户家庭主要耐用品拥有量(1982－2005 年)

POSSESSION OF MAJOR DURABLE CONSUMER GOODS PER 100 RURAL HOUSEHOLDS(1982－2005)

年份 Year	自行车(辆) Bicycle	电风扇(台) ElectricFans	洗衣机(台) Washing Machine	电冰箱(台) Household Refrigerator	黑白电视机(台) Black/WhiteTV Set	彩色电视机(台) ColorTV Set	收录机(台) Recorder	照相机(架) Camera
1982	94	0.3	–	–	3	–	–	–
1983	119	0.2	–	–	8	–	–	–
1984	137	1.3	–	–	15	–	4	–
1985	147	5.1	0.3	–	22	3	8	1
1986	165	10.5	1.1	0.3	36.5	4.5	13	1
1987	148	16.3	2.4	0.5	39	7	17	2
1988	154	23	2.4	1	48	9	20	2
1989	170	30	3	1	55	12	23	2
1990	164	37	4	2	57	13	25	2
1991	173	52	5	4	63	16	25	2
1992	178	62	5	7	65	20	26	2
1993	203	75	7	14	76	26	34	2
1994	204	100	9	21	69	35	35	7
1995	203	105	16	28	67	43	41	6
1996	198	113	13	33	62	46	41	8
1997	191	122	15	36	51	56	42	13
1998	184	123	17	39	46	63	43	15
1999	185	121	20	42	41	74	40	10
2000	165	128	28	47	38	86	32	13
2001	153	137	28	53	24	92	32	13
2002	152	143	36	58	18	98	33	16
2003	137	142	39	60	14	100	25	16
2004	142	147	48	68	8	105	32	21
2005	138	159	57	77	4	109	23	21

注:抽样调查资料

Note:The date is from sampling.

8－16 农村住户平均每百户购买生产资料和建筑材料

PURCHASES OF PRODUCTION AND CONSTRUCTION MATERIAL PER 100 RURAL HOUSEHOLD

商品名称	Name	计量单位	Unit	2005年 数 量 Amount	2005年 金额（元）Sum(yuan)	2004年 数 量 Amount	2004年 金额（元）Sum(yuan)
化肥	Chemical Fertilizer	千克	kg	64 908	117 436	62 044	103 112
饼肥	Cake Fertilizer	千克	kg	931.00	855.00	701.63	497.37
农药	Farm Pesticides	千克	kg	907.59	17 815.00	872.44	15 527
农用薄膜	Plastic Fim	千克	kg	1 175.26	13 444.84	1 103	10 784
生产用燃料(生产用柴油、汽油及用煤合并)	Fuel for Production	千克	kg	8 962.03	28 550.90	9 058	28 606
汽车	Automobile	辆	vehicle	0.35	3 370.69	0.12	2 326
大中型拖拉机	Large and Medium Tractors	台	set	0.81	5 439.59	0.8	8 079
小型和手扶拖拉机	Small and Walking Tractors	台	set	2.6	10 725.6	0.6	1 582
机动脱粒机	Motorized Thresher	台	set	0.1	65.5	0.3	343
胶轮大车	Cart with Rubber Tires	辆	vehicle	–	–	–	–
胶轮手推车	Trolley with Rubber Tires	辆	vehicle	–	–	–	–
抽水机	Water Pump	台	set	–	–	–	–
水泵	Pump	台	set	1.63	448.05	2	489
役畜	Draught Animal	头	head	3.45	3 263.85	1.5	1 559
产品畜	Commodity Animal	头	head	15.02	7 606.69	2.4	2 217
水泥	Cement	千克	kg	4 057	1 083	9 640	1 674
木材	Wood	立方米	cu. m	1	758	0.7	401
维修房屋用木材	Wood for House Mending	立方米	cu. m	–	–	–	–
钢材	Steel	千克	kg	310	1 121	166	421
玻璃	Glass	平方米	sq. m	–	–	–	–
维修房屋用玻璃	Glass for Housing Mending	平方米	sq. m	–	–	–	–
砖瓦	Brick and Tile	块	piece	9 437	1 565	4 360	801

注:抽样调查资料。

Note:The data is from sampling

8－17 农村住户人均主要食品消费量(1990－2005 年)

CONSUMPTION OF MAJOR FOOD OF RURAL HOUSEHOLD PER CAPITA(1990－2005)

项　目	Items	单位	Unit	1990 年	1995 年	2000 年	2004 年	2005 年
1. 粮食	Grain	千克	kg	248.33	185.01	216.45	153.12	155.79
2. 蔬菜	Vegetables	千克	kg	135.38	129.66	103.98	72.77	69.51
3. 食用油	Edible Oil	千克	kg	6.56	7.54	9.03	6.74	6.01
(1)植物油	Vegetable Oil	千克	kg	5.75	7.36	8.93	6.7	5.95
(2)动物油	Animal Fats	千克	kg	0.81	0.18	0.07	0.04	0.06
4. 肉类	Meat	千克	kg	9.22	9.62	12.36	12.46	23.53
(1)猪肉	Pork	千克	kg	8.55	9.08	11.85	11.82	12.82
(2)牛羊肉	Beef and Mutton	千克	kg	0.67	0.54	0.51	0.64	0.76
5. 牛羊奶	Milk	千克	kg	0.09	0.62	1.79	7.21	8.29
6. 家禽	Poultries	千克	kg	0.91	1.31	2.55	3.69	3.81
7. 蛋类	Eggs	千克	kg	4.79	9.29	14.41	11.85	11.52
8. 水产品	Aquatic Products	千克	kg	4.44	10.77	12.7	13.48	14.28
9. 食糖	Sugar	千克	kg	0.76	0.83	0.86	0.48	0.52
10. 卷烟	Cigarette	盒	case	23.21	22.43	23.18	20.03	24.36
11. 酒	Liquor	千克	kg	8.97	14.07	22.81	17.82	20.13
12. 茶叶	Tea	千克	kg	0.43	0.61	0.06	0.5	0.51
13. 糖果	Sweet	千克	kg	0.6	0.58	0.52	0.44	0.41
14. 糕点	Pastry	千克	kg	2.91	3.65	4.51	3.01	3.1
15. 水果及水果制品	Fruits and Fruit Products	千克	kg	7.75	28.11	39.73	17.28	20.11

注:抽样调查资料

Note:The data is from sampling.

CHAPTER 9
第九篇

城市建设、环境保护

CITY CONSTRUCTION AND ENVIRONMENT PROTECTION

编辑单位:	固定资产投资统计处	工业交通统计处	人口和社会科技统计处
编　　委:	王金峰	吴加琪	高明辉
编　　辑:	刘　芹	董　青	王　磊
校　　对:	刘　芹	董　青	关　静
电　　话:	85912252	85912257	85912263

9-1 主要年份城市建设和公用事业
MAJOR YEAR'S CITY CONSTRUCTION AND PUBLIC UTILITIES

年份 Year	建成区面积(平方公里) Constructed Area (sq. km)	房屋建筑面积(万平方米) Construction Area of Buildings (10000 sq. m)	住宅建筑面积(万平方米) Living Area of Residence (10000 sq. m)	道路长度(公里) Road Length (km)	道路面积(万平方米) Road Area (10000 sq. m)	汽车、电车线路(条) Bus and Tram Route (line)	汽车、电车线路长度(公里) Length of Bus and Tram Route (km)
1949	27	759	355	243	206	3	26.4
1952	29	796	388	245	213	10	124.4
1957	36	937	491	248	217	13	232.3
1962	55	925	496	266	235	14	252.8
1965	57	992	496	266	235	16	308.1
1970	59	1 063	520	374	346	19	358.5
1975	63	1 296	546	392	355	23	389.3
1978	66	1 463	628	408	368	24	422.1
1980	72	1 630	736	408	377	26	474.1
1985	79	2 559	1 157	462	464	34	611.3
1987	81	2 905	1 421	578	575	37	581
1989	92.5	3 379	1 653	541	583	42	661
1990	94.3	3 529	1 734	667	786	46	777
1991	94.7	3 798	1 856	673	826	48	922
1992	95.4	4 156	1 993	683	840	50	988
1993	99.9	4 468	2 125	764	944	51	1 094
1994	103.9	4 653	2 230	811	985	64	1 372
1995	106	4 888	2 391	936	1 177	64	1 101
1996	110	5 185	2 588	991	1 339	71	1 211
1997	112	5 457	2 750	1 047	1 436	77	1 492
1998	114	5 706	2 900	1 106	1 436	95	1 859
1999	116	6 065	3 153	1 171	1 698	123	2 339
2000	119.1	6 358	3 366	1 192	1 789	140	2 711
2001	123	6 748	3 622	1 248	2 169	145	2 521
2002	133	7 601	3 991	1 426	2 594	145	896
2003	145.9	8 062	4 290	1 595	2 816	164	973
2004	154.8	8 491	4 586	1 755	3 254	187	1 185
2005	178.8	9 022	4 896	1 862	3 547	187	1 159

注：供电量中1989年以后为居民生活用电量。汽车、电车线路长度2002年以后按路网不重复计算。

Note: Electricity Supply refers to residential consumption since 1989.

Repeated parts of roads net are not contained in length of bus and tram route since 2002.

9－1 续表 1
continued

年 份 Year	自来水管道长度(公里) Length of Tap Water Pipelines (km)	全年供水总量(万吨) Annual Supply Volume of Water (10000 tons)	全年售水总量(万吨) Annual Sales Volume of Water (10000 tons)	#居民家庭用水 Residential Use	生活用水普及率(%) Popularity Rate of Water for Residential Use(%)	下水管道长度(公里) Length of Sewer Pipe Lines(km)	全年用电量(亿千瓦时) Annual Electricity Supply (100 million kwh)	#居民生活用电 Urban Facilities and Residential Consumption
1949	308	721	456	331	89	200	0.88	0.14
1952	341	778	612	310	90	227	1.85	0.14
1957	412	1 392	1 296	606	93	273	2.61	0.26
1962	483	2 700	2 512	937	98	290	3.77	0.57
1965	500	3 220	2 979	929	98	295	5.92	0.68
1970	521	4 503	4 106	1 085	99	350	9.83	1.02
1975	564	6 726	6 302	1 950	99	361	12.41	1.43
1978	572	5 334	4 975	1 314	99	382	16.34	1.62
1980	588	8 224	7 874	2 577	99	394	21.48	2.78
1985	685	7 557	7 038	2 628	99.9	505	26.39	2.87
1987	749	10 716	9 155	3 691	99.9	569	34.15	4.01
1989	853	10 349	8 606	3 666	97	620	38.36	3.38
1990	873	1 1896	10 211	4 270	96.9	645	41.08	4.32
1991	908	13 865	11 760	4 990	96.6	649	44.51	5.34
1992	1 035	16 385	13 070	5 931	96.5	672	51.78	6.84
1993	1 123	16 137	14 027	6 124	99.1	734	55.02	7.66
1994	1 124	17 367	14 716	6 405	100	811	60.74	8.78
1995	1 046	22 513	15 810	7 050	100	990	67.23	10.16
1996	1 182	23 277	16 566	7 731	100	1 051	72.87	12.23
1997	1 266	24 130	17 215	8 787	100	1 167	77.82	13.73
1998	1 390	23 845	17 271	9 115	100	1 210	79.65	14.28
1999	1 471	23 849	18 558	10 032	100	1 301	88.12	15.31
2000	1 524	25 414	20 642	11 405	100	1 460	106.8	16
2001	1 665	22 225	18 556	10 555	100	1539	116.1	17.62
2002	1 781	27 662	21 684	10 129	100	1 641	131.44	18.31
2003	2 060	27 594	21 483	10 142	100	1 884	147.68	19.88
2004	2 566	30 877	23 864	11 695	100	2 002	167.95	23.63
2005	2 876	33 265	25 874	12 536	100	2 309	193.81	33.76

注:1990 年以前公共营运车辆不包括系统外及个体。

Note: Vehicles not belonging to system and individual vehicles are not contained in public operating vehicles before 1990.

9－1 续表2
continued

年份 Year	营运车辆（辆）Operating Vehicles (vehicle)	全年客运量（万人次）Annual Passenger Traffic Volume (10000 person-times)	出租汽车（辆）Taxi (vehicle)	使用液化气、煤气天然气人数（万人）Users of Liquefied Gas and Gas (10000 persons)	液化气 Liquefied Gas	煤气 Gas	天然气 Natural Gas	液化气售气量(吨) Sales Volume of Liquefied Gas(ton)
1949	32	298	–	–	–	–	–	–
1952	76	932	–	–	–	–	–	–
1957	112	4 110	–	–	–	–	–	–
1962	127	4 747	–	–	–	–	–	–
1965	173	6 092	–	–	–	–	–	–
1970	224	13 002	–	–	–	–	–	–
1975	324	14 426	–	2	2	–	–	184.9
1978	409	27 351	–	17	17	–	–	3 246
1980	485	38 981	48	24	24	–	–	4 345
1985	621	48 852	219	42.1	42.1	–	–	10 619
1987	679	56 102	652	56.4	45.4	11	–	12 947
1989	751	63 212	782	62.5	47.5	15	–	14 503
1990	801	63 495	832	75	57.4	17.6	–	17 512
1991	1 372	67 552	1 070	76.2	57.4	18.8	–	17 963
1992	1 470	73 529	1828	82.8	62	20.8	–	19 565
1993	1 875	72 427	4 874	88.4	64.6	23.8	–	22 224
1994	1 850	78 231	5 806	103.6	77.4	26.2	–	24 684
1995	1 891	71 867	5 887	116.2	82.9	33.3	–	32 443
1996	2 012	49 077	6 660	126	88	38	–	4 065
1997	2 148	55 642	6 861	133.6	92.9	40.7	–	38 717
1998	2 184	51 042	7 469	146.8	97.8	49	–	45 381
1999	2 470	55 414	7 839	154.9	98.3	56.6	–	40 537
2000	3 141	59 879	7 933	164.1	93.3	70.8	–	46 951
2001	3 453	60 167	8 110	168.8	87.5	81.3	–	45 295
2002	3 681	61 713	8 376	224.2	133.8	90.4	–	60 123
2003	3 648	58 792	8 109	246.7	138.3	93.1	15.3	67 803
2004	3 848	66 463	8 144	258.4	140.6	78.8	39	58 548
2005	4 039	68 776	8 121	265	132.6	45.7	86.7	78 000

注:1990 年以前公共营运车辆不包括系统外及个体。

Note: Vehicles not belonging to system and individual vehicles are not contained in public operating vehicles before 1990.

9 -1 续表3
continued

年 份 Year	煤气售气量（万立方米）Sales Volume of Gas (10000 cu. m)	天然气售气量（万立方米）Sales Volume of Natural Gas (10000 cu. m)	燃气普及率(%) Popularity Rate of Liquefied Gas and Gas(%)	园林绿地面积(公顷) Area of Parks, Gardens and Green Areas(hectare)	公共绿地面积(公顷) Public Green Area(hectare)	人均公共绿地面积(平方米) Per Capita Public Green Areas(sq. m)	建成区绿化覆盖率(%) Coverage Rate of Green Areas(%)	公园、动物园(个) Park and Zoo (place)	公园、动物园面积(公顷) Area of Parks and Zoos (hectare)
1949	–	–	–	133	42	0.7	4.9	3	43
1952	–	–	–	134	43	0.7	4.4	4	45
1957	–	–	–	245	132	1.7	6.9	10	122
1962	–	–	–	771	184	2.2	14	12	174
1965	–	–	–	777	184	2.1	13.7	12	174
1970	–	–	–	772	184	2.1	13	6	117
1975	–	–	2.3	465	162	1.8	7.6	5	134
1978	–	–	18.6	469	162	1.7	7.6	6	165
1980	–	–	24.5	625	206	2.1	10.4	6	152
1985	–	–	36.3	1 072	255	2.3	17.3	7	153
1987	491	–	47	1 790	427	3.6	21.8	20	372
1989	2 585	–	47.3	1 941	459	3.5	21.7	22	381
1990	3 073	–	56.2	2 120	492	3.7	22.8	26	404
1991	3 439	–	56.5	2 318	500	3.7	24.4	28	443
1992	3 824	–	60	2 471	515	3.7	25.9	28	417
1993	4 215	–	63.1	2 488	543	3.9	26.5	31	453
1994	4 116	–	63.1	2 866	572	4	27.9	31	463
1995	4 734	–	79.2	4 547	771	5.3	30.1	33	675
1996	5 447	–	83.9	4 679	836.2	5.6	30.4	33	675
1997	5 920	–	87.3	4 717	924.1	6	31.3	34	730.1
1998	5 959	–	92.5	6 812	1 047.3	6.6	35	35	774.5
1999	7 319	–	96	7 007	1 185.6	7.35	35.9	36	790.9
2000	9 567	–	98	7 439	1 422.5	8.5	37	37	790.1
2001	11 814	–	99	7 688	1 588.0	9.3	37.5	39	832.4
2002	13 500	–	99.5	7 967	1 791.0	8.07	36.4	43	926
2003	14 826	1 181	100	8 829	2 305.3	9.34	37.5	45	1 033.5
2004	15 503	2 710	100	10 047	2 842.3	11	38	48	1 421.4
2005	16 573	7 456	100	11 137	3 131.9	11.82	38.78	47	1 109.9

注：自 2002 年起人均公共绿地面积按辖区内全部人口计算。

Note: Per capita public green areas is calculated at total Population in the area under jurisdiction since 2002.

9-2 全年供电
ANNUAL ELECTRICITY SUPPLY

全年供电 项目	Items	单位	Unit	2005年 2005	2004年 2004	2005年比2004年增(+)减(-)% 2005 Compared to 2004(+/-)
发电设备总容量	Total Capacity of Generation Equipment	万千瓦	10 000 kw	214	184	16.3
#青岛电厂	Qingdao Power Plant	万千瓦	10 000 kw	96	66	45.5
黄岛电厂	Huangdao Power Plant	万千瓦	10 000 kw	73	73	持平
全年发电量	Annual Power Generation	万千瓦时	10 000 kwh	986 346	890 089	10.8
#青岛电厂	Qingdao Power Plant	万千瓦时	10 000 kwh	378 773	350 782	8
黄岛电厂	Huangdao Power Plant	万千瓦时	10 000 kwh	407 933	387 738	5.2
全年实际用电量	Annual Real Consumption	亿千瓦时	100 million kwh	193.81	167.95	15.4
#工　业	Industrial Consumption	亿千瓦时	100 million kwh	127.84	112.63	13.5
农　业	Agricultural Consumption	亿千瓦时	100 million kwh	2.4	6.55	-63.4
生　活	Residential Consumption	亿千瓦时	100 million kwh	33.76	23.63	42.9
平均每日用电量	Average Daily Consumption	万千瓦时	10 000 kwh	5 383.6	4 665.3	15.4

9-3 城市住宅
URBAN RESIDENCE

项目	Items	单位	Unit	2005年 2005	2004年 2004	2005年比2004年增(+)减(-)% 2005 Compared to 2004(+/-)
年末实有房屋建筑面积	Construction Area of Buildings Year-end	万平方米	10000 sq. m	9 022	8 491	6.3
年末住宅建筑面积	Construction Area of Residence Year-end	万平方米	10000 sq. m	4 896	4 586	6.8
#私有住宅	Private Residence	万平方米	10000 sq. m	4 373	4 063	7.6
本年新建竣工房屋面积	Floor Space Newly Completed During the Year	万平方米	10000 sq. m	527.27	438.42	20.3
#住宅	Residence	万平方米	10000 sq. m	329.7	297.25	10.9
本年减少房屋建筑面积	Floor Space Reduced During the Year	万平方米	10000 sq. m	27.73	9.35	196.6
#住宅	Residence	万平方米	10000 sq. m	19.38	1.46	1 227.4
城市居住人口	Population of Residents	万人	10000 persons	195.77	189.26	3.4
平均每人住宅建筑面积	Construction Area Per Capita	平方米	sq. m	25.01	24.22	3.3

9 -4 城市供水
URBAN WATER SUPPLY

项　目	Items	单位	Unit	2005 年 2005	2004 年 2004	2005 年比 2004 年增(+)减(-)% 2005 Compared to 2004(+/-)
自来水管道长度	Length of Tap Water Pipelines	公里	km	2 876	2 566	12.1
供水能力	Supply Capacity	万吨/日	10000 tons/day	124	120.9	2.6
全年供水量	Annual Supply Volume of Water	万吨	10000 tons	33 265	30 877	7.7
#生产用	Industrial Use	万吨	10000 tons	10 819	9 752	10.9
公共服务用	Public Services Use	万吨	10000 tons	4 999	5 222	-4.3
生活用	Residential Use	万吨	10000 tons	12 536	11 695	7.2
消防及其他用	Fire Control and Other Uses	万吨	10000 tons	4 911	4 208	16.7
平均每日供水量	Average Daily Supply	万吨	10000 tons	91.14	84.59	7.7
#生产用	Industrial Use	万吨	10000 tons	29.64	26.72	10.9
生活用	Residential Use	万吨	10000 tons	34.35	32.04	7.2
用水户数	Households with Access to Water	户	household	413 674	390 603	5.9
用水人口	Persons with Access to water	万人	10000 persons	265	258.39	2.6
工业用水量重复利用率	Recycling Rate of Industrial Use Water	%	%	83.39	82.24	1.4

9 -5 城市公共交通
URBAN PUBLIC TRAFFIC

项　目	Items	单位	Unit	2005 年 2005	2004 年 2004	2005 年比 2004 年增(+)减(-)% 2005 Compared to 2004(+/-)
线路长度	Route Length	公里	km	1 159	1 185	-2.2
公共电、汽车营运车辆	Operating Trams and Buses	辆	vehicle	4 039	3 848	4.9
#电车	Tram	辆	vehicle	102	102	持平
汽车	Bus	辆	vehicle	3 937	3 746	5.1
公共电、汽车客运量	Passenger Traffic Volume of Trams and Buses	万人次	10000 person - times	68 776	66 463	3.5
#电车	Tram	万人次	10000 person-times	2 891	3 120	-7.3
汽车	Bus	万人次	10000 person-times	65 885	63 343	4
公共电、汽车平均每日客运量	Average Daily Passenger Traffic Volume of Trams and Buses	万人	10000 persons	188.43	182.09	3.5
出租汽车数	Taxi	辆	vehicle	8 121	8 144	-0.3
轮渡运营船数	Operating Ferry Boats	艘	ship	15	15	持平
轮渡客运总量	Passenger Traffic Volume of Ferry Boats	万人次	10000 person-times	949	861.71	10.1
轮渡平均每日客运量	Average Daily Passenger Traffic Volume of Ferry Boats	万人	10000 persons	2.6	2.36	10.2

9 -6 城市供气
URBAN GAS SUPPLY

项　目	Items	单位	Unit	2005 年 2005	2004 年 2004	2005 年比 2004 年增(+)减(-)% 2005 Compared to 2004(+/-)
煤气供应总量	Supply Volume of Gas	万立方米	10000 cu. m	16 573	15 503	6.9
#家庭用量	Household Consumption	万立方米	10000 cu. m	8 708	10 016	-13.1
煤气用气户数	Households with Access to Gas	户	household	157 798	274 220	-42.5
#家庭用户	Household Users	户	household	157 255	273 506	-42.5
液化石油气供应总量	Supply Volume of Liquefied Gas	吨	ton	78 000	58 548	33.2
#家庭用量	Household Consumption	吨	ton	47 680	38 607	23.5
液化石油气用气户数	Households with Access to Liquefied Gas	户	household	640 637	518 396	23.6
#家庭用户	Household Users	户	household	632 247	511 515	23.6
天然气供应总量	Supply Volume of Natural Gas	万立方米	10000 cu. m	16 573	2 710	511.5
#家庭用量	Household Consumption	万立方米	10000 cu. m	8 708	1 101	690.9
天然气用气户数	Households with Access to Natural Gas	户	household	157 798	130 782	20.7
#家庭用户	Household Users	户	household	157 255	130 488	20.5
燃气普及率	Popularity Rate of Liquefied Gas and Gas	%	%	100	100	-

9 -7 城市环境卫生
URBAN ENVIRONMENTAL SANITATION

项　目	Items	单位	Unit	2005 年 2005	2004 年 2004	2005 年比 2004 年增(+)减(-)% 2005 Compared to 2004(+/-)
市容环卫专用车辆总数	Special Vehicles for Environmental Sanitation	辆	vehicle	394	315	25.1
生活垃圾清运量	Residential Garbage Disposal Cleared	万吨	10000 tons	96.6	91.3	5.8
生活垃圾无害化处理厂(场)数	Plant of Bio-safety Disposal of Residential Garbage	座	place	2	2	持平
生活垃圾无害化处理能力	Handling Capacity of Bio-safety Disposal of Residential Garbage	吨/日	ton/day	2 650	2 650	持平
生活垃圾无害化处理量	Handling Volume of Bio-safety Disposal of Residential Garbage	万吨	10000 tons	96.6	91.3	5.8
道路清扫保洁面积	Area of Roads Cleared	万平方米	10000 sq. m	2 380	2 342.9	1.6
#机械化	Mechanization	万吨	10000 tons	229.8	213.3	7.7
粪便清运量	Night Soil Disposal Cleared	万吨	10000 tons	11.3	8.4	34.5
粪便无害化处理量	Handling Volume of Bio-safety Disposal of Night Soil	万吨	10000 tons	11.3	8.4	34.5
公共厕所	Public Toilets	个	place	428	338	26.6
城市清洁卫生工作人员数	Number of Cleaners	人	person	5 919	5 035	17.6

9－8 城市道路、下水道及绿化
URBAN ROADS, DRAINAGES AND GREEN AREA

项　目	Items	单位	Unit	2005 年 2005	2004 年 2004	2005 年比 2004 年增(＋)减(－)% 2005 Compared to 2004(＋/－)
道路	**Roads**					
年末市政道路长度	Year-end Length of Civil Roads	公里	km	1 862	1 755	6.1
年末铺装道路面积	Year-end Area of Paved Roads	万平方米	10000 sq. m	3 546.6	3 253.8	9
#人行道面积	Area of Pavements	万平方米	10000 sq. m	777.3	733.3	6
下水道总长度	Length of Sewer Pipelines	公里	km	2 309	2 001.71	15.4
园林绿化	**Garden Afforestation**					
绿化覆盖面积	Coverage Area of Green Areas	公顷	hectare	11 743	10 940	7. 3
园林绿地面积	Area of Parks, Gardens and Green Areas	公顷	hectare	11 137	10 047	10.8
公共绿地	Public Green Area	公顷	hectare	3 131.9	2 842	10.2
公园数	Park	个	place	47	48	－2.1
公园面积	Area of Parks	公顷	hectare	1 109.9	1 421.42	－21.9
游人量	Visitors to Parks and Zoos	万人次	10000 person-times	2 467	2 307.64	6.9
城市每人平均公共绿地面积	Per Capita Urban Public Green Areas	平方米	sq. m	11.82	11	7.5
绿化覆盖率	Coverage Rate of Green Areas	%	%	38.78	38	2.1

9－9 环境保护基本情况
BASIC CONDITIONS OF ENVIRONMENTAL PROTECTION

项 目	Items	单位	Unit	2005年 2005	2004年 2004	2005年比2004年增(+)减(-)% 2005 Compared to 2004(+/-)
二氧化硫排放总量	Emission Volume of Sulphur of Dioxide	吨	ton	155 350.96	151 664.3	2.4
烟尘排放总量	Emission Volume of Soot	吨	ton	43 500.03	42 485.6	2.4
工业粉尘排放总量	Emission Volume of Industrial Dust	吨	ton	9 956.56	9 275.2	7.3
工业固体废物排放总量	Emission Volume of Industrial Solid Waste	吨	ton	500	800	-37.5
化学需氧量排放总量	Emission Volume of Chemical Oxygen Demand	吨	ton	54 201.58	55 882.6	-3.0
氨氮排放总量	Emission Volume of Ammonia and Nitrogen	吨	ton	6 019.32	5 802.2	3.7
废水排放总量	Emission Volume of Waste Water	万吨	10 000 tons	25 444.28	24 183.4	5.2

9－10 环境质量状况
ENVIRONMENT CONDITION

项 目	Items	单 位	Unit	2005年 2005	2004年 2004	2005年比2004年增(+)减(-)% 2005 Comparedto 2004(+/-)
市区空气质量优良率	The Percentages of Excellent Or Good Air Quality of Urban Area	%	%	90.7	90.4	0.3
空气质量按功能区达标率	The Reaching Rate of Air Quality For Corresponding Functional Regions	%	%	100	100	0
市区饮用水源地水质达标率	The Reaching Rate of Water Quality for Urban Drinking Water	%	%	97	97	0
近岸海域功能区达标率	The Reaching Rate of The Offshore Sea Water for Corresponding Functional Regions	%	%	75.9	79.3	-3.4
市区区域环境噪声平均等效声级	The Average Equivalent Sound Level of the Urban Regional Environmental Noise	分贝(A)	db(A)	53.4	53.6	-0.2
市区道路交通噪声平均等效声级	The Average Equivalent Sound Level of the Urban Road Traffic Noise	分贝(A)	db(A)	68.3	68.3	0

9－11 工业“三废”排放情况
DISCHARGE CONDITIONS OF INDUSTRIAL WASTE WATER, WASTE GAS AND SOLID WASTE

项　目	Items	单 位	Unit	2005 年 2005	2004 年 2004	2005 年比 2004 年增(＋)减(－)% 2005 Comparedto 2004(＋/－)
工业废水排放总量	Emission Volume of Industrial Waste Water	万吨	10 000 tons	8 956.28	9 130.38	－1.9
废水治理设施数	Number of Facilities for Waste Water Improvement	套	set	457	459	－0.4
废水治理设施处理能力	Handing Capacity of Facilities for Waste Water Improvement	万吨/日	10 000 tons/day	72.97	60.97	19.7
进入城市污水处理厂量	Volume Handled by Sewage Treatment Plant	万吨	10 000 tons	3 809.18	3 265.96	16.6
工业废水排放达标量	Volume of Meeting Standard for Industrial Waste Water Emission	万吨	10 000 tons	8 948.85	9 123.33	－1.9
化学需氧量排放量	Emission Volume of Chemical Oxygen Demand	吨	ton	14 094.68	16 049.18	－12.2
氨氮排放量	Emission Volume of Ammonia and Nitrogen	吨	ton	757.12	689.4	9.8
工业废气排放总量	Emission Volume of Industrial Waste Gas	万标立方米	10 000 cu. m	15 561 131	13 688 122	13.7
废气治理设施数	Number of Facilities for Waste Gas Improvement	套	set	816	874	－6.6
其中:脱硫设施数	of which: Desulphurization Facilities	套	set	105	86	22.1
废气治理设施处理能力	Handling Capacity of Facilities for Waste Gas Improvement	万标立方米/时	10 000 cu. m/hr	3 136.65	2 499.49	25.5
其中:脱硫能力	of which: Desulphurization Capacity	吨/时	ton/hr	4.13	2.72	51.8
二氧化硫去除量	Removing Volume of Sulphur of Dioxide	吨	ton	36 205.85	32 426.58	11.7
二氧化硫排放量	Demission Volume of Sulphur of Dioxide	吨	ton	123 491.96	114 990.27	7.4
其中:达标排放量	of which: Inline with Standard	吨	ton	123 452.61	114 932.27	7.4
烟尘排放量	Emission Volume of Soot	吨	ton	28 154.03	29 748.61	－5.4
其中:达标排放量	of which: Inline with Standard	吨	ton	28 154.03	29 726.11	－5.3
工业粉尘排放量	Emission Volume of Industrial Dust	吨	ton	9 956.56	9 275.2	7.3
其中:达标排放量	of which: Inline with Standard	吨	ton	9 956.56	9 268.91	7.4
工业固体废物产生量	Production Volume of Industrial Solid Waste	万吨	10 000 tons	568.31	509.91	11.5
其中:危险废物	of which: Hazardous Waste	吨	ton	17 347.37	14 243.57	21.8
工业固体废物综合利用量	Comprehensive Use Volume of Industrial Solid Waste	万吨	10 000 tons	622.86	500.65	24.4
工业固体废物排放量	Emission Volume of Industrial Solid Waste	万吨	10 000 tons	0.05	0.08	－37.5
其中:危险废物	of which: Hazardous Waste	吨	ton	0	0	0
污染治理项目完成投资	Completed Investment of Pollution Improvement Projects	万元	10 000 yuan	68 664.9	15 512	342.7
污染治理项目数	Number of Pollution Improvement Projects	个	item	72	56	28.6
当年竣工治理项目数	Number of Completed Improvement Projects of the Year	个	item	72	56	28.6

9－12 分市、区工业“三废”排放情况(2005 年)

DISCHARGE CONDITIONS OF INDUSTRIAL WASTE WATER, WASTE GAS AND SOLID WASTE BY REGION(2005)

市、区名称	Region	废水排放总量(万吨) Emission Volume of Industrial Waste Water (10 000 tons)	废水排放达标量(万吨) Volume of Meeting Standard for Industrial Waste Water Emission (10 000 tons)	化学需氧量排放总量(吨) Emission Volume of Chemical Oxygen Demand (ton)	氨氮排放量(吨) Emission Volume of Ammonia and Nitrogen (ton)	废水治理设施数(套) Number of Facilities for Waste Water Improvement (set)	二氧化硫排放量(吨) Emission Volume of Sulphur of Dixide (ton)	其中:达标排放量(吨) of which: Inline with Standard (ton)	烟尘排放量(吨) Emission Volumeof Soot (ton)
总计	**Total**	**8 956.28**	**8 948.85**	**14 094.68**	**757.12**	**457**	**123 491.96**	**123 452.61**	**28 154.03**
市区	Urban Area	5 980.69	5 973.79	9 107.57	548.09	240	104 073.26	104 053.25	23 724.31
#城阳区	Chengyang District	805.34	805.33	864.44	38.98	55	4 088.48	4 088.48	731.9
黄岛区	Huangdao District	1 008.8	1 008.35	1 199.91	73.52	57	34 417.13	34 417.13	4 795.44
崂山区	Laoshan District	322.05	317.73	587.74	58.69	31	1 354.9	1 334.9	312.86
胶州市	Jiaozhou	354.32	354.31	687.85	46.48	59	1 920.58	1 901.23	423.44
即墨市	Jimo	518.88	518.87	776.89	13.11	35	2 760.54	2 760.54	851.63
平度市	Pingdu	383.15	383.14	592.25	52.92	52	3 940.57	3 940.58	818.34
胶南市	Jiaonan	977.64	977.15	1 942.86	32.41	40	5 399.02	5 399.02	1 377.64
莱西市	Laixi	741.6	741.59	987.26	64.11	31	5 397.99	5 397.99	958.67

9－12 续表

continued

市、区名称	Region	其中:达标排放总量(吨) of which: Inline with Standard(ton)	粉尘排放量(吨) Emission Volume of Industrial Dust(ton)	其中:达标排放总量(吨) of which: Inlinewith Standard(ton)	工业固体废物产生量(万吨) Production Volum of Industrial Solid Waste (10000 tons)	其中:危险废物(吨) of which: Hazardous Waste(ton)	工业固体废物综合利用量(万吨) Comprehensive Use Volume of Industrial Solid Waste (10000 tons)	工业固体废物排放量(万吨) Emission Volume of Industrial Solid Waste (10000 tons)	其中:危险废物排放量(吨) of which: Hazardous Waste (ton)
总　计	**Total**	**28 154.03**	**9 956.56**	**9 956.56**	**568.31**	**17 347.37**	**622.86**	**0.05**	**0**
市　区	Urban Area	23 724.31	9 363.24	9 363.24	425.66	11 633.46	487.82	0.05	0
#城阳区	Chengyang District	731.9	246	246	6.87	721.4	6.68	0	0
黄岛区	Huangdao District	4 795.44	48.87	48.87	90.76	665.08	89.49	0	0
崂山区	Laoshan District	312.86	0	0	4.84	234.4	4.81	0	0
胶州市	Jiaozhou	423.44	74.64	74.64	7.29	1 131	5.24	0	0
即墨市	Jimo	851.63	2.45	2.45	9.69	263.32	9.25	0	0
平度市	Pingdu	818.34	405.38	405.38	81	3 475.97	76.93	0	0
胶南市	Jiaonan	1 377.64	0	0	27.8	45.42	27.7	0	0
莱西市	Laixi	958.67	110.85	110.85	16.87	798.2	15.92	0	0

CHAPTER 10

第十篇

农　业

AGRICULTURE

编辑单位：农村社会经济调查队

编　　委：纪中锐

编　　辑：魏　岗　宋舒平　武　斌

校　　对：魏　岗　宋舒平　武　斌

电　　话：82869379

10－1 农村基本情况(1980－2005 年)

BASIC STATISTICS OF RURAL AREA(1980－2005)

项目	Items	单位	Unit	1980 年	1990 年	1995 年	2000 年	2004 年	2005 年
一、农村基层组织	**RuralBasic Organizations**								
乡政府	Village Government	个	unit	159	93	31	11	–	–
镇政府(含市辖办事处)	Town Government(including offices administered by municipality)	个	unit	2	68	122	145	124	123
村民委员会	Villager Neighborhood Committee	个	unit	6 039	6 081	6 085	6 026	6 018	5 990
二、乡村户数人口、劳动力	**Households, Population and Labor Force of Village**								
乡村户数	Households of Village	万户	10 000 households	110.56	133.73	145.71	148.2	150.57	151.06
乡村人口	Population of Village	万人	10 000 persons	477.53	495.45	496.93	483.39	479.75	478.78
乡村劳动力	Labor Force of Village	万人	10 000 persons	194.1	247.29	258.66	254.62	258.91	257.87
男劳动力	Male Laborer	万人	10 000 persons	113.67	137.28	139.62	137.09	138.47	137.66
女劳动力	Female Laborer	万人	10 000 persons	80.43	110.01	119.04	117.53	120.44	120.21
三、年末实有耕地面积	**Cultivated Area Year-end**	**万公顷**	**10 000 hectares**	**53.13**	**49.84**	**48.65**	**47.75**	**42.26**	**42.1**
四、农用机械总动力	**Total Power of Agricultural Machinery**	**万千瓦**	**10 000 kw**	**110.44**	**253.52**	**289.23**	**459.21**	**598.87**	**619.69**
拖拉机	Tractors	台	set	24 278	55 363	56 391	126 981	168 061	163 032
农用汽车	Automobile for Agricultural Use	辆	vehicle	728	388 0	6 314	9 613	11 085	11 552
五、农村用电量	**Electricity Consumption in Rural Area**	**万千瓦时**	**10 000 kwh**	**20 492**	**67 616**	**134 284**	**189 651**	**330 609**	**372 645**
六、农用化肥施用量(折纯)	**Chemical Fertilizer Consumption(convert to pure amount)**	**万吨**	**10 000 tons**	**12.06**	**20.47**	**31.45**	**32.53**	**32.45**	**33.01**
七、有效灌溉面积	**Effective Irrigated Area**	**万公顷**	**10 000 hectares**	**29.66**	**27.47**	**28.7**	**29.52**	**29.25**	**29.65**

10－2 农村劳动力(1985－2005 年)

RURAL LABOR FORCE(1985－2005)

单位:万人(10 000 persons)

年　份 Year	合　计 Total	农林牧渔业 Farming, Forestry, Animal Husbandry and Fishery	工　业 Industry	建 筑 业 Construction
1985	225.09	147.89	32.92	15.62
1988	238.93	146	44.46	17.51
1989	242.7	151.16	44.65	16.46
1990	247.29	155.2	44.48	16.17
1991	253.01	160.31	45.49	15.87
1992	258.23	160.04	47	17.25
1993	259.18	159.22	44.04	20.2
1994	258.34	155.74	43.7	21.52
1995	258.66	154.08	44.06	22.33
1996	256.34	151.1	43.08	21.8
1997	258.6	153.07	41.66	22.02
1998	258.5	152.79	40.79	21.68
1999	256.82	149.11	42.18	22.32
2000	254.62	143.59	42.76	22.99
2001	253.98	132.46	47.76	24.66
2002	254.08	119.98	53.66	26.52
2003	257.67	118.27	55.65	26.65
2004	258.91	112.05	60.32	28.36
2005	257.87	103.03	65.59	29.03

10－2 续表

continued

单位:万人(10 000 persons)

年　份 Year	交通运输仓储和邮电业 Transportation, Storage, Postal and Telecommunications	批发零售贸易、餐饮业 Wholesale, Retail and Catering Business	金融保险业 Banking and Insurance	其他劳动力 Other Labor Force
1985	5.23	0.06	19.76	3.61
1988	5.89	0.09	20.4	4.58
1989	6	0.12	19.95	4.36
1990	6.11	0.12	20.71	4.5
1991	6.09	0.13	20.52	4.6
1992	7.02	0.16	21.74	5.02
1993	8.93	0.16	20.65	5.98
1994	6.48	10.1	–	20.8
1995	7.11	10.71	–	20.37
1996	7.33	11.78	–	21.25
1997	7.62	12.4	–	21.83
1998	8.02	13.32	–	21.9
1999	8.19	14.03	–	20.99
2000	8.39	16.1	–	20.79
2001	9.02	17.8	–	22.28
2002	10	20.07	–	23.85
2003	9.96	20.6	–	26.54
2004	10.2	24.08		22.96
2005	10.7	25.88		22.34

10－3 分市、区乡村户数、人口、劳动力(2005 年)

RURAL HOUSEHOLDS, POPULATION AND LABOR FORCE BY REGION(2005)

市、区名称	Region	乡村户数(万户) Households of Village (10000 households)	乡村人口(万人) Population of Village (10000 persons)	乡村劳动力(万人) Labor Force of Village (10000 persons)	男劳动力 Male Laborer	女劳动力 Female Laborer	农林牧渔业 Farming, Forestry, Animal Husbandry and Fishery	#林牧渔业 Forestry, Animal Husbandry and Fishery
总计	**Total**	**151.06**	**478.78**	**257.87**	**137.66**	**120.21**	**103.03**	**15.79**
市区	Urban Area	25.01	70.83	38.66	20.45	18.21	7.46	3.04
#城阳区	Chengyang District	13.55	38.14	20.15	10.48	9.67	3.42	1.43
黄岛区	Huangdao District	4.88	15.03	8.47	4.5	3.97	1.59	0.82
崂山区	Laoshan District	6.53	17.54	9.99	5.44	4.55	2.45	0.79
胶州市	Jiaozhou	19.22	62.96	31.63	16.94	14.69	9.6	1.31
即墨市	Jimo	29.16	94.59	55.69	29.33	26.36	17.39	2.38
平度市	Pingdu	36.49	119.96	64.49	34.8	29.69	36.44	5.53
胶南市	Jiaonan	21.66	67.68	33.53	18.04	15.49	13.94	2.51
莱西市	Laixi	19.52	62.76	33.87	18.1	15.77	18.2	1.02

10－3 续表

continued

市、区名称	Region	工业 Industry	建筑业 Construction	交通运输仓储和邮电业 Transportation, Storage, Postal and Telecommunications	批发零售贸易、餐饮业 Wholesale, Retail and Catering Business	其他劳动力 Other Labor Force	#外出合同工临时工 of which: Contracted and Temporary Labor
总计	**Total**	**65.59**	**29.03**	**10.7**	**25.88**	**22.34**	**12.28**
市区	Urban Area	13.87	5.6	2.42	4.68	4.29	2.2
#城阳区	Chengyang District	8.42	2.47	1.29	2.55	1.86	0.83
黄岛区	Huangdao District	2.3	1.8	0.5	1.01	1.14	0.82
崂山区	Laoshan District	3.11	1.33	0.63	1.12	1.28	0.55
胶州市	Jiaozhou	9.76	4.59	1.45	3.95	2.13	0.99
即墨市	Jimo	18.74	6.35	2.23	5.42	5.32	2.54
平度市	Pingdu	9.97	5.45	2.42	6.09	3.9	1.98
胶南市	Jiaonan	7.91	4.22	0.9	2.37	4.01	2.99
莱西市	Laixi	5.34	2.82	1.28	3.37	2.69	1.58

10－4 主要年份农、林、牧、渔业总产值（按1990年不变价格计算）
MAJOR YEAR'S GROSS OUTPUT VALUE OF FARMING, FORESTRY, ANIMAL HUSBANDRY AND FISHERY (1990 CONSTANT PRICE)

单位：万元(10 000 yuan)

年份 Year	农、林、牧、渔业总产值 Gross Output Value of Farming, Forestry, Animal Husbandry and Fishery	农业产值 Output Value of Farming	林业产值 Output Value of Forestry	牧业产值 Output Value of Animal Husbandry	渔业产值 Output Value of Fishery
1949	69 724	58 301	1 645	6 236	3 542
1952	102 401	80 257	2 287	9 324	10 533
1957	110 458	87 019	3 126	11 195	9 118
1962	69 659	52 677	1 204	6 557	9 221
1965	113 953	87 787	4 270	11 626	10 270
1970	168 225	124 678	7 652	17 330	18 565
1975	273 588	202 380	7 453	27 404	36 351
1978	304 715	224 213	7 641	31 101	41 760
1980	357 241	264 444	5 801	43 301	43 695
1985	516 165	331 174	14 237	102 110	686 644
1987	578 323	351 617	9 791	114 104	102 811
1989	593 516	359 872	11 166	115 159	107 319
1990	652 388	384 389	9 241	122 278	136 480
1991	738 720	410 790	10 578	148 070	169 282
1992	785 207	376 945	11 434	161 920	234 908
1993	963 045	449 125	9 896	204 865	299 159
1994	1 042 513	469 486	9 933	245 933	317 161
1995	1 182 266	501 906	10 680	312 312	357 368
1996	1 329 810	522 290	11 801	382 286	413 433
1997	1 266 050	482 742	10 175	344 936	428 197
1998	1 521 325	620 890	12 387	411 632	476 416
1999	1 627 859	666 577	11 738	436 971	512 573
2000	1 729 572	690 283	13 038	485 957	540 294
2001	1 778 928	700 333	13 684	524 290	540 621
2002	1 838 803	707 342	14 057	553 037	564 367
2003	1 783 451	602 867	20 434	578 720	581 430
2004	1 799 463	596 493	19 632	610 548	572 790
2005	1 812 328	601 130	14 867	648 829	547 502

10－5 主要年份农、林、牧、渔业总产值构成(以农林牧渔业总产值为100)

COMPOSITION OF MAJOR YEAR'S GROSS OUTPUT VALUE OF FARMING, FORESTRY, ANIMAL HUSBANDRY AND FISHERY (GROSS OUTPUT VALUE = 100)

年份 Year	农业产值 Output Value of Farming	林业产值 Output Value of Forestry	牧业产值 Output Value of Animal Husbandry	渔业产值 Output Value of Fishery
1949	83.62	2.36	8.94	5.08
1952	78.38	2.23	9.10	10.29
1957	78.78	2.83	10.14	8.25
1962	75.62	1.73	9.41	13.24
1965	77.04	3.75	10.20	9.01
1970	74.11	4.55	10.31	11.03
1975	73.97	2.72	10.02	13.29
1978	73.58	2.51	10.21	13.7
1980	74.02	1.62	12.13	12.23
1985	64.16	2.76	19.78	13.3
1987	60.8	1.69	19.73	17.78
1989	60.63	1.88	19.40	18.09
1990	58.92	1.42	18.74	20.92
1991	55.61	1.43	20.04	22.92
1992	48.01	1.46	20.62	29.91
1993	46.64	1.03	21.27	31.06
1994	45.03	0.95	23.59	30.43
1995	42.45	0.9	26.42	30.23
1996	39.28	0.89	28.75	31.08
1997	38.13	0.8	27.75	33.82
1998	40.81	0.81	27.06	31.32
1999	40.95	0.72	26.84	31.49
2000	39.91	0.75	28.10	31.24
2001	39.37	0.77	29.47	30.39
2002	38.47	0.76	30.08	30.69
2003	33.8	1.15	32.45	32.60
2004	33.15	1.09	33.93	31.83
2005	33.17	0.82	35.80	30.21

10－6 主要年份农、林、牧、渔业总产值指数（以1949年为100）
INDEX OF MAJOR YEAR'S GROSS OUTPUT VALUE OF FARMING, FORESTRY, ANIMAL HUSBANDRY AND FISHERY (1949 = 100)

年　份 Year	农、林、牧、渔业总产值 Gross Output Value of Farming, Forestry, Animal Husbandry and Fishery	农业产值 Output Value of Farming	林业产值 Output Value of Forestry	牧业产值 Output Value of Animal Husbandry	渔业产值 Output Value of Fishery
1949	100	100	100	100	100
1952	146.87	137.66	139.03	149.52	297.37
1957	158.42	149.26	190.03	179.52	257.43
1962	99.91	90.35	73.19	105.15	260.33
1965	163.43	150.58	259.57	186.43	289.95
1970	241.27	213.85	465.17	277.9	524.14
1975	392.39	347.13	453.07	439.45	1 026.28
1978	437.03	384.58	464.5	498.73	1 178.99
1980	512.36	453.58	352.64	694.37	1 233.63
1985	740.3	568.04	865.47	1 637.43	1 938.00
1987	829.45	603.11	595.2	1 829.76	2 902.63
1989	851.24	617.27	678.78	1 846.68	3 029.90
1990	935.67	659.32	561.76	1 960.84	3 853.19
1991	1 059.49	704.6	643.04	2 374.44	4 779.28
1992	1 126.16	646.55	695.08	2 596.54	6 632.07
1993	1 381.22	770.36	601.58	3 285.20	8 446.05
1994	1 495.20	805.28	603.83	3 943.76	8 954.29
1995	1 695.64	860.89	649.24	5 008.21	10 089.44
1996	1 907.25	895.85	717.39	6 130.31	11 672.30
1997	1 815.80	828.02	618.54	5 531.37	12 089.13
1998	2 181.92	1 064.97	753.01	6 600.90	13 450.48
1999	2 334.72	1 143.33	713.56	7 007.23	14 471.29
2000	2 480.60	1 184.00	792.58	7 792.77	15 253.92
2001	2 552.39	1 201.24	831.85	8 407.47	15 263.16
2002	2 637.26	1 213.26	854.53	8 868.46	15 933.57
2003	2 557.87	1 034.06	1 242.19	9 280.31	16 415.30
2004	2 580.84	1 023.13	1 193.43	9 790.7	16 171.37
2005	2 599.29	1 031.08	903.77	10 404.57	15 457.43

10－7 分市、区农、林、牧、渔业总产值(2005 年,现价)

GROSS OUTPUT VALUE OF FARMING, FORESTRY, ANIMAL HUSBANDRY AND FISHERY BY REGION(2005, CURRENT PRICE)

单位:万元(10 000 yuan)

市、区名称	Region	农、林、牧、渔业总产值 Gross Output Value of Farming, Forestry, Animal Husbandry and Fishery	农 业 Output Value of Farming	林 业 Output Value of Forestry	牧 业 Output Value of Animal Husbandry	渔 业 Output Value of Fishery
总计	**Total**	**3 205 057**	**1 265 695**	**25 246**	**1 070 831**	**843 285**
市区	Urban Area	406 881	29 432	2170	43 227	332 052
#城阳区	Chengyang District	227 615	15 367	698	23 582	18 7968
黄岛区	Huangdao District	63 291	9 173	626	7 213	46 279
崂山区	Laoshan District	108 583	4 592	296	9 800	93 895
胶州市	Jiaozhou	444 320	189 332	3 884	150 924	100 180
即墨市	Jimo	532 711	170 045	3 472	167 772	191 422
平度市	Pingdu	840 718	494 748	3 566	330 603	11 801
胶南市	Jiaonan	515 593	161 855	9 857	146 506	197 375
莱西市	Laixi	464 834	220 283	2 297	231 799	10 455

注:本表按当年价格计算。

Note: Data in this form are calculated at current prices.

10－8 分市、区农、林、牧、渔业总产值(2005 年,不变价)

GROSS OUTPUT VALUE OF FARMING, FORESTRY, ANIMAL HUSBANDRY AND FISHERY BY REGION(2005, CONSTANT PRICE)

单位:万元(10 000 yuan)

市、区名称	Region	农、林、牧、渔业总产值 Gross Output Value of Farming, Forestry, Animal Husbandry and Fishery	农 业 Output Value of Farming	林 业 Output Value of Forestry	牧 业 Output Value of Animal Husbandry	渔 业 Output Value of Fishery
总计	**Total**	**1 812 328**	**601 130**	**14 867**	**648 829**	**547 502**
市区	Urban Area	255 902	16 528	1 235	29 981	208 158
#城阳区	Chengyang District	155 315	6 784	471	18 639	129 421
黄岛区	Huangdao District	27 153	4 449	409	4 045	18 250
崂山区	Laoshan District	69 069	5 006	137	5 627	58 299
胶州市	Jiaozhou	251 505	85 261	2 681	88 619	74 944
即墨市	Jimo	313 464	76 515	2 054	98 881	136 014
平度市	Pingdu	421 787	226 090	2 199	188 381	5 117
胶南市	Jiaonan	306 645	95 534	5 372	87 680	118 059
莱西市	Laixi	263 025	101 202	1 326	155 287	5 210

注:本表按 1990 年不变价计算。

Note: Data in this form are calculated at constant prices of 1990.

10－9 农、林、牧、渔业增加值(2005 年)
VALUE－ADDED OF FARMING, FORESTRY, ANIMAL HUSBANDRY AND FISHERY(2005)

单位:万元(10 000 yuan)

		总计 Total	农业 Farming	#种植业 Planting	林业 Forestry	牧业 Animal Husbandry	渔业 Fishery
一、总产值	**Gross Output Value**	**3 205 057**	**1 265 695**	**1 265 695**	**25 246**	**1 070 831**	**843 285**
二、中间消耗	**Intermediate Expenditure**	**1 458 675**	**471 535**	**471 535**	**12 808**	**645 893**	**328 439**
中间物质消耗	Intermediate Expenditure of Matter	1 263 824	425 161	425 161	105 49	574 849	253 265
对非农生产部门的劳动支出	Expenditure of Labor Services to Nonagricultural Production Development	194 851	46 374	46 374	2 259	71 044	75 174
三、增加值	**Added Value**	**1 746 382**	**794 160**	**794 160**	**12 438**	**424 938**	**514 846**

10－10 分市、区农、林、牧、渔业增加值(2005 年)
VALUE-ADDED OF FARMING, FORESTRY, ANIMAL HUSBANDRY FISHERY BY REGION(2005)

单位:万元(10 000 yuan)

市、区名称	Region	增加值 Added Value	农业 Farming	林业 Forestry	牧业 Husbandry	渔业 Fishery
总计	**Total**	**1 746 382**	**794 160**	**12 438**	**424 938**	**514 846**
市区	Urban Area	231 500	17 928	1 150	17 140	195 282
#城阳区	Chengyang District	139 119	9 220	418	8 256	121 225
黄岛区	Huangdao District	35 982	5 810	301	3 029	26 842
崂山区	Laoshan District	54 792	2 678	152	4 747	47 215
胶州市	Jiaozhou	236 004	110 541	1 858	61 655	61 950
即墨市	Jimo	290 442	110 989	1 912	63 398	114 143
平度市	Pingdu	447 474	318 501	2 323	119 598	7 052
胶南市	Jiaonan	293 123	98 045	3 994	61 450	129 634
莱西市	Laixi	247 839	138 156	1 201	101 697	6 785

10－11 主要年份耕地面积与播种面积
MAJOR YEAR'S CULTIVATED AND SOWN AREA

单位:万公顷(10 000 hectares)

年份 Year	年末实有耕地面积 Cultivated Area Year-end	农作物播种面积 Sown Area of Farm Crops	#粮食作物 Grain Crops	#经济作物 Economic Crops
1949	65.7	93.47	84	7.2
1952	67.87	97.53	85.07	10.8
1957	59.67	97.87	87.07	10.53
1962	59.67	81.47	72.53	5.8
1965	59.53	82.8	71.8	8.33
1970	57.47	80.73	68.27	10.07
1975	55.25	79.82	65.84	11.01
1978	53.53	77.6	63.6	10.4
1980	53.13	75.87	60.33	12
1985	50.53	78.27	57.33	15.73
1987	50	76.67	55.87	15.93
1989	49.88	74.78	54.28	16.06
1990	49.84	76.85	56.99	15.53
1991	49.64	76.98	56.89	15.69
1992	49.23	76.96	56.37	15.64
1993	49	77.75	56.22	15.71
1994	48.81	76.61	54.08	16.2
1995	48.65	76.54	53.71	15.65
1996	48.46	77.26	54.81	14.9
1997	48.46	75.04	52.32	14.4
1998	48.33	77.18	53.05	14.54
1999	48.1	77.56	50.61	13.24
2000	47.75	76.47	45.07	13.98
2001	46.74	73.69	41.91	14.54
2002	45.45	72.32	40.83	13.95
2003	42.69	67.82	36.05	14.5
2004	42.26	71.33	41.4	14.11
2005	42.1	75.02	49.93	11.89

10－12 分市、区耕地面积(2005 年)
CULTIVATED AREA BY REGION(2005)

单位:公顷(hectare)

市、区名称	Region	年末耕地面积 Cultivated AreaYear-end	#旱田 Dry Farmland	当年增加的耕地 Cultivated Area Increased in the Year	#新开荒地 Wasteland Newly Opened up
总计	**Total**	**421 006**	**420 963**	**1 631**	**424**
市区	Urban Area	8 476	8 476	80	11
#城阳区	Chengyang District	4 293	4 293	64	11
黄岛区	Huangdao District	2 387	2 387	6	
崂山区	Laoshan District	1 693	1 693	10	
胶州市	Jiaozhou	54 839	54 839	22	15
即墨市	Jimo	76 329	76 329	123	13
平度市	Pingdu	158 374	158 374	1 091	273
胶南市	Jiaonan	53 418	53 375	23	7
莱西市	Laixi	69 570	69 570	292	105

10－12 续表
continued

单位:公顷(hectare)

市、区名称	Region	当年减少的耕地 Cultivated Area Decreased in the Year	国家基建占地 Government Capital Construction	乡镇集体基建占地 Rural Capital Construction	农民个人建房占地 Private Building
总计	**Total**	**3 234**	**2 011**	**694**	**45**
市区	Urban Area	471	171	122	1
#城阳区	Chengyang District	69		42	
黄岛区	Huangdao District	258	120		
崂山区	Laoshan District	74	51	10	1
胶州市	Jiaozhou	200	179	10	1
即墨市	Jimo	1 446	836	415	30
平度市	Pingdu	548	525	4	5
胶南市	Jiaonan	386	295	85	
莱西市	Laixi	183	5	58	8

10 –13 分市、区农作物播种面积(2005 年)
SOWN AREA OF FARM CROPS BY REGION(2005)

单位:公顷(hectare)

市、区名称	Region	总播种面积 Total Sown Area	粮食 Grain	#夏粮 Summer Crops	#小麦 Wheat	秋粮 Autumn Crops	谷子 Cereal	玉米 Corn
总计	**Total**	**750 239**	**499 255**	**256 413**	**256 405**	**242 842**	**298**	**214 726**
市区	Urban Area	7 709	3 177	1 200	1 200	1 977		1 347
#城阳区	Chengyang District	2 58	609	257	257	352		266
黄岛区	Huangdao District	3 728	2 249	943	943	1 306		960
崂山区	Laoshan District	1 020	316			316		120
胶州市	Jiaozhou	110 216	70 797	42 346	42 346	28 451	179	23 402
即墨市	Jimo	130 613	94 793	47 520	47 520	47 273	29	39 208
平度市	Pingdu	278 329	190 238	94 465	94 457	95 773	13	91 802
胶南市	Jiaonan	93 876	55 108	26 393	26 393	28 715	12	20 568
莱西市	Laixi	129 496	85 142	44 489	44 489	40 653	65	38 399

10 –13 续表
continued

单位:公顷(hectares)

市、区名称	Region	高粱 Sorghum	地瓜 Sweet Potato	大豆 Soybean	棉花 Cotton	花生 Peanut	烟叶 Tobacco	蔬菜 Vegetable
总计	**Total**	**684**	**9 663**	**16 544**	**3 637**	**102 856**	**2297**	**129 369**
市区	Urban Area		323	292	47	1 396		2 832
#城阳区	Chengyang District		16	70	47	42		2 004
黄岛区	Huangdao District		109	222		1 095		300
崂山区	Laoshan District		196			259		428
胶州市	Jiaozhou	100	1 143	3 205	172	8 802	515	27 722
即墨市	Jimo	160	3 724	4 031		21 012	1	13 571
平度市	Pingdu	273	958	2 520	3 418	33 191	125	45 942
胶南市	Jiaonan		2 986	5 088		18 011	1 656	17 852
莱西市	Laixi	151	529	1 408		20 444		21 450

10－14 分市、区农作物总产量(2005 年)

TOTAL YIELD OF FARM CROPS BY REGION(2005)

单位:吨(ton)

市、区名称	Region	粮食 Grain	#夏粮 Summer Crops	#小麦 Wheat	秋粮 Autumn Crops	谷子 Cereal	玉米 Corn	高粱 Sorghum
总计	**Total**	**3 150 203**	**1 535 490**	**1 535 471**	**1 614 713**	**1 195**	**1 478 616**	**2 721**
市区	Urban Area	19 392	6 250	6 250	13 142		9 686	
#城阳区	Chengyang District	3 340	1 271	1 271	2 069		1 812	
黄岛区	Huangdao District	13 791	4 979	4 979	8 812		7 142	
崂山区	Laoshan District	2 240			2 240		726	
胶州市	Jiaozhou	427 530	250 900	250 900	176 630	806	155 997	500
即墨市	Jimo	533 084	255 895	255 895	277 189	97	235 860	519
平度市	Pingdu	1 314 209	620 601	620 582	693 608	46	671 991	1 116
胶南市	Jiaonan	325 333	142 918	142 918	182 415	41	143 009	
莱西市	Laixi	530 655	258 926	258 926	271 729	205	262 073	586

10－14 续表

continued

单位:吨(ton)

市、区名称	Region	地瓜 Sweet Potato	大豆 Soybean	棉花 Cotton	花生 Peanut	烟叶 Tobacco	蔬菜 Vegetable
总计	**Total**	**80 738**	**48 007**	**4 042**	**503 941**	**6 668**	**5 792 110**
市区	Urban Area	2 645	746	66	5 529		126 541
#城阳区	Chengyang District	118	139	66	153		95 347
黄岛区	Huangdao District	998	607		4 596		11 878
崂山区	Laoshan District	1 514			780		14 248
胶州市	Jiaozhou	9 371	8 019	228	34 491	1 318	1 171 255
即墨市	Jimo	28 361	11 819		99 743	2	623 227
平度市	Pingdu	9 705	10 503	3 748	175 224	426	2 032 919
胶南市	Jiaonan	26 784	12 364		91 586	4 922	833 064
莱西市	Laixi	3 872	4 556		97 368		1 005 104

10 -15 分市、区农作物播公顷单产量(2005 年)
YIELD OF FARM CROPS PER HECTARE BY REGION(2005)

单位:千克(kg)

市、区名称	Region	粮食 Grain	#夏粮 Summer Crops	#小麦 Wheat	秋粮 Autumn Crops	谷子 Cereal	玉米 Corn	高粱 Sorghum
总计	**Total**	**6 310**	**5 988**	**5 988**	**6 649**	**4 010**	**6 886**	**3 978**
市区	Urban Area	6 104	5 208	5 208	6 647		7 191	
#城阳区	Chengyang District	5 484	4 946	4 946	5 878		6 812	
黄岛区	Huangdao District	6 132	5 280	5 280	6 747		7 440	
崂山区	Laoshan District	7 089			7 089		6 050	
胶州市	Jiaozhou	6 039	5 925	5 925	6 208	4 503	6 666	5000
即墨市	Jimo	5 624	5 385	5 385	5 864	3 345	6 016	3 244
平度市	Pingdu	6 908	6 570	6 570	7 242	3 538	7 320	4 088
胶南市	Jiaonan	5 904	5 415	5 415	6 353	3 417	6 953	
莱西市	Laixi	6 233	5 820	5 820	6 684	3 154	6 825	3 881

10 -15 续表
continued

单位:千克(kg)

市、区名称	Region	地瓜 Sweet Potato	大豆 Soybean	棉花 Cotton	花生 Peanut	烟叶 Tobacco	蔬菜 Vegetable
总计	**Total**	**8 355**	**2 902**	**1 111**	**4 899**	**2 903**	**44 772**
市区	Urban Area	8 189	2 555	1 404	3 961		47 154
#城阳区	Chengyang District	7 375	1 986	1 404	3 643		47 578
黄岛区	Huangdao District	9 156	2 734		4 197		39 593
崂山区	Laoshan District	7 724			3 012		33 290
胶州市	Jiaozhou	8 199	2 502	1 326	3 919	2 559	42 250
即墨市	Jimo	7 616	2 932		4 747	2 000	45 923
平度市	Pingdu	10 130	4 168	1 097	5 279	3 408	44 250
胶南市	Jiaonan	8 970	2 430		5 085	2 972	46 665
莱西市	Laixi	7 319	3 236		4 763		46 858

10－16 主要年份农作物总产量
MAJOR YEAR'S TOTAL YIELD OF FARM CROPS

单位：吨(ton)

年份 Year	粮食 Grain	#小麦 Wheat	#玉米 Corn	棉花 Cotton	花生 Peanut	水果 Fruit	蔬菜 Vegetable
1949	723 190	158 815	25 810	1 280	71 080	9 955	356 015
1952	967 640	200 380	58 130	6 025	115 585	13 468	284 050
1957	921 920	210 690	141 540	3 520	90 445	18 869	625 220
1962	628 930	104 340	53 010	1 280	35 470	8 366	524 455
1965	917 635	180 610	135 595	6 090	88 390	16 034	465 850
1970	1 175 985	243 945	244 530	16 490	96 280	33 907	541 145
1975	1 899 540	430 135	420 095	15 390	98 495	59 206	693 970
1978	1 900 850	514 570	510 635	8 720	114 370	82 819	921 140
1980	2 164 415	520 045	819 930	19 630	160 670	80 840	996 565
1985	2 331 060	961 055	739 455	19 335	475 270	200 515	1 253 075
1987	2 626 029	996 165	1 030 926	13 819	394 296	249 655	1 489 250
1989	2 654 334	993 406	1 084 441	14 638	391 782	288 757	1 664 238
1990	2 998 246	1 265 157	1 210 687	17 490	413 636	292 366	1 786 041
1991	3 180 893	1 421 143	1 285 043	25 965	446 880	294 349	1 837 265
1992	2 675 641	1 235 755	981 490	8 160	321 145	341 415	2 030 327
1993	3 164 812	1 463 759	1 248 780	15 344	419 109	383 368	2 705 349
1994	3 106 562	1 392 977	1 252 952	8 326	494 827	423 024	3 002 318
1995	3 291 587	1 480 385	1 365 167	8 177	510 662	478 685	3 221 507
1996	3 390 033	1 513 479	1 466 668	4 001	486 574	505 711	3 405 056
1997	2 523 064	1 584 478	743 199	2 000	308 233	438 398	3 333 181
1998	3 469 821	1 627 261	1 484 182	4 159	546 786	529 592	4 036 992
1999	3 331 124	1 501 182	1 499 775	3 668	572 941	606 800	5 459 140
2000	2 780 481	1 353 445	1 169 649	2 077	534 174	651 591	6 649 322
2001	2 539 257	1 143 679	1 178 851	3 409	579 441	675 244	6 250 361
2002	2 238 802	1 085 936	1 094 731	3 755	557 714	579 703	6 847 570
2003	2 221 697	931 787	1 117 704	5 324	568 798	677 361	7 305 618
2004	2 650 952	1 301 791	1 202 063	7 216	580 290	748 516	6 720 886
2005	3 150 203	1 535 471	1 478 616	4 042	503 941	737 300	5 792 110

10－17 分市、区大牲畜头数(2005 年)

NUMBER OF LARGE LIVESTOCK BY REGION(2005)

单位:万头(10 000 head)

市、区名称	Region	年末大牲畜头数 Number of Large Livestock Year-end	牛 Cattle and Buffaloes	#奶　牛 Cows	马 Horses	驴 Donkeys	骡 Mules
总计	**Total**	**83.07**	**82.40**	**14.53**	**0.19**	**0.26**	**0.23**
市区	Urban Area	0.56	0.56	0.56	—	—	—
#李沧区	Licang District	0.01	0.01	0.01	—	—	—
#城阳区	Chengyang District	0.55	0.55	0.55	—	—	—
黄岛区	Huangdao District	0.03	0.03	0.01	—	—	—
崂山区	Laoshan District	0.15	0.15	0.15	—	—	—
胶州市	Jiaozhou	18.11	17.70	1.35	0.10	0.15	0.16
即墨市	Jimo	11.62	11.60	1.72	0.01	0.01	0.00
平度市	Pingdu	16.00	15.82	1.10	0.07	0.04	0.06
胶南市	Jiaonan	16.80	16.75	1.60	—	0.05	—
莱西市	Laixi	19.80	19.78	8.02	0.01	0.01	—

10－18 分市、区猪、羊及家禽存养量(2005 年)

STOCKS OF HOGS,SHEEP AND POULTRY BY REGION(2005)

单位:万只(10 000 head)

市、区名称	Region	年末生猪存养量 Hog in Pens By Year-end	年末羊存养量 Sheep and Goats In Pens By Year-end	#山　羊 Goat	绵　羊 Sheep	家　禽 Poultry
总计	**Total**	**199.56**	**86.93**	**80.04**	**6.89**	**6 253.22**
市区	Urban Area	3.88	0.53	0.53	—	177.47
#李沧区	Licang District	1.10	0.01	0.01	—	22.00
#城阳区	Chengyang District	2.78	0.52	0.52	—	155.47
黄岛区	Huangdao District	1.34	0.46	0.46	—	—
崂山区	Laoshan District	2.63	0.08	0.08	—	43.93
胶州市	Jiaozhou	36.70	19.50	18.95	0.55	905.00
即墨市	Jimo	27.17	10.27	9.79	0.49	1 029.75
平度市	Pingdu	44.98	10.06	4.21	5.85	1 726.30
胶南市	Jiaonan	43.86	31.02	31.02	—	670.76
莱西市	Laixi	39.00	15.00	15.00	—	1 700.00

10－19 分市、区肉、蛋、奶、蜂蜜产量(2005年)
OUTPUT OF MEAT, EGG, MILK AND HONEY BY REGION(2005)

单位:吨(ton)

市、区名称	Region	肉类产量 Meat	#猪肉 Pork	#牛肉 Beef	#羊肉 Mutton	#禽肉 Poultry Meat	禽蛋 Egg	牛羊奶 Milk	蜂蜜 Honey
总计	**Total**	**819 437.55**	**280 703.51**	**63 792.90**	**11 034.54**	**455 489.91**	**386 280.01**	**508 193.19**	**72.7**
市区	Urban Area	13 781.85	5 856.06	75.63	32.76	7 768.15	27 210.10	17 290.00	10.00
#李沧区	Licang District	1 614.50	1 606.00	—	—	8.50	1 980	380.80	—
#城阳区	Chengyang District	12 167.35	4 250.06	75.63	32.76	7 759.65	25 230.10	16 909.20	10.00
黄岛区	Huangdao District	2 930.21	1 792.95	45.21	84.75	995.49	3 051.31	1 036.72	—
崂山区	Laoshan District	6 969.05	5 504.49	153.44	16.73	1 294.39	4 431.34	4 539.65	11.27
胶州市	Jiaozhou	91 648.50	45 114.00	12 437.00	2 298.50	30 430.00	7 1852.00	58 765.26	—
即墨市	Jimo	136 502.84	41 036.76	7 360.45	1 577.88	86 023.69	63 757.00	75 827.74	36.00
平度市	Pingdu	268 157.18	71 302.05	29 703.34	1 908.10	164 959.13	67 534.60	36 200.42	15.43
胶南市	Jiaonan	114 942.93	55 347.19	8 537.84	3 615.81	41 619.06	49 593.66	88 848.40	—
莱西市	Laixi	184 505.00	54 750.00	5 480.00	1 500.00	122 400.00	98 850.00	225 685.00	—

10－20 分市、区渔业养殖面积
BREEDING AREA OF FISHERY BY REGION

单位:公顷(hectare)

市、区名称	Region	2005年			2004年		
		养殖面积 Cultivation Area	海水 Seawater	淡水 Fresh Water	养殖面积 Cultivation Area	海水 Seawater	淡水 Fresh Water
总计	**Total**	**64 679**	**46 258**	**18 421**	**63 424**	**44 789**	**18 635**
市区	Urban Area	16 410	15 012	1 398	16 722	14 837	1 885
#城阳区	Chengyang District	10 281	9 204	1 077	10 214	8 638	1 576
黄岛区	Huangdao District	4 195	3 942	253	4 303	4 050	253
崂山区	Laoshan District	1 934	1 866	68	2 205	2 149	56
胶州市	Jiaozhou	8 578	4 297	4 281	8 513	4 290	4 223
即墨市	Jimo	16 960	15 476	1 484	16 676	15 311	1 365
平度市	Pingdu	3 718	—	3 718	3 639	—	3 639
胶南市	Jiaonan	14 208	11 473	2 735	13 099	10 351	2 748
莱西市	Laixi	4 805	—	4 805	4 775	—	4 775

10 –21 分市、区水产品总产量(2005 年)
TOTAL OUTPUT OF AQUATIC PRODUCTS BY REGION(2005)

单位:吨(ton)

市、区名称	Region	水产品总产量 Total Output of Aquatic Products	#养殖产量 Breeding Output	#鱼　类 Fish	#甲壳类 Crust	#贝　类 Shell-fish	#藻　类 Algae
总计	**Total**	**1 272 669**	**872 109**	**283 227**	**118 592**	**816 113**	**9 582**
市区	Urban Area	467 231	313 474	100 958	28 212	311 269	8 236
#城阳区	Chengyang District	316 108	238 154	56 601	8 698	241 775	1 933
黄岛区	Huangdao District	52 023	38 120	12 926	794	37 711	
崂山区	Laoshan District	91 200	37 200	23 531	18 720	31 783	6 303
胶州市	Jiaozhou	137 772	105 702	41 423	8 091	83 262	
即墨市	Jimo	329 447	213 413	28 252	60 691	231 123	36
平度市	Pingdu	13 020	13 020	12 663	279		
胶南市	Jiaonan	313 670	214 971	88 835	20 914	190 459	1 310
莱西市	Laixi	11 529	11 529	11 096	405		

10 –22 分市、区植树及造林面积(2005 年)
FORESTATION AREA BY REGION(2005)

市、区名称	Region	当年造林面积(公顷) Forested Area in the Year(hectare)	育苗面积(公顷) Nursery Garden Area(hectare)	幼林抚育面积(公顷) Laid out Area of Young Trees(hectare)	成林抚育面积(公顷) Laid out Area of Grown-up Trees (hectare)	零星(四旁)植树(万株) Surrounding Tree Planting(10 000)
总计	**Total**	**16 085**	**2 842**	**22 934**	**61 763**	**523**
市区	Urban Area	1 325	397	1 236	4 510	15
#城阳区	Chengyang District	538	260	450		3
黄岛区	Huangdao District	340	107	340	2 510	2
崂山区	Laoshan District	447	30	446	2 000	10
胶州市	Jiaozhou	1 685	296	3 400	22 453	50
即墨市	Jimo	3 560	887	3 560	9 000	100
平度市	Pingdu	3 405	479	5 405	11 210	106
胶南市	Jiaonan	3 667	443	6 000	8 970	130
莱西市	Laixi	2 443	340	3 333	5 620	122

10 -23 分市、区果园面积、水果总产量(2005 年)
AREA OF FRUIT RANCHES AND TOTAL OUTPUT OF FRUITS BY REGION(2005)

单位:吨(ton)

市、区名称	Region	果园总面积(公顷) Total Area of Fruit Ranches(hectare)	水果总产量(吨) Total Output of Fruits(ton)	#苹果 Apple	#梨 Pear	#桃 Peach	#葡萄 Grape	#杏 Apricot	#山楂 Hawthorn
总计	**Total**	**49 316**	**737 300**	**455 955**	**59 720**	**100 045**	**82 030**	**4 307**	**7 929**
市区	Urban Area	2 631	23 750	3 806	1 044	11 318	3 161	2 006	192
#城阳区	Chengyang District	1 174	10 465	1 477	580	3 470	2 805	1 010	40
黄岛区	Huangdao District	303	2 449	752	31	1 254	55	49	1
崂山区	Laoshan District	1 104	10 066	1 577	433	5 824	301	947	151
胶州市	Jiaozhou	5 038	64 541	24 669	3 375	24 068	9 735	91	629
即墨市	Jimo	3 845	38 905	20 403	603	10 147	1 991	267	386
平度市	Pingdu	12 795	237 824	129 346	14 234	24 053	58 608	338	1 089
胶南市	Jiaonan	11 690	217 293	182 499	8 005	17 518	600	1 053	1 095
莱西市	Laixi	13 317	154 987	95 232	32 459	12 941	7 935	552	4 538

10 -24 分市、区茶园、桑园面积和茶叶、蚕茧产量(2005 年)
AREA OF TEA AND MULBERRY GARDENS AND OUTPUTOF TEA AND SILK COCOON BY REGION(2005)

市、区名称	Region	茶园面积(公顷) Area of Tea Gardens(hectare)	茶叶产量(吨) Output of Tea(ton)	桑园面积(公顷) Area of Mulberry Gardens(hectare)	蚕茧产量(吨) Output of Silk Cocoon(ton)
总计	**Total**	**5 749**	**1 425**	**5 440**	**8 409**
市区	Urban Area	1 083	490		
#城阳区	Chengyang District	167	18		
黄岛区	Huangdao District	80	17		
崂山区	Laoshan District	828	453		
胶州市	Jiaozhou				
即墨市	Jimo	496	380		
平度市	Pingdu	16	7	3 007	7 429
胶南市	Jiaonan	4 154	548	1 178	500
莱西市	Laixi			1 255	480

10－25 主要年份主要农业机械拥有量
POSSESSION OF MAJOR YEAR'S MAJOR AGRICULTURAL MACHINERY

年 份 Year	农业机械总动力(万千瓦) Total Power of Agricultural Machinery(10 000 kw)	农用拖拉机 Agricultural Tractors		大、中型机引农具(万台) Large and Medium Towing Farm Machinery(10 000 sets)	农用汽车(辆) Agricultural Camion	排灌机械 Drainage and Irrigation Machinery	
		混合台 set	千瓦 kw			台 set	万千瓦 10 000 kw
1949	–	–	–	–	–	–	–
1952	–	–	–	–	1	–	–
1957	0.22	59	2.2	0.01	2	–	–
1962	2.47	254	11.47	0.06	13	–	–
1965	3.49	296	13.2	0.08	15	–	–
1970	10.4	602	7 963	0.07	12	–	–
1975	43.94	6 447	103 476	0.48	90	–	–
1978	75.45	15 576	309 287	1.02	261	–	–
1980	110.44	24 278	502 731	1.72	728	–	–
1985	174.76	33 097	506 217	1.71	2 645	67 794	54.92
1987	228	50 904	649 340	1.91	3 961	86 314	62.9
1989	241	53 556	661 400	1.96	3 982	93 437	70.46
1990	253.52	55 363	680 903	2.03	3 880	105 574	74.63
1991	250.58	57 404	691 332	2.2	3 706	134 900	73.77
1992	253.94	57 182	684 182	2.28	3 948	124 800	82.68
1993	261.24	56 335	678 161	2.34	4 378	144 460	78.96
1994	278.41	58 698	688 886	2.39	5 474	147 259	80.81
1995	289.23	56 391	657 025	2.28	6 314	138 625	73.98
1996	303.57	59 698	680 447	2.32	7 263	148 313	81.53
1997	326.72	66 841	744 424	2.42	8 085	155 629	88.09
1998	364.21	87 226	894 985	2.48	8 409	156 565	86.68
1999	411.44	105 743	1 075 907	3.06	9 363	170 875	96.2
2000	459.21	126 981	1 253 210	3.3	9 613	182 646	108.26
2001	496.27	141 409	1 394 114	4.33	10 212	178 437	104.18
2002	534.92	152 920	1 537 544	4.79	10 411	182 799	107.35
2003	560.94	160 676	1 666 185	5.07	11 201	192 930	109.44
2004	598.87	168 061	1 818 276	5.31	11 085	192 144	110.38
2005	619.69	163 032	1 757 177	5.66	11 552	188 689	112.16

10－26 主要年份农业机械化、用电量、化肥施用量

MAJOR YEAR'S MECHANIZATION, ELECTRICITY AND CHEMICAL FERTILIZER CONSUMPTION

年份 Year	有效灌溉面积(公顷) Effective Irrigated Area(hectare)	配套机电井(眼) Number of Electromechanical Well(well)	机耕面积(公顷) Area of Motorized Cultivation (hectare)	机播面积(公顷) Area of Motorized Planting (hectare)	机收面积(公顷) Area of Motorized Harvesting (hectare)	农村用电量(万千瓦时) Electricity Consumption in Rural Area (10 000 kwh)	化肥施用量(折纯万吨) Chemical Fertilizer Consumption (convert to 10 000 tons)
1949	8 340	-	-	-	-	-	-
1952	14 980	-	-	-	-	-	-
1957	59 353	-	12 800	13	-	-	0.19
1962	55 213	191	65 680	927	927	55	0.1
1965	80 000	125	11 433	573	247	128	0.55
1970	147 613	3 947	143 700	2 527	133	1 208	1.76
1975	233 980	12 820	248 867	54 507	953	2 522	2.77
1978	276 660	21 017	329 213	178 533	15 060	13 975	3.64
1980	296 606	22 472	444 800	187 980	55 333	20 492	12.06
1985	302 647	42 925	366 786	148 433	56 447	41 524	11.66
1987	260 800	48 497	410 820	187 680	104 240	58 280	13.87
1989	267 440	61 570	540 413	208 527	107 320	62 859	17.91
1990	274 680	56 821	426 680	220 593	143 133	67 616	20.47
1991	281 500	58 987	431 293	254 266	192 946	81 200	22.53
1992	281 610	62 100	438 533	270 453	207 780	88 024	22.6
1993	284 080	63 954	439 300	260 287	225 807	102 501	28.04
1994	286 750	64 877	436 820	262 846	238 693	121 307	28.73
1995	287 020	64 651	435 213	271 707	250 267	134 284	31.45
1996	289 320	65 237	438 947	280 480	235 933	143 740	31.36
1997	292 130	66 783	442 213	308 267	266 147	150 971	28.99
1998	294 120	64 109	442 920	359 447	285 513	153 113	31.95
1999	294 790	64 734	440 967	396 180	286 367	169 337	32.58
2000	295 190	65 179	439 980	346 480	292 787	189 651	32.53
2001	296 980	65 547	436 576	382 870	265 730	228 069	31.73
2002	294 310	65 588	433 660	364 680	267 690	256 453	31.07
2003	292 410	65 406	415 790	404 980	256 600	299 425	31.89
2004	292 520	65 501	415 220	454 800	314 680	330 609	32.45
2005	296 450	65 303	409 610	493 240	367 740	372 644.0	33.01

10 -27 分市、区农业机械化和电气化(2005 年)
MECHANIZATION AND ELECTRIFICATION IN AGRICULTURE BY REGION(2005)

市、区名称	Region	机耕地面积 Area of Motorized Cultivation		机播地面积 Area of Motorized Planting	
		面积(公顷) Area(hectare)	占耕地面积比重(%) Rate in Total(%)	面积(公顷) Area(hectare)	占播种面积比重(%) Rate in Total(%)
总计	**Total**	**409 610**	**97.29**	**493 240**	**65.74**
市区	Urban Area	5 840	68.9	1 490	19.33
#城阳区	Chengyang District	3 140	73.14	1 230	43.04
黄岛区	Huangdao District	2 300	96.36	260	6.97
崂山区	Laoshan District	400	23.63		
胶州市	Jiaozhou	54 600	99.56	70 550	64.01
即墨市	Jimo	74 000	96.95	104 040	79.66
平度市	Pingdu	156 000	98.5	174 320	62.63
胶南市	Jiaonan	52 600	98.47	47 790	50.91
莱西市	Laixi	66 570	95.69	95 050	73.4

10 -27 续表
continued

市、区名称	Region	机收面积 Area of Motorized Harvesting		农村用电量(万千瓦小时) Electricity Consumption in Rural Area(10 000 kwh)
		面积(公顷) Area(hectare)	占播种面积比重(%) Rate in total Planting	
总计	**Total**	**367 740**	**49.02**	**372 644.64**
市区	Urban Area	2 680	34.77	71 183
#城阳区	Chengyang District	1 950	68.23	48 884
黄岛区	Huangdao District	730	19.58	7574
崂山区	Laoshan District			14 725
胶州市	Jiaozhou	68 950	62.56	80 600
即墨市	Jimo	74 930	57.37	60 069
平度市	Pingdu	108 450	38.97	92 546.6
胶南市	Jiaonan	44 620	47.53	31 984.04
莱西市	Laixi	68 110	52.6	36 262

10 -28 分市、区农用化肥施用量(2005 年)
CHEMICAL FERTILIZER CONSUMPTION BY REGION(2005)

单位:折纯吨(ton converted to pure amount)

市、区名称	Region	农用化肥施用量 Chemical Fertilizer Consumption	氮　肥 Nitrogenous Fertilizer	磷　肥 Phosphate Fertilizer	钾　肥 Potassium Fertilizer	复合肥 Compound Fertilizer	附:平均每公顷耕地施用化肥量(*) Annotation:Chemical Fertilizer Consumption Per Hectare
总计	**Total**	**330 121**	**102 723**	**21 835**	**31 877**	**173 686**	**784.12**
市区	Urban Area	4 117	1 294	304	283	2 236	485.72
#城阳区	Chengyang District	1 836	690	209	187	750	427.67
黄岛区	Huangdao District	1 064	282	13	36	733	445.75
崂山区	Laoshan District	1 217	322	82	60	753	718.84
胶州市	Jiaozhou	46 403	13 311	1 370	5 989	25 733	846.17
即墨市	Jimo	54 212	28 882	3 167	1 817	20 346	710.24
平度市	Pingdu	108 826	17 959	4 488	11 139	75 240	687.15
胶南市	Jiaonan	53 323	18 263	6 029	7 676	21 355	998.22
莱西市	Laixi	63 240	23 014	6 477	4 973	28 776	909.01

注:(*)单位为[折纯千克]Note:The(*)mark refers to kilogram converted to pure amount

10 -29 分市、区农田水利(2005 年)
FARM WATER CONSERVANCY BY REGION(2005)

市、区名称	Region	灌溉面积(公顷) Irrigated Area (hectare)	#机、电排灌面积 of which:Area with Motorized Irrigation Facilities	灌溉面积占耕地面积比重(%) Rate in Total(%)	农业排灌机械拥有量(万台/万千瓦) Possession of Drainage and Irrigation Machinery (10 000 sets/10 000kw)	农用水泵(万台) Agricultural Pump (10 000 sets)	喷灌机械(套) Spraying Irrigation Machinery (set)	机电井数(眼) Number of Electromechanical Well
总计	**Total**	**339 363**	**269 010**	**80.73**	**17.62/114.36**	**13.76**	**71 842**	**74 131**
市区	Urban Area	8 053	7 200	95.01	0.53/2.55	0.57	1 843	2 333
#城阳区	Chengyang District	4 290	4 470	99.93	0.33/1.38	0.4	1 605	1 424
黄岛区	Huangdao District	2 380	1 860	99.71	0.08/0.57	0.13	237	376
崂山区	Laoshan District	1 280	670	75.61	0.05/0.29	0.04	1	335
胶州市	Jiaozhou	36 200	30 400	66.01	1.66/11.95	0.66	12 561	6 487
即墨市	Jimo	50 080	45 010	65.61	1.9/13.75	2.11	15 903	5 279
平度市	Pingdu	129 810	110 380	81.96	9.14/57.92	7.13	14 573	42 717
胶南市	Jiaonan	53 060	31 900	99.33	1.03/7.36	1.15	7 487	4 375
莱西市	Laixi	62 160	44 120	89.35	3.35/20.84	2.15	19 475	12 940

10－30 分市、区主要农业机械拥有量(2005 年)

POSSESSION OF MAJOR AGRICULTURAL MACHINERY BY REGION(2005)

市、区名称	Region	农业机械总动力(万千瓦) Total Power of Agricultural Machinery(10 000 kw)	平均每公顷耕地拥有量(千瓦) Power Per Hectare of Cultivated Land(kw)	柴油机 Diesel motors		电动机 Electric motors	
				台 set	千瓦 kw	台 set	千瓦 kw
总计	**Total**	**619.69**	**14.72**	**137 440**	**1 084 025**	**133 172**	**737 949**
市区	Urban Area	48.97	57.77	5 112	45 247	7 923	70 180
#城阳区	Chengyang District	33.44	77.9	4 324	39 842	4 705	44 273
黄岛区	Huangdao District	12.24	51.27	678	4 746	2 600	20 800
崂山区	Laoshan District	3.29	19.44	110	659	618	5 107
胶州市	Jiaozhou	85.49	15.59	15 698	118 205	11 146	94 780
即墨市	Jimo	97.61	12.79	22 330	170 128	14 050	106 019
平度市	Pingdu	248.73	15.71	57 223	472 610	77 741	332 614
胶南市	Jiaonan	55.84	10.45	7 481	65 138	7 037	63 540
莱西市	Laixi	83.04	11.94	29 596	212 697	15 275	70 816

10－30 续表 1

continued

市、区名称	Region	汽油机 Petrol Motors		大中型拖拉机 Large and Medium Tractors		小型拖拉机 Small Tractors	
		台 set	千瓦 kw	台 set	千瓦 kw	台 set	千瓦 kw
总计	**Total**	**9 359**	**32 599**	**24 603**	**685 588**	**138 429**	**1 071 589**
市区	Urban Area	1 632	12 190	453	15 157	2 204	20 720
#城阳区	Chengyang District	1 330	11 298	420	13 817	1 701	2 919
黄岛区	Huangdao District	12	45	33	1 340	171	16 279
崂山区	Laoshan District	290	847			332	1 522
胶州市	Jiaozhou	1 411	3 294	3 184	105 304	13 752	116 695
即墨市	Jimo	5 504	13 321	5 226	140 419	25 836	206 057
平度市	Pingdu	455	2 104	10 020	250 583	35 016	312 284
胶南市	Jiaonan	80	680	1 885	60 973	34 719	221 072
莱西市	Laixi	277	1 010	3 835	113 152	26 902	194 761

10－30 续表 2
continued

市、区名称	Region	农用汽车 Agricultural Camion 辆 vehicle	农用汽车 Agricultural Camion 千瓦 kw	大、中、小播种机(部) Large, Medium and Small Seeders(set)	机引犁(部) Towing Ploughs(set)	机引耙(部) Towing Rakes(set)	脱粒机(部) Threshers (set)
总计	**Total**	**11 552**	**445 274**	**50 066**	**123 484**	**31 944**	**37 632**
市区	Urban Area	1 392	72 750	592	2 465	204	674
#城阳区	Chengyang District	910	47 732	567	915	61	202
黄岛区	Huangdao District	397	18 818	25	1 505	91	472
崂山区	Laoshan District	85	6 200		45	52	
胶州市	Jiaozhou	2 094	100 001	7 089	13 792	2 369	4 945
即墨市	Jimo	2 096	98 845	9 945	20 854	918	5 648
平度市	Pingdu	2 712	72 742	22 780	26 070	13 480	14 361
胶南市	Jiaonan	1 069	30 889	3 534	29 450	11 110	7 346
莱西市	Laixi	2 189	70 047	6 126	30 853	3 863	4 658

10－30 续表 3
continued

市、区名称	Region	粮食加工机械(台) Grain Processing Machinery(set)	棉花加工机械(部) Cotton Processing Machinery(set)	油料加工机械(部) Oil Processing Machinery(set)	饲料粉碎机(部) Pulverizers (set)
总计	**Total**	**24 779**	**562**	**9 225**	**23 655**
市区	Urban Area	1 541	19	537	401
#城阳区	Chengyang District	1 340	19	402	285
黄岛区	Huangdao District	193		135	116
崂山区	Laoshan District	8			
胶州市	Jiaozhou	2 887	89	2 006	3 611
即墨市	Jimo	4 359	162	1 357	3 639
平度市	Pingdu	4 411	190	1 281	7 865
胶南市	Jiaonan	2 404	11	1 185	3 664
莱西市	Laixi	9 177	91	2 859	4 475

CHAPTER 11

第十一篇

工　业

INDUSTRY

编辑单位：	工业交通统计处	企业调查队产业调查处
编　　委：	吴加琪	孙昭信
编　　辑：	王福临　于泳洋	蒲永杰
校　　对：	王福临　于泳洋	蒲永杰
电　　话：	85912257	82869521

11－1 规模以上工业企业单位数

NUMBER OF INDUSTRIAL ENTERPRISES ABOVE THE SET SCALE

单位:个(unit)

项　目	Items	1985 年	1990 年	1995 年	2000 年	2004 年	2005 年
总　计	**Total**	**2 411**	**2 997**	**4 987**	**1 504**	**2 885**	**3 697**
一、按隶属关系分	**Grouped by Subordination**						
中央工业	Central Industry	24	16	102	18	21	26
省属工业	Provincial Industry	26	22	64	7	11	37
地方工业	Local Industry	2 361	2 959	4 821	1 479	2 853	3 634
二、按经济类型分	**Grouped by Economy Categories**						
国有企业	State-owned	502	568	1 084	179	81	76
集体企业	Collective-owned	1 907	2 386	2 731	226	123	87
其他经济类型企业	Other Economy Categories	2	43	1 172	1 099	2 681	3534
#“三资”企业	Three Kinds of Foreign-invested Enterprises or Ventures	–	35	1 027	593	1 299	1658
三、按轻重工业分	**Grouped by Light and Heavy Industries**						
轻工业	Light Industry	1 398	1 730	2 858	891	1 568	1942
以农产品为原料	Using Farm Products as Raw Materials	943	1 238	1 920	608	–	–
以非农产品为原料	Using Non-farm Products as Raw Materials	455	492	938	283	–	–
重工业	Heavy Industry	1 013	1 267	2 129	613	1 317	1755
采掘工业	Excavation	50	81	91	36	–	–
原料工业	Raw Materials	110	189	312	117	–	–
加工工业	Processing	853	997	1 726	460	–	–
四、按企业规模分	**Grouped by size of Enterprises**						
大型企业	Large	26	42	89	202	43	51
中型企业	Medium	80	168	216	229	327	441
小型企业	Small	2 305	2 787	4 480	1 073	2 515	3 205
五、按工业行业分	**Grouped by Sectors**						
黑色金属矿采选业	Ferrous Metals Mining and Dressing	–	4	6	1	6	2
有色金属矿采选业	Nonferrous Metals Mining and Dressing	2	7	9	7	5	5
非金属矿采选业	Nonmetal Minerals Mining and Dressing	43	70	87	29	23	34
自来水生产和供应业	Tap Water Production and Supply	8	12	12	8	11	10
食品加工制造业	Food Processing and Manufacturing	244	324	437	170	93	121
#粮食及饲料加工	Grain and Fodder Processing	62	57	60	27	–	–
饮料制造业	Beverage Manufacturing	31	44	74	23	31	29
#饮料酒	Beverage Liquor	20	28	27	19	16	20

注:1. 规模以上工业企业为国有及年产品销售收入500万元以上的非国有工业企业。
2. 本表1998年以前为乡及乡以上工业企业单位数。

Note:1. Industial enterprises above the set scale refers to state-owned enterprises or non-state-owned enterprises whose annual revenue of products sales is above 5,000,000 yuan.
2. Before 1998, number of industial enterprises refer to those at village level and above.

11－1 续表
continued

单位:个(unit)

项　　目	Items	1985 年	1990 年	1995 年	2000 年	2004 年	2005 年
烟草加工业	Tobacco Processing	2	2	5	3	2	2
纺织业	Textile Industry	169	225	330	132	233	300
#棉纺织业	Cotton Textile Industry	89	119	169	64	70	76
毛纺织业	Wool Textile Industry	7	18	25	17	16	20
针织品业	Knitwear Industry	50	58	82	33	74	115
服装业	Garments	171	194	322	95	218	272
皮革、毛皮制造	Leathers, Furs and Related Products	56	64	161	64	137	167
木材加工制品	Timber Processing Products	71	89	116	19	29	40
家具制造业	Furniture Manufacturing	61	72	88	10	45	72
造纸及纸制品业	Papermaking and Paper Products	66	74	110	56	87	102
印刷业	Printing	61	81	215	23	40	44
文教体育用品制造	Stationery, Education and Sports Goods	31	27	93	48	74	89
电力、蒸汽、热水	Electric Power, Steam and Hot Water	10	16	20	17	21	27
石油加工及炼焦业	Petroleum Processing and Coking	2	3	13	5	7	10
煤气生产和供应	Gas Production and Supply	1	4	3	2	3	5
化学工业	Chemical Industry	106	156	278	81	158	178
#有机	Organic	36	57	84	28	–	–
日用	Daily Used	25	31	42	4	8	5
医药工业	Medical and Pharmaceutic Industry	16	14	39	20	19	30
化纤工业	Chemical Fibers Industry	2	4	26	15	14	14
橡胶制品业	Rubber Products	53	57	143	48	103	116
塑料制品业	Plastic Products	103	131	237	64	118	153
非金属矿物制品业	Nonmetal Mineral Products	230	245	275	62	122	161
黑色金属压延加工	Smelting and Processing of Ferrous Metals	11	13	31	15	18	41
有色金属压延加工	Smelting and Processing of Nonferrous Metals	6	8	19	9	13	28
金属制品业	Metal Products	161	186	372	88	136	186
普通机械制造业	Ordinary Machinery Manufacturing	320	398	320	94	221	299
交通运输制造业	Transportation Equipment Manufacturing	104	114	358	52	123	151
电气机械制造业	Electric Equipment and Machinery Manufacturing	86	96	211	79	140	214
电子及通讯制造业	Electronic and Telecommunications Equipments Manufacturing	32	31	79	34	96	123
仪器仪表制造业	Instruments, Meters, Culture and Office Equipments Manufacturing	28	33	70	20	32	40
其他工业	Others	46	48	209	63	507	166

11－2 分市、区全部工业企业单位数(2005年)

NUMBER OF TOTAL INDUSTRIAL ENTERPRISES BY REGION(2005)

单位:个(unit)

市、区名称	Region	合计 Total	规模以上 Above Scale	按轻重工业分 Grouped by Light and Heavy Industries		按企业规模分 Grouped by Size of enterprises		
				轻工业 Light Industry	重工业 Heavy Industry	大型企业 Large	中型企业 Medium	小型企业 Small
总　计	**Total**	**69 948**	**3 697**	**1 942**	**1 755**	**51**	**441**	**3 205**
市　区	Urban Area	13 843	1 438	736	702	36	206	1 196
#城阳区	Chengyang District	4 056	591	353	238	9	65	517
黄岛区	Huangdao District	1 813	244	96	148	5	46	193
崂山区	Laoshan District	2 843	167	79	88	2	22	143
胶州市	Jiaozhou	10 467	466	271	195	4	64	398
即墨市	Jimo	12 851	531	337	194	4	52	475
平度市	Pingdu	12 409	411	179	232	0	60	351
胶南市	Jiaonan	9 886	463	185	278	4	39	420
莱西市	Laixi	10 492	388	234	154	3	20	365

11－2 续表

continued

单位:个(unit)

市、区名称	Region	按经济类型分 Grouped by Economy Categories				规模以下 Under Scale	#个体 Individual
		国有企业 State-owned	集体企业 Collectiv e-owned	乡镇企业 Township	三资工业 Three Kinds of Foreign-invested Enterprises or Ventu		
总　计	**Total**	**76**	**87**	**120**	**1 658**	**66 251**	**47 094**
市　区	Urban Area	53	46	4	811	12 405	5 050
#城阳区	Chengyang District	11	4	4	398	3 465	1 082
黄岛区	Huangdao District	4	3	0	150	1 569	756
崂山区	Laoshan District	4	11	0	86	2 676	1 567
胶州市	Jiaozhou	3	5	74	199	10 001	7 677
即墨市	Jimo	5	18	2	199	12 320	9 108
平度市	Pingdu	9	7	9	162	11 998	9 835
胶南市	Jiaonan	2	4	23	126	9 423	7 056
莱西市	Laixi	4	7	8	161	10 104	8 368

11－3 历年全部工业总产值

GROSS OUTPUT VALUE OF INDUSTRY OVER THE YEARS

单位:万元(10 000 yuan)

年　份 Year	工业总产值 Gross Output Value of Industry	轻工业产值 Light Industry	重工业产值 Heavy Industry
1949	21 605	18 494	3 111
1950	34 010	28 720	5 290
1951	53 538	44 600	8 938
1952	84 295	69 258	15 037
1953	115 222	74 716	40 506
1954	126 064	80 604	45 460
1955	118 935	86 956	31 979
1956	144 833	93 809	51 024
1957	142 920	101 202	41 718
1958	217 648	92 407	125 241
1959	282 610	84 376	198 234
1960	291 451	77 043	214 408
1961	164 628	70 347	94 281
1962	120 738	64 233	56 505
1963	139 542	83 630	55 912
1964	177 273	108 884	68 389
1965	215 536	141 765	73 771
1966	252 896	152 304	100 592
1967	287 739	163 627	124 112
1968	299 814	175 791	123 489
1969	296 814	188 860	107 954
1970	345 212	202 903	142 309

注:本表按当年价格计算,1995 年开始工业总产值按新规定计算。

Note: The data in this form are calculated at current prices. Since 1995, new regulations have been adopted in calculating gross output value of industry.

11 -3 续表1
continued

单位:万元(10000 yuan)

年　份 Year	工业总产值 Gross Output Value of Industry	轻工业产值 Light Industry	重工业产值 Heavy Industry
1971	365 770	216 172	149 598
1972	378 266	230 309	147 957
1973	377 943	245 371	132 572
1974	237 219	154 054	83 165
1975	402 541	261 418	141 123
1976	439 793	278 514	161 279
1977	490 669	296 728	193 941
1978	565 503	336 817	228 686
1979	625 227	379 276	245 951
1980	677 690	442 078	235 612
1981	707 434	479 954	227 480
1982	732 705	474 767	257 938
1983	816 793	513 759	303 034
1984	918 364	569 080	349 284
1985	1 113 891	699 524	414 367
1986	1 316 230	833 864	482 366
1987	1 703 830	1 065 873	637 957
1988	2 481 594	1 451 215	1 030 379
1989	3 191 643	1 857 019	1 334 624
1990	3 571 845	2 057 968	1 513 878

11－3 续表 2
continued

单位:万元(10 000 yuan)

年　份	Year	工业总产值 Gross Output Value of Industry	轻工业产值 Light Industry	重工业产值 Heavy Industry
1991	1991	3 986 427	2 318 257	1 668 170
1992	1992	4 826 834	2 835 728	1 991 106
1993	1993	5 929 236	3 422 107	2 507 129
1994	1994	8 456 974	4 931 262	3 525 712
1995	1995	9 412 635	5 579 637	3 832 998
1996	1996	11 173 672	6 793 007	4 380 665
1997	1997	13 704 735	8 620 710	5 084 025
1998	1998	15 794 106	10 153 634	5 640 472
1999	1999	16 822 436	10 918 827	5 903 609
2000	2000	19 408 338	12 433 214	6 975 124
2001	2001	22 398 464	14 368 582	8 029 882
2002	2002	25 794 324	14 811 106	10 983 218
2003	2003	31 195 595	17 306 539	13 889 056
2004	2004	39 590 783	21 473 202	18 117 581
2005	2005	50 017 829	24 697 792	25 320 037
"一五"时期合计	"First Five-Year Plan" Period	647 974	437 287	210 687
"二五"时期合计	"Second Five-Year Plan" Period	1 077 075	388 406	688 669
1963-1965 年合计	1963-1965	532 351	334 279	198 072
"三五"时期合计	"Third Five-Year Plan" Period	1 481 941	883 485	598 456
"四五"时期合计	"Fourth Five-Year Plan" Period	1 761 739	1 107 324	654 415
"五五"时期合计	"Fifth Five-Year Plan" Period	2 798 882	1 733 413	1 065 469
"六五"时期合计	"Sixth Five-Year Plan" Period	4 289 187	2 737 084	1 552 103
"七五"时期合计	"Seventh Five-Year Plan" Period	12 265 142	7 265 939	4 999 204
"八五"时期合计	"Eighth Five-Year Plan" Period	32 612 106	19 087 323	13 524 783
"九五"时期合计	"Ninth Five-Year Plan" Period	76 903 287	48 919 392	27 983 895
"十五"时期合计	"Tenth Five-Year Plan" Period	168 996 995	92 657 221	76 339 774

11－4 分市、区全部工业总产值(2005 年)
GROSS OUTPUT VALUE OF TOTAL INDUSTRY BY REGION(2005)

单位:万元(10000 yuan)

市、区名称	Region	工业总产值 Gross Output Value of Industry	规模以上工业 Above Scale	乡属企业 Township	三资企业 Three Kinds of Foreign-invested Enterprises or Ventures	规模以下工业 Under Scale
总计	**Total**	**50 017 829**	**43 166 129**	**12 378**	**12 859 575**	**6 851 700**
市区	Urban Area	26 690 125	24 784 025	0	6 557 109	1 906 100
#城阳区	Chengyang District	5 937 506	5 190 906	0	2 368 056	746 600
黄岛区	Huangdao District	7 929 785	7 668 485	0	2 582 962	261 300
崂山区	Laoshan District	3 871 322	3 581 222	0	489 536	290 100
胶州市	Jiaozhou	5 623 443	4 693 143	1 607	1 574 324	930 300
即墨市	Jimo	5 225 279	4 034 379	0	1 784 089	1 190 900
平度市	Pingdu	4 368 793	3 321 793	0	1 320 319	1 047 000
胶南市	Jiaonan	5 449 762	4 556 462	10 771	833 802	893 300
莱西市	Laixi	2 660 426	1 776 326	0	789 933	884 100

11－5 分市、区规模以上工业总产值(2005 年)

GROSS OUTPUT VALUE OF INDUSTRY ABOVE THE SET SCALE BY REGION(2005)

指　　标	Indicators	总计 Total	市内四区 Urban Area	黄岛区 Huangdao District	崂山区 Laoshan District	城阳区 Chengyang District
总　　计	**Total**	**43 166 129**	**8 343 412**	**7 668 485**	**3 581 222**	**5 190 906**
一、按隶属关系分	**Grouped by Subordination**					
中　央	Centrality	3 008 484	2 821 038	175 087	1 724	3 210
省(自治区、直辖市)	Province(Autonomous Region, Municipality)	290 867	153 586	15 550	6 413	33 783
市(地级)	Municipality(local level)	12 404 820	4 082 075	4 415 174	2 514 632	161 012
县级市(区)	Municipality at County Level(District)	3 529 645	179 449	302 128	277 567	440 049
城(镇)街道	Subdistrict in Town	4 140 904	0	1 685	93 742	1 229 556
乡	Country	12 378	0	0	0	0
其它	Others	19 779 032	1 107 264	2 758 862	687 144	3 323 296
二、按登记注册类型分	**Grouped by Registration Categories**					
国有经济	State-owned	2 259 827	1 504 053	132 542	9 007	114 673
集体经济	Collective-owned	5 729 986	114 505	2 542 089	2 374 441	223 608
#城市(镇)街道工业	Subdistrict Industry	253 242	0	0	10 461	212 337
乡办工业	Country Industry	0	0	0	0	0
其他经济	Others	35 176 316	6 724 854	4 993 855	1 197 773	4 852 625
#三资企业	Sino-foreign Joint Ventures, Cooperative Businesses and Exclusively Foreign-owned Enterprises	12 859 575	1 116 554	2 582 962	489 536	2 368 056
三、按轻重工业分	**Grouped by Light and Heavy Industries**					
轻工业	Light Industry	21 172 092	1 865 188	4 911 914	2 809 527	2 054 278
重工业	Heavy Industry	21 994 037	6 478 224	2 756 571	771 695	3 136 628
四、按企业规模分	**Grouped by Size of Enterprises**					
大型企业	Large	17 576 100	4 554 536	4 507 049	2 529 847	2 080 749
中型企业	Medium	12 716 333	2 618 796	1 745 904	567 000	1 499 073
小型企业	Small	12 873 695	1 170 081	1 415 532	484 375	1 611 084

单位:万元(10000 yuan)

胶州市 Jiaozhou	即墨市 Jimo	平度市 Pingdu	胶南市 Jiaonan	莱西市 Laixi
4 693 143	**4 034 379**	**3 321 793**	**4 556 462**	**1 776 326**
3 610	0	628	3 186	0
0	0	27 820	1 818	51 898
207 470	127 271	494 815	390 770	11 600
674 549	438 453	256 139	767 859	193 452
1 481 054	18 676	58 730	995 499	261 962
1 607	0	0	10 771	0
2 324 853	3 449 980	2 483 660	2 386 560	1 257 414
93 448	91 326	190 090	63 486	61 202
95 448	151 753	133 409	89 478	5 256
0	12 596	2 905	14 943	0
0	0	0	0	0
4 504 248	3 791 301	2 998 294	4 403 499	1 709 868
1 574 324	1 784 089	1 320 319	833 802	789 933
2 461 182	2 840 445	1 631 280	1 252 546	1 345 730
2 231 962	1 193 934	1 690 512	3 303 916	430 595
604 795	815 573	464 012	1 436 318	583 222
1 898 978	1 159 601	1 243 029	1 574 472	409 480
2 189 371	2 059 206	1 614 752	1 545 672	783 624

11 -5 续表 1
continued

指　标	Indicators	总计 Total	市内四区 Urban Area	黄岛区 Huangdao District	崂山区 Laoshan District
五、按工业行业大类分	**Grouped by Industrial Sectors**				
煤炭开采和洗选业	Coal Mining and Dressing	0	0	0	0
石油和天然气开采业	Petroleum and Natural Gas Extraction	0	0	0	0
黑色金属矿采选业	Ferrous Metals Mining and Dressing	9 276	0	0	0
有色金属矿采选业	Nonferrous Metals Mining and Dressing	57 134	0	0	0
非金属矿采选业	Nonmetal Minerals Mining and Dressing	321 016	0	0	0
其他采矿业	Other Minerals Mining	1 912	0	0	0
农副食品加工业	Agricultural Non - staple Food Processing	3 341 259	118 681	341 247	23 293
食品制造业	Food Production	930 518	32 098	44 294	51 214
饮料制造业	Beverage Production	566 735	263 386	0	140 321
烟草制品业	Tobacco Production	516 694	509 998	6 696	0
纺织业	Textile Industry	2 109 131	325 301	37 981	6 913
纺织服装、鞋、帽制造业	Textile Clothing and Footwear Production	1 291 841	81 978	45 840	20 035
皮革、毛皮、羽毛(绒)及其制品业	Leathers Furs Down and Related Products	1 463 174	21 494	9 637	9 683
木材加工及木、竹、藤、棕、草制品业	Timber Processing Bamboo Cane Palm Fiber and Straw Products	322 993	5 052	5 634	5 733
家具制造业	Furniture Manufacturing	358 653	54 137	2 897	1 479
造纸及纸制品业	Papermaking and Paper Products	507 778	53 274	37 421	38 075
印刷业和记录媒介的复制	Printing and Record Processing	144 998	76 634	2 737	0
文教体育用品制造业	Stationery Education and Sports Goods	545 927	13 821	31 563	16 541
石油加工、炼焦及核燃料加工业	Petroleum Processing Coking and Nuclear Fuel Processing	678 779	663 180	0	6 374
化学原料及化学制品制造业	Raw Chemical Materials and Chemical Products	2 198 769	752 486	275 401	53 360
医药制造业	Medicine Manufacturing	234 367	11 212	61 005	48 918
化学纤维制造业	Chemical Fiber Manufacturing	102 462	31 305	59 046	0
橡胶制品业	Rubber Products	1 423 331	116 185	107 823	7 326
塑料制品业	Plastic Products	667 012	66 917	145 391	50 918
非金属矿物制品业	Nonmetal Mineral Products	1 589 512	105 073	197 080	41 390
黑色金属冶炼及压延加工业	Smelting and Pressing of Ferrous Metals	2 338 718	1 991 394	147 078	0
有色金属冶炼及压延加工业	Smelting and Pressing of Nonferrous Metals	510 663	2 656	259 693	1 284
金属制品业	Metal Products	1 388 608	55 353	455 327	38 734
通用设备制造业	General - purpose Equipment Manufacturing	2 206 581	297 313	57 125	22 565
专用设备制造业	special - purpose Equipment Manufacturing	903 745	205 124	25 688	7 128
交通运输设备制造业	Transportation Equipment manufacturing	2 316 312	785 649	138 151	206 217
电气机械及器材制造业	Electric Equipments and Machinery Manufacturing	7 272 433	264 241	2 722 912	2 409 184
通信设备、计算机及其他电子设备	Communication Equipment Computers and Other Electronic Equipment Production	4 012 580	183 609	2 273 708	312 250
仪器仪表及文化、办公用机械制造业	Instruments Meters Culture and Office Equipments Manufacturing	243 184	19 026	0	41 009
工艺品及其他制造业	Handicraft Articles and Other Goods Production	747 273	112 967	42 394	18 911
废弃资源和废旧材料回收加工业	Discarded Resources and Waste Materials Recovery and Processing	113 483	0	0	0
电力、热力的生产和供应业	Power Steam Production and Supply	1 568 637	992 776	125 222	2 366
燃气生产和供应业	Gas Production and Supply	95 128	86 557	3 876	0
水的生产和供应业	Tap Water Production and Supply	65 514	44 537	5 620	0

单位:万元(10000 yuan)

城阳区 Chengyang District	胶州市 Jiaozhou	即墨市 Jimo	平度市 Pingdu	胶南市 Jiaonan	莱西市 Laixi
0	0	0	0	0	0
0	0	0	0	0	0
0	0	0	9 276	0	0
0	0	0	57 134	0	0
5 599	22 135	1 584	267 692	0	24 006
0	0	0	0	0	1 912
543 585	672 776	326 210	533 259	110 725	671 483
85 412	116 578	13 530	114 737	318 030	154 625
0	7 971	12 503	27 351	100 670	14 534
0	0	0	0	0	0
355 816	243 577	710 070	205 766	126 845	96 863
325 351	301 577	341 160	36 625	112 067	27 207
137 064	349 233	443 754	13 632	196 935	281 742
22 089	241 129	3 978	17 509	17 876	3 994
69 065	186 089	2 849	29 570	8 864	3 704
95 571	78 810	100 972	28 731	60 883	14 041
16 551	2 990	31 657	2 610	11 819	0
151 432	58 078	209 703	47 964	2 887	13 938
237	1 774	0	0	4 317	2 897
120 031	248 654	66 463	74 781	521 550	86 042
13 649	41 204	17 232	987	25 699	14 461
1 633	906	0	0	8 117	1 454
98 792	93 539	162 797	234 809	593 040	9 020
149 134	68 523	71 902	5 065	57 279	51 883
811 719	150 804	38 919	126 467	66 871	51 190
145 167	12 980	2 280	13 863	2 068	23 889
7 345	102 341	12 546	124 798	0	0
171 004	311 559	187 981	60 402	89 167	19 081
287 845	399 548	260 162	216 181	632 326	33 517
157 932	148 058	44 377	24 018	282 039	9 382
172 803	38 316	25 709	109 939	827 895	11 634
494 473	443 033	611 277	128 276	175 675	23 361
472 099	17 601	143 323	555 127	31 286	23 577
39 882	38 243	14 806	67 623	15 777	6 819
130 592	180 679	97 572	93 348	37 035	33 774
95 604	17 879	0	0	0	0
9 310	92 535	72 955	92 994	115 489	64 990
0	2 102	2 594	0	0	0
4 121	1 921	3 515	1 261	3 233	1 307

11 -6 规模以上工业企业主要指标(2005 年)
MAIN INDICATORS OF INDUSTRIAL ENTERPRISES ABOVE THE SET SCALE(2005)

项　　目	Indicators	企业单位数(个) Number of Enterprises (unit)
总　计	**Total**	**3 697**
一、按注册登记类型分	**Grouped by Economy Categories**	
国有及国有控股企业	State-owned	180
集体企业	Collective-owned	87
股份有限公司	Share-holding	117
外商投资企业	Foreign Funded Enterprises	259
港澳台商投资企业	Invested by HongKong, Macao and Taiwan	1 399
二、按轻重工业分	**Grouped by Light and Heavy Industries**	
轻工业	Light Industry	1 942
重工业	Heavy Industry	1 755
三、按企业规模分	**Grouped by size of Enterprises**	
大型企业	Large	51
中型企业	Medium	441
小型企业	Small	3 205
四、按所在地分	**Grouped by Region**	
市区	Urban Area	1 438
#城阳区	Chengyang District	591
黄岛区	Huangdao District	244
崂山区	Laoshan District	167
胶州市	Jiaozhou	466
即墨市	Jimo	531
平度市	Pingdu	411
胶南市	Jiaonan	463
莱西市	Laixi	388
五、按行业分	**Grouped by Sectors**	
煤炭开采和洗选业	Grouped by Light and Heavy Industries	0
石油和天然气开采业	Light Industry	0
黑色金属矿采选业	Heavy Industry	2
有色金属矿采选业	Grouped by Sectors	5
非金属矿采选业	Coal Mining and Dressing	34
其他采矿业	Other Minerals Mining	1

工业总产值 Gross Output Value of Industry (current price)(10000 yuan)	工业增加值 Added Value of Industry (production approach)	资产合计 Assets	流动资产年平均余额 Annual Average Balance of Circulating Funds	固定资产净值年平均余额 Annual Average Balance of Net Value of Fixed Assets
43 166 128	**13 595 333**	**30 722 539**	**16 142 632**	**8 641 750**
10 271 113	2 586 001	10 113 524	5 089 332	2 877 282
5 729 986	1 439 937	3 630 742	2 046 932	5 150 79
3 855 603	1 283 563	2 775 072	1 516 266	751 317
1 959 632	680 314	1 207 827	687 672	374 580
10 899 943	3 858 748	7 478 463	3 840 639	2 582 483
21 172 092	6 719 747	14 149 138	7 567 351	3 584 553
21 994 037	6 875 586	16 573 401	8 575 281	5 057 196
17 576 100	4 351 938	13 391 009	7 120 533	3 204 683
12 716 333	4 491 902	9 264 109	4 776 185	2 881 607
12 873 695	4 751 493	8 067 421	4 245 914	2 555 460
24 784 025	7 204 037	21 497 027	11 515 403	5 462 914
5 190 906	1 897 696	3 922 873	2 149 524	963 057
7 668 485	2 068 797	5 812 354	3 227 837	1 362 481
3 581 222	1 033 008	2 347 916	1 268 537	519 250
4 693 143	1 809 398	2 322 091	1 324 581	683 593
4 034 379	1 356 275	2 015 705	916 845	788 459
3 321 793	1 046 483	1 728 856	719 244	758 438
4 556 462	1 518 958	2 273 471	1 117 191	690 375
1 776 326	660 182	1 219 153	593 836	513 253
0	0	0	0	0
0	0	0	0	0
9 276	4 151	5 014	3 400	158
57 134	15 426	36 845	11 248	23 331
321 016	116 910	118 170	46 610	56 693
1 912	1 333	100	95	6

11 -6 续表 1
continued

项　　目	Indicators	产品销售收入 Revenue of Products Sales
总　计	**Total**	**41 878 690**
一、按注册登记类型分	**Grouped by Economy Categories**	
国有及国有控股企业	State-owned	10 539 502
集体企业	Collective-owned	5 677 926
股份有限公司	Share-holding	3 489 964
外商投资企业	Foreign Funded Enterprises	1 771 218
港澳台商投资企业	Invested by HongKong Macao and Taiwan	10 590 632
二、按轻重工业分	**Grouped by Light and Heavy Industries**	
轻工业	Light Industry	21 430 680
重工业	Heavy Industry	20 448 010
三、按企业规模分	**Grouped by size of Enterprises**	
大型企业	Large	18 170 788
中型企业	Medium	11 356 411
小型企业	Small	12 351 491
四、按所在地分	**Grouped by Region**	
市区	Urban Area	25 315 014
#城阳区	Chengyang District	4 854 899
黄岛区	Huangdao District	7 944 317
崂山区	Laoshan District	3 650 017
胶州市	Jiaozhou	4 400 025
即墨市	Jimo	3 870 111
平度市	Pingdu	3 306 362
胶南市	Jiaonan	4 077 286
莱西市	Laixi	1 701 652
五、按行业分	**Grouped by Sectors**	
煤炭开采和洗选业	Grouped by Light and Heavy Industries	0
石油和天然气开采业	Light Industry	0
黑色金属矿采选业	Heavy Industry	11 472
有色金属矿采选业	Grouped by Sectors	53 185
非金属矿采选业	Coal Mining and Dressing	274 234
其他采矿业	Other Minerals Mining	1 957

产品销售成本 Cost of Products Sales	产品销售税金及附加 Tax and Extra Charges of Products Sales	利润总额 Total After-tax Profits	本年应交增值税 Value-added Tax Payable	全部从业人员年平均人数（万人） Average Number of Total Employees（10000 persons）
35 952 402	**544 977**	**1 935 531**	**1 390 554**	**112**
				0
9 116 559	312 559	225 374	352 273	15
4 889 479	21 600	161 888	131 918	4
3 019 796	24 320	165 273	149 398	9
1 480 418	11 903	138 683	61 927	5
9 053 470	54 398	583 364	286 133	48
				0
17 977 197	377 720	1 028 272	719 811	62
17 975 205	167 257	907 258	670 743	50
				0
16 139 163	110 492	423 207	431 180	25
9 533 435	310 299	640 962	441 479	34
10 279 803	124 187	871 362	517 895	52
21 509 777	353 551	1 126 818	588 172	50
4 306 134	17 013	158 239	40 231	20
6 919 840	19 409	265 344	172 564	9
3 055 737	18 582	125 642	92 008	5
3 846 971	78 774	226 891	245 843	15
3 208 795	39 008	363 830	143 780	14
2 728 863	38 774	272 521	149 967	10
3 560 068	29 176	214 607	203 500	13
1 424 278	7 915	95 005	59 293	9
0	0	0	0	0
0	0	0	0	0
8 714	313	1 901	918	0
35 020	1 081	10 568	1 615	0
200 708	6 150	33 155	13 362	1
1 169	347	402	102	0

11 −6 续表 2
continued

项　　目	Indicators	企业单位数(个) Number of Enterprises (unit)
农副食品加工业	Agricultural Non-staple Food Processing	308
食品制造业	Food Production	121
饮料制造业	Beverage Production	29
烟草制品业	Tobacco Products	2
纺织业	Textile Industry	300
纺织服装、鞋、帽制造业	Textile, Clothing and Footwear Production	272
皮革、毛皮、羽毛(绒)及其制品业	Leathers, Furs, Down and Related Products	167
木材加工及木、竹、藤、棕、草制品业	Timber Processing, Bamboo, Cane, Palm Fiber and Straw Products	40
家具制造业	Furniture Manufacturing	72
造纸及纸制品业	Papermaking and Paper Products	102
印刷业和记录媒介的复制	Printing and Record Processing	44
文教体育用品制造业	Stationery, Education and Sports Goods	89
石油加工、炼焦及核燃料加工业	Petroleum Processing, Coking and Nuclear Fuel Processing	10
化学原料及化学制品制造业	Raw Chemical Materials and Chemical Products	178
医药制造业	Medicine Manufacturing	30
化学纤维制造业	Chemical Fiber Manufacturing	14
橡胶制品业	Rubber Products	116
塑料制品业	Plastic Products	153
非金属矿物制品业	Nonmetal Mineral Products	161
黑色金属冶炼及压延加工业	Smelting and Pressing of Ferrous Metals	41
有色金属冶炼及压延加工业	Smelting and Pressing of Nonferrous Metals	28
金属制品业	Metal Products	186
通用设备制造业	General-purpose Equipment Manufacturing	299
专用设备制造业	Special-purpose Equipment Manufacturing	154
交通运输设备制造业	Transportation Equipment Manufacturing	151
电气机械及器材制造业	Electric Equipments and Machinery Manufacturing	214
通信设备、计算机及其他电子设备制造业	Communication Equipment, Computers and Other Electronic Equipment Production	123
仪器仪表及文化、办公用机械制造业	Instruments, Meters, Culture and Office Equipments Manufacturing	40
工艺品及其他制造业	Handicraft Articles and Other Goods Production	166
废弃资源和废旧材料回收加工业	Discarded Resources and Waste Materials Recovery and Processing	3
电力、热力的生产和供应业	Power, Steam Production and Supply	27
燃气生产和供应业	Gas Production and Supply	5
水的生产和供应业	Tap Water Production and Supply	10

工业总产值 Gross Output Value of Industry (current price) (10000 yuan)	工业增加值 Added Value of Industry (production approach)	资产合计 Assets	流动资产年平均余额 Annual Average Balance of Circulating Funds	固定资产净值年平均余额 Annual Average Balance of Net Value of Fixed Assets
3 341 259	1 177 941	1 775 717	956 105	535 216
930 518	336 596	584 583	278 360	203 784
566 735	228 858	888 871	458 084	214 548
516 694	324 430	682 328	387 884	90 781
2 109 132	702 038	1 688 549	756 432	576 752
1 291 841	465 708	981 081	501 853	270 610
1 463 174	536 761	672 094	383 321	193 282
322 993	123 685	113 479	66 102	26 660
358 653	126 995	226 324	134 218	62 526
507 779	185 550	360 294	203 052	120 541
144 998	52 731	142 458	75 469	52 053
545 927	193 847	322 299	206 696	58 143
678 779	155 905	377 539	221 360	139 187
2 198 769	727 910	2 270 904	1 042 658	778 011
234 367	111 805	358 325	159 370	109 376
102 462	28 486	110 389	50 369	47 248
1 423 331	485 004	1 303 283	687 971	399 335
667 012	230 553	488 637	266 362	162 864
1 589 512	589 327	1 206 128	586 663	380 038
2 338 718	318 878	1 393 595	765 299	349 706
510 663	118 372	240 251	92 074	126 738
1 388 608	481 276	775 221	415 301	271 740
2 206 581	751 254	1 536 069	895 599	429 903
903 745	314 028	539 566	298 766	195 743
2 316 312	644 328	2 368 636	1 339 938	498 843
7 272 433	2 010 186	4 587 903	2 684 631	729 763
4 012 580	1 082 858	2 014 836	1 282 153	449 517
243 185	89 624	182 983	103 597	46 174
747 273	275 957	396 957	231 510	112 362
113 483	50 298	43 631	5 212	825
1 568 637	478 249	1 275 088	359 443	579 660
95 128	29 978	358 248	100 449	177 868
65 514	28 099	296 146	84 980	171 767

11 -6 续表3
continued

项　　目	Indicators	产品销售收入 Revenue of Products Sales
农副食品加工业	Agricultural Non-staple Food Processing	3 178 497
食品制造业	Food Production	906 893
饮料制造业	Beverage Production	649 508
烟草制品业	Tobacco Products	600 960
纺织业	Textile Industry	2 212 106
纺织服装、鞋、帽制造业	Textile Clothing and Footwear Production	1 217 220
皮革、毛皮、羽毛(绒)及其制品业	Leathers Furs Down and Related Products	1 352 607
木材加工及木、竹、藤、棕、草制品业	Timber Processing Bamboo Cane Palm Fiber and Straw Products	251 998
家具制造业	Furniture Manufacturing	340 969
造纸及纸制品业	Papermaking and Paper Products	470 378
印刷业和记录媒介的复制	Printing and Record Processing	142 116
文教体育用品制造业	Stationery Education and Sports Goods	554 590
石油加工、炼焦及核燃料加工业	Petroleum Processing Coking and Nuclear Fuel Processing	680 328
化学原料及化学制品制造业	Raw Chemical Materials and Chemical Products	2 131 951
医药制造业	Medicine Manufacturing	234 989
化学纤维制造业	Chemical Fiber Manufacturing	97 359
橡胶制品业	Rubber Products	1 479 968
塑料制品业	Plastic Products	644 758
非金属矿物制品业	Nonmetal Mineral Products	1 446 800
黑色金属冶炼及压延加工业	Smelting and Pressing of Ferrous Metals	2 635 825
有色金属冶炼及压延加工业	Smelting and Pressing of Nonferrous Metals	473 419
金属制品业	Metal Products	1 232 655
通用设备制造业	General-purpose Equipment Manufacturing	2 063 650
专用设备制造业	Special-purpose Equipment Manufacturing	839 304
交通运输设备制造业	Transportation Equipment Manufacturing	2 209 114
电气机械及器材制造业	Electric Equipments and Machinery Manufacturing	7 059 081
通信设备、计算机及其他电子设备制造业	Communication Equipment Computers and Other Electronic Equipment Production	4 506 334
仪器仪表及文化、办公用机械制造业	Instruments Meters Culture and Office Equipments Manufacturing	256 447
工艺品及其他制造业	Handicraft Articles and Other Goods Production	681 388
废弃资源和废旧材料回收加工业	Discarded Resources and Waste Materials Recovery and Processing	32 088
电力、热力的生产和供应业	Power Steam Production and Supply	767 314
燃气生产和供应业	Gas Production and Supply	121 128
水的生产和供应业	Tap Water Production and Supply	66 103

产品销售成本 Cost of Products Sales	产品销售税金及附加 Tax and Extra Charges of Products Sales	利润总额 Total After-tax Profits	本年应交增值税 Value-added Tax Payable	全部从业人员年平均人数(万人) Average Number of Total Employees (10000 persons)
2 780 007	20 345	184 203	106 381	8
714 100	10 877	81 230	44 290	2
410 430	27 462	63 123	46 196	1
243 937	228 478	75 749	63 078	0
1 924 148	15 533	97 655	71 445	9
1 030 937	7 693	64 476	37 201	11
1 171 727	10 489	68 754	46 088	10
223 602	1 474	15 687	16 102	1
300 607	2 181	10 751	11 397	2
397 691	3 659	33 043	20 711	2
111 576	910	13 309	7 861	1
479 394	1 576	32 205	13 773	4
671 857	26 288	-20 402	4 221	0
1 864 800	17 843	63 842	72 658	5
167 155	6 810	12 439	14 744	1
87 423	132	3 787	3 034	0
1 268 119	13 931	75 676	49 903	5
569 846	2 685	30 744	19 908	3
1 283 929	14 861	60 436	42 075	3
2 480 256	4 399	29 648	49 261	2
455 570	4 717	-2 943	6 846	1
1 058 519	11 123	86 219	37 253	3
1 760 940	14 635	124 397	88 932	6
703 828	11 134	70 470	34 192	3
1 941 940	9 733	78 054	67 284	6
6 061 200	39 717	273 330	170 104	8
3 849 288	13 096	194 731	105 344	7
218 228	3 587	13 713	11 286	1
570 177	5 212	46 631	29 316	4
29 940	49	621	675	0
706 104	4 993	4 448	72 626	2
105 877	1 064	4 001	7 259	0
63 643	402	-521	3 113	0

11 -7 按行业分国有及国有控股工业企业主要指标 (2005 年)

MAIN INDICATORS OF STATE-OWNED AND STATE-HOLDING INDUSTRIAL ENTERPRISES BY SECTORS(2005)

项　　目	Indicators	企业单位数(个) Number of Enterprises(unit)
总　　计	**Total**	**180**
煤炭开采和洗选业	Coal Mining and Dressing	0
石油和天然气开采业	Petroleum and Natural Gas Extraction	0
黑色金属矿采选业	Ferrous Metals Mining and Dressing	0
有色金属矿采选业	Nonferrous Metals Mining and Dressing	3
非金属矿采选业	Nonmetal Minerals Mining and Dressing	0
其他采矿业	Other Minerals Mining	0
农副食品加工业	Agricultural Non-staple Food Processing	0
食品制造业	Food Production	0
饮料制造业	Beverage Production	0
烟草制品业	Tobacco Products	1
纺织业	Textile Industry	15
纺织服装、鞋、帽制造业	Textile, Clothing and Footwear Production	3
皮革、毛皮、羽毛(绒)及其制品业	Leathers, Furs, Down and Related Products	2
木材加工及木、竹、藤、棕、草制品业	Timber Processing, Bamboo, Cane, Palm Fiber and Straw Products	0
家具制造业	Furniture Manufacturing	2
造纸及纸制品业	Papermaking and Paper Products	2
印刷业和记录媒介的复制	Printing and Record Processing	6
文教体育用品制造业	Stationery, Education and Sports Goods	2
石油加工、炼焦及核燃料加工业	Petroleum Processing, Coking and Nuclear Fuel Processing	1
化学原料及化学制品制造业	Raw Chemical Materials and Chemical Products	13
医药制造业	Medicine Manufacturing	4
化学纤维制造业	Chemical Fiber Manufacturing	2
橡胶制品业	Rubber Products	5
塑料制品业	Plastic Products	1
非金属矿物制品业	Nonmetal Mineral Products	10
黑色金属冶炼及压延加工业	Smelting and Pressing of Ferrous Metals	3
有色金属冶炼及压延加工业	Smelting and Pressing of Nonferrous Metals	1
金属制品业	Metal Products	7
通用设备制造业	General-purpose Equipment Manufacturing	17
专用设备制造业	Special-purpose Equipment Manufacturing	5
交通运输设备制造业	Transportation Equipment Manufacturing	20
电气机械及器材制造业	Electric Equipments and Machinery Manufacturing	5
通信设备、计算机及其他电子设备制造业	Communication Equipment, Computers and Other Electronic Equipment Production	3
仪器仪表及文化、办公用机械制造业	Instruments, Meters, Culture and Office Equipments Manufacturing	2
工艺品及其他制造业	Handicraft Articles and Other Goods Production	2
废弃资源和废旧材料回收加工业	Discarded Resources and Waste Materials Recovery and Processing	0
电力、热力的生产和供应业	Power, Steam Production and Supply	18
燃气生产和供应业	Gas Production and Supply	1
水的生产和供应业	Tap Water Production and Supply	10

工业总产值 Gross Output Value of Industry(current price) (10000 yuan)	工业增加值 Added Value of Industry (production approach)	资产合计 Assets	流动资产年平均余额 Annual Average Balance of Circulating Funds	固定资产净值年平均余额 Annual Average Balance of Net Value of Fixed Assets
10 271 113	**2 586 001**	**10 113 524**	**5 089 332**	**2 877 282**
0	0	0	0	0
0	0	0	0	0
0	0	0	0	0
23 154	9 606	24 438	6 124	15 492
0	0	0	0	0
0	0	0	0	0
0	0	0	0	0
0	0	0	0	0
0	0	0	0	0
509 998	320 083	666 015	378 970	87 193
122 146	34 302	249 694	131 587	84 589
60 124	21 302	81 446	43 869	17 148
17 539	6 002	16 124	8 385	4 085
0	0	0	0	0
1 512	529	2 963	1 599	1 066
4 017	1 354	14 038	8 071	5 353
56 553	19 048	55 282	33 143	19 168
3 089	1 261	2 063	1 705	328
642 708	145 122	354 571	209 265	135 590
800 865	278 441	1 330 335	601 783	418 320
10 448	2 892	31 406	13 399	5 822
37 035	9 869	38 050	13 728	21 732
503 228	143 457	756 524	406 257	193 561
22 992	4 019	26 365	10 363	15 007
95 696	33 604	129 044	57 401	42 017
1 993 597	207 685	1 220 817	637 659	311 709
2 656	916	10 912	1 932	8 913
44 355	17 388	62 075	29 908	20 738
110 508	38 877	148 118	80 716	40 498
155 880	35 744	110 960	65 659	24 614
747 892	177 802	1 239 570	739 479	229 379
26 909	8 359	20 724	11 268	2 340
2 195 250	406 413	890 740	585 684	166 842
7 629	3 263	6 213	5 820	941
9 452	1 022	9 397	5 949	2 585
0	0	0	0	0
1 500 495	455 843	1 169 843	335 411	528 786
86 557	27 900	336 383	90 840	166 589
65 514	28 099	296 146	84 980	171 767

11－7 续表1
continued

项　　目	Indicators	产品销售收入 Revenue of Products Sales
总计	**Total**	**10 539 502**
煤炭开采和洗选业	Coal Mining and Dressing	0
石油和天然气开采业	Petroleum and Natural Gas Extraction	0
黑色金属矿采选业	Ferrous Metals Mining and Dressing	0
有色金属矿采选业	Nonferrous Metals Mining and Dressing	20 476
非金属矿采选业	Nonmetal Minerals Mining and Dressing	0
其他采矿业	Other Minerals Mining	0
农副食品加工业	Agricultural Non-staple Food Processing	0
食品制造业	Food Production	0
饮料制造业	Beverage Production	0
烟草制品业	Tobacco Products	593 694
纺织业	Textile Industry	148 389
纺织服装、鞋、帽制造业	Textile Clothing and Footwear Production	59 741
皮革、毛皮、羽毛(绒)及其制品业	Leathers Furs Down and Related Products	13 378
木材加工及木、竹、藤、棕、草制品业	Timber Processing Bamboo Cane Palm Fiber and Straw Products	0
家具制造业	Furniture Manufacturing	1 282
造纸及纸制品业	Papermaking and Paper Products	5 699
印刷业和记录媒介的复制	Printing and Record Processing	59 319
文教体育用品制造业	Stationery Education and Sports Goods	4 320
石油加工、炼焦及核燃料加工业	Petroleum Processing Coking and Nuclear Fuel Processing	646 426
化学原料及化学制品制造业	Raw Chemical Materials and Chemical Products	729 273
医药制造业	Medicine Manufacturing	9 576
化学纤维制造业	Chemical Fiber Manufacturing	35 553
橡胶制品业	Rubber Products	578 716
塑料制品业	Plastic Products	23 295
非金属矿物制品业	Nonmetal Mineral Products	90 727
黑色金属冶炼及压延加工业	Smelting and Pressing of Ferrous Metals	2 286 270
有色金属冶炼及压延加工业	Smelting and Pressing of Nonferrous Metals	2 106
金属制品业	Metal Products	37 524
通用设备制造业	General-purpose Equipment Manufacturing	101 974
专用设备制造业	Special-purpose Equipment Manufacturing	148 678
交通运输设备制造业	Transportation Equipment Manufacturing	747 706
电气机械及器材制造业	Electric Equipments and Machinery Manufacturing	21 723
通信设备、计算机及其他电子设备制造业	Communication Equipment Computers and Other Electronic Equipment Production	2 788 645
仪器仪表及文化、办公用机械制造业	Instruments Meters Culture and Office Equipments Manufacturing	5 058
工艺品及其他制造业	Handicraft Articles and Other Goods Production	9 519
废弃资源和废旧材料回收加工业	Discarded Resources and Waste Materials Recovery and Processing	0
电力、热力的生产和供应业	Power Steam Production and Supply	695 451
燃气生产和供应业	Gas Production and Supply	111 470
水的生产和供应业	Tap Water Production and Supply	66 103

产品销售成本 Cost of Products Sales	产品销售税金及附加 Tax and Extra Charges of Products Sales	利润总额 Total After-tax Profits	本年应交增值税 Value-added Tax Payable	全部从业人员年平均人数(万人) Average Number of Total Employees(10000 persons)
9 116 559	**312 559**	**225 374**	**352 273**	**15**
0	0	0	0	0
0	0	0	0	0
0	0	0	0	0
11 417	95	5 436	8	0
0	0	0	0	0
0	0	0	0	0
0	0	0	0	0
0	0	0	0	0
0	0	0	0	0
239 990	228 371	73 801	62 278	0
133 127	622	-326	2 972	1
54 705	94	37	512	1
11 209	51	-930	523	0
0	0	0	0	0
1 298	2	-175	18	0
4 798	10	67	164	0
46 654	82	6 597	3 403	0
3 655	21	-53	0	0
646 031	26 251	-23 151	3 212	0
636 668	7 413	1 490	28 045	2
6 904	47	-2 976	627	0
32 577	3	1 231	1 470	0
529 094	5 164	7 926	8 230	2
23 006	0	-488	0	0
82 147	462	3 222	3 827	0
2 154 915	3 189	20 836	43 845	1
1 953	12	1	118	0
34 152	280	-2 030	1 020	0
78 653	1 579	10 981	4 837	1
129 862	2 725	4 487	4 375	0
674 326	1 794	23 502	10 014	2
18 097	58	1 324	626	0
2 437 907	10 094	45 851	58 981	1
4 744	39	-21	374	0
8 632	39	53	170	0
0	0	0	0	0
639 702	3 942	2 539	69 658	1
100 020	879	2 373	6 901	0
63 643	402	-521	3 113	0

11－8 按行业分规模以上三资工业企业主要指标（2005 年）

MAIN INDICATORS OF FOREIGN FUNDED INDUSTRIAL ENTERPRISES ABOVE THE SET SCALE BY SECTORS(2005)

项　目	Indicators	企业单位数(个) Number of Enterprises(unit)
总　计	**Total**	**1 658**
煤炭开采和洗选业	Coal Mining and Dressing	0
石油和天然气开采业	Petroleum and Natural Gas Extraction	0
黑色金属矿采选业	Ferrous Metals Mining and Dressing	1
有色金属矿采选业	Nonferrous Metals Mining and Dressing	0
非金属矿采选业	Nonmetal Minerals Mining and Dressing	10
其他采矿业	Other Minerals Mining	0
农副食品加工业	Agricultural Non-staple Food Processing	151
食品制造业	Food Production	72
饮料制造业	Beverage Production	9
烟草制品业	Tobacco Products	0
纺织业	Textile Industry	158
纺织服装、鞋、帽制造业	Textile, Clothing and Footwear Production	165
皮革、毛皮、羽毛(绒)及其制品业	Leathers, Furs, Down and Related Products	140
木材加工及木、竹、藤、棕、草制品业	Timber Processing, Bamboo, Cane, Palm Fiber and Straw Products	14
家具制造业	Furniture Manufacturing	31
造纸及纸制品业	Papermaking and Paper Products	34
印刷业和记录媒介的复制	Printing and Record Processing	7
文教体育用品制造业	Stationery, Education and Sports Goods	78
石油加工、炼焦及核燃料加工业	Petroleum Processing, Coking and Nuclear Fuel Processing	4
化学原料及化学制品制造业	Raw Chemical Materials and Chemical Products	56
医药制造业	Medicine Manufacturing	9
化学纤维制造业	Chemical Fiber Manufacturing	10
橡胶制品业	Rubber Products	32
塑料制品业	Plastic Products	73
非金属矿物制品业	Nonmetal Mineral Products	41
黑色金属冶炼及压延加工业	Smelting and Pressing of Ferrous Metals	9
有色金属冶炼及压延加工业	Smelting and Pressing of Nonferrous Metals	10
金属制品业	Metal Products	66
通用设备制造业	General-purpose Equipment Manufacturing	89
专用设备制造业	Special-purpose Equipment Manufacturing	31
交通运输设备制造业	Transportation Equipment Manufacturing	51
电气机械及器材制造业	Electric Equipments and Machinery Manufacturing	83
通信设备、计算机及其他电子设备制造业	Communication Equipment, Computers and Other Electronic Equipment Production	93
仪器仪表及文化、办公用机械制造业	Instruments, Meters, Culture and Office Equipments Manufacturing	19
工艺品及其他制造业	Handicraft Articles and Other Goods Production	108
废弃资源和废旧材料回收加工业	Discarded Resources and Waste Materials Recovery and Processing	0
电力、热力的生产和供应业	Power, Steam Production and Supply	1
燃气生产和供应业	Gas Production and Supply	3
水的生产和供应业	Tap Water Production and Supply	0

工业总产值 Gross Output Value of Industry(current price) (10000 yuan)	工业增加值 Added Value of Industry (production approach)	资产合计 Assets	流动资产年平均余额 Annual AverageBalance of Circulating Funds	固定资产净值年平均余额 Annual Average Balance of Net Value of Fixed Assets
12 859 576	**4 539 062**	**8 686 289**	**4 528 311**	**2 957 062**
0	0	0	0	0
0	0	0	0	0
5 878	2 082	1 757	1 599	145
0	0	0	0	0
77 993	33 156	28 891	7 227	13 768
0	0	0	0	0
1 385 534	497 484	813 674	410 102	257 479
541 697	202 963	388 706	187 250	136 068
130 545	45 069	108 815	35 787	61 689
0	0	0	0	0
777 835	281 930	617 014	283 711	246 860
727 254	261 916	515 975	242 003	158 309
1 267 125	463 755	558 230	311 404	167 501
27 628	8 706	29 029	10 810	10 454
169 938	55 704	114 828	76 638	32 125
223 624	75 287	175 534	98 527	59 734
53 119	18 445	46 217	27 294	16 659
424 950	152 169	280 206	176 521	50 427
26 846	7 240	15 988	10 027	2 291
535 042	188 381	419 914	188 200	186 409
50 790	19 117	61 138	27 740	25 361
86 368	25 560	101 695	45 983	44 384
220 549	80 143	147 900	76 327	54 721
440 363	154 106	311 721	156 755	119 480
236 532	77 302	278 237	103 910	112 336
163 737	58 753	99 368	68 131	18 850
339 309	64 271	191 830	65 803	106 785
717 603	230 982	491 037	273 341	189 659
667 376	227 845	529 277	274 937	190 068
270 686	96 837	171 253	79 486	103 602
320 108	120 272	385 481	169 120	98 357
727 808	254 350	479 142	301 365	152 064
1 678 056	623 398	924 277	592 904	225 902
143 965	51 975	85 498	48 181	22 433
411 209	156 840	279 189	166 217	70 151
0	0	0	0	0
2 559	1 342	14 283	2 088	12 088
7 552	1 681	20 187	8 929	10 904
0	0	0	0	0

11－8 续表1
continued

项　目	Indicators	产品销售收入 Revenue of Products Sales
总　计	**Total**	**12 361 850**
煤炭开采和洗选业	Coal Mining and Dressing	0
石油和天然气开采业	Petroleum and Natural Gas Extraction	0
黑色金属矿采选业	Ferrous Metals Mining and Dressing	5 878
有色金属矿采选业	Nonferrous Metals Mining and Dressing	0
非金属矿采选业	Nonmetal Minerals Mining and Dressing	57 068
其他采矿业	Other Minerals Mining	0
农副食品加工业	Agricultural Non-staple Food Processing	1 326 772
食品制造业	Food Production	524 808
饮料制造业	Beverage Production	141 346
烟草制品业	Tobacco Products	0
纺织业	Textile Industry	749 281
纺织服装、鞋、帽制造业	Textile, Clothing and Footwear Production	711 295
皮革、毛皮、羽毛(绒)及其制品业	Leathers, Furs, Down and Related Products	1 179 994
木材加工及木、竹、藤、棕、草制品业	Timber Processing, Bamboo, Cane, Palm Fiber and Straw Products	27 015
家具制造业	Furniture Manufacturing	160 578
造纸及纸制品业	Papermaking and Paper Products	199 719
印刷业和记录媒介的复制	Printing and Record Processing	55 322
文教体育用品制造业	Stationery, Education and Sports Goods	443 389
石油加工、炼焦及核燃料加工业	Petroleum Processing, Coking and Nuclear Fuel Processing	27 422
化学原料及化学制品制造业	Raw Chemical Materials and Chemical Products	545 164
医药制造业	Medicine Manufacturing	47 929
化学纤维制造业	Chemical Fiber Manufacturing	82 551
橡胶制品业	Rubber Products	236 310
塑料制品业	Plastic Products	419 992
非金属矿物制品业	Nonmetal Mineral Products	212 810
黑色金属冶炼及压延加工业	Smelting and Pressing of Ferrous Metals	156 438
有色金属冶炼及压延加工业	Smelting and Pressing of Nonferrous Metals	317 812
金属制品业	Metal Products	627 919
通用设备制造业	General-purpose Equipment Manufacturing	688 050
专用设备制造业	Special—purpose Equipment Manufacturing	260 876
交通运输设备制造业	Transportation Equipment Manufacturing	298 102
电气机械及器材制造业	Electric Equipments and Machinery Manufacturing	709 474
通信设备、计算机及其他电子设备制造业	Communication Equipment, Computers and Other Electronic Equipment Production	1 585 323
仪器仪表及文化、办公用机械制造业	Instruments, Meters, Culture and Office Equipments Manufacturing	160 876
工艺品及其他制造业	Handicraft Articles and Other Goods Production	386 961
废弃资源和废旧材料回收加工业	Discarded Resources and Waste Materials Recovery and Processing	0
电力、热力的生产和供应业	Power, Steam Production and Supply	6 741
燃气生产和供应业	Gas Production and Supply	8 639
水的生产和供应业	Tap Water Production and Supply	0

产品销售成本 Cost of Products Sales	产品销售税金及附加 Tax and Extra Charges of Products Sales	利润总额 Total After-tax Profits	本年应交增值税 Value - added Tax Payable	全部从业人员年平均人数(万人) Average Number of Total Employees(10000 persons)
10 533 888	**66 301**	**722 047**	**348 061**	**54**
0	0	0	0	0
0	0	0	0	0
4 503	26	1 095	574	0
0	0	0	0	0
40 315	2 070	6 076	3 378	0
0	0	0	0	0
1 149 828	10 740	84 453	48 817	4
392 091	5 573	53 582	22 728	1
89 814	4 213	12 269	7 782	0
0	0	0	0	0
636 402	4 451	36 723	23 051	4
612 101	3 450	31 094	17 962	8
1 032 135	7 541	57 079	36 309	9
24 306	93	-315	751	0
144 424	125	3 599	3 110	1
165 219	1 069	15 987	6 077	1
42 446	90	8 194	3 579	0
384 149	642	20 899	8 911	3
21 029	22	2 052	647	0
483 617	1 036	23 121	10 640	1
37 801	3 233	2 512	1 201	0
73 761	52	3 228	2 467	0
185 940	2 273	15 630	9 279	2
371 384	964	20 155	11 871	2
177 933	821	9 365	6 794	1
145 018	55	2 511	2 826	0
324 317	787	-13 197	1 559	0
533 456	1 106	53 578	12 456	1
601 887	1 023	25 148	14 427	2
216 713	472	32 442	4 616	1
257 527	1 665	3 994	12 974	1
607 646	9 087	45 567	17 419	3
1 311 238	1 192	131 353	38 786	5
138 454	952	9 165	6 236	0
317 754	1 297	22 616	10 043	3
0	0	0	0	0
5 450	48	657	498	0
5 232	134	1 416	296	0
0	0	0	0	0

11－9 按行业分大中型工业企业主要指标（2005年）

MAIN INDICATORS OF LARGE-SCALE AND MEDIUM-SCALE INDUSTRIAL ENTERPRISES BY SECTORS(2005)

项　目	Indicators	企业单位数(个) Number of Enterprises(unit)
总计	**Total**	**492**
煤炭开采和洗选业	Coal Mining and Dressing	0
石油和天然气开采业	Petroleum and Natural Gas Extraction	0
黑色金属矿采选业	Ferrous Metals Mining and Dressing	0
有色金属矿采选业	Nonferrous Metals Mining and Dressing	4
非金属矿采选业	Nonmetal Minerals Mining and Dressing	8
其他采矿业	Other Minerals Mining	0
农副食品加工业	Agricultural Non－staple Food Processing	36
食品制造业	Food Production	14
饮料制造业	Beverage Production	9
烟草制品业	Tobacco Products	1
纺织业	Textile Industry	39
纺织服装、鞋、帽制造业	Textile, Clothing and Footwear Production	31
皮革、毛皮、羽毛(绒)及其制品业	Leathers, Furs, Down and Related Products	23
木材加工及木、竹、藤、棕、草制品业	Timber Processing, Bamboo, Cane, Palm Fiber and Straw Products	3
家具制造业	Furniture Manufacturing	7
造纸及纸制品业	Papermaking and Paper Products	8
印刷业和记录媒介的复制	Printing and Record Processing	4
文教体育用品制造业	Stationery, Education and Sports Goods	13
石油加工、炼焦及核燃料加工业	Petroleum Processing, Coking and Nuclear Fuel Processing	1
化学原料及化学制品制造业	Raw Chemical Materials and Chemical Products	29
医药制造业	Medicine Manufacturing	7
化学纤维制造业	Chemical Fiber Manufacturing	2
橡胶制品业	Rubber Products	29
塑料制品业	Plastic Products	11
非金属矿物制品业	Nonmetal Mineral Products	20
黑色金属冶炼及压延加工业	Smelting and Pressing of Ferrous Metals	2
有色金属冶炼及压延加工业	Smelting and Pressing of Nonferrous Metals	4
金属制品业	Metal Products	16
通用设备制造业	General-purpose Equipment Manufacturing	32
专用设备制造业	Special-purpose Equipment Manufacturing	10
交通运输设备制造业	Transportation Equipment Manufacturing	31
电气机械及器材制造业	Electric Equipments and Machinery Manufacturing	36
通信设备、计算机及其他电子设备制造业	Communication Equipment, Computers and Other Electronic Equipment Production	23
仪器仪表及文化、办公用机械制造业	Instruments, Meters, Culture and Office Equipments Manufacturing	4
工艺品及其他制造业	Handicraft Articles and Other Goods Production	15
废弃资源和废旧材料回收加工业	Discarded Resources and Waste Materials Recovery and Processing	1
电力、热力的生产和供应业	Power, Steam Production and Supply	16
燃气生产和供应业	Gas Production and Supply	1
水的生产和供应业	Tap Water Production and Supply	2

工业总产值 Gross Output Value of Industry(current price) (10000 yuan)	工业增加值 Added Value of Industry (production approach)	资产合计 Assets	流动资产年平均余额 Annual AverageBalance of Circulating Funds	固定资产净值年平均余额 Annual Average Balance of Net Value of Fixed Assets
30 292 433	**8 843 840**	**22 655 118**	**11 896 718**	**6 086 289**
0	0	0	0	0
0	0	0	0	0
0	0	0	0	0
53 953	13 794	33 300	10 388	20 768
166 990	56 628	58 549	25 182	23 425
0	0	0	0	0
1 938 406	669 513	1 012 237	563 572	324 066
367 074	115 336	205 643	86 221	72 013
466 095	186 744	814 046	427 553	177 039
509 998	320 083	666 015	378 970	87 193
1 278 927	401 764	1 113 732	512 560	405 882
593 327	211 423	584 804	295 189	148 539
968 277	343 656	481 706	284 965	125 508
188 999	67 373	37 845	30 874	8 375
165 347	59 267	103 743	59 671	32 523
146 370	57 445	79 633	47 341	23 606
55 236	20 373	56 001	30 116	19 537
271 738	94 499	192 487	126 530	30 450
642 708	145 122	354 571	209 265	135 590
140 0781	450 574	1 746 559	765 264	603 054
150 424	80 052	246 558	117 919	67 597
43 809	12 293	43 309	16 028	23 974
1 095 520	364 865	1 101 283	586 112	319 544
198 781	69 945	166 175	81 485	62 825
1 023 091	371 174	822 017	405 585	241 226
2 066 488	233 216	1 280 305	679 930	317 669
413 704	93 896	198 879	70 313	108 681
699 444	221 045	351 517	211 916	127 388
1 292 354	419 726	949 870	591 221	224 134
399 456	131 016	292 087	165 583	114 859
1 901 740	488 286	2 045 750	1 166 167	398 284
6 392 031	1 695 487	4 174 377	2 439 352	608 431
3 356 256	787 542	1 519 541	924 763	352 534
97 932	30 991	31 962	18 326	10 463
215 388	80 249	153 650	97 663	42 255
84 060	36 213	37 412	738	50
1 513 353	464 850	1 151 324	322 361	537 966
86 557	27 900	336 383	90 840	166 589
47 820	21 503	211 850	56 760	124 256

11 -9 续表 1
continued

项　　目	Indicators	产品销售收入 Revenue of Products Sales
总　　计	**Total**	**29 527 199**
煤炭开采和洗选业	Coal Mining and Dressing	0
石油和天然气开采业	Petroleum and Natural Gas Extraction	0
黑色金属矿采选业	Ferrous Metals Mining and Dressing	0
有色金属矿采选业	Nonferrous Metals Mining and Dressing	49 934
非金属矿采选业	Nonmetal Minerals Mining and Dressing	154 148
其他采矿业	Other Minerals Mining	0
农副食品加工业	Agricultural Non – staple Food Processing	1 842 929
食品制造业	Food Production	359 064
饮料制造业	Beverage Production	564 335
烟草制品业	Tobacco Products	593 694
纺织业	Textile Industry	1 268 316
纺织服装、鞋、帽制造业	Textile Clothing and Footwear Production	570 360
皮革、毛皮、羽毛(绒)及其制品业	Leathers Furs Down and Related Products	943 186
木材加工及木、竹、藤、棕、草制品业	Timber Processing Bamboo Cane Palm Fiber and Straw Products	155 638
家具制造业	Furniture Manufacturing	160 956
造纸及纸制品业	Papermaking and Paper Products	123 213
印刷业和记录媒介的复制	Printing and Record Processing	57 322
文教体育用品制造业	Stationery Education and Sports Goods	294 731
石油加工、炼焦及核燃料加工业	Petroleum Processing Coking and Nuclear Fuel Processing	646 426
化学原料及化学制品制造业	Raw Chemical Materials and Chemical Products	1 301 359
医药制造业	Medicine Manufacturing	158 191
化学纤维制造业	Chemical Fiber Manufacturing	42 334
橡胶制品业	Rubber Products	1 163 767
塑料制品业	Plastic Products	206 280
非金属矿物制品业	Nonmetal Mineral Products	936 276
黑色金属冶炼及压延加工业	Smelting and Pressing of Ferrous Metals	2 357 673
有色金属冶炼及压延加工业	Smelting and Pressing of Nonferrous Metals	377 774
金属制品业	Metal Products	591 947
通用设备制造业	General – purpose Equipment Manufacturing	1 193 297
专用设备制造业	Special – purpose Equipment Manufacturing	381 753
交通运输设备制造业	Transportation Equipment Manufacturing	1 810 767
电气机械及器材制造业	Electric Equipments and Machinery Manufacturing	6 236 418
通信设备、计算机及其他电子设备制造业	Communication Equipment Computers and Other Electronic Equipment Production	3 806 318
仪器仪表及文化、办公用机械制造业	Instruments Meters Culture and Office Equipments Manufacturing	94 165
工艺品及其他制造业	Handicraft Articles and Other Goods Production	206 532
废弃资源和废旧材料回收加工业	Discarded Resources and Waste Materials Recovery and Processing	13 353
电力、热力的生产和供应业	Power Steam Production and Supply	703 537
燃气生产和供应业	Gas Production and Supply	111 470
水的生产和供应业	Tap Water Production and Supply	49 740

产品销售成本 Cost of Products Sales	产品销售 税金及附加 Tax and Extra Charges of Products Sales	利润总额 Total After- tax Profits	本年应交 增值税 Value-added Tax Payable	全部从业人员 年平均人数(万人) Average Number of Total Employees(10000 persons)
25 672 598	**420 791**	**1 064 169**	**872 659**	**60**
0	0	0	0	0
0	0	0	0	0
0	0	0	0	0
33 258	1 069	9 573	1 615	0
114 512	2 454	18 182	6 467	0
0	0	0	0	0
1 654 155	11 960	85 132	50 456	5
296 225	1 965	26 387	17 131	1
355 264	25 681	52 391	40 779	1
239 990	228 371	73 801	62 278	0
1 112 320	6 716	48 473	37 904	5
482 838	1 567	27 369	12 107	5
826 442	4 380	47 055	26 924	5
140 155	1 026	11 185	11 747	0
140 208	499	6 310	3 088	1
107 214	320	8 007	3 098	1
43 563	65	7 758	3 807	0
257 931	356	18 421	7 222	1
646 031	26 251	-23 151	3 212	0
1 162 603	8 360	21 554	44 306	4
108 646	5 898	8 872	1 1282	0
39 041	0	606	1 439	0
999 557	11 250	49 361	33 699	4
180 936	1 075	13 180	4 628	1
862 216	6 913	19 450	14 998	2
2 222 316	3 205	21 679	44 306	1
368 270	4 078	-7 783	3 888	0
512 464	1 452	54 394	12 934	1
1 044 788	7 043	59 031	46 935	3
319 076	5 062	39 371	11 782	1
1 614 464	6 445	48 317	49 400	4
5 370 666	27 301	205 713	140 080	5
3 349 683	10 571	88 978	73 991	4
87 108	838	1 089	3 500	0
175 256	3 448	11 332	7 856	1
13 291	3	2	0	0
643 157	4 040	7 645	70 643	1
100 020	879	2 373	6 901	0
48 937	251	2 113	2 259	0

11－10 按行业分规模以上工业企业主要经济效益指标（2005 年）

MAIN INDICATORS ON ECONOMIC BENEFIT OF INDUSTRIAL ENTERPRISES ABOVE THE SET SCALE BY SECTORS(2005)

行　业	Indicators	总资产贡献率(%) Ratio of Total Assets to Industrial Output Value
总　计	**Total**	**13.59**
按轻重工业分	**Grouped by Light and Heavy Industries**	
轻工业	Light Industry	15.93
重工业	Heavy Industry	11.59
按行业分	**Grouped by Sectors**	
煤炭开采和洗选业	Coal Mining and Dressing	0
石油和天然气开采业	Petroleum and Natural Gas Extraction	0
黑色金属矿采选业	Ferrous Metals Mining and Dressing	62.47
有色金属矿采选业	Nonferrous Metals Mining and Dressing	37.75
非金属矿采选业	Nonmetal Minerals Mining and Dressing	45.48
其他采矿业	Other Minerals Mining	849.7
农副食品加工业	Agricultural Non-staple Food Processing	18.62
食品制造业	Food Production	24.11
饮料制造业	Beverage Production	16.01
烟草制品业	Tobacco Products	54.13
纺织业	Textile Industry	11.81
纺织服装、鞋、帽制造业	Textile, Clothing and Footwear Production	11.97
皮革、毛皮、羽毛(绒)及其制品业	Leathers, Furs, Down and Related Products	19.9
木材加工及木、竹、藤、棕、草制品业	Timber Processing, Bamboo, Cane, Palm Fiber and Straw Products	29.97
家具制造业	Furniture Manufacturing	11.56
造纸及纸制品业	Papermaking and Paper Products	16.73
印刷业和记录媒介的复制	Printing and Record Processing	16.75
文教体育用品制造业	Stationery, Education and Sports Goods	15.59
石油加工、炼焦及核燃料加工业	Petroleum Processing, Coking and Nuclear Fuel Processing	7.23
化学原料及化学制品制造业	Raw Chemical Materials and Chemical Products	8.1
医药制造业	Medicine Manufacturing	10.75
化学纤维制造业	Chemical Fiber Manufacturing	7.82
橡胶制品业	Rubber Products	12.03
塑料制品业	Plastic Products	11.81
非金属矿物制品业	Nonmetal Mineral Products	11.45
黑色金属冶炼及压延加工业	Smelting and Pressing of Ferrous Metals	7.36
有色金属冶炼及压延加工业	Smelting and Pressing of Nonferrous Metals	5.91
金属制品业	Metal Products	18.35
通用设备制造业	General-purpose Equipment Manufacturing	15.6
专用设备制造业	Special-purpose Equipment Manufacturing	21.98
交通运输设备制造业	Transportation Equipment Manufacturing	7.06
电气机械及器材制造业	Electric Equipments and Machinery Manufacturing	11.47
通信设备、计算机及其他电子设备制造业	Communication Equipment, Computers and Other Electronic Equipment Production	16.32
仪器仪表及文化、办公用机械制造业	Instruments, Meters, Culture and Office Equipments Manufacturing	16.23
工艺品及其他制造业	Handicraft Articles and Other Goods Production	21.16
废弃资源和废旧材料回收加工业	Discarded Resources and Waste Materials Recovery and Processing	3.19
电力、热力的生产和供应业	Power, Steam Production and Supply	7.29
燃气生产和供应业	Gas Production and Supply	3.68
水的生产和供应业	Tap Water Production and Supply	1.48

资产负债率 (%) Assets Liability Ratio	流动资产周转次数(次/年) Number of times of Annual of Turnover Circulating Funds(Times/year)	工业成本费用利润率(%) Ratio of Profits to Industrial Cost	全员劳动生产率(元/人.年) Overall Labor Productivity (yuan/person-year)	产品销售率(%) Proportion of Products Sold
57.76	**2.59**	**4.92**	**121 550**	**98.12**
53.46	2.83	5.15	108 361	98.77
61.43	2.38	4.69	137 961	97.49
0	0	0	0	0
0	0	0	0	0
24.16	3.37	20.55	192 194	96.37
52.4	4.73	25.39	52 775	98.2
42.87	5.88	14.29	122 419	95.46
48.3	20.51	33.31	444 333	100
60.24	3.32	6.26	143 396	96.43
47.68	3.26	10.05	168 357	98.95
36.05	1.42	11.78	190 335	114.81
38.13	1.55	24.56	1 748 948	102.71
59.01	2.92	4.69	78 437	96.88
52.4	2.43	5.66	41 990	96.5
70.46	3.53	5.44	54 671	96.62
43.25	3.81	6.69	206 383	95.96
68.3	2.54	3.31	80 002	97.51
51.1	2.32	7.67	93 190	96.42
48.73	1.88	10.43	87 116	102.77
63.52	2.68	6.17	50 660	101.83
68.51	3.07	-2.92	535 205	99.98
58.94	2.04	3.1	141 038	99.4
48.1	1.47	5.84	144 338	97.05
50.86	1.93	4	116 841	97.9
65.92	2.15	5.5	89 905	94.78
57.2	2.42	5.03	84 641	97.1
56.29	2.47	4.4	193 635	97.81
70.51	3.44	1.15	187 388	99.15
77.13	5.14	-0.62	191 912	95.43
51.92	2.97	7.65	143 067	97.06
62.81	2.3	6.45	123 336	95.85
46.98	2.81	9.25	104 917	95.12
68.63	1.65	3.67	106 319	96.35
52.97	2.63	4.04	247 868	99.46
52.97	3.51	4.56	163 214	98.9
51.61	2.48	5.73	110 592	100.39
47.59	2.94	7.43	66 621	94.55
15.43	6.16	2.02	1 081 684	99.32
72.91	2.13	0.58	297 789	99.65
42.07	1.21	3.35	102 210	107.15
58.84	0.78	-0.69	69 519	98.51

11－11 按行业分国有及国有控股工业企业主要经济效益指标（2005 年）
MAIN INDICATORS ON ECONOMIC BENEFIT OF STATE-OWNED AND STATE-HOLDING INDUSTRIAL ENTERPRISES BY SECTORS(2005)

行　业	Indicators	总资产贡献率(%) Ratio of Total Assets to Industrial Output Value
总　计	**Total**	**9.83**
煤炭开采和洗选业	Coal Mining and Dressing	0
石油和天然气开采业	Petroleum and Natural Gas Extraction	0
黑色金属矿采选业	Ferrous Metals Mining and Dressing	0
有色金属矿采选业	Nonferrous Metals Mining and Dressing	24.38
非金属矿采选业	Nonmetal Minerals Mining and Dressing	30.47
其他采矿业	Other Minerals Mining	0
农副食品加工业	Agricultural Non-staple Food Processing	4.08
食品制造业	Food Production	0.81
饮料制造业	Beverage Production	13.5
烟草制品业	Tobacco Products	55.03
纺织业	Textile Industry	1.93
纺织服装、鞋、帽制造业	Textile, Clothing and Footwear Production	1.47
皮革、毛皮、羽毛(绒)及其制品业	Leathers, Furs, Down and Related Products	0.74
木材加工及木、竹、藤、棕、草制品业	Timber Processing, Bamboo, Cane, Palm Fiber and Straw Products	0
家具制造业	Furniture Manufacturing	-5.24
造纸及纸制品业	Papermaking and Paper Products	1.84
印刷业和记录媒介的复制	Printing and Record Processing	19.1
文教体育用品制造业	Stationery, Education and Sports Goods	-1.55
石油加工、炼焦及核燃料加工业	Petroleum Processing, Coking and Nuclear Fuel Processing	6.55
化学原料及化学制品制造业	Raw Chemical Materials and Chemical Products	4.21
医药制造业	Medicine Manufacturing	-4.91
化学纤维制造业	Chemical Fiber Manufacturing	9.15
橡胶制品业	Rubber Products	3.77
塑料制品业	Plastic Products	0.37
非金属矿物制品业	Nonmetal Mineral Products	6.52
黑色金属冶炼及压延加工业	Smelting and Pressing of Ferrous Metals	7.01
有色金属冶炼及压延加工业	Smelting and Pressing of Nonferrous Metals	1.44
金属制品业	Metal Products	1.25
通用设备制造业	General-purpose Equipment Manufacturing	12.34
专用设备制造业	Special-purpose Equipment Manufacturing	10.4
交通运输设备制造业	Transportation Equipment Manufacturing	3.04
电气机械及器材制造业	Electric Equipments and Machinery Manufacturing	9.82
通信设备、计算机及其他电子设备制造业	Communication Equipment, Computers and Other Electronic Equipment Production	14.36
仪器仪表及文化、办公用机械制造业	Instruments, Meters, Culture and Office Equipments Manufacturing	6.34
工艺品及其他制造业	Handicraft Articles and Other Goods Production	3.48
废弃资源和废旧材料回收加工业	Discarded Resources and Waste Materials Recovery and Processing	0
电力、热力的生产和供应业	Power, Steam Production and Supply	7.35
燃气生产和供应业	Gas Production and Supply	3.21
水的生产和供应业	Tap Water Production and Supply	1.48
国有控股	State-holding Enterprises	9.83
三　资	Foreign Funded Enterprises	6.68
大中型	Large-scale and Medium-scale Enterprises	10.24

资产负债率(%) Assets Liability Ratio	流动资产周转次数(次/年) Number of times of Annual of Turnover Circulating Funds(Times/year)	工业成本费用利润率(%) Ratio of Profits to Industrial Cost	全员劳动生产率(元/人.年) Overall Labor Productivity (yuan/person-year)	产品销售率(%) Proportion of Products Sold
60.7	**2.07**	**2.24**	**175 533**	**100.76**
0	0	0	0	0
0	0	0	0	0
0	0	0	0	0
55.02	3.34	36.39	104 524	98.64
79.3	3.54	9.54	43 839	96.1
0	0	0	0	0
84.13	0.92	2.04	348 982	96.33
73.12	1.01	-6.76	36 315	98.19
25.1	0.96	13.34	303 848	134.43
37.99	1.57	24.35	1 803 282	102.72
67.09	1.13	-0.22	28 944	99.86
67.22	1.36	0.06	42 452	100.77
71.3	1.6	-6.75	86 986	101.44
0	0	0	0	0
75.78	0.8	-12.41	24 701	100
50.68	0.71	1.15	21 872	88.08
46.31	1.79	12.45	180 204	104.04
98.77	2.53	-1.2	18 138	100
68.67	3.09	-3.46	722 359	100.14
59.93	1.21	0.21	134 597	99.03
95.1	0.71	-27.11	20 466	91.87
56.86	2.59	3.49	157 899	96.66
67.9	1.42	1.39	91 549	96.22
54.81	2.25	-2.05	279 097	101.32
65.58	1.58	3.66	103 749	99.21
70.45	3.59	0.93	171 018	99.32
119.19	1.09	0.04	74 472	100.27
71.06	1.25	-5.27	136 806	91.62
59.65	1.26	11.78	60 954	98.27
52.17	2.26	3.15	90 216	94.3
70.69	1.01	3.2	106 641	100.53
59.4	1.93	6.72	195 311	104.63
55.67	4.76	1.67	354 512	101.19
68.69	0.87	-0.42	134 851	94.85
77.71	1.6	0.56	22 363	96.71
0	0	0	0	0
72.09	2.07	0.37	322 949	99.36
40.55	1.23	2.11	113 552	107.88
58.84	0.78	-0.69	69 519	98.51
60.7	2.07	2.24	175 533	100.76
62.84	1.78	2.1	121 396	99.33
59.83	2.12	2.35	187 533	100.95

11－12 按行业分规模以上三资工业企业主要经济效益指标（2005 年）

MAIN INDICATORS ON ECONOMIC BENEFIT OF FOREIGN FUNDED INDUSTRIAL ENTERPRISESABOVE THE SET SCALE BY SECTORS(2005)

行　业	Indicators	总资产贡献率(%) Ratio of Total Assets to Industrial Output Value
总　计	**Total**	**13.84**
煤炭开采和洗选业	Coal Mining and Dressing	0
石油和天然气开采业	Petroleum and Natural Gas Extraction	0
黑色金属矿采选业	Ferrous Metals Mining and Dressing	96.49
有色金属矿采选业	Nonferrous Metals Mining and Dressing	0
非金属矿采选业	Nonmetal Minerals Mining and Dressing	40.64
其他采矿业	Other Minerals Mining	0
农副食品加工业	Agricultural Non-staple Food Processing	18.71
食品制造业	Food Production	21.72
饮料制造业	Beverage Production	22.7
烟草制品业	Tobacco Products	0
纺织业	Textile Industry	11.06
纺织服装、鞋、帽制造业	Textile, Clothing and Footwear Production	10.7
皮革、毛皮、羽毛(绒)及其制品业	Leathers, Furs, Down and Related Products	19.26
木材加工及木、竹、藤、棕、草制品业	Timber Processing, Bamboo, Cane, Palm Fiber and Straw Products	2.06
家具制造业	Furniture Manufacturing	6.88
造纸及纸制品业	Papermaking and Paper Products	14.04
印刷业和记录媒介的复制	Printing and Record Processing	26.05
文教体育用品制造业	Stationery, Education and Sports Goods	11.74
石油加工、炼焦及核燃料加工业	Petroleum Processing, Coking and Nuclear Fuel Processing	18.43
化学原料及化学制品制造业	Raw Chemical Materials and Chemical Products	9.2
医药制造业	Medicine Manufacturing	11.98
化学纤维制造业	Chemical Fiber Manufacturing	7.28
橡胶制品业	Rubber Products	19.03
塑料制品业	Plastic Products	11.53
非金属矿物制品业	Nonmetal Mineral Products	6.74
黑色金属冶炼及压延加工业	Smelting and Pressing of Ferrous Metals	6.21
有色金属冶炼及压延加工业	Smelting and Pressing of Nonferrous Metals	-3.86
金属制品业	Metal Products	14.6
通用设备制造业	General-purpose Equipment Manufacturing	8.36
专用设备制造业	Special-purpose Equipment Manufacturing	22.28
交通运输设备制造业	Transportation Equipment Manufacturing	5.65
电气机械及器材制造业	Electric Equipments and Machinery Manufacturing	15.85
通信设备、计算机及其他电子设备制造业	Communication Equipment, Computers and Other Electronic Equipment Production	18.68
仪器仪表及文化、办公用机械制造业	Instruments, Meters, Culture and Office Equipments Manufacturing	19.86
工艺品及其他制造业	Handicraft Articles and Other Goods Production	12.94
废弃资源和废旧材料回收加工业	Discarded Resources and Waste Materials Recovery and Processing	0
电力、热力的生产和供应业	Power, Steam Production and Supply	9.04
燃气生产和供应业	Gas Production and Supply	10.01
水的生产和供应业	Tap Water Production and Supply	0
国有控股	State-holding Enterprises	6.68
三　资	Foreign Funded Enterprises	13.84
大中型	Large-scale and Medium-scale Enterprises	11.14

资产负债率（%） Assets Liability Ratio	流动资产周转次数（次/年） Number of times of Annual of Turnover Circulating Funds（Times/year）	工业成本费用利润率（%） Ratio of Profits to Industrial Cost	全员劳动生产率（元/人.年） Overall Labor Productivity（yuan/person-year）	产品销售率（%） Proportion of Products Sold
55.98	**2.73**	**6.3**	**84 287**	**97.59**
0	0	0	0	0
0	0	0	0	0
45.74	3.68	23.03	173 467	94.28
0	0	0	0	0
36.19	7.9	12.51	104 394	96.84
0	0	0	0	0
59.48	3.24	6.87	141 588	97.09
43.8	2.8	11.77	180 444	99.4
59.58	3.95	10.52	127 820	97.1
0	0	0	0	0
64.71	2.64	5.29	72 242	94.93
42.89	2.94	4.62	33 804	98.45
71.67	3.79	5.16	52 174	96.56
45.61	2.5	-1.16	44 465	100.54
77.44	2.1	2.3	75 778	98.38
51.71	2.03	8.74	89 297	100.45
29.48	2.03	17.32	123 298	113.41
62.84	2.51	4.94	43 670	103.47
67.33	2.73	8.32	164 170	98.09
48.98	2.9	4.32	179 736	102.82
34.64	1.73	6.01	91 996	93.3
49.26	1.8	4.02	125 851	98.91
52.67	3.1	7.74	50 011	98.92
55.23	2.68	5.06	89 790	98.27
43.17	2.05	4.65	123 525	92.98
66.78	2.3	1.65	212 413	98.78
78.35	4.83	-3.99	206 392	95.14
50.53	2.3	9.39	156 928	98.83
54.09	2.5	3.79	143 651	100.21
48	3.28	14.06	100 735	95.21
72.73	1.76	1.38	90 601	91.04
65.1	2.35	6.97	91 051	97.88
49.14	2.67	9.37	128 287	96.06
42.14	3.34	6.1	113 433	104.82
47.74	2.33	6.23	51 175	93.31
0	0	0	0	0
55.72	3.23	10.88	2 684 000	100
68.31	0.97	22.44	65 155	99.67
0	0	0	0	0
62.84	1.78	2.1	121 396	99.33
55.98	2.73	6.3	84 287	97.59
62.42	2.81	4.7	93 396	97.5

11－13 按行业分大中型工业企业主要经济效益指标（2005年）

MAIN INDICATORS ON ECONOMIC BENEFIT OF LARGE-SCALE AND MEDIUM-SCALE INDUSTRIAL ENTERPRISES BY SECTORS(2005)

行　业	Indicators	总资产贡献率(%) Ratio of Total Assets to Industrial Output Value
总　计	**Total**	**11.48**
煤炭开采和洗选业	Coal Mining and Dressing	0
石油和天然气开采业	Petroleum and Natural Gas Extraction	0
黑色金属矿采选业	Ferrous Metals Mining and Dressing	0
有色金属矿采选业	Nonferrous Metals Mining and Dressing	38.62
非金属矿采选业	Nonmetal Minerals Mining and Dressing	47.21
其他采矿业	Other Minerals Mining	0
农副食品加工业	Agricultural Non-staple Food Processing	15.86
食品制造业	Food Production	23.05
饮料制造业	Beverage Production	15.21
烟草制品业	Tobacco Products	55.03
纺织业	Textile Industry	9.36
纺织服装、鞋、帽制造业	Textile, Clothing and Footwear Production	7.92
皮革、毛皮、羽毛(绒)及其制品业	Leathers, Furs, Down and Related Products	17.61
木材加工及木、竹、藤、棕、草制品业	Timber Processing, Bamboo, Cane, Palm Fiber and Straw Products	63.31
家具制造业	Furniture Manufacturing	10.62
造纸及纸制品业	Papermaking and Paper Products	15.34
印刷业和记录媒介的复制	Printing and Record Processing	21.47
文教体育用品制造业	Stationery, Education and Sports Goods	14.4
石油加工、炼焦及核燃料加工业	Petroleum Processing, Coking and Nuclear Fuel Processing	6.55
化学原料及化学制品制造业	Raw Chemical Materials and Chemical Products	5.69
医药制造业	Medicine Manufacturing	11.77
化学纤维制造业	Chemical Fiber Manufacturing	6.71
橡胶制品业	Rubber Products	9.98
塑料制品业	Plastic Products	12.62
非金属矿物制品业	Nonmetal Mineral Products	7.17
黑色金属冶炼及压延加工业	Smelting and Pressing of Ferrous Metals	6.83
有色金属冶炼及压延加工业	Smelting and Pressing of Nonferrous Metals	2.82
金属制品业	Metal Products	20.7
通用设备制造业	General-purpose Equipment Manufacturing	12.55
专用设备制造业	Special-purpose Equipment Manufacturing	19.45
交通运输设备制造业	Transportation Equipment Manufacturing	5.56
电气机械及器材制造业	Electric Equipments and Machinery Manufacturing	9.9
通信设备、计算机及其他电子设备制造业	Communication Equipment, Computers and Other Electronic Equipment Production	12.44
仪器仪表及文化、办公用机械制造业	Instruments, Meters, Culture and Office Equipments Manufacturing	18.81
工艺品及其他制造业	Handicraft Articles and Other Goods Production	15.22
废弃资源和废旧材料回收加工业	Discarded Resources and Waste Materials Recovery and Processing	0.01
电力、热力的生产和供应业	Power, Steam Production and Supply	8.06
燃气生产和供应业	Gas Production and Supply	3.21
水的生产和供应业	Tap Water Production and Supply	2.61
国有控股	State-holding Enterprises	10.24
三　资	Foreign Funded Enterprises	11.14
大中型	Large-scale and Medium-scale Enterprises	11.48

资产负债率（%） Assets Liability Ratio	流动资产周转次数（次/年） Number of times of Annual of Turnover Circulating Funds (Times/year)	工业成本费用利润率（%） Ratio of Profits to Industrial Cost	全员劳动生产率（元/人.年） Overall Labor Productivity (yuan/person-year)	产品销售率（%） Proportion of Products Sold
59.3	**2.48**	**3.79**	**148 554**	**98.8**
0	0	0	0	0
0	0	0	0	0
0	0	0	0	0
54.9	4.81	24.3	49 125	98.09
37.56	6.12	13.64	123 535	95.18
0	0	0	0	0
62.37	3.27	4.9	135 209	96.37
53.36	4.16	7.92	158 450	97.9
33.67	1.32	11.26	199 662	119.78
37.99	1.57	24.35	1 803 282	102.72
65.75	2.47	4.03	81 087	97.87
51.67	1.93	5.07	45 158	95.11
76.51	3.31	5.31	66 965	97.23
22.7	5.04	7.8	452 775	95.84
68.87	2.7	4.2	82 844	96.76
56.8	2.6	6.93	91 269	94.38
44.37	1.9	15.6	139 923	104.02
68.67	2.33	6.66	63 508	109.92
68.67	3.09	-3.46	722 359	100.14
61.36	1.7	1.67	125 229	100.44
46.13	1.34	6.18	219 984	97.89
54.32	2.64	1.43	138 278	97.19
67.14	1.99	4.53	93 011	94
64.01	2.53	6.73	73 572	98.07
56.01	2.31	2.13	244 370	98.5
70.41	3.47	0.94	166 002	99.34
78.91	5.37	-2.04	363 375	94.2
54.02	2.79	10.14	228 376	98.09
69.17	2.02	5.2	164 058	95.76
42.53	2.31	11.52	119 869	95.87
70.17	1.55	2.74	112 139	96.72
52.76	2.56	3.41	330 537	100.2
55.55	4.12	2.4	180 059	98.79
47.25	5.14	1.18	161 579	101.08
49.6	2.11	5.91	68 349	95.32
3.35	18.1	0.01	1 043 602	100
70.93	2.18	1.1	328 632	99.33
40.55	1.23	2.11	113 552	107.88
59.38	0.88	3.73	82 482	100
59.83	2.12	2.35	187 533	100.95
62.42	2.81	4.7	93 396	97.5
59.3	2.48	3.79	148 554	98.8

11－14 主要年份主要工业产品产量

MAJOR YEAR'S OUTPUT OF MAJOR INDUSTRIAL PRODUCTS

年　份 Year	原　盐（万吨）Salt (10000 tons)	发电量（亿千瓦小时）Electricity (100 million kwh)	饮料酒（万吨）Beverage Liquor (10000 tons)	#啤　酒 Beer	卷　烟（万箱）Cigarette (10000 cases)	罐　头（吨）Cans (ton)	化学纤维（吨）Chemical Fibers (ton)	纱（吨）Yarn (ton)
1949	15.16	1.21	0.18	0.12	2.36	–	–	27 447
1952	35.08	2.11	0.37	0.18	12.27	–	–	59 674
1957	44.34	2.92	0.96	0.58	23.41	–	–	50 699
1962	38.6	3.86	1.58	0.79	16.59	–	28	17 939
1965	41.34	6.8	2.04	1.34	31.34	–	205	68 082
1970	29.96	10.57	3.39	2.55	42.16	–	621	85 591
1975	34.52	10.98	5.3	2.98	36	–	357	79 516
1978	60.68	13.63	6.25	3.75	44	4 743	1 413	85 233
1980	41.19	12.5	8.49	4.84	48.79	3 521	2 116	83 389
1985	47.34	26.97	13.76	10.05	51.81	6 400	1 747	91 839
1987	50.64	28.97	23.4	13.85	55.84	16 000	3 442	108 003
1988	53.28	29.35	26.61	15.58	57.01	27 200	3 393	107 720
1989	55.37	29.87	24.57	15.4	58.64	13 200	3 700	118 379
1990	35.7	40.22	29.18	19.61	61.94	–	2 900	100 381
1991	31.39	54.6	36.75	27.38	56.19	130 510	5 200	96 271
1992	46.24	58.63	44.59	37.01	59.37	3 200	6 000	99 043
1993	48.88	59.39	54.74	45.92	63.46	1 900	27 100	91 351
1994	53.02	59.62	60	50.92	69.2	2 300	21 400	86 744
1995	50.84	64.69	60.85	54.16	70.96	4 609	20 973	79 492
1996	41.39	83.02	61.79	54.4	73.04	1 719	22 945	66 832
1997	34.11	95.12	66.64	56.06	88.32	554	26 300	70 402
1998	19.08	79.65	47.33	42.79	77.1	–	23 858	66 504
1999	30.3	82	126.21	120.1	149	379	29 967	56 431
2000	41.83	90.84	211.47	206.5	148.1	225	65 362	69 560.6
2001	31.4	85.73	279.37	274.28	142.95	99	89 989	72 932.5
2002	42.5	89.7	323.2	320.6	138.1	11 690	91 394	70 888
2003	36.85	87.69	353.9	351.8	148	–	101 752	65 919.4
2004	34.36	89.01	393.3	390.6	147.1	10 889	115 187	71 930.61
2005	10	98.63	439.7	435.2	150.7	10 097	95 887	72 140.45

注：本表为规模以上工业。1998 年以前为乡及乡以上工业。

Note: The data in the form refer to industry above scale.

Befor 1998, the data refer to those at village level and above.

11 -14 续表 1
continued

年　份 Year	布 （万米） Cloth （10000 m）	印染布 （万米） Printed Fabric （10000 m）	呢　绒 （万米） Wool Fabric （10000 m）	丝织品 （万米） Silk Products （10000 m）	机制纸及纸板 （万吨） Paperboard （10000 tons）	硫　酸 （万吨） Sulphuric Acid （10000 tons）	烧　碱 （万吨） Caustic Soda （10000 tons）	纯　碱 （万吨） Soda （10000 tons）
1949	10 608	2 947	–	–	0.98	–	0.01	–
1952	30 069	13 658	–	–	0.44	–	0.17	–
1957	27 806	16 053	–	–	1.54	–	0.74	–
1962	7 444	7 375	–	243	1.45	0.06	0.89	–
1965	29 538	13 670	–	425	2.22	–	1.66	5.32
1970	33 660	21 994	–	371	3.14	0.04	2.14	12.01
1975	31 242	22 828	4	351	3.1	0.53	2.36	9.15
1978	36 877	25 797	27	395	4.55	1.32	3.61	14.04
1980	34 937	22 900	67	451	5.25	4.11	4.33	18.18
1985	34 998	17 679	164	716	6.2	3.34	5.52	26.03
1987	38 155	21 833	375	644	6.52	4.4	6.15	29.53
1988	35 890	21 213	400	626	7.42	4.88	6.62	31.12
1989	36 188	19 842	325	648	6.2	4.3	6.95	32.25
1990	34 066	21 446	306	563	6.02	4.86	6.73	30.48
1991	34 076	19 999	277	592	5.99	5.62	5.99	29.5
1992	33 682	21 534	239	367	5.95	6.7	5.62	34.6
1993	35 912	16 606	244	715	8.84	6.96	6.07	40.43
1994	43 241	16 387	259	123	12.36	8.33	6.48	43.36
1995	41 170	17 864	350	1713	11.06	9.69	7.9	43.2
1996	39 023	16 881	684	1 682	11.31	10.12	7.3	46.91
1997	43 615	15 722	524	415	7.78	10.16	8.45	50.55
1998	40 440	9 864	97	125	6.91	10.33	9.25	52.8
1999	39 576	4 340	–	140	7.77	12.56	8.96	53.7
2000	41 783	3 526	93	164	10.96	12.96	10.24	56.2
2001	40 640	3 402	130	219	23.05	13.03	11.44	58.47
2002	47 609	5 592	53	437	29.92	5.0	13.8	60.7
2003	35 922	10 131	77	1 379	31.76	4.5	13.53	62.5
2004	50 111	7 718	14	1 182	36.38	14.7	14.86	60.8
2005	51 307	16 027	–	–	31.95	14.8	16.1	62.5

11－14 续表 2
continued

年份 Year	合成氨（万吨） Synthetic Ammonia (10000 tons)	化学肥料（万吨） Chemical Fertilizer (10000 tons)	化学农药（吨） Chemical Pesticides (ton)	油漆（吨） Paint (ton)	染料（吨） Dye (ton)	肥皂（吨） Soap (ton)
1949	–	–	–	30	599	300
1952	–	–	–	480	2 855	2 000
1957	–	–	1 226	1 247	4 307	4 200
1962	–	0.45	213	910	3 560	3 000
1965	–	1.42	2	4 727	8 667	5 600
1970	0.98	5.89	2 313	6 380	9 347	11 300
1975	3.46	12.46	4 439	7 016	5 967	13 000
1978	7.17	23.66	9 714	8 786	5 877	13 200
1980	7.24	7.82	8 333	14 556	2 159	20 100
1985	6.31	5.16	2 000	26 055	4 448	23 244
1987	8.2	8.32	2 200	28 323	5 316	27 698
1988	8.72	9.41	2 400	28 943	5 527	28 136
1989	8.47	8.84	2 500	27 713	5 784	26 150
1990	7.56	7.55	2 500	29 075	5 119	24 009
1991	8.52	8.04	2 800	33 548	5 263	21 340
1992	10.45	7.85	3 400	35 058	4 821	20 862
1993	10.7	8.02	3 600	33 054	4 550	22 903
1994	13.04	12.39	3 600	29 437	5 097	27 905
1995	14.98	12.62	4 934	37 772	7 185	27 084
1996	18.67	12.62	4 976	26 762	7 668	26 578
1997	16.94	12.52	4 600	19 743	11 189	27 039
1998	22.36	15.3	6 755	17 594	8 274	26 355
1999	26.09	20.19	4 480	3 730	7 866	16 811
2000	24.64	20.04	3 758	693	9 306	15 585
2001	35.53	28.07	3 915	1 349	9 757	15 378
2002	20.3	9.8	4 020	1 701	9 826	13 804
2003	21.55	9.7	2 039	2 106	10 734	15 201
2004	30.3	19.6	5 061	1 955	3 961	14 670
2005	33.8	22.1	6 524	1 687	13 979	–

11 –14 续表 3
continued

年 份 Year	化学原料药 （吨） Chemical Raw Materials (ton)	水 泥 （万吨） Cement (10000 tons)	平板玻璃 （万重量箱） Plate Glass (10000 cases)	耐火材料 （万吨） Refractory Material (10000 tons)	钢 （万吨） Steel (10000 tons)	钢 材 （万吨） Rolled-steel (10000 tons)	日用精铝制品 （吨） Daily Use Aluminum Products (ton)
1949	–	–	–	–	0.0031	0.06	–
1952	–	–	–	0.78	0.36	0.41	–
1957	–	–	–	3.39	1.77	4.3	–
1962	–	2.09	–	2.41	4.59	2.94	–
1965	–	6.59	–	2.91	11.72	8.43	450
1970	–	7.35	16.31	3.23	19.38	14.56	927
1975	55.45	20.93	19.44	4.88	21.25	20.01	671
1978	184.59	35.4	8.86	5.93	31.06	27.61	1 706
1980	123.1	44.66	70.13	5.38	37.14	32.82	2 227
1984	7 228.21	70.27	91.25	7.98	37.81	32.43	2 880
1985	4 222	82.7	77	4.35	37.51	32.63	2 652
1987	7 457	117.2	87	4.9	46.51	38.09	3 292
1988	7 655	140.81	108.81	4.56	50.17	38.26	2 610
1989	8 348	135	96.49	3.68	54.64	39.38	2 112
1990	6 913	139.48	83.13	3.91	54.55	38.04	2 813
1991	4 754	165.66	96.9	3.71	56.96	39.02	1 988
1992	5 743	191.5	120	3.86	63.75	50.09	1 400
1993	6 566	221.3	148.71	3.55	61.75	44.88	882
1994	4 238	246.5	145.12	3.06	60.82	46.95	328
1995	1 993	213.82	426.4	3.88	67.27	49.6	689
1996	5 505	181.45	423.6	3.54	72.02	50.6	1 375
1997	1 693	208.04	570.85	2.45	75.71	51.06	859
1998	909.7	131.51	509.38	0.991	84.02	64.93	–
1999	1 691.47	149.41	576.5	0.59	108.1	86.58	–
2000	2 130.73	137.52	556.58	0.62	101.17	93.35	–
2001	2 534.17	148.67	421.51	0.51	124.45	119.77	–
2002	2 711.74	140.3	405.4	0.45	145.9	142.2	–
2003	3 287.91	154.9	361.4	0.47	204.8	204.3	–
2004	4 393.9	181.19	163.3	0.69	225.7	230.97	–
2005	4 430	210.8	297.5	1.04	309.7	330.3	–

11－14 续表 4
continued

年　份 Year	金属切削机床（台） Metal-cutting Machines(set)	锻压机械（台） Metal forming Machinery(set)	拖拉机（台） Tractors (set)	照相机（万架） Cameras (10000 sets)	汽　车（辆） Motor Vehicles (vehicle)	交流电动机（万千瓦） AC Motors (10000 kw)
1949	–	–	–	–	–	0.02
1952	105	–	–	–	–	0.5
1957	76	–	–	–	–	3.61
1962	167	77	–	–	–	3.85
1965	526	111	–	–	13	6.48
1970	2 353	531	16 400	–	120	14.53
1975	3 213	788	2 987	0.03	490	15.56
1978	2 558	379	309	0.07	22	21.72
1980	595	444	3 540	0.1	1 644	20.11
1985	900	607	10 661	2.72	4 575	26.08
1987	1 175	887	16 107	10	2 304	27.02
1988	1 336	737	21 031	17.1	3 722	39.6
1989	1 107	1 010	27 755	14.23	3 404	38.6
1990	1 049	440	18 456	14.7	2 317	34.28
1991	869	764	13 905	24.6	1 514	44.17
1992	1 018	982	16 800	35.2	3 287	61.08
1993	1 532	919	4 051	36.03	4 828	64.13
1994	1 505	860	8 478	35.02	2 793	37.71
1995	972	2 563	17 918	67.25	5 210	39.18
1996	1 084	584	21 308	84.554	12 247	22.65
1997	449	416	27 569	81.41	13 020	20.74
1998	280	–	10 016	44.48	15 475	6.43
1999	251	–	21 186	19.58	20 038	11.1
2000	384	–	3 702	7.04	30 053	38.7
2001	472	2 477	2 129	–	40 658	42.72
2002	588	–	50	–	70 079	68.25
2003	990	–	–	–	65 612	95.63
2004	1 287	–	–	–	62 572	96.13
2005	1 347	–	–	–	31 055	63.5

11 -14 续表 5
continued

年　份 Year	钢芯铝绞线 （吨）Steel-cored Aluminum Stranded Wire(ton)	家用电冰箱 （万台）Household Refrigerators (10000 sets)	家用洗衣机 （万台）Household Washing Machines (10000 sets)	电视机 （万部）Television Sets (10000 sets)	#彩　电 Color TV Sets	显像管 （万只）Tubes (10000 units)	手　表 （万只）Watches (10000 units)
1949	–	–	–	–	–	–	–
1952	–	–	–	–	–	–	–
1957	–	–	–	–	–	–	–
1962	–	–	–	–	–	–	0.39
1965	250	–	–	–	–	–	0.85
1970	34	–	–	–	–	0.05	5.01
1975	188	–	–	0.05	–	0.07	17.07
1978	684	–	–	0.25	–	0.39	53.25
1980	1 232	–	–	4	–	2.8	80.03
1985	2 327	1.66	0.48	17.06	6.6	38.44	150
1987	2 849	9.08	22.08	26.05	14.2	38.95	145
1988	1 571	15.22	42.38	36.5	17	44.5	177.2
1989	2 805	21.65	35.02	41.23	18.11	47.47	194
1990	1 880	7.41	45.86	50.5	18.5	52.86	202
1991	2 463	31.51	45.7	48.13	22.27	33.04	220
1992	2 248	54.84	46.31	32.33	28.07	11.43	199.9
1993	1 144	50.48	56.59	43.53	36.08	–	283.58
1994	287	62.5	71.34	73.41	60.15	4.84	275.03
1995	1 659	107.91	64.34	76.78	60.53	15.86	283.83
1996	2 265	193.8	100.94	62.27	56.68	25.82	233.09
1997	2 616	257.1	171.95	137.11	124.86	22.84	140.77
1998	1 725.3	219.23	183.67	97.5	96.83	–	–
1999	2 805.2	259.6	256.3	297.7	285.2	–	–
2000	4 201.5	311.1	318.5	383.8	379.4	–	–
2001	4 498	396.3	367.89	458.2	455.4	–	–
2002	5 825	518.2	408.6	596.2	593.2	–	–
2003	4 940	598.3	471.5	673.7	671.7	–	–
2004	6 608	815.03	575.06	958.8	957.9	–	–
2005	116 592	908.8	614.9	1 324.3	1 324.3	–	–

11－15 主要工业产品产量(2005年)
OUTPUT OF MAJOR INDUSTRIAL PRODUCTS(2005)

产品名称	Name	计量单位	Unit	2005年 2005	2005年比2004年(±%) 2005/2004(±%)
冶金工业产品	**Products of Metallurgical Industry**				
钢	steel	万吨	10000 tons	309.7	37.2
钢材	Rolled-steel	万吨	10000 tons	330.3	43.9
耐火材料制品	Refractory Material	万吨	10000 tons	1.03	50.2
电力工业产品	**Products of Electricity Industry**				
发电量	Electricity	亿千瓦小时	100 million kwh	98.6	11.01
化学工业产品	**Products of Chemical Industry**				
原油加工量	Processing Amount of Crude Oil	万吨	10000 tons	378.9	-21.9
汽　油	Petrol	万吨	10000 tons	55.6	-12.1
煤　油	Kerosene	万吨	10000 tons		
柴　油	Diesel Oil	万吨	10000 tons	88.4	-15.5
燃烧油	Fuel Oil	万吨	10000 tons	145.6	-7.1
硫　酸	Sulphuric Acid	万吨	10000 tons	14.8	1.03
纯　碱	Soda	万吨	10000 tons	62.5	2.6
烧　碱	Caustic Soda	万吨	10000 tons	14.8	1.03
农用化肥(100%)	Ag-fertilizer(100%)	万吨	10000 tons	22.1	12.7
合成氨	Synthetic Ammonia	万吨	10000 tons	33.8	3.9
化学农药	Chemical Pesticides	万吨	10000 tons	0.65	74.5
染　料	Dye	吨	ton	13 979	17.7
油　漆	Paint	吨	ton	1 687	-0.4
塑　料	Plastic	吨	ton	77 215.7	23.5
化学药品(原料)	Chemical Medicines(Raw Materials)	吨	ton	4 430	52.3
轮胎外胎	Tires	万条	10000 lines	3 967.3	96.9
机械工业产品	**Machinery Industry**				
工业锅炉	Industrial Boiler	蒸发量吨	ton(evaporation amount)	1 894	8
交流电动机	AC Motors	万千瓦	10000 kw	63.5	-33.9
钢芯铝绞线	Steel-cored Aluminum Stranded Wire	吨	ton	116 592	34.9
金属切削机床	Metal-cutting Machines	台	set	1 347	4.7
汽　车	Motor Vehicles	辆	vehicle	31 055	-50.4
改装汽车	Refitted Motor Vehicles	辆	vehicle	6 144	-28.8

11 -15 续表 1
continued

产品名称	Name	计量单位	Unit	2005 年 2005	2005 年比 2004 年（±%） 2005/2004（±%）
客　车	Passenger Buses	辆	vehicle	408	-15.7
民用钢质船舶	Civil Steel Ships	综合吨	syn-ton	22 641	226.2
电子产品	**Electronic Products**				
电视机	Television Sets	万部	10000 sets	1 324.3	38.3
#彩　电	Color TV Sets	万部	10000 sets	1 324.3	38.3
程控交换机	Program-controlled Exchanges	万线	10000 lines	151.16	-50
电子元件	Electronics	万只	10000 units	4	16.6
半导体集成电路	Semiconductor Integrated Circuits	万块	10000 pieces	0.9	32.4
建材工业产品	**Products of Construction Industry**				
水　泥	Cement	万吨	10000 tons	210.8	19.9
平板玻璃	Plate Glass	万重量箱	10000 cases	297.5	100.6
砖（折标准砖）	Bricks	万块	10000 pieces	995	-5.3
纺织工业产品	**Products of Textile Industry**				
纱	Yarn	吨	ton	72 140.5	4.04
布	Cloth	万米	10000 m	51 307.2	-0.75
印染布	Printed Fabric	万米	10000 m	16 027.4	55.2
帘子布	Cord Fabrics	吨	ton	0	0
毛　线	Knitting Wool	吨	ton	12 560	0.34

11 -15 续表 2
continued

产品名称	Name	计量单位	Unit	2005 年 2005	2005 年比 2004 年 (±%) 2005/2004 (±%)
呢　绒	Wool Fabric	万米	10000 m	0	0
化学纤维	Chemical Fibers	万吨	10000 tons	9.6	10
丝织品	Silk Products	万米	10000 m	0	0
针棉织品折用纱线	Cotton Products	万吨	10000 tons	2.54	-0.9
轻工产品	**Products of Light Industry**				
机制纸及纸板	Paperboard	万吨	10000 tons	31.95	45.2
洗衣机	Washing Machines	万台	10000 sets	61.5	6.9
原　盐	Salt	万吨	10000 tons	10	-16.7
糖　果	Sweets	万吨	10000 tons	248	9.7
卷　烟	Cigarette	万箱	10000 cases	150.7	2.42
食用植物油	Vegetable Oil	万吨	10000 tons	27.5	14.4
饮料酒	Beverage Liquor	万吨	10000 tons	439.7	12.5
#白　酒	White Spirit	万吨	10000 tons	1.16	-1.6
#啤　酒	Beer	万吨	10000 tons	435.2	11
塑料制品	Plastic Products	吨	ton	77 215.8	23.7
家　具	Furniture	万件	10000 units	332.4	-28.1
电冰箱	Household Refrigerator	万台	10000 sets	908.8	11.5
皮　鞋	Leather Shoes	万双	10000 pairs	2 985	12.1
服　装	Garments	万件	10000 articles	53 033.64	24.4

11－16 主要工业产品生产能力(2005 年)

PRODUCTION CAPACITY OF MAJOR INDUSTRIAL PRODUCTS(2005)

产品名称	Name	计算单位	Unit	年初生产能力 Year-beginning Production Capacity	年末生产能力 Year-end Production Capacity
冶金工业产品	**Products of Metallurgical Industry**				
钢	Steel	万吨/年	10000 tons/year	362	362
转炉钢	Shifting Furnace Steel	万吨/年	10000 tons/year	361	361
钢　材	Rolled-steel	万吨/年	10000 tons/year	906.8	906.8
电力工业产品	**Products of Electricity Industry**				
发电设备装机容量	Installed Capacity of Power Generating Equipments	万千瓦/年	10000 kw/year	184	214
石油工业产品	**Products of Petroleum Industry**				
原油加工量	Processing Amount of Crude Oil	万吨/年	10000 tons/year	333	333
化学工业产品	**Products of Chemical Industry**				
硫　酸(100%)	Sulphuric Acid(100%)	吨/年	ton/year	190 500	190 500
盐　酸	Hydrochloric Acid	吨/年	ton/year	140 000	140 000
纯　碱	Soda	吨/年	ton/year	60 000	60 000
烧　碱	Caustic Soda	吨/年	ton/year	142 000	142 000
小苏打	Sodium Bicarbonate	吨/年	ton/year	30 000	30 000
合成氨	Synthetic Ammonia	吨/年	ton/year	369 000	369 000
农用化肥	Ag-fertilizer	吨/年	ton/year	470 360	470 360
化学农药(100%)	Chemical Pesticides(100%)	吨/年	ton/year	7 100	7 100
塑　料	Plastic	吨/年	ton/year	123 000	123 000
染　料	Dye	吨/年	ton/year	10 460	10 460
油　漆	Paint	吨/年	ton/year	20 000	20 000
轮胎外胎	Tires	万条/年	10000 lines/year	478 500	478 500
手推车外胎	Handcart Tires	万条/年	10000 lines/year	3 580	3 580
运输带	Conveyer Belts	万平方米/年	10000 sq. m/year	5 217	5 217

11 －16 续表
continued

产品名称	Name	计算单位	Unit	年初 生产能力 Year-beginning Production Capacity	年末 生产能力 Year-end Production Capacity
胶　管	Rubber Pipeline	万标米/年	10000 m/year	831	831
化学原料药	Chemical Raw Materials	吨/年	ton/year	12 520	12 520
建材工业产品	**Products of Construction Industry**				
水　泥	Cement	万吨/年	10000 tons/year	872	872
平板玻璃	Plate Glass	万重箱/年	10000 cases/year	815	820
机械工业产品	**Machinery Industry**				
汽　车	Motor Vehicles	辆/年	vehicle/year	97 000	97 000
内燃机车	Internal Combustion Engines	台/年	set/year	150	150
电子工业产品	**Electronic Products**				
彩　电	Color TV Sets	万台/年	10000 sets/year	1 282	1 282
电度表	Electricity Meters	万只/年	10000 units/year	430	430
电冰箱	Household Refrigerator	万台/年	10000 sets/year	1 532	1 532
洗衣机	Washing Machines	万台/年	10000 sets/year	620	620
纺织工业产品	**Products of Textile Industry**				
化学纤维	Chemical Fibers	吨/年	ton/year	103 000	103 000
轻工产品	**Products of Light Industry**				
原　盐	Salt	万吨/年	10000 tons/year	269	269
卷烟(三班)	Cigarette	万箱/年	10000 cases/year	256	260.3
啤　酒	Beer	万吨/年	10000 tons/year	82	82

CHAPTER 12

第十二篇

建筑业

CONSTRUCTION

编辑单位：固定资产投资统计处
编　　委：王金峰
编　　辑：钱孝高
校　　对：钱孝高
电　　话：85912252

12－1 建筑业企业生产情况(2005 年)
PRODUCTING STATISTICS OF CONSTRUCTION ENTERPRISES(2005)

项 目	Items	单位	Unit	合计 Total	国有企业 State-owned Enterprises	#中央 of which: Central Enterprises	集体企业 Collective-owned Enterprises	其他所有制企业 Other Ownership Enterprises
一、施工企业单位数	**Number of Construction Enterprises**	**个**	**unit**	**602**	**36**	**6**	**42**	**518**
二、建筑业总产值	**Gross Output Value of Construction**	**万元**	**10000 yuan**	**3 484 664**	**901 684**	**628 863**	**171 312**	**1 782 805**
#建筑工程	Construction Projects	万元	10000 yuan	3 031 232	759 403	494 528	153 320	1 623 981
安装工程	Installation Projects	万元	10000 yuan	327 118	113 183	108 955	16 598	88 382
三、建筑业增加值*	**Added Value of Construction**	**万元**	**10000 yuan**	**1 329 600**				
四、全年竣工产值	**Gross Output Value of Building Completed of the Year**	**万元**	**10000 yuan**	**2 073 378**	**518 094**	**304 955**	**111 604**	**1 138 725**
五、施工房屋面积	**Floor Space of Building under Construction**	**万平方米**	**10000 sq. m**	**3 864**	**1 008**	**312**	**166**	**2 378**
#新开工	of which: Newly Operating	万平方米	10000 sq. m	2 044	380	99	116	1 449
投标承包	Bidding and Contracting	万平方米	10000 sq. m	3 431	1 002	311	152	1 966
六、竣工房屋面积	**Floor Space of Building Completed**	**万平方米**	**10000 sq. m**	**1 517**	**282**	**41**	**74**	**1 120**
#住 宅	of which: Residence	万平方米	10000 sq. m	826	161	8	48	609
七、年末自有施工机械设备台数	**Machinery and Equipment(year-end)**	**台**	**set**	**65 996**	**12 241**	**3 500**	**5 916**	**44 339**
八、年末自有施工机械设备净值	**Net Value of Machinery and Equipment (year-end)**	**万元**	**10000 yuan**	**179 876**	**51 560**	**45 874**	**9 745**	**72 697**
九、年末自有施工机械设备总功率	**Power of Machinery and Equipment(year-end)**	**万千瓦**	**10000 kw**	**112**	**18**	**18**	**10**	**66**
十、计算建筑业劳动生产率平均人数	**Average Number of Persons for Calculating the Labor Productivity**	**人**	**person**	**336 705**	**57 454**	**22 211**	**26 178**	**230 862**

注:建筑业增加值指标与2004年之前计算方法和口径不一致。现指标为省局反馈建筑业全行业增加值。

Note: The calculation and calibre of the added value of construction are diffierent from those in 2004. Now the indicator is fedback by Shandong Statistical Bureau and refers to the added value of all sectors of construction.

12－2 建筑业企业财务状况(2005 年)

FINANCIAL POSITION OF CONSTRUCTION ENTERPRISES(2005)

项　目	Items	单位	Unit	合计 Total
一、流动资产	**Circulation Funders**	**万元**	**10000 yuan**	**2 698 265**
#存货	of which:Stock	万元	10000 yuan	645 168
二、年末固定资产原价	**Original Value of Fixed Assets(year-end)**	**万元**	**10000 yuan**	**783 923**
#生产经营用	of which:for Business	万元	10000 yuan	579 973
三、本年固定资产折旧	**Depreciation of Fixed Assets in the Year**	**万元**	**10000 yuan**	**43 591**
四、年末固定资产净值	**Net Value of Fixed Assets(year-end)**	**万元**	**10000 yuan**	**560 802**
五、年末资产合计	**Total Assets(year-end)**	**万元**	**10000 yuan**	**3 591 099**
六、年末负债合计	**Total Liabilities(year-end)**	**万元**	**10000 yuan**	**2 547 758**
七、所有者权益合计	**Total Owners Right and Interests**	**万元**	**10000 yuan**	**1 043 341**
#实收资本	Paid-up Capital	万元	10000 yuan	824 195
八、工程结算收入	**Revenue of Engineering Settlement Accounts**	**万元**	**10000 yuan**	**3 087 720**
工程结算成本	Cost of Engineering Settlement Accounts	万元	10000 yuan	2 725 127
工程结算税金及附加	Tax and Extra Charges of Engineering Settlement Accounts	万元	10000 yuan	103 723
工程结算利润	After-tax Profits of Engineering Settlement Accounts	万元	10000 yuan	219 492
九、管理费用	**Management Costs**	**万元**	**10000 yuan**	**135 780**
十、利润总额	**Total After-tax Profits**	**万元**	**10000 yuan**	**68 749**
十一、利税总额	**Total Profit and Tax**	**万元**	**10000 yuan**	**177 340**
十二、年末应收工程款	**Year-end Receivable Project Funds**	**万元**	**10000 yuan**	**747 376**
#其中:竣工工程	of which:Completed Project	万元	10000 yuan	401 405

12 -2 续表
continued

国有企业 State-owned	#中央 of which: Central Enterprises	集体企业 Collective-owned Enterprises	其他所有制企业 Other Ownership Enterprises
723 719	**334 824**	**108 493**	**1 866 053**
66 108	33 393	35 705	543 355
185 195	**121 519**	**70 626**	**406 583**
120 377	84 156	58 567	316 873
11 458	**8 740**	**1 717**	**21 676**
112 783	**70 111**	**59 662**	**318 246**
915 076	**466 964**	**175 432**	**2 033 627**
773 398	**413 435**	**131 983**	**1 228 942**
141 678	**53 529**	**43 449**	**804 685**
133 189	51 319	41 122	598 565
1 050 174	**658 549**	**95 661**	**1 283 336**
947 567	604 663	84 591	1 088 306
33 859	21 368	2 828	45 668
54 062	31 913	6 247	127 270
42 506	**20 977**	**4 612**	**67 685**
12 495	**9 918**	**1 203**	**45 133**
47 438	**31 654**	**4 301**	**93 947**
286 268	**126 176**	**20 227**	**314 705**
161 472	60 094	12 896	166 943

12－3 建筑业企业主要经济效益指标(2005 年)

MAIN INDICATORS ON ECONOMIC BENEFIT OF CONSTRUCTION ENTERPRISES(2005)

项 目	Items	单位	Unit	合计 Total	国有企业 State-owned	#中央企业 of which: Central Enterprises	集体企业 Collective-owned Enterprises	其他所有制企业 Other Ownership Enterprises
一、建筑业劳动生产率	**Labor Productivity of Construction**							
按总产值计算	In Term of Gross Output Value	元/人	yuan/person	103 493	156 940	283 131	65 441	77 224
二、竣工率	**Rate of Building Completed**							
按产值计算	In Term of Output Value	%	%	59.5	57.5	48.5	65.1	63.9
三、产值工资率	**Rate of Wage/Gross Output Value**	%	%	**13.9**	**12.9**	**7.4**	**19.6**	**15.4**
四、资金利润率	**Rate of Profit/Fund**	%	%	**2.1**	**1.5**	**2.2**	**0.7**	**2.5**
五、产值利润率	**Rate of Profit/Gross Output Value**	%	%	**2.0**	**1.4**	**1.6**	**0.7**	**2.5**
六、技术装备率	**Per Capita Machinery**	元/人	yuan/person	**5 776**	**9 669**	**18 615**	**3 773**	**3 528**
七、流动比率	**Current Rate**	%	%	**111.4**	**101.5**	**95.6**	**87.3**	**125.3**
八、资产负债率	**Rate of Liabilities/Assets**	%	%	**70.9**	**84.5**	**88.5**	**75.2**	**60.4**

12 -4 建筑业增加值(2005 年)
ADDED VALUE OF CONSTRUCTION(2005)

单位:万元(10 000 yuan)

市、区名称	Region	增加值 Added Value
总　计	**Total**	**1 329 600**
市南区	Urban Area	98 100
市北区	Shibei District	83 800
四方区	Sifang District	29 900
李沧区	Licang District	51 000
黄岛区	Huangdao District	169 000
崂山区	Laoshan District	100 300
城阳区	Chengyang District	122 900
胶州市	Jiaozhou	155 000
即墨市	Jimo	176 700
平度市	Pingdu	98 000
胶南市	Jiaonan	141 000
莱西市	Laixi	103 900

12 -5 重点建筑企业一览表(2005 年)
LIST OF IMPORTANT CONSTRUCTION CORPORATION(2005)

序号 Precedence	企业单位名称	Name	所在地区 Location	资质等级 Class
1	青岛建设集团公司	Qingdao Construction Group Corporation	市北区	1001
2	中港第一航务工程局第二工程公司	No. 2 Engineering Company CHEC	市南区	1104
3	中铁二十局集团第四工程有限公司	China Railway 20 Bureau Group No. 4 Project Co. ,Ltd.	崂山区	1103
4	山东莱钢建设有限公司	Shandong Laigang Construction Co. ,Ltd.	市南区	1108
5	中国石油天然气第七建设公司	Petro China No. 7 Construction Corp.	胶州市	1109
6	中国建筑第八工程局青岛分公司	China Construction Qingdao Branch Bureau	市南区	1001
7	青岛市胶州建设集团有限公司	Qingdao Jiaozhou Construction Group Co. ,Ltd.	胶州市	1101
8	山东省筑港总公司	Shandong Ports Construction Corp.	四方区	1104
9	中国建筑土木工程公司第四建筑公司	China Construction Project Corp. No. 4 Corp.	市南区	1101
10	莱西市建筑总公司	Laixi Construction Corp.	莱西市	1101
11	山东兴华建设集团有限公司	Shandong Xinghua Construction Group Co. ,Ltd.	黄岛区	1101
12	青岛第一市政工程有限公司	Qingdao No. 1 Municipal Administration Project Co. ,Ltd.	四方区	1110
13	青岛市第二建筑工程公司	Qingdao No. 2 Construction Project Corp.	市北区	1101
14	青岛瑞源工程集团有限公司	Qingdao Ruiyuan Project Group Co. ,Ltd.	黄岛区	1201
15	青岛海尔家居集成股份有限公司	Qingdao Haier Home Decoration Co. ,Ltd.	崂山区	2103
16	青岛建设集团零零一工程有限公司	Qingdao Construction Group 001 Project Co. ,Ltd.	市北区	1101
17	青岛胶城建设集团有限公司	Qingdao Jiaocheng Construction Group Co. ,Ltd.	胶州市	1101
18	青岛一宅建筑集团股份有限公司	Qingdao No. 1 Residence Construction Group Co. ,Ltd.	市北区	1101
19	青岛恒源电力股份有限公司	Qingdao Hengyuan Electricity Co. ,Ltd.	市南区	2249
20	青岛经济技术开发区城市建设集团有限公司	Qingdao Development Zone City Construction Group Co. ,Ltd.	黄岛区	1201
21	青岛福瀛建设集团有限公司	Qingdao Fuying Construction Group Co. ,Ltd.	黄岛区	1101
22	青岛亿联集团股份有限公司	Qingdao Yilian Group Co. ,Ltd.	胶南市	1101
23	青岛市华鲁公路工程有限公司	Qingdao Hualu Highway Project Co. ,Ltd.	胶南市	1202
24	青岛市泽惠建设集团有限公司	Qingdao Zehui Construction Group Co. ,Ltd.	城阳区	1101
25	胶南市市政工程管理公司	Jiaonan Municipal Administration Project Co. ,Ltd.	胶南市	1301
26	平度市建筑安装集团公司	Pingdu Construction and Installation Group Co. ,Ltd.	平度市	1101
27	青岛市城阳区院后庄建筑公司	Qingdao Chengyang Yuanhouzhuang Construction Corp.	城阳区	2203
28	胶南市自来水供水工程公司	Jiaonan Tap Water Supply Project Corp.	胶南市	1301
29	青岛铁路工程建筑有限公司	Qingdao Railway Project Construction Co. ,Ltd.	市南区	1203
30	青岛通广建工集团有限公司	Qingdao Tongguang Construction Project Co. ,Ltd.	即墨市	1101
31	青岛市神州建筑工程有限公司	Qingdao Shenzhou Construction Project Co. ,Ltd.	胶州市	1201
32	青岛安装建设股份有限公司	Qingdao Installation and Construction Co. ,Ltd.	四方区	1112
33	青岛立中建筑工程有限公司	Qingdao Lizhong Construction Project Co. ,Ltd.	胶州市	1201

12 -5 续表
continued

序号 Precedence	企业单位名称	Name	所在地区 Location	资质等级 Class
34	青岛城建集团有限公司	Qingdao City Construction Group Co. ,Ltd.	四方区	1110
35	青岛青房建安集团有限公司	Qingdao Qingfang Construction Group Co. ,Ltd.	市南区	1201
36	青岛市第一建筑工程公司	Qingdao No. 1 Construction Project Corp.	四方区	1101
37	即墨市泰康建筑工程有限公司	Jimo Taikang Construction Project Co. ,Ltd.	即墨市	1201
38	青岛宏远建筑工程有限公司	Qingdao Hongyuan Construction Project Co. ,Ltd.	莱西市	1201
39	青岛荣昌基础建设工程有限公司	Qingdao Rongchang Construction Project Co. ,Ltd.	黄岛区	2205
40	青岛港务局港务工程公司	Qingdao Port Project Corp.	黄岛区	1204
41	青岛胶州湾建设集团有限公司	Qingdao Jiaozhou Bay Construction Group Co. ,Ltd.	胶州市	1101
42	青岛八方路桥工程有限公司	Qingdao Bafang Highway & Bridge Project Co. ,Ltd.	胶南市	1302
43	即墨恒生源建筑工程有限公司	Jimo Hengshengyuan Construction Project Co. ,Ltd.	即墨市	1101
44	青岛金沙滩建设集团有限公司	Qingdao Jinsha Beach Construction Co. ,Ltd.	黄岛区	1201
45	即墨市温泉建筑工程有限公司	Jimo Hot Spring Construction Project Co. ,Ltd.	即墨市	1101
46	青岛正东建设集团有限公司	Qingdao Zhengdong Construction Co. ,Ltd.	黄岛区	1204
47	青岛胶州南关建安股份有限公司	Qingdao Jiaozhou Nanguan Construction and Installation Co. ,Ltd.	胶州市	1201
48	青岛市盈鑫建筑集团有限公司	Qingdao Yingxin Construction Group Co. ,Ltd.	城阳区	1201
49	青岛胶南海天建筑工程有限公司	Qingdao Jiaonan Haitian Construction Project Co. ,Ltd.	胶南市	1301
50	青岛金茂建设工程有限公司	Qingdao Jinmao Construction Project Co. ,Ltd.	胶南市	1301
51	青岛建国工程集团有限公司	Qingdao Jianguo Project Group Co. ,Ltd.	黄岛区	1201
52	青岛联晟建筑工程有限公司	Qingdao Liansheng Construction Project Co. ,Ltd.	胶州市	1201
53	青岛福海洋建设工程有限公司	Qingdao Fusea Construction Project Co. ,Ltd.	胶州市	1201
54	青岛武晓铁塔安装有限公司	Qingdao Wuxiao Iron Tower Installation Co. ,Ltd.	黄岛区	2208
55	胶南市宏华建筑安装工程公司	Jiaonan Honghua Construction and Installation Co. ,Ltd.	胶南市	1301
56	青岛福盛建设集团有限公司	Qingdao Fusheng Construction Group Co. ,Ltd.	城阳区	1201
57	青岛泰华集团有限公司	Qingdao Taihua Group Co. ,Ltd.	胶南市	1201
58	青岛中兴建设集团有限责任公司	Qingdao Zhongxing Construction Group Co. ,Ltd.	平度市	1201
59	青岛胜利兄弟建筑有限公司	Qingdao Victory Brother Construction Co. ,Ltd.	胶州市	1201
60	青岛九龙建设工程有限公司	Qingdao Jiulong Construction Project Co. ,Ltd.	胶州市	1201
61	青岛公路建设集团有限公司	Qingdao Highway Construction Group Co. ,Ltd.	四方区	1102
62	青岛新世纪路桥工程有限公司	Qingdao New Century Highway & Bridge Project Co. ,Ltd.	即墨市	1302
63	青岛德泰建筑工程有限公司	Qingdao Detai Construction Project Co. ,Ltd.	黄岛区	1201
64	青岛万通公路工程有限公司	Qingdao Wantong Highway Project Co. ,Ltd.	胶南市	2327
65	山东杭萧钢构有限公司	Shandong hangxiao Co. ,Ltd.	胶州市	2208
66	青岛经济技术开发区建筑安装工程总公司	Qingdao Development Zone City Construction Group Co. ,Ltd.	黄岛区	1201

12 –5 续表
continued

序号 Precedence	企业单位名称	Name	所在地区 Location	资质等级 Class
67	青岛三林建筑工程有限公司	Qingdao Sanlin Construction Project Co. ,Ltd.	胶南市	1301
68	青岛洋河建设工程有限公司	Qingdao Yanghe Construction Project Co. ,Ltd.	胶州市	1201
69	胶南市大场镇建筑工程公司	Jiaonan Dachangzhen Construction Corp.	胶南市	1301
70	胶南市圣海建筑工程公司	Jiaonan Shenghai Construction Project Co. ,Ltd.	胶南市	1301
71	青岛环城置业集团有限公司	Qingdao Huancheng Group Co. ,Ltd.	黄岛区	1201
72	青岛东方恒升集团有限公司	Qingdao East Hengsheng Group Co. ,Ltd.	胶南市	1201
73	青岛四机建筑安装有限公司	Qingdao Siji Construction Project Co. ,Ltd.	四方区	2201
74	青岛星火建筑工程有限公司	Qingdao Spark Construction Project Co. ,Ltd.	胶南市	1301
75	青岛东恒建筑工程有限公司	Qingdao dongheng Construction Project Co. ,Ltd.	胶南市	1201
76	青岛市胶南镇东建筑工程公司	Qingdao Jiaonan Zhendong Construction Project Co. ,Ltd.	胶南市	1301
77	青岛市城阳区仙家寨建筑工程公司	Qingdao Chengyang District Xianjiazhai Construction Project Co. ,Ltd.	城阳区	1201
78	胶州市广厦建筑安装有限公司	Jiaozhou Guangsha Construction and Installation Co. ,Ltd.	胶州市	1201
79	青岛营海建设集团有限公司	Qingdao Yinghai Construction Group Co. ,Ltd.	胶州市	1201
80	青岛光大集团工程有限公司	Qingdao Guangda Group Project Co. ,Ltd.	胶南市	1201
81	胶南市隐珠镇建筑工程公司	Jiaonan Yinzhuzhen Construction Co. ,Ltd.	胶南市	1301
82	青岛城阳太阳城建筑有限公司	Qingdao Chengyang Suncity Construction Co. ,Ltd.	城阳区	1301
83	胶州市阳光建筑有限公司	Jiaozhou Sunshine Construction Co. ,Ltd.	胶州市	1201
84	青岛城阳兴源建筑工程有限公司	Qingdao Chengyang Construction Project Co. ,Ltd.	城阳区	1301
85	青岛城阳城建有限公司	Qingdao Chengyang Chengjian Co. ,Ltd.	城阳区	1201
86	青岛富华泰建筑有限公司	Qingdao Fuhuatai Construction Co. ,Ltd.	胶州市	1201
87	胶南市建筑工程公司	Jiaonan Construction Project Corp.	胶南市	1201
88	平度市金泰建筑有限公司	Pingdu Jintai Construction Co. ,Ltd.	平度市	1201
89	平度市李园建筑安装有限责任公司	Pingdu Liyuan Construction and Installation Co. ,Ltd.	平度市	1201
90	青岛莱西市通达公路工程有限公司	Qingdao Laixi Tongda Highway Project Co. ,Ltd.	莱西市	1202
91	青岛河南建筑工程有限公司	Qingdao Henan Construction Project Corp.	即墨市	1201
92	青岛弘海建设有限公司	Qingdao Honghai Construction Co. ,Ltd.	市南区	1201
93	青岛昶德建设工程有限公司	Qingdao Changde Construction Project Co. ,Ltd.	胶州市	1201
94	青岛市李沧建筑安装工程有限公司	Qingdao Licang Construction and Installation Project Co. ,Ltd.	李沧区	1201
95	青岛经济技术开发区市政工程总公司	Qingdao Economic Development Zone Municipal Administration Project Co. ,Ltd.	黄岛区	1210
96	青岛胶南万德建筑工程有限公司	Qingdao Jiaonan Wande Construction Project Co. ,Ltd.	胶南市	1301
97	青岛施运机械施工有限责任公司	Qingdao Shiyun Machinery Construction Co. ,Ltd.	四方区	2201
98	青岛岳海建筑工程有限公司	Qingdao Yuehai Construction Project Corp.	崂山区	1301
99	胶南市新兴建筑工程公司	Jiaonan Xinxing Construction Project Corp.	胶南市	1301

12 -5 续表
continued

序号 Precedence	企业单位名称	Name	所在地区 Location	资质等级 Class
100	青岛新城发展建筑工程有限公司	Qingdao Xincheng Development Construction Project Co. ,Ltd.	市北区	1201
101	青岛鑫隆建设集团有限公司	Qingdao Xinlong Construction Group Co. ,Ltd.	黄岛区	1201
102	青岛凌云建设工程有限公司	Qingdao Lingyun Construction Project Co. ,Ltd.	胶州市	1201
103	胶南市琅琊建筑工程公司	Jiaonan Langya Construction Corp.	胶南市	1301
104	青岛圣达建筑工程有限公司	Qingdao Shengda Construction Project Co. ,Ltd.	平度市	1301
105	青岛工业设备安装工程公司	Qingdao Industrial Equipment and Installation Project Corp.	四方区	2253
106	青岛胶东建筑有限公司	Qingdao Jiaodong Construction Co. ,Ltd.	胶州市	1201
107	青岛城阳恒泰建筑有限公司	Qingdao Chengyang Hengtai Construction Co. ,Ltd.	城阳区	1301
108	青岛建设装饰集团有限公司	Qingdao Construction and Decoration Group Co. ,Ltd.	崂山区	2103
109	青岛高新建筑安装工程有限公司	Qingdao Gaoxin Construction and Installation Co. ,Ltd.	崂山区	2201
110	青岛新德隆建筑安装有限公司	Qingdao Xindelong Construction and Installation Co. ,Ltd.	胶州市	1201
111	青岛市益水工程股份有限公司	Qingdao Yishui Project Co. ,Ltd.	市南区	1210
112	青岛市沙子口建设工程有限公司	Qingdao Xiazikou Construction Project Co. ,Ltd.	崂山区	1201
113	山东省即墨市第二建筑工程公司	Shandong Jimo No. 2 Construction Project Corp.	即墨市	1201
114	即墨市灵山建筑工程公司	Jimo Lingshan Construction Project Co. ,Ltd.	即墨市	1301
115	青岛凯盛源建筑安装工程有限公司	Qingdao Kaishengyuan Construction and Installation Co. ,Ltd.	平度市	1201
116	青岛海都建筑安装工程有限公司	Qingdao Haidu Construction and Installation Project Co. ,Ltd.	城阳区	1301
117	青岛豪斯建设工程有限公司	Qingdao Haosi Construction Project Co. ,Ltd.	崂山区	1301
118	青岛燃通达股份有限公司	Qingdao Rantongda Co. ,Ltd.	四方区	1210
119	青岛建设集团华友建设发展有限公司	Qingdao Construction Group Huayou Construction and Development Co. ,Ltd.	市北区	1201
120	青岛永祥建筑工程公司	Qingdao Yongxiang Construction Project Co. ,Ltd.	即墨市	1301
121	青岛水集建筑有限公司	Qingdao Shuiji Construction Co. ,Ltd.	莱西市	1201
122	青岛城阳恒升建筑安装工程有限公司	Qingdao Chengyang Hengsheng Construction Co. ,Ltd.	城阳区	1301
123	平度市鲁兴建筑工程有限公司	Pingdu Luxing Construction Project Co. ,Ltd.	平度市	1201
124	青岛隆海集团建筑安装有限公司	Qingdao Longhai Group Construction and Installation Co. ,Ltd.	胶南市	1301
125	平度市伟达建筑有限责任公司	Pingdu Weida Construction Co. ,Ltd.	平度市	1301
126	胶南市张家楼建筑公司	Jiaonan Zhangjialou Construction Co. ,Ltd.	胶南市	1301
127	青岛恒源达建设工程有限公司	Qingdao Hengyuanda Construction Project Co. ,Ltd.	城阳区	1301
128	青岛安建热力设备安装工程有限公司	Qingdao Anjian Power Equipment Installation Co. ,Ltd.	胶州市	2318
129	平度市华伟建筑有限责任公司	Pingdu Huawei Construction Co. ,Ltd.	平度市	1301
130	青岛鸿润建设集团有限公司	Qingdao Hongrun Construction Group Co. ,Ltd.	黄岛区	1201
131	青岛经济技术开发区黄岛建筑工程有限公司	Qingdao Huangdao Construction Project Co. ,Ltd.	黄岛区	1201
132	青岛华天建设工程有限公司	Qingdao Huatian Construction Project Co. ,Ltd.	胶州市	1201

12 -5 续表

continued

序号 Precedence	企业单位名称	Name	所在地区 Location	资质等级 Class
133	青岛崂峰市政工程有限公司	Qingdao Laofeng Municipal Project Co. ,Ltd.	崂山区	1210
134	青岛市城阳区夏庄建筑工程有限公司	Qingdao Chengyang District Xiazhuang Construction Project Co. ,Ltd.	城阳区	1301
135	青岛隆昌达建筑安装有限公司	Qingdao Longchangda Construction and Installation Co. ,Ltd.	胶州市	1301
136	青岛东方铁塔安装工程有限公司	Qingdao East Iron Tower Installation Project Co. ,Ltd.	胶州市	2108
137	青岛胶南市康大建筑工程有限公司	Qingdao Jiaonan Kangda Construction Project Co. ,Ltd.	胶南市	1301
138	平度市宏伟建筑工程有限公司	Pingdu Hongwei Construction Project Co. ,Ltd.	平度市	1201
139	平度市粮食局建筑公司	Pingdu Grain Bureau Construction Corp.	平度市	1301
140	青岛易通建安有限公司	Qingdao Yitong Construction and Installation Co. ,Ltd.	黄岛区	1201
141	青岛市城阳区东葛建筑工程公司	Qingdao Chengyang Dongge Construction Project Corp.	城阳区	1301
142	平度市西城建筑安装有限公司	Pingdu Xicheng Construction and Installation Co. ,Ltd.	平度市	1301
143	青岛金原建筑工程有限公司	Qingdao Jinyuan Construction Project Co. ,Ltd.	胶南市	1301
144	青岛宏东建设工程有限公司	Qingdao Hongdong Construction Project Co. ,Ltd.	莱西市	1301
145	山东红建建安集团公司	Shandong Hongjian Jian' an Group Corp.	黄岛区	1201
146	青岛泓鑫源建筑安装工程有限公司	Qingdao Hongxinyuan Construction and Installation Project Co. ,Ltd.	胶州市	1301
147	青岛鳌山建筑工程有限公司	Qingdao Aoshan Construction Project Co. ,Ltd.	即墨市	1301
148	青岛多元建设集团有限公司	Qingdao Duoyuan Construction Group Co. ,Ltd.	黄岛区	1201
149	青岛汇泰建安工程有限公司	Qingdao Huitai Construction and Installation Co. ,Ltd.	李沧区	1301
150	即墨市金口建筑工程有限公司	Jimo Jinkou Construction Project Co. ,Ltd.	即墨市	1301
151	青岛海盛源修建工程有限公司	Qingdao Haishengyuan Maintenance and Construction Co. ,Ltd.	崂山区	2301
152	青岛鲁通通信工程有限责任公司	Qingdao Lutong Communication Project Co. ,Ltd.	市南区	2222
153	青岛城阳城建有限公司	Qingdao Chengyang Chengjian Co. ,Ltd.	城阳区	1201
154	青岛建泰建筑工程有限公司	Qingdao Jiantai Construction Project Co. ,Ltd.	黄岛区	1201
155	青岛市热电工程公司	Qingdao Heat and Electricity Project Co. ,Ltd.	市北区	1210
156	平度市东苑建筑工程有限公司	Pingdu Dongyuan Construction Project Co. ,Ltd.	平度市	1201
157	青岛市崂山区古建建筑工程有限公司	Qingdao Laoshan Gujian Construction Co. ,Ltd.	崂山区	1201
158	青岛市房产工程公司	Qingdao Real Estate Project Corp.	市南区	2203
159	青岛市崂山区北宅镇建筑公司	Qingdao Laoshan Beizhaizhen Construction Corp.	崂山区	1301
160	青岛永鑫幕墙有限公司	Qingdao Yongxin Co. ,Ltd.	崂山区	2104
161	青岛中天伟业建设工程有限公司	Qingdao Zhongtian Weiye Construction Project Co. ,Ltd.	黄岛区	1201
162	青岛清华园建筑安装工程有限公司	Qingdao Qinghuayuan Construction and Installation Co. ,Ltd.	平度市	1301
163	青岛市政道桥实业有限公司	Qingdao Municipal Administration Road&Bridge Co. ,Ltd.	市南区	1210
164	青岛顺源建设工程有限公司	Qingdao Shunyuan Construction Project Co. ,Ltd.	黄岛区	2114
165	青岛营上建设集团有限公司	Qingdao Yingshang Construction Group Co. ,Ltd.	即墨市	1201

12 -5 续表
continued

序号 Precedence	企业单位名称	Name	所在地区 Location	资质等级 Class
166	青岛东电电力工程有限公司	Qingdao Dongdian Electric Power Project Co. ,Ltd.	崂山区	2349
167	青岛通盛达建筑工程有限公司	Qingdao Tongshengda Construction Project Co. ,Ltd.	即墨市	1201
168	莱西市九州建设工程有限公司	Laixi Jiuzhou Construction Project Co. ,Ltd.	莱西市	1301
169	青岛腾达建筑装饰公司	Qingdao Tengda Construction and Decoration Corp.	即墨市	1301
170	青岛昊金德建设有限公司	Qingdao Haojinde Construction Co. ,Ltd.	胶州市	1301
171	青岛崂建建筑工程有限责任公司	Qingdao Laojian Construction Project Co. ,Ltd.	崂山区	1301
172	青岛市城阳区朝阳建筑工程有限公司	Qingdao Chengyang Chaoyang Construction Project Co. ,Ltd.	城阳区	1301
173	青岛恒浩建安发展有限公司	Qingdao Henghao Construction and Installation Co. ,Ltd.	城阳区	1301
174	青岛鲁泽置业集团建设工程有限公司	Qingdao Luze Group Construction Co. ,Ltd.	黄岛区	1201
175	青岛光明建筑工程有限公司	Qingdao Guangming Construction Project Co. ,Ltd.	胶州市	1301
176	青岛莱西九联建筑工程有限公司	Qingdao Laixi Jiulian Construction Project Co. ,Ltd.	莱西市	1301
177	青岛爱华工程有限公司	Qingdao Aihua Project Co. ,Ltd.	市北区	1301
178	青岛旭泰建设工程有限公司	Qingdao Xutai Construction Project Co. ,Ltd.	胶州市	1301
179	青岛市城阳区东城建筑安装有限公司	Qingdao Chengyang Dongcheng Co. ,Ltd.	城阳区	1301
180	青岛城阳建筑有限公司	Laiyang Agriculture College Chengyang Construction Co. ,Ltd.	城阳区	1201
181	青岛长青建筑安装有限公司	Qingdao Changqing Construction and Installation Co. ,Ltd.	胶州市	1201
182	青岛望城三宝建设有限公司	Qingdao Wangcheng Sanbao Construction Co. ,Ltd.	莱西市	1201
183	胶州市市政工程处	Jiaozhou Municipal Engineering Department	胶州市	1210
184	青岛华夏建设有限公司	Qingdao Huaxia Construction Co. ,Ltd.	莱西市	1301
185	青岛田横建筑工程有限公司	Qingdao Tianheng Construction Project Co. ,Ltd.	即墨市	1301
186	青岛桃林建筑工程有限公司	Qingdao Taolin Construction Project Co. ,Ltd.	城阳区	1301
187	青岛九鼎峰建筑工程公司	Qingdao Jiudingfeng Construction Project Co. ,Ltd.	黄岛区	1301
188	青岛德瑞建筑装饰有限公司	Qingdao Derui Construction and Decoration Co. ,Ltd.	崂山区	2103
189	青岛新隆安建筑安装有限公司	Qingdao Xinlongan Construction and Installation Co. ,Ltd.	四方区	1201
190	青岛嘉和建造有限公司	Qingdao Jiahe Construction Co. ,Ltd.	即墨市	1301
191	胶南市信阳建筑公司	Jiaonan Xinyang Construction Corp.	胶南市	1301
192	即墨市金家建筑工程有限公司	Jimo Jinjia Construction Project Co. ,Ltd.	即墨市	1301
193	青岛热电安装有限公司	Qingdao Thermal Power Installation Co. ,Ltd.	四方区	2318
194	莱西市海星建设有限公司	Laixi Haixing Construction Co. ,Ltd.	莱西市	1301
195	青岛市平度康峰建筑工程有限公司	Qingdao Pingdu Kangfeng Construction Project Co. ,Ltd.	平度市	1301
196	青岛鑫鸿泰建设工程有限公司	Qingdao Xinhongtai Construction Project Co. ,Ltd.	胶州市	1301
197	青岛豪第建筑工程有限公司	Qingdao Haodi Construction Project Co. ,Ltd.	即墨市	1201
198	青岛海利源建设工程有限公司	Qingdao Hailiyuan Construction Project Co. ,Ltd.	胶州市	1201
199	即墨市七级建筑工程有限公司	Jimo Seven Class Construction Project Co. ,Ltd.	即墨市	1201
200	青岛前湾建筑工程有限公司	Qingdao Qianwan Construction Project Co. ,Ltd.	黄岛区	1301

CHAPTER 13

第十三篇

运输、邮电

TRANSPORTATION,POSTAL AND TELECOMMUNICATIONS SERVICES

编辑单位：工业交通统计处
编　　委：吴加琪
编　　辑：童文菁
校　　对：童文菁
电　　话：85912257

13-1 主要年份客货运输及港口吞吐量
MAJOR YEAR'S PASSENGER & FREIGHT TRAFFIC AND CARGO HANDLED AT PORTS

年份 Year	客运量(万人) Passenger Traffic(10000 persons)				货运量(万吨) Freight Traffic(10000 tons)				港口吞吐量(万吨) Cargo Handled at Ports (10000 tons)	集装箱吞吐量(万标箱) Containers (10000 TEU)
	铁路 Railways	公路 Highways	海运 Waterways	航空 Civil Aviation	铁路 Railways	公路 Highways	海运 Waterways	航空 Civil Aviation		
1949	327	14	9	–	386	162	22	–	73	–
1952	571	49	13	–	447	399	44	–	181	–
1957	1 054	149	13	–	747	548	118	–	269	–
1962	3 100	141	39	–	909	524	97	–	391	–
1965	1 424	230	19	–	1 257	690	158	–	524	–
1970	1 329	373	20	–	1 856	736	232	–	695	–
1975	1 803	159	30	–	2 325	817	282	–	1 542	–
1978	1 986	274	49	–	2 917	1 561	528	–	2 081	–
1980	1 896	713	73	–	2 596	1 642	941	–	1 779	–
1985	2 063	1 894	86	1	3 009	2 303	919	0.03	2 610	–
1987	2 019	2 133	159	7	3 288	4 948	1 085	0.04	3 070	–
1988	2 083	3 300	234	8.8	3 418	6 486	1 160	0.04	3 153	–
1989	1 802	3 441	308	11.3	3 717	8 926	1 450	0.1	3 145	–
1990	1 488	3 639	316	14.1	3 741	6 433	1 556	0.2	3 068	–
1991	1 453	4 144	366	19	3 774	6 896	1 789	0.31	3 194	–
1992	1 488	4 965	437	27	3 899	6 822	1 981	0.45	3 240	–
1993	1 499	6 436	499	35.3	4 044	7 685	1 910	0.64	3 650	–
1994	1 564	6 787	–	47	4 112	8 336	1 804	–	4 331	–
1995	1 480	9 785	–	66.6	4 205	11 788	2 185	–	5 165	–
1996	1 230	10 738	–	79.9	4 415	10 749	474	–	6 056	81.1
1997	1 308	11 855	–	–	4 466	11 232	544	–	6 944	103.3
1998	1 549	11 754	–	–	4 028	14 311	1 792	1.44	7 044	121.3
1999	1 674	12 103	–	–	3 919	14 550	1 926	1.96	7 282	154.3
2000	1 780	12 145	–	124.1	4 256	17 234	2 998	2.3	8 661	212
2001	1 678	13 686	–	143	4 778	20 906	3 432	2.4	10 423	264
2002	1 530	14 516	777	163.7	5 079	24 480	2 530	3	12 252	341
2003	1 366	13 132	786	174.7	4 929	27 241	2 773	3.6	14 135	424
2004	1 496	16 420	862	241.9	5 119	29 937	3 503	5.3	16 303	514
2005	551.6	17 212	971.5	280.9	2 299	31 009	4 471	4.6	18 726.5	630.7

注:2004 年底青岛铁路分局撤销,以上数据为济南铁路局反馈数据,与 2004 年口径不同。
航空货运量为货邮离港量,与 2004 年口径不同,2004 年为行、货、邮离港量。

Note: Qingdao railway station had been withdrawn by the end of 2004. The data in 2005 is fed back by Jinan railway station, and different from the data in 2004 in calibre. Freight traffic volume of civil aviation refers to outward volume of cargo and postal parcel. And the data in 2004 refers to outward volume of baggage, cargo and postal parcel.

13－2 民用车辆拥有量(2005 年底)

POSSESSION OF CIVIL MOTOR VEHICLES(END OF 2005)

项 目	Items	合计 Total 辆数 Number	#个人 Private 辆数 Number
一、汽车	**Automobile**	**373 807**	**146 825**
1. 载客汽车	Passenger Vehicles	272 003	130 536
其中:轿车	of which: Sedan	134 962	61 553
2. 载货汽车	Freight Trucks	93 632	15 912
3. 其他汽车	Others	8 172	337
二、电车	**Tram**	**81**	**-**
三、摩托车	**Motorcycle**	**715 141**	**705 201**
四、农用运输车	**Agricultural Camion**	**110 821**	**105 400**
五、挂车	**Trailer Trucks**	**10 269**	**425**
六、其他类型车	**Other Vehicles**	**152**	**3**

补充资料:机动车驾驶员 1 174 901 人　其中:汽车驾驶员 833 844 人

Motor vehicle drivers(person): 1 174 901　of which: Automobile drivers(person): 833 844

13 –3 客货运输及港口吞吐量(2005 年)

PASSENGER & FREIGHT TRAFFIC AND CARGO HANDLED AT PORTS(2005)

项　目	Items	货运量（万吨）Freight Traffic Volume（10000 tons）	货物周转量（亿吨公里）Freight Ton-kilometers(100 million tons. km)	客运量（万人）Passenger Traffic Volume(10000 persons)	旅客周转量（亿人公里）Passenger-Kilometers(100 million persons · km)	旅客吞吐量（万人）Passenger Handled Volume（10000 persons）	货物吞吐量（万吨）Cargo Handled Volume（10000 tons）	集装箱（万标箱）Containers（10000 TEU）
总　计	**Total**	**37 779.22**	**3 314.07**	**18 735.1**	**72.51**	**568.74**	**18 735.41**	**630.7**
铁路	Railways	2 299	69.89	551.6	16.82	–	–	–
公路	Highways	31 009	88.83	17 212	54.6	–	–	–
水运	Waterways	4 471.22	3 155.36	971.5	1.1	–	–	–
民航	Civil Aviation	–	–	–	–	555.04	8.91	–
港口	Ports	–	–	–	–	13.7	18 726.5	630.7

13 –4 独立核算运输邮电单位主要财务指标(2005 年)

MAIN FINANCIAL INDICATORS OF INDEPENDENT ACCOUNTING UNITS OF TRANSPORTATION, POSTS AND TELECOMMUNICATIONS(2005)

单位:万元(10 000 yuan)

项　目	Items	营业收入 Revenue of Business	营业成本 Cost of Business	营业利润 After-tax Profits of Business	营业税金及附加 Tax and Extra Charges of Business	利润总额 Total After-tax Profits
总　计	**Total**	**1 760 097.8**	**1 021 859.8**	**270 571.6**	**50 169.3**	**368 195.1**
铁路	Railways	–	–	–	–	–
公路	Highways	211 671.1	174 407.1	2 153.2	8 535	2 993.1
水运	Waterways	325 467.4	281 296.5	25 416.7	2 417.1	30 190.6
民航	Civil Aviation	36 477.4	20 525.9	8 627.4	1 432.1	7 468.5
港口	Ports	571 953	316 914	1 145 44.6	19 729.7	108 443.2
邮政	Post	48 442.2	35 274.5	291.3	1 617.3	291.3
电信	Telecommunications	566 086	193 441	119 538	16 438	218 808

13 –5 邮电通讯基本情况(2005 年)

BASIC STATISTICS OF POST AND TELECOMMUNICATION SERVICES(2005)

市、区名称	Region	邮电局(处) Post Office (place)	#提供邮政全功能服务的 of which: Providing All Kinds of Services	邮路总长度(公里) Length of Postal Routes(km)	邮运汽车(辆) Vehicles for Postal Services(vehicle)	固定电话长话电路(路) Fixed Telephone Circuit(line)
总　计	**Total**	**718**	**208**	**76 488**	**413**	**44 819**
市　区	Urban Area	240	63	70 428	305	42 929
#黄岛区	Huangdao District	48	8	223	28	600
崂山区	Laoshan District	51	6	105	15	300
胶州市	Jiaozhou	124	26	341	34	360
即墨市	Jimo	97	33	642	20	360
平度市	Pingdu	128	33	568	14	180
胶南市	Jiaonan	54	29	4 255	20	180
莱西市	Laixi	75	24	254	20	180

13 –5 续表 1

continued

市、区名称	Region	固定电话市话交换机容量(门) Fixed telephone switchboard capacity of the city(uint)	固定电话市话用户数(户) Telephone Users in Urban Area (household)	固定电话农村交换机容量(门) Fixed telephone switchboard capacity of the rural(uint)	固定电话农村用户数(户) Telephone Users in Rural Area (household)	信筒、信箱(个) Pillar-boxes (unit)	邮电业务总量(万元,2000 年价) Business Volume of Post and Telecommunication Services(10000 yuan at 2000 price)
总　计	**Total**	**3 201 494**	**2 274 770**	**1 429 577**	**1 263 923**	**1 530**	**9 701 50.5**
市　区	Urban Area	2 728 700	1 576 700	326 112	269 914	920	567 589.6
#黄岛区	Huangdao District	100 721	180 094	61 396	48 437	28	663 21.9
崂山区	Laoshan District	187 156	246 337	59 624	46 100	32	69 221.52
胶州市	Jiaozhou	126 012	156 477	145 892	152 845	210	86 694.57
即墨市	Jimo	118 431	180 561	285 151	233 174	46	90 525.72
平度市	Pingdu	74 276	119 470	309 460	298 106	112	93 224.01
胶南市	Jiaonan	89 827	139 952	184 315	160 202	26	74 341.73
莱西市	Laixi	64 248	101 610	178 647	149 682	216	57 774.79

13 -5 续表2
continued

市、区名称	Region	函件（出口）（万件）Number of Letter (10000 pcs)	包件（出口）（万件）Number of Parcels (10000 pcs)	汇票（出口）（万张）Number of Draft (10000 pcs)	报纸期发份数（万份）Number of Newspapers Circulation (10000 pcs)	杂志期发份数（万份）Number of Magazines Circulation (10000 pcs)
总　计	**Total**	**8 011.8**	**82.5**	**156.2**	**899.6**	**67.9**
市　区	Urban Area	5561.1	63.2	108	428.65	45.16
#黄岛区	Huangdao District	358.3	7.7	9.4	53.08	2.36
崂山区	Laoshan District	478.3	15.2	15	76.94	5.26
胶州市	Jiaozhou	521.8	4.4	15	74.53	4.18
即墨市	Jimo	480.1	4.6	14.7	104.77	3.51
平度市	Pingdu	666.7	3.7	6.1	102.98	4.82
胶南市	Jiaonan	447.6	4.3	6.6	131.94	2.96
莱西市	Laixi	334.5	2.5	5.8	56.73	7.27

CHAPTER 14

第十四篇

国内贸易

CIVIL TRADE

编辑单位：外经贸易统计处
编　　委：刘　伟
编　　辑：王维周　刘兰英　张砚慧
校　　对：王维周　刘兰英　张砚慧
电　　话：85912241 85912243

14 –1 社会消费品零售总额(1985 –2005 年)
TOTAL RETAIL SALES OF CONSUMER GOODS(1985-2005)

单位:万元(10 000 yuan)

年份 Year	消费品零售总额 Total Retail Sales of Consumer Goods	批发和零售业 Wholesale and Retail Trade	住宿和餐饮业 Accommodation and Catering Trade	其他行业 Others
1985	30 222	231 477	16 996	18 753
1986	364 091	269 418	21 384	27 118
1987	432 569	310 658	23 319	32 617
1988	590 538	434 572	32 304	45 449
1989	619 941	450 812	34 083	56 303
1990	658 264	484 770	35 568	67 863
1991	760 562	566 767	4 320	56 812
1992	888 411	666 911	53 045	67 392
1993	1 294 962	965 043	74 896	90 499
1994	1 701 513	1 223 282	115 186	183 606
1995	2 108 064	145 2235	164 996	271 357
1996	2 402 309	1 661 252	195 413	284 997
1997	2 668 794	1 867 660	214 576	320 407
1998	2 987 876	2 059 666	246 300	364 720
1999	3 337 347	2 408 613	279 660	347 139
2000	3 812 241	2 764 592	344 084	358 196
2001	4 356 427	3 159 051	449 690	384 801
2002	4 944 142	3 692 055	566 187	357 131
2003	6 323 490	5 175 849	831 720	315 922
2004	7 475 022	6 266 750	1 017 193	191 079
2005	8 659 065	7 269 407	1 170 861	218 797

注：1、自 2003 年开始消费品零售总额不再包括制造业零售额和农民对非农居民的销售额分组。
Note:Since 2003,retail sales of manufacture and retail sales of rural residents to urban residents are excluded in total retail sales.

2、自 2005 年起,住宿业从其它行业调整到住宿餐饮业中。Note:Since 2005,accommodation trade is adjusted to accommodation and Catering trade from the others.

3、根据经济普查结果,对 1993 年以来的历史数据进行了调整。Note:Historical data since 1993 have been adjusted according to cata of economic census.

14 –2 分市、区社会消费品零售总额(2005 年)
TOTAL RETAIL SALES OF CONSUMER GOODS BY REGION(2005)

单位:万元(10 000 yuan)

市、区名称	Region	消费品零售总额 Total Retail Sales of Consumer Goods	按经济类型分 Grouped By Economy Categories			按行业分 Grouped By Sectors		
			#国有及国有控股 State-owned and State-holding	#私营 Private	#个体 Individual	批发零售贸易业 Wholesale and Retail Trade	住宿餐饮业 Accommodation and Catering Trade	其他 Others
总　计	**Total**	**8 659 065**	**468 089**	**1 769 593**	**4 234 258**	**7 269 407**	**1 170 861**	**218 797**
市　区	Urban Area	4 880 750	242 948	1 144 316	1 808 213	4 041 421	759 742	79 587
市南区	Shinan District	1 245 869	60 098	283 300	264 567	993 736	232 340	19 793
市北区	Shibei District	1 084 339	95 319	307 042	387 463	936 653	128 914	18 772
四方区	Sifang District	522 318	28 624	97 265	186 317	460 172	55 019	7 127
李沧区	Licang District	739 912	15 253	110 762	262 109	641 168	84 273	14 471
城阳区	Chengyang District	460 004	21 574	121 184	265 480	361 710	86 699	11 595
黄岛区	Huangdao District	446 393	16 250	97 677	262 162	340 552	102 114	3 727
崂山区	Laoshan District	381 915	5 830	127 086	180 115	307 430	70 383	4 102
胶州市	Jiaozhou	752 641	46 725	145 685	528 104	629 713	97 095	25 833
即墨市	Jimo	907 669	52 521	148 118	581 397	797 616	79 997	30 056
平度市	Pingdu	845 633	74 288	110 716	521 215	719 861	87 690	38 082
胶南市	Jiaonan	667 021	20 797	124 063	414 493	573 259	69 056	24 706
莱西市	Laixi	605 351	30 810	96 695	380 836	507 537	77 281	205 33

14－3 限额以上批发和零售业商品购销存总额(2005 年)

PURCHASES, SALES AND INVENTORY OF WHOLESALE AND RETAIL TRADE ABOVE LEVEL(2005)

项　目	Items
总计	**Total**
国有企业	State-owned
集体企业	Collective-owned
其它企业	Others
农畜产品批发业	Wholesale of Agricultural Animal and Products
食品饮料及烟草制品批发业	Wholesale of Food, Beverage and Tabacco Products
纺织服装及日用品批发业	Wholesale of Textile Products, Garments and Daily Use Goods
文化体育用品及器材批发业	Wholesale of Culture&Sports Articles and Equipments
医药及医疗器械批发业	Wholesale of Medicine and Medical Appliance
矿产品建材及化工产品批发业	Wholesale of Mineral Products Building Materials and Chemical Products
机械设备五金交电及电子产品批发业	Wholesale of Machine Equipments Hardware, Electrical Appliance and Electronic Products
贸易经济与代理	Business Brokerage
其它批发业	Wholesale of Others
综合零售业	Multiple Retail Trade
食品饮料及烟草制品专门零售业	Retail Sales of Food, Beverage and Tabacco Products
纺织服装及日用品专门零售业	Retail Sales of Textile Products, Garments and Daily Use Goods
文化体育用品及器材专门零售业	Retail Sales of Culture&Sports Articles and Equipments
医药及医疗器械专门零售业	Retail Sales of Medicine and Medical Appliance
汽车摩托车燃料及零配件专门零售业	Retail Sales of Spare and Component Parts for Automobiles, Motorcycles
家用电器及电子产品专门零售业	Retail Sales of Electrical Equipment and Electronic Products
五金家具及室内装潢材料专门零售业	Retail Sales of Hardware, Electrical Appliance and Decoration Materials
无店铺及其他零售业	Retail Sales of Having No Shop and Others

单位:万元(10 000 yuan)

商品销售总额 Sales of Commodities	批发 Wholesale Trade	零售 Retail Trade	库存总额 Inventory
12 406 689	**9 949 652**	**2 457 038**	**689 940**
2 992 902	2 907 758	85 144	173 237
1 490 130	1 445 343	44 787	32 878
7 923 658	5 596 551	2 327 107	483 824
333 724	333 724	0	30 462
977 497	974 744	2 753	39 445
1 149 931	1 149 931	0	47 864
33 542	29 122	4 420	4 953
178 951	177 770	1 181	10 541
3 435 935	3 268 205	167 730	104 079
3 034 929	2 974 274	60 655	125 297
0	0	0	0
576 509	576 509	0	37 057
1 509 453	374 712	1 134 741	167 069
20 798	5 371	15 427	2 855
36 995	3 969	33 025	7 066
59 490	19 619	39 871	15 672
43 110	3 426	39 684	6 825
729 682	43 206	686 477	59 297
230 583	13 887	216 696	21 108
45 869	210	45 659	9 762
9 692	973	8 720	588

14－4 限额以上批发和零售业商品分类销售额(2005 年)

SALES OF WHOLESALE AND RETAIL TRADE ABOVE LEVEL BY CATEGORY OF COMMODITIES(2005)

单位:万元(10 000 yuan)

项　目	Items	销售总额 Total Sales	批发总额 Wholesale	零售总额 Retail Sales
分类合计	**Total**	**11 696 990**	**9 343 130**	**2 353 860**
食品、饮料、烟酒类	Food, Beverage, Tabacco and Liquor	1 500 430	1 090 925	409 505
粮油类	Grain and Oil	65 412	32 219	33 193
肉禽蛋类	Meat, Poultry and Eggs	103 908	45 568	58 340
其他食品类	Other Food	500 266	278 585	221 681
饮料类	Beverage	48 445	17 502	30 943
烟酒类	Tabacco and Liquor	782 399	717 051	65 348
服装鞋帽、针、纺织品类	Garments, Shoes, Hats and Knitwear	1 221 202	886 046	335 156
服装类	Garments	667 678	417 589	250 089
鞋帽类	Shoes and Hats	114 066	57 762	56 304
针、纺织品类	Knitwear	439 458	410 695	28 763
化妆品类	Cosmetics	93 434	35 184	58 250
金银珠宝类	Jewelry	42 722	5 145	37 577
日用品类	Articles for Daily Use	246 555	137 271	109 284
洗涤用品类	Detergents and Cleaning Products	36 245	8 028	28 217
儿童玩具类	Children Toys	13 748	6 221	7 527
五金、电料类	Hardware and Electrical Appliance	125 731	113 107	12 624
体育、娱乐用品类	Recreation and Sports Articles	19 930	5 589	14 341
书报杂志类	Books and Newspapers	53 007	16 555	36 452
电子出版物及音像制品类	Electric Publication and Sound-video Materials	10 748	3 207	7 541
家用电器和音像器材类	Household Electric Appliances and Sound-video Equipments	1 664 251	1 388 431	275 820
中西药品类	Medicines	143 221	105 173	38 048
西药	Western Medicines	90 785	65 126	25 659
中草药及中成药	Traditional Chinese Medicines	44 209	31 997	12 212
文化办公用品类	Culture and Office Articles	210 665	144 923	65 742
家俱类	Furnitures	29 583	15 848	13 735
通讯器材类	Telecommunication Appliances	204 732	95 893	108 839
煤炭及制品类	Coal and Coal Products	251 815	248 553	3 262
木材及制品类	Timber	18 042	15 534	2 508
石油及制品类	Petroleum and Products	1 374 351	1 220 488	153 863
化工材料及制品类	Chemical Materials and Products	475 347	475 033	314
化肥类	Fertilizer	30 272	30 272	0
金属材料类	Metal Materials	1 211 173	1 209 889	1 284
建筑及装潢材料类	Materials for Construction and Ornament	104 686	74 467	30 219
机电产品及设备类	Mechanical and Electrical Instruments	1 119 143	1 114 956	4 187
农机类	Agricultural Machinery	11 295	11 295	0
汽车类	Automobile	853 904	230 945	622 959
种子饲料类	Seeds and Forage	51 290	51 290	0
棉麻类	Cotton and Flax Products	39 161	39 161	0
其他类	Others	631 867	619 518	12 349

14－5 限额以上批发业财务状况(2005 年)
FINANCIAL POSITION OF WHOLESALE TRADE ABOVE LEVEL(2005)

指标	Indicators	合计 Total	国有经济 State-owned	集体经济 Collective-owned	外商及港澳台经济 With Funds from Foreign and Hong Kong, Macao and Taiwan Funded	其它 Others
单位数	**Number of Enterprises**	**297**	**46**	**12**	**6**	**233**
一、年末资产负债	**Year-end Assets-liability**					
资产合计	Total Assets	3 189 448	1 091 960	506 147	62 983	1 528 358
流动资产小计	Circulation Funds	2 690 133	857 562	462 388	58 150	1 312 034
负债合计	Liabilities	2 860 379	1 031 521	485 098	57 651	1 286 109
所有者权益合计	Total Owners Rights and Interests	329 069	60 439	21 050	5 332	242 248
二、损益及分配	**Loss, Profits and Distribution**					
主营业务收入	Income from Major Business	7 593 634	2 324 162	1 278 850	182 537	3 808 085
主营业务成本	Major Business Costs	7 173 375	2 175 412	1 254 207	162 914	3 580 841
主营业务税金及附加	Tax and Extra Charges of Major Business	6 225	2 567	967	25	2 666
主营业务利润	Profits from Major Business	342 813	142 873	22 504	19 598	157 838
其他业务利润	Profits from Other Business	16 912	6 348	2 123	281	8 160
营业费用	Operating Costs	201 467	48 879	7 735	17 142	127 711
管理费用	Cost of Management	124 003	53 424	13 799	4 652	52 128
财务费用	Financial Expenses	31 048	10 974	1 889	876	17 310
利润总额	Total Profits	71 234	55 048	2 606	－2 723	16 302
三、经济效益	**Economic Efficiency**					
商品经营费用率%	Rate of Business Expenses	2. 65	2. 10	0. 60	9. 39	3. 35
商品销售利润率%	Rate of Sales Profits	0. 84	2. 17	0. 15	－1. 51	0. 38

14－6 限额以上零售业财务状况(2005 年)
FINANCIAL POSITION OF RETAIL TRADE ABOVE LEVEL(2005)

指标	Indicators	合计 Total
单位数	**Number of Enterprises**	**240**
一、年末资产负债	**Year-end Assets-Liability**	
资产合计	Total Assets	1 297 486
流动资产小计	Circulation Funds	763 311
负债合计	Liabilities	944 705
所有者权益合计	Total Owners Rights and Interests	352 781
二、损益及分配	**Loss, Profits and Distribution**	
主营业务收入	Income from Major Business	2 166 137
主营业务成本	Major Business Costs	1 941 248
主营业务税金及附加	Tax and Extra Charges of Major Business	5 552
主营业务利润	Profits from Major Business	148 640
其他业务利润	Profits from other Business	39 065
营业费用	Operating Costs	91 122
管理费用	Management Costs	105 310
财务费用	Financial Expenses	15 558
利润总额	Total Profits	33 294
三、经济效益	**Economic Efficiency**	
商品经营费用率%	Rate of Business Expenses	4.21
商品销售利润率%	Rate of Sales Profits	1.32

单位:万元(10 000 yuan)

国有经济 State-owned	集体经济 Collective - owned	外商及港澳台经济 With Funds from Foreign and Hong Kong, Macao and Taiwan Funded	其它 Others
6	**9**	**9**	**216**
25 658	20 074	191 646	1 060 108
6 281	12 102	91 004	653 924
21 733	16 428	97 092	809 451
3 925	3 645	94 554	250 656
15 612	27 450	228 239	1 894 836
13 966	25 661	187 520	1 714 101
29	67	207	5 250
1 542	760	36 958	109 380
756	295	12 334	25 681
2 054	1 110	16 763	71 195
2 238	477	19 887	82 709
668	169	163	14 558
-385	136	16 260	17 283
13.15	4.04	7.34	3.76
-7.67	0.31	7.05	0.72

14 -7 批发业营业收入、实现利润前30位企业(2005年)

THE TOP 30 ENTERPRISEES OF WHOLESALE TRADE AT OPERATING REVENUE AND TOTAL PROFITS(2005)

营业收入前30位企业	Name of the Top 30 at Operating Revenue	所在地区	Address
海尔集团电器产业有限公司	Haier Group Electric Appliance Industry Limited Company	崂山区	Laoshan District
山东省机械进出口集团公司	Shandong Province Mechanical Import And Export Group Company	市南区	Shinan District
青岛海尔国际贸易有限公司	Qingdao Haier International Trade Limited Company	崂山区	Laoshan District
青岛钢铁进出口公司	Qingdao Steel And Iron Import And Export Company	市南区	Shinan District
青岛市烟草专卖局青岛烟草有限公司	Qingdao Tobacco Monopoly Bureau Qingdao Tobacco Limited Company	市北区	Shibei District
青岛益佳国际贸易集团有限公司	Qingdao Yijia International Trade Group Limited Company	市南区	Shinan District
青岛海信进出口有限责任公司	Qingdao Hisense Import And Export Limited Liability Company	市南区	Shinan District
中国船舶燃料供应青岛公司	China Marine Bunker(Petro China) Qingdao Company	市北区	Shibei District
中国中煤能源集团公司青岛分公司	China National Coal Group Company Qingdao Subsidiary Company	黄岛区	Huangdao District
山东绮丽集团公司	Shandong Cherry Group Company	市南区	Shinan District
青岛欧美进出口有限公司	Qingdao Europe And America Import And Export Limited Company	市南区	Shinan District
青岛海尔工贸有限公司	Qingdao Haier Industry And Trade Limited Company	崂山区	Laoshan District
青岛浩华通信产品有限公司	Qingdao Haohua Correspondence Product Limited Company	城阳区	chengyang District
青岛润升石油有限公司	Qingdao Runsheng Petroleum Limited Company	黄岛区	Huangdao District
青岛海润投资集团有限公司	Qingdao Hairun Investment Group Limited Company	市南区	Shinan District
山东省东方国际贸易有有限公司	Shandong Province East International Trade Limited Company	市南区	Shinan District
山东莱钢国际贸易有限公司	Shandong Laigang International Trade Limited Company	市南区	Shinan District
青岛欧美投资集团有限公司	Qingdao Europe And America Investment Group Limited Company	市南区	Shinan District
青岛中油油品销售有限公司	China Petroleum Sales Qingdao Limited Company	市南区	Shinan District
五矿钢铁青岛有限公司	Fifth Ores Steel And Iron Qingdao Limited Company	市南区	Shinan District
山东六和集团有限公司	Shandong Liuhe group Limited Company	崂山区	Laoshan District
山东三利源经贸有限公司	Shandong Sanliyuan Economics And Trade Limited Company	平度市	Pingdu
青岛圣元乳业有限公司	Qingdao Shengyuan Dairying Limited Company	黄岛区	Huangdao District
新华锦集团山东锦宜纺织有限公司	Hiking Group Shandong Jinyi Gaintex Limited Company	市南区	Shinan District
新华锦集团山东盈商针棉织品进出口有限公司	Hiking Group Shandong Welltrade Knitwears And Home Textiles Import And Export Limited Company	市南区	Shinan District
青岛华青进出口有限公司	Qingdao Huaqing Import And Export Limited Company	市南区	Shinan District
山东美赫尔国际贸易有限公司	Shandong Meiher International Trade Limited Company	市南区	Shinan District
青岛保税区龙舒洋国际贸易有限公司	Qingdao Bonded Area Long Shuyang International Trade Limited Company	黄岛区	Huangdao District
山东省五金矿产进出口公司	Shandong Province Hardware Minerals Import－export Company	市南区	Shinan District
新华锦集团山东海川发制品进出口有限公司	Hiking Group Shandong Haichuan Wig Ware Import And Export Limited Company	市南区	Shinan District

14 -7 续表
continued

实现利润前30位企业	Name of the Top 30 at Operating Profits	所在地区	Address
青岛市烟草专卖局青岛烟草有限公司	Qingdao Tobacco Monopoly Bureau Qingdao Tobacco Limited Company	市北区	Shibei District
山东莱钢国际贸易有限公司	Shandong Laigang International Trade Limited Company	市南区	Shinan District
青岛欧美进出口有限公司	Qingdao Europe And America import And Export Limited Company	市南区	Shinan District
山东省机械进出口集团公司	Shandong Province Mechanical Import And Export Group Company	市南区	Shinan District
青岛欧美投资集团有限公司	Qingdao Europe And America Investment Group Limited Company	市南区	Shinan District
中国烟草山东进出口公司	China Tobacco Shandong Import And Export Company	市南区	Shinan District
青岛保税区济钢国际物流有限公司	Qingdao Bonded Area Jigang Works International Flows The Limited Company	黄岛区	Huangdao District
青岛保税区首益物流有限公司	Qingdao Bonded Area Shouyi Flows Limited Company	黄岛区	Huangdao District
青岛钢铁进出口公司	Qingdao Steel And Iron Import And Export Company	市南区	Shinan District
青岛保税区龙舒洋国际贸易有限公司	Qingdao Bonded Area Long Shuyang International Trade Limited Company	黄岛区	Huangdao District
青岛鲍德经贸有限公司	Qingdao Baud Economics And Trade Limited Company	平度市	Pingdu
中国船舶燃料供应青岛公司	China Marine Bunker(Petro China) Qingdao Company	市北区	Shibei District
青岛海尔国际贸易有限公司	Qingdao Haier International Trade Limited Company	崂山区	Laoshan District
中国中煤能源集团公司青岛分公司	China National Coal Group Company Qingdao Subsidiary Company	黄岛区	Huangdao District
青岛海润投资集团有限公司	Qingdao Hairun Investment Group Limited Company	市南区	Shinan District
伊藤忠(青岛)有限公司	Itochu(Qingdao) Limited Company	市南区	Shinan District
青岛胜利石化产品销售有限公司	Qingdao Shengli Petrified Product Sale Limited Company	市北区	Shibei District
山东机械设备进出口集团公司	Shandong Mechanical Device Import And Export Group Company	市南区	Shinan District
青岛波导电子有限公司	Qingdao Bird Electron Limited Company	市北区	Shibei District
青岛胜世嘉工贸有限公司	Qingdao Shengshijia Industry And Trade Limited Company	四方区	Sifang District
青岛国运集团有限公司	Qingdao Guoyun Group Limited Company	李沧区	Licang District
青岛世纪新科啤酒开发有限公司	Qingdao Century Shinco Beer Development Limited Company	市南区	Shinan District
青岛世纪瑞丰国际贸易有限公司	Qingdao Century Ruifeng International Trade Limited Company	市南区	Shinan District
新华锦集团山东锦岳国际经贸有限责任公司	Hiking Group Shandong Jinyue International Economics And Trade Limited Liability Company	市南区	Shinan District
青岛青汽汽车销售有限公司	Qingdao Qingqi Auto Sale Limited Company	市南区	Shinan District
山东省东方国际贸易有有限公司	Shandong Province East International Trade Limited Company	市南区	Shinan District
青岛即发进出口有限公司	Qingdao Jesfeel Import And Export Limited Company	即墨市	Jimo
青岛中油油品销售有限公司	China Petroleum Sales Qingdao Limited Company	市南区	Shinan District
青岛鑫雷音电子有限公司	Qingdao Xinleiyin Electron Limited Company	市北区	Shibei District
青岛贵生商贸有限公司	Qingdao Guisheng Business Trade Limited Company	崂山区	Laoshan District

14－8 零售业营业收入、实现利润前30位企业(2005年)
THE TOP 30 ENTERPRISES OF RETAIL TRADE AT OPERATING REVENUE AND TOTAL PROFITS(2005)

营业收入前30位企业	Name of the Top 30 at Operating Revenue	所在地区	Address
青岛利群集团股份有限公司	Qingdao Liqun Group Inc.	市北区	Shibei District
青岛维客集团股份有限公司	Qingdao Weekly Group Inc.	市南区	Shinan District
青岛国美电器有限公司	Qingdao Gome Electric Appliance Limited Company	四方区	Sifang District
青岛永旺东泰商业有限公司	Qingdao AEON JUSCO Commercial Limited Company	市南区	Shinan District
青岛家乐福商业有限公司	Qingdao Carrefour Commercial Limited Company	市南区	Shinan District
青岛北方国贸大厦股份有限公司	Qingdao North Trade Building Inc.	李沧区	Licang District
青岛第一百盛有限公司	Qingdao No. 1 Parkson Limited Company	市南区	Shinan District
青岛海信实业股份有限公司	Qingdao Hisense Industry Inc.	市南区	Shinan District
青岛苏宁电器有限公司	Qingdao Suning Electric Appliance Limited Company	市南区	Shinan District
青岛利客来商贸股份有限公司	Qingdao Likelai Trade Inc.	李沧区	Licang District
青岛日产汽车销售服务有限公司	Qingdao Japan – made Auto Sale And Service Limited Company	市北区	Shibei District
青岛国货城阳购物中心有限公司	Qingdao Guohuo Chengyang Shopping Center Limited Company	城阳区	Chengyang District
青岛阳光百货股份有限公司	Qingdao Sunshine Department Store Co. , Ltd	市南区	Shinan District
青岛福日汽车销售有限公司	Qingdao Furi Auto Sale Limited Company	李沧区	Licang District
青岛通宝汽车有限公司	Qingdao Tongbao Automobile Limited Company	市南区	Shinan District
青岛成达汽车销售服务有限公司	Qingdao Dacheng Auto Sale And Service Limited Company	崂山区	Laoshan District
青岛佳恒汽车销售有限公司	Qingdao Jiaheng Auto Sale Limited Company	市南区	Shinan District
青岛六和汽车销售有限公司	Qingdao Liuhe Auto Sale Limited Company	四方区	Sifang District
青岛安华机电设备有限公司	Qingdao Anwar Electromechanical Device Limited Company	市南区	Shinan District
青岛新华书店有限责任公司	Qingdao Xinhua Bookstore Limited Liability Company	市南区	Shinan District
青岛润泰事业有限公司	Qingdao Runtai Limited Company	市南区	Shinan District
青岛国货集团新世纪购物中心有限公司	Qingdao Guohuo Group New Century Shopping Center Limited Company	胶州市	Jiaozhou
山东省城市车辆青岛有限公司	Shandong Province City Vehicles Qingdao Limited Company	市南区	Shinan District
青岛万事达汽车销售有限公司	Qingdao Wanshida Auto Sale Limited Company	李沧区	Licang District
青岛喜盈门集团喜盈门商场	Qingdao Xiyingmen Group Xiyingmen Shopping Mall	城阳区	Chengyang District
青岛润华汽车销售服务有限公司	Qingdao Runhua Auto Sale And Service Limited Company	城阳区	Chengyang District
青岛名流车行有限公司	Qingdao Celebrities Car Dealership Limited Company	即墨市	Jimo
青岛安利捷丰田汽车销售有限公司	Qingdao ALJ Toyota Auto Sale Limited Company	四方区	Sifang District
青岛国货商厦有限公司	Qingdao Guohuo Commercial Building Limited Company	市南区	Shinan District
青岛世泰丰田汽车销售服务有限公司	Qingdao Shitai Toyota Auto Sale And Service Limited Company	四方区	Sifang District

14 -8 续表
continued

实现利润前 30 位企业	Name of the Top 30 at Operating Profits	所在地区	Address
青岛利群集团股份有限公司	Qingdao Liqun Group Inc.	市北区	Shibei District
青岛永旺东泰商业有限公司	Qingdao AEON JUSCO Commercial Limited Company	市南区	Shinan District
青岛家乐福商业有限公司	Qingdao Carrefour Commercial Limited Company	市南区	Shinan District
青岛国货城阳购物中心有限公司	Qingdao Guohuo Chengyang Shopping Center Limited Company	城阳区	Chengyang District
青岛第一百盛有限公司	Qingdao No. 1 Parkson Limited Company	市南区	Shinan District
青岛欧海家居有限公司	Qingdao Ouhai Home Limited Company	市北区	Shibei District
青岛苏宁电器有限公司	Qingdao Suning Electric Appliance Limited Company	市北区	Shibei District
青岛国货集团新世纪购物中心有限公司	Qingdao Guohuo Group New Century Shopping Center Limited Company	胶州市	Jiaozhou
青岛华洲实业有限公司	Qingdao Huazhou Industry Limited Company	李沧区	Licang District
青岛新华书店有限责任公司	Qingdao Xinhua Bookstore Limited Liability Company	市南区	Shinan District
青岛世泰丰田汽车销售服务有限公司	Qingdao Shitai Toyota Auto Sale And Service Limited Company	四方区	Sifang District
青岛维客集团股份有限公司	Qingdao Weekly Group Inc.	李沧区	Licang District
青岛阳光百货股份有限公司	Qingdao Sunshine Department Store Co. , Ltd	市南区	Shinan District
青岛美森置业有限公司	Qingdao Meisen Real Estate Limited Company	平度市	Pingdu
青岛平度维克购物中心有限公司	Qingdao Pingdu Weekly Shopping Center Limited Company	平度市	Pingdu
青岛安利捷丰田汽车销售有限公司	Qingdao ALJ Toyota Auto Sale Limited Company	四方区	Sifang District
青岛润泰事业有限公司	Qingdao Runtai Limited Company	市南区	Shinan District
青岛国货商厦有限公司	Qingdao Guohuo Commercial Building Limited Company	黄岛区	Huangdao District
青岛国美电器有限公司	Qingdao Gome Electric Appliance Limited Company	四方区	Sifang District
青岛北方国贸大厦股份有限公司	Qingdao North Trade Building Inc.	李沧区	Licang District
青岛海信实业股份有限公司	Qingdao Hisense Industry Inc.	市南区	Shinan District
青岛协亨通讯设备有限公司	Qingdao Xieheng Communication Equipment Limited Company	市北区	Shibei District
青岛宏祥液化气有限公司	Qingdao Hongxiang Liquid Gas Limited Company	莱西市	Laixi
青岛佳恒汽车销售有限公司	Qingdao Jiaheng Auto Sale Limited Company	市南区	Shinan District
青岛北星汽车销售有限公司	Qingdao North - star Auto Sale Limited Company	四方区	Sifang District
青岛平度市新华书店有限责任公司	Qingdao Pingdu Xinhua Bookstore Limited Liability Company	平度市	Pingdu
胶南市糖酒副食品总公司	Jiaona Rum And Non - staple Food Product Main Corporation	胶南市	Jiaonan
青岛利客来商贸股份有限公司	Qingdao Likelai Trade Inc.	李沧区	Licang District
青岛中百佳乐家超市有限公司	Qingdao Zhongbai Jialejia Supermarket Limited Company	平度市	Pingdu
青岛医保药品城有限公司	Qingdao Medical Insurance Drugs City Limited Company	市北区	Shibei District

14 -9 分市、区城乡亿元商品交易市场分布情况(2005 年)
DISTRIBUTION OF BILLION COMMODITY MARKETS OF URBAN AND RURAL AREA BY REGION(2005)

市、区名称	Region	亿元商品交易市场数量(个) Number of Billion Commodity Market(unit)			亿元商品交易市场成交额(亿元) Turnover of Billion Commodity Market(100 million yuan)		
		合计 Total	#综合市场 Comprehensive Market	#专业市场 Specialized Market	合计 Total	#综合市场 Comprehensive Market	#专业市场 Specialized Market
总　计	**Total**	**46**	**16**	**30**	**440. 68**	**189. 84**	**250. 84**
市　区	Urban Area	23	9	14	197. 35	113. 77	83. 58
#黄岛区	Chengyang District	3	2	1	4. 68	3. 45	1. 23
崂山区	Huangdao District	1	–	1	1. 24	–	1. 24
城阳区	Laoshan District	2	1	1	90. 67	70. 31	20. 36
胶州市	Jiaozhou	4	2	2	14. 59	10. 47	4. 12
即墨市	Jimo	9	1	8	175. 66	43. 43	132. 23
平度市	Pingdu	7	2	5	38. 44	15. 96	22. 48
胶南市	Jiaonan	2	2	–	6. 21	6. 21	–
莱西市	Laixi	1	–	1	8. 43	–	8. 43

14－10 批发和零售业网点(2005 年底)
OUTLETS OF WHOLESALE AND RETAIL TRADE(END OF 2005)

单位:个(unit)

区市名称	Region	批发和零售业 Wholesale and Retail Trade	分经济类型 Grouped by Economy Categories				
			国有及控股 State-owned and State-holding	私营 Private	外商投资 Foreign	个体 Individual	其他 Others
全市总计	**Total**	**198 911**	**917**	**13 901**	**269**	**180 406**	**3 418**
市区	Urban Area	68 885	419	10 580	257	55 276	2 353
市南区	Shinan District	9 909	157	2 897	152	6 062	641
市北区	Shibei District	14 253	88	3 300	42	10 489	334
四方区	Sifang District	9 849	45	1 802	15	7 269	718
黄岛区	Huangdao District	9 387	71	836	26	8 274	180
崂山区	Laoshan District	6 041	18	570	3	5 324	126
李沧区	Licang District	10 171	20	793	4	9 197	157
城阳区	Chengyang District	9 275	20	382	15	8 661	197
胶州市	Jiaozhou	26 492	67	1 169	2	25 012	242
即墨市	Jimo	34 032	41	762	4	32 990	235
平度市	Pingdu	23 947	248	466		23 105	128
胶南市	Jiaonan	23 085	120	477	3	22 180	305
莱西市	Laixi	22 470	22	447	3	21 843	155

14－11 批发和零售业从业人员(2005 年底)
EMPLOYMENT OF WHOLESALE AND RETAIL TRADE(END OF 2005)

单位:人(person)

区市名称	Region	批发和零售业 Wholesale and Retail Trade	分经济类型 Grouped by Economy Categories				
			国有及控股 State-owned and State-holding	私营 Private	外商投资 Foreign	个体 Individual	其他 Others
全市总计	**Total**	**528 202**	**19 353**	**108 416**	**8 717**	**344 514**	**47 202**
市区	Urban Area	263 956	13 551	83 111	8 307	124 057	34 930
市南区	Shinan District	54 015	5 630	20 750	3 960	11 940	11 735
市北区	Shibei District	80 802	4 977	30 050	2 473	33 367	9 935
四方区	Sifang District	32 895	345	13 190	340	16 446	2 574
黄岛区	Huangdao District	19 444	607	4 479	876	12 026	1 456
崂山区	Laoshan District	16 918	931	5 011	108	9 165	1 703
李沧区	Licang District	34 472	550	6 100	402	22 850	4 570
城阳区	Chengyang District	25 410	511	3 531	148	18 263	2 957
胶州市	Jiaozhou	59 131	359	6 167	50	51 143	1 412
即墨市	Jimo	66 578	1 242	5 574	202	56 014	3 546
平度市	Pingdu	47 894	1 998	4 576		40 133	1 187
胶南市	Jiaonan	39 466	1 768	4 868	96	29 138	3 596
莱西市	Laixi	51 177	435	4 120	62	44 029	2 531

14－12 批发业网点(2005 年底)

OUTLETS OF WHOLESALE TRADE(END OF 2005)

单位:个(unit)

区市名称	Region	批发业 Wholesale Trade	#个体 of which:Individual	农畜产品 Wholesale of Agricultural Animal and Products	食品饮料烟草制品 Food,Beverage and Tabacco Products	纺织服装及日用品 Textile Products,Garments and Daily Use Goods
全市总计	**Total**	**47 547**	**36 892**	**8 517**	**7 047**	**13 013**
市区	Urban Area	13 736	5 239	491	1 815	2 956
市南区	Shinan District	2 666	322	58	335	705
市北区	Shibei District	4 765	2 328	18	822	1 748
四方区	Sifang District	2 383	608	10	209	113
黄岛区	Huangdao District	905	238	8	79	104
崂山区	Laoshan District	417	99	14	36	61
李沧区	Licang District	1 303	739	313	159	44
城阳区	Chengyang District	1 297	905	70	175	181
胶州市	Jiaozhou	4 545	4 016	273	1 719	1 632
即墨市	Jimo	10 668	10 174	1 285	820	6 738
平度市	Pingdu	6 207	5 661	3 408	486	426
胶南市	Jiaonan	5 928	5 619	693	922	358
莱西市	Laixi	6 463	6 183	2 367	1 285	903

14－12 续表

continued

单位:个(unit)

区市名称	Region	文化体育用品及器材 Culture,Sports Articles and Equipments	医药及医疗器械 Medicine and Medical Appliance	矿产品建材及化工产品 Wholesale of Mineral Products,Building Materials and Chemical Products	机械设备五金交电及电子产品 Wholesale of Machine Equipments,Hardware,Electrical Appliance and Electronic Products	其他批发 Wholesale of Others
全市总计	**Total**	**796**	**538**	**6 916**	**7 569**	**3 151**
市区	Urban Area	434	255	2 518	4 068	1 199
市南区	Shinan District	126	88	430	539	385
市北区	Shibei District	136	83	511	1 312	135
四方区	Sifang District	48	24	442	1 304	233
黄岛区	Huangdao District	33	11	324	279	67
崂山区	Laoshan District	11	7	158	92	38
李沧区	Licang District	17	7	358	316	89
城阳区	Chengyang District	63	35	295	226	252
胶州市	Jiaozhou	67	161	382	190	121
即墨市	Jimo	188	12	593	631	401
平度市	Pingdu	16	36	410	515	910
胶南市	Jiaonan	75	62	2 113	1 355	350
莱西市	Laixi	16	12	900	810	170

14 –13 批发业从业人员(2005 年底)

EMPLOYMENT OF WHOLESALE TRADE(END OF 2005)

单位:人(person)

区市名称	Region	批发业 Wholesale Trade	#个体 of which:Individual	农畜产品 Wholesale of Agricultural Animal and Products	食品饮料烟草制品 Food,Beverage and Tabacco Products	纺织服装及日用品 Textile Products,Garments and Daily Use Goods
全市总计	**Total**	**194 345**	**87 000**	**20 367**	**30 311**	**42 947**
市区	Urban Area	103 541	18 816	3 000	13 909	21 506
市南区	Shinan District	26 187	520	1 405	2 463	8 619
市北区	Shibei District	37 835	11 467	260	7 173	9 558
四方区	Sifang District	15 576	1 734	62	1 957	1 533
黄岛区	Huangdao District	5 316	439	35	797	529
崂山区	Laoshan District	5 034	193	143	170	278
李沧区	Licang District	6 762	1 460	478	587	293
城阳区	Chengyang District	6 831	3 003	617	762	696
胶州市	Jiaozhou	18 900	13 178	1 498	8 088	3 316
即墨市	Jimo	24 947	20 358	2 698	1 852	14 854
平度市	Pingdu	15 283	11 081	6 113	1 457	897
胶南市	Jiaonan	12 493	8 148	1 282	1 678	595
莱西市	Laixi	19 181	15 419	5 776	3 327	1 779

14 –13 续表

continued

单位:人(person)

区市名称	Region	文化体育用品及器材 Culture,Sports Articles and Equipments	医药及医疗器械 Medicine and Medical Appliance	矿产品建材及化工产品 Wholesale of Mineral Products,Building Materials and Chemical Products	机械设备五金交电及电子产品 Wholesale of Machine Equipments,Hardware,Electrical Appliance and Electronic Products	其他批发 Wholesale of Others
全市总计	**Total**	**3 340**	**4 323**	**37 192**	**42 493**	**13 372**
市区	Urban Area	2 252	2 574	20 303	31 918	8 079
市南区	Shinan District	934	1 250	3 278	5 222	3 016
市北区	Shibei District	306	699	6 578	11 995	1 266
四方区	Sifang District	231	124	2 543	7 175	1 951
黄岛区	Huangdao District	191	103	1 915	1 474	272
崂山区	Laoshan District	70	150	1 562	2 561	100
李沧区	Licang District	89	117	2 571	2 085	542
城阳区	Chengyang District	431	131	1 856	1 406	932
胶州市	Jiaozhou	281	358	2 099	1 813	1 447
即墨市	Jimo	411	71	2 533	1 535	993
平度市	Pingdu	39	539	3 333	1 959	946
胶南市	Jiaonan	142	130	5 493	2 303	870
莱西市	Laixi	215	651	3 431	2 965	1 037

14－14 零售业网点(2005 年底)
OUTLETS OF RETAIL TRADE(END OF 2005)

单位:个(unit)

区市名称	Region	零售业 Retail Trade	#个体 of which: Individual	综合零售 Multiple Retail Trade	食品饮料烟草制品 Food, Beverage and Tabacco Products	纺织服装及日用品 Textile Products, Garments and Daily Use Goods	文化体育用品及器材 Culture, Sports Articles and Equipments
全市总计	**Total**	**151 364**	**143 004**	**31 461**	**54 795**	**33 961**	**5 043**
市区	Urban Area	55 149	49 545	12 438	17 499	11 853	1 852
市南区	Shinan District	7 243	5 740	1 290	2 895	1 671	320
市北区	Shibei District	9 488	7 669	1 880	1 866	2 804	524
四方区	Sifang District	7 466	6 661	1 082	3 218	1 195	209
黄岛区	Huangdao District	8 482	8 036	2 478	2 397	2 058	268
崂山区	Laoshan District	5 624	5 225	1 608	1 906	800	248
李沧区	Licang District	8 868	8 458	2 477	3 281	1 719	30
城阳区	Chengyang District	7 978	7 756	1 623	1 936	1 606	253
胶州市	Jiaozhou	21 947	20 996	5 608	6 672	4 329	531
即墨市	Jimo	23 364	22 816	2 331	10 649	6 510	1 018
平度市	Pingdu	17 740	17 444	3 502	8 582	3 922	531
胶南市	Jiaonan	17 157	16 563	3 739	6 349	3 973	631
莱西市	Laixi	16 007	15 640	3 843	5 044	3 374	480

14－14 续表
continued

单位:个(unit)

区市名称	Region	医药及医疗器械 Medicine and Medical Appliance	汽车摩托车燃料及零配件 Spare and Component Part for Automobiles, Motorcycles	家用电器及电子产品 Electrical Equipment and Electronic Products	五金家具及室内装潢材料 Hardware, Electrical Appliance, Furniture and Decoration Materials	无店铺及其他零售 Retail Sales of Having No Shop and Others
全市总计	**Total**	**1 545**	**3 810**	**4 457**	**9 075**	**7 217**
市区	Urban Area	690	1 827	1 766	4 482	2 742
市南区	Shinan District	145	80	260	190	392
市北区	Shibei District	164	367	724	905	254
四方区	Sifang District	41	265	130	415	911
黄岛区	Huangdao District	139	220	206	355	361
崂山区	Laoshan District	60	72	44	600	286
李沧区	Licang District	36	227	191	789	118
城阳区	Chengyang District	105	596	211	1 228	420
胶州市	Jiaozhou	169	329	798	1 910	1 601
即墨市	Jimo	156	370	185	1 405	740
平度市	Pingdu	164	58	172	225	584
胶南市	Jiaonan	273	201	883	448	660
莱西市	Laixi	93	1 025	653	605	890

14－15 零售业从业人员(2005 年底)

EMPLOYMENT OF RETAIL TRADE(END OF 2005)

单位:人(person)

区市名称	Region	零售业 Retail Trade	#个体 of which:Individual	综合零售 Multiple Retail Trade	食品饮料烟草制品 Food, Beverage and Tabacco Products	纺织服装及日用品 Textile Products, Garments and Daily Use Goods	文化体育用品及器材 Culture, Sports Articles and Equipments
全市总计	**Total**	**333 857**	**258 554**	**86 098**	**93 714**	**75 811**	**9 538**
市区	Urban Area	160 415	105 241	48 731	37 799	30 793	6 050
市南区	Shinan District	27 828	11 420	7 050	7 825	6 956	1 452
市北区	Shibei District	42 967	21 900	15 324	6 378	8 206	2 006
四方区	Sifang District	17 319	14 712	5 290	5 614	2 568	607
黄岛区	Huangdao District	14 128	11 587	5 291	2 794	2 647	461
崂山区	Laoshan District	11 884	8 972	3 100	3 308	2 180	636
李沧区	Licang District	27 710	21 390	9 144	8 065	5 207	95
城阳区	Chengyang District	18 579	15 260	3 532	3 815	3 029	793
胶州市	Jiaozhou	40 231	37 965	9 240	10 408	10 124	609
即墨市	Jimo	41 631	35 656	6 685	18 068	10 293	194
平度市	Pingdu	32 611	29 052	7 706	10 149	11 366	828
胶南市	Jiaonan	26 973	22 029	6 057	8 889	5 443	898
莱西市	Laixi	31 996	28 611	7 679	8 401	7 792	959

14－15 续表

continued

单位:人(person)

区市名称	Region	医药及医疗器械 Medicine and Medical Appliance	汽车摩托车燃料及零配件 Spare and Component Part for Automobiles, Motorcycles	家用电器及电子产品 Electrical Equipment and Electronic Products	五金家具及室内装潢材料 Hardware, Electrical Appliance, Furniture and Decoration Materials	无店铺及其他零售 Retail Sales of Having No Shop and Others
全市总计	**Total**	**7 340**	**12 984**	**12 950**	**24 913**	**10 509**
市区	Urban Area	4 678	6 956	6 707	14 543	4 158
市南区	Shinan District	1 029	645	1 176	935	760
市北区	Shibei District	2 218	1 768	3 369	3 389	309
四方区	Sifang District	279	536	329	947	1 149
黄岛区	Huangdao District	239	425	557	1 002	712
崂山区	Laoshan District	246	1 000	101	938	375
李沧区	Licang District	331	1 247	633	2 657	331
城阳区	Chengyang District	336	1 335	542	4 675	522
胶州市	Jiaozhou	766	1 995	1 403	3 975	1 711
即墨市	Jimo	658	1 011	796	2 635	1 291
平度市	Pingdu	302	108	538	891	723
胶南市	Jiaonan	656	865	1 571	1 255	1 339
莱西市	Laixi	280	2 049	1 935	1 614	1 287

14－16 零售业营业面积(2005 年底)

BUSINESS AREA OF RETAIL TRADE(END OF 2005)

单位:平方米(sq. m)

区市名称	Region	零售业 Retail Trade	#个体 of which: Individual	综合零售 Multiple Retail Trade	食品饮料烟草制品 Food, Beverage and Tabacco Products	纺织服装及日用品 Textile Products, Garments and Daily Use Goods	文化体育用品及器材 Culture, Sports Articles and Equipments
全市总计	**Total**	**5 964 633**	**3 179 310**	**1 838 171**	**1 464 826**	**1 157 596**	**165 195**
市区	Urban Area	2 624 018	1 291 068	973 865	551 864	415 569	70 689
市南区	Shinan District	584 618	127 950	248 680	105 435	89 550	19 100
市北区	Shibei District	514 692	224 086	242 646	38 950	84 465	18 860
四方区	Sifang District	319 238	196 757	82 341	128 703	46 378	4 605
黄岛区	Huangdao District	281 387	184 077	113 969	64 769	48 998	6 604
崂山区	Laoshan District	218 760	116 800	69 584	50 250	23 060	10 000
李沧区	Licang District	367 790	206 635	147 876	81 706	56 275	987
城阳区	Chengyang District	337 533	234 763	68 769	82 051	66 843	10 533
胶州市	Jiaozhou	570 630	360 216	172 034	109 876	170 001	17 680
即墨市	Jimo	535 637	278 438	17 806	248 098	180 796	17 639
平度市	Pingdu	790 904	395 202	359 226	166 127	96 952	16 889
胶南市	Jiaonan	578 454	430 638	127 126	184 121	111 681	19 566
莱西市	Laixi	864 990	423 748	188 114	204 740	182 597	22 732

14－16 续表

continued

单位:平方米(sq. m)

区市名称	Region	医药及医疗器械 Medicine and Medical Appliance	汽车摩托车燃料及零配件 Spare and Component Part for Automobiles, Motorcycles	家用电器及电子产品 Electrical Equipment and Electronic Products	五金家具及室内装潢材料 Hardware, Electrical Appliance, Furniture and Decoration Materials	无店铺及其他零售 Retail Sales of Having No Shop and Others
全市总计	**Total**	**109 667**	**339 239**	**304 288**	**440 277**	**145 374**
市区	Urban Area	45 003	154 515	109 159	227 211	76 143
市南区	Shinan District	14 820	41 520	23 613	22 760	19 140
市北区	Shibei District	13 522	23 996	44 551	43 991	3 711
四方区	Sifang District	2 095	9 712	6 348	15 917	23 139
黄岛区	Huangdao District	3 489	10 222	8 749	18 168	6 419
崂山区	Laoshan District	4 605	20 790	1 496	35 000	3 975
李沧区	Licang District	2 153	22 563	15 606	38 834	1 790
城阳区	Chengyang District	4 319	25 712	8 796	52 541	17 969
胶州市	Jiaozhou	6 042	27 765	18 169	30 864	18 199
即墨市	Jimo	6 334	18 224	15 418	27 735	3 587
平度市	Pingdu	17 418	18 220	70 085	32 045	13 942
胶南市	Jiaonan	19 519	19 598	32 229	38 215	26 399
莱西市	Laixi	15 351	100 917	59 228	84 207	7 104

14－17 餐饮业网点(2005 年底)
OUTLETS OF CATERING TRADE(END OF 2005)

单位:个(unit)

区市名称	Region	餐饮业 CateringTrade	分经济类型 Grouped by Economy Categories				
			国有及控股 State-holding	私营 Private	外商投资 Foreign Invested	个体 Individual	其他 Others
全市总计	**Total**	**24 728**	**89**	**671**	**93**	**23 516**	**359**
市区	Urban Area	11 732	67	467	81	10 842	275
市南区	Shinan District	1 573	20	170	50	1 273	60
市北区	Shibei District	1 578	13	82	9	1 412	62
四方区	Sifang District	1 181	28	52		1 024	77
黄岛区	Huangdao District	1 976	2	59	4	1 896	15
崂山区	Laoshan District	1 222	3	40	2	1 161	16
李沧区	Licang District	1 674		20	4	1 632	18
城阳区	Chengyang District	2 528	1	44	12	2 444	27
胶州市	Jiaozhou	2 883	1	48	4	2 807	23
即墨市	Jimo	2 278	0	42	1	2 227	8
平度市	Pingdu	3 286	18	16		3 219	33
胶南市	Jiaonan	2 387	2	40	2	2 330	13
莱西市	Laixi	2 162	1	58	5	2 091	7

14－18 餐饮业从业人员(2005 年底)
EMPLOYMENT OF CATERING TRADE(END OF 2005)

单位:人(person)

区市名称	Region	餐饮业 Catering Trade	分经济类型 Grouped by Economy Categories				
			国有及控股 State-holding	私营 Private	外商投资 Foreign Invested	个体 Individual	其他 Others
全市总计	**Total**	**115 031**	**3 554**	**16 924**	**3 707**	**83 768**	**7 078**
市区	Urban Area	70 751	2 470	13 136	3 325	46 343	5 477
市南区	Shinan District	20 986	1 652	6 010	2 246	8 768	2 310
市北区	Shibei District	10 859	155	2 462	352	7 024	866
四方区	Sifang District	5 619	184	404		4 226	805
黄岛区	Huangdao District	8 746	187	1 356	216	6 821	166
崂山区	Laoshan District	6 267	125	1 238	22	4 761	121
李沧区	Licang District	7 834		1 081	102	6 313	338
城阳区	Chengyang District	10 440	167	585	387	8 430	871
胶州市	Jiaozhou	10 449	209	863	49	9 010	318
即墨市	Jimo	8 748	0	1 137	25	7 432	154
平度市	Pingdu	10 354	790	265		8 902	397
胶南市	Jiaonan	7 227	17	712	15	5 872	611
莱西市	Laixi	7 502	68	811	293	6 209	121

14－19 限额以上批发法人企业一览表(2005 年)

SCHEDULE OF WHOLESALE TRADE CORPORATE ENTERPRISES ABOVE LEVEL(2005)

序号 Serial Number	单位名称	Name	所在地区	Location
1	青岛市市南区江西路加油站	Qingdao Jiangxi Road Gas Station At Shinan District	市南区	Shinan District
2	青岛海润投资集团有限公司	Qingdao Hairun Investment Group Limited Company	市南区	Shinan District
3	青岛富轩进出口有限公司	Qingdao Fuxuan Import And Export Limited Company	市南区	Shinan District
4	青岛海珊进出口有限责任公司	Qingdao Haishan Import And Export Limited Liability Company	市南区	Shinan District
5	青岛嘉德汽车有限公司	Qingdao Jiade Automobile Sales Limited Company	市南区	Shinan District
6	中土畜东方进出口有限责任公司	China National Native Produce And Animal By-products East Import And Export Limited Liability Company	市南区	Shinan District
7	山东机械设备进出口集团公司	Shandong Mechanical Device Import Snd Export Group Company	市南区	Shinan District
8	青岛经济开发区进出口公司	Qingdao Economic Development Zone Import And Export Company	市南区	Shinan District
9	青岛亚萌贸易有限公司	Qingdao Yameng Trade Limited Company	市南区	Shinan District
10	青岛保税区韩亚国际贸易有限公司	Qingdao Bonded Area Hanya International Trade Limited Company	市南区	Shinan District
11	仪征化纤青岛康祺有限责任公司	Icheng Chemical Fiber Qingdao Kangqi Limited Liability Company	市南区	Shinan District
12	青岛华青进出口有限公司	Qingdao Huaqing Import And Export Limited Company	市南区	Shinan District
13	新华锦集团山东锦岳国际经贸有限责任公司	Hiking Group Shandong Jinyue International Economics And Trade Limited Liability Company	市南区	Shinan District
14	新华锦集团山东海诚进出口有限公司	Hiking Group Shandong Haicheng Import And Export Limited Company	市南区	Shinan District
15	青岛中联油国际贸易公司	Qingdao China United Oil International Trade Company	市南区	Shinan District
16	五矿钢铁青岛有限公司	Fifth Ores Steel And Iron Qingdao Limited Company	市南区	Shinan District
17	青岛新兴东方进出口总公司	Qingdao Xinxing East import And Export Main Corporation	市南区	Shinan District
18	山东省华隆进出口公司	Shandong Province Hualong Import-export Company	市南区	Shinan District
19	青岛莱钢经贸有限公司	Qingdao Laigang Economics And Trade Limited Company	市南区	Shinan District
20	青岛南北通商贸有限公司	The Qingdao North And South Trade Limited Company	市南区	Shinan District
21	山东省五金矿产进出口公司	Shandong Province Hardware Minerals Import-export Company	市南区	Shinan District
22	青岛欧美进出口有限公司	Qingdao Europe And America Import And Export Limited Company	市南区	Shinan District
23	青岛金绣纺织品有限公司	Qingdao Jinxiu Textile Limited Company	市南区	Shinan District
24	新华锦集团山东海川发制品进出口有限公司	Hiking Group Shandong Haichuan Wig Ware Import And Export Limited Company	市南区	Shinan District
25	青岛新华锦集团山东海润工艺品进出口有限公司	Hiking Group Shandong Hairun Arts and Crafts Import And Export Limited Company	市南区	Shinan District
26	新华锦集团山东海锦国际贸易有限公司	Hiking Group Shandong Haijin International Trade Limited Company	市南区	Shinan District
27	山东省纺织品进出口公司青岛华锐贸易公司	Shandong Province Textile Import And Export Company Qingdao Huarui Trade Company	市南区	Shinan District
28	青岛卓琴实业发展有限公司	Qingdao Zhuoqin Industry Limited Company	市南区	Shinan District
29	伊藤忠(青岛)有限公司	Itochu(Qingdao) Limited Company	市南区	Shinan District
30	青岛红玺国际贸易有限公司	Qingdao Redseal International Trade Limited Company	市南区	Shinan District
31	青岛邦联通达贸易有限公司	Qingdao Banglian Tongda Trade Limited Company	市南区	Shinan District
32	山东绮丽集团公司	Shandong Cherry Group Company	市南区	Shinan District
33	金光纸业(青岛)有限公司	APP Qingdao Limited Company	市南区	Shinan District
34	青岛卓信工贸有限公司	Qingdao Zhuoxin Industry And Trade Limited Company	市南区	Shinan District
35	山东嘉源进出口有限公司	Shandong Jiayuan Import And Export Limited Company	市南区	Shinan District
36	青岛欧美投资集团有限公司	Qingdao Europe And America Investment Group Limited Company	市南区	Shinan District
37	青岛瑞祥抽纱有限公司	Qingdao Ruixiang Artex Limited Company	市南区	Shinan District

14－19 续表
continued

序号 Serial Number	单位名称	Name	所在地区	Location
38	青岛双星集团燃料有限公司	Qingdao Doublestar Group Fuel Limited Company	市南区	Shinan District
39	中国包装进出口山东公司	China Packs Import And Export Shandong Corporation	市南区	Shinan District
40	青岛双星化工工贸有限公司	Qingdao Doublestar Chemical Industry And Trade Limited Company	市南区	Shinan District
41	山东省机械进出口集团公司	Shandong Province Mechanical Import And Export Group Company	市南区	Shinan District
42	青岛海湾集团进出口有限公司	Qingdao Bay Group Import And Export Limited Company	市南区	Shinan District
43	新华锦集团山东海川对外贸易有限公司	Hiking Group Shandong Haichuan Foreign Trade Limited Company	市南区	Shinan District
44	青岛农资实业有限公司	Qingdao Agricultural Goods And Material Industry Limited Company	市南区	Shinan District
45	中国烟草山东进出口公司	China Tobacco Shandong Import And Export Company	市南区	Shinan District
46	青岛市纺织纱布市场有限责任公司	Qingdao Spinning And Weaving Gauze Market Limited Liability Company	市南区	Shinan District
47	山东省医药保健品进出口公司	Shandong Province Medicine Healthy Product Import And Export Company	市南区	Shinan District
48	青岛世纪瑞丰国际贸易有限公司	Qingdao Century Ruifeng International Trade Limited Company	市南区	Shinan District
49	青岛丰利茶叶有限公司	Qingdao Fengli Tea Limited Company	市南区	Shinan District
50	山东新英大国际贸易有限公司	Shandong Xinyingda International Trade Limited Company	市南区	Shinan District
51	青岛海亨达商贸有限公司	Qingdao Haihengda Trade Limited Company	市南区	Shinan District
52	山东省金富林进出口有限公司	Shandong Province Jinfulin Import And Export Limited Company	市南区	Shinan District
53	山东省物产进出口公司	Shandong Province Native Product Import – export Company	市南区	Shinan District
54	山东美赫尔国际贸易有限公司	Shandong Meiher International Trade Limited Company	市南区	Shinan District
55	山东对外经贸华通公司	Shandong Foreign Economics And Trade Huatong Company	市南区	Shinan District
56	新华锦集团山东锦立泰进出口有限公司	Hiking Group Shandong Jintel Import And Export Limited Company	市南区	Shinan District
57	新华锦集团山东锦丰纺织有限公司	Hiking Group Shandong Jinfeng Gaintex Limited Company	市南区	Shinan District
58	山东中粮花生制品进出口有限公司	COFCO Shandong Peanut Product Import And Export Limited Company	市南区	Shinan District
59	新华锦集团山东锦宜纺织有限公司	Hiking Group Shandong Jinyi Gaintex Limited Company	市南区	Shinan District
60	山东三川贸易有限公司	Shandong Sanchuan Trade Limited Company	市南区	Shinan District
61	中粮山东粮油进出口公司	COFCO Shandong Grain And Oil Import And Export Company	市南区	Shinan District
62	山东欣中基国际贸易有限公司	Shandong Xinzhongji International Trade Limited Company	市南区	Shinan District
63	新华锦集团山东盈商针棉织品进出口有限公司	Hiking Group Shandong Welltrade Knitwears And Home Textiles Import And Export Limited Company	市南区	Shinan District
64	青岛东方同祥经贸有限公司	Qingdao East Tongxiang Economics And Trade Limited Company	市南区	Shinan District
65	山东省东方国际贸易有有限公司	Shandong Province East International Trade Limited Company	市南区	Shinan District
66	青岛包装印刷物资公司	Qingdao Packing And Printing Materials Company	市南区	Shinan District
67	青岛华辰化工供销公司	Qingdao Huachen Chemical Industry Supply And Sales Company	市南区	Shinan District
68	青岛钢铁进出口公司	Qingdao Steel And Iron Import And Export Company	市南区	Shinan District
69	青岛疗养区供应有限公司	Qingdao Convalesces Area Supply Limited Company	市南区	Shinan District
70	青岛市化学石油供销有限责任公司	Qingdao Chemistry Petroleum Supply And Sales Limited liability Company	市南区	Shinan District
71	青岛菲尔特商务有限公司	Qingdao Feierte Commerce Limited Company	市南区	Shinan District
72	中国化工建设青岛公司	China Chemical Industry Constructs Qingdao Corporation	市南区	Shinan District
73	青岛银储物资发展公司	Qingdao Yinchu Materials Development Company	市南区	Shinan District
74	山东省荣鑫进出口有限公司	Shandong Province Rongxin Import And Export Limited Company	市南区	Shinan District

14 –19 续表
continued

序号 Serial Number	单位名称	Name	所在地区	Location
75	青岛世纪新科啤酒开发有限公司	Qingdao Century Shinco Beer Development Limited Company	市南区	Shinan District
76	青岛德隆纺织有限公司	Qingdao Delong Gaintex Limited Company	市南区	Shinan District
77	青岛锦纬时装有限公司	Qingdao Jinwei Fashion Clothing Limited Company	市南区	Shinan District
78	青岛施蒂特经贸有限公司	Qingdao State Economics And Trade Limited Company	市南区	Shinan District
79	山东莱钢国际贸易有限公司	Shandong Laigang International Trade Limited Company	市南区	Shinan District
80	青岛国药医药有限公司	Qingdao Statemedicine Medicine Limited Company	市南区	Shinan District
81	青岛益佳国际贸易集团有限公司	Qingdao Yijia International Trade Group Limited Company	市南区	Shinan District
82	青岛海利尔商贸发展有限公司	Qingdao Hailir Trade Development Limited Company	市南区	Shinan District
83	山东金蜂星电子科技有限公司	Shandong King Cellstar Electronics Technology Limited Company	市南区	Shinan District
84	青岛华讯泰普通讯器材有限公司	Qingdao Huaxun Taipu Communications Equipment Limited Company	市南区	Shinan District
85	青岛京青联合石油公司	Qingdao Jingqing United Petroleum Company	市南区	Shinan District
86	青岛中油油品销售有限公司	China Petroleum Sales Qingdao Limited Company	市南区	Shinan District
87	攀钢集团国际经济贸易有限公司青岛分公司	Pangang Group International Economy Trade Limited Company Qingdao Subsidiary Company	市南区	Shinan District
88	青岛华氏国风医药有限公司	Qingdao Growful Medicine Limited Company	市南区	Shinan District
89	青岛汽车进出口有限公司	Qingdao Automobile Import Snd Export Limited Company	市南区	Shinan District
90	青岛嘉翔经贸有限公司	Qingdao Jiaxiang Economics And Trade Limited Company	市南区	Shinan District
91	山东省交通进出口有限公司	Shandong Province Transportation Import And Export Limited Company	市南区	Shinan District
92	山东成套设备国际贸易有限公司	Shandong Complete Eets Of Equipment International Trade Limited Company	市南区	Shinan District
93	青岛海信进出口有限责任公司	Qingdao Hisense Import And Export Limited Liability Company	市南区	Shinan District
94	青岛吉利汽车销售服务有限公司	Qingdao Jili Auto Sale Service Limited Company	市南区	Shinan District
95	青岛庆铃汽车销售有限公司	Qingdao Qingling Auto Sale Limited Company	市南区	Shinan District
96	青岛太阳石圣邦医药有限公司	Qingdao Sunstone Shengbang Medicine Limited Company	市南区	Shinan District
97	中国化工青岛橡胶公司	China Chemical Industry Qingdao Rubber Company	市南区	Shinan District
98	青岛源丰实业集团有限公司	Qingdao Yuanfeng Industry Group Limited Company	市南区	Shinan District
99	青岛纵横纺织品有限责任公司	Qingdao Zongheng Textile Limited Liability Company	市南区	Shinan District
100	山东省食品进出口公司	Shandong Province Food Import – export Company	市南区	Shinan District
101	青岛富利达实业有限公司	Qingdao Freedom Industry Limited Company	市南区	Shinan District
102	青岛怡远汽车销售服务有限公司	Qingdao Yiyuan Auto Sale And Service Limited Company	市南区	Shinan District
103	青岛凯元物产有限公司	Qingdao Kaiyuan Product Limited Company	市南区	Shinan District
104	中国船舶燃料供应青岛公司	China Marine Bunker(Petro China) Qingdao Company	市北区	Shibei District
105	青岛第一粮库	Qingdao No. 1 Grain Storage	市北区	Shibei District
106	青岛中然实业公司	Qingdao Zhongran Industrial Corporation	市北区	Shibei District
107	青岛纺联集团进出口股份有限公司	Qingdao Textiles Import And Export Limited Liability Company	市北区	Shibei District
108	青岛红星化工集团进出口有限公司	Qingdao Red – star Chemical Industry Group Import And Export Limited Company	市北区	Shibei District
109	青岛市棉麻有限公司	Qingdao Cotton And Kapok Hemp Limited Company	市北区	Shibei District
110	青岛飞讯电子工程公司	Qingdao Feixun Electronic Engineering Company	市北区	Shibei District
111	青岛索电数码科技有限公司	Qingdao Suodian Digital Science And Technology Limited Company	市北区	Shibei District

14 −19 续表
continued

序号 Serial Number	单位名称	Name	所在地区	Location
112	青岛海四达办公设备有限公司	Qingdao Haisida Office Equipment Limited Company	市北区	Shibei District
113	青岛三业电脑科技有限公司	Qingdao Sanye Computer Science And Technology Limited Company	市北区	Shibei District
114	青岛博君电脑有限公司	Qingdao Bojun Computer Limited Company	市北区	Shibei District
115	青岛新月商用电脑有限公司	Qingdao Xinyue Computer Limited Company	市北区	Shibei District
116	青岛卓海电子资讯有限公司	Qingdao Zhuohai Electron Information Limited Company	市北区	Shibei District
117	青岛志伟创达科贸有限公司	Qingdao Zhiwei Chuangda Technology And Trade Limited Company	市北区	Shibei District
118	青岛旭海正洋电子咨讯有限公司	Qingdao Xuhai Zhengyang Electron Consults The news Limited Company	市北区	Shibei District
119	青岛凯健经贸有限公司	Qingdao Kaijian Economics And Trade Limited Company	市北区	Shibei District
120	青岛鑫雷音电子有限公司	Qingdao Xinleiyin Electron Limited Company	市北区	Shibei District
121	青岛波导电子有限公司	Qingdao Bird Electron Limited Company	市北区	Shibei District
122	青岛凯沃贸易有限公司	Qingdao Kaiwo Trade Limited Company	市北区	Shibei District
123	青岛华金针纺织品进出口有限公司	Qingdao Huatin Knitting And Textile Inp& Exp Corp. , Ltd.	市北区	Shibei District
124	青岛工贸商业发展有限公司	Qingdao Industry And Trade Commercial Development Limited Company	市北区	Shibei District
125	青岛市烟草专卖局青岛烟草有限公司	Qingdao Tobacco Monopoly Bureau Qingdao Tobacco Limited Company	市北区	Shibei District
126	青岛基建物资配套有限责任公司	Qingdao Construction Goods Attachment Limited Liability Company	市北区	Shibei District
127	青岛远洋船舶供应公司	Qingdao Open Sea Ships Supply Company	市北区	Shibei District
128	青岛华孚石油有限公司	Qingdao Huafu Petroleum Limited Company	市北区	Shibei District
129	青岛康悦电子科技有限公司	Qingdao Kangyue Electron Science And Technology Limited Company	市北区	Shibei District
130	青岛东正经贸有限公司	Qingdao Dongzheng Economics And Trade Limited Company	市北区	Shibei District
131	青岛新中印物资有限公司	Qingdao Xinzhongyin Materials Limited Company	市北区	Shibei District
132	青岛双蝶实业有限公司	Qingdao Double Butterfly Industry Limited Company	市北区	Shibei District
133	青岛探索科技有限公司	Qingdao Exploration Science And Technology Limited Company	市北区	Shibei District
134	青岛胜利石化产品销售有限公司	Qingdao Shengli Petrified Product Sale Limited Company	市北区	Shibei District
135	青岛世纪阳光油气有限公司	Qingdao Century Sunlight Petroleum Limited Company	市北区	Shibei District
136	青岛统力星商贸有限公司	Qingdao Tongli Star Business Trade Limited Company	市北区	Shibei District
137	青岛恒源电业物资有限责任公司	Qingdao Hengyuan Electricity Materials Limited Liability Company	市北区	Shibei District
138	青岛双峰钢管有限公司	Qingdao Split-blip Steel Pipe Limited Company	市北区	Shibei District
139	青岛嘉瑞动力装备有限公司	Qingdao Jiarui Power Equipment Limited Company	四方区	Sifang District
140	青岛盐业专营有限公司	Qingdao Salt-industry Monopolizes The Limited Company	四方区	Sifang District
141	青岛杜森商贸有限公司	Qingdao Dusen Business Trade Limited Company	四方区	Sifang District
142	青岛倍力商贸有限公司	Qingdao Beili Business Trade Limited Company	四方区	Sifang District
143	青岛同发商贸有限公司	Qingdao Tongfa Business Trade Limited Company	四方区	Sifang District
144	青岛好源粮油食品有限公司	Qingdao Haoyuan Oil Food Limited Company	四方区	Sifang District
145	青岛胜世嘉工贸有限公司	Qingdao Shengshijia Industry And Trade Limited Company	四方区	Sifang District
146	青岛四方华晨橡塑销售中心	Qingdao Sifang Huachen Rubber And Plastic Sale Center	四方区	Sifang District
147	青岛华丰玻璃销售有限公司	Qingdao Huafeng Glass Sale Limited Company	四方区	Sifang District
148	青岛建设机械材料有限公司	Qingdao Construction Machinery And Material Corporation	四方区	Sifang District

14 –19 续表
continued

序号 Serial Number	单位名称	Name	所在地区	Location
149	青岛中基机床设备有限公司	Qingdao Zhongji Machine Tool Equipment Limited Company	四方区	Sifang District
150	青岛广丰棉麻有限公司	Qingdao Guangfeng Cotton And Gunny Limited Company	四方区	Sifang District
151	青岛四机物资经营有限公司	Qingdao Siji Materials Managements Limited Company	四方区	Sifang District
152	青岛北方钢管有限公司	Qingdao North Steel Pipe Limited Company	四方区	Sifang District
153	青岛一棉纺织品进出口有限公司	Qingdao A – cotton Textile Import And Export Limited company	四方区	Sifang District
154	青岛世泰实业有限公司	Qingdao Shitai Industry Limited Company	四方区	Sifang District
155	青岛第三粮库	Qingdao No. 3 Grain Storage	四方区	Sifang District
156	青岛市华纺物资有限公司	Qingdao Huafang Materials Limited Company	四方区	Sifang District
157	青岛华亿诚物资有限公司	Qingdao Huayicheng Materials Limited Companies	四方区	Sifang District
158	青岛富纺商贸有限公司	Qingdao Fufang Business Trade Limited Company	四方区	Sifang District
159	青岛健泰化工有限公司	Qingdao Jiantai Chemical Industry Limited Company	四方区	Sifang District
160	青岛华龙盛集团有限公司	Qingdao Hualongsheng Group Limited Company	四方区	Sifang District
161	青岛沃尔富金属材料有限公司	Qingdao Wef Metal Material Limited Company	四方区	Sifang District
162	青岛五菱汽车销售有限公司	Qingdao Wuling Auto Sale Limited Company	四方区	Sifang District
163	青岛中豪达汽车销售有限公司	Qingdao Zhonghaoda Auto Sale Limited Company	四方区	Sifang District
164	青岛经济技术开发区银达加油站	Qingdao Economic Development Zone Yinda Gas Station	黄岛区	Huangdao District
165	青岛佳宝元经贸有限公司	Qingdao Jiabaoyuan Economics And Trade Limited Company	黄岛区	Huangdao District
166	中国中煤能源集团公司青岛分公司	China National Coal Group Company Qingdao Subsidiary Company	黄岛区	Huangdao District
167	中国煤炭工业进出口集团青岛有限公司	China Coal Industry Import And Export group Qingdao Limited Company	黄岛区	Huangdao District
168	青岛铁盟国际贸易有限公司	Qingdao Tiemeng International Trade Limited Company	黄岛区	Huangdao District
169	青岛润升石油有限公司	Qingdao Runsheng Petroleum Limited Company	黄岛区	Huangdao District
170	青岛塞轮子午线轮胎销售有限公司	Qingdao Sailun Noon – mark Tire Sale Limited Company	黄岛区	Huangdao District
171	青岛怡群进出口有限公司	Qingdao Yiqun Import And Export Limited Company	黄岛区	Huangdao District
172	青岛沿海热电燃料有限公司	Qingdao Coast Thermoelectricity Fuel Limited Company	黄岛区	Huangdao District
173	青岛安福德经贸有限公司	Qingdao Anfude Economics And Trade Limited Company	黄岛区	Huangdao District
174	青岛鑫金来实业有限公司	Qingdao Xinjinlai Industry Limited Company	黄岛区	Huangdao District
175	青岛丰硕源工贸有限公司	Qingdao Fengshuoyuan Industry And Trade Limited Company	黄岛区	Huangdao District
176	青岛保税区泉盛源国际贸易有限公司	Qingdao Bonded Area Quanshengyuan International Trade Limited Company	黄岛区	Huangdao District
177	青岛保税区济钢国际物流有限公司	Qingdao Bonded Area Jigang Works International Flows The Limited Company	黄岛区	Huangdao District
178	青岛保税区容博国际贸易有限公司	Qingdao Bonded Area Rongbo International Trade Limited Company	黄岛区	Huangdao District
179	青岛保税区瀛寰盛国际贸易有限公司	Qingdao Bonded Area Yinghuansheng International Trade Limited Company	黄岛区	Huangdao District
180	青岛瑞易通化工有限公司	Qingdao Ruiyitong Chemical Limited Company	黄岛区	Huangdao District
181	青岛文瑞接通物流有限公司	Qingdao Wenrui Flows The Limited Company	黄岛区	Huangdao District
182	青岛保税区美丰贸易有限公司	Qingdao Bonded Area Meifeng Trade Limited Company	黄岛区	Huangdao District
183	青岛保税区百思得尔国际贸易有限公司	Qingdao Bonded Area Best International Trade Limited Company	黄岛区	Huangdao District
184	青岛保税区信华德国际贸易有限公司	Qingdao Bonded Srea Xin Huade International Trade Limited Company	黄岛区	Huangdao District
185	青岛保税区尧舜国际贸易有限公司	Qingdao Bonded Area Yao And Shun International Trade Limited Company	黄岛区	Huangdao District

14－19 续表

continued

序号 Serial Number	单位名称	Name	所在地区	Location
186	青岛佳思瑞科贸有限公司	Qingdao Jiasiyui Technology And Trade Limited Company	黄岛区	Huangdao District
187	青岛圣元乳业有限公司	Qingdao Shengyuan Dairying Limited Company	黄岛区	Huangdao District
188	青岛天方商务有限公司	Qingdao Tianfang Commerce Limited Company	黄岛区	Huangdao District
189	青岛金中汇贸易有限公司	Qingdao Jin Zhonghui Trade Limited Company	黄岛区	Huangdao District
190	青岛保税区龙舒洋国际贸易有限公司	Qingdao Bonded Area Long Shuyang International Trade Limited Company	黄岛区	Huangdao District
191	青岛保税区首益物流有限公司	Qingdao Bonded Area Shouyi Flows Limited Company	黄岛区	Huangdao District
192	青岛三剑线业工贸中心	Qingdao Three Swords Lines Industry And Trade Center	崂山区	Laoshan District
193	青岛东大行工贸有限公司	Qingdao Dongdaxing Industry And Trade Limited Company	崂山区	Laoshan District
194	青岛维奥斯商贸有限公司	Qingdao Welsh Business Trade Limited Company	崂山区	Laoshan District
195	青岛金盛世化工有限公司	Qingdao Jin Shengshi Chemical Industry Limited Company	崂山区	Laoshan District
196	青岛辉煌电讯器材有限公司	Qingdao Magnificent Telecommunication Equipment Limited Company	崂山区	Laoshan District
197	青岛海尔工贸有限公司	Qingdao Haier Industry And Trade Limited Company	崂山区	Laoshan District
198	海尔集团电器产业有限公司	Haier Group Electric Appliance Industry Limited Company	崂山区	Laoshan District
199	青岛海尔国际贸易有限公司	Qingdao Haier International Trade Limited Company	崂山区	Laoshan District
200	青岛荣岩商贸有限公司	Qingdao Rongyan Trade Limited Company	崂山区	Laoshan District
201	中棉集团(青岛)棉花有限公司	China National Cotton Group (Qingdao) Cotton Limited Company	崂山区	Laoshan District
202	青岛麦迪科技有限公司	Qingdao Maidi Technical Limited Company	崂山区	Laoshan District
203	青岛金长江集团有限公司	Qingdao Gold－Yangtze River Group Limited Company	崂山区	Laoshan District
204	青岛舜和牧业有限公司	Qingdao Shunhe Animal Husbandry Limited Company	崂山区	Laoshan District
205	青岛佳诺商务有限公司	Qingdao Jianuo Commerce Limited Company	崂山区	Laoshan District
206	青岛亿利中兴进出口有限公司	Qingdao Yili Zhongxing Import And Export Limited Company	崂山区	Laoshan District
207	青岛中垦进出口有限公司	Qingdao Zhongken Import And Export Limited Company	崂山区	Laoshan District
208	青岛广安实业有限公司	Qingdao Quangan Industry Limited Company	崂山区	Laoshan District
209	青岛汇能物资有限公司	Qingdao Huineng Materials Limited Company	崂山区	Laoshan District
210	青岛科信石油化工有限公司	Qingdao Kexin Petroleum Chemical Industry Limited Company	崂山区	Laoshan District
211	青岛高科技工业园联谊石化有限公司	Qingdao High－tech Industry Garden Lianyi Petrochemical Limited Company	崂山区	Laoshan District
212	青岛银泉科技发展有限公司	Qingdao Silver Spring Science And Technology Development Limited Company	崂山区	Laoshan District
213	青岛贵生商贸有限公司	Qingdao Guisheng Business Trade Limited Company	崂山区	Laoshan District
214	山东六和集团有限公司	Shandong Liuhe Group Limited Company	崂山区	Laoshan District
215	青岛地恩地贸易有限公司	Qingdao Graciousness Trade Limited Company	崂山区	Laoshan District
216	青岛天发工贸有限公司	Qingdao Tianfa Industry And Trade Limited Company	崂山区	Laoshan District
217	青岛世展科技有限公司	Qingdao Shizhan Technical Limited Company	崂山区	Laoshan District
218	青岛中商华天溶剂油有限公司	Qingdao China Commerce Crown Solvent Limited Company	崂山区	Laoshan District
219	青岛东展经贸有限公司	Qingdao Dongzhan Economics And Trade Limited Company	李沧区	Licang District
220	青岛金属股份有限公司	Qingdao Metal Limited Liability Company	李沧区	Licang District
221	青岛旭辉经贸有限公司	Qingdao Xuhui Economics And Trade Limited Company	李沧区	Licang District
222	青岛盛欣纺织品有限公司	Qingdao Shengxin Textile Limited Company	李沧区	Licang District

14 –19 续表
continued

序号 Serial Number	单位名称	Name	所在地区	Location
223	山东海王银河医药有限公司青岛分公司	Shandong Sea – king Milky Way Medicine Limited Company Qingdao Subsidiary Company	李沧区	Licang District
224	山东合力叉车销售有限公司	Shandong Heli Forklift sale Limited Company	李沧区	Licang District
225	青岛国运集团有限公司	Qingdao Guoyun Group Limited Company	李沧区	Licang District
226	青岛路路通轮胎配套销售有限公司	Qingdao Lu Lutong Tire Matching Sale Limited Company	李沧区	Licang District
227	青岛颂宏电力实业有限公司	Qingdao Songhong Electric Power Industry Limited Company	李沧区	Licang District
228	青岛吉化化工有限公司	Qingdao Jihua Chemical Industry Limited Company	李沧区	Licang District
229	青岛祥源化工有限公司	Qingdao Xiangyuan Chemical Industry Limited Company	李沧区	Licang District
230	青岛广运五金电器有限公司	Qingdao Guangyun Hardware Electric Appliance Limited Company	李沧区	Licang District
231	青岛奥旭电器有限公司	Qingdao Ausoul Electric Appliance Limited Company	李沧区	Licang District
232	青岛三和世纪医药有限公司	Qingdao Sanhe Century Medicine Limited Company	李沧区	Licang District
233	青岛星火大地化工有限公司	Qingdao Spark Earth Chemical Industry Limited Company	李沧区	Licang District
234	青岛永安化学品有限公司	Qingdao Yongan Chemical Limited Company	李沧区	Licang District
235	浙江杭叉工程股份有限公司青岛分公司	Zhejiang Hangcha Project Limited Liability Company Qingdao Subsidiary Company	李沧区	Licang District
236	青岛圣通华汽车销售服务有限公司	Qingdao Shengtonghua Auto Sale And Service Limited Company	李沧区	Licang District
237	青岛林达汽车销售有限公司	Qingdao Linda Auto Sale Limited Company	李沧区	Licang District
238	青岛世达机械有限公司	Qingdao Shida Machinery Limited Company	李沧区	Licang District
239	青岛华裕通汽车销售有限公司	Qingdao Hua Yutong Auto Sale Limited Company	李沧区	Licang District
240	青岛市李沧区十梅庵燃料公司	Qingdao Licang District Shimei Buddhist Nunnery Fuel Company	李沧区	Licang District
241	青岛鲁能物资有限公司	Qingdao Luneng Materials Limited Company	李沧区	Licang District
242	青岛市瑞金废纸收购站有限公司	Qingdao Ruijin Scrap Paper Purchasing Station Limited Company	李沧区	Licang District
243	青岛石化液化气公司	Qingdao Petrification And Liquid Gas Company	李沧区	Licang District
244	青岛环海石钢钢材贸易有限公司	Qingdao Link Coral Shigang Steel Products Trade Limited Company	李沧区	Licang District
245	青岛恒丰利商贸有限公司	Qingdao Hengfengli Business Trade Limited Company	李沧区	Licang District
246	青岛云华汽车销售有限公司	Qingdao Yunhua Auto Sale Limited Company	李沧区	Licang District
247	青岛青汽汽车销售有限公司	Qingdao Qingqi Auto Sale Limited Company	李沧区	Licang District
248	青岛吉运汽车销售服务有限公司	Qingdao Jiyun Auto Sale And Service Limited Company	李沧区	Licang District
249	青岛德天舜汽车销售有限公司	Qingdao Detianshun Auto Sale Limited Company	李沧区	Licang District
250	青岛润玉物资有限公司	Qingdao Runyu Materials Limited Company	李沧区	Licang District
251	青岛太钢销售有限公司	Qingdao Taigang Sale Limited Company	城阳区	Chengyang District
252	青岛邯青物资有限公司	Qingdao Hanqing Materials Limited Company	城阳区	Chengyang District
253	湖北汇通钢铁工贸有限公司青岛分公司	Hubei Huitong Steel And Iron Industry And Trade Limited Company Qingdao Subsidiary Company	城阳区	Chengyang District
254	青岛森泰达橡胶有限公司	Qingdao Sentaida Rubber Limited Company	城阳区	Chengyang District
255	山东义庭现代汽车销售有限公司	Shandong Yiting Modern Auto Sale Limited Company	城阳区	Chengyang District
256	青岛市城阳区石油有限公司	Qingdao Chengyang District Petroleum Limited Company	城阳区	Chengyang District
257	青岛浩华通信产品有限公司	Qingdao Haohua Correspondence Product Limited Company	城阳区	Chengyang District
258	青岛银丰不锈钢材料有限公司	Qingdao Yinfeng Stainless Steel Material Limited Company	城阳区	Chengyang District
259	青岛宝冠工贸有限公司	Qingdao Baoguan Industry Snd Trade Limited Company	城阳区	Chengyang District

14－19 续表
continued

序号 Serial Number	单位名称	Name	所在地区	Location
260	青岛攀鑫平板有限公司	Qingdao Panxin Plate Limited Company	城阳区	Chengyang District
261	青岛诚阳钢联物资有限公司	Qingdao Chengyang Ganglian Commodity Limited Company	城阳区	Chengyang District
262	青岛市城阳区云海物资贸易有限公司	Qingdao Chengyang District Commodity Trade Limited Company	城阳区	Chengyang District
263	青岛昊润达国际贸易有限公司	Qingdao Haorunda International Trade Limited Company	胶州市	Jiaozhou
264	青岛九州金属材料有限公司	Qingdao Jiuzhou Metal Material Limited Company	胶州市	Jiaozhou
265	青岛龙洲酒业有限公司	Qingdao Longzhou Wine Business Limited Company	胶州市	Jiaozhou
266	青岛市胶州农业生产资料有限公司	Qingdao Jiaozhou Agricultural Means Of Production Limited Company	胶州市	Jiaozhou
267	青岛即墨市电力物资材料公司	Qingdao Jimo Electric Power Commodity Material Company	即墨市	Jimo
268	青岛华纺纱布有限公司	Qingdao Huafang Gauze Limited Company	即墨市	Jimo
269	青岛即墨市深化外贸包装材料有限公司	Qingdao Jimo Shenhua Foreign Trade Packing Material Limited Company	即墨市	Jimo
270	山东省即墨市福田农业机械有限公司	Shandong Province Jimo Futian Farm Machinery Limited Company	即墨市	Jimo
271	青岛即发进出口有限公司	Qingdao Jesfeel Import And Export Limited Company	即墨市	Jimo
272	山东省即墨市金盾石化有限公司	Shandong Province Jimo Goldenshield Petrification Limited Company	即墨市	Jimo
273	青岛群益金属制品有限公司	Qingdao Qunyi Metal Product Limited Company	即墨市	Jimo
274	青岛青威地方工业金属有限公司	Qingdao Qingwei Local Industry Metal Limited Company	即墨市	Jimo
275	青岛平度市供销社农业生产资料有限公司	Qingdao Pingdu Supply And Marketing Cooperative Agricultural Means Of Production Limited Company	平度市	Pingdu
276	青岛平度市宏远民用爆破器材专营有限公司	Qingdao Pingdu Hongyuan Civil Demolition Equipment Monopolizes Limited Company	平度市	Pingdu
277	青岛市源盛金属回收有限公司	Qingdao Yuansheng Metal Recycling Limited Company	平度市	Pingdu
278	山东三利源经贸有限公司	Shandong Sanliyuan Economics And Trade Limited Company	平度市	Pingdu
279	青岛鲍德经贸有限公司	Qingdao Baud Economics And Trade Limited Company	平度市	Pingdu
280	胶南市绿洲农资油业有限公司	Jiaona Lvzhou Agriculture Materials And Oil limited Company	胶南市	Jiaonan
281	胶南市粮食储备库	Jiaona Grain Reservoir Depot	胶南市	Jiaonan
282	青岛琅琊台酒销售有限公司	Qingdao Langyatai Liquor Sale Limited Company	胶南市	Jiaonan
283	山东省胶南市农业机械总公司	Shandong Province Jiaonan Farm Machinery Main Corporation	胶南市	Jiaonan
284	青岛国风集团胶南医药有限责任公司	Qingdao Growful Group Jiaonan Medicine Limited Liability Company	胶南市	Jiaonan
285	胶南市灵山物资有限公司	Jiaonan Lingshan Materials Limited Company	胶南市	Jiaonan
286	胶南市水产供销公司	Jiaonan Aquatic Product Supply And Sale Company	胶南市	Jiaonan
287	青岛国风药业莱西医药有限责任公司	Qingdao Growful Group Laixi Medicine Limited Liability Company	莱西市	Laixi
288	青岛海奥植保服务有限公司	Qingdao Haiao Zhibao Service Limited Company	莱西市	Laixi
289	山东省莱西市农业机械公司	Shandong Province Laixi Farm Machinery Company	莱西市	Laixi
290	山东省莱西市再生资源公司	Shandong Province Laixi Regeneration Resources Company	莱西市	Laixi
291	青岛天勤石墨有限公司	Qingdao Tianqin Graphite Limited Company	莱西市	Laixi
292	青岛祥运达商贸有限公司	Qingdao Xiangyunda Business Trade Limited Company	莱西市	Laixi
293	青岛莱西市南岚粮食管理所	Qingdao Laixi Nanlan Grain Administration Center	莱西市	Laixi
294	莱西市店埠粮食管理所	Laixi Dianbu Grain Administration Center	莱西市	Laixi
295	青岛红夕阳蔬菜服务有限公司	Qingdao Red－sunset Vegetables Service Limited Company	莱西市	Laixi
296	青岛纳新食品有限公司	Qingdao Nangxin Food Limited Company	莱西市	Laixi
297	青岛东生进出口有限公司	Qingdao Dongsheng Import And Export Limited Company	莱西市	Laixi

14－20 限额以上零售法人企业一览表(2005 年)

SCHEDULE OF RETAIL TRADE CORPORATE ENTERPRISES ABOVE LEVEL(2005)

序号 Serial Number	单位名称	Name	所在地区	Location
1	青岛安华机电设备有限公司	Qingdao Anwar Electromechanical Device Limited Company	市南区	Shinan District
2	青岛亨得利有限公司	Qingdao Hengdeli Limited Company	市南区	Shinan District
3	青岛飞利汽车贸易有限公司	Qingdao Feili Automobile Trade Limited cCmpany	市南区	Shinan District
4	青岛麒龙科技发展有限公司	Qingdao Qilong Science And Technology Development Limited Company	市南区	Shinan District
5	青岛苏宁电器有限公司	Qingdao Suning Electric Appliance Limited Company	市南区	Shinan District
6	青岛金大友汽车销售有限公司	Qingdao Jin Dayou Auto Sale Limited Company	市南区	Shinan District
7	青岛阳光百货股份有限公司	Qingdao Sunshine Department Store Co. , Ltd	市南区	Shinan District
8	青岛家乐福商业有限公司	Qingdao Carrefour Commercial Limited Company	市南区	Shinan District
9	统杰(青岛)食品加工有限责任公司	Tongjie(Qingdao)Food Process Co. ,Ltd.	市南区	Shinan District
10	青岛国货有限公司	Qingdao Guohuo Limited Company	市南区	Shinan District
11	青岛工艺美术品有限责任公司	Qingdao Craft Artwork Limited Liability Company	市南区	Shinan District
12	青岛海滨食品有限公司	Qingdao Haibin Food Limited Company	市南区	Shinan District
13	青岛第一百盛有限公司	Qingdao No. 1 Parkson Limited Company	市南区	Shinan District
14	青岛华联商厦股份有限公司	Qingdao Hualian Commercial Building Inc.	市南区	Shinan District
15	青岛国风大药房连锁有限公司	Qingdao Growful Co. ,Ltd.	市南区	Shinan District
16	青岛天秦超市有限公司	Qingdao Tianqin Supermarket Limited Company	市南区	Shinan District
17	青岛百安居装饰建材有限公司	Qingdao B&Q Decoration Building Materials Limited Company	市南区	Shinan District
18	青岛海信实业股份有限公司	Qingdao Hisense Industry Inc.	市南区	Shinan District
19	青岛润泰事业有限公司	Qingdao Runtai Limited Company	市南区	Shinan District
20	青岛博达汽车销售有限公司	Qingdao Boda Auto Sale Limited Company	市南区	Shinan District
21	青岛金麦园经贸有限公司	Qingdao Jin Maiyuan Economics And Trade Limited Company	市南区	Shinan District
22	青岛通宝汽车有限公司	Qingdao Tongbao Automobile Limited Company	市南区	Shinan District
23	青岛神龙达实业有限公司	Qingdao Shenlongda Industry Limited Company	市南区	Shinan District
24	青岛海马汽车销售有限公司	Qingdao Seahorse Auto Sale Limited Company	市南区	Shinan District
25	青岛华世通实业有限公司	Qingdao Hua Shitong Industry Limited Company	市南区	Shinan District
26	青岛华泰现代汽车销售有限公司	Qingdao Huatai Modern Suto Sale Limited Company	市南区	Shinan District
27	青岛福泰汽车销售公司	Qingdao Futai Auto Sale Company	市南区	Shinan District
28	山东省城市车辆青岛有限公司	Shandong Province City Vehicles Qingdao Limited Company	市南区	Shinan District
29	青岛机动车辆服务汽车展销处	Qingdao Motor Vehicle Service Automobile Selling Place	市南区	Shinan District
30	青岛佳恒汽车销售有限公司	Qingdao Jiaheng Auto Sale Limited Company	市南区	Shinan District
31	青岛永旺东泰商业有限公司	Qingdao AEON JUSCO Commercial Limited Company	市南区	Shinan District
32	青岛新华书店有限责任公司	Qingdao Xinhua Bookstore Limited Liability Company	市南区	Shinan District
33	青岛市三聚成蔬菜副食品连锁有限公司	Qingdao Sanjucheng Vegetables And Non－staple Food Product Chain－like Limited Company	市南区	Shinan District
34	青岛特种油品公司	Qingdao Special Oil Quality Company	市南区	Shinan District

14-20 续表
continued

序号 Serial Number	单位名称	Name	所在地区	Location
35	上海大众汽车青岛销售服务有限公司	Shanghai Volkswagen Automobile Qingdao Sale And Service Limited Company	市北区	Shibei District
36	青岛市燃料运销公司	Qingdao Fuel Transportation And Sale Company	市北区	Shibei District
37	青岛横店东方贸易大厦有限公司	Qingdao Hengdian East Trade Building Limited Company	市北区	Shibei District
38	青岛伊都锦商厦有限公司	Qingdao Itokin Limited Company	市北区	Shibei District
39	青岛千川百货有限公司	Qingdao Qianchuan Department Store Limited Company	市北区	Shibei District
40	青岛杏林医药连锁有限公司	Qingdao Xinglin Medicine Chain – like Limited Company	市北区	Shibei District
41	青岛宝利捷计算机系统公司	Qingdao Baolijie Computer System Company	市北区	Shibei District
42	青岛澳深计算机技术服务有限公司	Qingdao Aoshen Computer Technology Service Limited Company	市北区	Shibei District
43	青岛信大慧通数码科技有限公司	The Qingdao Xinda Huitong Digital Science And Technology Limited Company	市北区	Shibei District
44	山东五星电器有限公司	Shandong Five – star Electric Appliance Limited Company	市北区	Shibei District
45	青岛众生大药房连锁有限公司	Qingdao Zhongsheng Drugstore Chain – like Limited Company	市北区	Shibei District
46	青岛恒生堂大药房有限公司	Qingdao Hengshengtang Drugstore Limited Company	市北区	Shibei District
47	北京同仁堂青岛药店有限责任公司	Beijing Tongrentang Qingdao Drugstore Limited Liability Company	市北区	Shibei District
48	青岛法宝有限公司	Qingdao Bonjour Limited Company	市北区	Shibei District
49	青岛兰盾消防有限责任公司	Qingdao Blue Shield Fire Prevention Limited Liability Company	市北区	Shibei District
50	青岛市军队粮油供应站	Qingdao Army Grain And Oil Supply Station	市北区	Shibei District
51	青岛星月缝制设备商行	The Qingdao Star – month Sewing Equipment Firm	市北区	Shibei District
52	青岛市市北区贵和针车有限公司	Qingdao Shibei District Guihe Sewing Equipment Limited Company	市北区	Shibei District
53	青岛启运商贸有限公司	Qingdao Qiyun Trade Limited Company	市北区	Shibei District
54	青岛协亨通讯设备有限公司	Qingdao Xieheng Communication Equipment Limited Company	市北区	Shibei District
55	利群集团股份有限公司	Liqun Group Inc.	市北区	Shibei District
56	青岛苏宁电器有限公司	Qingdao Suning Electric Appliance Limited Company	市北区	Shibei District
57	青岛医保药品城有限公司	Qingdao Medical Insurance Drugs City Limited Company	市北区	Shibei District
58	青岛金粮食业有限责任公司	Qingdao Jinliang Industry Limited Liability Company	市北区	Shibei District
59	青岛台东五金商店	Qingdao Taidong Hardware Store	市北区	Shibei District
60	青岛瑞泰电器有限公司	Qingdao Ruitai Electric Appliance Limited Company	市北区	Shibei District
61	青岛神力威商贸有限公司	Qingdao Shenliwei Business Trade Limited Company	市北区	Shibei District
62	青岛施乐办公设备有限公司	Qingdao Shile Office Equipment Limited Company	市北区	Shibei District
63	青岛鲜京新兴能源有限公司	Qingdao Xianjing Xinxing Energy Limited Company	市北区	Shibei District
64	青岛家世界超市有限公司	Qingdao Home – world Supermarket Limited Company	市北区	Shibei District
65	青岛一木集团营销有限公司	Qingdao Yimu Group Marketing Limited Company	市北区	Shibei District
66	青岛家世界家居建材有限公司	Qingdao Home – world Home Building Materials Limited Company	市北区	Shibei District
67	青岛昌龙汽车销售有限公司	Qingdao Changlong Auto Sale Limited Company	市北区	Shibei District
68	青岛欧海家居有限公司	Qingdao Ouhai Home Limited Company	市北区	Shibei District

14 –20 续表
continued

序号 Serial Number	单位名称	Name	所在地区	Location
69	青岛海滨超市连锁有限责任公司	Qingdao Haibin Supermarket Chain – like Limited Liability Company	市北区	Shibei District
70	青岛元丰汽车贸易有限公司	Qingdao Yuanfeng Automobile Trade Limited Company	市北区	Shibei District
71	青岛市市北区海城加油站	Qingdao Shibei District Haicheng Gas Station	市北区	Shibei District
72	青岛华泰汽车销售有限公司	Qingdao Huatai Auto Sale Limited Company	市北区	Shibei District
73	青岛恒瑞汽车销售有限公司	Qingdao Hengrui Auto Sale Limited Company	市北区	Shibei District
74	青岛日产汽车销售服务有限公司	Qingdao Japan – made Auto Sale And Service Limited company	市北区	Shibei District
75	青岛海伦商贸有限公司	Qingdao Helen Business Trade Limited Company	四方区	Sifang District
76	青岛四百购物中心	Qingdao 4rd Department Stores Shopping Centers	四方区	Sifang District
77	青岛交运行通汽车服务有限公司	Qingdao Jiaoyun Xingtong Auto Service Limited Company	四方区	Sifang District
78	东方家园(青岛四方)装饰建材有限公司	Eastern Homeland (Qingdao Sifang) Building Materials Limited Company	四方区	Sifang District
79	青岛泰能汽车燃气发展有限公司	Qingdao Taineng Automobile Fuel Gas Development Limited Company	四方区	Sifang District
80	青岛长青股份有限公司	Qingdao Changqing Inc.	四方区	Sifang District
81	山东真维斯服饰有限公司	Shandong Jewest Garment Limited Company	四方区	Sifang District
82	青岛国美电器有限公司	Qingdao Gome Electric Appliance Limited Company	四方区	Sifang District
83	青岛世泰丰田汽车销售服务有限公司	Qingdao Shitai Toyota Auto Sale And Service Limited Company	四方区	Sifang District
84	青岛中机汽车销售有限公司	Qingdao Zhongji Auto Sale Limited Company	四方区	Sifang District
85	青岛昌青贸易有限公司	Qingdao Changqing Trade Limited Company	四方区	Sifang District
86	青岛众铃汽车贸易有限公司	Qingdao Zhongling Automobile Trade Limited Company	四方区	Sifang District
87	青岛新建达汽车销售有限公司	Qingdao Xinjianda Auto Sale Limited Company	四方区	Sifang District
88	青岛明盛工贸有限公司	Qingdao Mingsheng Industry And Trade Limited Company	四方区	Sifang District
89	青岛华之杰汽车销售服务有限公司	Qingdao Huazhijie Auto Sale And Service Limited Company	四方区	Sifang District
90	青岛全顺江铃汽车销售服务有限公司	Qingdao Quanshun JMC Auto Sale And Service Limited Company	四方区	Sifang District
91	青岛神龙达汽车销售服务有限公司	Qingdao Shenlongda Auto Sale And Service Limited Company	四方区	Sifang District
92	青岛骏濠汽车贸易有限公司	Qingdao Junhao Automobile Trade Limited Company	四方区	Sifang District
93	青岛六和汽车销售有限公司	Qingdao Liuhe Auto Sale Limited Company	四方区	Sifang District
94	青岛宝狮汽车销售有限公司	Qingdao Baoshi Auto Sale Limited Company	四方区	Sifang District
95	青岛福日机电设备有限公司	Qingdao Furi Electromechanical Device Limited Company	四方区	Sifang District
96	青岛鑫泰达汽车销售服务有限公司	Qingdao Xintaida Auto Sale And Service Limited Company	四方区	Sifang District
97	青岛新濠汽车贸易有限公司	Qingdao Xinhao Automobile Trade Limited Company	四方区	Sifang District
98	青岛北星汽车销售有限公司	Qingdao North – star Auto Sale Limited Company	四方区	Sifang District
99	青岛安利捷丰田汽车销售有限公司	Qingdao ALJ Toyota Auto Sale Limited Company	四方区	Sifang District
100	青岛东联汽车销售有限公司	Qingdao Donglian Auto Sale Limited Company	四方区	Sifang District
101	青岛大栏汽车销售有限公司	Qingdao Dalan Auto Sale Limited Company	四方区	Sifang District
102	青岛福鑫源汽车销售有限公司	Qingdao Fuxinyuan Auto Sale Limited cCmpany	四方区	Sifang District

14－20 续表
continued

序号 Serial Number	单位名称	Name	所在地区	Location
103	青岛圣豪汽车销售服务有限公司	Qingdao Shenghao Auto Sale And Service Limited Company	四方区	Sifang District
104	青岛北方建达汽车销售服务有限公司	Qingdao North Jianda Auto Sale And Service Limited Company	四方区	Sifang District
105	青岛市黄岛区新华书店有限责任公司	Qingdao Huangdao Xinhua Bookstore Limited Liability Company	黄岛区	Huangdao District
106	青岛国货商厦有限公司	Qingdao Guohuo Commercial Building Limited Company	黄岛区	Huangdao District
107	青岛经济技术开发区华光机电化工公司	Qingdao Economic Development Zone Huaguang Electromechine And Chemical Industry Company	黄岛区	Huangdao District
108	青岛真诺汽车有限公司	Qingdao Zhennuo Automobile Limited Company	黄岛区	Huangdao District
109	青岛惠驰汽车贸易有限公司	Qingdao Huichi Automobile Trade Limited Company	黄岛区	Huangdao District
110	青岛保税区瑞友国际东城有限公司	Qingdao Bonded Area Ruiyou International East - city Limited Company	黄岛区	Huangdao District
111	青岛安康汽车销售有限公司	Qingdao Ankang Suto Sale Limited Company	黄岛区	Huangdao District
112	青岛家佳源购物中心有限责任公司	Qingdao Jiajiayuan Shopping Center Limited Liability Company	黄岛区	Huangdao District
113	青岛华成汽车服务有限公司	Qingdao Car Service Limited Company	崂山区	Laoshan District
114	青岛成达汽车销售服务有限公司	Qingdao Dacheng Auto Sale And Service Limited Company	崂山区	Laoshan District
115	青岛信立达科技发展有限公司	Qingdao Xinlida Science And Technology Development Limited Company	崂山区	Laoshan District
116	青岛嘉业汽车进出口有限公司	Qingdao Jiaye Automobile Import And Export Limited Company	崂山区	Laoshan District
117	青岛成胜达汽车销售服务有限公司	Qingdao Cheng Shengda Auto Sale And Service Limited Company	崂山区	Laoshan District
118	青岛奥达汽车销售服务有限公司	The Qingdao Aoda Auto Sale And Service Limited Company	崂山区	Laoshan District
119	青岛成汇达汽车销售服务有限公司	Qingdao Cheng Huida Auto Sale And Service Limited Company	崂山区	Laoshan District
120	青岛深蓝汽车网络投资股份有限公司	Qingdao Dark - blue Automobile Network Investment Limited Liability Company	崂山区	Laoshan District
121	青岛黑马车行有限公司	Qingdao Black Horse Car Dealership Limited Company	崂山区	Laoshan District
122	青岛奥华汽车销售有限公司	Qingdao Aohua Auto Sale Limited Company	崂山区	Laoshan District
123	青岛泰宁实业有限公司	Qingdao Taining Industry Limited Company	崂山区	Laoshan District
124	青岛大学海源汽车销售服务有限公司	Qingdao University Haiyuan Auto Sale And Service Limited Company	崂山区	Laoshan District
125	青岛移通通信技术服务有限公司	Qingdao Yitong Telecommunication Service Limited Company Entirely	崂山区	Laoshan District
126	青岛市崂山区登瀛加油站	Qingdao Laoshan District Dengying Gas Station	崂山区	Laoshan District
127	青岛华洲实业有限公司	Qingdao Huazhou Industry Limited Company	李沧区	Licang District
128	青岛宏益加油站有限公司	Qingdao Hongyi Gas Station Limited Company	李沧区	Licang District
129	青岛中商百盛有限公司	Qingdao Zhongshang Parkson Limited Company	李沧区	Licang District
130	山东新华鲁抗药业零售有限公司李沧医药商城	Shandong Xinhua Lukang Pharmaceutical Sales Limited Company Licang Medicine Mall	李沧区	Licang District
131	青岛爱特蒙罗服饰发展有限公司	Qingdao Aitemengluo Dress Development Limited Company Especially	李沧区	Licang District
132	青岛维客集团股份有限公司	Qingdao Weekly Group Inc.	李沧区	Licang District
133	青岛康视商贸有限公司	Qingdao Kangshi Trade Limited Company	李沧区	Licang District
134	青岛利客来商贸股份有限公司	Qingdao Likelai Trade Inc.	李沧区	Licang District
135	青岛北方国贸大厦股份有限公司	Qingdao North Trade Building Inc.	李沧区	Licang District
136	青岛大中电器有限公司	Qingdao Dahzong Electric Appliance Limited Company	李沧区	Licang District

14 –20 续表
continued

序号 Serial Number	单位名称	Name	所在地区	Location
137	青岛百富德商贸有限公司	Qingdao Baifude Business Trade Limited Company	李沧区	Licang District
138	青岛海易通电讯发展有限公司	Qingdao Haiyitong Telecommunication Development Limited Company	李沧区	Licang District
139	青岛金超汽车销售有限公司	Qingdao Jinchao Auto Sale Limited Company	李沧区	Licang District
140	青岛新时代汽车销售有限公司	Qingdao New Times Auto Sale Limited Company	李沧区	Licang District
141	青岛荣青实业有限公司	Qingdao Rongqing Industry Limited Company	李沧区	Licang District
142	青岛万事达汽车销售有限公司	Qingdao Wanshida Auto Sale Limited Company	李沧区	Licang District
143	青岛天合医药股份有限公司	Qingdao Tianhe Medicine Inc.	李沧区	Licang District
144	青岛中达燕宝汽车销售有限公司	Qingdao Zhongda Yanbao Auto Sale Limited Company	李沧区	Licang District
145	青岛好美家装潢建材有限公司	Qingdao Homemart Decoration Materials Limited Company	李沧区	Licang District
146	青岛福日汽车销售有限公司	Qingdao Furi Auto Sale Limited Company	李沧区	Licang District
147	青岛帅潮商贸有限公司	Qingdao Shuaichao Business Trade Limited Company	李沧区	Licang District
148	青岛刘家加油站有限公司	Qingdao Liujia Gas Station Limited Company	李沧区	Licang District
149	青岛市城阳区新华书店有限责任公司	Qingdao Chengyang District Xinhua Bookstore Limited Liability Company	城阳区	Chengyang District
150	青岛市城阳区新城石化有限公司	Qingdao Chengyang District New – town Petrochemical Limited Company	城阳区	Chengyang District
151	青岛喜盈门集团喜盈门商场	Qingdao Xiyingmen Group Xiyingmen Shopping Mall	城阳区	Chengyang District
152	青岛国货城阳购物中心有限公司	Qingdao Guohuo Chengyang Shopping Center Limited Company	城阳区	Chengyang District
153	青岛家佳源(城阳)购物中心有限公司	Qingdao Jiajiayuan (Chengyang) Shopping Center Limited Company	城阳区	Chengyang District
154	青岛太阳城商场有限责任公司	Qingdao Sun – city Shopping Mall Limited Liability Company	城阳区	Chengyang District
155	青岛润华汽车销售服务有限公司	Qingdao Runhua Auto Sale And Service Limited Company	城阳区	Chengyang District
156	青岛亚马逊数码广场有限公司	Qingdao Amazon Digital Square Limited Company	胶州市	Jiaozhou
157	青岛鲁汇商业集团有限公司	Qingdao Luhui Commercial Group Limited Company	胶州市	Jiaozhou
158	胶州市金州贸易大厦	Jiaozhou Jinzhou Trade Building	胶州市	Jiaozhou
159	青岛永春工贸有限公司	Qingdao Yongchun Industry And Trade Limited Company	胶州市	Jiaozhou
160	青岛长丰汽车销售有限公司	Qingdao Changfeng Auto Sale Limited Company	胶州市	Jiaozhou
161	胶州市同兴摩托车销售有限公司	Jiaozhou Tongxing Motorcycle Sale Limited Company	胶州市	Jiaozhou
162	胶州市新远摩托车销售有限公司	Jiaozhou Xinyuan Motorcycle Sale Limited Company	胶州市	Jiaozhou
163	青岛狮龙工贸有限公司	Qingdao Shilong Industry And Trade Limited Company	胶州市	Jiaozhou
164	青岛国货集团新世纪购物中心有限公司	Qingdao Guohuo Group New Century Shopping Center Limited Company	胶州市	Jiaozhou
165	青岛嘉恒摩托车销售有限公司	Qingdao Jiaheng Motorcycle Sale Limited Company	胶州市	Jiaozhou
166	胶州市新华书店	Jiaozhou Xinhua Bookstore	胶州市	Jiaozhou
167	青岛双信液化气销售有限公司	Qingdao Shuangxin Liquid Gas Sale Limited Company	胶州市	Jiaozhou
168	青岛鑫源丰燃料有限公司	Qingdao Xinyuanfeng Fuel Limited Company	胶州市	Jiaozhou
169	青岛开顺汽车销售有限公司	Qingdao Kaishun Auto Sale Limited Company	胶州市	Jiaozhou
170	青岛万僖龙汽车销售有限公司	Qingdao Wanxilong Auto Sale Limited Company	胶州市	Jiaozhou

14 -20 续表
continued

序号 Serial Number	单位名称	Name	所在地区	Location
171	青岛志源汽车销售有限公司	Qingdao Zhiyuan Auto Sale Limited Company	胶州市	Jiaozhou
172	青岛宏林源汽车销售有限公司	Qingdao Honglinyuan Auto Sale Limited Company	胶州市	Jiaozhou
173	青岛利客来商贸(有)李哥庄超市	Qingdao Likelai Trade Limited Company Ligezhuang Supermarket	胶州市	Jiaozhou
174	青岛即墨市新华书店有限责任公司	Qingdao Jimo Xinhua Bookstore Limited Liability Company	即墨市	Jimo
175	青岛紫光药业有限公司	Qingdao Ziguang Pharmaceutical Limited Company	即墨市	Jimo
176	青岛大成汽车服务有限公司	Qingdao Dacheng Car Service Limited Company	即墨市	Jimo
177	青岛名流车行有限公司	Qingdao Celebrities Car Dealership Limited Company	即墨市	Jimo
178	青岛飞利汽车贸易有限公司即墨分公司	Qingdao Feili Auto Trade Limited Company Jimo Subsidiary Company	即墨市	Jimo
179	青岛国风集团祥泰药庄连锁有限公司	Qingdao Growful Group Xiangtai Drug Store Chain - like Limited Company	即墨市	Jimo
180	青岛龙宇木业有限公司	Qingdao Longyu Wooden Industry Limited Company	即墨市	Jimo
181	青岛喜盈门顺利达超市有限公司	Qingdao Xiyinmen Shunlida Supermarket Limited Company	即墨市	Jimo
182	青岛即墨市新世界大厦	Qingdao Jimo New World Building	即墨市	Jimo
183	青岛亨通汽车销售服务有限公司	Qingdao Hengtong Auto Sale And Service Limited Company	即墨市	Jimo
184	青岛三联家电有限公司	Qingdao Sanlian Electrical Appliance Limited Company	即墨市	Jimo
185	青岛圣帝亚服饰中心	Qingdao Shengdiya Dress Center	即墨市	Jimo
186	青岛中豪汽车销售有限公司	Qingdao Zhonghao Auto Sale Limited Company	即墨市	Jimo
187	青岛新雅泰电器有限公司	Qingdao Xinyatai Electric Appliance Limited Company	即墨市	Jimo
188	青岛亚泰大药房	Qingdao Yatai Drug Stone	即墨市	Jimo
189	青岛即墨市液化气公司	Qingdao Jimo Liquid Gas Company	即墨市	Jimo
190	青岛平度市新华书店有限责任公司	Qingdao Pingdu Xinhua Bookstore Limited Liability Company	平度市	Pingdu
191	青岛中百佳乐家超市有限公司	Qingdao Zhongbai Jialejia Supermarket Limited Company	平度市	Pingdu
192	青岛爱客电器有限公司	Qingdao Aiek Electric Appliance Limited Company	平度市	Pingdu
193	平度市燃料总公司	Pingdu Fuel Main Corporation	平度市	Pingdu
194	青岛美森置业有限公司	Qingdao Meisen Real Estate Limited Company	平度市	Pingdu
195	青岛平度新时代商贸有限公司	Qingdao Pingdu New Times Business Trade Limited Company	平度市	Pingdu
196	青岛平度东方大厦股份有限公司	Qingdao Pingdu East Building Inc.	平度市	Pingdu
197	青岛平度维克购物中心有限公司	Qingdao Pingdu Weekly Shopping Center Limited Company	平度市	Pingdu
198	青岛国风集团平度医药有限责任公司	Qingdao Groeful Group Pingdu Medicine Limited Liability Company	平度市	Pingdu
199	青岛宝威车行有限公司	Qingdao Baowei Car Dealership Limited Company	平度市	Pingdu
200	青岛宝凯超市有限公司	Qingdao Baokai Supermarket Limited Company	平度市	Pingdu
201	青岛世达机械有限公司平度汽车公司	Qingdao Shida Machinery Limited Company Pingdu Car Company	平度市	Pingdu
202	胶南市百货批发总公司	Jiaonan General Merchandise Wholesale Main Corporation	胶南市	Jiaonan
203	青岛胶南振兴日用杂品有限公司	Qingdao Jiaonan Daily Use Sundries Limited Company	胶南市	Jiaonan
204	胶南汇众汽车销售有限公司	Jiaonan Huizhong Auto Sale Limited Company	胶南市	Jiaonan

14－20 续表
continued

序号 Serial Number	单位名称	Name	所在地区	Location
205	青岛鑫海洋电脑技术有限公司	Qingdao Xinhaiyang Computer Technology Limited Company	胶南市	Jiaonan
206	胶南市糖酒副食品总公司	Jiaona Rum And Non－staple Food Product Main Corporation	胶南市	Jiaonan
207	胶南市华盛五交化批发商场	Jiaona Huasheng Hardware, Electric Apparatus & Chemical Industry Wholesale Market	胶南市	Jiaonan
208	山东省胶南市大世界商乐城	Shandong Province Jiaonan Great World business And Entertainment Centre	胶南市	Jiaonan
209	青岛金华达摩托销售有限公司	Qingdao Jinhuada Motorized Sale Limited Company	胶南市	Jiaonan
210	胶南三联电器有限公司	Jiaonan Sanlian Electric Appliance Limited Company	胶南市	Jiaonan
211	胶南市亚飞汽车连锁有限公司	Jiaonan Yafei Automobile Chain－like Limited Company	胶南市	Jiaonan
212	青岛胶南市新华书店有限责任公司	Qingdao Jiaonan Xinhua Bookstore Limited Liability Company	胶南市	Jiaonan
213	青岛瑞源汽车销售有限公司	Qingdao Ruiyuan Auto Sale Limited Company	胶南市	Jiaonan
214	青岛维客胶南购物中心有限公司	Qingdao Weekly Jiaonan Shopping Center Limited Company	胶南市	Jiaonan
215	青岛大富隆摩托车销售有限公司	Qingdao Dafulong Motorcycle Sale Limited Company	莱西市	Laixi
216	上海大众汽车莱西销售服务有限公司	Shanghai Volkswagen Automobile Laixi Sale And Service Limited Company	莱西市	Laixi
217	莱西市外贸大厦有限公司	Laixi Foreign Trade Building Limited Company	莱西市	Laixi
218	青岛利客来莱西购物有限公司	Qingdao Likelai Laixi Shopping Limited Company	莱西市	Laixi
219	青岛莱西市新华书店有限责任公司	Qingdao Laixi Xinhua Bookstore Limited Liability Company	莱西市	Laixi
220	青岛莱西市粮贸大厦有限公司	Qingdao Laixi Grain Trade Building Limited Company	莱西市	Laixi
221	青岛清洗防腐公司	Qingdao Washing & Antisepsis Company	莱西市	Laixi
222	青岛科信商贸有限公司	Qingdao Kexin Business Trade Limited Company	莱西市	Laixi
223	青岛麦琦女子美容健身俱乐部	Qingdao Maggie Female Beauty And Fitness Club	莱西市	Laixi
224	青岛景顺商贸有限公司	Qingdao Jingshun Trade Limited Company	莱西市	Laixi
225	青岛莱西市月宫食品商场有限责任公司	Qingdao Laixi Yuegong Food Shopping Mall limited Liability Company	莱西市	Laixi
226	青岛晓华啤酒销售有限公司	Qingdao Xiaohua Beer Sale Limited Company	莱西市	Laixi
227	莱西市五金交电化工总公司	Laixi Hardware, Electric Apparatus & Chemical Industry Main Corporation	莱西市	Laixi
228	青岛莱西万客来商贸有限公司	Qingdao Laixi Wankelai Trade Limited Company	莱西市	Laixi
229	青岛神龙潮汽车销售有限公司	Qingdao Shenlongchao Auto Sale Limited Company	莱西市	Laixi
230	青岛通达资源开发有限公司	Qingdao Tongda Resources Development Limited Company	莱西市	Laixi
231	青岛豪特汽车有限公司	Qingdao Haote Automobile Limited Company	莱西市	Laixi
232	青岛兴良家具有限公司	Qingdao Xingliang Furniture Limited Company	莱西市	Laixi
233	青岛宏祥液化气有限公司	Qingdao Hongxiang Liquid Gas Limited Company	莱西市	Laixi
234	青岛顺好加油站	Qingdao Shunhao Gas Station	莱西市	Laixi
235	青岛海诺大药房连锁有限公司	Qingdao Hainuo Drug Store Chain－like Limited Company	莱西市	Laixi
236	青岛大成汽车服务有限公司莱西分公司	Qingdao Dacheng Car Service Limited Company Laixi Subsidiary Company	莱西市	Laixi
237	青岛和立盛加油站	Qingdao Helisheng Gas Station	莱西市	Laixi
238	青岛周君百货有限公司	Qingdao Zhoujun General Merchandise Limited Company	莱西市	Laixi
239	青岛利客来李权庄购物有限公司	Qingdao Likelai Li Quanzhuang Shopping Limited Company	莱西市	Laixi
240	莱西市李权庄镇万友商场	Laixi Li Quanzhuang Town Wanyou Shopping Mall	莱西市	Laixi

CHAPTER 15

第十五篇

对外经济贸易和旅游

FOREIGN TRADE AND TOURISM

编辑单位：	外经贸易统计处	企业调查队产业调查处
编　　委：	刘　伟	孙昭信
编　　辑：	孙　明　任庆利	贾洪泰
校　　对：	孙　明　任庆利	贾洪泰
电　　话：	85912241 85912243	82869521

15-1 青岛口岸进出口总额(1985-2005年)

TOTAL VALUE OF IMPORTS AND EXPORTS THROUGH QINGDAO CUSTOM(1985-2005)

单位:万美元(10000 USD)

年 份 Year	青岛口岸进出口总额 Total Value of Imports and Exports through Qingdao Custom	出口 Exports	进口 Imports
1985	414 448	234 652	179 796
1986	382 840	191 926	190 914
1987	445 090	259 458	185 632
1988	474 516	259 176	215 340
1989	506 152	268 397	237 755
1990	477 117	304 011	173 106
1991	519 273	332 949	186 324
1992	581 495	350 163	231 332
1993	678 013	360 297	317 716
1994	888 574	510 760	377 814
1995	1 307 508	705 245	602 263
1996	1 391 323	760 566	629 757
1997	1 542 284	936 142	609 142
1998	1 463 718	933 392	530 326
1999	1 696 514	1 063 768	632 746
2000	2 520 420	1 423 266	1 097 154
2001	2 797 085	1 636 888	1 160 197
2002	3 128 048	1 889 612	1 238 436
2003	4 088 096	2 366 046	1 722 050
2004	5 677 570	3 197 697	2 479 873
2005	6 932 944	3 959 947	2 972 997

15-2 进出口总额(1988-2005年)

TOTAL VALUE OF IMPORTS AND EXPORTS (1988-2005)

单位:万美元(10000 USD)

年 份 Year	进出口总额(含中央、省公司) Total Value of Imports and Exports (including central and provincial companies)	出口 Exports	进口 Imports	进出口总额(不含中央、省公司) Total Value of Imports and Exports (decluding central and provincial companies)	出口 Exports	进口 Imports
1988	-	-	-	28 097	21 731	6 366
1989	-	-	-	39 327	27 797	11 530
1990	-	-	-	41 649	33 529	8 120
1991	-	-	-	54 624	44 746	9 878
1992	-	-	-	88 600	66 291	22 309
1993	517 643	346 288	171 355	139 048	100 201	38 847
1994	633 213	434 102	199 111	234 978	164 135	70 843
1995	858 560	536 386	322 174	376 372	245 072	131 300
1996	863 521	516 317	347 204	461 950	287 123	174 827
1997	916 269	579 261	377 008	521 967	338 535	183 432
1998	882 042	573 020	309 022	595 826	382 657	213 169
1999	1 009 885	631 072	378 813	775 565	446 260	329 305
2000	1 353 222	826 891	526 331	1 083 133	611 426	471 707
2001	1 541 564	950 160	591 404	1 235 781	712 024	523 757
2002	1 692 567	1 057 141	635 426	1 409 598	850 420	559 178
2003	2 065 912	1 239 199	826 713	1 784 556	1 035 528	749 028
2004	2 698 781	1 578 167	1 120 614	2 433 188	1 391 171	1 042 017
2005	3 302 230	1 942 242	1 359 988	3 045 542	1 758 834	1 286 708

15 –3 分国别外贸出口总额(含中央、省公司)

VALUE OF EXPORTS BY MAJOR TRADING PARTNERS
(INCLUDING CENTRAL AND PROVINCIAL COMPANIES)

单位:万美元(10000 USD)

国别(地区)	Country and Region	2005 年 2005	2004 年 2004	2005 年比 2004 年 ± % 2005/2004(± %)
总计	**Total**	**1 942 242**	**1 578 167**	**23.1**
#亚洲	Asia	885 041	772 083	14.6
香港	Hong Kong	71 062	69 171	2.7
日本	Japan	367 467	318 478	15.4
韩国	Korea	248 075	208 786	18.8
台湾	Taiwan	13 803	13 555	1.8
非洲	Africa	50 445	37 510	34.5
南非	South Africa	9 723	8 032	21.1
欧洲	Europe	447 195	340 510	31.3
欧盟	EU	402 014	289 667	30.6
南美洲	South America	58127	41 949	38.6
北美洲	North America	464 383	358 617	29.5
美国	United States	422 611	326 365	29.5
大洋洲	Oceanica	37 048	27 498	34.7
澳大利亚	Australia	28 888	22 595	27.9

注:2005 年欧盟成员国较 2004 年增加 5 个,因此将 2004 年基数由 289667 万美元调整为 307821 万美元。

Note: The figure in 2004 that the calculation based on had been adjusted for 3.07821 billion U.S. dollars from 2.89667 billion U.S. dollars. Because there are 5 EU member states newly increased in 2005.

15 –4 分国别外贸出口总额(不含中央、省公司)

VALUE OF EXPORTS BY MAJOR TRADING PARTNERS
(DECLUDING CENTRAL AND PROVINCIAL COMPANIES)

单位:万美元(10000 USD)

国别(地区)	Country and Region	2005 年 2005	2004 年 2004	2005 年比 2004 年 ± % 2005/2004(± %)
总计	**Total**	**1 758 834**	**1 391 171**	**26.4**
#亚洲	Asia	811 141	691 201	17.4
香港	Hong Kong	68 738	65 365	5.2
日本	Japan	337 920	286 669	17.9
韩国	Korea	233 743	194 518	20.2
台湾	Taiwan	13 035	11 139	17
非洲	Africa	44 763	31 862	40.5
南非	South Africa	8 271	6 473	27.8
欧洲	Europe	393 887	287 951	36.8
欧盟	EU	358 648	263 532	36.1
南美洲	South America	54 334	38 190	42.3
北美洲	North America	421 690	319 205	32.1
美国	United States	384 989	291 003	32.3
大洋洲	Oceanica	33 012	22 762	45
澳大利亚	Australia	25 641	18 753	36.7

15 -5 外贸出口商品构成(不含中央、省公司)

COMPOSITION OF EXPORT COMMODITIES(DECLUDING CENTRAL AND PROVINCIAL COMPANIES)

单位:%

项　目	Items	2005 年 2005	2004 年 2004	2005 年比 2004 年 ± % 2005/2004(± %)
总值	**Total Value**	**100**	**100**	
一、初级产品	**Primary Products**	**13.3**	**13.9**	**-0.6**
食品及活动物	Food and Livestock	10	10.2	-0.2
饮料及烟类	Drinks and Tobacco	0.2	0.2	0.0
非食用原料(燃料除外)	Non-edible Raw Materials	1.2	1.4	-0.2
矿物燃料、润滑油及有关原料	Mineral Fuel, Lubricant and Related Raw Materials	1.8	1.9	-0.1
动植物油、脂及蜡	Animal and Plant Oil, Fat and Wax	0.1	0.2	-0.1
二、工业制品	**Industrial Products**	**86.7**	**86.1**	**0.6**
#机电产品	Mechanical and Electronic Products	35.4	34.9	0.5
化学成品及有关产品	Chemicals and Related Products	3.7	3.2	0.5
按原料分类的制成品	Raw Material Products	19.4	18.2	1.2
机械及运输设备	Machinery and Transportation Equipment	29.8	29.3	0.5
杂项制品	Assorted Products	33.8	35.4	-1.6
未分类的商品	Other Commodities	–	–	–

15 -6 主要出口商品总值(不含中央、省公司)

EXPORT VALUE OF MAJOR COMMODITIES(DECLUDING CENTRAL AND PROVINCIAL COMPANIES)

单位:万美元(10000 USD)

商品名称	Name	2005 年 2005	2004 年 2004	2005 年比 2004 年 ± % 2005/2004(± %)
服装及衣着附件	Garments and Clothing Accessories	239 994	197 855	21.3
电器及电子类产品	Electronic Products	222 146	167 082	33
机械设备	Machinery & Equipment	155 947	116 989	33.3
运输工具	Transport Instruments	143 910	123 926	16.1
纺织纱线、织物及制品	Textile Yarn Fabrics and Make-up Articles	118 163	89 833	31.5
鞋类	Shoes	81 866	71 213	15
金属制品	Metal Products	72 562	47 235	53.6
水海产品	Aquatic Products	71 183	53 719	32.5
化工产品	Products of Chemical Industry	62 859	45 334	38.7
食品	Foods	62 743	50 998	23

15 -7 利用外资情况(1990 -2005 年)
UTILIZATION FOREIGN CAPITAL(1990 - 2005)

单位:万美元(10000 USD)

		单位	Unit	1990 年	1995 年	2000 年	2004 年	2005 年
批准项目个数	**Projects Permitted**	**个**	**unit**	**16**	**1 148**	**1 132**	**2 423**	**2 530**
一、外商直接投资	Direct Foreign Investments	个	unit	64	718	1 128	2 423	2 530
#中外合资企业	Sino-foreign Joint Ventures	个	unit	40	260	303	318	274
中外合作企业	Sino-foreign Cooperative Businesses	个	unit		45	5	19	18
外商独资企业	Foreign Funded	个	unit	1	412	76	2 086	2 236
其它	Others	个	unit	-	1	1	-	2
二、外商其他投资	Other Foreign Investments	个	unit	103	430	4	-	-
合同外资金额	**Utilization of Foreign Capital through Signed Agreements**	**万美元**	**10000 USD**	**8 137**	**165 402**	**269 081**	**676 621**	**954 486**
一、外商直接投资	Direct Foreign Investments	万美元	10000 USD	6 900	146 734	266 221	671 723	954 486
#中外合资企业	Sino-foreign Joint Ventures	万美元	10000 USD	3 265	52 118	69 889	47 772	112 777
中外合作企业	Sino-foreign Cooperative Businesses	万美元	10000 USD	346	14 774	26 835	7 382	17 588
外商独资企业	Foreign Funded	万美元	10000 USD	3 289	79 842	169 370	616 473	813 485
其它	Others	万美元	10000 USD	-	-	12	96	10 636
二、外商其他投资	Other Foreign Investments	万美元	10000 USD	1 237	18 668	2 860	4 898	-
实际外资金额	**Actual Foreign Capital**	**万美元**	**10000 USD**	**7 770**	**86 573**	**128 171**	**381 698**	**365 625**
一、外商直接投资	Direct Foreign Investments	万美元	10000 USD	4 839	70 310	126 132	379 917	365 625
#中外合资企业	Sino-foreign Joint Ventures	万美元	10000 USD	4 161	22 640	39 224	54 798	77 636
中外合作企业	Sino-foreign Cooperative Businesses	万美元	10000 USD	19	2 671	3 886	7 319	5 654
外商独资企业	Foreign Funded	万美元	10000 USD	659	44 999	82 992	317 088	280 130
其它	Others	万美元	10000 USD	-	-	30	712	2 205
二、外商其他投资	Other Foreign Investments	万美元	10000 USD	2 931	16 263	2 039	1 781	-

15－8 外商直接投资项目数和投资额(2005 年)
DIRECT FOREIGN PROJECTS AND INVESTMENT(2005)

单位:万美元(10000 USD)

项　目	Items	批准项目数（个）Project Permitted (unit)	合同外资金额（万美元）Utilization of Foreign Capital through Signed Agreements(10000 USD)	实际外资金额（万美元）Actual Foreign Capital (10000 USD)
外商直接投资	**Direct Foreign Investments**	**2 530**	**954 486**	**365 625**
一、按投资方式分	**Grouped by Investment Ways**			
中外合资企业	Sino-foreign Joint Ventures	274	112 777	77 636
中外合作企业	Sino-foreign Cooperative Business	18	17 588	5 654
外商独资企业	Foreign Funded	2 236	813 485	280 130
外商投资股份制企业	Foreign Investment Share Enterprises	2	10 636	2 205
其他	Other			
二、按行业分	**Grouped by Sector**			
农、林、牧、渔业	Farming, Forestry, Animal Husbandry and Fishery	48	29 184	13 180
采矿业	Excavation	7	1 765	168
制造业	Manufacturing	2 110	798 190	314 439
电力、燃气及水的生产和供应业	Power, Gas and Water Production and Supply	4	3 871	1 102
建筑业	Construction	21	11 653	1 894
交通运输、仓储和邮政业	Transportation, Storage and Postal	21	15 738	5 475
信息传输、计算机服务和软件业	Information Transmission, Computer Service and Software Service	9	1 402	135
批发和零售业	Wholesale and Retail Trade	115	12 608	5 785
住宿和餐饮业	Accommodation and Catering Trade	66	11 835	3 414
房地产业	Real Estate	39	45 827	11 661
租赁和商务服务业	Lease and Commercial Service	46	9 414	4 904
科学研究、技术服务和地质勘查业	Scientific Research, Technical service and Geological Prospecting	5	1 055	883
水利、环境和公共设施管理业	Water Conservancy, Enviroment and Public Facilities administration	1	3 751	945
居民服务和其他服务业	Resident Services and Other Services	12	867	256
教育	Education	3	170	26
卫生、社会保障和社会福利业	Health Care, Social Protection and Social Walfare	2	607	7
文化、体育和娱乐业	Culture, Sports and Entertainment	21	6 549	1 351
三、按主要国别(地区)分	**Grouped by Country and Region**			
韩国	Korea	1 691	498 754	179 853
香港	Hong Kong	187	136 008	47 120
日本	Japan	199	95 144	42 012
美国	United States	112	38 842	17 288
台湾省	Taiwan	86	21 687	12 192
维尔京群岛	Virgin Islands	42	34 753	18 038
新加坡	Singapore	19	13 027	7 208
英国	United Kingdom	20	9 823	2 166
加拿大	Canada	28	8 549	2 293
澳大利亚	Australia	21	11 786	2 515

15 -9 外商投资企业生产经营状况(2005 年)
PRODUCTION AND OPERATION OF FOREIGN INVESTMENT ENTERPRISES(2005)

		单位	Unit	总计 Total	中外合资企业 Sino-foreign Joint Ventures	中外合作企业 Sino-foreign cooperative Operation Enterprises	外商独资企业 Foreign-owned Enterprises
实有企业数	Number of Enterprises	个	unit	3 982	613	82	2 565
#亏损企业	of which: Loss-making Enterprises	个	unit	1 985	314	40	1 243
主营业务收入	Income from Major Business	万元	10000 yuan	16 543 623	4 335 040	246 830	7 767 689
#出口销售收入	of which: Sales Revenue of Exports	万元	10000 yuan	8 290 596	1 677 494	107 470	5 386 958
从业人员	Employment	人	person	767 006	114 724	14 267	535 488
#外籍人员	Foreign Employees	人	person	13 676	848	84	11 587
企业资产总计	Total Assets	万元	10000 yuan	15 572 560	4 172 192	340 375	6 732 949
#流动资产合计	Total Circulating Funds	万元	10000 yuan	9 292 443	2 250 321	174 666	4 018 715
固定资产合计	Total Fixed Assets	万元	10000 yuan	4 932 481	1 309 722	102 717	2 413 788
费用总额	Total Expenses	万元	10000 yuan	1 660 566	437 641	32 441	496 264
利润总额	Total Profits	万元	10000yuan	690 289	245 435	13 172	273 471
税金总额	Total Tax	万元	10000 yuan	420 228	115 973	10 403	153 253
可供分配利润	Profits for Assigned	万元	10000yuan	691 115	274 951	7 238	331 687
已分配股利	Assigned Dividends	万元	10000 yuan	163 700	98 262	0	53 717
负债合计	Total Liabilities	万元	10000 yuan	9 023 108	2 435 102	254 154	3 775 702

15 -9 续表
continued

		单位	Unit	港澳台与大陆合资经营企业 Joint Ventures (Hong Kong, Macao and Taiwan)	港澳台与大陆合作经营企业 Cooperative Businesses (Hong Kong, Macao and Taiwan)	港澳台独资企业 Hong Kong, Macao Taiwan Funded	中外股份制 Sino-foreign Share Holding
实有企业数	Number of Enterprises	个	unit	297	36	367	22
#亏损企业	Number of Enterprises	个	unit	148	71	200	4
主营业务收入	Income from Major Business	万元	10000 yuan	2 131 024	927 492	653 891	481 658
#出口销售收入	of which: Sales Revenue of Exports	万元	10000 yuan	613 436	38 638	340 375	126 225
从业人员	Employment	人	person	46 105	8 043	37 784	10 595
#外籍人员	Foreign Employees	人	person	131	11	525	490
企业资产总计	Total Assets	万元	10000 yuan	1 720 063	686 469	1 161 711	758 801
#流动资产合计	Total Circulating Funds	万元	10000 yuan	1 168 506	396 153	860 003	424 079
固定资产合计	Total Fixed Assets	万元	10000 yuan	461 556	259 858	259 288	125 552
费用总额	Total Expenses	万元	10000 yuan	197 116	39 554	83 968	96 744
利润总额	Total Profits	万元	10000yuan	86 820	13 194	13 787	44 410
税金总额	Total Tax	万元	10000 yuan	56 258	26 221	9 463	48 657
可供分配利润	Profits for Assigned	万元	10000yuan	56 721	3 739	15 016	1 763
已分配股利	Assigned Dividends	万元	10000 yuan	9 463	3	2 258	0
负债合计	Total Liabilities	万元	10000 yuan	1 032 602	458 499	832 410	234 638

15－10 分行业外商投资企业生产经营状况(2005 年)

PRODUCTION AND OPERATION OF FOREIGN INVESTMENT ENTERPRISES BY SECTOR(2005)

		主营业务收入(万元) Income from Major Business(10000 yuan)
农、林、牧、渔业	Farming, Forestry, Animal Husbandry and Fishery	38 661
其中:农业	Farming	5 922
采矿业	Excavation	23 756
制造业	Manufacturing	14 897 547
其中:农副食品加工业	Agricultural Non-staple Food Processing	915 571
食品制造业	Food Manufacturing	973 958
饮料制造业	Beverage Manufacturing	474 022
纺织业	Textile Industry	839 740
纺织服装、鞋、帽制造业	Textile, Clothing and Footwear Production	1 031 096
皮革、皮衣、羽毛(绒)及其制造品业	Leathers, Furs, Down and Related Products	1 090 974
家具制造业	Furniture Maunufacturing	125 448
石油加工、炼焦及核燃料加工业	PetroLeum Processing, Coking and Nuclear Fuel Processing	18 172
化学原料及化学制品制造业	Raw Chemical Material and Chemical Products	443 550
医药制造业	Medical and Pharmaceutic Products	30 087
化学纤维制造业	Chemical Fibers	181 991
塑料制造业	Plastic Products	556 909
非金属矿物制造业	Nonmetal Mineral Products	556 909
黑色金属冶炼及压延加工业	Smelting and Processing of Ferrous Metals	1 031 253
通用设备制造业	General-purpose Equipment Manufacturing	687 138
交通运输设备制造业	Transportation Equipment Manufacturing	272 131
电气机械及器材制造业	Electric Equipment and Machinery Manufacturing	1 126 144
通信设备、计算机及其他电子设备	Communication Equipment, Computers and Other Electric Equipment Production	1 898 581
电力、燃气及水的生产和供应	Electric Power, Gas, Water Production and Supply	13 191
建筑业	Construction	13 177
交通运输、仓储和邮政业	Transportation , Storage, Postal and Telecommunications	392 432
信息传输、计算服务和软件业	Information Transmission, Computer Service and Software Service	10 338
批发与零售业	Wholesale and Retail Trade	540 133
其中:批发业	Wholesale Trade	442 679
零售业	Retail Trade	97 455
住宿和餐饮业	Accommodation and Catering Trade	155 972
其中:住宿业	Accommodation Trade	86 681
餐饮业	Catering Trade	69 291
金融业	Financial	42 937
其中:银行业	Banking	42 803
房地产业	Real Estate	263 946
租赁和商务服务	Leasing Trade and Commercial Service	5 091
科学研究、技术服务与地质勘查业	Scientific Research, Technical Service and Geological Prospecting	99 614
水利、环境和公共设施管理业	Water Conservancy, Environment and Administration of Public Facilities	2 100
居民服务和其他服务业	Residents Services and Other Social Services	0
教育	Education	29 134
卫生、社会保障和社会福利业	Health Care, Social Protection and Social Walfare	2 141
文化、体育和娱乐业	Culture, Sports and Recreation	482
公共管理和社会组织	Public Administration and Social Orgnization	12 363
国际组织	International Orgnization	0

出口销售收入(万元) Sales Revenue of Exports(10000 yuan)	税金总额(万元) Total Tax (10000 yuan)	利润总额(万元) Total Profits (10000 yuan)	从业人员(人) Employment (person)
25 225	1 991	225	2 034
2 712	195	251	725
9 621	1 339	1 215	1 435
8 090 400	341 332	496 635	731 097
438 261	12 634	31 154	31 730
681 090	15 451	33 818	19 902
26 869	57 632	46 863	5 998
475 257	19 074	14 978	44 060
779 847	16 482	21 740	128 000
991 910	6 357	-8 631	105 950
105 145	463	-370	10 430
	484	-1 883	410
193 635	10 334	26 761	12 982
14 687	1 072	1 440	1 859
61 753	4 039	-3 456	3 853
219 293	15 186	17 883	23 398
219 293	15 186	17 883	23 398
16 183	19 277	-14 486	5 364
445 047	11 484	28 216	22 204
112 940	7 841	19 249	14 632
464 589	23 737	167 34	29 050
870 890	49 849	119 973	64 504
118	894	1 997	414
2 714	457	2 786	497
24 618	9 026	97 164	5 275
551	727	26	953
119 275	15 337	878	7 737
119 081	11 608	349	5 286
194	3 728	529	2 451
2 284	13 140	16 125	11 324
2 147	6 872	8 152	4 813
138	6 268	7 972	6 511
0	2 610	12 877	197
0	2 604	11 627	191
272	14 232	20 397	2 260
0	234	763	243
10 929	17 300	36 423	874
0	8	6	220
4 139	347	128	532
123	21	1 120	161
109	52	160	50
0	1 116	1 430	1 649
0	0	0	0
0	0	0	0

15－11 分国别外商投资企业生产经营状况(2005 年)

PRODUCTION AND OPERATION OF FOREIGN INVESTMENT ENTERPRISES BY COUNTRY AND REGION(2005)

		主营业务收入(万元) Income from Major Business (10000 yuan)	出口销售收入(万元) Sales Revenue of Exports (10000 yuan)	税金总额(万元) Total Tax (10000 yuan)	利润总额(万元) Total Profits (10000 yuan)	从业人员(人) Employment (person)
按投资国别、地区分组	Grouped by Country and Region					
1、亚洲	Asia	122 444 62	6 885 877	230 149	252 666	667 012
#香港	Hong Kong	3 426 079	941 210	84 636	107 733	67 271
澳门	Macao	20 392	11 283	903	1 554	1 043
台湾	Taiwan	503 539	214 917	10 112	15 667	28 638
印度尼西亚	Indonesia	10 610	5 968	515	933	641
日本	Japan	1 673 327	988 508	48 111	87 766	79 177
马来西亚	Malaysia	154 586	14 410	5 539	3 997	4 320
菲律宾	Philippines	10 728	3 947	509	537	411
新加坡	Singapore	260 675	54 309	8 956	12 368	7 469
韩国	Korea	6 155 649	4 635 607	69 633	19 055	476 444
泰国	Thailand	12 309	10 951	708	1 661	879
2、非洲	Africa	165 308	1 218	4 890	87 010	1 620
3、欧洲	Europe	1 529 641	454 049	81 978	99 835	35 206
#比利时	Belgium	4 314	532	201	-89	70
丹麦	Denmark	189 020	188 873	-	-3 828	2 837
英国	United Kingdom	186 640	56 610	5 186	20 739	9 744
德国	Germany	124 117	46 558	5 935	9 866	2 718
法国	France	174 735	26 718	8 224	7 454	3 327
爱尔兰	Ireland	4 074	4 074	18	-217	339
意大利	Italy	148 959	15 169	1 891	3 996	1 564
卢森堡	Luxemburg	1 462	-	138	5700	43
荷兰	Netherlands	108 637	637	6 324	10 770	5 458
希腊	Greece	95	-	3	-	-
葡萄牙	Portugal	-	-	-	-	-
西班牙	Spain	14 527	6 013	-5	711	387
芬兰	Finland	253	253	-	-56	130
瑞士	Switzerland	128 139	45 401	4 704	8 020	1 443
4、拉丁美洲	Latin America	321 037	211 402	7 249	25 389	8 044
#开曼群岛	Cayman Islands	38 447	606	1 528	1 514	634
英属维尔京群岛	British Virgin Islands	235 184	193 063	3 896	20 893	2 244
5、北美洲	North America	1 897 051	633 865	81 052	202 672	47 082
#加拿大	Canada	90 746	56 848	880	1 080	4 968
美国	United States	1 805 157	576 524	80 094	201 661	41 893
6、大洋洲	Oceanica	386 125	104 186	14 911	22 698	8 042
#澳大利亚	Australia	54 875	24 982	2 845	532	2 303
新西兰	New Zealand	6 206	741	80	-182	138
7、其他	Others	-	-	-	-	-

15－12 分市、区外商投资企业生产经营状况(2005年)

PRODUCTION AND OPERATION OF FOREIGN INVESTMENT ENTERPRISES BY REGION(2005)

单位:万元(10 000 yuan)

市、区名称	Region	资产总计 Total Assets	流动资产合计 Total Circulating Funds	固定资产合计 Total Fixed Assets	无形资产合计 Total Intangible Assets
合计	**Total**	**15 572 560**	**9 292 443**	**4 932 481**	**780 684**
市 区	Urban Area	4 440 416	2 994 104	913 259	114 723
#崂山区	Chengyang District	1 596 774	1 184 723	318 851	48 796
黄岛区	Huangdao District	2 705 287	1 206 722	1 016 036	425 262
城阳区	Laoshan District	2 196 855	1 344 687	789 868	62 152
胶州市	Jiaozhou	1 368 884	762 266	538 508	46 084
即墨市	Jimo	1 302 946	685 733	503 441	41 537
平度市	Pingdu	885 116	516 229	425 115	19 058
胶南市	Jiaonan	463 619	259 046	173 233	13 678
莱西市	Laixi	612 663	338 935	254 169	9 395

15－12 续表1

continued

单位:万元(10 000 yuan)

市、区名称	Region	负债合计 Total Liabilities	流动负债合计 Total Circulating Liabilities	长期负债合计 Total Long-term Liabilities	所有者权益合计 Total Owners Rights and Interests
合 计	**Total**	**9 023 108**	**8 028 956**	**986 622**	**6 549 592**
市 区	Urban Area	2 882 537	2 665 525	214 536	1 557 879
#崂山区	Chengyang District	844 041	811 018	32 055	752 733
黄岛区	Huangdao District	1 486 241	1 051 351	434 853	1 219 050
城阳区	Laoshan District	1 264 219	1 169 923	93 824	932 637
胶州市	Jiaozhou	740 589	710 282	30 220	628 295
即墨市	Jimo	713 327	612 288	99 510	589 620
平度市	Pingdu	398 162	375 734	22 093	486 954
胶南市	Jiaonan	264 673	244 350	19 623	198 707
莱西市	Laixi	429 321	388 487	39 909	183 718

15－12 续表2
continued

单位:万元(10 000 yuan)

市、区名称	Region	主营业务收入 Income from Major Business	出口销售收入 Sales Revenue of Exports	费用总额 Total Expenses	利润总额 Total Profits
合　计	**Total**	**16 543 623**	**8 290 596**	**2 483 422**	**690 289**
市　区	Urban Area	3 089 628	588 560	367 819	138 759
#崂山区	Chengyang District	1 807 879	318 348	212 623	178 760
黄岛区	Huangdao District	2 763 696	1 091 211	385 491	179 368
城阳区	Laoshan District	3 145 283	2 542 147	568 743	106 638
胶州市	Jiaozhou	1 912 975	1 499 193	341 217	10 481
即墨市	Jimo	1 554 769	913 207	246 798	56 509
平度市	Pingdu	1 056 289	538 827	159 512	22 911
胶南市	Jiaonan	494 916	312 485	80 740	13 957
莱西市	Laixi	718 190	486 620	74 999	－17 095

15－12 续表3
continued

单位:万元(10 000 yuan)

市、区名称	Region	税金总额 Total Tax	可供分配利润 Profits for Assigned	已分配股利 Assigned Dividends	从业人员(人) Employment(person)
合　计	**Total**	**420 228**	**691 115**	**163 700**	**767 006**
市　区	Urban Area	140 455	74 740	15 416	69 701
#崂山区	Chengyang District	86 154	257 693	59 536	27 994
黄岛区	Huangdao District	57 630	241 017	75 103	83 728
城阳区	Laoshan District	34 192	12 362	917	235 511
胶州市	Jiaozhou	19 661	14 433	1 448	117 243
即墨市	Jimo	33 339	46 496	98 200	104 841
平度市	Pingdu	23 865	25 213	381	43 593
胶南市	Jiaonan	13 733	13 051	1 016	33 735
莱西市	Laixi	11 300	6 111	64	50 660

15－13 主营业务收入前60位的外商投资企业(2005年)
MAJOR BUSINESS INCOME OF THE TOP 60 FOREIGN INVESTED ENTERPRISES(2005)

名次 Precedence	企业名称	Name	所在地区	Location
1	青岛颐和针织有限公司	Qingdao Yihe Knitting Co. ,Ltd	即墨市	Jimo
2	金光纸业(青岛)有限公司	APP (Qingdao) Co. ,Ltd	市南区	Shinan District
3	青岛福生食品有限公司	Qingdao Fusheng Food Co. ,Ltd	胶州市	Jiaozhou
4	青岛开必思工贸有限公司	Qingdao Kaibisi Industry and Trade Co. ,Ltd	黄岛区	Huangdao District
5	青岛华棉水洗制衣有限公司	Qingdao Huamian Co. ,Ltd.	即墨市	Jimo
6	海尔百汇(青岛)实业有限公司	Haier Baihui(Qingdao) Industry Co. ,Ltd	黄岛区	Huangdao District
7	青岛三莹电子有限公司	Qingdao Sanying Electronic Co. ,Ltd.	平度市	Pingdu
8	海尔梅洛尼(青岛)电器有限公司	Haier Meiluoni(Qingdao) Appliance Co. ,Ltd	崂山区	Laoshan District
9	青岛家乐福商业有限公司	Qingdao Carrefour Co. ,Ltd	市南区	Shinan District
10	浦铁(青岛)钢材加工有限公司	Posteel (Qingdao) Steel Processing Co. ,Ltd	城阳区	Chengyang District
11	艾默生(中国)电机有限公司	Amerson(China) Co. ,Ltd.	胶州市	Jiaozhou
12	青岛圣乔治乳业有限公司	Qingdao St. George Milk Co. ,Ltd.	胶南市	Jiaonan
13	青岛可口可乐饮料有限公司	Qingdao Coca Cola Co. ,Ltd.	崂山区	Laoshan District
14	青岛交河技工塑料有限公司	Qingdao Jiaohe Plastic Co. ,Ltd	城阳区	Chengyang District
15	青岛肯德基有限公司	Qingdao KFC Co. ,Ltd.	市南区	Shinan District
16	三菱重工海尔(青岛)空调机有限公司	Sanling(Qingdao) Air Conditioner Co. ,Ltd	崂山区	Laoshan District
17	青岛永昌因特皮革有限公司	Qingdao Yongchang yinte Leather Co. ,Ltd	莱西市	Laixi
18	青岛永昌皮革	Qingdao Yongchang Leather Co. ,Ltd	莱西市	Laixi
19	青岛高丽钢线有限公司	Qingdao Kiswire & Arcelor Co. ,Ltd	即墨市	Jimo
20	青岛世正乐器有限公司	Qingdao Shizheng Instrumental Co. ,Ltd	城阳区	Chengyang District
21	青岛华天车辆有限公司	Qingdao Huatian Vehicle Co. ,Ltd.	胶南市	Jiaonan
22	青岛新宇化工有限公司	Qingdao Xinyu Co. ,Ltd	市南区	Shinan District
23	海程邦达国际货运代理有限公司	Qingdao Haicheng Bangda Co. ,Ltd.	市南区	Shinan District
24	青岛华诺针织有限公司	Qingdao Huanuo Knitting Co. ,Ltd	即墨市	Jimo
25	青岛圣元乳业有限公司	Qingdao Shengyuan Milk Co. ,Ltd.	黄岛区	Huangdao District
26	青岛第一百盛有限公司	Qingdao No. 1 Parkson Co. ,Ltd	市南区	Shinan District
27	青岛朗讯科技通讯设备服务有限公司	Qingdao Lucent Telecommunication Equipment Co. ,Ltd.	崂山区	Laoshan District
28	青岛昌新鞋业有限公司	Qingdao Changxin Shoes corp	胶州市	Jiaozhou
29	海尔梅洛尼(青岛)洗衣机有限公司	Haier Meiluoni(Qingdao) Washing Machine Co. ,Ltd	崂山区	Laoshan District
30	青岛大明皮革有限公司	Qingdao Daming Leather Co. ,Ltd	胶州市	Jiaozhou

15 –13 续表
continued

名次 Precedence	企业名称	Name	所在地区	Location
31	青岛雀巢有限公司	Qingdao Nestle Co. ,Ltd	莱西市	Laixi
32	青岛红领制衣有限公司	Qingdao Hongling Garment Co. ,Ltd.	即墨市	Jimo
33	青岛三美电机有限公司	Qingdao Sanmei Co. ,Ltd.	黄岛区	Huangdao District
34	青岛永旺东泰商业有限公司	Qingdao Yingwang Dongtai Co. ,Ltd	市南区	Shinan District
35	青岛世原鞋业有限公司	Qingdao Shiyuan Shoes Corp	胶州市	Jiaozhou
36	青岛高合有限公司	Qingdao Gaohe Co. ,Ltd	黄岛区	Huangdao District
37	青岛海尔电冰箱(国际)有限公司	Qingdao Haier Refrigerator(International) Co. ,Ltd	平度市	Pingdu
38	青岛太平货柜有限公司	Qingdao Taiping Goods Counter Co. ,Ltd.	黄岛区	Huangdao District
39	青岛嘉里花生油有限公司	Qingdao Jiali Vegetable Oil Co. ,Ltd	黄岛区	Huangdao District
40	新都理光(青岛)有限公司	Sindouicoh (Qingdao) Co. ,Ltd.	黄岛区	Huangdao District
41	青岛泰光制鞋有限公司	Qingdao Taiguang Shoes Co. ,Ltd.	莱西市	Laixi
42	青岛中集冷藏箱制造有限公司	Qingdao CIMC Refrigerant Container Co. ,Ltd.	胶州市	Jiaozhou
43	青岛嘉里植物油有限公司	Qingdao Jiali Vegetable Oil Co. ,Ltd	黄岛区	Huangdao District
44	青岛安普泰科电子有限公司	Qingdao Amp Tyco Electronics Co. ,Ltd	城阳区	Chengyang District
45	青岛松下电子部品(保税区)有	Qingdao Matsushita Components (Free Trade Zone) Co. , Ltd.	黄岛区	Huangdao District
46	青岛海尔特种电冰箱有限公司	Qingdao Haier Special Refrigerator Co. ,Ltd.	黄岛区	Huangdao District
47	青岛前湾集装箱码头有限责任	Qingdao Qianhaiwan Container Co. ,Ltd.	黄岛区	Huangdao District
48	青岛中集集装箱制造有限公司	Qingdao CIMC Container Co. ,Ltd.	黄岛区	Huangdao District
49	青岛马士基集装箱工业有限公司	Qingdao Maersk Container Co. ,Ltd.	城阳区	Chengyang District
50	青岛银钢烧结有限公司	Qingdao Yingang Co. ,Ltd.	李沧区	Licang District
51	飞马通讯(青岛)有限公司	Feima(Qingdao)Co. ,Ltd.	崂山区	Laoshan District
52	青岛浦项不锈钢有限公司	Qingdao POSCO Stainless Steel Co. ,Ltd.	黄岛区	Huangdao District
53	青岛三湖制鞋有限公司	Qingdao Sanhu Shoes Corp	即墨市	Jimo
54	青岛乐金浪潮数字通信有限公司	Qingdao Lejin Langchao Digital Communication Co. ,Ltd.	城阳区	Chengyang District
55	青岛海信电器有限公司	Qingdao Hisense Co. ,Ltd.	平度市	Pingdu
56	朗讯科技通讯企业有限公司	Qingdao Lucent Telecommunication Co. ,Ltd.	崂山区	Laoshan District
57	青岛啤酒股份有限公司	Tsingtao Beer Co. ,Ltd.	市南区	Shinan District
58	青岛朗讯科技通讯设备有限公司	Qingdao Lucent Telecommunication Equipment Co. ,Ltd.	崂山区	Laoshan District
59	青岛大韩食品有限公司	Qingdao Dahan Food Co. ,Ltd.	胶州市	Jiaozhou
60	青岛银钢炼铁有限公司	Qingdao Yingang Co. ,Ltd.	李沧区	Licang District

15－14 实现利润总额前60位的外商投资企业(2005年)
TOTAL PROFITS OF THE TOP 60 FOREIGN INVESTED ENTERPRISES(2005)

名次 Precedence	企业名称	Name	所在地区	Location
1	保赫曼(青岛)有限公司	Baoheman (Qingdao) Co. ,Ltd.	胶南市	Jiaonan
2	青岛利百时纺织有限公司	Qingdao Libaishi textile Co. ,Ltd.	城阳区	Chengyang District
3	青岛林河水产食品有限公司	Qingdao Linhe aquatic product food Co. ,Ltd.	城阳区	Chengyang District
4	青岛住友商事有限公司	Qingdao Sumitomo trading Co. ,Ltd.	黄岛区	Huangdao District
5	青岛高丽体育用品有限公司	Qingdao Korea sporting goods Co. ,Ltd.	城阳区	Chengyang District
6	青岛荏原环境设备有限公司	Qingdao Renyuan environmental equipment Co. ,Ltd.	四方区	Sifang District
7	青岛韩一华瑞纺织有限公司	Qingdao Hanyi Huarui textile Co. ,Ltd.	四方区	Sifang District
8	青岛巴斯莱恩包装制品有限公司	Qingdao Buss Ryan packing product Co. ,Ltd.	城阳区	Chengyang District
9	希杰(青岛)食品有限公司	Xijie(Qingdao) food Co. ,Ltd.	莱西市	Laixi
10	青岛星华粮油食品有限公司	Qingdao Xinghua Grain and cooking oil food Co. ,Ltd.	胶南市	Jiaonan
11	青岛菱达机械有限公司	Qingdao Lingda machinery Co. ,Ltd.	即墨市	Jimo
12	青岛荣花边有限公司	Qingdao Sakae Lace Co. ,Ltd.	李沧区	Licang District
13	青岛海尔丰彩包装有限公司	Qingdao Haier Fengcai packing Co. ,Ltd.	黄岛区	Huangdao District
14	莱茵化学(青岛)有限公司	Rhine chemistry (Qingdao) Co. ,Ltd.	李沧区	Licang District
15	青岛环海房地产发展有限公司	Qingdao Huanhai real estate development Co. ,Ltd.	市南区	Shinan District
16	青岛晶腾家具有限公司	Qingdao Jingteng furniture Co. ,Ltd.	胶州市	Jiaozhou
17	青岛美善柳轻工制品有限公司	Qingdao Meishanliu light industry product Co. ,Ltd.	黄岛区	Huangdao District
18	裕富(青岛)食品公司	Yufu (Qingdao) food company	胶州市	Jiaozhou
19	青岛扶庆鞋业有限公司	Qingdao Fuqing shoe industry Co. ,Ltd.	城阳区	Chengyang District
20	青岛统一农牧有限公司	Qingdao unification farming and animal husbandry Co. ,Ltd.	平度市	Pingdu
21	青岛台励福机器设备有限公司	Qingdao Tailifu machine equipment Co. ,Ltd.	胶州市	Jiaozhou
22	青岛喜爱海游艇有限公司	Qingdao Love－sea yacht Co. ,Ltd.	城阳区	Chengyang District
23	青岛吉母皮亚珠宝有限公司	Qingdao Jimu Piya jewelry Co. ,Ltd.	黄岛区	Huangdao District
24	青岛欧特美交通设备有限公司	Qingdao Outemei Communication Equipment Co. ,Ltd.	崂山区	Laoshan District
25	青岛黄海集装箱有限公司	Qingdao Yellow Sea container Co. ,Ltd.	即墨市	Jimo
26	青岛三硕钢塑制品有限公司	Qingdao Sansuo steel model product Co. ,Ltd.	城阳区	Chengyang District
27	青岛金龙包装有限公司	Qingdao Jinlong packing Co. ,Ltd.	平度市	Pingdu
28	青岛顶益食品有限公司	Qingdao Dingyi food Co. ,Ltd.	崂山区	Laoshan District
29	青岛水星化学有限公司	Qingdao Mercury chemistry Co. ,Ltd.	城阳区	Chengyang District
30	青岛二和化纤有限公司	Qingdao Erhe chemical fiber Co. ,Ltd.	莱西市	Laixi

15－14 续表
continued

名次 Precedence	企业名称	Name	所在地区	Location
31	青岛昌隆文具有限公司	Qingdao Changlong stationery Co. ,Ltd.	黄岛区	Huangdao District
32	青岛吉明美机械制造有限公司	Qingdao Jimingmei machine manufacture the Co. ,Ltd.	莱西市	Laixi
33	鲁丰航运有限公司	Lufeng shipping Co. ,Ltd.	市北区	Shibei District
34	青岛宝库光学有限公司	Qingdao Baoku optics Co. ,Ltd.	城阳区	Chengyang District
35	捷城地毯(青岛)有限公司	Jiecheng Carpet (Qingdao) Co. ,Ltd.	即墨市	Jimo
36	青岛海尔开利冷冻设备有限公司	Qingdao Haier Kaili Co. ,Ltd.	崂山区	Laoshan District
37	青岛盛林电子有限公司	Qingdao Shenglin electron Co. ,Ltd.	平度市	Pingdu
38	青岛巨光厨具机械有限公司	Qingdao Juguang kitchenware machinery Co. ,Ltd.	城阳区	Chengyang District
39	青岛阔尔佳物流有限公司	Qingdao Kuoerjia flows the Co. ,Ltd.	黄岛区	Huangdao District
40	青岛京信电子有限公司	Qingdao Jingxin electron Co. ,Ltd.	黄岛区	Huangdao District
41	创新科技(中国)有限公司	Innovation science and technology (China) Co. ,Ltd.	即墨市	Jimo
42	青岛德固萨化学有限公司	Qingdao Degusa chemistry Co. ,Ltd.	胶州市	Jiaozhou
43	青岛润德粮油制品有限公司	Qingdao Runde Grain and cooking oil product Co. ,Ltd.	即墨市	Jimo
44	青岛东亚轮胎公司	Qingdao East Asia tire company	胶南市	Jiaonan
45	青岛格林玛特礼品有限公司	Qingdao Gelin Mate present Co. ,Ltd.	城阳区	Chengyang District
46	青岛佑映纤维有限公司	Qingdao Youying textile fiber Co. ,Ltd.	城阳区	Chengyang District
47	青岛二和纤维有限公司	Qingdao Erhe textile fiber Co. ,Ltd.	胶南市	Jiaonan
48	青岛韩申工艺品有限公司	Qingdao Hanshen handicraft Co. ,Ltd.	城阳区	Chengyang District
49	青岛成昌因特皮包有限公司	Qingdao Chengchang Yinte handbag Co. ,Ltd.	莱西市	Laixi
50	青岛彗重人造毛皮有限公司	Qingdao Huizhong man－made fur Co. ,Ltd.	城阳区	Chengyang District
51	青岛南南有限公司	Qingdao Nannan Co. ,Ltd.	李沧区	Licang District
52	青岛东海玩具有限公司	Qingdao East Sea toy Co. ,Ltd.	城阳区	Chengyang District
53	青岛丰昌制帽有限公司	Qingdao Fengchang cap Co. ,Ltd.	胶州市	Jiaozhou
54	青岛韩信鞋业有限公司	Qingdao Hanxin shoe industry Co. ,Ltd.	城阳区	Chengyang District
55	青岛伟胜电子塑胶有限公司	Qingdao Weisheng electron revertex Co. ,Ltd.	黄岛区	Huangdao District
56	德瑞皮革科技(青岛)有限公司	Derui leather science and technology (Qingdao) Co. ,Ltd.	崂山区	Laoshan District
57	青岛美特容器有限公司	Qingdao Meire vessel Co. ,Ltd.	李沧区	Licang District
58	青岛三进餐具有限公司	Qingdao Sanjin Tableware Co. ,Ltd.	城阳区	Chengyang District
59	青岛藤华纺织有限公司	Qingdao Tenghua Textile Co. ,Ltd.	城阳区	Chengyang District
60	青岛香格里拉大饭店有限公司	Qingdao Shangrila hotel Co. ,Ltd.	市南区	Shinan District

15－15 实现税金总额前60位的外商投资企业(2005年)

TOTAL TAX OF THE TOP 60 FOREIGN INVESTED ENTERPRISES(2005)

名次 Precedence	企业名称	Name	所在地区	Location
1	青岛奇奥制衣有限公司	Qingdao Qi Ao clothes Co. ,Ltd.	城阳区	Chengyang District
2	青岛宏盛琴豪肉牛有限公司	Qingdao Hongsheng Qinhao Meat cow Co. ,Ltd.	平度市	Pingdu
3	青岛耐丝克医材有限公司	Qingdao Naisike medicine material Co. ,Ltd.	城阳区	Chengyang District
4	青岛仁义工艺品有限公司	Qingdao Renyi handicraft Co. ,Ltd.	即墨市	Jimo
5	青岛天秀制衣有限公司	Qingdao Tianxiu clothes Co. ,Ltd.	崂山区	Laoshan District
6	青岛帝杰运动用品有限公司	Qingdao Dijie Sport Goods Co. ,Ltd.	即墨市	Jimo
7	青岛福得味食品有限公司	Qingdao Fudewei food Co. ,Ltd.	胶南市	Jiaonan
8	青岛罗道服装有限公司	Qingdao Luodao clothing Co. ,Ltd.	即墨市	Jimo
9	青岛天地箱包有限公司	Qingdao Tiandi box and package Co. ,Ltd.	胶州市	Jiaozhou
10	青岛飞驰工具有限公司	Qingdao Feichi tool Co. ,Ltd.	黄岛区	Huangdao District
11	青岛勃鲁尼克工艺品有限公司	Qingdao Blue Nike handicraft Co. ,Ltd.	黄岛区	Huangdao District
12	青岛纽新元塑料有限公司	Qingdao Niuxinyuan plastic Co. ,Ltd.	城阳区	Chengyang District
13	青岛三州塑料制品有限公司	Qingdao Sanzhou plastics product Co. ,Ltd.	胶州市	Jiaozhou
14	青岛保税区泰星高宇工贸公司	Qingdao bonded area Taixing Gaoyu trade company	黄岛区	Huangdao District
15	青岛富兰德设备有限公司	Qingdao Fulande equipment Co. ,Ltd.	城阳区	Chengyang District
16	青岛哈比斯特有限公司	Qingdao Habi Site Co. ,Ltd.	胶州市	Jiaozhou
17	青岛桃园玩具有限公司	Qingdao Taoyuan toy Co. ,Ltd.	莱西市	Laixi
18	青岛桃园工艺品有限公司	Qingdao Taoyuan handicraft Co. ,Ltd.	莱西市	Laixi
19	青岛金浦工艺品有限公司	Qingdao kimpo handicraft Co. ,Ltd.	崂山区	Laoshan District
20	青岛大原化学有限公司	Qingdao Dayuan chemistry Co. ,Ltd.	城阳区	Chengyang District
21	青岛宇星针织服装有限公司	Qingdao Yuxing knitting clothing Co. ,Ltd.	莱西市	Laixi
22	青岛高科技产业开发有限公司	Qingdao high tech industry development Co. ,Ltd.	崂山区	Laoshan District
23	青岛金富工艺品有限公司	Qingdao Jinfu handicraft Co. ,Ltd.	平度市	Pingdu
24	青岛阿丽亚斯皮革制品有限公司	Qingdao Alias leather product Co. ,Ltd.	即墨市	Jimo
25	青岛研煌电子有限公司	Qingdao Yanhuang electronic Co. ,Ltd.	黄岛区	Huangdao District
26	青岛优钢铸造有限公司	Qingdao Yougang casting Co. ,Ltd.	胶州市	Jiaozhou
27	青岛民乐食品有限公司	Qingdao Minle food Co. ,Ltd.	莱西市	Laixi
28	青岛韩美来珠宝有限公司	Qingdao Hanmeilai jewelry Co. ,Ltd.	城阳区	Chengyang District
29	青岛扶桑贸易有限公司	Qingdao Chinese hibiscus trade Co. ,Ltd.	黄岛区	Huangdao District
30	青岛大珉服装有限公司	Qingdao Daming clothing Co. ,Ltd.	胶州市	Jiaozhou

15 -15 续表
continued

名次 Precedence	企业名称	Name	所在地区	Location
31	青岛鲜明电子有限公司	Qingdao bright electron Co. ,Ltd.	胶州市	Jiaozhou
32	青岛发仁服装有限公司	Qingdao Faren clothing Co. ,Ltd.	即墨市	Jimo
33	青岛海派机绣有限公司	Qingdao Haipai machine embroiders Co. ,Ltd.	崂山区	Laoshan District
34	青岛华林服饰有限公司	Qingdao Hualin clothing Co. ,Ltd.	胶南市	Jiaonan
35	青岛贝事达食品有限公司	Qingdao Beishida food Co. ,Ltd.	平度市	Pingdu
36	青岛大现皮革有限公司	Qingdao Daxian leather Co. ,Ltd.	胶州市	Jiaozhou
37	青岛三莹服装有限公司	Qingdao Sanying clothing Co. ,Ltd.	胶南市	Jiaonan
38	青岛伟利制帽有限公司	Qingdao Weili cap Co. ,Ltd.	胶州市	Jiaozhou
39	青岛嘉原得精密模具机械有限公司	Qingdao Jiayuande precision mold machinery Co. ,Ltd.	城阳区	Chengyang District
40	青岛可定文化用品有限公司	Qingdao Keding cultural item Co. ,Ltd.	胶州市	Jiaozhou
41	青岛光洋电子有限公司	Qingdao Guangyang electron Co. ,Ltd.	城阳区	Chengyang District
42	青岛成元箱包有限公司	Qingdao ChengyuanBox and package of Co. ,Ltd.	即墨市	Jimo
43	青岛佰佳得服装有限公司	Qingdao Baijiade clothing Co. ,Ltd.	胶南市	Jiaonan
44	青岛巨山制鞋有限公司	Qingdao great mountain shoemaking Co. ,Ltd.	即墨市	Jimo
45	青岛大昌泰克机械有限公司	Qingdao Dachang Taike machinery Co. ,Ltd.	莱西市	Laixi
46	青岛多元纤维有限公司	Qingdao Duoyuan textile fibers Co. ,Ltd.	莱西市	Laixi
47	青岛希思希运动用品有限公司	Qingdao Xisixi Sport Goods Co. ,Ltd.	即墨市	Jimo
48	青岛大荣中青服装有限公司	Qingdao Darong Zhongqing clothing Co. ,Ltd.	莱西市	Laixi
49	青岛成玟电子有限公司	Qingdao Chengwen electronic Co. ,Ltd.	平度市	Pingdu
50	青岛广轮国际贸易有限公司	Qingdao Guanglun international trade Co. ,Ltd.	黄岛区	Huangdao District
51	青岛亿华金属有限公司	Qingdao Yihua metal Co. ,Ltd.	崂山区	Laoshan District
52	青岛格力特乐器有限公司	Qingdao Gelite musical instrument Co. ,Ltd.	胶州市	Jiaozhou
53	青岛俪徕精细化工有限公司	Qingdao Lilai fine chemical industry Co. ,Ltd.	黄岛区	Huangdao District
54	青岛富岗包装有限公司	Qingdao Fugang packing Co. ,Ltd.	胶州市	Jiaozhou
55	青岛东友服饰有限公司	Qingdao Dongyou clothing Co. ,Ltd.	即墨市	Jimo
56	青岛大华农产有限公司	Qingdao Dahua agricultural production Co. ,Ltd.	平度市	Pingdu
57	青岛南炅塑料有限公司	Qingdao Nanjiong plastic Co. ,Ltd.	即墨市	Jimo
58	青岛绣城工艺品有限公司	Qingdao Xiucheng handicraft Co. ,Ltd.	李沧区	Licang District
59	青岛相垣包装有限公司	Qingdao Xiangyuan packing Co. ,Ltd.	胶南市	Jiaonan
60	青岛金富资工艺品有限公司	Qingdao Jin Fuzi handicraft Co. ,Ltd.	城阳区	Chengyang District

15－16 国际旅游人数(1990－2005年)

NUMBER OF OVERSEAS TOURISTS(1990－2005)

单位:人次(person-time)

项　目	Items	1990年	1995年	2000年	2001年	2002年	2003年	2004年	2005年
总计	**Total**	**72 019**	**177 797**	**260 592**	**323 079**	**417 452**	**341 158**	**522 498**	**68 4407**
#接待过夜游客	Overnight Tourists	52 392	120 146	237 465	294 756	390 547	328 214	508 175	668 580
一、外国人	**Foreigner**	**22 329**	**79 469**	**177 098**	**263 018**	**356 156**	**295 637**	**458 358**	**596 177**
#日本	Japan	9 426	34 296	67 215	95 424	130 816	94 359	156 374	177 121
美国	United States	2 454	5 607	10 384	10 571	12 389	9 568	14 130	23 284
德国	Germany	1 494	2 660	3 820	4 379	4 242	3 748	5 165	10 646
新加坡	Singapore	626	2 998	6 321	4 646	4 623	3 801	4 650	6 060
英国	United Kingdom	712	1 545	2 798	2 562	2 669	2 272	2 955	5 744
加拿大	Canada	556	930	1 865	2 167	2 473	1 700	2 531	4 397
法国	France	461	825	2 491	2 021	1 981	1 807	2 619	5 166
意大利	Italy	437	746	1 555	1 414	1 665	1 508	1 774	3 963
澳大利亚	Australia	351	1 009	1 817	2 111	2 577	2 337	2 811	4 257
俄罗斯	Russia	163	449	4 820	5 587	6 707	4 544	5 509	12 062
菲律宾	Philippines	270	558	7 947	6 818	7 468	2 630	3 613	3 459
泰国	Thailand	406	299	780	906	1 393	749	2 089	3 261
印尼	Indonesia	237	670	1 241	1 727	2 379	1 273	1 846	2 349
新西兰	New Zealand	68	192	442	598	610	488	425	710
韩国	Korea	－	20 330	69 878	103 136	152 530	150 456	204 779	295 111
二、港澳和台湾同胞	**Hong Kong and Macao Chinese and Taiwanese**	**29 276**	**39 223**	**60 367**	**60 061**	**61 296**	**45 521**	**64 140**	**88 230**

15－17 涉外旅游收入(1990－2005年)

REVENUE OF FOREIGN-RELATED TOURISM(1990－2005)

单位:万元(10 000 yuan)

项　目	Items	1990年	1995年	2000年	2001年	2002年	2003年	2004年	2005年
总计	**Total**	**13 534**	**48 320**	**118 164**	**146 907**	**198 993**	**130 073**	**237 771**	**34 0899**
商品销售	Commodity Sales	4 409	5 933	20 742	26 513	40 209	28 512	41 372	67 047
住宿费	Accommodation Expenditure	3 267	18 509	17 443	21 147	25 825	15 980	26 868	3 7277
餐饮业	Catering Income	1 160	5 361	11 223	13 951	18 655	14 361	23 302	33 557
交通费	Traffic Expenditure	3 619	11 404	35 252	43 955	64 734	54 730	88 689	12 8112
邮电费	Posts and Teleconmunications Spending	585	3 246	5 502	6 547	6 945	7 810	11 175	18 394
文化娱乐费	Entertainment Cost	89	1 302	6 894	8 712	11 918	8 680	15 217	20 240
其他	Other	－	－	－	－	－	－	31 148	36 272

15－18 国内旅游人数(2005 年)

NUMBER OF DOMESTIC TOURISTS(2005)

指　标	Indicators	单　位	unit
国内旅游人数	**Number of Domestic Tourists**	**万人**	**10000 persons**
1. 过夜旅游者人数	Number of Overnight Tourists	万人	10000 persons
(1)旅游住宿设施国内旅游人数	Domestic Tourists Staying Overnight at Hotels	万人	10000 persons
(2)住亲友家去景点的国内旅游人数	Domestic Tourists Staying Overnight at Relatives and Friends' s Home	万人	10000 persons
2. 不过夜旅游者(一日游)人数	Number of One-day Tourists	万人	10000 persons
旅游景点接待一日游人数	One-day Tourists Received by Tour Scenes	万人	10000 persons
(1)本地一日游人数	Number of One-day Local Tourists	万人	10000 persons
(2)外地一日游人数	Number of One-day Outside Tourists	万人	10000 persons
国内旅游人均花费	**Average Per Capita Spending on Domestic Tour**	**元**	**yuan**
其中:旅游住宿设施国内旅游者人均花费	of which:Staying Overnight at Hotels	元	yuan
住亲友家去景点的国内旅游者人均花费	Staying Overnight at Relatives and Friends' s Home	元	yuan
一日游旅游者人均花费	Average Per Capita Spending of One-day Tourists	元	yuan
国内旅游收入	**Domestic Tour Income**	**万元**	**10000 yuan**
1. 接待过夜旅游者收入	From Overnight Tourists	万元	10000 yuan
(1)旅游住宿设施接待国内旅游者收入	of which:Staying Overnight at Hotels	万元	10000 yuan
(2)住亲友家去景点的国内旅游者旅游花费	Staying Overnight at Relatives and Friends' s Home	万元	10000 yuan
2. 接待不过夜旅游者(一日游)收入	From One-day Tourists	万元	10000 yuan

注:抽样调查资料。

Note:The data is from sampling.

一季度 1st Quarter	二季度 2nd Quarter	三季度 3rd Quarter	四季度 4th Quarter	全年 Annual Total
375.23	**637.21**	**995.39**	**441.2**	**2 449.03**
329.37	519.49	841.69	387.86	2 078.41
315.18	485.56	651.04	364.73	1 816.51
14.19	33.93	190.65	23.13	261.90
45.86	117.72	153.70	53.34	370.62
45.86	117.72	153.70	53.34	370.62
14.48	53.28	74.77	32.23	174.76
31.38	64.43	78.93	21.11	195.85
907.85	**840.51**	**834.30**	**1 176.81**	**908.89**
1 010.25	983.29	1 066.23	1 340.37	1 089.39
866.12	797.38	598.30	705.27	648.04
216.97	264.01	144.64	262.91	208.52
340 651.28	**535 575.06**	**830 453.88**	**519 210.41**	**2 225 890.63**
330 701.05	504 497.08	808 223.49	505 187.1	2 148 608.72
318 410.78	477 444.42	694 157.25	488 874.1	1 978 886.55
12 290.27	27 052.66	114 066.24	16 313	169 722.17
9 950.23	31 077.98	22 230.39	14 023.31	77 281.91

CHAPTER 16

第十六篇

教育、科技和文化

EDUCATION,SCIENCE AND CULTURE

编辑单位：人口和社会科技统计处
编　　委：高明辉
编　　辑：王　磊
校　　对：关　静
电　　话：85912263

16 -1 各级各类学校基本情况(2005 年)

BASIC STATISTICS OF VARIOUS SCHOOLS(2005)

项　目	Items	学校数（所） Schools (place)	毕业生数（人） Graduates (person)	招生数（人） New Students Enrollment(person)	在校学生数（人） Students Enrollment(person)	教职工数（人） Staff and Workers(person)	#专任教师 of which: Full-time Teachers
研究生	Postgraduates	–	1 725	4 768	10 775	–	2 908
普通高等学校	Institution of Higher Education	25	46 114	79 725	239 761	23 078	13 894
中等专业学校	Specialized Secondary School	7	8 312	12 129	33 522	956	545
#中师	of which: Secondary Normal School	3	696	786	2 192	428	235
技工学校	Technical Worker Schools	22	5 925	15 667	38 160	1 303	966
职业学校	Vocational Schools	49	27 097	35 162	106 400	8 121	5 677
普通中学	Regular Secondary Schools	317	150 168	112 870	391 148	36 848	29 697
初中	Junior Schools	250	108 255	66 938	251 724	–	20 756
高中	Senior Schools	67	41 913	45 932	139 424	–	8 941
小学	Primary Schools	1 004	66 717	72 595	479 781	34 641	31 733
特殊教育学校	Special Education Schools	13	204	189	1 372	557	395
幼儿园	Kindergartens	2 235	59 642	52 280	154 736	12 470	8 972
成人高等学校	Adult Higher Education Schools	3	20 813	28 120	64 585	1 775	938
成人中等学校	Adult Secondary Education Schools	23	4 722	5 460	14 050	1 002	695
成人初等学校	Adult Primary Education Schools	–	–	–	–	–	–

注：1. 研究生栏中专任教师指的是指导教师。2. 成人中等学校仅包括成人中学和成人中专。

Note: 1. Full-time teachers of postgraduates refer to instructors.

2. Adult higher education school refer to adult secondary schools and adult specialized secondary schools.

16 –2 主要年份各级各类学校在校学生数
MAJOR YEAR'S STUDENTS ENROLLMENT OF VARIOUS SCHOOLS

单位：人(person)

年份 Year	普通高等学校 Institutions of Higher Education	中等学校 Secondary Schools	中等专业学校 Specialized Secondary Schools	普通中学 Regular Secondary Schools	职业中学 Vocational Schools	技工学校 Technical Worker Schools	小学 Primary Schools
1949	1 007	13 804	1 600	12 204	–	–	213 470
1952	2 761	27 951	3 770	24 181	–	–	413 286
1957	3 133	56 689	4 985	51 604	100	–	482 397
1962	4 381	62 646	2 791	58 639	243	973	522 921
1965	2 987	99 605	9 405	88 187	1 490	523	788 485
1970	320	222 521	105	220 262	2 154	–	728 433
1975	1 151	350 309	3 144	346 403	–	762	928 153
1978	3 465	464 584	4 269	457 460	2 000	865	634 905
1980	6 783	325 935	5 195	318 193	1 344	1 203	816 970
1985	10 631	327 446	11 475	279 915	33 945	2 111	691 341
1988	14 408	352 576	11 819	306 943	28 933	4 881	629 212
1989	15 183	348 367	14 401	296 318	32 283	5 365	634 794
1990	15 433	351 365	15 118	296 163	34 568	5 516	632 314
1991	15 491	353 410	14 618	298 568	34 421	5 803	612 772
1992	16 470	367 480	14 763	307 903	38 242	6 572	585 381
1993	23 858	383 043	16 877	318 179	40 743	7 244	583 585
1994	25 018	420 077	20 582	347 667	43 734	8 094	593 419
1995	24 908	450 212	23 744	372 335	46 044	8 089	595 891
1996	26 076	468 561	26 951	382 760	50 131	8 719	607 284
1997	27 434	463 619	28 543	362 305	61 640	11 131	626 749
1998	29 507	442 525	28 757	336 918	65 989	10 861	625 308
1999	33 681	459 520	26 955	352 238	70 236	10 091	583 594
2000	46 131	497 391	25 192	398 458	63 894	9 847	534 922
2001	60 728	542 400	25 358	443 693	62 003	11 346	499 147
2002	82 539	575 599	27 421	467 628	67 085	13 465	478 634
2003	168 439	586 704	28 948	461 435	75 221	211 00	467 560
2004	201 739	598 804	30 881	436 117	101 553	30 253	476 897
2005	239 761	569 230	33 522	391 148	106 400	38 160	479 781

16－3 普通高等学校普通本专科教育基本情况(2005年)

BASIC STATISTICS OF REGULAR UNDERGRADUATE AND TRAIN COURSE IN INSTITUTIONS OF HIGHER EDUCATION(2005)

单位:人(person)

学校名称	Name of School	招生数 New Students Enrollment	毕业生数 Graduates	在校学生数 Students Enrollment	教职工数 Staff and Workers	#专任教师 of which: Full-time Teachers	在校研究生数 Postgraduates Enrollment
总　计	**Total**	**72 635**	**41 235**	**221 564**	**23 078**	**13 894**	**10 775**
中国海洋大学	Ocean University of China	2 988	2 513	10 992	2 262	1 044	4 584
青岛大学	Qingdao University	7 450	7 894	31 115	4 049	2 019	1 952
青岛理工大学	Qingdao Technological University	4 729	4 492	15 909	1 771	985	496
青岛科技大学	Qingdao University of Science & Technology	5 798	4 775	19 985	1 870	1 172	898
青岛职业技术学院	Qingdao University Technical College	2 504	2 473	7 987	688	441	–
山东外贸职业学院	Shangdong Foreign Trade Vocational College	2 377	318	6 482	374	298	–
莱阳农学院	Laiyang Agriculture College	5 719	3 379	20 960	1 693	1 103	417
山东科技大学	Shangdong University of Science & Technical College	6 239	7 889	25 617	2 995	1 934	1 421
石油大学青岛校区	China University of Petroleum(Qingdao)	2 200	1 531	4 902	488	314	1 007
青岛酒店管理职业技术学院	Qingdao Hotel Management Vocational Technical College	3 211	409	6 680	351	248	–
青岛港湾职业技术学院	Qingdao Harbour Vocational Technical College	2 398	441	5 806	361	290	–
青岛远洋船员学院	Qingdao Ocean Shipping Mariners College	1 892	459	4 322	–	–	–
青岛广播电视大学	Qingdao Broadcasting and TV University	2 273	1 444	6 402	–	–	–
青岛滨海学院	Qingdao Binhai College	4 120	2 173	12 011	1 159	788	–
青岛理工大学琴岛学院	Qingdao Technological University Qindao College	2 971	208	6 354	620	297	–
青岛科技大学四方学院	Qingdao Sifang College of QUST	–	–	945	–	–	–
青岛飞洋职业技术学院	Qingdao Feiyang Vocational and Technical College	5 124	429	1 4828	1 260	990	–
青岛恒星职业技术学院	Qingdao Hengxing Vocational and Technical College	5 250	408	10 380	1 167	713	–
青岛求实职业技术学院	Qingdao Qiushi Vocational and Technical college	2 348	–	4 224	482	315	–
青岛黄海职业学院	Qingdao Huanghai Vocational College	3 044	–	5 663	739	547	–
青岛海川商务专修学院	Qingdao Haichuan Commercial Management College	–	–	–	140	74	–
青岛华侨理工专修学院	Qingdao Haichuan Commercial Management College	–	–	–	234	138	–
青岛海达科技专修学院	Qingdao Haida Science and Technology College	–	–	–	64	44	–
私立青岛东方外国语专修学院	Qingdao Dongfang Foreign Language College	–	–	–	93	48	–
青岛中鲁工商专修学院	Qingdao Zhonglu Business College	–	–	–	61	30	–
青岛长城计算机工程专修学院	Qingdao Changcheng Computer College	–	–	–	81	32	–
青岛现代经贸专修学院	Qingdao Xiandai Economy and Trade College	–	–	–	11	7	–
青岛科大技术专修学院	Technical College in Qingdao University of Science & Technology	–	–	–	65	23	–

16 –4 普通高等学校学历文凭考试、电大注册视听生、自考助学班学生数(2005 年)

STUDENTS JOINING IN DIPLOMA EXAMS, REGISTERED IN TV UNIVERSITIES AND GOING TO TEACH – YOURSELF TEST CLASSES(2005)

学校名称	Name of School	毕(结)业生数 Graduates			
		合计 Total	学历文凭考试 Joining in Diploma Exams	电大注册视听生 Registered in TV Universities	自考助学班 Tech-yourself Test Classes
总　计	**Total**	**4 879**	**4 608**	**–**	**271**
青岛大学	Qingdao University	96	–	–	96
青岛职业技术学院	Qingdao University Technical College	–	–	–	–
青岛滨海学院	Qingdao Binhai College	397	397	–	–
青岛飞洋职业技术学院	Qingdao Feiyang Vocational and Technical College	1 558	1 558	–	–
青岛恒星职业技术学院	Qingdao Hengxing Vocational and Technical College	50	50	–	–
青岛求实职业技术学院	Qingdao Qiushi Vocational and Technical college	232	232	–	–
青岛黄海职业学院	Qingdao Huanghai Vocational College	775	775	–	–
青岛海川商务专修学院	Qingdao Haichuan Commercial Management College	606	606	–	–
青岛华侨理工专修学院	Qingdao Haichuan Commercial Management College	226	226	–	–
青岛海达科技专修学院	Qingdao Haida Science and Technology College	220	45	–	175
私立青岛东方外国语专修学院	Qingdao Dongfang Foreign Language College	308	308	–	–
青岛中鲁工商专修学院	Qingdao Zhonglu Business College	126	126	–	–
青岛长城计算机工程专修学院	Qingdao Changcheng Computer College	130	130	–	–
青岛现代经贸专修学院	Qingdao Xiandai Economy and Trade College	26	26	–	–
青岛科大技术专修学院	Technical College in Qingdao University of Science & Technology	129	129	–	–

单位:人(person)

入学数 New Students Enrollment				在校(学)学生数 Students Enrollment			
合计 Total	学历文凭考试 Joining in Diploma Exams	电大注册视听生 Registered in TV Universities	自考助学班 Tech-yourself Test Classes	合计 Total	学历文凭考试 Joining in Diploma Exams	电大注册视听生 Registered in TV Universities	自考助学班 Tech-yourself Test Classes
7 090	**1 797**	**–**	**5 293**	**18 197**	**9 628**	**–**	**8 569**
422	–	–	422	943	–	–	943
–	–	–	–	1 743	–	–	1 743
402	–	–	402	1 527	1 125	–	402
1 516	1 516	–	–	2 019	2 019	–	–
–	–	–	–	50	50	–	–
–	–	–	–	529	529	–	–
3 309	–	–	3 309	5 586	2 277	–	3 309
99	–	–	99	971	872	–	99
–	–	–	–	504	504	–	–
88	–	–	88	1 182	82	–	1 100
113	–	–	113	588	475	–	113
102	–	–	102	607	505	–	102
581	281	–	300	581	281	–	300
–	–	–	–	43	43	–	–
458	–	–	458	1 324	866	–	458

16 –5 主要年份普通高等学校基本情况

MAJOR YEAR'S BASIC STATISTICS OF INSTITUTIONS OF HIGHER EDUCATION

单位：人（person）

年　份 Year	学校数（所） Schools （place）	毕业生数 Graduates	招生数 New Students Enrollment	在校学生数 Students Enrollment	教职工数 Staff and Workers	#专任教师 of which： Full-time Teachers
1949	1	–	250	1 007	779	226
1952	2	262	565	2 761	12 530	308
1957	2	356	755	3 133	1 308	622
1962	5	647	653	4 381	1 866	749
1965	3	741	529	2 987	1 539	623
1970	2	684	–	320	1 178	486
1975	2	460	473	1 151	1 353	582
1978	4	739	1 782	3 465	2 829	1 176
1980	6	431	1 717	6 783	4 182	1 606
1985	7	1 828	3 823	10 631	5 561	2 181
1988	7	3 496	4 687	14 408	6 875	2 499
1989	7	3 891	4 567	15 183	7 174	2 554
1990	7	4 495	4 745	15 433	7 305	2 624
1991	7	4 880	4 954	15 491	7 282	2 489
1992	7	4 458	5 428	16 470	7 344	2 523
1993	7	3 140	9 449	23 858	7 366	2 520
1994	4	7 059	8 042	25 018	7 466	2 650
1995	4	7 828	7 978	24 908	7 545	2 682
1996	4	6 691	7 956	26 076	7 606	2 745
1997	4	7 091	8 503	27 434	7 790	2 813
1998	4	6 912	8 849	29 507	7 662	2 907
1999	4	7 202	11 584	33 681	7 662	2 928
2000	6	7 128	18 427	46 131	8 030	3 278
2001	6	8 991	22 787	60 728	8 706	4 058
2002	7	13 053	29 731	82 539	9 517	4 723
2003	25	25 747	61 975	168 439	18 911	10 293
2004	25	34 860	70 022	201 739	21 437	12 347
2005	25	46 114	79 725	239 761	23 078	13 894

16－6 中等专业学校分校基本情况(2005 年)

BASIC STATISTICS OF SPECIALIZED SECONDARY SCHOOLS(2005)

单位:人(person)

学校名称	Name of Schools	毕业生数 Graduates	招生数 New Students Enrollment	在校学生数 Students Enrollment	教职工数 Staff and Workers	#专任教师 of which: Full-time Teachers
总　计	**Total**	**8 312**	**12 129**	**33 522**	**956**	**545**
平度师范学校	Pingdu Normal School	254	280	628	129	81
青岛师范学校	Qingdao Normal School	242	241	847	128	80
青岛幼儿师范学校	Qingdao Children Normal School	200	265	717	171	74
青岛市体育运动学校	Qingdao Sport School	108	81	211	85	53
青岛卫生学校	Qingdao Health School	813	1 140	3 458	163	83
山东省轻工工程学校	Shandong Light Industry & Engineering School	1 266	1 517	4 353	184	106
青岛市第二卫生学校	Qingdao No. 2 Health School	416	610	1 927	96	68
其他学校(附设)	Others	5 013	7 995	21 381	-	-

16－7 技工学校分校基本情况(2005年)

BASIC STATISTICS OF TECHNICAL WORKER SCHOOL(2005)

学校名称	Name of School	毕业生数 Graduates
总　计	**Total**	**5 925**
青岛市高级技工学校	Qingdao Senior Technical Worker School	741
四方机车车辆技术学校	Technical School of Sifang Locomotive And Rolling Stock	400
青岛市电子信息技术学校	Qingdao Electronic Technology School	479
青岛机电技术学校	Qingdao Mechanical & Electronic Technology School	391
青岛海洋技术学校	Qingdao Ocean Technology School	449
青岛市化工技术学校	Qingdao Chemical Technology School	202
青岛市经济贸易技术学校	Qingdao Commerce & Trade Technology School	489
青岛北海船舶技术学校	Qingdao Beihai Ship Technology School	40
青岛市房产技术学校	Qingdao Real Estate Technology	313
青岛市建设技术学校	Qingdao Construction Technology School	59
青岛市捷能技术学校	Qingdao Jieneng Technology School	173
青岛市冶金技术学校	Qingdao Metallurgy Technology School	231
青岛市园林环卫技术学校	Qingdao Gardens & Environmental Sanitation Technology School	115
青岛橡胶技术学校	Qingdao Rubber Technology School	107
青岛市铸造机械集团公司技术学校	Technical Worker School of Qingdao Casting Machinery Group Corporation	4
山东省饮食服务技工学校	Shandong Catering Service Technical Worker School	2
中国人民解放军海军第六职业技术学校	PLA Navy No. 6 Vocational Technical School	163
中国石油天然气第七建设公司技工学校	Technical Workers School of No. 7 Corporation CNPC	345
平度市技术学校	Pingdu Technology School	342
青岛市第二技术学校	Qingdao No. 2 Technology School	557
青岛市第三技术学校	Qingdao No. 3 Technology School	323
青岛市工业技术学校	Qingdao Industrial Technology School	–

单位：人(person)

招生数 New Students Enrollment	在校学生数 Students Enrollment	教职工数 Staff and Workers	#专任教师 of which: Full-time teachers
15 667	**38 160**	**1 303**	**966**
4 018	9 869	130	99
1 278	2 993	117	84
1 061	2 720	65	50
641	1 831	77	77
1 763	3 714	80	52
492	1 583	47	47
298	1 189	70	46
–	35	15	11
314	1 507	40	40
85	239	20	20
414	902	34	23
378	791	31	19
78	252	33	33
70	136	19	9
166	305	19	19
–	53	62	24
252	448	48	23
500	1 112	47	34
1 994	3 894	80	69
621	2 203	89	62
919	1 754	129	93
325	630	51	32

16－8 各类成人教育基本情况(2005 年)

BASIC STATISTICS OF VARIOUS ADULT EDUCATION(2005)

单位:人(person)

各类学校	Items	学校数(所) Schools (place)	毕业生数 Graduates	招生数 New Students Enrollment	在校学生数 Students Enrollment	教职工数 Staff and Workers	#专任教师 of which: Full-time Teachers
总　计	**Total**	**26**	**25 535**	**33 580**	**78 635**	**2 777**	**1 633**
成人高等教育	Adult Higher Education	3	20 813	28 120	64 585	1 775	938
广播电视大学	Broadcasting and TV Universities	1	83	20	95	803	504
职工、农民大学	Staff and Peasants Higher Education Schools	1	168	426	819	463	207
函授、夜大学	Correspondence and Evening College Education	–	18 606	23 548	57 062	–	–
管理干部学校	Cadre Management Schools	1	1 956	4 126	6 609	509	227
成人中等教育	Adult Secondary Education	23	4 722	5 460	14 050	1 002	695
成人中等专业学校	Specialized Secondary Schools	23	4 722	5 460	14 050	1 002	695

注:本年度成人高等自学考试毕业 2 740 人;参加成人高等单科班、进修班、短训班、专业证书班学习毕业(结业)20 905 人。

Note:2 740 persons have been graduated from adult higher tech-oneself tests in the year,20 905 persons have been graduated from adult higher single subject courses,training courses,short-term training course and specialized diploma courses.

16－9 分市、区普通中学情况(2005 年)
BASIC STATISTICS OF REGULAR SECONDARY SCHOOLS BY REGION(2005)

市、区名称	Region	普通高中 Senior Schools				普通初中 Junior Schools			
		学校数 Schools	毕业生数 Graduates	招生数 New Students Enrollment	在校生数 Students Enrollment	学校数 Schools	毕业生数 Graduates	招生数 New Students Enrollment	在校生数 Students Enrollment
总 计	**Total**	**67**	**41 913**	**45 932**	**139 424**	**250**	**108 255**	**66 938**	**251 724**
市 区	Urban Area	33	13 481	14 735	46 139	76	30 601	24 143	77 912
#城阳区	Chengyang District	3	2 967	2 485	8 728	15	5 498	4 264	14 018
黄岛区	Huangdao District	2	1 310	1 724	5 320	8	3 612	2 884	9 615
崂山区	Laoshan District	7	1 307	1 506	4 602	9	2 599	1 778	6 207
胶州市	Jiaozhou	5	4 143	6 100	16 366	26	13 347	6 956	28 661
即墨市	Jimo	9	6 593	5 993	19 146	38	15 411	9 741	32 183
平度市	Pingdu	8	7 616	8 136	24 390	49	22 954	11 583	52 907
胶南市	Jiaonan	6	5 854	6 281	19 193	25	13 817	6 705	27 278
莱西市	Laixi	6	4 226	4 687	14 190	36	12 125	7 810	32 783

16－10 分市、区职业中学、小学情况(2005 年)
BASIC STATISTICS OF SECONDARY VOCATIONAL SCHOOLS AND PRIMARY SCHOOLS REGION(2005)

市、区名称	Region	职业中学 Secondary Vocational Schools				小学 Primary Schools			
		学校数 Schools	毕业生数 Graduates	招生数 New Students Enrollment	在校生数 Students Enrollment	学校数 Schools	毕业生数 Graduates	招生数 New Students Enrollment	在校生数 Students Enrollment
总 计	**Total**	**49**	**27 097**	**35 162**	**106 400**	**1 004**	**66 717**	**72 595**	**479 781**
市 区	Urban Area	28	14 213	17 586	55 246	270	23 516	24 628	155 971
#城阳区	Chengyang District	2	1 414	185	2 102	72	4 248	4 468	31 656
黄岛区	Huangdao District	7	6 768	10 293	31 819	31	2 608	3 641	22 370
崂山区	Laoshan District	1	1 021	613	2 228	33	1 856	1 765	12 899
胶州市	Jiaozhou	3	1 869	2 598	7 105	124	6 910	8 430	56 950
即墨市	Jimo	6	2 014	2 961	10 118	194	10 413	10 604	76 966
平度市	Pingdu	6	2 872	5 900	13 722	212	11 574	14 565	92 774
胶南市	Jiaonan	3	4 480	4 261	14 115	101	6 416	8 023	55 766
莱西市	Laixi	3	1 649	1 856	6 094	103	7 888	6 345	41 354

16－11 分市、区中小学教职工情况(2005 年)

BASIC STATISTICS OF STAFF AND WORKERS IN SECONDARY AND PRIMARY SCHOOLS BY REGION(2005)

单位:人(person)

市、区名称	Region	普通中学 Regular Secondary Schools		职业中学 Secondary Vocational Schools		小学 Primary Schools	
		教职工数 Staff and Workers	#专任教师 of which: Full-time Teachers	教职工数 Staff and Workers	#专任教师 of which: Full-time Teachers	教职工数 Staff and Workers	#专任教师 of which: Full-time Teachers
总 计	**Total**	**36 848**	**29 697**	**8 121**	**5 677**	**34 641**	**31 733**
市 区	Urban Area	12 524	9 411	4 867	3 272	11 567	10 269
#城阳区	Chengyang District	2 366	2 183	699	418	2 190	2 041
黄岛区	Huangdao District	1 326	1 186	1 638	1 244	1 230	1 185
崂山区	Laoshan District	1 335	989	237	144	1 044	917
胶州市	Jiaozhou	3 979	3 301	549	411	3 991	3 748
即墨市	Jimo	5 042	4 114	767	536	5 619	5 113
平度市	Pingdu	6 686	5 543	869	635	6 269	5 795
胶南市	Jiaonan	4 367	3 879	572	465	4 192	4 016
莱西市	Laixi	4 250	3 449	497	358	3 003	2 792

16－12 分市、区幼儿园基本情况(2005 年)

BASIC STATISTICS OF KINDERGARTENS BY REGION(2005)

单位:人(person)

市、区名称	Region	幼儿园(所) Kindergartens(place)	幼儿数 Children	教职工数 Staff and Workers	#专任教师 of which: Full-time teachers
总 计	**Total**	**2 235**	**154 736**	**12 470**	**8 972**
市 区	Urban Area	470	55 029	6 037	3 919
#城阳区	Chengyang District	141	11 429	1 118	853
黄岛区	Huangdao District	86	7 038	838	570
崂山区	Laoshan District	73	4 188	472	337
胶州市	Jiaozhou	436	14 955	1 332	1 016
即墨市	Jimo	362	31 219	1 541	1 157
平度市	Pingdu	509	27 197	1 610	1 297
胶南市	Jiaonan	199	14 429	1 209	991
莱西市	Laixi	259	11 907	741	592

16－13 科研机构基本情况(1978－2005年)

BASIC STATISTICS OF INSTITUTIONS OF SCIENTIFIC RESEARCH(1978－2005)

年 份 Year	独立自然科研机构(个) Independent Institutions of Natural Scientific Research(unit)	独立自然科研机构中科技人员(人) Personnel of Independent Institutions of Natural Scientific Research(person)	完成科研项目(项) Number of Projects completed(item)	取得科技成果(项) Number of Achievements in Scientific Research(item)
1978	31	2 701	306	306
1980	–	–	481	297
1982	41	2 345	451	451
1983	48	3 182	530	530
1984	53	3 312	507	507
1985	52	3 673	552	552
1986	63	3 998	577	577
1987	76	4 629	579	579
1988	101	5 199	544	510
1989	111	5 885	544	688
1990	141	6 046	414	931
1991	72	5 665	753	753
1992	71	5 726	659	659
1993	69	5 545	546	546
1994	69	5 540	467	467
1995	59	5 286	441	441
1996	58	4 738	613	613
1997	54	4 577	418	418
1998	52	4 142	517	517
1999	58	3 771	606	606
2000	54	3 637	621	621
2001	50	3 191	457	457
2002	52	3 248	406	406
2003	53	3 246	589	589
2004	50	3 226	506	506
2005	50	3 234	438	438

注:1991年以后不包括民办科研机构。

Note: Institutions of scientific research run by the local people are not contained since 1991.

16－14 独立科学研究机构情况(2005 年)

BASIC STATISTICS OF INDEPENDENT INSTITUTIONS OF SCIENTIFIC RESEARCH(2005)

		计量单位	Unit	总计 Total	中央属 Central	省属 Provincial	地市属 Local	县级市属 County
机构数	Number of Institutions	个	unit	50	7	8	32	3
职工人数	Staff and Workers	人	person	5 249	2 352	729	2 130	38
科技人员	Personnel Engaged in Science and Technology	人	person	3 234	1 627	491	1 091	25
经费收入	Funding for Scientific and Technical Research	万元	10 000 yuan	106 361.9	73 165.9	14 153.2	18 978.9	63.9
经费支出	Expenditures of Scientific and Technical Research Funds	万元	10 000 yuan	95 622.0	67 021.3	10 962.5	17 523.7	114.5

16－15 科学技术奖励情况(2005 年)

AWARD STATISTICS OF SCIENCE AND TECHNOLOGY(2005)

项目	Items	单位	Unit	自然科学奖 Natural Science Prizes Awarded	技术发明奖 Invention Prizes Awarded	科技进步奖 Science And Technological Progress Prizes Awarded	科学技术功勋奖 Science And Technological Credit Prizes Awarded	国际科技合作奖 International Science And Technological Cooperation Prizes Award	最高奖 Highest Prizes Award
国家级	National Level	项	item	–	1	3	–	–	–
#一等	First Grade	项	item	–	–	–	–	–	–
二等	Second Grade	项	item	–	1	3	–	–	–
三等	Third Grade	项	item	–	–	–	–	–	–
省级	Provincial Level	项	item	4	3	63	–	–	1
#一等	First Grade	项	item	1	–	4	–	–	–
二等	Second Grade	项	item	–	1	19	–	–	–
三等	Third Grade	项	item	3	2	40	–	–	–
市级	Municipal Level	项	item	19	5	152	–	3	–
#一等	First Grade	项	item	3	–	15	–	–	–
二等	Second Grade	项	item	7	3	57	–	–	–
三等	Third Grade	项	item	9	2	80	–	–	–

注:国际科技合作奖、最高奖不分等级。

Note:There is no grade in international science and technological cooperation prizes award and highest prizes award.

16－16 大中型工业企业技术开发主要相对指标(1990－2005年)

MAJOR RELATIVE INDICATORS OF TECHNICAL DEVELOPMENT OF LARGE AND MEDIUM INDUSTRIAL ENTERPRISES (1990－2005)

项目	Items	单位	Unit	1990年	1995年	2000年	2004年	2005年
企业技术开发人员占全部职工比重	Technical Development Personnel/Staff and Workers	%	%	2.3	2.6	5.7	4.5	4.4
科学家工程师占技术开发人员比重	Scientists and Engineers/Technical Development Personnel	%	%	32.4	39.0	62.3	59.7	66.1
设有开发机构的企业占企业总数比重	Enterprises Owned Technical Development Institutions/Total Enterprises	%	%	59.5	59.3	29.7	24.6	20.8
科学家工程师占开发机构人员比重	Scientists and Engineers/Personnel in Development Institutions	%	%	37.1	48.1	77.6	61.4	-
平均每个企业技术开发经费筹集额	Average Funds for Development Owned by Each Enterprises	万元	10 000yuan	144.0	118.2	873.0	1 550.4	1 535.8
平均每个企业技术开发经费支出额	Average Expenditures of Development Spent by Each Enterprises	万元	10 000yuan	125.0	114.5	812.0	1 675.5	1 626.0
开发新产品用款占经费支出比重	Expenditures of New Products/Total Funds	%	%	81.9	50.8	52.6	49.7	55.9
技术开发经费支出占产品销售收入比重	Expenditures of Development/Revenue of Products Sales	%	%	2.1	1	3.1	3.0	2.7
新产品产值比重	Rate of Output Value of New Products	%	%	8.2	-	35.5	34.4	31.3
新产品销售额比重	Rate of Sales Volume of New Products	%	%	8.0	12.2	32.7	36.4	32.5
新产品利税额比重	Rate of Profits and Tax of New Products	%	%	7.4	18.7	30.6	-	-

16－17 主要年份文化事业机构数
MAJOR YEAR'S INSTITUTIONS OF CULTURE

单位:个(unit)

年份 Year	合计 Total	#剧院 Theatres	#影剧院 Cinemas and Theatres	#电影队 Film Teams	#文化馆 Cultural Palaces	#艺术表演团体 Art Performance Troupes
1949	24	8	9	1	3	3
1952	50	9	11	7	15	8
1957	99	8	16	39	11	15
1962	103	8	17	51	12	13
1965	117	8	18	64	13	13
1970	121	7	20	67	12	13
1975	249	5	21	188	12	16
1978	402	5	24	276	13	15
1980	661	4	24	372	12	17
1985	1 290	3	81	934	12	11
1988	1 473	2	84	924	12	11
1989	1 308	2	106	773	12	11
1990	1 323	2	106	773	12	11
1991	1 185	–	108	634	12	11
1992	1 167	–	108	634	12	11
1993	1 079	–	103	561	12	11
1994	964	–	78	487	12	11
1995	767	–	61	367	13	11
1996	761	–	61	367	13	11
1997	634	–	61	260	12	11
1998	491	–	51	125	12	11
1999	638	–	43	279	12	11
2000	637	–	45	280	12	11
2001	614	–	44	279	12	11
2002	590	–	44	279	11	11
2003	492	–	50	189	11	11
2004	476	–	29	214	12	11
2005	478	–	39	205	12	12

16－18 文化、文物事业机构、人员数(2005 年)

INSTITUTIONS AND PERSONNEL OF CULTURE AND HISTORICAL RELIC(2005)

项　目	Items	文化机构数(个) Institutions of Culture(unit)		文化人员数(人) Personnel Engaged in Culture(person)	
		2005 年 2005	2004 年 2004	2005 年 2005	2004 年 2004
总　计	**Total**	**221**	**219**	**2 052**	**2 002**
文化事业合计	**Culture**	**205**	**204**	**1 805**	**1 773**
一、艺术事业	**Art**	**27**	**26**	**928**	**903**
1. 艺术表演团体	Art Performance Troupes	12	11	740	653
2. 艺术表演场所	Art Performance Places	10	11	160	227
3. 艺术创作机构	Institutions of Art Creation	3	2	10	7
4. 艺术研究机构	Institutions of Art Research	2	2	18	16
5. 艺术展览机构	Institutions of Art Exhibition	-	-	-	-
6. 其他	Others	-	-	-	-
二、图书馆事业	**Libraries**	**13**	**13**	**267**	**265**
公共图书馆	Public Libraries	13	13	267	265
#县(区)级图书馆	County Libraries	12	12	162	165
三、群众文化事业	**Mass Culture**	**160**	**160**	**505**	**509**
1. 群众艺术馆	Mass Art Centers	1	1	47	53
2. 文化馆	Cultural Palaces	12	12	191	191
3. 文化站	Cultural Centers	147	147	267	265
4. 其他	Others	-	-	-	-
四、教育事业	**Education**	**-**	**-**	**-**	**-**
1. 高等院校	Institutions of Higher Education	-	-	-	-
2. 中等专业学校	Specialized Secondary School	-	-	-	-
3. 其他教育机构	Other Institutions of Education	-	-	-	-
五、其他文化事业	**Others**	**5**	**5**	**105**	**96**
文物事业合计	History Relic	16	15	247	229
1. 文物机构	Institutions of History Relic	6	6	36	35
2. 博物馆纪念馆	Museums and Memorial Halls	8	8	185	175
3. 文物商店	History Relic Shops	1	1	19	19
4. 文物科研机构	Scientific Research Institutions of History Relic	1	-	7	-

16－19 分市、区艺术表演、电影发行及放映机构数(2005 年)
INSTITUTIONS OF ART PERFORMANCE, FILMS DISTRIBUTION AND PROJECTION BY REGION(2005)

单位:个(unit)

市、区名称	Region	合计 Total	影剧院 Cinemas and Theatres	电影发行机构 Institutions of Films Distribution	电影院 Cinemas	#乡镇 of which: Township	电影放映队 Film Teams	俱乐部 Clubs
总 计	**Total**	**257**	**15**	**9**	**24**	**16**	**205**	**4**
市 区	Urban Area	40	10	4	9	2	15	2
#城 阳 区	Chengyang District	8	–	–	–	–	8	–
黄 岛 区	Huangdao District	9	–	1	2	–	6	–
崂 山 区	Laoshan District	2	–	–	2	2	–	–
胶 州 市	Jiaozhou	10	1	1	–	–	8	–
即 墨 市	Jimo	29	2	1	6	6	20	–
平 度 市	Pingdu	123	1	1	–	–	121	–
胶 南 市	Jiaonan	22	–	1	1	–	20	–
莱 西 市	Laixi	33	1	1	8	8	21	2

16－20 艺术表演、电影放映情况(2005 年)
ART PERFORMANCE AND FILMS PROJECTION(2005)

项 目	Items	机构数(个) Institutions(unit)	座位数(个) Seats(unit)	演出场次(场) Times of Performance(time)	观众人数(万人次) Audiences (10000 person-times)	票款收入(万元) Income (10000 yuan)
艺术表演总计	Art Performances	10	6 245	472	19.6	171.9
电影放映总计	Films Projection	248	29 221	49 814	302	1 307
#影 剧 院	Cinemas and Theatres	15	9 742	22 146	81	844
电 影 院	Cinemas	24	13 985	14 287	16	342
电 影 队	Films Teams	205	–	13 344	202	110
俱 乐 部	Clubs	4	5 494	37	3	11

16－21 文化部门艺术剧团情况(2005 年)
ART TROUPES OF CULTURE DEPARTMENT(2005)

项　目	Items	剧团数(个) Troupes (unit)	职工人数(人) Staff and Workers (person)	演出场次(场) Times of Performance (time)	观众人数(万人次) Audiences (10000 person-times)	演出收入(万元) Performance Income (10000 yuan)	拨款经费(万元) Appropriation (10000 yuan)
总　计	**Total**	**12**	**740**	**2 379**	**377.9**	**554.7**	**4 095.1**
一、按隶属关系分	**By Administrative Relationship**						
国营剧团	State－run Troupes	12	740	2 379	377.9	554.7	4 095.1
集体经营剧团	Collective－owned Troupes	－	－	－	－	－	－
二、按剧种分	**By Type of Drama**						
1. 话剧团	Drama Troupes	1	105	286	37.6	58.3	610.1
2. 歌舞团	Song and Dance Troupes	1	134	173	34.6	151.6	759.4
3. 戏曲剧团	Local Opera Troupes	6	304	1 512	253.7	280.2	1 148.5
#京剧	of which: Beijing Opera	1	82	274	23.9	76.5	482.9
4. 曲艺团	Recitation and Ballad Troupes	1	24	98	9.8	13.9	118.2
5. 文工团(艺术团)	Art Troupes	3	173	310	42.2	50.7	1 458.9

16－22 图书馆、博物馆、文化馆情况
LIBRARIES, MUSEUMS AND CULTURAL PALACES

项　目	Items	单位	Unit	2005 年 2005 全市合计 Total	2005 年 2005 #市区 Urban Area	2004 年 2004 全市合计 Total	2004 年 2004 #市区 Urban Area
公共图书馆	Public Libraries	个	unit	13	8	13	8
工作人员	Staff and Workers	人	person	267	201	265	198
藏书册数	Collection Books	千册	1000 copies	3 294	2 369	2 938	2 216
阅览席位	Seats in Reading Room	张	seat	4 488	3 526	5 011	3 941
读者人数	Readers	万人次	10 000 person-times	253.6	189.2	211.8	150.8
博物馆、纪念馆	Museums and Memorial Halls	个	unit	8	4	8	4
工作人员	Staff and Workers	人	person	185	135	175	128
藏品数量	Collection	万件	10 000 copies	14.1	10.8	14.1	10.8
参观人数	Visitors	万人次	10 000 person－times	91.0	86.2	58.0	55.6
文化馆	Cultural Palaces	个	unit	12	7	12	7

16－23 图书、杂志、报纸出版情况(1990－2005年)
PUBLICATIONS OF BOOK,MAGAZINE AND NEWSPAPER(1990－2005)

项 目	Items	单 位	Unit	1990年	1995年	2000年	2004年	2005年
图书出版	**Publications of Book**							
种数	Number of Publications	种	kind	292	530	572	771	896
总印数	Total Printed	万册	10 000 copies	1 626	2 109	1 542	3 156	2 873
总印张数	Total Printed Signatures	千印张	1 000 signatures	40 358	75 242	71 826	171 232	191 671
杂志出版	**Publications of Magazine**							
种数	Number of Publications	种	kind	32	34	35	43	44
每期平均印数	Average Publication Issued	万册(份)	10 000 copies	41.71	37.42	75.41	79.66	76.95
总印数	Total Printed	万册	10 000 copies	452	409	1 249	1 750	1 755
总印张数	Total Printed Signatures	千印张	1 000 signatures	6 422	5 630	31 946	65 632	69 635
报纸出版	**Publications of Newspaper**							
种数	Number of Publications	种	kind	4	8	14	12	12
每期平均印数	Average Publication Issued	万份	10 000 copies	64.25	81.51	84.74	208.2	174.16
总印数	Total Printed	万份	10 000 copies	7 127	16 318	21 309	64 593	53 947
总印张数	Total Printed Signatures	千印张	1 000 signatures	56 670	231 642	555 503	4 843 795	4 188 151

16 -24 广播电视业基本情况(1990 -2005 年)
BASIC STATISTICS OF BROADCASTING AND TELEVISION(1990 - 2005)

项 目	Items	单 位	Unit	1990 年	1995 年	2000 年	2004 年	2005 年
一、广播基本情况	**Basic Statistics of Broadcasting**							
电台个数	Number of Broadcasting Stations	座	place	6	8	1	1	1
发射台个数	Number of Launching Stations	座	place	7	9	9	11	11
节目套数	Number of Programs	套	set	7	10	10	11	12
平均日播音时间	Program Time Per Day	时:分	hour: minute	53:35	126:35	119:15	146:21	174:01
#自办节目	of which: Self-programs of the Year	时:分	hour: minute	41:15	117:05	107:50	80:30	111:12
本年制作广播节目时间	Time of Making Programs of the Year	小时	hour	-	-	-	-	-
#自制广播节目	of which: Self-programs of the Year	小时	hour	-	-	-	23 842	36 964
加工广播节目	Time of Processing Programs	小时	hour	-	-	-	-	-
节目被中央台采用时间	Time of Programs Used by CBS	时:分	hour: minute	-	-	-	21:49	18:26
广播人口覆盖率	Population Coverage Rate	%	%	94	94	96.02	97.87	97.9
二、电视基本情况	Basic Statistics of Television							
电视台个数	Number of Television Stations	座	place	4	8	1	1	1
发射台个数	Number of Launching Stations	座	place	42	48	29	11	11
节目套数	Number of Programs	套	set	4	9	9	15	15
平均每周播出时间	Program Time Per Week	时:分	hour: minute	129:10	382:18	489:20	1443:48	1522:38
#自办节目	of which: Self-Produced Programs	时:分	hour: minute	38:25	327:35	410:54	552:35	597:55
本年制作电视节目时间	Time of Making Programs of the Year	小时	hour	-	-	-	-	-
#自制电视节目	of which: Self-programs of the Year	小时	hour	-	-	-	9 917	11 977
加工电视节目	Time of Processing Programs	小时	hour	-	-	-	-	-
节目被中央台采用时间	Time of Programs Used by CCTV	时:分	hour: minute	-	-	-	17:16	33:06
电视人口覆盖率	Population Coverage Rate	%	%	90.87	92	95.04	97.46	97.7
三、有线电视基本情况	**Basic Statistics of Cable Television**							
总用户数	Total Users	万户	10 000 households	-	-	-	155.6	176.6
有线电视入户率	Use Rate of Cable Television	%	%	-	-	-	66.99	75.05
网络总长	Length of the Network	公里	km	-	-	-	43 376	44 827
广播电视卫星收转系统	Satellite Systems of Broadcasting and Television	座	place	-	-	-	947	1 062

CHAPTER 17

第十七篇

体育、卫生和民政、司法

SPORTS,HEALTH CARE,
CIVIL ADMINISTRATION AND LAW

编辑单位：人口和社会科技统计处
编　　委：高明辉
编　　辑：王　磊
校　　对：关　静
电　　话：85912263

17 -1 体育事业情况(1985 -2005 年)

STATISTICS OF SPORT(1985-2005)

项目	Items	单位	Unit	1985 年	1990 年	1995 年	2000 年	2004 年	2005 年
体育部门职工人数	Staff and Workers of Sport Department	人	person	464	714	902	849	710	834
#运动员	Athletes	人	person	31	88	121	90	56	87
教练员	Coaches	人	person	129	166	175	174	229	235
重点体校	Key and Sparetime Physical Schools	人	person	6	70	141	126	106	117
业余体校	Regular and Sparetime Physical Schools	人	person	83	174	117	142	200	223
体育专业队	Professional Teams	人	person	31	120	158	135	121	132
优秀运动员	Excellent Athletes	人	person	31	82	121	90	56	87
优秀运动队专职教练员	Full-time Coaches of Excellent Teams	人	person	3	14	15	18	37	23
等级裁判员发展人数	Certified Referees	人	person	977	827	223	1 114	305	275
#二　级	Second Grades	人	person	381	402	50	451	305	275
三　级	Third Grades	人	person	596	425	136	616	-	-
等级运动员发展人数	Certified Athletes	人	person	1 115	868	249	343	320	260
#二　级	Second Grades	人	person	-	7	135	209	320	260
三　级	Third Grades	人	person	682	454	114	46	-	-
少年级	Juvenile	人	person	433	395	-	88	-	-

17 -1 续表
continued

项目	Items	单位	Unit	1985 年	1990 年	1995 年	2000 年	2004 年	2005 年
全年获得奖牌数	Items	枚	unit	184	281	278	347.5	567.5	669
#国家级金牌	Golden Medals at National Level	枚	unit	28	20	34	45	37	62
国家级银牌	Silver Medal at National Level	枚	unit	36	23	18	28	37	48
省级金牌	Golden Medals at Provincial Level	枚	unit	-	83	94	116.5	183.5	187
省级银牌	Silver Medals at Provincial Level	枚	unit	-	79	47	62	139	174
体育运动破全国记录	Records Broken the National Records								
项　目	Item	项	item	-	5	2	-	3	2
人　数	Persons	人	person	-	8	2	-	3	2
次　数	Time	人次	person-time	-	7	2	-	3	4
体育运动破全省记录	Records Broken the Provincial Records								
项　目	Item	项	item	-	3	4	7	-	3
人　数	Persons	人	person	-	3	5	7	-	1
次　数	Time	人次	person-time	-	2	5	7	-	3

17 –2 主要年份卫生事业基本情况
MAJOR YEAR'S BASIC STATISTICS OF HEALTH CARE

年份 Year	卫生机构数(个) Health Care Institutions(unit)	#医院 of which: Hospitals	医疗床位数(张) Hospital Beds(bed)	#医院 of which: Hospitals	卫生技术人员(人) Medical Professionals (person)	#医生 of which: doctors	每千人口拥有医生数(人) Doctors Owned by Every 1000 Persons(person)	每千人口拥有床位数(张) Hospital Beds Owned by Every 1000 Persons(bed)
1949	80	26	1 079	970	2 637	1 292	0.32	0.27
1952	260	34	2 943	1 691	3 748	1 559	0.37	0.7
1957	624	45	5 163	2 656	6 941	2 578	0.53	1.07
1962	849	149	7 167	4 526	8 279	2 972	0.64	1.55
1965	912	162	8 428	5 003	9 051	3 586	0.73	1.72
1970	712	170	8 613	6 603	9 591	3 761	0.7	1.6
1975	959	181	10 902	9 078	13 558	4 566	0.8	1.9
1978	1 192	212	13 084	10 709	16 921	5 893	1.01	2.24
1980	1 253	212	14 170	11 345	19 265	6 781	1.14	2.38
1985	1 517	219	18 469	13 214	23 413	9 694	1.55	2.95
1987	1 553	228	21 667	15 463	26 669	11 738	1.81	3.34
1989	1 566	232	22 668	15 670	27 195	13 555	2.06	3.46
1990	1 563	235	23 541	16 586	27 932	13 761	2.08	3.56
1991	1 579	235	23 727	16 796	27 772	13 227	1.98	3.54
1992	1 562	236	24 765	17 269	28 305	13 157	1.95	3.67
1993	1 540	237	24 885	17 469	28 705	13 312	1.97	3.68
1994	1 335	242	24 732	17 882	28 938	13 535	1.99	3.64
1995	1 347	228	25 282	18 126	29 816	13 840	2.02	3.69
1996	2 216	228	24 334	18 344	30 048	13 790	2	3.53
1997	2 193	239	25 201	19 046	31 121	14 400	2.07	3.62
1998	2 190	237	24 887	19 083	31 623	14 327	2.05	3.56
1999	2 185	235	25 481	19 798	31 965	14 453	2.06	3.62
2000	2 911	231	24 392	20 057	32 160	14 860	2.1	3.45
2001	3 199	217	24 755	20 313	32 765	15 772	2.22	3.48
2002	3 050	213	21 370	20 662	31 469	13 371	1.87	2.99
2003	3 111	213	23 980	21 605	32 337	13 452	1.87	3.33
2004	2 923	219	25 432	23 465	32 937	13 953	1.91	3.48
2005	2 609	235	30 627	28 564	33 942	15 008	2.03	4.13

17－3 各类卫生机构、床位、人员数(2005 年底)

VARIOUS HEALTH CARE INSTITUTIONS, HOSPITAL BEDS AND PERSONNEL(END OF 2005)

项　　目	Items	机构数(个) Institutions (unit)	床位数(张) Hospital Beds (bed)	人员数(人) Personnel (person)
总　　计	**Total**	**2 609**	**30 627**	**40 227**
一、医院合计	**Total Hospitals**	**235**	**28 564**	**31 505**
1. 医院	Hospitals	145	24 651	27 585
#综合医院	Comprehensive hospitals	104	19 274	22 719
中医医院	hospitals of Traditional Chinese Medicine	10	1 880	1 831
中西医结合医院	Hospitals of Combination of Chinese and Western Medicine	1	60	2
专科医院	Specialized Hospitals	30	3 437	3 033
#口腔医院	Stomatological Hospitals	2	40	119
眼科医院	Ophthalmology Hospitals	3	180	134
肿瘤医院	Tumor Hospitals	1	336	354
心血管病医院	Cardiovascular Diseases Hospitals	2	114	64
精神病医院	Mental Hospitals	7	1 115	631
传染病医院	Infectious Disease Hospitals	1	370	378
皮肤病医院	Dermatology Hospitals	2	30	62
结核病医院	Tuberculosis Hospitals	1	80	45
骨科医院	Orthopaedics Hospitals	4	180	59
其它专科医院	Other Specialized Hospitals	7	992	1 187
2. 卫生院	Sanitation Stations	90	3 913	3 920
二、社区卫生服务中心	**Neighborhood Service Centers**	**1**	**80**	**41**
三、门诊部	**Outpatient Service Stations**	**3**	**2**	**29**
四、诊所	**Clinics**	**1 290**	**–**	**2 323**
五、卫生所、医务室	**Medical Houses**	**535**	**–**	**1 160**
六、社区卫生服务站	**Neighborhood Service Stations**	**467**	**–**	**1 942**
七、急救中心	**First Aid Centers**	**2**	**–**	**130**
八、采供血机构	**Institutions of Blood Collection and Supply**	**7**	**–**	**152**
九、妇幼保健院(所、站)	**Maternity and Child Care Centers**	**10**	**216**	**441**
十、专科疾病防治院(所、站)	**Specialized Disease Centers**	**6**	**90**	**184**
十一、疾病预防控制中心(防疫站)	**Diseases Control Centers**	**20**	**–**	**910**
十二、卫生监督所	**Sanitation Control Stations**	**13**	**–**	**529**
十三、卫生监督检验所(站)	**Sanitation Control and Test Stations**	**–**	**–**	**–**
十四、医学科学研究机构	**Institutions of Medical Science**	**–**	**–**	**–**
十五、医学在职培训机构	**Institutions of Medical Training for Working Personnel**	**1**	**–**	**13**
十六、健康教育所(站、中心)	**Health Education Stations**	**1**	**–**	**32**
十七、其它卫生机构	**Other Health Care Institutions**	**10**	**22**	**111**
十八、疗养院	**Sanatoriums**	**8**	**1 653**	**725**

#卫生技术人员 Medical Professionals	#医生 Doctors	注册护士 Nurses	药剂人员 Pharmacists	检验人员 Laboratory Technicians
33 942	**15 008**	**10 851**	**2 344**	**1 381**
26 254	**10 967**	**9 961**	**2 131**	**1 137**
22 732	9 272	9 168	1 761	972
18 836	7 713	7 616	1 465	782
1 597	724	540	135	61
2	2	–	–	–
2 297	833	1 012	161	129
100	80	7	5	1
101	28	28	5	5
260	102	133	13	12
49	14	14	5	6
454	132	258	34	14
273	90	133	23	23
53	17	12	5	8
34	22	7	4	1
46	24	12	6	3
927	324	408	61	56
3 522	1 695	793	370	165
32	**9**	**8**	**3**	**2**
24	**13**	**7**	**3**	**1**
2 323	**1 648**	**399**	**52**	**14**
1 160	**680**	**153**	**50**	**21**
1 942	**501**	**42**	**34**	**2**
34	**16**	**9**	**2**	**3**
101	**17**	**17**	**2**	**54**
356	**214**	**37**	**12**	**33**
152	**76**	**38**	**16**	**10**
697	**366**	**26**	**17**	**78**
384	**291**	**2**	**4**	**12**
–	**–**	**–**	**–**	**–**
–	**–**	**–**	**–**	**–**
3	**–**	**–**	**–**	**–**
10	**2**	**–**	**–**	**–**
99	**52**	**16**	**4**	**3**
371	**156**	**136**	**14**	**11**

17－4 分市、区各类卫生机构、床位、人员数(2005 年底)

VARIOUS HEALTH CARE INSTITUTIONS, HOSPITAL BEDS
AND PERSONNEL BY REGION(END OF 2005)

市、区名称	Region	机构数（个）Institutions (unit)	医院小计 Sub-total of Hospitals	#医院 Hospitals	#卫生院 Sanitation Stations	社区卫生服务中心 Neighborhood Service Centers
总　计	**Total**	**2 609**	**235**	**145**	**90**	**1**
市　　区	Urban Area	1 416	98	88	10	1
#城 阳 区	Chengyang District	108	9	7	2	–
黄 岛 区	Huangdao District	227	6	2	4	–
崂 山 区	Laoshan District	111	10	6	4	1
胶 州 市	Jiaozhou	346	22	9	13	–
即 墨 市	Jimo	488	34	16	18	–
平 度 市	Pingdu	152	39	15	24	–
胶 南 市	Jiaonan	109	19	8	11	–
莱 西 市	Laixi	98	23	9	14	–

17－4 续表 1

continued

市、区名称	Region	采供血机构 Institutions of Blood Collection and Supply	妇幼保健院(所、站) Maternity and Child Care Centers	专科疾病防治院(所、站) Specialized Disease Centers
总　计	**Total**	**7**	**10**	**6**
市　　区	Urban Area	2	7	1
#城 阳 区	Chengyang District	–	1	–
黄 岛 区	Huangdao District	1	1	–
崂 山 区	Laoshan District	–	1	–
胶 州 市	Jiaozhou	1	1	–
即 墨 市	Jimo	1	1	1
平 度 市	Pingdu	1	–	2
胶 南 市	Jiaonan	1	–	2
莱 西 市	Laixi	1	1	–

门诊部 Outpatient Service Stations	诊所 Clinics	卫生所、医务室 Medical Houses	社区卫生服务站 Neighborhood Service Stations	急救中心 First Aid Centers
3	**1 290**	**535**	**467**	**2**
3	1 005	228	35	1
–	65	25	3	–
–	147	53	12	–
–	75	22	–	–
–	134	182	–	–
–	12	6	428	1
–	63	44	–	–
–	43	39	2	–
–	33	36	2	–

疾病预防控制中心(防疫站) Diseases Control Centers	卫生监督所 Sanitation Control Stations	卫生监督检疫所(站) Sanitation Control and Test stations	医学科学研究机构 Institutions of Medical Science
20	**13**	**–**	**–**
12	8	–	–
3	1	–	–
1	1	–	–
1	1	–	–
4	1	–	–
1	1	–	–
1	1	–	–
1	1	–	–
1	1	–	–

17 –4 续表 2
continued

市、区名称	Region	医学在职培训机构 Institutions of Medical Training for Working Personnel	健康教育所(站、中心) Health Education Station	其他卫生机构 Other Health Care Institutions	床位数(张) Hospital Beds (bed)
总　计	**Total**	**1**	**1**	**10**	**30 627**
市　　区	Urban Area	–	1	7	16 605
#城 阳 区	Chengyang District	–	–	1	1 659
黄 岛 区	Huangdao District	–	–	5	755
崂 山 区	Laoshan District	–	–	–	1 111
胶 州 市	Jiaozhou	1	–	–	2 534
即 墨 市	Jimo	–	–	1	3 820
平 度 市	Pingdu	–	–	1	3 780
胶 南 市	Jiaonan	–	–	1	2 009
莱 西 市	Laixi	–	–	–	1 879

17 –4 续表 3
continued

市、区名称	Region	专科疾病防治院(所、站) Specialized Disease Centers	人员数(人) Personnel (person)	卫生技术人员 Medical Professionals
总　计	**Total**	**90**	**40 227**	**33 942**
市　　区	Urban Area	25	23 760	19 392
#城 阳 区	Chengyang District	–	1 910	1 700
黄 岛 区	Huangdao District	–	1 621	1 482
崂 山 区	Laoshan District	–	1 173	971
胶 州 市	Jiaozhou	–	3 511	3 047
即 墨 市	Jimo	–	4 625	4 318
平 度 市	Pingdu	30	3 228	2 841
胶 南 市	Jiaonan	35	2 711	2 326
莱 西 市	Laixi	–	2 392	2 018

医院小计 Sub-total of Hospitals	#医院 Hospitals	#卫生院 Sanitation Stations	门诊部 Outpatient Service Stations	妇幼保健院(所、站) Maternity and Child Care Centers
28 564	**24 651**	**3 913**	**2**	**216**
15 145	14 656	489	2	48
1 659	1 375	284	–	–
755	630	125	–	–
1 001	921	80	–	30
2 486	1 860	626	–	48
3 390	2 506	884	–	80
3 750	2 862	888	–	–
1 954	1 487	467	–	–
1 839	1 280	559	–	40

执业医师 Doctors	执业助理医师 Assistant Doctors	注册护士 Nurses	药剂人员 Pharmacists	检验人员 Laboratory Technicians	其他人员 Other Personnel
13 071	**1 937**	**10 851**	**2 344**	**1 381**	**4 358**
7 955	703	7 118	1 310	801	1 505
561	290	541	99	62	147
714	82	398	91	63	134
371	51	331	57	37	124
957	216	1 073	195	113	493
1 327	489	701	218	106	1 477
1 149	247	752	251	125	317
907	134	683	192	109	301
776	148	524	178	127	265

17 –5 收养性社会福利单位情况(2005 年)
ADOPTION UNITS OF SOCIAL WELFARE(2005)

市、区名称	Region	单位数(个) Number (unit)	年末职工人数(人) Year-end Staff and Workers(person)	医护人员 Medical Personnel and Nurses	年末床位数(张) Year-end Beds (bed)
总　计	**Total**	**212**	**2 059**	**619**	**14 371**
市　　区	Urban Area	126	1 680	523	8 730
#城 阳 区	Chengyang District	17	86	25	1 234
黄 岛 区	Huangdao District	4	21	8	152
崂 山 区	Laoshan District	9	87	16	400
胶 州 市	Jiaozhou	15	64	15	2 500
即 墨 市	Jimo	23	130	27	883
平 度 市	Pingdu	22	56	22	1 213
胶 南 市	Jiaonan	8	32	7	290
莱 西 市	Laixi	18	97	25	755

17 –6 社会救济情况(2005 年)
STATISTICS OF SOCIAL RELIEF(2005)

市、区名称	Region	城镇居民最低生活保障人数(人) Urban Residences under Basic Provision Protection(person)	城镇居民最低生活保障家庭数(户) Urban Households under Basic Provision Protection (household)	城镇低保资金计划支出(万元) Urban Program of Basic Provision Protection (10 000 yuan)	城镇临时救济人数(人次) Urban Residences Enjoying Temporal Relief (person-time)
总　计	**Total**	**39 688**	**17 603**	**8 805.6**	**21 010**
市　　区	Urban Area	34 644	15 247	8 027.5	19 850
#城 阳 区	Chengyang District	720	297	141.0	50
黄 岛 区	Huangdao District	573	236	98.5	90
崂 山 区	Laoshan District	581	235	64.5	168
胶 州 市	Jiaozhou	804	409	158.0	210
即 墨 市	Jimo	1393	719	256.5	320
平 度 市	Pingdu	711	353	101.0	–
胶 南 市	Jiaonan	1 584	664	193.0	300
莱 西 市	Laixi	552	211	69.6	330

年末在院人数(人) Year-end Residences (person)	优抚对象 Persons Enjoying Commiseration	"三无"对象 Persons Having No House, No Child and No Living Resource	自费人员 Persons at One's Own Expense
8 092	**118**	**3 797**	**4 177**
5 225	57	1 223	3 945
383	–	383	–
76	2	74	–
341	–	141	200
1 043	–	846	197
465	13	417	35
529	–	529	–
165	–	165	–
665	48	617	–

农村居民最低生活保障人数(人) Rural Residences under Basic Provision Protection(person)	农村居民最低生活保障家庭数(户) Rural Households under Basic Provision Protection(household)	农村低保资金计划支出(万元) Rural Program of Basic Provision Protection(10 000 yuan)	农村临时救济人数(人次) Rural Residences Enjoying Temporal Relief(person-time)
61 709	**33 444**	**3 334.1**	**15 068**
12 662	6 136	814.4	7 905
6 178	3 222	321.2	6 230
2 813	1 438	153.8	–
3 671	1 476	339.4	1 675
8 206	3 480	393.7	–
9 748	6 167	633.9	3 063
11 870	6 306	569.4	–
10 732	7 310	523.9	–
8 491	4 045	398.8	4 100

17－7 分市、区婚姻登记情况(2005 年)

STATISTICS OF MARRIAGE REGISTRATION BY REGION(2005)

市、区名称	Region	准予登记结婚 Marriage Registration Permitted					准予登记离婚(对) Divorce Registration Permitted(couple)	涉外婚姻登记(对) Chinese-Foreign Marriage(couple)
		合计(对) Total(couple)	初婚(人) First marriage (person)	恢复结婚(对) Resumed Marriage (couple)	再婚(人) Remarriage(person) 男 Male	女 Female		
总　计	**Total**	**53 706**	**92 402**	**494**	**7 033**	**7 977**	**6 894**	**366**
市　　区	Urban Area	20 779	34 529	302	3 484	3 545	4 205	366
#城阳区	Chengyang District	3 367	5 926	6	422	386	329	–
黄岛区	Huangdao District	2 654	4 691	295	322	295	381	–
崂山区	Laoshan District	3 710	6 642	–	401	377	154	–
胶州市	Jiaozhou	5 634	10 131	48	559	578	488	–
即墨市	Jimo	7 704	13 644	16	831	933	550	–
平度市	Pingdu	8 427	14 339	115	997	1 518	891	–
胶南市	Jiaonan	6 217	11 021	–	632	781	448	–
莱西市	Laixi	4 945	8 738	13	530	622	312	–

17－8 律师、公证、调解、社会治安基本情况(1985－2005 年)

BASIC STATISTICS OF LAWYERS, NOTARIZATIONS, MEDIATIONS AND LAW-AND-ORDER SITUATION(1985-2005)

项 目	Items	单位	Unit	1985 年	1990 年	1995 年	2000 年	2004 年	2005 年
一、律师工作	**Lawyer**								
律师事务所	Law Office	个	unit	13	16	61	76	109	116
律师工作者	Lawyers	人	person	152	278	783	1 439	1 924	1 941
专 职	Full-time Lawyers	人	person	68	111	458	971	1 463	1 542
兼 职(含特邀)	Part-time Lawyers	人	person	84	167	325	150	63	73
聘请常年法律顾问单位	Units with Permanent Legal Advisors	个	unit	162	731	2 028	2 508	3 397	3 564
全年办理民事代理	Civil Lawsuit Annual Transacted	件	case	309	1 512	1 650	5 571	9 624	11 104
刑事辩护	Criminal Lawsuit	件	case	275	1 172	1 009	1 755	2 789	3 003
非诉讼事件	Non-litigation Action	件	case	128	252	3 885	5 251	8 034	6 501
解答法律询问	Legal Advisory Services	件	case	8 305	15 489	23 758	58 385	32 699	27 880
代写法律事务文书	Legal Documents Written on Behalf of Clients	件	case	1 460	2 237	4 635	9 335	7 826	8 595
二、公证工作	**Notarizations**								
公证处	Notarial Office	个	unit	13	13	15	15	15	15
公证人员	Notarial Personnel	人	person	71	103	111	152	178	196
公证员	Notaries	人	person	46	56	89	106	121	112
办理公证文书	Documents Notarized	件	case	22 627	68 954	106 205	120 849	119 303	105 787
三、人民调解	**People's Mediation**								
人民调解委员会	People's Mediation Committees	个	unit	8 009	8 718	9 631	9 750	11 055	11 480
调解人员	Mediators(person)	人	person	38 721	41 061	64 806	34 714	31 962	46 735
调解民间纠纷	Civil Disputes Mediated(case)	件	case	22 409	21 175	17 552	18 501	17 579	13 658
四、社会治安	**Law-and-order Situation**								
交通事故发生次数	Traffic Accidents	次	time	360	1 047	917	15 601	9 340	7 051
死亡人数	Deaths	人	person	90	345	600	1 371	973	776
受伤人数	Injuries	人	person	282	409	329	8 620	6 967	6 639
经济损失	Losses	万元	10 000 yuan	32.7	125.3	381.55	4 815.70	3 040.7	2 208.2
火灾发生次数	Fires	次	time	206	422	221	3 088	2 199	1 948
死亡人数	Deaths	人	person	18	12	18	10	8	3
受伤人数	Injuries	人	person	15	18	33	43	9	3
经济损失	Losses	万元	10 000 yuan	77.96	401.62	3 542.29	1 531.06	557.9	550.4

注：火灾发生次数自 1997 年统计方法及口径范围发生变化，与往年不可比。
交通事故发生次数自 1998 年统计方法及口径范围发生变化，与往年不可比。

Note: The statistical method and coverage have been adopted in fires since 1997 and in traffic accidents since 1998.
The data are not comparable with those in preceding year.

CHAPTER 18

第十八篇

企业调查

ENTERPRISES SURVEY

编辑单位：企业调查队专项调查处
编　　委：庞　昕
编　　辑：王淑玉　赵施雯　尹正德　郭芳芳
校　　对：王淑玉　赵施雯　尹正德　郭芳芳
电　　话：82869521　82869531

18－1 企业家信心指数(2005 年)
ENTERPRENEUR CONFIDENCE INDEX(2005)

单位:点(point)

		1季度 First Quarter	2季度 Second Quarter	3季度 Third Quarter	4季度 Fourth Quarter
总体状况	**Total Condition**	**128.62**	**132.17**	**124.48**	**130.37**
一、按行业门类分	**Grouped by Sectors**				
(一)工业	Industry	111.51	119.1	100.74	120.97
1. 采掘业	Excavation	163.53	152.02	140.3	160.97
2. 制造业	Manufacturing	107.42	115.35	96.27	117.65
3. 电力、煤气及水的生产和供应业	Power, Gas and Tap Water Production and Supply	158.33	153.82	158.33	153.07
(二)建筑业	Construction	167.96	170.01	167.75	168.33
(三)交通运输、仓储和邮政业	Transportation, Storage, Postal and Telecommunication Services	137.43	131.12	143.85	129.84
(四)批发和零售业	Wholesale and Retail Trade	169.67	158.99	153.78	144.02
(五)房地产业	Real Estate	165.87	146.31	140.44	136.17
(六)社会服务业	Social Services	128.2	143.75	175	131.25
(七)信息传输、计算机服务和软件	Information Transmission, Computer Service and Software	162.5	150	162.5	162.5
(八)住宿和餐饮业	Accommodation and Catering Trade	141.62	156.12	159.98	139.09
二、按企业登记注册类型分	**Grouped by Registration Categories**				
1. 国有企业	State-owned Enterprises	149.29	128.27	122.37	123.83
2. 集体企业	Collective-owned Enterprises	148.57	157.01	145.04	135.5
3. 股份合作企业	Share Holding Enterprises	143.22	118.96	152.5	137.3
4. 联营企业	Joint State-owned Enterprises	200	200	200	200
5. 有限责任公司	Companies with Limited Liabilities	147.31	131.21	137.87	126.31
6. 股份有限公司	Stock-holding Companies with Limited Liabilities	79.37	116.01	76.14	123.51
7. 私营企业	Private Enterprises	127.27	136.36	145.45	127.27
8. 其它内资企业	Other domestic investment Enterprises	100	50	150	100
9. 外商及港、澳、台投资企业	Foreign and Hong Kong, Macao and Taiwan Funded Companies	148.38	150.06	145.11	139.89
三、按企业规模分	**Grouped by Size of Enterprises**				
总大型	Large	110.42	121.17	93.48	123.29
中型	Medium	141.72	135.58	138.04	128.83
小型	Small	118.03	126.23	122.95	119.67

18－2 企业景气指数(2005年)
BUSINESS CLIMATE INDEX(2005)

单位:点(point)

		1季度 First Quarter	2季度 Second Quarter	3季度 Third Quarter	4季度 Fourth Quarter
总体状况	**Total Condition**	**143.39**	**147.05**	**147.06**	**147.65**
一、按行业门类分	**Grouped by Sectors**				
(一)工业	Industry	147.2	145.96	145.16	145.83
1.采掘业	Excavation	132.4	152.02	114.29	132.4
2.制造业	Manufacturing	147.4	143.8	144.11	145.47
3.电力、煤气及水的生产和供应业	Power, Gas and Tap Water Production and Supply	142.39	160.92	159.69	153.71
(二)建筑业	Construction	119.19	159.9	153.12	164.73
(三)交通运输、仓储和邮政业	Transportation, Storage, Postal and Telecommunication Services	126.2	139.35	137.3	142.72
(四)批发和零售业	Wholesale and Retail Trade	171.36	152.19	156.37	156.38
(五)房地产业	Real Estate	150.44	137.11	133.78	137.11
(六)社会服务业	Social Services	134.45	140.7	153.2	143.75
(七)信息传输、计算机服务和软件	Information Transmission, Computer Service and Software	162.5	175	162.5	165.72
(八)住宿和餐饮业	Accommodation and Catering Trade	135.06	152.13	168.2	145.66
二、按企业登记注册类型分	**Grouped by Registration Categories**				
1.国有企业	State-owned Enterprises	129.73	123.88	122.23	132.92
2.集体企业	Collective-owned Enterprises	150.33	156.3	122.14	130.87
3.股份合作企业	Share Holding Enterprises	122.72	104.68	130.81	119.38
4.联营企业	Joint State-owned Enterprises	100	100	200	200
5.有限责任公司	Companies with Limited Liabilities	157.88	149.78	152.25	147.17
6.股份有限公司	Stock-holding Companies with Limited Liabilities	164.77	162.76	166.09	176.86
7.私营企业	Private Enterprises	145.45	163.64	145.45	145.45
8.其它内资企业	Other domestic investment Enterprises	100	100	100	100
9.外商及港、澳、台投资企业	Foreign and Hong Kong, Macao and Taiwan Funded Companies	140.65	139.76	143.05	113.94
三、按企业规模分	**Grouped by Size of Enterprises**				
总大型	Large	177.97	167.39	165.77	168.91
中型	Medium	141.72	135.58	138.04	128.83
小型	Small	118.03	129.51	124.59	127.87

18－3 企业盈利(亏损)变化景气指数(2005 年)
PROFIT AND LOSS OF ENTERPRISES INDEX(2005)

单位:点(point)

		1 季度 First Quarter	2 季度 Second Quarter	3 季度 Third Quarter	4 季度 Fourth Quarter
盈利(亏损)变化景气指数	**Profit and Loss Index**	**116.79**	**127.36**	**127.16**	**123.75**
一、按行业门类分	**Grouped by Sectors**				
(一)工业	Industry	128.81	135	129.68	128.01
1. 采掘业	Excavation	112.78	137.73	162.48	118.11
2. 制造业	Manufacturing	129.45	132.71	127.36	125.38
3. 电力、煤气及水的生产和供应业	Power, Gas and Tap Water Production and Supply	126.17	154.1	149.53	164.09
(二)建筑业	Construction	72.02	134.59	120.68	129.82
(三)交通运输、仓储和邮政业	Transportation, Storage, Postal and Telecommunication Services	96.9	116.23	122.91	115.69
(四)批发和零售业	Wholesale and Retail Trade	132.33	122.09	135.7	130.06
(五)房地产业	Real Estate	123.81	104.51	97.84	113.62
(六)社会服务业	Social Services	100	87.5	140.55	99.86
(七)信息传输、计算机服务和软件	Information Transmission, Computer Service and Software	123.5	112.5	112.5	125
(八)住宿和餐饮业	Accommodation and Catering Trade	81.28	134.17	126.05	109.57
二、按企业登记注册类型分	**Grouped by Registration Categories**				
1. 国有企业	State-owned Enterprises	98.06	120.32	110.98	122.24
2. 集体企业	Collective-owned Enterprises	146.69	151.12	84.21	105.34
3. 股份合作企业	Share Holding Enterprises	79.81	102.09	103	94.43
4. 联营企业	Joint State-owned Enterprises	100	100	100	200
5. 有限责任公司	Companies with Limited Liabilities	126.03	115.65	132.57	104.05
6. 股份有限公司	Stock-holding Companies with Limited Liabilities	153.15	150.35	155.93	165.7
7. 私营企业	Private Enterprises	72.73	100	90.91	90.91
8. 其它内资企业	Other domestic investment Enterprises	150	150	150	150
9. 外商及港、澳、台投资企业	Foreign and Hong Kong, Macao and Taiwan Funded Companies	108.44	108.47	119.37	90.83
三、按企业规模分	**Grouped by Size of Enterprises**				
总大型	Large	148.62	148.72	148.07	137.01
中型	Medium	101.84	107.98	115.34	115.95
小型	Small	111.48	124.59	113.11	116.39

18－4 企业货款拖欠景气指数(2005 年)

LOANS OF ENTERPRISES IN APPEARS INDEX(2005)

单位:点(point)

		1 季度 First Quarter	2 季度 Second Quarter	3 季度 Third Quarter	4 季度 Fourth Quarter
总 体 状 况	**Total Condition**	**120.76**	**118.61**	**111.63**	**112.81**
一、按行业门类分	**Grouped by Sectors**				
(一)工业	Industry	124.96	126.47	125.48	119.66
1. 采掘业	Excavation	102.77	140.3	140.3	114.29
2. 制造业	Manufacturing	126.22	124.93	124.06	119.15
3. 电力、煤气及水的生产和供应业	Power, Gas and Tap Water Production and Supply	120.1	141.98	136.07	120.32
(二)建筑业	Construction	141.77	109.89	55.8	98.86
(三)交通运输、仓储和邮政业	Transportation, Storage, Postal and Telecommunication Services	87.17	110.66	83.66	96.35
(四)批发和零售业	Wholesale and Retail Trade	118.48	114.09	119.12	130.12
(五)房地产业	Real Estate	119.49	120.33	127.8	120.72
(六)社会服务业	Social Services	125	100	93.75	75
(七)信息传输、计算机服务和软件	Information Transmission, Computer Service and Software	134.28	117.22	104.72	131.44
(八)住宿和餐饮业	Accommodation and Catering Trade	98.77	81.78	102.35	96.77
二、按企业登记注册类型分	**Grouped by Registration Categories**				
1. 国有企业	State-owned Enterprises	123.05	113.52	111.38	113.62
2. 集体企业	Collective-owned Enterprises	123.08	103.5	107.48	122.09
3. 股份合作企业	Share Holding Enterprises	98.39	103.54	103.61	93.45
4. 联营企业	Joint State-owned Enterprises	100	100	0	0
5. 有限责任公司	Companies with Limited Liabilities	107.26	118.81	114.75	99.28
6. 股份有限公司	Stock-holding Companies with Limited Liabilities	147.79	145.21	141.85	154.1
7. 私营企业	Private Enterprises	109.09	81.82	100	90.91
8. 其它内资企业	Other domestic investment Enterprises	100	100	100	50
9. 外商及港、澳、台投资企业	Foreign and Hong Kong, Macao and Taiwan Funded Companies	98.65	106.95	114.62	122.19
三、按企业规模分	**Grouped by Size of Enterprises**				
总大型	Large	143.99	144.44	142.6	144.69
中型	Medium	108.59	102.45	102.45	101.23
小型	Small	91.8	108.2	108.2	88.52

18 -5 企业流动资金景气指数(2005 年)
CIRCULATING CAPITAL OF ENTERPRISES INDEX(2005)

单位:点(point)

		1季度 First Quarter	2季度 Second Quarter	3季度 Third Quarter	4季度 Fourth Quarter
总体状况	**Total Condition**	**73.65**	**72.61**	**87.86**	**79.98**
一、按行业门类分	**Grouped by Sectors**				
(一)工业	Industry	66.34	65.39	80.39	78.4
1.采掘业	Excavation	68.87	97.44	68.87	97.44
2.制造业	Manufacturing	61.14	57.96	76.53	72.83
3.电力、煤气及水的生产和供应业	Power, Gas and Tap Water Production and Supply	126.63	141.66	126.05	131.32
(二)建筑业	Construction	68.99	83.87	98.13	64.22
(三)交通运输、仓储和邮政业	Transportation, Storage, Postal and Telecommunication Services	95.99	89.87	90.06	88.4
(四)批发和零售业	Wholesale and Retail Trade	103.7	100.03	106.62	97.73
(五)房地产业	Real Estate	83.14	73.06	64.7	62.04
(六)社会服务业	Social Services	43.89	43.89	112.64	65.7
(七)信息传输、计算机服务和软件	Information Transmission, Computer Service and Software	70.28	47	59.5	72
(八)住宿和餐饮业	Accommodation and Catering Trade	113.26	117.73	141.37	127.34
二、按企业登记注册类型分	**Grouped by Registration Categories**				
1.国有企业	State-owned Enterprises	117.07	103.94	93.5	100.01
2.集体企业	Collective-owned Enterprises	39.62	75.17	37.03	53.98
3.股份合作企业	Share Holding Enterprises	81.57	74.34	100.35	87.19
4.联营企业	Joint State-owned Enterprises	0	0	0	0
5.有限责任公司	Companies with Limited Liabilities	91.48	88.99	96.33	78.63
6.股份有限公司	Stock-holding Companies with Limited Liabilities	44.07	43.3	86.98	89.29
7.私营企业	Private Enterprises	72.73	63.64	81.82	72.73
8.其它内资企业	Other domestic investment Enterprises	50	50	0	50
9.外商及港、澳、台投资企业	Foreign and Hong Kong, Macao and Taiwan Funded Companies	88.06	84.4	83.57	80.11
三、按企业规模分	**Grouped by Size of Enterprises**				
总大型	Large	81.62	74.11	104.12	97.24
中型	Medium	71.78	73.01	76.07	73.01
小型	Small	60.66	63.93	67.21	63.93

18－6 企业劳动力需求景气指数(2005年)

REQUIREMENT FOR ENTERPRISES LABOR INDEX(2005)

单位:点(point)

		1季度 First Quarter	2季度 Second Quarter	3季度 Third Quarter	4季度 Fourth Quarter
总体状况	**Total Condition**	**112.37**	**125.73**	**129.78**	**116.1**
一、按行业门类分	**Grouped by Sectors**				
(一)工业	Industry	122.64	130.25	125.43	125.17
1.采掘业	Excavation	108.95	76.76	102.77	91.05
2.制造业	Manufacturing	124.73	134.82	129.76	127.76
3.电力、煤气及水的生产和供应业	Power, Gas and Tap Water Production and Supply	101.95	87.89	84.03	96.14
(二)建筑业	Construction	84.61	176.15	173.63	126.82
(三)交通运输、仓储和邮政业	Transportation, Storage, Postal and Telecommunication Services	103.56	106.69	127.98	102.94
(四)批发和零售业	Wholesale and Retail Trade	113.18	91.63	111.71	104.46
(五)房地产业	Real Estate	81.06	96.74	96.6	86.27
(六)社会服务业	Social Services	106.25	106.25	162.5	100
(七)信息传输、计算机服务和软件	Information Transmission, Computer Service and Software	123.5	100	135.78	100
(八)住宿和餐饮业	Accommodation and Catering Trade	86.1	136.74	122.61	87.9
二、按企业登记注册类型分	**Grouped by Registration Categories**				
1.国有企业	State-owned Enterprises	103.28	97.69	107.29	98.08
2.集体企业	Collective-owned Enterprises	148.18	133.72	74.21	80.36
3.股份合作企业	Share Holding Enterprises	114.32	105.64	128.79	108.17
4.联营企业	Joint State-owned Enterprises	100	100	200	100
5.有限责任公司	Companies with Limited Liabilities	128.55	113.53	114.48	104.04
6.股份有限公司	Stock-holding Companies with Limited Liabilities	106.92	148.42	154.29	155.92
7.私营企业	Private Enterprises	109.09	109.09	127.27	100
8.其它内资企业	Other domestic investment Enterprises	50	50	150	0
9.外商及港、澳、台投资企业	Foreign and Hong Kong, Macao and Taiwan Funded Companies	110.98	130.08	144.87	109.42
三、按企业规模分	**Grouped by Size of Enterprises**				
总大型	Large	119.81	135.89	140.24	137.63
中型	Medium	106.75	107.98	111.04	95.09
小型	Small	113.11	116.39	118.03	106.56

18 –7 企业固定资产投资景气指数(2005 年)
INVESTMENT OF ENTERPRISES IN FIXED ASSETS INDEX(2005)

单位:点(point)

		1 季度 First Quarter	2 季度 Second Quarter	3 季度 Third Quarter	4 季度 Fourth Quarter
总体状况	**Total Condition**	**114.2**	**122.5**	**123.93**	**118.27**
一、按行业门类分	**Grouped by Sectors**				
(一)工业	Industry	123.53	132.86	133.03	125.98
1. 采掘业	Excavation	111.72	88.49	110.67	117.06
2. 制造业	Manufacturing	123.26	132.14	132.26	124.48
3. 电力、煤气及水的生产和供应业	Power, Gas and Tap Water Production and Supply	138.28	158.97	153.89	149.2
(二)建筑业	Construction	69.93	125.45	109.74	87.96
(三)交通运输、仓储和邮政业	Transportation, Storage, Postal and Telecommunication Services	131.99	114.43	107.72	107.15
(四)批发和零售业	Wholesale and Retail Trade	107.88	108.64	113.09	111.96
(五)房地产业	Real Estate	103.48	103.67	106.67	104.32
(六)社会服务业	Social Services	84.45	87.5	109.45	131.25
(七)信息传输、计算机服务和软件	Information Transmission, Computer Service and Software	95.28	86	148.28	114
(八)住宿和餐饮业	Accommodation and Catering Trade	103.38	107.74	110.29	109.88
二、按企业登记注册类型分	**Grouped by Registration Categories**				
1. 国有企业	State-owned Enterprises	118.14	124.27	128.1	117.5
2. 集体企业	Collective-owned Enterprises	147.16	140.48	117.25	95.45
3. 股份合作企业	Share Holding Enterprises	104.15	108.58	122.29	119.03
4. 联营企业	Joint State-owned Enterprises	100	100	100	100
5. 有限责任公司	Companies with Limited Liabilities	98.01	111.02	112.24	100.31
6. 股份有限公司	Stock-holding Companies with Limited Liabilities	145.22	153.21	145.77	149.31
7. 私营企业	Private Enterprises	90.91	100	118.18	127.27
8. 其它内资企业	Other domestic investment Enterprises	50	50	150	100
9. 外商及港、澳、台投资企业	Foreign and Hong Kong, Macao and Taiwan Funded Companies	114.25	96.01	126.94	132.92
三、按企业规模分	**Grouped by Size of Enterprises**				
总大型	Large	132.94	148.92	145.29	136.55
中型	Medium	107.98	103.68	112.88	111.04
小型	Small	111.48	111.48	109.84	108.2

18 –8 企业集团一览表(2005 年)

LIST OF ENTERPRISES GROUP(2005)

序号 SerialNumber	企业集团名称	Name of Corporation	规模	Dimension
1	青岛万年集团	Qingdao Wannian Group	中型	Medium
2	青岛崂塑建材集团公司	Qingdao Laosu Construction Material Group Corporation	中型	Medium
3	青岛朗讯科技通讯企业有限公司	Qingdao Lucent Telecommunication Equipment Co. ,Ltd.	大型	Large
4	青岛崂发包装制品集团有限公司	Qingdao Laofa Packing Products Co. ,Ltd.	中型	Medium
5	青岛天泰集团	Tiantai Co. ,Ltd.	大型	Large
6	青岛天林集团有限公司	Qingdao Tianlin Group Co. ,Ltd.	其他	Others
7	裕龙集团有限公司	Yulong Co. ,Ltd.	中型	Medium
8	青岛金长江集团有限公司	Qingdao Jinchangjiang Group Co. ,Ltd.	大型	Large
9	青岛融商投资发展集团有限公司	Qingdao Absorbing Business and Investment Production Group Co. ,Ltd.	其他	Others
10	利群集团	Liqun Group	大型	Large
11	青岛汉缆集团	Qingdao Hanhe Cable Co. ,Ltd.	中型	Medium
12	南车四方机车车辆股份有限公司	CSR Sifang Locomotive and Rolling Stock Co. ,Ltd.	大型	Large
13	海尔集团	Haier Group	大型	Large
14	青岛亨达集团有限公司	Qingdao Humand Group Co. ,Ltd.	中型	Medium
15	青岛中泰集团有限责任公司	Qingdao Zhongtai Group Co. ,Ltd.	中型	Medium
16	青岛恒大实业集团公司	Qingdao Hengda Group Co. ,Ltd.	小型	Small
17	青岛亿路发集团有限公司	Qingdao Yilufa Co. ,Ltd.	大型	Large
18	青岛一木集团有限责任公司	Qingdao Yimu Group Co. ,Ltd.	中型	Medium
19	青岛长生集团股份有限公司	Qingdao Changsheng Group	中型	Medium
20	青岛华金集团	Qingdao Huajin Group	中型	Medium
21	青岛铸造机械集团公司	Qingdao Casting Machinery Co. ,Ltd.	中型	Medium
22	青岛海润自来水集团	Qingdao HighRunWater Supply Group	大型	Large
23	青岛热电集团	Qingdao Heat&Electricity Group	大型	Large
24	青岛华欧集团有限责任公司	Qingdao Huaou Group Co. ,Ltd.	中型	Medium
25	青岛开源集团	Qingdao Kaiyuan Group Co. ,Ltd.	中型	Medium
26	青岛亨达玻璃集团公司	Qingdao Hengda Glass Group Co. ,Ltd.	中型	Medium
27	青岛三元集团股份有限公司	Qingdao Sanyuan Co. ,Ltd.	小型	Small
28	青岛良木集团有限公司	Qingdao Liangmu Co. ,Ltd.	中型	Medium
29	青岛文昌企业(集团)公司	Qingdao Wenchang (Group) Corporation	中型	Medium
30	青岛万德集团股份有限公司	Qingdao Wande Co. ,Ltd.	中型	Medium
31	山东天象集团公司	Shandong Tianxiang Group Corporation	中型	Medium
32	青岛中大集团股份有限公司	Qingdao Zhongda Group Inc.	中型	Medium
33	青岛昌华集团股份有限公司	Qingdao Changhua Co. ,Ltd.	中型	Medium
34	青岛立大集团股份有限公司	Qingdao Lida Group Co. ,Ltd.	中型	Medium
35	青岛琅琊台酒业集团	Qingdao Lanyatai Group Co. ,Ltd.	中型	Medium
36	青岛三恩集团有限公司	Qingdao Sanen Group	大型	Large
37	青岛东生集团公司	Qingdao Dongsheng Group Corporation	中型	Medium
38	青岛英派斯集团有限公司	Qingdao Yingpaisi Group	小型	Small
39	山东大洋食品集团有限公司	Shandong Dayang Foods Co. ,Ltd.	中型	Medium
40	青岛雪达集团有限公司	Qingdao Xueda Co. ,Ltd.	中型	Medium
41	青岛红领集团有限公司	Qingdao Red Collar Group	中型	Medium
42	青岛中能集团有限公司	Qingdao Zhongneng Group Co. ,Ltd.	中型	Medium
43	青岛东佳纺机集团有限公司	Qingdao Dongjia Textile Machinery Group Co. ,Ltd.	中型	Medium
44	青岛迎春乐集团	Qingdao Yingchunle Group	小型	Small

经济类型	Economical Type	所在地区	Location
其他有限责任公司	Other Companies with Limited Liabilities	崂山区	Laoshan District
其他有限责任公司	Other Companies with Limited Liabilities	崂山区	Laoshan District
其他	Others	崂山区	Laoshan District
其他有限责任公司	Other Companies with Limited Liabilities	崂山区	Laoshan District
股份有限公司	Stock-holding Companies with Limited Liabilities	崂山区	Laoshan District
其他有限责任公司	Other Companies with Limited Liabilities	崂山区	Laoshan District
其他有限责任公司	Other Companies with Limited Liabilities	崂山区	Laoshan District
其他有限责任公司	Other Companies with Limited Liabilities	崂山区	Laoshan District
其他有限责任公司	Other Companies with Limited Liabilities	崂山区	Laoshan District
股份有限公司	Stock-holding Companies with Limited Liabilities	崂山区	Laoshan District
其他有限责任公司	Other Companies with Limited Liabilities	崂山区	Laoshan District
股份有限公司	Stock-holding Companies with Limited Liabilities	崂山区	Laoshan District
其他	Others	崂山区	Laoshan District
其他有限责任公司	Other Companies with Limited Liabilities	即墨市	Jimo
其他有限责任公司	Other Companies with Limited Liabilities	四方区	Sifang District
其他	Others	市南区	Shinan District
其他有限责任公司	Other Companies with Limited Liabilities	城阳区	Chengyang District
其他	Others	四方区	Sifang District
股份有限公司	Stock-holding Companies with Limited Liabilities	市北区	Shibei District
股份有限公司	Stock-holding Companies with Limited Liabilities	市北区	Shibei District
国有企业	State-owned	市北区	Shibei District
国有独资企业	Sole Funded Companies of State - owned	市南区	Shinan District
国有独资企业	Sole Funded Companies of State - owned	市北区	Shibei District
其他有限责任公司	Other Companies with Limited Liabilities	黄岛区	Huangdao District
其他有限责任公司	Other Companies with Limited Liabilities	市南区	Shinan District
其他有限责任公司	Other Companies with Limited Liabilities	市北区	Shibei District
股份有限公司	Stock-holding Companies with Limited Liabilities	市北区	Shibei District
其他有限责任公司	Other Companies with Limited Liabilities	城阳区	Chengyang District
其他	Others	李沧区	Licang District
股份有限公司	Stock-holding Companies with Limited Liabilities	胶南市	Jiaonan
其他	Others	平度市	Pingdu
股份有限公司	Stock-holding Companies with Limited Liabilities	四方区	Sifang District
股份有限公司	Stock-holding Companies with Limited Liabilities	莱西市	Laixi
股份有限公司	Stock-holding Companies with Limited Liabilities	平度市	Pingdu
股份有限公司	Stock-holding Companies with Limited Liabilities	胶南市	Jiaonan
中外合资企业	Sino-foreign joint Ventures	城阳市	Chengyang District
其他	Others	莱西市	Laixi
其他	Others	城阳区	Chengyang District
其他有限责任公司	Other Companies with Limited Liabilities	胶州市	Jiaozhou
其他有限责任公司	Other Companies with Limited Liabilities	即墨市	Jimo
其他	Others	即墨市	Jimo
其他	Others	李沧区	Licang District
其他有限责任公司	Other Companies with Limited Liabilities	胶南市	Jiaonan
其他有限责任公司	Other Companies with Limited Liabilities	城阳区	Chengyang District

18 –8 续表 1
continued

序号 SerialNumber	企业集团名称	Name of Corporation	规模	Dimension
45	青岛十梅庵集团公司	Qingdao Shimeian Group Corporation	其他	Others
46	青岛巴龙集团有限公司	Qingdao baron Co. ,Ltd.	中型	Medium
47	青岛海丰集团	Qingdao Haifeng Group	中型	Medium
48	青岛琴畅集团股份有限公司	Qingdao Qinchang Co. ,Ltd.	中型	Medium
49	青岛开达实业集团有限公司	Qingdao Kaida Co. ,Ltd.	其他	Others
50	青岛利客来商贸集团股份有限公司	Qingdao Likelai trade Inc.	大型	Large
51	青岛银河集团	Qingdao Yinhe Group Co. ,Ltd.	其他	Others
52	青岛雁山集团有限公司	Qingdao Yanshan Group Co. ,Ltd.	中型	Medium
53	青岛中房集团股份有限公司	Qingdao Zhongfang Group Co. ,Ltd.	大型	Large
54	青岛麦迪绅集团股份有限公司	Qingdao Maidishen Group Co. ,Ltd.	小型	Small
55	青岛万福集团	Qingdao Wanfu Group	中型	Medium
56	青岛物华集团股份有限公司	Qingdao Wuhua Group Co. ,Ltd.	大型	Large
57	青岛振华工业集团有限公司	Qingdao Zhenhua Industry Co. ,Ltd.	中型	Medium
58	山东绮丽集团	Shandong Qili Group Corporation	大型	Large
59	山东机械设备进出口集团公司	Shandong Mechanical Equipment Group Corporation	大型	Large
60	青岛市新华书店(集团)有限责任公司	Qingdao Xinhua Bookstore(Group)	大型	Large
61	青岛泰能燃气集团	Qingdao Taineng Gas Group	大型	Large
62	青岛园林集团有限公司	Qingdao Yunlin Group Co. ,Ltd.	中型	Medium
63	山东集力集团有限公司	Shandong Jili Group Co. ,Ltd.	小型	Small
64	青岛银海旅游集团公司	Qingdao Yinhai Travel Group Corporation	其他	Others
65	青岛华和天润集团	Qingdao Huahe Tianrun Group	小型	Small
66	青岛喜盈门集团	Qingdao Xiyingmen Group Corporation	大型	Large
67	青岛正进集团	Qingdao Zhengjin Import & Export Co. ,Ltd.	大型	Large
68	山东红建建安集团公司	Shandong Hongjian Jianan Group Co. ,Ltd.	大型	Large
69	青岛裕源集团公司	Qingdao Yuyuan Group Corporation	其他	Others
70	青岛交运集团	Qingdao Transport Group	大型	Large
71	华仁世纪集团有限公司	Huaren Shiji Group Co. ,Ltd.	其他	Others
72	青岛国人集团有限公司	Qingdao Sinoer Group Co. ,Ltd.	大型	Large
73	青岛信达荣昌置业集团股份有限公司	Qingdao Reachamp Real Estate Group Inc.	其他	Others
74	青岛益佳国际贸易有限公司	Qingdao Yijia Group Co. ,Ltd.	大型	Large
75	青岛磊鑫集团有限公司	Qingdao Leixin Group Co. ,Ltd.	中型	Medium
76	青岛创统科技集团有限公司	Qingdao Chuang Tong Science&Technology Group Co. ,Ltd.	中型	Medium
77	青岛市胶州建设集团有限公司	Qingdao Jiaozhou Construction Group Co. ,Ltd.	大型	Large
78	欧美投资集团	Europe and United States Investment Group	大型	Large
79	青岛金王集团	Qingdao Jinwang Group	中型	Medium
80	青岛康大外贸集团有限公司	Qingdao Kangda Foreign Trade Co. ,Ltd.	小型	Small
81	青岛亚星集团有限公司	Qingdao Yaxing Group Co. ,Ltd.	其他	Others
82	青岛工艺美术集团公司	Qingdao Art and Craft Group Co. ,Ltd.	中型	Medium
83	青岛福瀛建设集团	Qingdao Fuying Construction Group	中型	Medium
84	青岛亿联集团股份有限公司	Qingdao Yilian Group Co. ,Ltd.	中型	Medium
85	青岛九联集团股份有限公司	Qingdao Jiulian Group Co. ,Ltd.	大型	Large
86	青岛建设集团	Qingdao Construction Group	大型	Large
87	青岛红福集团有限公司	Qingdao Hongfu Group Co. ,Ltd.	中型	Medium
88	山东六和集团有限公司	Shandong Liuhe Co. ,Ltd.	中型	Medium

经济类型	Economical Type	所在地区	Location
其他	Others	李沧区	Licang District
其他有限责任公司	Other Companies with Limited Liabilities	市南区	Shinan District
股份有限公司	Stock-holding Companies with Limited Liabilities	市南区	Shinan District
股份有限公司	Stock-holding Companies with Limited Liabilities	莱西市	Laixi
其他有限责任公司	Other Companies with Limited Liabilities	市北区	Shibei District
股份有限公司	Stock-holding Companies with Limited Liabilities	李沧区	Licang District
其他有限责任公司	Other Companies with Limited Liabilities	市南区	Shinan District
其他有限责任公司	Other Companies with Limited Liabilities	四方区	Sifang District
股份有限公司	Stock-holding Companies with Limited Liabilities	市南区	Shinan District
股份有限公司	Stock-holding Companies with Limited Liabilities	市南区	Shinan District
股份有限公司	Stock-holding Companies with Limited Liabilities	莱西市	Laixi
股份有限公司	Stock-holding Companies with Limited Liabilities	市北区	Shibei District
其他有限责任公司	Other Companies with Limited Liabilities	胶南市	Jiaonan
国有企业	State-owned	市南区	Shinan District
国有企业	State-owned	市南区	Shinan District
国有独资企业	Sole Funded Companies of State-owned	市南区	Shinan District
国有独资企业	Sole Funded Companies of State-owned	市南区	Shinan District
国有独资企业	Sole Funded Companies of State-owned	市南区	Shinan District
其他有限责任公司	Other Companies with Limited Liabilities	黄岛区	Huangdao District
其他	Others	市南区	Shinan District
其他有限责任公司	Other Companies with Limited Liabilities	市南区	Shinan District
其他有限责任公司	Other Companies with Limited Liabilities	城阳区	Chengyang District
其他有限责任公司	Other Companies with Limited Liabilities	城阳区	Chengyang District
其他	Others	黄岛区	Huangdao District
国有企业	State-owned	市南区	Shinan District
国有企业	State-owned	市北区	Shibei District
港澳台合资企业	Hongkong, Macao and Taiwan joint Ventures	市南区	Shinan District
其他有限责任公司	Other Companies with Limited Liabilities	市北区	Shibei District
股份有限公司	Stock-holding Companies with Limited Liabilities	市南区	Shinan District
国有独资企业	Sole Funded Companies of State-owned	市南区	Shinan District
其他有限责任公司	Other Companies with Limited Liabilities	城阳区	Chengyang District
其他	Others	黄岛区	Huangdao District
其他有限责任公司	Other Companies with Limited Liabilities	胶州市	Jiaozhou
其他有限责任公司	Other Companies with Limited Liabilities	市南区	Shinan District
其他有限责任公司	Other Companies with Limited Liabilities	市北区	Shibei District
其他有限责任公司	Other Companies with Limited Liabilities	胶南市	Jiaonan
中外合资企业	Sino-foreign joint Ventures	市南区	Shinan District
其他	Others	四方区	Sifang District
其他有限责任公司	Other Companies with Limited Liabilities	黄岛区	Huangdao District
股份有限公司	Stock-holding Companies with Limited Liabilities	胶南市	Jiaonan
股份有限公司	Stock-holding Companies with Limited Liabilities	莱西市	Laixi
国有企业	State-owned	市南区	Shinan District
其他有限责任公司	Other Companies with Limited Liabilities	城阳区	Chengyang District
其他有限责任公司	Other Companies with Limited Liabilities	城阳区	Chengyang District

18-8 续表2
continued

序号 SerialNumber	企业集团名称	Name of Corporation	规模	Dimension
89	青岛营海建设集团有限公司	Qingdao Yinghai Construction Group Co. ,Ltd.	小型	Small
90	青岛浩源集团有限公司	Qingdao Haoyuan Group Co. ,Ltd.	中型	Medium
91	青岛市市政工程集团有限公司	Qingdao Municipal Administration Project Co. ,Ltd.	中型	Medium
92	青岛福日集团	Qingdao Furi Group	中型	Medium
93	青岛天一集团有限公司	Qingdao Tianyi Group Co. ,Ltd.	中型	Medium
94	新华锦集团	Jinyi Textile Co. ,Ltd.	大型	Large
95	青岛康太源集团有限公司	Qingdao Kantaiyuan Group Co. ,Ltd.	中型	Medium
96	青岛东李企业集团公司	Qingdao Dongli Group Co. ,Ltd.	其他	Others
97	青岛海悦集团有限公司	Qingdao Haiyue Group Co. ,Ltd.	小型	Small
98	青岛公交集团	Qingdao Public Bus Group Corporation	大型	Large
99	青岛金翔矿业集团公司	Qingdao Jinxiang Mining Group Corporation	中型	Medium
100	青岛市房产置业集团有限公司	Qingdao Real Estate Group Co. ,Ltd.	大型	Large
101	山东省机械进出口集团	Shandong Machinery Import & Export Group Corporation	大型	Large
102	一汽解放青岛汽车厂	Qingdao Auto Factory	大型	Large
103	青岛海晶化工集团	Qingdao Hygain Chemical Group	大型	Large
104	青岛捷能电工电子集团	Jieneng Electronic Co. ,Ltd.	大型	Large
105	双星集团	Doublestar Group	大型	Large
106	海信集团	Hisense Group Co. ,Ltd.	大型	Large
107	青岛黄海橡胶集团	Qingdao Huanghai Rubber Group	大型	Large
108	青岛即发集团	Qingdao Jifa Co. ,Ltd.	大型	Large
109	青岛双蝶集团	Qingdao Double Butterfly Co. ,Ltd.	中型	Medium
110	青岛变压器集团	Qingdao Transformer Co. ,Ltd.	大型	Large
111	颐中集团	ETSONG Group	大型	Large
112	青岛海湾集团	Qingdao Haiwan Group Co. ,Ltd.	大型	Large
113	青岛星火纺机纺织集团股份有限公司	Qingdao Xinghuo Textile Machinery Inc.	大型	Large
114	青岛红星化工集团	Qingdao RedStar Chemical Group	大型	Large
115	青特集团有限公司	Qingte Group Co. ,Ltd.	大型	Large
116	青岛中集集装箱制造有限公司	Qingdao Zhongji Container Making Co. ,Ltd.	大型	Large
117	青岛广源发集团	Qingdao Guangyuanfa corp	大型	Large
118	山东省对外贸易集团	Shandong Foreign trade Co. ,Ltd.	大型	Large
119	青岛纺联集团	Qingdao Textile Co. ,Ltd.	小型	Small
120	青岛海珊服装服饰集团	Qingdao Haishan Group	大型	Large
121	青岛啤酒集团	Tsingtao Brewery Co. ,Ltd.	大型	Large
122	青岛维客集团	Qingdao Weekly Co. ,Ltd.	大型	Large
123	青岛宏大纺织机械有限责任公司	Qingdao Hongda Weave Machinery Co. ,Ltd.	中型	Medium
124	青岛钢铁控股集团有限责任公司	Qingdao Iron and Steel Group Company	大型	Large
125	青岛澳柯玛集团	Qingdao AUCMA Group	大型	Large
126	青岛港集团	Qingdao Port Group	大型	Large
127	青岛泰发集团	Qingdao Taifa Group	大型	Large
128	山东海丰国际航运集团有限公司	Shandong Haifeng Co. ,Ltd.	小型	Small
129	中国石化集团青岛石油化工有限责任公司	Qingdao Petrochemical Co. ,Ltd.	大型	Large

经济类型	Economical Type	所在地区	Location
其他有限责任公司	Other Companies with Limited Liabilities	胶州市	Jiaozhou
其他有限责任公司	Other Companies with Limited Liabilities	城阳区	Chengyang District
国有独资企业	Sole Funded Companies of State-owned	市南区	Shinan District
其他有限责任公司	Other Companies with Limited Liabilities	市南区	Shinan District
其他有限责任公司	Other Companies with Limited Liabilities	胶南市	Jiaonan
国有独资企业	Sole Funded Companies of State-owned	市南区	Shinan District
其他有限责任公司	Other Companies with Limited Liabilities	李沧区	Licang District
其他	Others	李沧区	Licang District
其他有限责任公司	Other Companies with Limited Liabilities	即墨市	Jimo
国有独资企业	Sole Funded Companies of State-owned	市南区	Shinan District
其他	Others	平度市	Pingdu
国有独资企业	Sole Funded Companies of State-owned	市北区	Shibei District
国有企业	State-owned	市南区	Shinan District
国有企业	State-owned	李沧区	Licang District
其他有限责任公司	Other Companies with Limited Liabilities	四方区	Sifang District
股份有限公司	Stock-holding Companies with Limited Liabilities	四方区	Sifang District
国有独资企业	Sole Funded Companies of State-owned	市南区	Shinan District
国有独资企业	Sole Funded Companies of State-owned	市南区	Shinan District
国有独资企业	Sole Funded Companies of State-owned	李沧区	Licang District
股份有限公司	Stock-holding Companies with Limited Liabilities	即墨市	Jimo
股份有限公司	Stock-holding Companies with Limited Liabilities	市北区	Shibei District
其他有限责任公司	Other Companies with Limited Liabilities	城阳区	Chengyang District
国有独资企业	Sole Funded Companies of State-owned	市北区	Shibei District
国有独资企业	Sole Funded Companies of State-owned	市南区	Shinan District
股份有限公司	Stock-holding Companies with Limited Liabilities	胶南市	Jiaonan
国有独资企业	Sole Funded Companies of State-owned	市北区	Shibei District
其他有限责任公司	Other Companies with Limited Liabilities	城阳区	Chengyang District
中外合资企业	Sino-foreign joint Ventures	黄岛区	Huangdao District
其他有限责任公司	Other Companies with Limited Liabilities	城阳区	Chengyang District
国有独资企业	Sole Funded Companies of State-owned	市南区	Shinan District
其他有限责任公司	Other Companies with Limited Liabilities	市北区	Shibei District
其他有限责任公司	Other Companies with Limited Liabilities	市南区	Shinan District
国有独资企业	Sole Funded Companies of State-owned	市南区	Shinan District
股份有限公司	Stock-holding Companies with Limited Liabilities	李沧区	Licang District
其他有限责任公司	Other Companies with Limited Liabilities	四方区	Sifang District
其他有限责任公司	Other Companies with Limited Liabilities	李沧区	Licang District
其他	Others	黄岛区	Huangdao District
国有企业	State-owned	市北区	Shibei District
股份有限公司	Stock-holding Companies with Limited Liabilities	胶南市	Jiaonan
其他有限责任公司	Other Companies with Limited Liabilities	黄岛区	Huangdao District
其他有限责任公司	Other Companies with Limited Liabilities	李沧区	Licang District

18－9 企业集团主要经济指标(2005 年)

MAJOR ECONOMICAL INDICATORS OF ENTERPRISES GROUP(2005)

		单位数 Member of Company	从业人员 Laborers (person)	资产总计 Assets	固定资产原价本年实际 Original Value of Fixed Assets	长期投资 Long-time Investment
合计	**Total**	**129**	**448 503**	**25 274 085**	**9 270 991**	**2 091 076**
按审批部门分	**Grouped by Examining and Approving Department**					
国务院主管部门	Charged by State Council	1	8 214	1 346 089	481 740	254 662
省级人民政府	Charged by Provincial Government	23	223 839	15 137 477	6 144 507	1 182 358
省级政府主管部门	Charge by Department of Provincial Government	10	11 353	713 193	213 455	63 061
其他	Others	95	205 097	8 077 326	2 431 289	590 995
按控股情况分	**Grouped by Holding Stock**					
国有绝对控股	State Absolute Holding Stock	36	192 450	13 611 984	6 256 414	1 169 543
国有相对控股	State Relative Holding Stock	5	18 494	456 514	169 354	42 981
集体绝对控股	Collectivity Absolute Holding Stock	9	63 925	5 569 933	1 280 884	544 869
集体相对控股	Collectivity Relative Holding Stock	5	21 189	239 334	91 136	19 263
其他	Others	74	152 445	5 396 320	1 473 203	314 420
按企业集团主营行业分	**Grouped by Sectors**					
工业	Industry	88	347 491	19 482 976	7 070 343	1 766 801
建筑业	Construction	10	41 712	1 214 465	228 039	62 427
交通运输、仓储和邮政业	Transportation Post and Telecommunications	5	35 931	1 902 783	1 523 162	59 559
批发和零售业	Wholesale and Retail	12	19 076	1 590 231	331 993	127 044
金融业	Finance	2	1 425	142 632	38 458	19 518
房地产业	Real Estate Trade	11	2 721	934 962	77 994	55 100
其他	Others	1	147	6 036	1 002	627
按登记注册类型分	**Grouped by Economy Categories**					
国有企业	State-owned	9	38 381	3 071 805	1 570 863	98 652
国有独资公司	Sole Funded Companies of State-owned	18	126 027	8 159 725	3 663 275	959 060
其他有限责任公司	Other Companies with Limited Liabilities	53	136 203	5 431 176	1 862 211	323 265
股份有限公司	Stock-holding Companies with Limied Liabilities	27	64 663	2 440 305	803 534	150 595
中外合资企业	Sino-foreign Joint Ventures	3	2 553	221 081	39 649	8 644
港澳台合资企业	Hongkong, Macco and Taiwan Joint Ventures	1	421	73 655	17 868	0
其他	Others	18	80 255	5 876 338	1 313 591	550 860
按企业规模分	**Grouped by Size of Enterprises**					
大型	Large	55	345 607	21 903 429	8 289 107	1 878 434
中型	Medium	51	78 331	2 202 716	672 575	151 950
小型	Small	12	15 095	642 711	199 211	27 624
其他	Others	11	9 470	525 229	110 098	33 068

短期投资 Short-time Investment	存货 Inventory	流动资产年平均余额 Annual Average Balance of Circulating Funds	应收帐款 Loans Lending Abroad	年末负债合计 Year-end Totall Liabilities	其中:流动负债 of which:Circulating Liabilities
91 713	**4 109 060**	**14 865 359**	**2 884 712**	**15 917 176**	**14 431 645**
0	322 379	663 147	37 829	659 811	645 967
73 646	2 595 004	9 189 112	1 608 133	9 412 860	8 565 970
2 175	111 892	399 639	166 579	580 778	540 819
15 892	1 079 785	4 613 461	1 072 171	5 263 727	4 678 889
33 496	2 021 243	7 170 079	1 264 840	8 365 701	7 435 884
108	94 002	273 349	59 699	321 902	271 915
54 099	1 002 141	3 988 639	935 010	3 661 139	3 531 274
83	54 082	134 120	18 428	155 637	144 052
3 927	937 592	3 299 172	606 735	3 412 797	3 048 520
66 121	3 406 442	11 948 137	2 227 290	12 009 703	11 059 422
16 581	177 865	770 209	200 118	892 726	836 048
8 008	27 219	427 965	73 459	919 045	572 575
957	287 813	942 895	340 950	1 273 704	1 239 681
15	13 665	43 902	2 760	86 389	67 430
31	195 202	729 208	39 873	731 367	652 247
0	854	3 043	262	4 242	4 242
22 597	241 696	1 436 194	313 691	1 879 117	1 536 521
10 438	1 484 759	4 191 405	776 283	4 762 620	4 375 727
1 082	797 042	3 275 181	453 304	3 461 802	3 051 277
633	479 092	1 453 807	228 476	1 771 430	1 585 628
10	24 933	172 954	29 164	152 969	149 718
0	12 175	45 024	6 169	41 592	37 316
56 953	1 069 363	4 290 794	1 077 625	3 847 646	3 695 458
90 400	3 565 345	12 891 841	2 446 396	13 671 473	12 508 362
1 271	355 275	1 268 840	343 846	1 456 390	1 301 793
22	82 566	393 444	64 290	410 986	304 180
20	105 874	311 234	30 180	378 327	317 310

18－9 续表
continued

		年末少数股东权益(万元) Year-end Share-holder Liabilities	年末股东(所有者)权益 (万元) Year-end Share-holder Equity	主营业务收入 Major Business Income	主营业务税金及附加(万元) Pre-tax and Related Payment of Major Business	出口销售总额 Value of Exports
合计	**Total**	**1 019 011**	**8 337 898**	**33 377 966**	**634 073**	**4 581 195**
按审批部门分	**Grouped by Examining and Approving Department**					
国务院主管部门	Charged by State Council	0	686 278	811 071	304 502	631
省级人民政府	Charged by Provincial Government	894 089	4 830 528	23 929 672	243 535	2 552 310
省级政府主管部门	Charge by Department of Frovincial Government	59 704	72 711	928 969	3 208	638 842
其他	Others	65 218	2 748 381	7 708 254	82 828	1 389 412
按控股情况分	**Grouped by Holding Stock**					
国有绝对控股	State Absolute Holding Stock	334 777	4 911 506	13 852 740	546 400	2 093 260
国有相对控股	State Relative Holding Stock	0	134 612	305 906	1 607	105 500
集体绝对控股	Collectivity Absolute Holding Stock	585 124	1 323 670	11 401 309	24 622	1 119 889
集体相对控股	Collectivity Relative Holding Stock	0	83 697	764 814	4 439	82 306
其他	Others	99 110	1 884 413	7 053 197	57 005	1 180 240
按企业集团主营行业分	**Grouped by Sectors**					
工业	Industry	728 211	6 745 062	28 589 431	522 387	3 316 576
建筑业	Construction	3 386	318 353	934 014	30 134	258
交通运输、仓储和邮政业	Transportation Post and Telecommunications	228 916	754 822	755 715	53 651	0
批发和零售业	Wholesale and Retail	53 004	263 523	2 735 317	3 789	1 264 361
金融业	Finance	0	56 243	88 085	6 795	0
房地产业	Real Estate Trade	5 494	198 101	274 108	17 270	0
其他	Others	0	1 794	1 296	47	0
按登记注册类型分	**Grouped by Economy Categories**					
国有企业	State-owned	229 268	963 420	2 295 724	67 975	623 002
国有独资公司	Sole Funded Companies of State-owned	101 000	3 296 105	8 041 973	444 810	1 372 225
其他有限责任公司	Other Companies with Limited Liabilities	62 726	1 906 648	7 760 782	67 125	675 906
股份有限公司	Stock-holding Companies with Limied Liabilities	49 689	619 186	3 240 358	24 536	473 863
中外合资企业	Sino-foreign Joint Ventures	0	68 112	262 970	2 802	194 949
港澳台合资企业	Hongkong, Macco and Taiwan Joint Ventures	0	32 063	11 455	386	0
其他	Others	576 328	1 452 364	11 764 704	26 439	1 241 250
按企业规模分	**Grouped by Size of Enterprises**					
大型	Large	948 845	7 283 111	29 610 029	598 852	3 960 548
中型	Medium	50 226	696 100	3 058 648	13 958	494 138
小型	Small	15 483	216 242	468 905	5 943	90 564
其他	Others	4 457	142 445	240 384	15 320	35 945

职工教育费 Cost for Staff's Education	利润总额 Total Profits	应交所得税 Income Taxes Payable	应交增值税 Added Value Tax Payable	固定资产投资完成额 Investment of Fixed Assets	研究开发费用 Expenditure for Research and Development
9 342	**864 570**	**258 992**	**665 620**	**672 368**	**738 543**
609	62 128	23 644	86 028	47 537	5 995
4 564	408 626	140 731	469 052	404 022	684 338
250	46 157	9 327	3 435	5 626	806
3 919	347 659	85 290	107 105	215 183	47 404
4 831	324 422	144 965	377 894	396 792	213 947
109	-29	349	1 838	6 662	1 691
1 615	154 574	35 628	178 152	98 633	480 981
19	18 079	3 212	10 509	4 049	308
2 768	367 524	74 838	97 227	166 232	41 616
7 619	644 482	178 584	628 953	463 791	729 763
589	17 879	8 130	948	16 630	115
688	116 107	41 580	1 646	156 781	8 233
270	58 156	17 154	33 163	20 226	250
11	5 899	1 632	262	0	12
160	22 042	11 911	643	14 938	170
5	5	1	5	2	0
1 117	136 758	47 483	2 615	162 033	9 876
2 957	190 258	82 009	317 078	174 563	191 690
2 759	161 893	51 404	95 495	137 418	29 358
792	119 382	34 904	49 825	99 755	28 567
25	18 946	2 761	827	2 950	335
23	280	77	0	23	0
1 669	237 053	40 354	199 780	95 626	478 717
8 086	714 900	219 948	627 457	618 717	718 942
875	106 389	25 416	31 986	47 766	17 635
231	26 354	6 764	3 347	1 356	1 459
150	16 927	6 864	2 830	4 529	507

18－10 青岛市驰名商标和著名商标一览表
LIST OF QINGDAO FAMOUS BRANDS

序号 Precedence	商标名称	Brand Name	主要产品	Major Product	认定时间 Granted Time	所在地区	Location
1	海尔	Haier	电冰箱	Refrigerator	1991	崂山区	Laoshan District
2	利渤海尔	LIBHL	电冰箱	Refrigerator	1991	崂山区	Laoshan District
3	青岛啤酒	TSINGTAO BEER	啤酒	Beer	1991	市北区	Shibei District
4	双星	DOUBLESTAR	胶靴	Sports Shoes	1995	市南区	Shinan District
5	澳柯玛	AUCMA	冰柜	Freezer	1997	黄岛区	Huangdao District
6	海信	Hisense	电视机	Television	1999	市南区	Shinan District
7	即发	JASFEEL	针织服装	Knitting Garments	2002	即墨市	Jimo
8	喜盈门	XIYINGMEN	针织毛巾	Towel	2004	城阳区	Chengyang District
9	英派斯	IMPULSE	跑步机	Running Machine	2004	城阳区	Chengyang District
10	壹枝笔	A pen	香烟	Tobacco	2004	市北区	Shibei District
11	白雪	Snowhite	修正液	Correction Fluid	2004	黄岛区	Huangdao District
12	亨达	HUMAND	皮鞋	Leather Shoes	2005	即墨市	Jimo
13	红领	Rcollar	服装	Garments	2005	即墨市	Jimo
14	哈德门	Hatamen	香烟	Tobacco	2005	市北区	Shibei District
15	六合	LIUHE	饲料	Feed	2005	城阳区	Chengyang District

附　录

APPENDIX

附 录:

主要统计指标解释

1. 国内生产总值

指一个国家(或地区)所有常住单位在一定时期内生产活动的最终成果。它的英文全称 GrossDomesticProduct(GDP)，考虑到Domestic 一词有“国内、地区、当地、家里”等多种涵义，故国内外一些专家和学者认为，将全国和地区的 GDP 一律称为国内生产总值显然不恰当，香港特别行政区统计部门在使用这一概念时就是用的“本地生产总值”。我国习惯上将国家和地区的 GDP 统称为国内生产总值。为了更加准确和规范化地表述，国家统计局决定自 2004 年起将地区的 GDP 中文名称作如下调整：地区 GDP 的中文名称改为“地区生产总值”；特定地区的 GDP 用行政区的名字作定语，如“青岛市生产总值”简称为“青岛市 GDP”。各地 GDP 称为“各地生产总值”。

2. 人均 GDP

人均 GDP 是一定时期内 GDP 与同期人口平均数的比值。按照国际标准，人口平均数应该是同期平均常住人口。我国在核算制度中也规定，无论是国家还是地区，人口数都采用常住人口。国家统计局规定从 2004 年开始，过去采用户籍人口计算人均 GDP 的地区，作为过渡性措施，可在两年内同时计算两种口径的人均 GDP(数据后面必须注明是什么口径)，两年后取消按户籍人口计算的人均 GDP。我市采用常住人口计算人均 GDP。

3. 三次产业

根据社会生产活动历史发展的顺序对产业结构的划分，产品直接取自自然界的部门称为第一产业，对初级产品进行再加工的部门称为第二产业，为生产和消费提供各种服务的部门称为第三产业。它是世界上通用的产业结构分类，但各国的划分不尽一致。我国的三次产业划分是：

第一产业：农业(包括种植业、林业、牧业、副业和渔业)。

第二产业：工业(包括采掘工业、制造业、自来水、电力、蒸汽、热水、煤气)和建筑业。

第三产业：除第一、第二产业以外的其他各业。

4. 农业总产值

农业总产值是以货币表现的农、林、牧、渔业全部产品的总量，它反映一定时期内农业生产的总规模和总成果。

农、林、牧、渔业的统计范围是：

(1)农业包括农作物种植业和其他农业。

农作物种植业包括谷物、豆类、薯类、棉、油料、糖料、麻类、烟叶、蔬菜、药材、瓜类和其他农作物的种植，以及茶园、桑园、果园的生产经营。其他农业包括采集野生植物的果实、纤维、树胶、树脂、油料以及柴草、野生药材、菌类等及农民家庭兼营的商品性工业。

(2)林业包括林木的栽培(不包括茶园、桑园和果园的栽培、管理和收获等活动)、林产品的采集和村及村以下合作经济组织和农户的竹木采伐。

(3)牧业包括除渔业养殖以外的一切动物饲养和放牧，以及野生动物的捕猎和饲养。

(4)渔业包括水生动物和海藻类植物的养殖和捕捞。

5. 粮食产量

指稻谷、小麦、玉米、高粱等谷物及薯类和豆类的全社会产量。包括国有经济经营的、集体统一经营的和农民家庭经营的粮食产量，还包括工矿企业办的农场和其他生产单位的产量。其产量计算方法，豆类按去豆荚后的干豆计算；薯类(包括甘薯和马铃薯，不包括芋头和木薯)按 5 公斤鲜薯折 1 公斤粮食计算。城市郊区作为蔬菜的薯类(如马铃薯等)按鲜品计算，并且不作粮食统计。其他粮食一律按脱粒后的原粮计算。

6. 水产品产量

指人工养殖的水产品和天然生长的水产品的捕捞量.包括海水的鱼类、虾蟹类、贝类和藻类以及内陆水域的鱼类、虾蟹类和贝类，不包括淡水生植物。

7. 猪、牛、羊肉产量

指当年出栏并已屠宰、除去头蹄下水后带骨头肉(即胴体重)的重量。其统计范围为全社会。

8. 农用化肥施用量

指本年内实际用于农业生产的化肥数量，包括氮肥、磷肥、钾肥和复合肥。化肥施用量要求按折纯量计算数量。折纯量是指把氮肥、磷肥、钾肥分别按含氮、含五氧化二磷、含氧化钾的百分之百成分进行折算后的数量。复合肥按其所含主要成分折算。

公式：折纯量=实物量×某种化肥有效成分含量的百分比

9. 农业机械总动力

指用于农、林、牧、渔业生产的各种动力机械的动力总和。动力机械包括耕作、排灌、种植、植物保护、收获、农产品加工、运输、畜牧、渔业、农田水利等各种机械。不包括专门用于乡办工业、基本建设、非农业运输、科学试验和教学等非农业生产方面用的动力机械与作业机械的数量。

10. 工业总产值

是以货币表现的工业企业在一定日棚内生产的已出售或可供出售工业产品总量，它是反映一定时间内工业生产的总规模和总水平。

11. 工业销售产值

是以货币表现的工业企业在一定时期内销售的本企业生产的工业产品产量。包括已销售的成品、半成品价值，以及对外提供的工业性作业价值和对本单位基本建设部门、生活福利部门等提供的产品和工业性作业及自制设备的价值。

12. 工业增加值

指工业企业在报告期内以货币表现的工业生产活动的最终成果。

13. 货(客)运量

指在一定时期内，各运输部门实际运送的货物(旅客)数量。是反映运输业为国民经济和人民生活服务的数量指标，也是制定和检查运输生产计划，研究运输发展规模和速度的重要指标。货运按吨计算，客运按人计算。货物不论运输距离长短，货物类别，均按实际重量统计；旅客不论行程远近或票价多少，均按一人一次作为客运量统计。半价票、小孩票也按一人统计。

14. 货物(旅客)周转量

指在一定时期内，由各种运输工具运送的货物(旅客)数量与其相应运输距离的乘积之总和，是反映运输业生产总成果的重要指标，也是编制和检查运输生产计划，计算运输效益、劳动生产率以及核算运输单位成本的主要基础资料。通常以吨公里和人公里为计算单位。计算货物周转量通常按发出站与到达站之间的最短距离，也就是计费距离计算。

15. 邮电业务总量

指以货币表现的邮电部门用于传递信息和提供其他邮电服务的总数量。它综合反映了一定时期邮电工作的总成果，是研究邮电业务量构成和发展趋势的重要指标。根据邮电管理体制不同，分为中央国营业务总量和地方国营业务总量。它用各种邮电分类业务量，如函件件数、电报份数、长话张数、市内电话和农村电话的年均户数、订销报刊累计份数等，分别乘以相应的平均单位(不变价)，加总后再加上出租电路和设备的收入、代用户维护电话交换机和线路等设备的收入、其他业务收入求得。

16. 全社会固定资产投资

是国民经济再生产活动的一个重要部分。通过建造和购置固定资产的活动，国民经济不断采用先进技术装备，建立新兴部门，进一步调整经济结构和生产力的地区分布，增强经济实力，为改善人民物质文化生活创造物质条件。固定资产投资额是以货币形式表现的在一定时期内建造和购置固定资产的工作量以及与此有关的费用总称。它是反映固定资产投资规模、结构和发展速度的综合性指标。按照现行国家统计制度，全社会固定资产投资包括基本建设、更新改造、房地产开发、城乡集体经济单位、城乡私人建房和其他经济单位投资。

17. 新增固定资产

又称交付使用的固定资产，是指已经完成建造和购置过程，并已交付生产或使用单位的固定资产价值。新增固定资产是表示固定资产投资成果的价值量指标，也是反映建设进度、计算固定资产投资效果的必要数据。

18. 房屋施工面积

是指报告期内施工的全部房屋建筑面积。包括本期新开工的面积和上期开工跨入本期继续施工的房屋面积，以及上期已停缓建在本期恢复施工的房屋面积。本期竣工和本期施工后又停缓建的房屋，其建筑面积仍计入本期房屋施工面积中。

19. 房屋竣工面积

是指在报告期内房屋建筑按照设计要求全部完工，达到住人和使用条件，经验收鉴定合格(或达到竣工验收标准)，正式移交使用单位的各栋房屋建筑面积的总和。

20. 建筑业总产值

是以货币形式表现的建筑业企业在一定时期内生产的建筑业产品的总和。建筑业总产值包括：建筑工程产值、安装工程产值、房屋构筑物修理产值和非标准设备制造产值。

21. 建筑业增加值

指建筑业企业在报告期内以货币形式表现的建筑业生产经营活动的最终成果。具体计算方式为：[建筑业增加值=本年提取的固定资产折旧+主营业务应付工资+主营业务应付福利费、税金+工程结算税金及附加+工程结算利润]

22. 社会消费品零售总额

指各种经济类型的批发和零售业、住宿和餐饮业以及其他行业对城乡居民和社会集团的消费品零售额总和。该指标从2003年开始不再包括制造业零售额和农民对非农居民的零售额。

23. 商品购进总额

指从本企业(单位)以外的单位和个人购进(包括从国外直接进口)作为转卖或加工后转卖的商品。这个指标反映批发零售贸易业从国内、国外市场上购进商品的总量。商品购进总额包括：(1)从工农业生产者购进的商品；(2)从出版社、报社的出版发行部门购进的图书、杂志和报纸；(3)从各种类型的批发零售贸易企业(单位)购进的商品；(4)从其他单位购进的商品，如从机关、团体、企业、单位购进的剩余物资，从餐饮业、服务业购进的商品，从海关、市场管理部门购进的缉私和没收的商品，向居民收购的废旧商品等；(5)从国(境)外直接进口的商品，但不包括企业(单位)为自身经营用和未通过买卖行为而收入的商品以及销售退回、商品损益等。

24. 商品销售总额

指对本企业(单位)以外的单位和个人出售(包括对国(境)外直接出口)的商品。这个指标反映批发零售贸易业在国内市场上销售商品以及出口商品的总量。商品销售总额包括：(1)售给城乡居民和社会集团消费用的商品；(2)售给工业、农业、建筑业、运输邮电业、批发零售贸易业、餐饮业、服务业等作为生产、经营使用的商品；(3)售给批发零售贸易业作为转卖或加工后转卖的商品；(4)对国(境)外直接出口的商品。不包括：出售本企业(单位)自用的废旧包装用品，未通过买卖行为付出的商品，经本单位介绍，由买卖双方直接结算，本单位只收取手续费的业务，购货退出的商品以及商品损耗和损失等。

25. 批准企业(项目)个数

是指外商直接投资中批准设立的外商投资企业个数、批准的合作开发项目个数。

26. 合同外资金额

是指批准外商投资企业的合同、章程中规定的外国投资者认缴的出资额和企业投资总额内的应由外方投资者以自己的境外自有资金直接向企业提供的贷款。包括新批准企业合同外资和原有企业的增资减资，增资减资不对企业（项目）个数进行调整。

27. 实际使用外资金额

是指合同外资金额的实际执行金额。

28. 外商直接投资

是指外国企业和经济组织或个人(包括华侨、港澳台胞以及我国在境外注册的企业)按我国有关政策、法规，用现汇、实物、技术等在我国境内开办外商独资企业、与我国境内的企业或经济组织共同举办中外合资经营企业、合作经营企业或合作开发资源的投资(包括外商投资收益的再投资)以及经政府有关部门批准的项目投资总额内，企业从境外借入的资金。

29. 外商其它投资

是指除外商直接投资以外其他方式吸收的外资。

30. 旅游人数

指来我国参观、访问、旅行、探亲、访友、休养、考察、参加会议和从事经济、科技、文化、教育、体育、宗教等活动的外国人、华侨、港澳和台湾同胞的人数。不包括外国在我国的常驻机构，如领事馆、通讯社、企业办事处的工作人员；来我国常住的外国专家、留学生以及在岸逗留不过夜人员。

31. 进出口总额

指实际进出我国国境的货物总金额。包括对外贸易实际进出口货物，来料加工装配进出口货物，国家间、联合国及国际组织无偿援助物资和赠送品，华侨、港澳台同胞和外籍华人捐赠品，租赁期满归承租人所有的租赁货物，进料加工进出口货物，边境地方贸易及边境地区小额贸易进出口货物(边民互市贸易除外)，中外合资企业、中外合作经营企业、外商独资经营企业进出口货物和公用物品，到、离岸价格在规定限额以上的进出口货样和广告品(无商业价值、无使用价值和免费提供出口的除外)，从保税仓库提取在中国境内销售的进口货物，以及其他进出口货物。

32. 普通高等学校

指按照国家规定的设置标准和审批程序批准举办，通过国家统一招生考试，招收高中毕业生为主要培养对象，实施高等教育的全日制大学、独立设置的学院和高等专科学校、短期职业大学。

33. 成人高等学校

指按照国家有关规定审批，招收通过全国成人高教统一招生考试的具有高中毕业或同等学历的在职从业人员，利用脱产、半脱产、业余或函授等多种形式对其实施高等学历教育，培养高等教育专科或本科毕业水平的专门人才，修业年限、课程设置和总学时数均按高等学历教育要求付诸实施的学校。包括广播电视大学、职工高等学校、农民高等学校、管理干部学院；教育学院、独立设置的函授学院等。

34. 卫生技术人员

指卫生事业机构中现任职务为卫生技术工作的人员。包括中医师、西医师、中西医结合高级医师、护师、中药师、西药师、检验师、其他技师、中医士、西医士、护士、助产士、中药剂士、西药剂士、检验士、其他技士、其他中医、护理员、中药剂员、西药剂员、检验员、其他初级卫生技术人员。

35. 文化事业机构

指从事专业文化工作和为专业文化工作服务的独立建制的单独核算的单位。不包括这些单位另外举办独立核算的其他机构和各部门的业余文化组织。

36. 工业废水排放量

指经过企业厂区所有排放口排到企业外部的工业废水量。包括生产废水、外排的直接冷却水、超标排放的矿井地下水和与工业废水混排的厂区生活污水，不包括外排的间接冷却水(清污不分流的间按冷却水应计算在内)。

37. 工业废水排放达标量

指各项指标都达到国家或地方排放标准的外排工业废水量，包括未经处理外排达标的和经过处理后外排达标的和两部分。国家排放标准见 GB8978—88。

38. 工业固体废物产生量

指企业在生产过程中产生的固体状、半固体状和高浓度液体状废弃物的总量，包括危险废物、冶炼废渣、粉煤灰、炉渣、煤矸渣、尾矿、放射性废物和其他废物等；不包括矿山开采的剥离废石和掘进废石(煤矸石和呈酸性或碱性的废石除外)酸性或碱性废石是指采掘的废石其流经水、雨淋水的 pH 值小于 4 或 pH 值大于 10.5 者。

39. 社会从业人员

指从事一定社会劳动并取得劳动报酬或经营收入的全部劳动力。这一指标反映了一定时期内全部劳动力资源的实际利用情况，是研究我国基本国情国力的重要指标。各单位的从业人员是指在各级国家机关、政党机关、社会团体及企业、事业单位中工作，并取得劳动报酬的全部人员。包括在岗职工、再就业的离退休人员、民办教师以及在各单位工作的外方人员和港、澳、台方人员等。

40. 职工

指在内资(国有、集体、股份合作、联营、有限责任公司、股份有限公司)单位、港澳台商投资单位和外商投资单位及其附属机构工作，并由其支付工资的在岗人员以及不在岗但劳动关系仍在本单位的离岗人员。

41. 人口自然增长率

是指一定时期内人口自然增长数(出生人数减死亡人数)与人口总数之比，通常以一年为期计算，用千分数表示，表明人口自然增长的趋势或程度。其计算公式为：人口自然增长率；(全年出生人数—全年死亡人数)；年平均人数 x1000%。人口自然增长率等于出生率与死亡率之差。

42. 居民消费价格指数

是度量一组代表性消费商品及服务项目价格水平随着时间而变动的相对数，反映居民家庭购买的消费品及服务价格水平的变动情况。它是宏观经济分析和决策、价格总水平监测和调控以及国民经济核算的重要指标。其按年度计算的变动率通常被用来作为反映通货膨胀(或紧缩)程度的指标。

43. 商品零售价格指数

是商品流通过程中最后一个环节的价格，是工业、商业、餐饮业和其他零售企业向城乡居民、机关团体出售生活消费品和办公用品的价格。商品零售价格调查的任务是系统地调查、搜集和整理市场商品零售价格资料，编制商品联手价格指数，以此反映市场商品零售价格的变动趋势和变动程度。其目的在于掌握商品价格的变动趋势，为国家宏观调控提供参考依据。同时，还可以在此基础上编制其他各种派生价格指数。

44. 职工工资总额

指各单位在一定时期内直接支付给本单位全部职工的劳动报酬总额，即在岗职工工资总额和离岗职工生活费两部分。工资总额的计算原则应以直接支付给职工的全部劳动报酬为根据。各单位支付给职工的劳动报酬以及其他根据有关规定支付的工资，不论是计入成本的还是不计入成本的，不论是按国家规定列入计征奖金税项目的，还是未列入计征奖金税项目的，不论是以货币形式支付的还是以实物形式支付的，均包括在工资总额内。

45. 职工平均工资

指各单位一定时期内平均每人所得的工资。它表明一定时期职工工资收入的高低程度，是反映职工工资水平的主要指标。

全社会单位包括：国有经济、集体经济、联营经济、股份制经济、外商和港、澳、台投资经济、私营经济、其他内资。

城镇单位包括：国有经济、集体经济、联营经济、股份制经济、外商和港、澳、台投资经济。

46. 城市居民家庭总收入、可支配收入

城市家庭总收入指家庭成员得到的工薪收入、经营净收入、财产性收入、转移性收入之和，不包括出售财务收入和借贷收入。城市家庭可支配收入指家庭成员得到可用于最终消费支出和其他业务性支出以及储蓄的总和，即居民家庭可以用来自由支配的收入。它是家庭总收入扣除交纳所得税、个人交纳的社会保障费以及记帐补贴后的收入。计算公式为：

可支配收入=家庭总收入—交纳所得税—个人交纳的社会保障支出—记帐补贴

47. 城市居民消费性支出

指被调查的城市居民家庭用于日常生活的全部支出，包括购买商品支出和文化生活、服务等非商品性支出。不包括罚没、丢失款和缴纳的各种税款(如个人所得税、牌照税、房产税等)，也不包括个体劳动者生产经营过程中发生的各项费用。

48. 农村居民家庭总收入、纯收入

农村居民家庭总收入指调查期内农村住户和住户成员从各种来源渠道得到的收入总和。按收入的性质划分为工资性收入、家庭经营收入、财产性收入和转移性收入。农民人均纯收入指按人口平均的纯收入水平，反映的是一个地区或一个农户农村居民的平均收入水平。纯收入指农村住户当年从各个来源得到的总收入相应地扣除所发生的费用后的收入总和。纯收入主要用于再生产投入和当年生活消费支出，也可用于储蓄和各种非义务性支出。计算方法：

纯收入=总收入-家庭经营费用支出-税费支出-生产性固定资产折旧-赠送农村外部亲友支出

49. 农村居民家庭生活消费支出

指农村常住居民家庭用于日常生活的全部开支，是反映和研究农民家庭实际生活消费水平高低的重要指标。

50. 景气指数

又称景气度。它是对景气调查中定性经济指标的量化描述，以直观地反映经济所处状态。景气指数的数值介于 0-200 之间，当景气指数为 100 时，说明经济处于景气的边缘；大于 100 时，则表示经济状况处于景气状态，越接近 200，状态越好；小于 100 时，表示经济处于不景气状态，越接近于 0，状态越差。

EXPLANATORY NOTES TO MAJOR STATISTICAL INDICATORS

Gross Domestic Product Refers to the final products of all resident units in a country(or a region)during a certain period of time. There are many meanings of the word “Domestic”,so it is not proper to name GDP of the whole country and a certain region both as Gross Domestic Product.This conception is used as gross product of local area by statistical department in Hongkong Special Administrative Region. For the Correction and standardization of the expression,since 2004,the Chinese name of GDP of a certain region has been adopted as region gross product;GDP of a specified region has the name of administrative region name as attribute. For example, “Gross Product of Qingdao” is Called “Qingdao GDP” for short.

Per Capita GDP refers to the ratio of GDP in a certain term and average population in the same term.According to the international standard,average population should be average constant population in the same term.In the account regulation,population of both the country and the region should be constant population.In the after two yers since 2004,per capita GDP can be calculated at two coverage.i.e. at constant population and household registered population(the note of coverage should follow the data.)The per capita GDP calculated with household registered population will be abolished after two years.Per capita GDP of Qingdao is calculated at constant population.

Three Industries has been classfied according to the historical sequence of development.Primary industry refers to extraction of natural resources;secondary industry involves processing of primary products;and tertiary industry provides services of various kinds for production and consumption.The above classification is universal although it varies to some extent form country to country.Industry in China comprises:

Primary industry:agriculture(including farming,forestry,animal husbandry,sideline production and fishing).

Secondary industry:industry(including mining,manufacturing,water supply,electricity generation and supply,steam,hot water,gas)and construction.

Tertiary industry:all other industries not included in primary or secondary industries.

Gross Output Value of Agriculture refers to the total volume of products of farming,forestry,animal husbandry,and fishery expressed in the monetary terms. It reflects the overall scale and achievements of agricultural production during a given period of time.

The scope of statistics on farming,forestry,animal husbandry,and fishery are as follows:

Farming includes cultivation of farm crops and other agricultural activities.

Cultivation of farm crops include cultivation of grain crops, legume crops,tuber crops,cotton,oil bearing crops,sugar crops, and cultivation and management of tea plantations,mulberry fields and orchards.

Other agricultural activities include harvesting wild fruits,fiber,tree gum,resin,oil bearing plants,firewood,wild medicinal herbs,fungus,and rural household commodity industries.

Forestry refers to planting trees of various kinds (excluding tea plantations,mulberry fields and orchards), collection of forestry products and cutting and felling of bamboo and trees by villages and other cooperative organizations under village level.

Animal husbandry refers to raising and grazing of all kinds of farm animals except fishing and aquatic cultivating,and hunting and rising of wild animals.

Fishery refers to cultivation and catching of fish and other aquatic products and cultivation and collection of seaweed and other aquatic plants.

In terms of ownership,China's agriculture includes specialized state farms (for farming,forestry,animal husbandry, fishery),farms managed by various government agencies,organizations,organizations,schools,research institutions,and army;farms managed by rural collective organizations at levels of the township,town,and village;farming forestry,animal husbandry,fishery run by various rural collective organizations and farming run by collective family members' organizations of mining and industrial enterprises,farming,forestry,animal husbandry and fishery and some commodity industries run by individual farmer.

Gross output value of agriculture is obtained by first multiplying the output of products or by products by their unit price.For a small number of products,annual output of which is not available or difficult to get due to the long production/growing process involved,the output value will be estimated through an indirect approach.The sum of output value of all products of farming,forestry,animal husbandry and fishery will then and together to form gross output value of agriculture.

Grain Output refers to the total output of rice,wheat,corn,sorghum,millet and other miscellaneous grains as well as tubers and bean in the whole country including grains produced by states farms,collective unit,industrial enterprises and mines,output of beans refers to dry beans without pods,the output of tubers(sweet potatoes and potatoes, excluding taros and cassava) was converted into that of grain at the ratio 5：1,i.e. 5 kilograms of fresh tubers was equivalent to 1 kilogram of grain,tubers supplies as vegetable(such as potatoes) in cities and suburbs are calculated as fresh vegetables and their output is not included in the output of grain output of all other grains refers to husked grain.

Output of Aquatic products refers to catches of both artificially cultured and naturally grown aquatic products,including fish,shrimps,crabs and shellfish in sea and inland water as well as seaweed,freshwater plants are not included.

Output of Pork,Beef,and Mutton refers to the meat of slaughtered hogs,cattle,sheep and goats with head,feet,and offal taken away the statistical scope is of the whole society.

Consumption of Chemical Fertilizers In Agriculture refers to the quantity of chemical fertilizers applied in agriculture in the year,including nitrogenous fertilizer,phosphate fertilizer,potash fertilizer,and compound fertilizer,the consumption of chemical fertilizer is required in calculation to convert to gross weight into weight containing 100% effective component(e.g.100%nitrogen content in nitrogenous fertilizer,100% phosphorous pent oxide contents in phosphate fertilizer,100% phosphorous oxide contents in potash fertilizer).compound fertilizer is converted with its major component,the formula is:

Volume of effect component=physical quantity effective component of certain chemical fertilizer(%)

Total Power of Farm Machinery Refers to the total mechanical power of machinery used in farming forestry animal husbandry and fishery,including machines used for ploughing,irrigation and drainage,crop growing,plant protection,harvesting,farm product processing,transport,stock breeding,fishery and water conservancy,Machinery employed for non agricultural purposes such as township industry,capital construction,non agricultural transport,scientific experiments and for teaching is excluded.

Gross Output Value of Industry refer to the total volume,expressed in the monetary terms,of products turned out by industrial enterprises during a given period of time which are already sold or available for sale.It reflects the overall scale and level of the industrial production during a given period.

Sales Output Value of Industry refers to total sales of products produced by industrial enterprises during a given period,including sales of fished goods,value of semi products,value of industrial services provided to other units,value of products,industrial services provided for capital construction sector,welfare and self produced equipments within enterprise.

Added Value of Industry refers to the final results of industrial production of industrial enterprises in money terms during the reference period.

Freight(Passenger)Traffic refers to the physical volume of freight(passenger)transported.Freight transport is calculated by ton and passenger traffic by number of persons.Despite the type of freight and traveling distance,the freight transport is calculated by the actual weight;and despite the traveling distance and ticket price,the passenger traffic is calculated by one person per quantitative measure to reflect how the transport industry serves the national economy and people,and an important indicator for planning the transport industry and for studying the development scale and speed of the industry.

Freight(Passenger)Traffic Volume refers to the total of the product of the physical volume of transported cargo(passengers)by the transport distance,usually using ton/kilometer and person/kilometer as calculating unit.Normally,the shortest distance between the departure point and the destination is the basis to calculate the freight traffic volume,that is to say,the payable distance.This is an important indicator to show the total results of the transport industry,to prepare and examine the transport plan and to measure the efficiency,the labor productivity and the unit cost of transport.

Service Revenue of Posts and Telecommunications refers to the total amount of the information delivered and other post and telecommunication services provided by the post and telecommunication departments for the customers.It is arrived by first multiplying the business volume of different types,such as number of letters,telegrams,long distance calls,city and rural telephone(fixed price)and then adding these products together,plus the income from maintenance of telephone switchboards and lines,and the income from other business operations.The service revenue of posts and telecommunications reflects the total achievements by the post and telecommunication departments during a given period of time in a comprehensive way,and is an important indicator to study the composition and development of the post and telecommunication business.

Total Investment in Fixed Assets constitutes an important portion of the national economic reproduction.Through production and purchase of fixed assets,the advanced technology and equipment are constantly adopted and new industries are established to adjust the economic structure and reginal distribution of productive forces,enhance economic capacity,and prepare the material conditions for improving the nation' s material and cultural life.

Fixed assets investment is a general term for both the work volume of production and purchas of fixed assets and relevant expenditure,in the form of currency,during a certain period.It is a comprehensive indicator of scale,structure and development speed of fixed assets investment.As stipulated in the current national statistics regulations,the social fixed assets investment includes the investment into infrastructure,substitution and reformation,real estate development,urban and rural collective economic bodies,private house construction in urban and rural areas and other economic bodies.

Newly Increased Fixed Assets also called fixed assets put into operation,refers to the value of fixed assets that has been put into production or handed over to the production units after the completion of the process of construction and purchase.The newly increased fixed asset is an value indicator of the result of investment.It is also the necessary data for reflecting the construction process and the result of investment in fixed assets.

Floor Space under Construction refers to total floor space of all buildings under construction during the reference period,including floor space of newly started building during the reference period,floor space of construction extended from the previous period to the current period,floor space of construction suspended during the previous period and resumed in the current period,floor space of construction completed in the current period,and floor space of construction started and then suspended in the current period.

Floor Space of Buildings Completed refers to the floor space of buildings completed in the reference period,which have come up to the designed standards and have been put into use.

Gross Output Value Of Construction refers to total of construction products,expressed in money terms,completed by construction and installation enterprises during a given period of time.It includes:output Value of installation projects,output value of installation projects,out value of repair of buildings and structures and Output value of manufactured non standard equipment.

Added Value of Construction refers to the final result of the activities of production and management of production industry in monetary terms in the reference period.

The formula is as follows:Value added of construction=depreciation of fixed assets in the year+wages payable of the major operation+welfare expenses payable of major operation+insurance premium and tax for waiting of waiting for employment in the administrative expenses+taxes and surcharges on project settlement +profit gained from project settlement.

Total Retail Sales of Consumer Goods refers to the sum of retail sales of consumer goods sold by all sectors of the national economy to urban and rural residents and social groups.Sectors of the national economy include wholesale and retail trade, accommodation and catering trade and others.Since 2003,retail sales of manufacture and retail sales of rural residents to urban residents are excluded in total retail sales.

Total Purchase of Commodities refers to purchase of commodities from other establishments or individuals (including direct import from abroad)for the purpose of re selling,either with or without further processing of the commodities purchased.Reflecting the total value of purchases of commodities by wholesale and retail establishments from domestic and overseas markets,they include:(1)agricultural and industrial products purchased from producers;(2)books,magazines and newspapers purchased from distribution departments of the publishers;(3)commodities purchased from wholesale and retail establishments;(4)commodities purchased from other units,such as surplus materials purchased from government agencies,enterprises or institutions;commodities purchased from catering and service establishments;confiscated goods purchased from customs authorities or market management agencies;second hand goods and wastes purchased from households;(5)commodities directly imported from abroad.Excluded are commodities purchased by enterprises for their own operation,commodities obtained without buying or selling procedures,rejected commodities,etc.

Total Sales of Commodities refers to the selling of commodities to other establishments and individuals (including direct export).Reflecting the total value of sales of commodities at domestic markets and export,this indicator includes:(1)commodities sole to urban and rural households and institutions for their consumption;(2)commodities sole to establishments in industry,agriculture,construction,transportation,post and telecommunications,wholesale and retail trade,catering and service trade and public utility for their production and operation;(3)commodities sold to wholesale and retail establishments for re selling,with or without further processing ;and (4)commodities for direct export to other countries.Excluded are selling of waste packaging materials used by enterprises themselves commodities transferred without buying or selling procedures,commission income from brokerage in transactions whose settlement is directly handled by buyers and sellers,rejected commodities in the purchase,loss in commodities,etc.

Enterprises(Projects) Permitted refers to number of foreign invested enterprises and developed projects under cooperation through the permission.

Contracted Foreign Investment refers to expenditure promised by the foreign investor and loan stemed from broad innate fund of the foreign investor,according to the contract and regulation approved of enterprise invested by foreigner.

Actual Utilization of Foreign Investment refers to actual usage of contracted foreign investment,including cash,investment in kind and incorporeal agreed by the both sides as part of the investment,such as services and technology.

Foreign Direct Investment refers to the investments by foreign enterprises and economic organizations or individuals(including overseas Chinese,compatriots from Hong dong,Macao and Taiwan,and Chinese enterprises registered abroad),following the relevant policies and laws of China,for the establishment of ventures and cooperative enterprises or cooperative exploration of resources with enterprises or economic organizations in China,It includes the reinvestment of the foreign entrepreneurs with the profits gained from the investment and the funds that enterprises borrow from aboard in the total investment of projects which are approved by the relevant department of the government.

Other Investment by Foreign Entrepreneurs refers to all forms of utilization of foreign capitals other than foreign direct investment.

Number of Tourists refers to the number of foreigners,overseas Chinese,and compatriots from Hong Kong,Macao and Taiwan coming to the Chinese mainland for sightseeing,visits,tours,family reunions,meeting friends,vacations,study tours,attending meetings and other activities of an economic,scientific and technological,cultural,physical culture and religious nature.This does not include employees of foreign organizations stationed in China such as embassies,news agencies,representative offices of overseas firms and foreign experts and students residing in China and persons who enter the country but without staying over.

Total Imports and Exports refers to the value of commodities imported into and exported from the boundary of China.They include the actual imports and exports through foreign trade,imported and exported goods under the processing and assembling trades and materials,supplies and gifts as aid given gratis between governments and by the United Nations and other international organizations,and contributions donated by overseas Chinese,compatriots in Hong Kong and Macao and Chinese with foreign citizenship,leasing commodities owned by tenant at the expiration of leasing period,the imported and Macao and exported commodities processed with imported materiais,commodities trading in border areas(excluding mutual exchange goods),the imported and exported commodities and articles for public use of the Sino foreign joint ventures,cooperative enterprises and ventures exclusively with foreign own investment.Also included is import or export of samples and advertising goods for whose CLF or FOB value are beyond the permitted ceiling(excluding goods of no trading or use value and free commodities for export),imported goods sold in China from bonded warehouses and other imported or exported goods.

General Institutions of Higher Education refers to educational establishments which are set up according to government evaluation and approval procedures,enroll graduates from high schools who have passed the national college entrance examination and provide higher education courses and training for senior professionals.They include full time universities,colleges,high professional schools and short term professional universities.

Institutions of Higher Education for Adults refers to educational establishments which are set up in line with relevant rules and approved by government,enroll workers or staff with high school or equivalent education,and provide higher education courses in forms of full time,part time,spare time,or correspondence for adults.Professionals thus trained receive a qualification equivalent to graduates studying regular courses at general colleges,universities and professional colleges.Institutions of higher education for adults include radion and TV universities,schools of high education for staff and workers and peasants,colleges for management cadres,pedagogical,independent correspondence colleges.

Medical Technical Personnel refers to those medical workers employed institutions,including doctors of Chinese and Western medicine,senior doctors of integrated Chinese Western medicine,head nurses,pharmacists of Chinese and Western medicine,laboratory specialists,other specialists,junior doctors of Chinese and Western medicine,nurses,midwives,druggists of Chinese and Western medicine,laboratory technicians,other technicians,other practitioners of Chinese medicine,nursing attendants,pharmacological workers of Chinese and Western medicine,laboratory workers,and other primary medical personnel.

Cultural Institutions refers to units which have their own establishment and independent accounting system and specialize in cultural activities or serve cultural developments.Cultural Institutions exclude other establishments run by units under the cultural authorities and amateur cultural groups established by other departments.

Volume of Industrial Water Discharged refers to the volume of industrial waste discharged,through all outlets,to the outside of industrial enterprises,including waste water produced,direct cooling water,underground water from mines that does that does not meet the standard of discharge,and the domestic sewage mixed up with industrial waste water when discharged,but excluding discharged indirect cooling water.

Volume of Waste Water up to the Standard for Discharge refers to the volume of discharged industrial waste water that,with or without treatment,has come up to the national or local standards for discharge.

Volume of Industrial Solid Wastes Produced refers to the total volume of solid,semi solid or high concentration liquid residue produced by industrial enterprises in their production process,including dangerous wastes,residues from melting,slag,powdered coalash,gangue,chemical,tailings,radioactive and other residues,but excluding stripped or dug stones in mining(except gangue and acid or alkali stones which are stones washed or soaked by water with a pH value smaller than 4 or larger than100.5.)

Persons Employed refers to the total number of persons engaged in social labour which generates income.

This indicator reflects the actual utilization of total labor force during a certain period of time and is often used for the research of China' s economic affairs and power.

Persons Employed in Various Units refers to total staff working for government agencies of various levels,political and party organizations,social organizations,and enterprises and institutions receiving income,including working working staff staff and workers reemployed retirees,social organizations,and enterprises and institutions receiving income,including working staff and workers reemployed retirees,non government paid teachers.foreigners,and Chinese compatriots from Hong Kong,Macao,and Taiwan working in various units.

Natural Growth Rate of Population refers to the ratio of natural increase in population(number of births minus number of deaths) in a certain period of time(usually a year) to the average population (or mid year population) of the same period,which is often presented as perminvar.The following formula are applied:

Natural Growth of Population=(Number of Births Number of Deaths Average Number of Population) 1000

Natural Growth Rate of Population=Birth Rate Death Rate

Consumer Price Index is an index is an index that reflects the time based change of prices of a group of representative consumption commodities and services,It is an important reference factor for macro economic analysis and strategy,monitoring and adjustment of overall price level and the national economic budgeting.The year on year change of the index is often a norm reflecting the inflation or deflation.

Retail Price Index as the last link of the circle of commodities,is the price of daily consumption articles and office stationery sold to residents and organizations by the industrial,food and other retail sectors.It measures the change trend and variation degree of the retail prices in order to offer a reference for the national macro economic and compile derivative price indexes.

Total Wage Bill of Staff and Workers refers to total remuneration paid in line with relevant regulations to permanent staff and workers of various during a certain period of time.Total wage bill of staff and workers includes the total salary payment for the working staff and workers and the stipends for laid off workers.

The calculation of total wages hill is based on the total remuneration payment and therefore,wage and salaries and other payments to staff and workers regardless of its resources,category,in kind or cash,are included.